Witnessing America

Emigrants coming to "the land of promise," a stereo photograph by
William H. Rau, taken at the turn of the century.

Witnessing America

The Library of Congress Book of Firsthand
Accounts of Life in America 1600–1900

COMPILED AND EDITED BY NOEL RAE

A Stonesong Press Book

PENGUIN
REFERENCE

973
WIT

PENGUIN REFERENCE

Published by the Penguin Group

Penguin Books USA Inc., 375 Hudson Street, New York, New York 10014, U.S.A.

Penguin Books Ltd, 27 Wrights Lane, London W8 5TZ, England

Penguin Books Australia Ltd, Ringwood, Victoria, Australia

Penguin Books Canada Ltd, 10 Alcorn Avenue, Toronto, Ontario, Canada M4V 3B2

Penguin Books (N.Z.) Ltd, 182–190 Wairau Road, Auckland 10, New Zealand

Penguin Books Ltd, Registered Reference:
Harmondsworth, Middlesex, England

First published in 1996 by Penguin Reference,
an imprint of Penguin Books USA Inc.

10   9   8   7   6   5   4   3   2   1

Grateful acknowledgment is made for permission to reprint an excerpt from *Black Elk Speaks* by John G. Neihardt. Reprinted by permission of the University of Nebraska Press. Copyright 1932, 1959, 1972 by John G. Neihardt. Copyright © 1961 by the John G. Neihardt Trust.

LIBRARY OF CONGRESS CATALOGING-IN-PUBLICATION DATA
Witnessing America: the Library of Congress book of firsthand accounts of life in America,
   1600–1900 / compiled and edited by Noel Rae; with a foreword by James H. Billington and
   an introduction by Douglas Brinkley.
        p.   cm.
    Includes index.
    ISBN 0-670-86400-5
    1. United States—Social life and customs—Sources.   I. Rae, Noel (Noel Martin Douglas)
   II. Library of Congress.
   E161.W58   1996
   973—dc20   96–16201

This book is printed on acid-free paper.

A Stonesong Press Book

All illustrations courtesy of the Library of Congress
Printed in the United States of America
Set in New Baskerville

FOREWORD

"THE HISTORY OF EVERY COUNTRY," wrote Willa Cather in *O Pioneers!*, "begins in the heart of a man or a woman." In the pages of *Witnessing America,* you will find an engaging and informative collection of excerpts from the personal testaments of many men and women who helped create the United States we know today. In this volume you will encounter people of all stations in life, those who were born in America and those who came to America from all around the globe—eagerly or unwillingly, filled with hope or pushed by desperation. Their individual stories are pieces of the unique American mosaic. Reading them, we laugh, get angry, shake our heads at what should not have been, marvel at those who survived against long odds, and take heart at the many kinds of personal courage that have helped shape this young Republic.

Dutchman Johannes Megalopensis writes his impressions of the Mohawk Indians in 1644, and in 1879 Mohawk Ah-Nen-La-Dee-Ni tells of his experiences in "Indian school." Charles Dickens, visiting America, describes the trials caused by his literary celebrity; in 1889 the Reverend Thomas De Witt Talmage delivers a fiery sermon on "The Wickedness of Modern Society," excoriating contemporary novels as "unclean literature." Frontier settlers run out of food during harsh winters, Indian tribes are decimated by illness, women are tried for witchcraft, slave families are torn apart when parents and children are sold to different owners, reformers improve education and working conditions, births and marriages are celebrated, deaths are mourned. Behind all the testaments, and the lives they describe, we see a nation building, and we realize anew how appropriate is our national motto: "E Pluribus Unum"—From Many, One.

The Library of Congress is pleased to join The Stonesong Press and Penguin USA in publishing this lively compendium of the American experience. Preserving that experience and making it accessible to all is one of the Library's primary missions. Although we are an institution whose collections are international in scope, we are most particularly the Nation's Library. Among the more than 110 million items in our collections are rich troves of maps, photographs, drawings, recordings, rare books, broadsides, music, and motion pictures that track the course of the nation's history and cast light on the complexities of the American character. Our collections also include millions of published and unpublished accounts of what life was like for individuals, both celebrated and unsung, who contributed to the history and the enduring strength of the United States. The progress of the nation—from science to the theater, from its economic growth to manners and morals—can be traced through our holdings, reminding us of who we are, what we have done, what we have hoped to do. These elements resonate through the pages of *Witnessing America,* as well.

"All history is modern history," wrote American poet Wallace Stevens. And, in the pages of *Witnessing America,* we recognize that this is so. This very "human" book, ably compiled and annotated by Noel Rae, gives us the observations of people whose voices and experiences seem not all that dissimilar from those of our own time. Their words bring the past to life, and make the present more comprehensible. What you find in these pages will, I believe, stir as well as enlighten you. It may also draw you to your local library, or to the Library of Congress—in person or via the on-line resources made available through our National Digital Library—to find out more about the people you have encountered here, about others who have helped build the United States, and about the American experience as a whole. I hope that happens. It is an exciting quest. In the meantime, you have *Witnessing America* at hand: Its bright glimpses of American life, from the earliest days to the end of the nineteenth century, comprise a useful reference, an authentic narrative—and a "good read."

James H. Billington
The Librarian of Congress

INTRODUCTION

D R. SAMUEL JOHNSON ONCE REMARKED that "A man will turn over half a library to make one book." This seeming hyperbole turns to fact in the tome at hand: *Witnessing America,* an extraordinary selection of first-person narratives penned by an eclectic assemblage of native storytellers over the three centuries from 1600 to 1900. The ambitious compiler and annotator is Noel Rae, editor, writer, and translator, and the depository none other than the venerable Library of Congress. The combination is potent.

Tired of traditional textbooks and academic interpretations, Rae decided that an American history volume ringing with the actual voices of ordinary people would help the reader rediscover a collective heritage that grows cloudier with each passing sunset. Borrowing Davy Crockett's motto—"Be sure you're right, then go ahead"—Rae spent years scouring the labyrinthine corridors of the Library of Congress for the incandescent eyewitness anecdotes that could recapture the unadorned daily essence of the American past.

At face value, there is nothing novel about Rae's approach to history—after all, the prose excerpts included here stem from the same primary sources traditionally used by scores of other dedicated scholars: diaries, letters, newspapers, court records, travel journals, forgotten memoirs, popular broadsides, sermons, speeches and random stories left behind, in one printed form or another, for posterity to ponder. But instead of distilling these historical nuggets into his own narrative, Rae serves them up raw. This technique—recently popularized by PBS's "Civil War" series, in which diary entries were spoken to great dramatic effect—allows the student of history to feel more intimately what it was like to exist in an era when electricity was but a bright notion in Ben Franklin's restless mind. It is one thing, Rae contends, to read a contemporary historian's well-researched account of slave life on a Georgia plantation; it is quite another to read first-hand the anguish of an exhausted cotton picker who toiled daily under the crack of an oiled whip.

Rae's view of history is wonderfully simple: to understand the past, look directly at its leavings. Of course, few of us have the time to browse the Library of Congress for the odd historical insight, so Rae does a signal service by providing this lively sampler. For what makes *Witnessing America* such an impressive achievement is the meticulous care with which the editor made his prose selections, consciously rendering a "living history" in the plaintive words of our predecessors, speaking for themselves in chronological, turnstile-like succession.

Of course, no one volume can embrace the sum total of the American tradition. But this was not Rae's intention: he aimed instead to cobble an impressionistic mosaic. Read as a whole from beginning to end, this "historical anthology" echoes Thornton Wilder's Pulitzer Prize-winning play "Our Town," writ large. As in that quintessential American drama, common people step briefly into the spotlight to state the facts of their daily regimens. Rae's cast of characters ranges as far as America itself: Native Americans, religious dissenters, Spanish conquistadors, early naturalists, fire-and-brimstone clergymen, indentured servants, African slaves, plantation owners, Revolutionary War militiamen, editorial writers, yeoman farmers, Chinese coolies, rebellious lawyers, frontier teachers, etiquette mavens, prairie homesteaders, Kansas vigilantes, itinerant preachers, cow punchers, village idiots, Virginia aristocrats, Southern belles, fur trappers, railroad workers, New England tinkerers, labor anarchists, pioneer families, New York philanthropists, Texas Rangers, buffalo skinners—the roll goes on and on like a Carl Sandburg epic poem.

As the reader will soon discover, however, not all of the entries flow from the pens of private diarists or small-town scribes. Rae also excerpts skillfully from some of our nation's literary classics, such as Jack London's *The Road*, Francis Parkman's *The Oregon Trail*, and Mark Twain's *Roughing It*, among others. In fact, personal testaments from many of America's most celebrated and sophisticated chroniclers are mixed in with those of the common folk: Cotton Mather, Henry David Thoreau, Walt Whitman, Louisa May Alcott, Nathaniel Hawthorne, Richard Henry Dana, Laura Ingalls Wilder, Frederick Douglass, Jane Addams, Joaquin Miller, Emma Goldman. W. E. B. Du Bois, Black Elk, Frederick Law Olmsted, and other intellectual stars make untrumpeted appearances. Theirs are treated just as American voices—no more or less important than the words of an anonymous slave or a fugitive pirate.

Witnessing America thus blurs the academic distinctions between high and lowbrow culture. Rae is a stout egalitarian: he makes no apologies for including an erudite passage from Frenchman Alexis de Toqueville's famed 1831 American journal in the same chapter with the recipe for a home remedy for worms from Lydia Maria Child's 1829 self-improvement tract, *The American Frugal Housewife.* Rae presents history as called for by Ralph Ellison in *Invisible Man* (1952): "America is woven of many strands; I would recognize them and let it so remain. . . . Our fate is to become one, and yet many—This is not prophecy, but description."

Clearly, Rae's *modus operandi* as he wandered library stacks and rifled card catalogues was to dust off the cleverest yarn, best-honed letter, or starkest reportage of transcendent but largely forgotten moments. The result is a trove of Americana that reveals just what it was like to call a seventeenth-century Mohawk village or an eighteenth-century Virginia plantation, or a nineteenth-century Kentucky log cabin "home." These personal testaments make *Witnessing America* something of a timeless quilt that will never be outdated, no matter the scholarly trend. It will become a mainstay in public libraries everywhere, and in personal ones, too—the ideal book to dip into at leisure with no need for a bookmark.

Divided into eleven chapters under broad headings such as "Arriving," "Housing," and "Upbringing," *Witnessing America* leads the reader down a specific lane of memories that illustrate our progress as a nation. What shines through the pages most clearly is the hopeful notion of just how much easier life is at the end of the twentieth century than it was for our ancestors. Just reading about the past's fatal outbreaks of cholera, smallpox, yellow fever and malaria makes one grateful for modern medicine. By the same token, today's flawed judicial system looks Solomon-like compared with what Rae calls the "rough justice" of earlier America. And first hand accounts of the seventeenth century witchcraft trials prove anew that women really have come a long way in this country.

There is no question that America is the star of this production of "Our Country," and many of the epistolary testimonies will make the reader swell with patriotic pride. Whether it's William Bradford describing the harrowing Atlantic voyage of the *Mayflower* or George Armstrong Custer marveling at the herds of antelope on the Great Plains or Dorothea Dix crying for the rights of fellow citizens afflicted with mental illness, the steady drumbeat march of American dynamism is intoxicating. But this is hardly a compendium of chest-beating jingoism; no red-white-and-blue veneer glosses over America's dark underbelly here. Bigots, hatemongers, and criminals climb the soapbox for themselves in *Witnessing America,* and it hurts to realize that the warped rationales and racist rhetoric of the past still linger in our society no matter how much we amend the Constitution.

Witnessing America exalts by humbling. It illustrates that all our forbears—regardless of origin, race or religion—possessed a common attribute that we share: They were human beings. It is somehow comforting to have validated in black on white what we've instinctively known all along: that Americans of the past harbored the same hopes and fears we do today, and that they persevered through them to achieve remarkable goals—great and small.

Douglas Brinkley
Director
The Eisenhower Center
    for American Studies
University of New Orleans

Contents

School...Life at Harvard...The Academic Year

PREFACE

THIS IS A HISTORY of the American people, told by themselves. It is incomplete, of course, for what single book—what multi-volume encyclopedia—could possibly contain even a fraction of the stories of all those who have ever lived in this country and left some account of their lives? And who is to speak for the millions who had no written language or have left no written record?

These limitations acknowledged, it is still possible to tell the story of our country's past by using only the words of those who actually lived it. The contemporary interviewer extends his microphone and asks, "What happened? What was it like? What did you do then?" Our method has been to read through first-person accounts of long ago, looking for answers to such questions as "What was it like to cross the Atlantic on the *Mayflower*?" or "Why did you become a witch?" or "How do you build a log cabin?" or "Did you see the steamboat explode? The fornicator being whipped? The minstrel show? The war dance? The slave auction? The cattle stampede? The lynching? . . . "

In this list of implied questions, politics, economics, and military affairs have, as a matter of editorial policy, been largely excluded. So too have intellectual and cultural history and the carryings-on of high society. Instead, the focus is on those matters that have touched the everyday lives of large numbers of people—the struggle to make a living, for example, or going to school, or falling in and out of love. Sometimes space is given to a topic that might seem a bit remote, as with the account of life among the Shakers, who at their height never numbered more than a few thousand. But the Shakers were famous in their day, a "must-see" for every traveler and every visitor from abroad, Charles Dickens being one of them; and they have a wider significance as an example of the hundreds, perhaps thousands, of utopias that have flourished here, even if often only briefly, ever since the Pilgrim Fathers set up their community of "Saints" in Plymouth.

Of course, a single example, no matter how representative, cannot stand for the whole. Rather, our claim is that the several hundred stories and scenes presented here are probably as true a depiction of each particular topic as can be found, and that taken together they provide a fairly impartial—if highly selective—overview of the country's past.

When there are numerous versions of the same event, a guiding principle has been to choose the one that tells the best story. Another principle has been to rely on narrators who see things with the eyes of the ordinary person—the Yankee drover rather than the railroad baron, the private in the infantry rather than the general, the circuit-riding preacher rather than Ralph Waldo Emerson or William Ellery Channing; but no one who enjoys a well-told story would want to exclude Ben Franklin or Buffalo Bill or Frederick Douglass or Carry Nation, all of whom are represented.

The period covered begins with the first peopling of the continent as recorded in a number of Indian legends, and runs through to the end of the last century. Times after that are within the purview of living memory, that is, times we have experienced ourselves or have heard about directly from members of an older generation.

The book's organization follows the general progression of life from the cradle to the grave. Along the way there are chapters on the immigrant experience, schooling, love and marriage, working, housing and housekeeping, eating and drinking, enduring hard times and enjoying good times, following any one of many different religions, falling afoul of the law, falling sick, dying and the hereafter. This is by no means so tidy an arrangement as it sounds, and the book can just as easily be looked into here and there, at random, as read from the beginning to the end.

The texts used are in most cases from the standard published editions (rather than from manuscripts), as particularized in the bibliography. Some have been partially repunctuated, where the original punctuation was confusing. For the same reason, the spelling has also been updated here and there, and some abbreviations have been spelled out. In cases where narrators have strayed from the subject that is of primary interest, or repeated themselves, the text has been cut. These cuts, when they occur in the middle of a paragraph, have been indicated by ellipses; when a whole paragraph has been removed, the fact is indicated by a slightly wider spacing between paragraphs.

Finally, a word of caution. We are told not to judge the past by the standards of the present, but of course we do, and the past being what it was, there is something in this book to offend almost everyone. People in this country have written and spoken of others in terms that nowadays are considered unforgivable, and they have treated each other in ways that were callous and cruel. We can wish that they hadn't, but they did. But our obligation to the past is not to feel responsible for it but to learn from it, and we can only do that by acknowledging history in its entirety.

Doing so also honors all those men and women who saw the evils around them for what they were and, refusing to accept comforting justifications, led the way in setting things to rights. Religious persecution, slavery, child labor, slums and tenements, vicious punishments— these and other blights, once commonplace features of daily life, have now largely or entirely disappeared, not of themselves but through the human agency of first a few courageous and outspoken reformers and then the general will of an aroused people. The idea of progress has long been out of fashion, but as this book's implicit comparison between the present and the past makes clear, the American people have demonstrated a truly amazing readiness to cast off the unjust, the harsh, and the outworn and to move on to something better. The old ideal of building a more perfect society—what John Winthrop in 1630 called the "city upon a hill"—has long been a driving force; the city is still incomplete, but work continues.

Acknowledgments

My thanks to John Cole, Ralph Eubanks and Peggy Wagner at the Library of Congress for their sponsorship and helpful suggestions; to Gillian Speeth for her diligent picture research; to Edward Burlingame for his advice and early support; to Paul Fargis of The Stonesong Press for his energy and skill in guiding the book along to publication; to Hugh Rawson of Viking for his expert editorial guidance and oversight; and to Kerry Acker of The Stonesong Press, the hands-on, day-to-day editor, whose intelligence, intuition, hard work, tact and enthusiasm have made her an ideal collaborator.

Witnessing America

A Yuma Indian in Arizona watching the arrival of emigrants,
stereo photograph by E. Conklin, 1877.

CHAPTER

1

ARRIVING

VERY AMERICAN IS AN IMMIGRANT or the descendant of immigrants. This is as true of the American Indians whose forebears crossed the Bering Strait many thousands of years ago as it is of the newcomer who has just taken the oath of citizenship or the baby being born this very moment. In this, as indeed in many other ways, America is unique; and so although the great majority of those who have lived and died here were also born here, this first chapter is devoted to telling the story of the immigrants.

It is of course a very selective telling. Every person who came surely had a story to tell, but many were illiterate, unable even to write their names; and because most American Indians have until recently relied on an oral tradition, outsiders must be consulted for reports on their early legends and histories. So the testimony of a few will have to represent the experience of millions.

Of these, some came to escape religious persecution, others to see the wonders of the new world or escape a pinching life in the old; some fled the guillotine, others were brought over in shackles; some sought gold, others freedom. Whatever the reason, they came, by the millions and from every quarter of the globe, to make what Walt Whitman called "not merely a nation, but a teeming nation of nations."

IN THE BEGINNING: THREE NATIVE AMERICAN MYTHS.
Johannes Megalopensis, a dominie of the Dutch Reformed Church, spent several years as minister at Fort Orange (now Albany, New York). In 1644, he published Een Kort Ontwerp vande Mahakvase Indiaenen (A Short Account of the Mohawk Indians)*, from which this is taken.*

They have a droll theory of the Creation, for they think that a pregnant woman fell down from heaven, and that a tortoise (tortoises are plenty and large here, in this country, two, three and four feet long, some with two heads, very mischievous and addicted to biting) took this pregnant woman on its back, because every place was covered with water; and that the woman sat upon the tortoise, groped with her hands in the water, and scraped together some of the earth, whence it finally happened that the earth was raised above the water. They think that there are more worlds than one, and that we came from another world.

Fredrika Bremer, a Swedish novelist, spent two years traveling around this country in the middle of the last century. Here she is writing home from St. Paul, Minnesota, in October 1850. The Indians she mentions are Sioux.

The Indians, like the Greenlanders, look down upon the white race with a proud contempt, at the same time that they fear them; and their legend of what happened at the creation of the various races proves naively how they view the relationship between them.

Artist John White, who created this image between 1577 and 1590, identified his subjects as "Chief Herowars wife of Pomec and her daughter of the age of 8 or 10 years."

"The first man which Manitou baked," say they, "was not thoroughly done, and he came white out of the oven; the second was overdone, was burned in the baking, and he was black. Manitou now tried a third time, and with much better success; this third man was thoroughly baked, and came out of the oven a fine red brown—this was the Indian."

Another early observer was John Josselyn, an English naturalist who traveled here in 1638–39 and 1663–71. His book An Account of Two Voyages to New England *contains this story.*

Their Theologie is not much, but questionless they acknowledge a God and a Devil, and some small light they have of the Souls immortality; for ask them whither they go when they dye, they will tell you pointing with their finger to Heaven beyond the white mountains, and do hint at *Noah's* Floud, as may be conceived by a story they have received from Father to Son, time out of mind, that a great while agon their Countrey was drowned, and all the People and other Creatures in it, only one *Powaw* and his *Webb* [wife] foreseeing the Flood fled to the white mountains carrying a hare along with them and so escaped; after a while the *Powaw* sent the *Hare* away, who not returning emboldned thereby they descended, and lived many years after, and had many Children, from whom the Countrie was filled again with *Indians.* Some of them tell another story of the *Beaver,* saying that he was their Father.

THE WHITE MAN ARRIVES. *The Moravian missionary John Heckewelder records a story he once heard "from the mouth of an intelligent Delaware Indian." The islands he speaks of are Manhattan and its neighbors; the ship was probably the* Half Moon, *commanded by Henry Hudson, who was employed by the Dutch East India Company. The* Half Moon *arrived in 1609; Heckewelder published his* Account of the History, Manners and Customs of the Indian Nations *in 1819.*

A great many years ago, when men with a white skin had never yet been seen in this land, some Indians who were out a fishing, at a place where the sea widens, espied at a great distance something remarkably large floating on the water, and such as they had never seen before.

Some believed it to be an uncommonly large fish or animal, while others were of opinion it must be a very big house floating on the sea. At length the spectators concluded that this wonderful object was moving towards the land, and that it must be an animal or something else that had life in it; it would therefore be proper to inform all the

Indians on the inhabited islands of what they had seen, and put them on their guard. Accordingly they sent off a number of runners and watermen to carry the news to their scattered chiefs.

These arriving in numbers, and having themselves viewed the strange appearance, and observing that it was actually moving towards the entrance of the river or bay, concluded it to be a remarkably large house in which the Mannitto (the Great or Supreme Being) himself was present, and that he was probably coming to visit them. . . . bringing them some kind of game, such as he had not given them before. But other runners soon after arriving declare that it is positively a house full of human beings, of quite a different colour from that of the Indians, and dressed quite differently from them; that in particular one of them was dressed entirely in red, who must be the Mannitto himself.

The house, some say large canoe, at last stops, and a canoe of a smaller size comes on shore with the red man, and some others in it; some stay with his canoe to guard it. The chiefs and wise men, assembled in council, form themselves into a large circle, towards which the man in red clothes approaches with two others. He salutes them with a friendly countenance, and they return the salute after their manner. They are lost in admiration; the dress, the manners, the whole appearance of the unknown strangers is to them a subject of wonder; but they are particularly struck with him who wore the red coat all glittering with gold lace, which they could in no manner account for. He, surely, must be the great Mannitto, but why should he have a white skin?

Meanwhile a large *Hackhack* [glass bottle] is brought by one of his servants, from which an unknown substance is poured out into a small cup or glass, and handed to the supposed Mannitto. He drinks—has the glass filled again, and hands it to the chief standing next to him. The chief receives it, but only smells the contents and passes it on to the next chief, who does the same. The glass or cup thus passes through the circle, without the liquor being tasted by anyone, and is upon the point of being returned to the red clothed Mannitto, when one of the Indians, a brave man and a great warrior, suddenly jumps up and harangues the assembly on the impropriety of returning the cup with its contents. It was handed to them, says he, by the Mannitto, that they should drink out of it, as he himself had done. To follow his example would be pleasing to him; but to return what he had given them might provoke his wrath, and bring destruction on them.

He then took the glass, and . . . at once drank up its whole contents. Every eye was fixed on the resolute chief to see what effect the unknown liquor would produce. He soon began to stagger, and at last

Captain Smith ("C. S.") is led away a prisoner
(before Pocahontas saves him), while his captors dance
in triumph. Engraving by Robert Vaughan from
John Smith's *General Historie of Virginia,* 1624.

fell prostrate on the ground. His companions now bemoan his fate, he falls into a sound sleep, and they think he has expired. He wakes again, jumps up and declares that he has enjoyed the most delicious sensations, and that he never before felt himself so happy as after he had drunk the cup. He asks for more, his wish is granted; the whole assembly then imitate him, and all become intoxicated.

After this general intoxication had ceased, for they say that while it lasted the whites had confined themselves to their vessel, the man with the red clothes returned again, and distributed presents among them, consisting of beads, axes, hoes, and stockings such as the white people wear. They soon became familiar with each other, and began to converse by signs. The Dutch made them understand that they would not stay here, that they would return home again, but would pay them another visit the next year, when they would bring them more presents, and stay with them awhile; but as they could not live without eating, they should want a little land of them to sow seeds, in order to raise herbs and vegetables to put into their broth.

They went away as they had said, and returned in the following season, when both parties were much rejoiced to see each other; but the whites laughed at the Indians, seeing that they knew not the use of the axes and hoes they had given them the year before; for they had these hanging to their breasts as ornaments, and the stockings were made use of as tobacco pouches. The whites now put handles to the former for them, and cut trees down before their eyes, hoed up the ground, and put the stockings on their legs.

As the whites became daily more familiar with the Indians, they at last proposed to stay with them, and asked only for so much ground for a garden spot as, they said, the hide of a bullock would cover or encompass, which hide was spread before them. The Indians readily granted this apparently reasonable request; but the whites then took a knife, and beginning at one end of the hide, cut it up to a long rope, not thicker than a child's finger, so that by the time the whole was cut up it made a great heap; they then took the rope at one end and drew it gently along, carefully avoiding its breaking. It was drawn out into a circular form, and being enclosed at its ends, encompassed a large piece of ground. The Indians were surprised at the superior wit of the whites, but did not wish to contend with them about a little land, as they still had enough themselves.

The white and red men lived contentedly together for a long time, though the former from time to time asked for more land, which was readily obtained, and thus they gradually proceeded higher up the Mahicannittuck, until the Indians began to believe that they would soon want all their country, which in the end proved true.

THE PILGRIMS SET FORTH. *In 1609, the Pilgrims—a small band of religious dissenters who refused to conform to the laws of the Church of England—had left their homeland and settled in Holland. Eleven years later, they were finding life there so difficult that they decided to move on. William Bradford, who was to be governor of Plymouth Plantation for many years, was present on the day of departure, July 22, 1620, when the Pilgrims left Leyden en route for Southampton, where they were to transfer to the* Mayflower.

The time being come that they must depart, they were accompanied with most of their brethren out of the city, unto a town sundry miles off called Delftshaven, where the ship lay ready to receive them. So they left that goodly and pleasant city which had been their resting place near twelve years; but they knew they were pilgrims, and looked not much on those things, but lift up their eyes to the heavens, their dearest country, and quieted their spirits.

When they came to the place they found the ship and all things ready, and such of their friends as could not come with them followed after them, and sundry also came from Amsterdam to see them shipped and to take their leave of them. That night was spent with little sleep by the most, but with friendly entertainment and Christian discourse and other real expressions of true Christian love. The next day (the wind being fair) they went aboard and their friends with them, where truly doleful was the sight of that sad and mournful parting, to see what sighs and sobs and prayers did sound amongst them, what tears did gush from every eye, and pithy speeches pierced each heart; that sundry of the Dutch strangers that stood on the quay as spectators could not refrain from tears. Yet comfortable and sweet it was to see such lively and true expressions of dear and unfeigned love. But the tide, which stays for no man, calling them away that were thus loath to depart, their reverend pastor falling down on his knees (and they all with him) with watery cheeks commended them with most fervent prayers to the Lord and His blessing. And then with mutual embraces and many tears they took their leaves one of another, which proved to be the last leave to many of them.

GOD'S PROVIDENCE. *After several false starts, the* Mayflower *crossed the Atlantic in a voyage of sixty-five days. This account is also by William Bradford, governor of Plymouth.*

September 6. And now all being compact together in one ship [the Mayflower], they put to sea again with a prosperous wind, which continued divers days together, which was some encouragement unto them; yet, according to the usual manner, many were afflicted with seasickness. And I may not omit here a special work of God's providence. There was a proud and very profane young man, one of the seamen, of a lusty, able body, which made him the more haughty; he would alway be contemning the poor people in their sickness and cursing them daily with grievous execrations; and did not let to tell them that he hoped to help to cast half of them overboard before they came to their journey's end, and to make merry with what they had; and if he were by any gently reproved, he would curse and swear most bitterly. But it pleased God before they came half seas over, to smite this young man with a grievous disease, of which he died in a desperate manner, and so was himself the first that was thrown overboard. Thus his curses light on his own head, and it was an astonishment to all his fellows for they noted it to be the just hand of God upon him.

After they had enjoyed fair winds and weather for a season, they were encountered many times with cross winds and met with many fierce storms with which the ship was shrewdly shaken, and her upper works made very leaky. . . . In sundry of these storms the winds were so fierce and the seas so high, as they could not bear a knot of sail, but were forced to hull for divers days together. And in one of them, as they thus lay at hull in a mighty storm, a lusty young man called John Howland, coming upon some occasion above the gratings was, with a seele [lurch] of the ship, thrown into sea; but it pleased God that he caught hold of the topsail halyards which hung overboard and ran out at length. Yet he held his hold (though he was sundry fathoms under water) till he was hauled up by the same rope to the brim of the water, and then with a boat hook and other means got into the ship again and his life saved. And though he was something ill with it, yet he lived many years after and became a profitable member both in church and commonwealth. In all this voyage there died but one of the passengers, which was William Butten, a youth, servant to Samuel Fuller, when they drew near the coast.

But to omit other things (that I may be brief) after long beating at sea they fell with that land which is called Cape Cod; the which being made and certainly known to be it, they were not a little joyful. After some deliberation had amongst themselves and with the master of the ship, they tacked about and resolved to stand for the southward (the wind and weather being fair) to find some place about Hudson's River for their habitation. But after they had sailed that course about half the day, they fell amongst dangerous shoals and roaring breakers, and they were so far entangled therewith as they conceived themselves in great danger; and the wind shrinking upon them withal, they resolved to bear up again for the Cape and thought themselves happy to get out of those dangers before night overtook them, as by God's good providence they did. And the next day they got into the Cape Harbor where they rid in safety.

Being thus arrived in a good harbor, and brought safe to land, they fell upon their knees and blessed the God of Heaven who had brought them over the vast and furious ocean, and delivered them from all the perils and miseries thereof, again to set their feet on the firm and stable earth, their proper element.

THE HAND OF GOD. *Edward Johnson, the Puritan author of* Wonder-Working Providence of Sion's Saviour in New England, *explains why the Pilgrims met almost no opposition when they first settled in Cape Cod Bay.*

About the yeare 1618, a little before the removeall of that Church of Christ from Holland to Plimoth in New England, as the ancient Indians report, there befell a great mortality among them, the greatest that ever the memory of Father to Sonne tooke notice of, chiefly desolating those places, where the English afterward planted [settled]. The Country of Pockanoky, Agissawamg, it was almost wholly deserted, insomuch that the Neighbour Indians did abandon those places for feare of death. . . .

The Pecods (who retained the Name of a war-like people, till afterwards conquered by the English) were also smitten at this time. Their Disease being a sore Consumption, sweeping away whole Families, but chiefly young Men and Children, the very seeds of increase. Their Powwows, which are their Doctors, working partly by Charmes, and partly by Medicine, were much amazed to see their Wigwams lie full of dead Corpes, and that now neither Squantam nor Abbamocho could helpe, which are their good and bad God, and also their Powwows themselves were oft smitten with deaths stroke. Howling and much lamentation was heard among the living, who being possest with great feare, oftimes left their dead unburied, their manner being such, that they remove their habitations at death of any. This great mortality being an unwonted thing, feared them the more, because naturally the Country is very healthy. But by this meanes Christ (whose great and glorious workes the Earth throughout are altogether for the benefit of his Churches and chosen) not onely made roome for his people to plant; but also tamed the hard and cruell hearts of these barbarous Indians, insomuch that halfe a handfull of his people landing not long after in Plimoth-Plantation, found little resistance.

TAKING NO RISKS. *In October 1627, Isaack de Rasieres, chief commercial agent and secretary of the Dutch province of New Netherland, "a man of a fair and genteel behavior" in the words of Governor William Bradford, paid a friendly visit to Plymouth. Here is an extract from Rasieres' report on his visit, contained in a letter to a merchant in Amsterdam.*

New Plymouth lies on the slope of a hill stretching east towards the sea-coast, with a broad street about a cannon shot of 800 feet long, leading down the hill; with a crossing in the middle, northwards to the rivulet and southwards to the land. The houses are constructed of hewn planks, with gardens also enclosed behind and at the sides with hewn planks, so that their houses and court-yards are arranged in very good order, with a stockade against a sudden attack; and at the ends of the streets there are three wooden gates. In the centre, on the cross street, stands the governor's house, before which is a square stockade upon which four patereros [small, swivel-mounted cannon] are mounted, so as to enfilade the streets. Upon the hill they have a large square house, with a flat roof, made of thick sawn plank, stayed with oak beams, upon the top of which they have six cannon, which shoot iron balls of four and five pounds, and command the surrounding country. The lower part they use for their church, where they preach on Sundays and the usual holidays. They assemble by beat of drum, each with his musket or firelock, in front of the captain's door; they have their cloaks on, and place themselves in order, three abreast, and are led by a sergeant without beat of drum. Behind comes the governor, in a long robe; beside him, on the right hand, comes the preacher with his cloak on, and with a small cane in his hand; and so they march in good order, and each sets his arms down near him. Thus they are constantly on their guard night and day.

MASSACRE IN VIRGINIA. *Unlike the Pilgrims in Plymouth, the English who had settled at Jamestown, Virginia, were "placed stragglingly and scatteringly." This, in part, was because they believed they were on good terms with the local Indians, whose conversion to Christianity was one of the English colonists' professed purposes in coming to America. Captain John Smith tells what happened as a result of this overconfidence.*

On the Friday morning that fatall day, being the two and twentieth of March [1622], as also in the evening before, as at other times, they came unarmed into our houses, with Deere, Turkies, Fish, Fruits, and other provisions to sell us: yea in some places sat downe at breakfast with our people, whom immediatly with their owne tooles they slew most barbarously, not sparing either age or sex, man woman or childe; so sudden in their execution, that few or none discerned the weapon or blow that brought them to destruction. In which manner also they slew many of our people at severall works in the fields, well knowing in what places and quarters each of our men were, in regard of their familiaritie with us, for the effecting that great master-peece of worke their conversion: and by this meanes fell that fatall morning under the bloudy and barbarous hands of that perfidious and inhumane people, three hundred forty seven men, women and children; mostly by their own weapons. And not being content with their lives, they fell againe upon the dead bodies, making as well as they could a fresh murder, defacing, dragging, and mangling their dead carkases into many peeces, and carrying some parts away in derision, with base and brutish triumph. Neither yet did these beasts spare those amongst the rest well knowne unto them, from whom they had daily received many benefits; but spightfully also massacred them without any remorse or pitie. . . .

"That fatall morning," the Jamestown Massacre of March 22, 1622,
when there were killed "under the bloudy and barbarous hands of that perfidious
and inhumane people, three hundred forty-seven men, women and children,"
John Smith. Engraving by Theodore De Bry.

That worthy religious Gentleman Master George Thorp . . . did so
truly effect their conversion, that whosoever under him did them the
least displeasure, were punished severely. He thought nothing too
deare for them, he never denied them any thing; in so much that
when they complained that our Mastives did feare them, he to content
them in all things, caused some of them to be killed in their presence,
to the great displeasure of the owners, and would have had all the rest
gelt to make them the milder, might he have had his will. The King
[Opechancanough] dwelling but in a Cottage, he built him a faire
house after the English fashion, in which he tooke such pleasure,
especially in the locke and key, which he so admired, as locking and
unlocking his doore a hundred times a day, he thought no device in
the world comparable to it.

Thus insinuating himselfe into this Kings favour for his religious
purpose, he conferred oft with him about Religion; as many other in
this former Discourse had done; and this Pagan confessed to him (as
he did to them) our God was better than theirs, and seemed to be

much pleased with that Discourse, and of his company, and to requite all those courtesies. Yet this viperous brood did, as the sequel shewed, not onely murder him, but with such spight and scorne abused his dead corps as is unfitting to be heard with civill eares.

Captaine Nathaniel Powell one of the first Planters, a valiant Souldier . . . they not onely slew him and his family, but butcher-like hagled their bodies, and cut off his head, to expresse their uttermost height of cruelty. Another of the old company of Captaine Smith, called Nathaniel Causie, being cruelly wounded, and the Salvages about him, with an axe did cleave one of their heads, whereby the rest fled and he escaped: for they hurt not any that did either fight or stand upon their guard. In one place, where there was but two men that had warning of it, defended the house against sixty or more that assaulted it. Master Baldwin at Warraskoyack, his wife being so wounded, she lay for dead; yet by his oft discharging of his peece, saved her, his house, himselfe, and divers others. At the same time they came to one Master Harisons house, neere halfe a mile from Baldwines, where was Master Thomas Hamer with six men, and eighteene or nineteene women and children. Here the Salvages with many presents and faire perswasions, fained they came for Captain Ralfe Hamer to go to their King, then hunting in the woods: presently they sent to him, but he not comming as they expected, set fire of a Tobacco-house, and then came to tell them in the dwelling house of it to quench it; all the men ran towards it but Master Hamer, not suspecting any thing, whom the Salvages pursued, shot them full of arrowes, then beat out their braines. Hamer having finished a letter hee was a writing, followed after to see what was the matter, but quickly they shot an arrow in his back, which caused him to returne and barricade up the doores, whereupon the Salvages set fire on the house. Harisons Boy finding his Masters peece loaded, discharged it at randome, at which bare report the Salvages all fled. . . .

But for the better understanding of all things, you must remember these wilde naked natives live not in great numbers together; but dispersed, commonly in thirtie, fortie, fiftie, or sixtie in a company. Some places have two hundred, few places more, but many lesse; yet they had all warning given them one from another in all their habitations, though farre asunder, to meet at the day and houre appointed for our destruction at all our several Plantations; some directed to one place, some to another, all to be done at the time appointed, which they did accordingly. . . .

Six of the Counsell suffered under this treason, and the slaughter had beene universall, if God had not put it into the heart of an Indian, who lying in the house of one Pace, was urged by another Indian his

Brother, that lay with him the night before, to kill Pace, as he should doe Perry which was his friend, being so commanded from their King: telling him also how the next day the execution should be finished. Perrys Indian presently arose and reveales it to Pace, that used him as his sonne; and thus them that escaped was saved by this one converted Infidell. And though three hundred fortie seven were slaine, yet thousands of ours were by the meanes of this alone thus preserved; for which Gods name be praised for ever and ever.

Pace upon this, securing his house, before day rowed to James Towne, and told the Governor of it, whereby they were prevented, and at such other Plantations as possibly intelligence could be given: and where they saw us upon our guard, at the sight of a peece they ranne away; but the rest were most slaine, their houses burnt, such Armes and Munition as they found they took away, and some cattell also they destroied.

Thus have you heard the particulars of this massacre, which in those respects some say will be good for the Plantation, because now we have just cause to destroy them by all meanes possible. . . . Besides it is more easie to civilize them by conquest than faire meanes; for the one may be made at once, but their civilization will require a long time and much industry. The manner how to suppresse them is so often related and approved, I omit it here: And you have twenty examples of the Spaniards how they got the West-Indies, and forced the treacherous and rebellious Infidels to doe all manner of drudgery worke and slavery for them, themselves living like Souldiers upon the fruits of their labours.

THE CONQUISTADORS. *Among the "examples of the Spaniards" that Captain John Smith might have had in mind (in the previous entry) were those furnished by Francisco Vázquez de Coronado, who in 1540 led an expedition of three hundred Spanish cavalry and a thousand Indian allies north from Mexico in search of the fabulously rich Seven Cities of Cibola. In this extract from Pedro de Castañeda's account of the expedition, winter is just coming on as the army reaches Tiguex, a group of pueblo villages north of present-day Albuquerque. The "Turk" mentioned at the outset was a Pawnee guide from present-day Nebraska, so called because his headdress was thought to resemble a turban.*

The general went up the river from here, visiting the whole province, until he reached Tiguex, where he found Hernando de Alvarado and the Turk. He felt no slight joy at such good news, because the Turk said that in his country there was a river in the level country which was two leagues wide, in which there were fishes as big as horses, and large

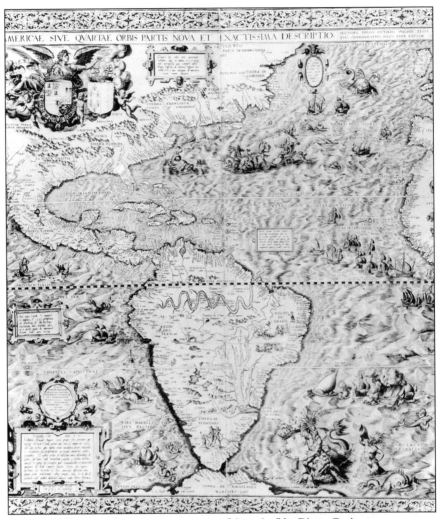

"A new and most accurate map of America" by Diego Gutierrez,
dated 1562—some twenty years after Coronado had explored
Texas and Kansas. Engraved by Hieronymous Cock.

numbers of very big canoes, with more than twenty rowers on a side,
and that they carried sails, and that their lords sat on the poop under
awnings, and on the prow they had a great golden eagle. He also said
that the lord of that country took his afternoon nap under a great tree
on which were hung a great number of little golden bells, which put
him to sleep as they swung in the air. He said also that everyone had
his ordinary dishes made of wrought plate, and the jugs and bowls
were of gold. He called gold *acochis*. For the present he was believed,
on account of the ease with which he told it and because they showed

him metal ornaments and he recognized them and said they were not gold, and he knew gold and silver very well and did not care anything about other metals.

The general sent Hernando de Alvarado back to Cicuye to demand some gold bracelets which this Turk said they had taken from him at the time they captured him. Alvarado went, and was received as a friend at the village, and when he demanded the bracelets they said they knew nothing at all about them, saying the Turk was deceiving him and was lying. Captain Alvarado, seeing that there were no other means, got the Captain Whiskers [probably a priest] and the governor to come to his tent, and when they had come he put them in chains. The villagers prepared to fight, and let fly their arrows, denouncing Hernando de Alvarado, and saying that he was a man who had no respect for peace and friendship. Hernando de Alvarado started back to Tiguex, where the general kept them prisoners for more than six months.

The people of Tiguex did not feel well about this seizure. In addition to this, the general wished to obtain some clothing to divide among his soldiers, and for this purpose he summoned one of the chief Indians of Tiguex. . . . The general told him that he must furnish about three hundred or more pieces of cloth, which he needed to give his people. The chief said that he was not able to do this, but that it pertained to the governors; and that besides this, they would have to consult together and divide it among the villages, and . . . make the demand of each town separately. The general did this, and ordered certain of the gentlemen who were with him to go and make the demand; and as there were twelve villages, some of them went on one side of the river and some on the other. As they were in very great need, they did not give the natives a chance to consult about it, but when they came to a village they demanded what they had to give, so that they could proceed at once. Thus these people could do nothing except take off their own cloaks and give them to make up the number demanded of them. And some of the soldiers who were in these parties, when the collectors gave them some blankets or cloaks which were not such as they wanted, if they saw any Indian with a better one on, they exchanged with him without more ado, not stopping to find out the rank of the man they were stripping, which caused not a little hard feeling.

Besides what I have just said, one whom I will not name, out of regard for him, left the village where the camp was and went to another village about a league distant, and seeing a pretty woman there he called her husband down to hold his horse by the bridle while he went up; and as the village was entered by the upper story, the Indian supposed he was going to some other part of it. While he was there the

Indian heard some slight noise, and then the Spaniard came down, took his horse, and went away. The Indian went up and learned that he had violated, or tried to violate, his wife, and so he came with the important men of the town to complain that a man had violated his wife, and he told how it had happened. When the general made all his soldiers and the persons who were with him come together, the Indian did not recognize the man, either because he had changed his clothes or for whatever other reason there may have been, but he said he could tell the horse, because he had held his bridle. So he was taken to the stables, and found the horse, and said that the master of the horse must be the man. He [the owner] denied doing it, seeing that he had not been recognized, and it may be that the Indian was mistaken in the horse; anyway, he went off without getting any satisfaction. The next day one of the Indians, who was guarding the horses of the army, came running in, saying that a companion of his had been killed, and that the Indians of the country were driving off the horses toward their villages. The Spaniards tried to collect the horses again, but many were lost, besides seven of the general's mules.

The next day Don Garcia Lopez de Cardenas went to see the villages and talk with the natives. He found the villages closed by palisades and a great noise inside, the horses being chased as in a bull fight and shot with arrows. They were all ready for fighting. Nothing could be done, because they would not come down on to the plain and the villages are so strong that the Spaniards could not dislodge them. The general then ordered Don Garcia Lopez de Cardenas to go and surround one village with all the rest of the force. This village was the one where the greatest injury had been done and where the affair with the Indian woman occurred. Several captains who had gone on in advance with the general, Juan de Saldivar and Barrionuevo and Diego Lopez and Melgosa, took the Indians so much by surprise that they gained the upper story, with great danger, for they wounded many of our men from within the houses. Our men were on top of the houses in great danger for a day and a night and part of the next day, and they made some good shots with their crossbows and muskets. The horsemen on the plain with many of the Indian allies from New Spain smoked them out from the cellars into which they had broken, so that they begged for peace.

Pablo de Melgosa and Diego Lopez . . . were left on the roof and answered the Indians with the same signs they were making for peace, which was to make a cross. The Indians then put down their arms and received pardon. They were taken to the tent of Don Garcia Lopez de Cardenas who, according to what he [later] said, did not know about the peace and thought that they had given themselves up of their own accord because they had been conquered. As he had been ordered by the general not to take them alive, but to make an example of them so that the other natives would fear the Spaniards, he ordered 200 stakes to be prepared at once to burn them alive. Nobody told him about the peace that had been granted them, for the soldiers knew as little as he, and those who should have told him about it remained silent. . . . When the enemies saw that the Spaniards were binding them and beginning to roast them, about a hundred men who were in the tent began to struggle and defend themselves with what there was there and with the stakes they could seize. Our men who were on foot attacked the tent on all sides, so that there was great confusion around it, and then the horsemen chased those who escaped. As the country was level, not a man of them remained alive, unless it was some who remained hidden in the village and escaped that night to spread throughout the country the news that the strangers did not respect the peace they had made, which afterward proved a great misfortune. After this was over, it began to snow, and they abandoned the village and returned to the camp.

THE NEW WORLD. *Although most Europeans spoke of the Indians as savages, there were many who were keenly interested in the customs and languages of a people who, some thought, might well be the Lost Tribes of Israel. One of these observers was Dominie Johannes Megalopensis of the Dutch Reformed Church, who, starting in 1642, was minister to the settlers at Fort Orange (now Albany, New York) and also served as missionary to the local Indians.*

The principal nation of all the savages and Indians hereabouts with which we have the most intercourse, is the Mahakuaas [Mohawks], who have laid all the other Indians near us under contribution. This nation has a very difficult language, and it costs me great pains to learn it, so as to be able to speak and preach in it fluently. There is no Christian here who understands the language thoroughly; those who have lived here long can use a kind of jargon just sufficient to carry on trade with it, but they do not understand the fundamentals of the language. I am making a vocabulary of the Mahakuaas' language, and when I am among them I ask them how things are called; but as they are very stupid, I sometimes cannot make them understand what I want. Moreover when they tell me, one tells me the word in the infinitive mood, another in the indicative; one in the first, another in the second person; one in the present, another in the preterit. So I stand oftentimes and look, but do not know how to put it down.

When I first observed that they pronounced their words so differently, I asked the commissary of the company what it meant. He answered me that he did not know, but imagined they changed their language every two or three years; I argued against this that it could never be that a whole nation should change its language with one consent;—and, although he has been connected with them here these twenty years, he can afford me no assistance.

The people and Indians here in this country are like us Dutchmen in body and stature; some of them have well formed features, bodies and limbs; they all have black hair and eyes, but their skin is yellow. In summer they go naked, having only their private parts covered with a patch. The children and young folks to ten, twelve and fourteen years of age go stark naked. In winter, they hang about them simply an undressed deer or bear or panther skin; or they take some beaver and otter skins, wild cat, raccoon, martin, otter, mink, squirrel or such like skins, which are plenty in this country, and sew some of them to others, until it is a square piece, and that is then a garment for them; or they buy of us Dutchmen two and a half ells of duffel, and that they hang simply about them, just as it was torn off, without sewing it, and walk away with it. They look at themselves constantly, and think they are very fine. They make themselves stockings and also shoes of deer skin, or they take leaves of their corn, and plait them together and use them for shoes. The women, as well as the men, go with their heads bare. The women let their hair grow very long, and tie it together a little, and let it hang down their backs. The men have a long lock of hair hanging down, some on one side of the head, and some on both sides. On the top of their heads they have a streak of hair from the forehead to the neck, about the breadth of three fingers, and this they shorten until it is about two or three fingers long, and it stands right on end like a cock's comb or hog's bristles; on both sides of this cock's comb they cut all the hair short, except the aforesaid locks, and they also leave on the bare places here and there small locks, such as are in sweeping-brushes, and then they are in fine array.

They likewise paint their faces red, blue, etc., and then they look like the Devil himself. They smear their heads with bear's-grease, which they all carry with them for this purpose in a small basket; they say they do it to make their hair grow better and to prevent their having lice. When they travel, they take with them some of their maize, a kettle, a wooden bowl, and a spoon; these they pack up and hang on their backs. Whenever they are hungry, they forthwith make a fire and cook; they can get fire by rubbing pieces of wood against one another, and that very quickly.

They generally live without marriage; and if any of them have wives, the marriage continues no longer than seems good to one of the parties, and then they separate, and each takes another partner. I have seen those who had parted, and afterwards lived a long time with others, leave these again, seek their former partners, and again be one pair. And, though they have wives, yet they will not leave off whoring; and if they can sleep with another man's wife, they think it a brave thing. The women are exceedingly addicted to whoring; they will lie with a man for the value of one, two, or three *schillings*, and our Dutchmen run after them very much.

The women, when they have been delivered, go about immediately afterwards, and be it ever so cold, they wash themselves and the young child in the river or the snow. They will not lie down (for they say that if they did they would soon die), but keep going about. They are obliged to cut wood, to travel three or four leagues with the child; in short, they walk, they stand, they work, as if they had not lain in, and we cannot see that they suffer any injury by it; and we sometimes try to persuade our wives to lie-in so, and that the way of lying-in in Holland is a mere fiddle-faddle. . . . The women are obliged to prepare the land, to mow, to plant, and do everything; the men do nothing, but hunt, fish, and make war upon their enemies. They are very cruel towards their enemies in time of war; for they first bite off the nails of the fingers of their captives, and cut off some joints, and sometimes even whole fingers; after that, the captives are forced to sing and dance before them stark naked; and finally, they roast their prisoners dead before a slow fire for some days, and then eat them up. The common people eat the arms, buttocks and trunk, but the chiefs eat the head and the heart.

Our Mahakas carry on great wars against the Indians of Canada, on the River Saint Lawrence, and take many captives, and sometimes there are French Christians among them. Last year, our Indians got a great booty from the French on the River Saint Lawrence, and took three Frenchmen, one of whom was a Jesuit. They killed one, but the Jesuit (whose left thumb was cut off, and all the nails and parts of his fingers were bitten,) we released, and sent him to France by a yacht which was going to our country. They spare all the children from ten to twelve years old, and all the women whom they take in war, unless the women are very old, and then they kill them too. Though they are so very cruel to their enemies, they are very friendly to us, and we have no dread of them. We go with them into the woods, we meet with each other, sometimes at an hour or two's walk from any houses, and think no more about it than as if we met with a Christian. They sleep by us, too, in our chambers before our beds. I have had eight at once lying and sleeping upon the floor near my bed, for it is their custom to sleep simply on the bare ground, and to have only a stone or a bit of wood under their heads. In the evening, they go to bed very soon after they have supped; but early in the morning, before day begins to break, they are up again. They are very slovenly and dirty; they wash neither their face nor hands, but let all remain upon their yellow skin, and look like hogs. Their bread is Indian corn beaten to pieces between two stones, of which they make a cake, and bake it in the ashes: their other victuals are venison, turkies, hares, bears, wild cats, their own dogs, etc. The fish they cook just as they get them out of the water without cleansing; also the entrails of deer with all their contents, which they cook a little; and if the intestines are then too tough, they take one end in their mouth, and the other in their hand, and between hand and mouth they separate and eat them. So they do commonly with the flesh, for they carve a little piece and lay it on the fire, as long as one would need to walk from his house to church, and then it is done; and then they bite into it so that the blood runs along their mouths. They can also take a piece of bear's-fat as large as two fists, and eat it clear without bread or anything else.

They are entire strangers to all religion, but they have a *Tharonhijouaagon* (whom they also otherwise call *Athzoockkuatoriaho*), that is, a Genius [spirit], whom they esteem in the place of God; but they do not serve him or make offerings to him. They worship and present offerings to the Devil, whom they call *Otskon,* or *Aireskuoni.* If they have any bad luck in war, they catch a bear, which they cut in pieces, and roast, and that they offer up to their *Aireskuoni,* saying in substance, the following words: "Oh! great and mighty Aireskuoni, we confess that we have offended against thee, inasmuch as we have not killed and eaten our captive enemies;—forgive us this. We promise that we will kill and eat all the captives we shall hereafter take as certainly as we have killed, and now eat this bear." Also when the weather is very hot, and there comes a cooling breeze, they cry out directly, *Asoronusi, asoronusi, Otskon aworouhsi reinnuha;* that is, "I thank thee, I thank thee, devil, I thank thee, little uncle!" If they are sick, or have a pain or soreness anywhere in their limbs, and I ask them what ails them they say that the Devil sits in their body, or in the sore places, and bites them there; so that they attribute to the Devil at once the accidents which befall them; they have otherwise no religion. When we pray they laugh at us. Some of them despise it entirely; and some, when we tell them what we do when we pray, stand astonished. When we deliver a sermon, sometimes ten or twelve of them, more or less, will attend, each having a long tobacco pipe, made by himself, in his mouth, and will stand awhile and look, and afterwards ask me what I am doing and what I want, that I stand there alone and make so many words, while none of the rest may speak. I tell them that I am admonishing the Christians, that they must not steal, nor commit lewdness, nor get drunk, nor commit murder, and that they too ought not to do these things; and that I intend in process of time to preach the same to them and come to them in their own country and castles (about three days' journey from here, further inland), when I am acquainted with their language. Then they say I do well to teach the Christians; but immediately add, *Diatennon jawij Assirioni, hagiouisk,* that is, "Why do so many Christians do these things?" They call us *Assirioni,* that is, cloth-makers, or *Charistooni,* that is, iron-workers, because our people first brought cloth and iron among them.

THE WONDERS OF NEW ENGLAND. *The English naturalist John Josselyn wrote two books:* An Account of Two Voyages to New England *and* New England's Rarities Discovered, *published in the seventeenth century. Here, drawn from both books, are some of his observations, first on the fauna and flora, then on the Indians.*

The *Wolf* seeketh his mate and goes a clicketing [mating] at the same season with *Foxes,* and bring forth their whelps as they do, but their kennels are under thick bushes by great Trees in remote places by the swamps; he is to be hunted as the *Fox* from *Holyrood* day till the *Annunciation.* . . . . Their eyes shine by night as a Lanthorn. The Fangs of a *Wolf* hung about childrens necks keep them from frighting, and are very good to rub their gums with when they are breeding of Teeth; the gall of a *Wolf* is soveraign for swelling of the sinews; the fiants or dung of a *Wolf* drunk with white-wine helpeth the *Collick.*

The *Turkie,* who is blacker than ours; I have heard several credible persons affirm, they have seen *Turkie Cocks* that have weighed forty, yea sixty pound; but out of my personal experimental knowledge I can assure you, that I have eaten my share of a *Turkie Cock,* that when he was pull'd and garbidg'd, weighed thirty pound; and I have also seen threescore broods of young *Turkies* on the side of a Marsh, sunning of themselves in a morning betimes, but this was thirty years since, the *English* and the *Indian* having now destroyed the breed, so that 'tis very rare to meet with a wild *Turkie* in the Woods; but some of the *English* bring up great store of the wild kind, which remain about their Houses as tame as ours in *England.*

The *Goose,* of which there are three kinds; the *Gray Goose,* the *White Goose,* and the *Brant:* the *Goose* will live a long time; I once found in a *White Goose* three Hearts, she was a very old one, and so tuff, that we gladly gave her over although exceeding well roasted.

The *Wobble,* an ill shaped Fowl, having no long Feathers in their Pinions, which is the reason they cannot fly, not much unlike the *Pengwin;* they are in the Spring very fat, or rather oyly, but pull'd and garbidg'd, and laid to the Fire to roast, they yield not one drop. . . . They are very soveraign for *Aches.*

A Narrow Escape from a Snake

In 1672, John Josselyn describes "The *Rattle Snake*, who poysons with a Vapour that comes through two crooked Fangs." Almost 200 years later, the snake is depicted in an engraving from *The Crockett Almanacks*, published 1835–1856, which featured the fabled adventures of Daniel Boone, Mike Fink and other frontiersmen, including David Crockett himself.

The *Moose Deer*, which is a very goodly Creature, some of them twelve foot high, with exceeding fair Horns with broad Palms, some of them two fathom from the tip of one Horn to the other; they commonly have three *Fawns* at a time; their flesh is not dry like Deers flesh, but moist and lushious somewhat like Horse flesh (as they judge that have tasted of both) but very wholsome. The flesh of their *Fawns* is an incomparable dish, beyond the flesh of an Asses Foal so highly esteemed by the *Romans,* or that of young Spaniel Puppies so much cried up in our days in *France* and *England.*

The *Soile or Sea Calf,* a Creature that brings forth her young ones upon dry land, but at other times keeps in the Sea preying upon Fish. The Oyl of it is much used by the *Indians,* who eat of it with their Fish, and anoint their limbs therewith, and their Wounds and Sores: It is very good for Scalds and Burns; and the fume of it, being cast upon Coals, will bring Women out of the Mother Fits. The Hair upon the young ones is white, and as soft as silk; the Skins, with the Hair on, are good to make Gloves for the Winter.

The *Rattle Snake,* who poysons with a Vapour that comes through two crooked Fangs in their Mouth; the hollow of these Fangs are as black as Ink: The *Indians,* when weary with travelling, will take them up with their bare hands, laying hold with one hand behind their Head, with the other taking hold of their Tail, and with their teeth tear off the Skin of their Backs, and feed upon them alive; which they say refresheth them.

They have Leafs of Fat in their Bellies, which is excellent to annoint frozen Limbs, and for Aches and Bruises wondrous soveraign. Their Hearts swallowed fresh is a good Antidote against their Venome, and their Liver (the Gall taken out) bruised and applied to their Bitings is a present Remedy.

The *Indesses* that are young, are some of them very comely, having good features, their faces plump and round, and generally plump of their Bodies, as are the men likewise, and as soft and smooth as a mole-skin, of reasonable good complexions, but that they dye themselves tawnie, many pretty Brownettos and spider finger'd Lasses may be seen amongst them. The *Vetula's* or old women are lean and uglie, all of them are of a modest demeanor, considering their Savage breeding; and indeed do shame our *English* rusticks whose rudeness in many things exceedeth theirs.

Wives they have two or three, according to the ability of their bodies and strength of their concupiscence, who have the easiest labours of any women in the world; they will go out when their time is come alone, carrying a board with them two foot long, and a foot and a half broad, bor'd full of holes on each side, having a foot beneath like a Jack that we pull Boots off with; on the top of the board a broad strap of leather which they put over their forehead, the board hanging at their back; when they are come to a Bush or a Tree that they fancy they lay them down and are delivered in a trice, not so much as groaning for it, they wrap the child up in a young *Beaver*-skin with his heels close to his britch, leaving a little hole if it be a Boy for his Cock to peep out at; and lace him down to the board upon his back, his knees resting upon the foot beneath, then putting the strap of leather upon their fore-head with the infant hanging at their back, home they trudge.

They acknowledge a God who they call *Squantam*, but worship him they do not, because (they say) he will do them no harm. But *Abbamocho* or *Cheepie* many times smites them with incurable Diseases, scares them with his Apparitions and panick Terrours, by reason whereof they live in a wretched consternation worshipping the Devil for fear. One black *Robin* an *Indian* sitting down in a Corn field belonging to the house where I resided, ran out of his *Wigwam* frighted with the apparition of two infernal spirits in the shape of *Mohawkes*. Another time two *Indians* and an *Indess*, came running into our house crying out they should all dye, *Cheepie* was gone over the field gliding in the Air with a long rope hanging from one of his legs: we askt them what he was like, they said all wone *Englishman,* clothed with hat and coat, shooes and stockins, &c.

A HEALTHFULL PLACE. *From the very first, the new settlers wrote home to encourage others to join them. One of these early promotional writers was the Reverend Francis Higginson, a Puritan clergyman who moved to Salem in 1629, where he died the following year.*

The Temper of the Aire of *New-England* is one speciall thing that commends this place. Experience doth manifest that there is hardly a more healthfull place to be found in the World that agreeth better with our English Bodyes. Many that have been weake and sickly in old *England,* by comming hither have beene thoroughly healed and growne healthfull and strong. For here is an extraordinarie cleere and dry Aire that is of a most healing nature to all such as are of a Cold, Melancholy, Flegmatick, Reumaticke temper of Body. None can more truly speake hereof by their owne experience than my selfe. My Friends that knew me can well tell how verie sickly I have been and continually in Physick, being much troubled with a tormenting paine through an extraordinarie weaknesse of my Stomacke, and aboundance of Melancholicke humors; but since I came hither on this Voyage, I thanke God I have had perfect health, and freed from paine and vomitings, having a Stomacke to digest the hardest and coarsest fare who before could not eat finest meat.

FREE LAND. *An extract from "Conditions propounded by the Lord Baltemore, to such as shall goe or adventure into Maryland." They were included in* A Relation of Maryland, *published in London in 1635, and for sale at "Master William Peasley, Esq., his house, on the back-side of Drury-Lane, neere the Cock-Pit Playhouse."*

Any married man that shall transport himselfe, his wife and children shall have assigned unto him, his heires and assignes for ever, in freehold, (as aforesaid) for himselfe 100 acres; and for his wife 100 acres; and for every child that he shall carry over, under the age of 16 yeares, 50 acres; paying for a quit rent 12 pence for every fifty acres.

Any woman that shall transport herselfe or any children, under the age of six yeeres, shall have the like Conditions as aforesaid.

SOME MORE WELCOME THAN OTHERS. *After spending several years at Fort Orange (now Albany, New York), Dominie Johannes Megalopensis moved down to New Amsterdam. From there, in 1655, he wrote home to his superiors "the Reverend, Pious and very Learned Deputies in the Classis of Amsterdam."*

Some Jews came from Holland last summer, in order to trade. Later some Jews came upon the same ship as Dominie Polheymius; they were healthy, but poor. It would have been proper, that they should have been supported by their own people, but they have been at our charge, so that we have had to spend several hundred guilders for their support. They came several times to my house, weeping and bemoaning their misery. When I directed them to the Jewish merchant, they said, that he would not lend them a single stiver. Some more have come from Holland this spring. They report that many more of that same lot would follow, and then they would build here a synagogue. This causes among the congregation here a great deal of complaint and murmuring. These people have no other God than the Mammon of unrighteousness, and no other aim than to get possession of Christian property, and to overcome all other merchants by drawing all trade towards themselves. Therefore we request your Reverences to obtain from the Messrs. Directors, that these godless rascals, who are of no benefit to the country, but look at everything for their own profit, may be sent away from here. For as we have here Papists, Mennonites and Lutherans among the Dutch; also many Puritans or Independents, and many atheists and various other servants of Baal among the English under this Government, who conceal themselves under the name of Christians; it would create a still greater confusion, if the obstinate and immovable Jews came to settle here.

In closing I commend your Reverences with your families to the protection of God, who will bless us and all of you in the service of the divine word.

PROSPERITY IN NEW YORK. *From* A Brief Description of New York, *by Daniel Denton, published in London in 1670. Denton was the son of the Reverend Richard Denton, the first minister in Hempstead, Long Island; in 1665 he was a member of the General Assembly of Deputies which drew up the "Duke's Laws"—English laws for the newly English colony of New York.*

I may say, & say truly, that if there be any terrestrial happiness to be had by people of all ranks, especially of an inferior rank, it must certainly be here: here any one may furnish himself with land, & live rent-free, yea, with such a quantity of Land, that he may weary himself with walking over his fields of Corn, and all sorts of Grain: & let his stock of Cattel amount to some hundreds, he needs not fear their want of pasture in the Summer or Fodder in the Winter, the Woods affording sufficient supply. For the *Summer* season, where you have grass as high as a man's knees, nay, as high as his waste, interlaced with Pea-vines and other weeds that Cattel much delight in, as much as a man can press through; and these woods also every mile or half-mile are furnished with fresh ponds, brooks or rivers, where all sorts of Cattel, during the heat of the day, do quench their thirst and cool themselves. . . . Here those which Fortune hath frown'd upon in *England,* to deny them an inheritance amongst their Brethren, or such as by their utmost labors can scarcely procure a living, I say such may procure here inheritances of lands & possessions, stock themselves with all sorts of Cattel, enjoy the benefit of them whilst they live, & leave them to the benefit of their children when they die.

What shall I say more? you shall scarce see a house, but the South side is begirt with Hives of Bees, which increase after an incredible manner: That I must needs say, that if there be any terrestrial *Canaans,* 'tis surely here, where all the Land floweth with milk & Honey. The inhabitants are blest with Peace & plenty, blessed in their Countrey, blessed in their Fields, blessed in the Fruit of their bodies, in the fruit of their grounds, in the increase of their Cattel, Horses and Sheep, blessed in their Basket, & in their store; In a word, blessed in whatsoever they take in hand, or go about, the Earth yielding plentiful increases to all their painful labours.

THE CHARMS OF PENNSYLVANIA. *Another writer of promotional literature was Gabriel Thomas, whose* Account of the Province and Country of Pensilvania *was published in London in 1698.*

Of Lawyers and Physicians I shall say nothing, because this Countrey is very Peaceable and Healt[h]y; long may it so continue and never have occasion for the Tongue of the one, nor the Pen of the other, both equally destructive to Mens Estates and Lives. . . . Labouring-Men have commonly here, between 14 and 15 Pounds a Year, and their Meat, Drink, Washing and Lodging; and by the Day their Wages is generally between Eighteen Pence and Half a Crown, and Diet also; But in Harvest they have usually between Three and Four Shillings each Day, and Diet. The Maid Servants Wages is commonly betwixt Six and Ten Pounds per Annum, with very good Accommodation. And for the Women who get their Livelihood by their own Industry, their Labour is very dear, for I can buy in London a Cheese-Cake for Two Pence, bigger than theirs at that price, when at the same time their Milk is as cheap as we can buy it in London, and their Flour cheaper by one half.

Corn and Flesh, and what else serves Man for Drink, Food and Rayment, is much cheaper here than in England, or elsewhere; but the chief reason why Wages of Servants of all sorts is much higher here than there, arises from the great Fertility and Produce of the Place; besides, if these large Stipends were refused them, they would quickly set up for themselves, for they can have Provision very cheap, and Land for a very small matter, or next to nothing in comparison of the Purchase of Lands in England.

The Christian Children born here are generally well-favoured, and Beautiful to behold; I never knew any come into the World with the least blemish on any part of its Body, being in the general, observ'd to be better Natur'd, Milder, and more tender Hearted than those born in England. . . . Jealousie among Men is here very rare, and Barrenness among Women hardly to be heard of, nor are old Maids to be met with; for all commonly Marry before they are Twenty Years of Age, and seldom any young Married Woman but hath a Child in her Belly, or one upon her Lap.

What I have delivr'd concerning this Province, is indisputably true, I was an Eye-Witness to it all, for I went in the first Ship that was bound from England for that Countrey, since it received the Name of Pensilvania, which was in the Year 1681.

A BONNY COUNTRY. *From a letter written by James Murray, a recent immigrant, dated November 7, 1737, and addressed "For the Kingdom of Ereland, in the North of Ereland, near to Aughnacloy, in the County of Tyrone, To Baptist Boyd, the Reverend Minister of the Gospel, in the Parish of Aughelow. Let aw Persons that see this, tak Care to send it to the Reverend Baptist Boyd, Minister of Gospel, in the Parish of Aughelow in the County of Tyrone, living near Aughnacloy. With Care."*

Reverend Baptist Boyd,

Read this Letter, and look, and tell aw the poor Folk of your Place, that God has open'd a Door for their Deliverance; for here is ne Scant of Bread here, and if your Sons *Samuel and James Boyd* wad but come here, they wad het [get] more Money in ane Year for teechin a Letin Skulle, nor ye yersell wad get for Three Years Preechin whar ye are. . . . Ye ken I had but sma Learning when I left ye, and now wad ye think it, I hea 20 Pund a Year for being a Clark to *York Meeting-House*, and I keep a Skulle for wee Weans: The young Foke in Ereland are aw but a Pack of Couards, for I will tell ye in short, this is a bonny Country, and aw Things grows here that ever I did see grow in Ereland; and wee hea Cows and Sheep and Horses plenty here, and Goats, and Deers, and Raccoons, and Moles, and Bevers, and Fish, and Fouls of aw Sorts: Trades are aw gud here, a Wabster gets 12 Pence a Yeard, a Labourer gets 4 Shillings and 5 Pence a Day, a Lass gets 4 Shillings and 6 Pence a Week for spinning on the Wee Wheel, a Carpenter gets 6 Shillings a Day, and a Tailor gets 20 Shillings for making a Suit of Cleaths. . . . Desire my Fether and Mether too, and my Three Sisters to come here,

and ye may acquaint them, there are Lads enough here, and bid my
Brether come, and I will pay their Passage; Desire *James Gibson* to sell
aw he has and come, and I weel help him too. . . .

A WARNING. *In 1750, Gottlieb Mittelberger, a professional organist, left his
native Württemberg and traveled to Philadelphia. After a fairly short stay, he
returned to Germany, where he wrote* Reise nach Pennsylvanien *(A Journey
to Pennsylvania) to warn his fellow countrymen of how harsh and expensive
the journey could be and of what was likely to happen to "redemptioners": those
who traveled on credit, which they redeemed on arrival by being sold off to masters for several years.*

When the ship finally weighs anchor in Cowes in Old England, then
the long voyage and the real misery begin. Unless they have a good
wind, the voyage can take eight, nine, ten or twelve weeks, and even
with a very good wind it lasts seven weeks.

During the voyage the ship is full of misery—foul smells, fumes, horror, vomiting, sea-sickness of every kind, fever, dysentery, headaches,
heat, constipation, boils, scurvy, cancers, mouth-rot and so on, all of it
caused by the old and highly-salted condition of the food, especially the
meat, and the foul water, so that many die wretchedly. Lice are so abundant, especially on sick people, that they have to be scraped off their
bodies. This misery reaches its climax when, in addition to everything
else, a storm rages for two or three nights in succession, and everyone is
convinced that the ship is about to sink.

It is impossible to describe what happens during the voyage to
women in childbirth and to their innocent offspring. Very few escape
with their lives. One day on board our ship, during a great storm, a
woman died while in labor. She was so far back in the stern of the ship
that it was impossible to bring her body forward, and it was pushed
through a porthole into the sea.

Few children between the ages of one and seven survive the voyage, and parents must often watch as their offspring suffer miserably
before dying and being thrown into the ocean. I myself saw this miserable fate overtake thirty-two children on board our vessel. The grief of
the parents is all the greater in that their children do not find repose
in the earth, but are devoured by the predatory fish of the sea.
Children who have not had measles or smallpox usually get them on
board and for the most part perish as a result. Accidents also often
happen on these ships, especially falls in which people become crippled for life.

When the ship finally arrives at Philadelphia only those who have
paid their passage or can give good security are allowed to disembark.
The others have to remain on board until they are purchased.

Passengers who are sick fare worst in this business; many of them remain on board and in sight of the city for another two or three weeks. During this time many of them die.

This is how the traffic in human beings is conducted. Every day Englishmen, Dutchmen, and High Germans come from the city of Philadelphia and other places and go on board the newly arrived ship. From among the healthy they pick out those who are suitable for their purposes and then negotiate with them the length of service needed to pay off the cost of their passage. When agreement is reached, adults bind themselves by written contract to serve for three, four, five, or six years, according to their age and health. Young people between the ages of ten and fifteen have to serve until they are twenty-one.

Many parents, to pay their fares in this way, have to barter away their children as if they were cattle. And since the fathers and mothers often do not know where their children's masters live, or even who they are, it often happens that parents and children do not see each other again for many years, and sometimes never.

A wife is responsible for her sick husband and a husband for his sick wife. If the husband or the wife should die after having come more than halfway, then the surviving spouse must pay not only his or her own fare, but also the fare of the deceased. If both parents die at sea having come more than halfway, then their children must be responsible for their own fares as well as those of their parents, and must serve a master until they are twenty-one years old. When their term of service is completed, they receive at parting a suit of clothing and, if it has been so stipulated in their contract, a man also gets a horse and a woman gets a cow.

If someone runs away from a master who has been treating him harshly, he cannot get far. Runaways are soon recaptured, and those who arrest and return them get a good reward. For every day that a runaway is absent from his master he must serve an extra week, for every week an extra month, and for every month half a year.

Work is hard in this new land. For the most part it involves cutting wood, felling oak trees, and clearing great tracts of forest, roots and all. Europeans who have been purchased must work hard all the time; and thus they learn that oak tree stumps are just as hard in America as they are in Germany.

So let him who wants to earn his bread honestly and like a Christian, and who in his native country can do so only by working with his hands, stay *there* rather than come to America. People who let themselves be talked into leaving home and crossing the ocean are complete fools if they really believe that in America or Pennsylvania roasted pigeons will fly into their mouths without their having to work for them.

THE SLAVE TRADE. *Much of the slave trade was in the hands of the English, who had established trading posts at Bonny and other ports on the west coast of Africa. From there the slave ships crossed to the West Indies, where their cargoes were usually sold wholesale to dealers, who in turn sold the slaves to plantations on the other islands or on the American mainland. Alexander Falconbridge, whose account was written as testimony for the Anti-Slavery Society, was an English physician who served as ship's doctor on various slave ships in the 1780s.*

After permission has been obtained for *breaking trade,* as it is termed, the captains go ashore . . . to examine the Negroes that are exposed to sale, and to make their purchases. The unhappy wretches thus disposed of, are bought by the black traders at fairs, which are held for that purpose, at the distance of upwards of two hundred miles from the sea coast; and these fairs are said to be supplied from an interior part of the country. Many Negroes, upon being questioned relative to the places of their nativity, have asserted, that they have travelled during the revolution of several moons (their usual method of calculating time), before they have reached the places they were purchased by the black traders. At these fairs, which are held at uncertain periods, but generally every six weeks, several thousands are frequently exposed to sale, who had been collected from all parts of the country for a very considerable distance round. While I was upon the coast, during one of the voyages I made, the black traders brought down, in different canoes, from twelve to fifteen hundred Negroes, which had been purchased at one fair. They consisted chiefly of men and boys, the women seldom exceeding a third of the whole number. . . .

There is great reason to believe, that most of the Negroes shipped off from the coast of Africa, are *kidnapped.* But the extreme care taken by the black traders to prevent the Europeans from gaining any intelligence of their modes of proceeding; the great distance inland from whence the Negroes are brought; and our ignorance of their language (with which, very frequently, the black traders themselves are equally unacquainted), prevent our obtaining such information on this head as we could wish. I have, however, by means of occasional inquiries, made through interpreters, procured some intelligence relative to the point. . . . From these I shall select the following striking instances: While I was in employ on board one of the slave ships, a Negro informed me that being one evening invited to drink with some of the black traders, upon his going away, they attempted to seize him. As he was very active, he evaded their design, and got out of their hands. He was, however, prevented from effecting his escape by a large dog, which laid hold of him, and compelled him to submit. These creatures

On average, one out of eight slaves died during the crossing. Slave ships were trailed by schools of man-eating sharks. Wood engraving from Mrs. A. M. French's *Slavery in South Carolina and the Ex-Slaves*, 1862.

are kept by many of the traders for that purpose; and being trained to the inhuman sport, they appear to be much pleased with it.

I was likewise told by a Negro woman that as she was on her return home, one evening, from some neighbors, to whom she had been making a visit by invitation, she was kidnapped; and, notwithstanding she was big with child, sold for a slave. This transaction happened a considerable way up the country, and she had passed through the hands of several purchasers before she reached the ship. A man and his son, according to their own information, were seized by professed kidnappers, while they were planting yams, and sold for slaves. This likewise happened in the interior parts of the country, and after passing through several hands, they were purchased for the ship to which I belonged. It frequently happens that those who kidnap others are themselves, in their turns, seized and sold.

Continual enmity is thus fostered among the Negroes of Africa, and all social intercourse between them destroyed, which most assuredly would not be the case, had they not these opportunities of finding a ready sale for each other.

During my stay on the coast of Africa, I was an eye-witness of the following transaction: a black trader invited a Negro, who resided a little way up the country, to come and see him. After the entertainment was over, the trader proposed to his guest, to treat him with a sight of one of the ships lying in the river. The unsuspicious countryman readily consented, and accompanied the trader in a canoe to the side of the ship, which he viewed with pleasure and astonishment. While he was thus employed, some black traders on board, who appeared to be in the secret, leaped into the canoe, seized the unfortunate man, and dragging him into the ship, immediately sold him.

The preparations made at Bonny by the black traders, upon setting out for the fairs which are held up the country, are very considerable. From twenty to thirty canoes, capable of containing thirty or forty Negroes each, are assembled for this purpose; and such goods put on board them as they expect will be wanted for the purchase of the number of slaves they intend to buy. When their loading is completed, they commence their voyage, with colours flying, and music playing; and in about ten or eleven days, they generally return to Bonny with full cargoes. As soon as the canoes arrive at the trader's landing-place, the purchased Negroes are cleaned, and oiled with palm-oil; and on the following day they are exposed for sale to the captains.

When the Negroes, whom the black traders have to dispose of, are shown to the European purchasers, they first examine them relative to their age. They then minutely inspect their persons, and inquire into the state of their healths, if they are afflicted with any infirmity, or are deformed, or have bad eyes or teeth; if they are lame, or weak in their joints, or distorted in the back, or of a slender make, or are narrow in the chest; in short, if they have been, or are afflicted in any manner, so as to render them incapable of much labour; if any of the foregoing defects are discovered in them, they are rejected. But if approved of, they are generally taken on board the ship the same evening. The purchaser has liberty to return on the following morning, but not afterwards, such as upon re-examination are found exceptionable.

The traders frequently beat those Negroes which are objected to by the captains, and use them with great severity. It matters not whether they are refused on account of age, illness, deformity, or for any other reason. At New Calabar, in particular . . . the traders, when any of their Negroes have been objected to, have dropped their canoes under the stern of the vessel, and instantly beheaded them, in sight of the captain.

Treatment of the Slaves. As soon as the wretched Africans, purchased at the fairs, fall into the hands of the black traders, they experience an earnest of those dreadful sufferings which they are doomed in future to undergo. . . . They are brought from the places where they are purchased to Bonny, etc. in canoes; at the bottom of which they lie, having their hands tied with a kind of willow twigs, and a strict watch is kept over them. Their usage in other respects, during the time of the passage, which generally lasts several days, is equally cruel. Their allowance of food is so scanty, that it is barely sufficient to support nature. They are, besides, much exposed to the violent rains which frequently fall here, being covered only with mats that afford but a slight defence; and as there is usually water at the bottom of the canoes, from their leaking, they are scarcely ever dry.

Nor do these unhappy beings, after they become the property of the Europeans (from whom, as a more civilised people, more humanity might naturally be expected), find their situation in the least amended. Their treatment is no less rigorous. The men Negroes, on being brought aboard the ship, are immediately fastened together, two and two, by handcuffs on their wrists, and by irons rivetted on their legs. They are then sent down between the decks, and placed in an apartment partitioned off for that purpose. The women likewise are placed in a separate apartment between decks, but without being ironed. And an adjoining room, on the same deck, is besides appointed for the boys. Thus are they all placed in different apartments.

But at the same time, they are frequently stowed so close, as to admit of no other posture than lying on their sides. Neither will the height between decks, unless directly under the grating, permit them the indulgence of an erect posture; especially where there are platforms, which is generally the case. These platforms are a kind of shelf, about eight or nine feet in breadth, extending from the side of the ship towards the centre. They are placed nearly midway between the decks, at the distance of two or three feet from each deck. Upon these the Negroes are stowed in the same manner as they are on the deck underneath.

In each of the apartments are placed three or four large buckets, of a conical form, being near two feet in diameter at the bottom, and only one foot at the top, and in depth about twenty-eight inches; to which, when necessary, the Negroes have recourse. It often happens that those who are placed at a distance from the buckets, in endeavouring to get to them, tumble over their companions, in consequence

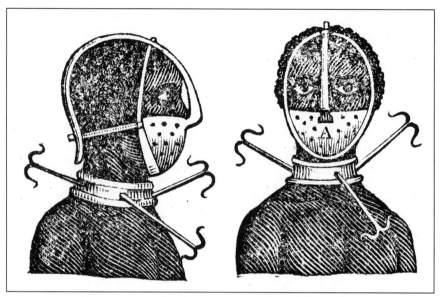

Iron mask and collar designed to restrain rebellious slaves.
From *The Penitential Tyrant*, by Thomas Branigan, 1807.

of their being shackled. These accidents, although unavoidable, are productive of continual quarrels, in which some of them are always bruised. In this distressed situation, unable to proceed, and prevented from getting to the tubs, they desist from the attempt; and, as the necessities of nature are not to be repelled, ease themselves as they lie. This becomes a fresh source of broils and disturbances, and tends to render the condition of the poor captive wretches still more uncomfortable. The nuisance arising from these circumstances, is not unfrequently increased by the tubs being much too small for the purpose intended, and their being usually emptied but once every day. . . .

About eight o'clock in the morning the Negroes are generally brought upon deck. Their irons being examined, a long chain, which is locked to a ring-bolt, fixed in the deck, is run through the rings of the shackles of the men, and then locked to another ring-bolt, fixed also in the deck. By this means fifty or sixty, and sometimes more, are fastened to one chain, in order to prevent them from rising, or endeavouring to escape. If the weather proves favourable, they are permitted to remain in that situation till four or five in the afternoon, when they are disengaged from the chain, and sent down.

The diet of the Negroes, while on board, consists chiefly of horse beans, boiled to the consistence of a pulp; of boiled yams and rice, and sometimes a small quantity of beef or pork. The latter are frequently taken from the provisions laid in for the sailors. They sometimes make use of a sauce, composed of palm oil, mixed with flour, water, and pepper, which the sailors call *slabber sauce*. Yams are the favourite food of the Eboe, or Bight Negroes, and rice or corn, of those from the Gold and Windward Coasts.

Most of the slaves have such an aversion to the horse beans that unless they are narrowly watched, when fed upon deck, they will throw them overboard, or in each other's faces when they quarrel.

Their food is served up to them in tubs, about the size of a small water bucket. They are placed round these tubs in companies of ten to each tub, out of which they feed themselves with wooden spoons. These they soon lose, and when they are not allowed others, they feed themselves with their hands. In favourable weather they are fed upon deck, but in bad weather their food is given them below. Numberless quarrels take place among them during their meals; more especially when they are put upon short allowance.

Upon the Negroes refusing to take sustenance, I have seen coals of fire, glowing hot, put on a shovel, and placed so near their lips, as to scorch and burn them. And this has been accompanied with threats, of forcing them to swallow the coals, if they any longer persisted in refusing to eat. These means have generally had the desired effect. I have also been credibly informed that a certain captain in the slave trade poured melted lead on such of the Negroes as obstinately refused their food.

Exercise being deemed necessary for the preservation of their health, they are sometimes obliged to dance, when the weather will permit their coming on deck. If they go about it reluctantly, or do not move with agility, they are flogged; a person standing by them all the time with a cat-o'-nine-tails in his hand for that purpose. Their music, upon these occasions, consists of a drum, sometimes with only one head; and when that is worn out, they do not scruple to make use of the bottom of one of the tubs before described. The poor wretches are frequently compelled to sing also; but when they do so, their songs are generally, as may naturally be expected, melancholy lamentations of their exile from their native country.

The women are furnished with beads for the purpose of affording them some diversion. But this end is generally defeated by the squabbles which are occasioned, in consequence of their stealing them from each another. On board some ships, the common sailors are allowed to have intercourse with such of the black women whose consent they can pro-cure. . . . The officers are permitted to indulge their passions among them at pleasure, and sometimes are guilty of such brutal excesses as disgrace human nature.

The hardships and inconveniences suffered by the Negroes during the passage are scarcely to be enumerated or conceived. They are far more violently affected by the seasickness than the Europeans. It frequently terminates in death, especially among the women. But the exclusion of the fresh air is among the most intolerable. For the purpose of admitting this needful refreshment, most of the ships in the slave trade are provided, between the decks, with five or six air-ports on each side of the ship of about six inches in length, and four in breadth; in addition to which, some few ships, but not one in twenty, have what they denominate *wind-sails*. But whenever the sea is rough and the rain heavy, it becomes necessary to shut these, and every other conveyance by which the air is admitted. The fresh air being thus excluded, the Negroes' rooms very soon grow intolerably hot. The confined air, rendered noxious by the effluvia exhaled from their bodies, and by being repeatedly breathed, soon produces fever and fluxes, which generally carries off great numbers of them.

During the voyages I made, I was frequently a witness to the fatal effects of this exclusion of fresh air. I will give one instance, as it serves to convey some idea, though a very faint one, of the sufferings of those unhappy beings whom we wantonly drag from their native country, and doom to perpetual labor and captivity. Some wet and blowing weather having occasioned the port-holes to be shut, and the grating to be covered, fluxes and fevers among the Negroes ensued. While they were in this situation, my profession requiring it, I frequently went down among them, till at length their apartments became so extremely hot, as to be only sufferable for a very short time. But the excessive heat was not the only thing that rendered their situation intolerable. The deck, that is, the floor of their rooms, was so covered with the blood and mucus which had proceeded from them in consequence of the flux, that it resembled a slaughter-house. It is not in the power of the human imagination to picture to itself a situation more dreadful or disgusting. Numbers of the slaves having fainted, they were carried upon deck, where several of them died. . . . It had nearly proved fatal to me also. The climate was too warm to admit the wearing of any clothing but a shirt, and that I had pulled off before I went down; notwithstanding which, by the continuing among them for about a quarter of an hour, I was so overcome with the heat, stench, and foul air, that I had nearly fainted; and it was not without assistance that I could get upon deck. The consequence was that I soon after fell sick of the same disorder, from which I did not recover for several months.

The loss of slaves through mortality, arising from the causes just mentioned, are frequently very considerable. In the voyage lately referred to . . . one hundred and five, out of three hundred and eighty, died in the passage—a proportion seemingly very great, but by no means uncommon. One half, sometimes two-thirds, and even beyond that, have been known to perish.

As very few of the Negroes can so far brook the loss of their liberty, and the hardships they endure, as to bear them with any degree of patience, they are ever upon the watch to take advantage of the least negligence in their oppressors. Insurrections are frequently the consequence; which are seldom suppressed without much bloodshed. Sometimes these are successful, and the whole ship's company is cut off. They are likewise always ready to seize every opportunity for committing some act of desperation to free themselves from their miserable state; and notwithstanding the restraints under which they are laid, they often succeed.

While a ship, to which I belonged, lay in Bonny River, one evening, a short time before our departure, a lot of Negroes, consisting of about ten, was brought on board; when one of them, in a favourable moment, forced his way through the network on the larboard side of the vessel, jumped overboard and was devoured by the sharks.

During the time we were there, fifteen Negroes belonging to a vessel from Liverpool, found means to throw themselves into the river; very few were saved; and the residue fell a sacrifice to the sharks. A similar instance took place in a French ship while we lay there.

The following circumstances also came within my knowledge. A young female Negro, falling into a desponding way, it was judged necessary, in order to attempt her recovery, to send her on shore, to the hut of one of the black traders. Elevated with the prospect of regaining her liberty by this unexpected step, she soon recovered her usual cheerfulness; but hearing, by accident, that it was intended to take her on board the ship again, the poor young creature hung herself.

It frequently happens that the Negroes, on being purchased by the Europeans, become raving mad, and many of them die in that state, particularly the women. While I was one day ashore at Bonny, I saw a middle-aged stout woman, who had been brought down from the fair the preceding day, chained to the post of a black trader's door, in a state of furious insanity. On board a ship in Bonny River, I saw a young Negro woman chained to the deck, who had lost her senses, soon after she was purchased and taken on board. In a former voyage, on board a ship to which I belonged, we were obliged to confine a female Negro, of about twenty-three years of age, on her becoming a lunatic. She was afterwards sold during one of her lucid intervals.

One morning, upon examining the place allotted for the sick Negroes, I perceived that one of them, who was so emaciated as scarcely to be able to walk, was missing, and was convinced that he must have gone overboard in the night, probably to put a more expeditious period to his sufferings. And, to conclude on this subject, I could not help being sensibly affected, on a former voyage, at observing with what apparent eagerness a black woman seized some dirt from off an African yam, and put it into her mouth, seeming to rejoice at the opportunity of possessing some of her native earth.

AN ARISTOCRAT EMIGRATES. *In 1793, at the height of the Reign of Terror in France, when aristocrats were being sent to the guillotine daily, La Marquise de La Tour du Pin, aged 24 and the mother of two small children, found herself trapped in Bordeaux, a city dominated by extremist revolutionaries.*

My situation became more alarming by the hour. Not a day went by without further executions. My lodgings were so close to the Place Dauphine that I could hear the drum-roll whenever a head fell. I knew the number of victims before the evening paper told me their names. My room looked out onto a garden which bordered the grounds of a former church which had been taken over as a club house by The Friends of the People, and when their evening meetings grew boisterous I could hear the wretches shouting and yelling and applauding.

The news from Tesson made me realize that my husband's position there was extremely risky. Repeatedly there was talk of using the château as a barracks or military hospital, which would have made it impossible for him to stay there, but I didn't know where else he could go with any degree of safety. Having him join me in Bordeaux was out of the question because of the girl I had hired to help me look after my little boy. I had been warned not to trust her, but I didn't dare get rid of her for fear of getting someone worse.

I was at the end of my tether. Several means of flight had been considered but rejected as impossible. Every day there were more executions of people who had thought they were safe. I couldn't sleep at night, the smallest sound making me think they were coming to arrest me. I hardly dared leave the house. My milk was drying up. I was afraid I was going to fall sick at the very moment that I needed my health more than ever, so that I could act if need be.

Finally, one morning when I had gone to visit M. de Brouquens, who was still under house arrest, I was leaning absent-mindedly over his table when I began mechanically reading the morning paper which was lying there open. Under Commercial News I read: "The ship Diana, of Boston, 150 tons, under ballast, has been authorized by the Secretary of the Navy to sail next week." At that time there were some eighty American ships rotting away in the harbor because they could not obtain official permission to set sail.

Without saying a word, I straightened up and started to leave. M. de Brouquens, who was still busy writing, looked up and asked: "Where are you off to in such a hurry?"

"America," I replied, and left.

FACTORY WORKERS. *Joseph Hollingworth, youngest son in a family of skilled textile workers and a recent immigrant, writes to his uncle and aunt back in Yorkshire.*

South Leicester, Dec. 7th, 1828

Respected Aunt & Uncle

This day being the 1st Anniversary of my landing in America I wanted to celebrate it by writing a Letter.

I have lived in America exactly one year. I have seen all the Seasons and must confess that I prefer the American weather far before the English. I have never seen in this Country a Beggar such as I used Daily to see in England, nor a tax gatherer with his *Red Book* as Impudent as the D-v-l, taking the last penny out of the poor Mans Pocket. In this country are no Lords, nor Dukes, nor Counts, nor Marquises, nor Earls, no Royal Family to support nor no King. The "President of the United States" is the highest Titled fellow in this Country. He is chosen by the People, out of the People; holds his station four years, and if not rechosen he is no more than the rest of the People. The President when he makes a speech does not begin with "My Lords and Gentlemen" but with "Fellow Citizens."

Give my respects to Old Haigh and tell him if you please that my Father has no occasion to hawk Nuts in America as every body can have them for gathering in this Country. Neither is he bound to carry Messrs. Haighs wet Peices up Mirylane on his back nor to go Roast himself in their stove every Sunday morning for Nothing. I have got a New Hat which cost 5 dollars and three quarters. I have a pair of Boots making which will be 4 dollars and an half. I am still working in the Gig Room at 17 $ per month. Father has been writing a letter for 6 months together to William Lockwood. He has not yet finished. It is to be so large, and so compleat with information, but I guess it will be like the Mountain in Labour, it may bring forth a Mouse. The more I live in this Country the better I like it. . . . You must excuse my Brothers James and Jabez for not writing as they are both deeply engaged in Sparking. Jabez Sparks a yankee Girl James Sparks a Saddleworth Girl, and on the 25th of Novbr. Joseph Kenyon took two English Girls to a Ball.

We are all in good Health at present hoping you are the same. Jabez & James are a little tickled at what I have Just written So I will conclude.

I Remain your most Inteligent
Affectionate & well Wishing Nephew

Joseph Hollingworth

WHO ARE WANTED IN MINNESOTA. *From an editorial under this title that appeared in the* St. Anthony Express *on June 21, 1851. Mostly it appealed for farmers and farm workers, but it also had this to say about some other groups.*

Lawyers are wanted in Minnesota—men of education, character and refinement, who thoroughly understand both the science and practice of their profession—men who adorn that profession by irreproachable lives and high moral virtues, men whose severe study, unswerving integrity and enlarged views evince their love for the noble science of the law, and afford security of their usefulness in society. A lawyer in Minnesota should be able to plead a cause in law, to advise a client of his rights, to wield an axe or handle the hoe. He will not have business in his profession to occupy all his time, and he must think no honest labor beneath him of whatever kind it may be. Our Territory is large, but there is no room for miserable pettifoggers, who gain a wretched subsistence by stirring up quarrels in the community—vampires, who drain the blood of society, too lazy to work, too ignorant to harbor an idea, too stupid to have a sense of shame, hated of the gods and despised of man.

Physicians who expect to live by the practice of their profession will find Minnesota a poor field for a location. If there is any one peculiar characteristic of this Territory, it is its exceedingly healthy climate. Life Insurance Companies are at a discount. There are already a goodly number of the disciples of Galen among us, who will find "their occupation gone," as soon as they have cured or killed such desperate cases as come here infected with the thousand dangerous and complicated diseases of other parts of the Union, and have been given over by the "regulars" of eastern and more southern states.

Last, but not least, **young ladies** are wanted. By this term, it is not meant that class to which it is usually misapplied—so-called genteel young misses, brought up to read yellow-covered literature, to idleness and tight lacing, to sing a sentimental song or play a tune on the piano, dance the polka and talk fashionable nonsense. There is no room for such in Minnesota. We use the term "young lady" in its legitimate sense, as meaning one who is ready to engage in any labor that

GRAND RUSH
FOR THE
INDIAN
TERRITORY!

Over 15,000,000 Acres ᵒꜰ Land
NOW OPEN FOR SETTLEMENT!

Being part of the Land bought by the Government in 1866 from the Indians for the Freedmen.

NOW IS THE CHANCE
TO
PROCURE A HOME
In this Beautiful Country!

THE FINEST TIMBER!
THE RICHEST LAND!
THE FINEST WATERED!
WEST OF THE MISSISSIPPI RIVER.

Every person over 21 years of age is entitled to 160 acres, either by pre-emption or homestead, who wishes to settle in the Indian Territory. It is estimated that over Fifty Thousand will move to this Territory in the next ninety days. The Indians are rejoicing to have the whites settle up this country.

The Grand Expedition will Leave Independence May 7, 1879

Independence is situated at the terminus of the Kansas City, Lawrence & Southern Railroad. The citizens of Independence have laid out and made a splendid road to these lands; and they are prepared to furnish emigrants with complete outfits, such as wagons, agricultural implements, dry goods, groceries, lumber and stock. They have also opened an office there for general information to those wishing to go to the Territory. IT COSTS NOTHING TO BECOME A MEMBER OF THIS COLONY.

Persons passing through Kansas City will apply at the office of K. C., L. & S. R. R., opposite Union Depot, for Tickets.

This 1879 broadside proclaims that "The Indians are rejoicing to have the whites settle up this country."

may be useful and necessary, whether it be to wash or bake, mop the floor, clean house, or patch a worn garment. These are your true ladies, more worthy of honor than those to whom armed knights of old paid homage—who give dignity to labor by a noble example, render homes happy, and become ornaments to society. Such can command two or three dollars per week for their work, break the hearts of industrious and enterprising young men by their charms, heal them by consenting to become happy wives and mothers, and become the founders of a great and prosperous commonwealth. Let **such** young ladies come to Minnesota.

STEPS FORWARD. *In an editorial under this title, the July 7, 1868, issue of the* New Mexican *celebrates the arrival of the telegraph in Santa Fe.*

Twenty years ago, New Mexico was an entirely isolated country. The nearest towns east were but small villages on the banks of the Missouri river, and the time required to traverse the dreary distance between, say, Santa Fe and Kansas City, was long, weary and sometimes dangerous. Then, no railroad penetrated even to St. Louis, nor was there a telegraphic line in operation to the Mississippi from the Atlantic slope.

Twenty years ago, all that vast area of country lying between the Rocky Mountains and the Missouri river was known on the maps as the "Great American Desert," a land fit only for the bison and Indian to inhabit. The idea that all this vast central half of the American continent was then or was ever to be valuable to man, had not gained much if any ground, and all west of the "Big Muddy," to most people, was a *terra incognita.*

But these twenty years past have wrought wonderful revolutions in the mysteries of the "Great American Desert." New Mexico was certainly known as *existing* twenty years ago,—that is all. Kansas, Nebraska, Colorado, Minnesota, Dakota, Arizona, Montana, Idaho, Nevada, California, Oregon, Washington Territory, aye, Alaska, who knew about these?

How is it now, after the lapse of these twenty past years? California, Kansas, Nebraska, Oregon, Minnesota, Nevada—these are now states. Colorado is a state, and requires only the last finishing touch of Congress. Montana, Utah, Idaho and New Mexico have already populations nearly or quite sufficient to become states in the Union. This is the progress of population, and the advance of civilization, where but a short time since was wilderness and savage life.

IOWA FARMERS. *Mary Stephenson, wife of Olagus Steffanson (who has changed his name to Oliver Stephenson), writes to her family back in Sweden.*

Mount Pleasant, Iowa, July 1868

Dear parents, brothers, and sisters:

The peace of God be with you! We send greetings to you all. . . .

Dear Brother-in-law Carl and Sister Johanna, you ask how you can put your money to the best advantage. You cannot buy a farm, because land is too high priced, but you can get a start by renting a farm. Renters get ahead much faster here than in Sweden. Those who want to own land go farther west, where the land is free. If you settle in this community, however, you can soon get started by buying colts and calves and harvesting fodder. . . . Oliver says he will help you all he can. You will not regret coming here if you do not encounter misfortunes—and misfortunes are met with in every country.

Day laborers are able to save money here—an impossibility in Sweden. I know of many who own farms who didn't even have gruel in Sweden. I am reminded of Jonas Peter, whose possessions on his arrival consisted only of his clothing. Now if his property were converted into money he could buy a good estate in Sweden, and this in spite of the fact that he married a poor girl, suffered misfortunes, and had no one to help him. But he is industrious and has a good wife. There are many similar cases. . . .

Double-yoked teams of oxen, guided by a woman and boy on foot, haul wagonloads of freight into the Black Hills. Photographed by J. C. H. Grabill, circa 1887.

A few weeks ago seventeen emigrants from Nydala parish arrived and made their headquarters with us. We housed and fed them, as they had no relatives or acquaintances. One family is still with us. The husband has been engaged to work two months for an American for twenty dollars per month, his wife and two children staying with us. She assists me in various ways. People are arriving from Sweden and from other countries and sections in large numbers; but do not worry over the danger of overpopulation, as Iowa is as large as Sweden and only half settled. Then think of the other states! People come and go constantly.

Now a few words with my parents. We are glad to know America is in your thoughts, but I am sorry that Mother is so reluctant. One of you will have to yield, and that of course will be difficult. But whatever you do, don't separate; if Father came without Mother, he would be so lonesome that he would see the dark side of everything and finally return. . . . I advise you to come together, and I believe you will spend a happy old age here.

NO CHINESE. *Chinese immigrants, mostly single men who came to work in California mines and on the railroads, were bitterly resented by white workers, who feared that the "coolies" would lower wages. Testifying before a congressional committee in 1876, a witness from California who described himself as "a minister of the Gospel," and editor of* The Pacific, *"the oldest weekly paper in the Far West," draws a parallel between slavery and coolieism.*

Slavery gave the master power to destroy all the distinctive heathenism which the African brought with him, and he did destroy it. But coolieism gives the employer no such power, and he does not do it. Slavery changed the whole early acquired character of the African, leaving almost or quite nothing of his idolatrous religion, language, customs, habits, morals, tastes, and prejudices, educating him and elevating him up to a whole new character, as an American Christian citizen, in the use of the American language, with American feelings, views, and aspirations.

Coolieism, with very slight exceptions, leaves the Chinese just what they were in their native land, with all their idolatry, immorality, vice, and heathen customs, habits, dress, tastes, prejudices, and most unacquirable language—a large, distinct class of people, adverse to all that is American. Slavery rendered impossible any clanship or race combination among Africans in conflict with our interests or our Government; but coolieism gives the Chinese full opportunity to unite all their energies in any schemes they may devise in their supposed interests, to enforce and perpetuate their numerical influence, their heathen worship, their idolatrous customs, their temple ceremonies, their degrading habits, immoralities, vices, dress, prostitution, language, and every feature of abomination so common in their own country.

Already they have a perfect government among themselves distinct from our own, with their laws, their secret courts of trial, and their police, executive, and other officers, the object of which is to perpetuate their race peculiarities, their clanship interests, and their religion, with terrible sanctions of law, even the death penalty, to enforce their regulations.

They are managing a perfect and increasingly efficient *"imperium in imperio,"* to enforce obedience to their requirements, however adverse to American interests or government. They now number full 150,000 in our country, of whom about 130,000 are in California, being nearly one-sixth of our whole population. Others in large numbers are coming, amounting (when unchecked by intimidation) to 25,000 a year. Very few of these ever change in character, to become Americanized. Only about 500 in the last twenty-five years have

"The Magic Washer; The Chinese Must Go."
Lithograph by Schober and Carquerville, 1886.

renounced their native heathenism to profess Christianity. Thus do they remain and rapidly increase in our country, a vast united class, distinct from us in all important characteristics, tastes, habits and language, exerting an influence adverse to our interests, soon, if unrestrained, to number 5,000,000 or even 10,000,000.

LATTER-DAY PILGRIMS. *In her book* The Promised Land, *which she wrote first in Yiddish and later translated into English, Mary Antin tells of growing up in Polotzk, in Russian-occupied Poland, and of the long-awaited day when the summons came to join her father, who had gone ahead to America and settled in Boston. This took place in 1894, when Mary was thirteen.*

On the day when our steamer ticket arrived, my mother did not go out with her basket, my brother stayed out of heder, and my sister salted the soup three times. . . .

Before sunset the news was all over Polotzk that Hannah Hayye had received a steamer ticket for America. Then they began to come. Friends and foes, distant relatives and new acquaintances, young and old, wise and foolish, debtors and creditors, and mere neighbors,—from every quarter of the city, from both sides of the Dvina, from over the Polota, from nowhere,—a steady stream of them poured into our street, both day and night, till the hour of our departure. And my mother gave audience. Her faded kerchief halfway off her head, her black ringlets straying, her apron often at her eyes, she received her guests in a rainbow of smiles and tears. She was the heroine of Polotzk, and she conducted herself appropriately. She gave her heart's thanks for the congratulations and blessings that poured in on her; ready tears for condolences; patient answers to monotonous questions; and handshakes and kisses and hugs she gave gratis.

What did they not ask, the eager, foolish, friendly people? They wanted to handle the ticket, and mother must read them what is written on it. How much did it cost? Was it all paid for? Were we going to have a foreign passport or did we intend to steal across the border? Were we not all going to have new dresses to travel in? Was it sure that we could get koscher food on the ship? And with the questions poured in suggestions, and solid chunks of advice were rammed in by nimble prophecies. Mother ought to make a pilgrimage to a "Good Jew"—say, the Rebbe of Lubavitch—to get his blessing on our journey. She must be sure and pack her prayer books and Bible, and twenty pounds of zwieback at the least. If they did serve trefah on the ship, she and the four children would have to starve, unless she carried provisions from home.—Oh, she must take all the featherbeds! Featherbeds are scarce in America. In America they sleep on hard mattresses, even in winter. Haveh Mirel, Yachne the dressmaker's daughter, who emigrated to

An Italian immigrant family photographed at Ellis
Island, near the turn of the century.

New York two years ago, wrote her mother that she got up from
childbed with sore sides, because she had no featherbed.—Mother
mustn't carry her money in a pocketbook. She must sew it into the lining of her jacket. . . .

And so on, and so on, till my poor mother was completely bewildered. And as the day set for our departure approached, the people
came oftener and stayed longer, and rehearsed my mother in long
messages for their friends in America, praying that she deliver them
promptly on her arrival, and without fail, and might God bless her for
her kindness, and she must be sure and write them how she found
their friends.

The last night in Polotzk we slept at my uncle's house, having disposed of all our belongings, to the last three-legged stool, except such
that we were taking with us. . . . I did not really sleep. Excitement kept
me awake, and my aunt snored hideously. In the morning I was going
away from Polotzk, forever and ever. I was going on a wonderful journey. I was going to America. How could I sleep?

Poised between old world and new, these turn-of-the-century
immigrants pause on their journey at Ellis Island.

My uncle gave out a false bulletin, with the last batch that the gossips carried away in the evening. He told them that we were not going to start till the second day. This he did in the hope of smuggling us quietly out, and so saving us the wear and tear of a public farewell. But his ruse failed. . . . Half of Polotzk was at my uncle's gate in the morning, to conduct us to the railway station, and the other half was aready there before we arrived.

The procession resembled both a funeral and a triumph. The women wept over us, reminding us eloquently of the perils of the sea, of the bewilderment of a foreign land, of the torments of homesickness that awaited us. They bewailed my mother's lot, who had to tear herself away from blood relations to go among strangers; who had to face gendarmes, ticket agents, and sailors, unprotected by a masculine escort; who had to care for four young children in the confusion of travel, and very likely feed them trefah or see them starve on the way. Or they praised her for a brave pilgrim, and expressed confidence in her ability to cope with gendarmes and ticket agents, and blessed her with every other word, and all but carried her in their arms.

At the station the procession disbanded and became a mob. My uncle and my tall cousins did their best to protect us, but we wanderers were almost torn to pieces. They did get us into a car at last, but the riot on the station platform continued unquelled. When the warning bell rang out, it was drowned in a confounding babel of voices—fragments of oft-repeated messages, admonitions, lamentations, blessings, farewells—"Don't forget!"—"Take care of—" "Keep your tickets—" "Moshele—newspapers!" "Garlick is best!" "Happy journey!" "God help you!" "Good-bye! Good-bye!" "Remember—"

Miss Blanche Lamont, shown with her unsmiling students outside her school at Hecla, Montana. Photographed by Henry W. Brown in October, 1893.

2

UPBRINGING

AR E T H E R E A N Y TA X PAY E R S or parents who have not felt—
at least on occasion—that the cost of schooling is excessive? Or
students who have not at times complained that their lives were
wasting away while they were stuck in class learning things they did not
want to know? Given the huge investment of time and money that almost
any educational system requires, it is fair to ask the question: Is the whole
thing worth it?

To the Puritans, the answer was clearly yes. Literacy was the road to
salvation. If people could not read they could not study the Scriptures,
which in turn could be properly expounded only by a college-educat-
ed ministry. Ignorance played straight into the hands of Satan—the
"Old Deluder."

To later and more pragmatic generations, the answer was also
obvious: Education was the way to make the world a better place.
Economically, because it enabled people to make a better living.
Morally, because the spread of prosperity would bring with it an
improvement in conduct—for "'Tis hard for an empty Bag to stand
upright," as Benjamin Franklin said in *The Way to Wealth*. And politi-
cally, because a well-informed electorate was essential to the working
of a democracy.

Puritans and pragmatists could agree on other benefits. Appropriate schooling would make young people "tractable or manageable,"
would teach Indians "the civility and religion of the prevailing nation,"
and turn the foreign-born into conforming citizens.

Within these areas of agreement there was plenty of room for
argument. Should everyone be taught? Might not learning—along
with bad books—destroy weak minds or lead to civil unrest? Who was
qualified to teach? What subjects should be taught? Who should pay?

To address these various concerns, the chapter falls into three parts: some theories, laws, suggestions, and cautionary tales; books and teachers; and student life from primary school through college—firsthand testimony to how much things have changed, and how much they have stayed the same.

SOME THEORIES, LAWS, SUGGESTIONS, AND CAUTIONARY TALES

SOME PROS AND CONS. *First, the Reverend Jeremiah Wise, a seventeenth-century New England minister.*

The Education of Youth is a great Benefit and Service to the Publick. This is that which civilizes them, takes down their Temper, Tames the Fierceness of their Natures, forms their minds to virtue, learns 'em to carry it with a Just Deference to Superiors; makes them tractable or manageable; and by learning and knowing what it is to be under Government, they will know the better how to govern others when it comes their Turn.

Governor William Berkeley of Virginia, in a letter written in 1671 to the Commissioners of Trade and Plantations in London.

I thank God, we have not free schools nor printing, and I hope we shall not have these hundred years. For learning has brought disobedience and heresy and sects into the world; and printing has divulged them and libels against the government. God keep us from both.

John Winthrop, first governor of the Massachusetts Bay Company, gives an instance of learning misapplied.

April 13, 1645. Mr. Hopkins, the governor of Hartford upon Connecticut, came to Boston, and brought his wife with him, (a godly young woman, and of special parts,) who was fallen into a sad infirmity, the loss of her understanding and reason, which had been growing upon her divers years, by occasion of her giving herself wholly to reading and writing, and had written many books. Her husband, being very loving and tender of her, was loath to grieve her; but he saw his error, when it was too late. For if she had attended her household affairs, and such things as belong to women, and not gone out of her way and calling to meddle in such things as are proper for men, whose minds are stronger, she had kept her wits, and might have improved them usefully and honorably in the place God had set her. He brought her to Boston, and left her with her brother, one Mr. Yale, a merchant, to try what means might be had here for her. But no help could be had.

Daniel Gookin, superintendent of the Indians in Massachusetts until 1687, on the many advantages of a free school for Indians.

I have advised with many judicious men of quality among us, who do very well approve of this contrivance as a very good expedient, not only to civilize, but to propagate religion among the Indians. And also most of the known and pious Indians earnestly desired it; and the reasons that do occur to encourage that there will be good in it, are: First, hereby the Indians will be able to converse with the English familiarly; and thereby learn civility and religion from them. Secondly, they will be able to read any English book, the better to teach them the knowledge of God and themselves. And likewise thereby they may sooner come to the understanding of several other arts and sciences, wherein English authors do abound. Thirdly, they will hereby be able to understand our English ministers, who are better fitted to instruct them in substantial and orthodox divinity, than teachers of their own nation, who cannot in reason be imagined to be so sufficient, as if they were learned men; for who is sufficient for these things? Fourthly, it hath been the observation of some prudent historians, that the changing of the language of a barbarous people, into the speech of a more civil and potent nation that have conquered them, hath been an approved experiment, to reduce such a people unto the civility and religion of the prevailing nation.

LAWS NORTH AND SOUTH. *Some extracts from a codification and summary of the laws of New England to the year 1700.*

All Parents to teach their Children to read, and all Masters to acquaint their Families with the capital Laws, on Penalty of 20 shillings, and to catechise them once a Week.

The Select Men may examine Children and Apprentices, and admonish Parents and Masters, if they find them ignorant, and with the consent of two Magistrates, or the next County-Court, put them into better Hands.

Children so removed by the Magistrate, shall serve the Masters they are plac'd with, Males 'till 21, Females 'till 18 Years of Age.

Magistrates may punish disorderly Children or Servants on complaint, by Whipping, or otherwise, as they see cause, and bind them over to the next County-Court.

Whoever gives credit, or lends Money to any under 21, shall lose his Money, and answer for the Mischief his doing so occasion'd.

Every Town having 50 House-holders, shall provide a School-master to teach to write and read; if it have 100, it shall have a Grammar-School, the Select Men to see them paid; whatever Town neglects it, pays 10 pounds. Every Master must be approv'd by the Minister, or two neighbouring Ministers.

A North Carolina law of 1831. Other states in the antebellum South had similar laws.

Whereas the teaching of slaves to read and write, has a tendency to excite dissatisfaction in their minds, and to produce insurrection and rebellion, to the manifest injury of the citizens of this State: Therefore, *Be it enacted by the General Assembly of the State of North Carolina, and it is hereby enacted by the authority of the same,* That any free person, who shall hereafter teach, or attempt to teach, any slave within the State to read or write, the use of figures excepted, or shall give or sell to such slave or slaves any books or pamphlets, shall be liable to indictment in any court of record in this State having jurisdiction thereof, and upon conviction, shall, at the discretion of the court, if a white man or woman, be fined not less than one hundred dollars, nor more than two hundred dollars, or imprisoned; and if a free person of color, shall be fined, imprisoned, or whipped, at the discretion of the court, not exceeding thirty nine lashes, nor less than twenty lashes.

Be it further enacted, That if any slave shall hereafter teach, or attempt to teach, any other slave to read or write, the use of figures excepted, he or she may be carried before any justice of the peace, and on conviction thereof, shall be sentenced to receive thirty nine lashes on his or her bare back.

EDUCATION FOR YOUNG FEMALES. *Recalling his early days as a printer in Philadelphia, Benjamin Franklin has a story to tell and a lesson to be derived from it.*

In 1733, I sent one of my Journeymen to Charleston South Carolina where a Printer was wanting. I furnish'd him with a Press and Letters, on an Agreement of Partnership, by which I was to receive One Third of the Profits. He was a Man of Learning and honest, but ignorant in Matters of Account; and tho' he sometimes made me Remittances, I could get no Account from him, nor any satisfactory State of our Partnership while he lived. On his Decease, the Business was continued by his Widow, who being born & bred in Holland, where as I have been inform'd the Knowledge of Accompts makes a Part of Female Education, she not only sent me as clear a State as she could find of the Transactions past, but continu'd to account with the greatest Regularity & Exactitude every Quarter afterwards; and manag'd the Business with such Success that she not only brought up reputably a Family of Children, but at the Expiration of the Term was able to

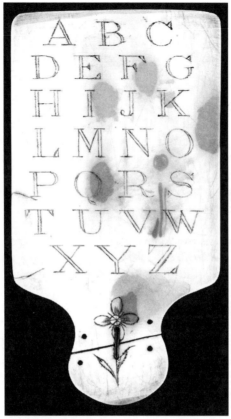

Slate alphabet board with handle,
seventeenth century.

purchase of me the Printinghouse and establish her Son in it. I mention this Affair chiefly for the Sake of recommending that Branch of Education for our young Females, as likely to be of more Use to them & their children in Case of Widowhood than either Music or Dancing, by preserving them from Losses by Imposition of crafty Men, and enabling them to continue perhaps a profitable mercantile House with establish'd Correspondence till a Son is grown up fit to undertake and go on with it, to the lasting Advantage and enriching of the Family.

MOTIVATION. *In his volume of memoirs,* Forty Years of American Life, *the journalist Thomas Low Nichols looks back on his school days in New Hampshire in the 1830s.*

The one perpetual incentive to hard study in our schools was ambition. Every boy knew that he might be governor of the State, or a member of Congress. There was nothing to hinder him from being

President; all he had to do was learn. No position was beyond his reach if he chose to work for it. Franklin was a printer's boy; General Putnam was a farmer, and left his plough in the furrow to take command of the troops that were so gloriously beaten at Bunker Hill; Roger Sherman was a shoemaker, and Andrew Jackson a poor boy who worked his way up from the humblest position. What was Patrick Henry, whose eloquence thrilled us as we spouted his famous speech in the Virginia Assembly? A country tavern-keeper. Our history was full of men who had risen from the ranks, and what in other countries would be called the lowest ranks of life. We knew that where there was a will there was a way, and our teachers constantly stimulated us by the glittering prizes of wealth, honors, offices, and distinctions which were certainly within our reach.

This constant stimulation of hope, emulation, and ambition, produced its natural result of feverish effort and discontent. Few were content to live at home and cultivate the niggard soil of New Hampshire. If we wished to be farmers, there were the fertile bottom lands and broad prairies of the West. But we could be doctors, lawyers, preachers, merchants; there were a hundred avenues to wealth and fame opening fair before us, if we only chose to learn our lessons. Of course we learnt them.

TRUE INDEPENDENCE. *In their 1869 book* The American Woman's Home or, Principles of Domestic Science; Being a Guide to the Formation and Maintenance of Economical, Healthful, Beautiful and Christian Homes, *the authors, Catharine Beecher and Harriet Beecher Stowe, have this advice for mothers.*

In forming the moral habits of children, it is wise to take into account the peculiar temptations to which they are to be exposed. The people of this nation are eminently a trafficking people; and the present standard of honesty, as to trade and debts, is very low, and every year seems sinking still lower. It is, therefore, preëminently important, that children should be trained to strict *honesty*, both in word and deed. It is not merely teaching children to avoid absolute lying, which is needed: *all kinds of deceit* should be guarded against; and all kinds of little dishonest practices be strenuously opposed. A child should be brought up with the determined principle, never to *run in debt*, but to be content to live in a humbler way, in order to secure that true independence, which should be the noblest distinction of an American citizen.

ADMISSION TO LAW SCHOOL. *Two entries from the diary of George Templeton Strong, a successful and well-established New York lawyer. Theodore Dwight was warden of Columbia Law School.*

1869 October 9. Application from three infatuated young women for admission to Law School. No woman shall degrade herself by practising law, in New York especially, if I can save her. Our committee will probably have to pass on the application, *pro forma,* but I think the clack of these possible Portias will never be heard at Dwight's moot courts. "Women's-Rights Women" are uncommonly loud and offensive of late. I loathe the lot. The first effect of their success would be the introduction into society of a third sex, without the grace of woman or the vigor of man; and then woman, being physically the weaker vessel and having thrown away the protection of her present honors and immunities, would become what the squaw is to the male of her species—a drudge and domestic animal.

1879 December 1. Law School Committee this evening at the School on Great Jones Street. Mr. Ruggles, Dwight, Nash, Ogden, and I. Two hours of close, relevant, businesslike talk. We recommend a third year and a test for admission—namely, either a college diploma or an examination, including Latin. This will keep out the little scrubs (German Jew boys mostly) whom the School now promotes from grocery counters in Avenue B to be "gentlemen of the bar." Dwight reluts at anything that tends to diminish the number of students and the aggregate of fees, but he was tractable and reasonable.

THE ACADEMIC MELTING POT. *This article appeared in the* New York Tribune, *September 2, 1900.*

The directory makers are experiencing less difficulty every year with the names of the Russian and Polish Jews on the East Side of New York. The names with which they are burdened when they come to this country are made pronounceable by the children or the teachers when the second generation goes to school.

An example of this kind was mentioned recently by a young woman who had been a teacher in a school where many Russian children were pupils. "A man came in one day," she said, "with two boys who could not say a word in English. . . . When the man was gone, I made one understand that his name would be John and the other that he would have to answer to the name William, and in some way or other the family name which was full of twists and turns, and ended with a 'witch,' became Holz. Within a few weeks John and William Holz made themselves understood in fair English, and within a year they were star pupils. One day the father called at the school to see me about his boys and introduced himself as Mr. Holz! He seemed to be as much at home with the name as though he had been born with it. . . . "

Students bent over their slate-boards in a New York City East Side classroom. Photograph by Jacob Riis, early 1890s.

In many instances a sign bought at a bargain has caused men to assume a new name, and the changes are made without the least feeling in the matter. One East Side patriarch said, "We honor our fathers just as much, even if we drop their names. Nothing good ever came to us while we bore them; possibly we'll have more luck with the new names."

SOME BOOKS AND TEACHERS

HOME EDUCATION. *In his diary for the year 1706, the Reverend Cotton Mather, minister of the Second Church in Boston and perhaps the most influential Puritan of his day, notes his methods of bringing up his children.*

I first begett in them an high Opinion of their Father's Love to them, and of his being best able to judge, what shall be good for them. Then I make them sensible, tis a Folly for them to pretend unto any Witt and Will of their own; they must resign all to me, who will be sure to do what is best; my word must be their Law.

The *first Chastisement*, which I inflict for an ordinary Fault, is, to lett the Child see and hear me in an Astonishment, and hardly able to beleeve that the Child could do so *base* a Thing, but beleeving that they will never do it again.

I would never come to give a child a *Blow;* except in Case of *Obstinacy;* or some gross Enormity. To be chased for a while out of *my Presence,* I would make to be look'd upon, as the sorest Punishment in the Family. . . .

I am not fond of proposing *Play* to them, as a Reward of any diligent Application to learn what is good; lest they should think *Diversion* to be a better and a nobler Thing than *Diligence.*

I would have them come to propound and expect, at this rate, *I have done well, and now I will go to my Father; He will teach me some curious Thing for it.* I must have them count it a *Priviledge,* to be taught; and I

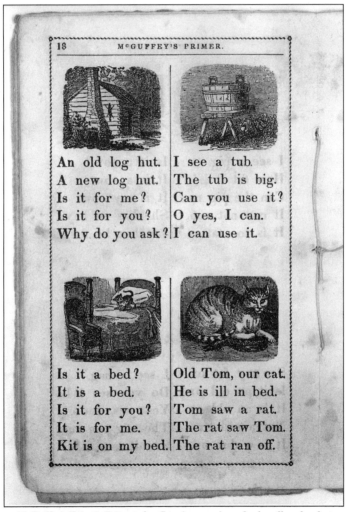

McGuffey's Eclectic Primer, the first in a series of schoolbooks that
sold more than a hundred million copies by the end of the century.
Cincinnati, 1849.

sometimes manage the Matter so, that my Refusing to teach them Something, is their *Punishment*.

The *slavish* way of *Education*, carried on with raving and kicking and scourging (in *Schools* as well as *Families*,) tis abominable; and a dreadful Judgment of God upon the World.

THE SCHOOL OF MANNERS. *Published in England in 1701 and widely distributed in the colonies, this little book was doubly didactic: Rules for children's behavior were set in English on one page and in Latin on the facing page. Here (in English only) are some of its precepts, most of them clearly aimed at boys.*

Of Behaviour at the Church:

Decently walk to thy Seat or Pew; run not, nor go wantonly. Fix thine eye upon the Minister; Let it not wildly wander to gaze upon any Person or Thing.

Attend diligently to the Words of the Minister; pray with him when he prayeth, at least in thy Heart; and while he preacheth, listen, that thou mayest remember.

Be not hasty to run out of the Church when the Worship is ended, as if thou wert weary of being there. Walk decently and soberly home, without hast or wantonness.

Of Behaviour at Home:

Never sit in the presence of thy Parents without bidding, though no Strangers be present.

If thou be going to speak to thy Parents, and see them engaged in Discourse or Company, draw back, and leave thy business till afterward; but if thou must speak, be sure to whisper.

Dispute not, nor delay to do thy Parents Commands.

Quarrel not, nor contend with thy Brethren or Sisters, but live in Love, Peace, and Unity.

Bear with Meekness and Patience, and without murmuring or sullenness, thy Parents Reproofs or Corrections, nay, though it should so happen that they be causeless or undeserved.

Of Behaviour at the Table:

Come not to the Table unwash'd or not comb'd.

Offer not to carve for thy self, or to take any thing, though it be what thou ever so much desirest.

Feed thy self with thy two Fingers, and the Thumb of the left hand.

Speak not at the Table; if thy Superiors be discoursing, meddle not with the matter.

Eat not too fast, or greedily.

Eat not too much, but moderately.

Eat not so slow as to make others wait for thee.

Make not a noise with thy tongue, mouth, lips, or breath, either in eating or drinking.

Stare not in the face of any one (especially thy Superior) at the Table.

Dip not thy Meat in the Sawce.

Take not salt with a greazy Knife.

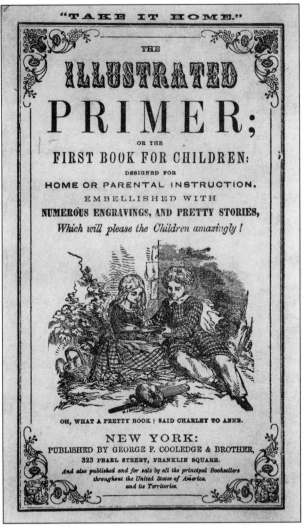

Cover of *The Illustrated Primer; or the First Book for Children.* "Designed for Home or Parental Instruction," the primer promises to "please the Children amazingly." Published by George F. Cooledge and Brother, New York.

Spit not, cough not, nor blow thy Nose at Table if it may be avoided; but if there be necessity, do it aside, and without much noise.

Lean not thy Elbow on the Table, or on the back of thy Chair.

Stuff not thy mouth so as to fill thy Cheeks; be content with smaller Mouthfuls.

Blow not thy Meat, but with patience wait till it be cool.

Smell not to thy Meat, nor move it to thy Nose; turn it not the other side upward to view it upon the Plate.

Throw not any thing under the Table.

Fix not thine eyes upon the plate or trencher of another, or upon the meat on the Table.

Lift not up thine eyes, nor roll them about, while thou art drinking.

Gnaw not Bones at the Table, but clean them with thy knife (unless they be very small ones) and hold them not with a whole hand, but with two fingers.

Pick not thy Teeth at the Table, unless holding up thy Napkin before thy mouth with thine other Hand.

Frown not, nor murmur if there be any thing at the Table which thy Parents or Strangers with them eat of, while thou thy self hast none given thee.

Rules for Behaviour in Company:

Put not thy hand in the presence of others to any part of thy body, not ordinarily discovered.

Sing not nor hum in thy mouth while thou art in company.

Play not wantonly like a Mimick with thy Fingers or Feet.

Spit not in the Room, but in a corner, and rub it out with thy Foot, or rather go out and do it abroad.

Let thy Countenance be moderately chearful, neither laughing nor frowning.

Stand not before Superiors with thine hands in thy pockets, scratch not thy Head, wink not with thine Eyes, but thine Eyes modestly looking straight before thee, and thine Hands behind thee.

Whisper not in company.

Strive not with Superiors in Argument or Discourse, but easily submit thine opinion to their assertions.

If thy Superior speak any thing wherein thou knowest he is mistaken, correct not, nor contradict him, nor grin at the hearing of it, but pass over the error without notice or interruption.

If thy Superior be relating a Story, say not, *I have heard it before;* but attend as if it were to thee altogether new; seem not to question the truth of it; if he tell it not right, snigger not, nor endeavour to help out or add to his relation.

Beware thou utter not any thing hard to be believed.

TOO TRUE TO BE DOUBTED. *One of the sacred texts in the educational canon, as conceived by Mason Locke Weems, who liked to style himself "Formerly Rector of Mount-Vernon Parish." The story is from the fifth edition (1806) of* The Life and Memorable Actions of George Washington, *where it makes its first appearance.*

Never did the wise Ulysses take more pains with his beloved Telemachus, than did Mr. Washington with George, to inspire him with an *early love of truth*. "Truth, George," said he, "is the loveliest quality of youth. I would ride fifty miles, my son, to see the little boy whose heart is so *honest,* and his lips so *pure,* that we may depend on every word he says. O how lovely does such a child appear in the eyes of everybody! his parents doat on him. His relations glory in him. They are constantly praising him to their children, whom they beg to imitate him. They are often sending for him to visit them; and receive him, when he comes, with as much joy as if he were a little angel, come to set pretty examples to their children.

"But, Oh! how different, George, is the case with the boy who is given to lying, that nobody can believe a word he says! He is looked at with aversion wherever he goes, and parents dread to see him coming among their children. Oh, George! my son! rather than see you come to this pass, dear as you are to my heart, gladly would I assist to nail you up in your little coffin, and follow you to your grave. Hard, indeed, would it be to me to give up my son, whose little feet are always so ready to run about with me, and whose fondly looking eyes, and sweet prattle make so large a part of my happiness. But still I would give him up, rather than see him a common liar."

"Pa," said George very seriously, "do I ever tell lies?"

"No, George, I *thank* God you do not, my son; and I rejoice in the hope you never will. At least, you shall never, from me, have cause to be guilty of so shameful a thing. Many parents, indeed, even compel their children to this vile practice, by barbarously beating them for every little fault: hence, on the next offence, the little terrified creature slips out a *lie!* just to escape the rod. But as to yourself, George, you know I have *always* told you, and now tell you again, that, whenever by accident, you do anything wrong, which must often be the case, as you are but a poor little boy yet, without *experience or knowledge,* you must never tell a falsehood to conceal it; but come *bravely* up, my son, like a *little* man, and tell me of it: and, instead of beating you, George, I will but the more honour and love you for it, my dear."

This, you'll say, was sowing good seed!—Yes, it was: and the crop, thank God, was, as I believe it ever will be, where a man acts the true parent, that is, the *Guardian Angel,* by his child.

The following anecdote is a *case in point.* It is too valuable to be lost, too true to be doubted; for it was communicated to me by the same excellent lady to whom I am indebted for the last.

"When George," said she, "was about six years old, he was made the wealthy master of a *hatchet!* of which, like most little boys, he was immoderately fond, and was constantly going about chopping every thing that came in his way. One day, in the garden, where he often amused himself hacking his mother's pea-sticks, he unluckily tried the edge of his hatchet on the body of a beautiful young English cherry-tree, which he barked so terribly, that I don't believe the tree ever got the better of it. The next morning the old gentleman, finding out what had befallen his tree, which, by the by, was a great favourite, came into the house; and with much warmth asked for the mischievous author, declaring at the same time, that he would not have taken five guineas for his tree. Nobody could tell him anything about it. Presently George and his hatchet made their appearance. *'George,'* said his father, 'do you know who killed that beautiful little cherry tree yonder in the garden?' This was a *tough question;* and George staggered under it for a moment; but quickly recovered himself: and looking at his father, with the sweet face of youth brightened with the inexpressible charm of all-conquering truth, he bravely cried out, 'I can't tell a lie, Pa; you know I can't tell a lie. I did cut it with my hatchet.'—'Run to my arms, you dearest boy,' cried his father in transports, 'run to my arms; glad I am, George that you killed my tree; for you have paid me for it a thousand fold. Such an act of heroism in my son is more worth than a thousand trees, though blossomed with silver, and their fruits of purest gold.'"

It was in this way by interesting at once both his *heart* and *head,* that Mr. Washington conducted George with great ease and pleasure along the happy paths of virtue.

BOARDING OUT. *In* Forty Years of American Life, *the journalist Thomas Low Nichols, who was born in 1815, explains how the system worked in New Hampshire when he was a boy.*

Every year, at town-meeting, the paupers of the town were sold at auction to those who would keep them cheapest, taking into account the work they were capable of doing. The pauper was a slave, sold for a year at a time, but sold yearly as long as he lived. The schoolmaster was treated in the same inglorious fashion. The cheaper he could be boarded, the longer the money would last, and the longer the school-term continue. A well-to-do farmer, with an abundance of food, and children who might have some extra assistance in their lessons, would be glad to board the master for a very trifling consideration. . . .

But even this amount was often saved to the district by the master or mistress boarding round—taking turns of a week or two at the houses of his or her pupils. This gave a pleasing variety to the life of the teacher, and enabled the people of the district to vie with each other in their hospitalities. I think that this was the most popular system. It gave all the young misses a fair chance at a possible admirer, and though the teacher might have long walks when boarding at the extremities of his district, he was treated everywhere with the attentions due to a transient and honoured guest. The best room in the house and the best fare that could be provided were ready for the schoolmaster.

END OF A TYRANT. *Charles Anthon was Rector of Columbia Grammar School and also Jay Professor of Greek and Latin Languages at Columbia College. The lawyer and diarist George Templeton Strong had been a student at both institutions.*

1867 July 29, Monday. I feel really much cut up by this news of poor old Bull Anthon's death. He did so tyrannize over all my boyhood from thirteen to nineteen! . . . How well I remember his style of work in the horrible old grammar school! *Scene:* twenty boys in a lecture room, no teacher yet in his place. Time, nine o'clock in the morning. Some little subdued talking and skylarking in progress. A wretched creature called "a monitor" in nominal charge, vainly beseeching his classmates to be quiet. The professor comes swiftly upstairs, full of business, with a big watch in his hand and twirling the big seal and the ribbon round his forefinger, and *loquitur:* " Too much noise here! Any names, monitor?" Monitor replies (distracted between his dread of discipline and his dread of lynching by his classmates), "No, sir. I didn't think—" Professor rejoins, Napoleonically, "I don't want to know what you think, sir. Take *this* down to Mr. Shea." *"This"* was a scrap of paper inscribed with the words "six blows" or "twelve blows," as the case might be. They were delivered by the rattan on the hand. Shea was lictor of the infernal old school and rattan-bearer. I do not think poor old James Shea liked his office much. So it was when we were in the "first Latin class" of the school. An imperfect recitation was punished by the order "Take *this* down to Mr. Shea." So was a bad weekly report. Shea was muscular, six-foot high, and I think kindhearted, though he did use to say, with the utmost aggravation of manner, as he flourished his rattan, "Now hold your hand straight, my sonny, or I may hurt your knuckles."

July 31. To St. Mark's Church at 10:30 a.m. for poor old Professor Bull (or Charles) Anthon's funeral. . . . I was invited to attend as *pall-bearer,* everybody being out of town. Before the coffin was taken out of the church it was opened and everybody looked at the professor's still, stern face. It was natural—not at all unlike his lecture-room face, only *whiter*. While I looked on it, there came on me the thought, "Suppose that figure should rise and say, 'Strong! You will now translate *Oedipus Tyrannus,* lines 213–227!' What answer should I give him?"

A THUNDERBOLT FROM THE PULPIT. *Some passages from* Social Dynamite; or, The Wickedness of Modern Society, *1889, by Thomas De Witt Talmage. A Presbyterian clergyman whose sermons attracted huge audiences, Talmage was also the author of* Crumbs Swept Up *and the editor of* The Christian at Work.

The greatest blessing that ever came to this nation is that of an elevated literature, and the greatest scourge has been that of unclean literature. This last has its victims in all occupations and departments. It has helped to fill insane asylums and penitentiaries and almshouses and dens of shame. The bodies of this infection lie in the hospitals and in the graves, while their souls are being tossed over into a lost eternity, an avalanche of horror and despair.

Alas for the impure literature that has come upon this country in the shape of novels, like a freshet overflowing all the banks of decency and common sense! They are coming from some of the most celebrated publishing houses of the country. They are coming with recommendation of some of our religious newspapers. They lie in your center table to curse your children, and blast with their infernal fires generations unborn. You find these books in the desk of the school miss, in the trunk of the young man, in the steamboat cabin, on the table of your hotel reception room. You see a light in your child's room late at night. You suddenly go in and say: "What are you doing?" "I am reading." "What are your reading?" "A book." You look at the book; it is a bad book. "Where did you get it?" "I borrowed it." Alas, there are always those abroad who would like to loan your son or daughter a bad book. Everywhere, everywhere an unclean literature.

"But," you say, "how can I find out whether a book is good or bad without reading it?" There is always something suspicious about a bad book. I never knew an exception—something suspicious in the index or style of illustration. This venomous reptile almost always carries a warning rattle. I charge you to stand off from all those books which corrupt the imagination and inflame the passions. I do not refer now to that kind of a book which the villain has under his coat waiting for the school to get out, and then, looking both ways to see that there is no policeman around the block, offers the book to your son on his way home. I do not speak of that kind of literature, but that which evades the law and comes out in polished style, and with acute plot sounds the tocsin that rouses up all the baser passions of the soul. To-day, under the nostrils of this land, there is a fetid, reeking unwashed literature, enough to poison all the fountains of public virtue, and smite your sons and daughters as with the wing of a destroying angel, and it is time that the ministers of the gospel blew the trumpet and rallied the forces of righteousness, all armed to the teeth, in this great battle against a depraved literature.

Cursed be the books that try to make impurity decent, and crime attractive, and hypocrisy noble! Cursed be the books that swarm with libertines and desperadoes, who make the brains of the young people whirl with villainy. Ye authors who write them, ye publishers who print them, ye booksellers who distribute them, shall be cut to pieces, if not by an aroused community, then, at last, by the hail of divine vengeance, which shall sweep to the lowest pit of perdition all ye murderers of souls. . . .

The clock strikes midnight. A fair form bends over a romance. The eyes flash fire. The breath is quick and irregular. Occasionally the color dashes in the cheeks, and then dies out. The hands tremble as though a guardian spirit were trying to shake the deadly book out of the grasp. Hot tears fall. She laughs with a shrill voice that drops dead at its own sound. The sweat on her brow is the spray dashed up from the river of death. The clock strikes four, and the rosy dawn soon after begins to look through the lattice upon the pale form that looks like a detained specter of the night. Soon in a mad-house she will mistake her ringlets for curling serpents, and thrust her white hand though the bars of the prison, and smite her head, rubbing it back as though to push the scalp from the skull, shrieking: "My brain! My brain!"

LADY'S ETIQUETTE. *Those not fortunate enough to have learned genteel manners in a ladies' academy could always improve themselves with the help of books such as* The Lady's Guide to Perfect Gentility *by Emily Thornwell (author also of* Home Cares Made Easy*), published in Cleveland in 1887.*

The Lady Abroad

Gait and carriage.—A lady ought to adopt a modest and measured gait; too great hurry injures the grace which ought to characterize her. She should not turn her head on one side and on the other, especially in large towns or cities, where this bad habit seems to be an invitation to the impertinent. A lady should not present herself alone in a library, or a museum, unless she goes there to study, or work as an artist.

Gentlemen's attendance.—After twilight, a young lady would not be conducting herself in a becoming manner, by walking alone; and if she passes the evening with any one, she ought, beforehand, to provide some one to come for her at a stated hour; but if this is not practicable, she should politely ask of the person whom she is visiting, to permit a servant to accompany her. But, however much this may be considered proper, and consequently an obligation, a married lady, well educated, will disregard it if circumstances prevent her being able, without trouble, to find a conductor.

Raising the dress.—When tripping over the pavement, a lady should gracefully raise her dress a little above her ancle. With the right hand, she should hold together the folds of her gown, and draw them towards the right side. To raise the dress on both sides, and with both

A page from *The Girl's Own Indoor Book*, a guide
that offers "Practical help to girls on all matters
relating to their material comfort and moral
well-being." Published in 1888.

hands, is vulgar. This ungraceful practice can only be tolerated for a moment, when the mud is very deep.

Receiving visitors.—When we see persons enter, whether announced or not, we rise immediately, advance towards them, request them to sit down, avoiding however the old form of, "Take the trouble to be seated." If it is a young man, we offer him an arm-chair, or a stuffed one; if an elderly man, we insist upon his accepting the arm-chair; if a lady, we beg her to be seated upon the ottoman.

In winter, the most honorable places are those at the corner of the fireplace; in proportion as they place you in front of the fire, your seat is considered inferior in rank. Moreover, when it happens to be a respectable married lady, and one to whom we wish to do honor, we take her by the hand and conduct her to the corner of the fireplace. If this place is occupied by a young lady, she should rise and offer her seat to the married lady, taking for herself a chair in the middle of the circle.

Propriety of movement and general demeanor in company.—To look steadily at any one, especially if you are a lady and are speaking to a gentleman; to turn the head frequently on one side and the other during conversation . . . to cross your legs . . . to admire yourself with complacency in a glass . . . to fold carefully your shawl, instead of throwing it with graceful negligence upon a table . . . to laugh immoderately . . . to place your hand upon the person with whom you are conversing; to take him by the buttons, the collar of his cloak, the cuffs, the waist, etc. . . . . to roll the eyes or raise them in affectation . . . to play continually with your chain or fan . . . to beat time with the feet and hands . . . to shake with your feet the chair of your neighbor; to rub your face or your hands; wink your eyes; shrug up your shoulders; stamp with your feet, &c.;—all these bad habits . . . are in the highest degree displeasing.

SUMMER SCHOOL TEACHER. *Born in Great Barrington, Massachusetts, in 1868, W. E. B. Du Bois was a student at Fisk University in Nashville, Tennessee, before going on to attend Harvard and then the University of Berlin. While at Fisk, Du Bois helped to make ends meet by working as a summer school teacher in rural Tennessee.*

There was a Teachers' Institute at the county seat; and there distinguished guests of the superintendent taught the teachers fractions and spelling and other mysteries—white teachers in the morning, Negroes at night. This was to supplement the wretched elementary training of the prospective teachers. . . .

There came a fine day when all the teachers left the Institute and began the hunt for schools. I learned from hearsay (for my mother was mortally afraid of fire-arms) that the hunting of ducks and bears and men is wonderfully interesting, but I am sure that the man who has never hunted a country school in the South has something to learn of the pleasures of the chase. I see now the white, hot roads lazily rise and wind and fall before me under the burning July sun; I feel the deep weariness of heart and limb as ten, eight, six miles stretch relentlessly ahead; I feel my heart sink heavily as I hear again and again "Got a teacher? Yes." So I walked on and on—horses were too expensive—until I had wandered beyond railways, beyond stage lines, to a land of "varmints" and rattlesnakes, where the coming of a stranger was an event, and men lived and died in the shadow of one blue hill.

Sprinkled over hill and dale lay cabins and farmhouses, shut out from the world by the forests and the rolling hills toward the east. There I found at last a little school. Josie told me of it; she was a thin, homely girl of 20, with a dark-brown face and thick, hard hair. I had crossed the stream at Watertown, and rested under the great willows; then I had gone to the little cabin in the lot, where Josie was resting on her way to town. The gaunt black farmer made me welcome and Josie, hearing my errand, told me anxiously that they wanted a school over the hill; that but once since the Civil War had a teacher been there; that she herself longed to learn—and thus she ran on, talking fast and loud, with much earnestness and energy.

Next morning I crossed the tall round hill, lingered to look at the blue and yellow mountains stretching toward the Carolinas, then plunged into the wood, and came out at Josie's home. It was a dull frame cottage with four rooms, perched just below the brow of the hill, amid peach trees. The father was a quiet, simple soul, calmly ignorant, with no touch of vulgarity. The mother was different—strong, bustling, and energetic, with a quick, restless tongue, and an ambition to live "like folks." There was a crowd of children. Two boys had gone away. There remained two growing girls; a shy midget of eight; John, tall, awkward and 18; Jim, younger, quicker and better looking; and two babies of indefinite age.

Then there was Josie herself. She seemed to be the center of the family; always busy at service, or at home, or berry-picking; a little nervous and inclined to scold, like her mother, yet faithful, too, like her father. She had about her a certain fineness, the shadow of an unconscious moral heroism that would willingly give all of life to make life broader, deeper and fuller for her and hers. I saw much of this family afterwards, and grew to love them for their honest efforts to be decent and comfortable, and for their knowledge of their own ignorance.

There was with them no affectation. The mother would scold the father for being so "easy"; Josie would roundly berate the boys for carelessness; and all knew that it was a hard thing to dig a living out of a rocky side-hill. I found a place where there had been a Negro public school only once since the Civil War; and there for two successive terms during the summer I taught at 28 and 30 dollars a month.

It was an enthralling experience. I remember the day I rode horseback out to the commissioner's house with a pleasant young white fellow who wanted the white school. The road ran down the bed of a stream; the sun laughed and the water jingled, and we rode on. "Come in," said the commissioner, "come in. Have a seat. Yes, that certificate will do." I was pleasantly surprised when the superintendent invited me to stay for dinner; and he would have been astonished if he had dreamed that I expected to eat at the table with him and not after he was through.

The schoolhouse was a log hut, where Colonel Wheeler used to store his corn. It sat in a lot behind a rail fence and thorn bushes, near the sweetest of springs. There was an entrance where a door once was, and within, a massive rickety fireplace; great chinks between the logs served as windows. Furniture was scarce. My desk was made of three boards reinforced at critical points, and my chair, borrowed from my landlady, had to be returned every night. Seats for the children— these puzzled me much. I was haunted by a New England vision of neat little desks and chairs, but, alas the reality was rough plank benches without backs, and at times without legs. They had the one virtue of making naps dangerous, possibly fatal, for the floor was not to be trusted. All the appointments of my school were primitive: a window-less log cabin; hastily manufactured benches; no blackboards; almost no books; long, long distances to walk. On the other hand, I heard the sorrow songs sung with primitive beauty and grandeur. I saw the hard, ugly drudgery of country life and the writhing of landless, ignorant peasants. I saw the race problem at nearly its lowest terms.

It was a hot morning late in July when the school opened. I trembled when I heard the patter of little feet down the dusty road, and saw the growing row of dark solemn faces and bright eager eyes facing me. First came Josie and her brothers and sisters. The longing to know, to be a student in the great school at Nashville, hovered like a star above this child-woman amid her work and worry, and she studied doggedly. There were the Dowells from their farm toward Alexandria—Fanny, with her smooth black face and wondering eyes; Martha, brown and dull; the pretty girl-wife of a brother, and the younger brood.

There were the Burkes—two brown and yellow lads, and a tiny haughty-eyed girl. Fat Reuben's little chubby girl came, with golden face and old-gold hair, faithful and solemn. 'Thonie was on hand early—a jolly, ugly, good-hearted girl, who slyly dipped snuff and looked after her little bow-legged brother. When her mother could spare her, 'Tildy came—a midnight beauty, with starry eyes and tapering limbs; and her brother, correspondingly homely. And the big boys—the hulking Lawrences; the lazy Neills, unfathered sons of mother and daughter; Hickman, with a stoop in his shoulders, and the rest.

There they sat, nearly 30 of them, on the rough benches, their faces shading from a pale cream to a deep brown, the little feet bare and swinging, the eyes full of expectation, with here and there a twinkle of mischief, and the hands grasping Webster's blue-back spelling book. I loved my school, and the fine faith the children had in the wisdom of their teacher was truly marvellous. We read and spelled together, wrote a little, picked flowers, sang, and listened to stories of the world beyond the hill.

At times the school would dwindle away, and I would start out. I would visit Mun Eddings, who lived in two very dirty rooms, and ask why little Lugene, whose flaming face seemed ever ablaze with the dark-red hair uncombed, was absent all last week, or why I missed so often the inimitable rags of Mack and Ed. Then the father, who worked Colonel Wheeler's farm on shares, would tell me how the crops needed the boys; and the thin slovenly mother, whose face was pretty when washed, assured me that Lugene must mind the baby. "But we'll start them again next week. . . . "

On Friday nights I often went home with some of the children— sometimes to Doc Burke's farm. He was a great, loud, thin black, ever working, and trying to buy the 75 acres of hill and dale where he lived; but people said that he would surely fail, and the "white folks would get it all." His wife was a magnificent Amazon, with saffron face and shining hair, uncorseted and barefooted, and the children were strong and beautiful. They lived in a one-and-a-half-room cabin in the hollow of the farm, near the spring. The front room was full of great fat white beds, scrupulously neat; and there were bad chromos on the walls, and a tired center table. In the tiny back kitchen I was often invited to "take out and help" myself to fried chicken and wheat biscuits, "meat" and corn pone, string-beans and berries.

On this visit, at first I was a little alarmed at the approach of bedtime in the one lone bedroom, but embarrassment was very deftly avoided. First, all the children nodded and slept, and were stowed away in one great pile of goose feathers; next, the mother and the father discreetly slipped away to the kitchen while I went to bed; then, blowing out the dim light, they retired in the dark. In the morning all were up and away before I thought of waking. Across the road, where fat Reuben lived, they all went outdoors while the teacher retired, because they did not boast the luxury of a kitchen.

I liked to stay with the Dowells, for they had four rooms and plenty of good country fare. Uncle Bird had a small, rough farm, all woods and hills, miles from the big road; but he was full of tales—he preached now and then—and with his children, berries, horses, and wheat he was happy and prosperous. . . . Best of all I loved to go to Josie's, and sit on the porch, eating peaches, while the mother bustled and talked; how Josie had bought the sewing machine; how Josie worked at house service in winter, but that four dollars a month was "mighty little" wages; how Josie longed to go away to school, but that it "looked like" they never could get far enough ahead to let her.

PRAIRIE SCHOOL. *Soon after she arrived in Kansas, where her parents were homesteaders, India Harris Simmons was appointed teacher in a brand-new school in Kearny County.*

School opened in October of 1888 with nineteen pupils. Not wishing to postpone the opening of school until a suitable building could be

A turn-of-the-century photograph by Joseph H. Young of "the only remaining Sod School House in Decatur County, Kansas."

secured, the patrons decided to use a dugout which had served as a dwelling for a pre-empter, who had 'proved up' and gone.

The outlook, or speaking more exactly, the inlook, was not reassuring. The floor and walls were just plain dirt, not even adobe plaster, and the one window and the cellar type of doorway gave scant illumination. Plain benches without backs ran around three sides of the room. There were no blackboards or other school equipment. Decorating it, or improving it in any substantial way would take at least a little money which could not be spared by the district until more land was 'proved up' and made taxable.

So, clean 'gunny bags,' a kind of coarse burlap bag, were ripped apart and fastened against the walls to keep the dirt away from the clothing. Use had somewhat packed and hardened the floor, which they cleared of loose dirt, and then laid down old rugs and pieces of carpet, on which the children's feet could rest. They cleaned the tiny four-paned window, at each side of which they hung a bright piece of cheap drapery, being careful not to obscure any of the precious light.

A small wooden box, with a clean paper on top, held the water jug and the common drinking cup. A taller box, with a shelf inside and a pretty stand cover on it, served as the teacher's desk, and her chair was one of the home-made kind with a broad board nailed on slantingly for a back, quite common in the dugout homes. A little Topsy stove, on which the bachelor claim holder had baked his morning flap-jacks, was the final piece of furniture.

When the little group had been called in, and nineteen happy expectant faces greeted her from the row of benches, the young teacher had a sense of misgiving as to her ability to change that crude little dirt-walled room into a hall of learning. . . . But breathing a prayer that plain surroundings, like plain living, might be conducive to high thinking, she began the opening exercises which dedicated the lowly dwelling to its new high use.

The nondescript supply of books which each pupil had brought from whatever state was 'back home' to him was placed on the bench by his side. Slates, which had to take the place of both blackboard and tablets, were of all sizes and descriptions, from Jimmy's tiny one with the red felt covered frame and pencil tied to it with a string, to Mary's big double one with the wide home-made frames fastened together with strong hinges and cut deep with initials and hearts. She had found it packed away among grandfather's books, which he had used away back in Ohio. There were histories from Illinois, spellers and writing books from Iowa, readers from St. Louis city schools, and even some old blue-backed spellers, with their five-syllabled puzzlers.

A history class learns about Captain John Smith.
Photograph by Frances Benjamin Johnson, circa 1902.

From this motley array the teacher made the assignments and
arranged the classifications, depending entirely upon her own judgment. The pupils had been without school privileges long enough to
be glad to have an opportunity to study, and their rapid progress
showed they came, for the most part, from intelligent families. True,
there was not a suspension globe for explaining mathematical geogra-
phy, but an apple and a ball did very well. There was no case of the lat-
est wall maps on rollers, but the large ones in the books answered the
purpose when care was taken to hold them correctly.

STUDENT LIFE

DAME'S SCHOOL. *Born in 1827, Laura Russell grew up in a ship captain's house that stands a stone's throw from Plymouth Rock. In her privately
printed memoir,* Laura Russell Remembers, *she looks back to her first academic experience.*

Our education began at a very early age, from twenty months to two
years being considered a proper time for us to enter the infant school.
As one child after another was added to the family and our mother's
cares increased, this school served as a sort of day-nursery. It was but a
short distance from our house and was taught by an old dame whom

we always addressed as "Marm." She was an excellent woman and fulfilled the duties of nurse as faithfully as those of teacher. She usually
wore an Indigo blue calico gown with small white spots, a mob cap
with a broad band of black ribbon tied into a large bow in front and
round-eyed spectacles, with heavy iron frames. The house was old and
small and there seemed to be a perpetual colony of skunks under it
which occasionally caused great excitement among us and was a
source of much annoyance to the old lady who tried in vain to get
some one to rout them. She used to say that if needle, thimble and
scissors would do it she need not call upon anybody for help. . . .

The schoolroom was small and of irregular shape with an open
fireplace in one corner. . . . Next to the fireplace was a closet where
among the dishes always stood a little black teapot whose supply of the
drink which cheers seemed to be as unfailing as that of the widow's
cruse, for though "Marm" made frequent demands upon it, the contents were never exhausted. Her method of drinking was somewhat
primitive and would hardly meet with favor at a fashionable afternoon
tea. She considered a cup quite unnecessary preferring the simpler
way of taking the spout into her mouth.

The old lady began each morning's session by reading a chapter
from the Bible, rapping on its cover with her steel tailor's thimble as a
signal for us to range ourselves in a semicircle about her chair and listen to the Holy Word. It is doubtful if these lessons had the intended
effect for the only recollection of them which I retain is the frequent
repetition of the word "Selah" from which it may be inferred that the
Psalms were her favorite selection. In after years when asked the
meaning of the word, she frankly replied that she did not know, and
being further questioned as to why she read it, she answered, "Because
it's in the Bible, dear." The great Bible lay upon a table under the
looking-glass between the windows and, with the Old Farmer's
Almanac, constituted the old lady's entire library. On the sacred volume and the almanac was a small wooden box into which at the close
of each day we dropped our little brass thimbles and our bit of patch-
work with its irregular, blackened stitches piled one upon another
after having been many times picked out and re-sewed with squeaking,
crooked needle and tear-dimmed eyes.

The white unpainted floor of the schoolroom was bare with the
exception of a braided mat in front of "Marm's" chair, but in place of
a carpet there was a liberal sprinkling of beach sand which was
renewed every week, and ornamented by being herring-boned with a
broom. The only school furniture was a number of low wooden crickets which were placed in a row through the middle of the room, and
which were sometimes supplemented with a block or two under the

windows, when the school was crowded. The crickets were worn smooth and shiny from long wriggling of the little unsupported forms daily seated upon them, the knots being conspicuous for their high polish. Each child carried its cricket at night into the adjoining room, and returned it to its place the next morning, the school room serving also for parlor and bedroom.

Occasionally we got a slight rap on the head from the tailor's thimble, but the only other punishment that I remember was when an aggravated offence brought from "Marm" the command, "Take your cricket and go down to Bantam," Bantam being the farther corner of the room occupied by an old roundabout chair. I have never been able to trace the origin of this word nor do I know whether it referred to the corner or the chair, but the punishment was resorted to as an extreme measure and to us meant not only deep disgrace but almost Siberian exile.

Into this seminary we were initiated at the tender age before-mentioned and sent with undeviating regularity twice a day with the exception of Saturday when we were allowed a half-holiday. No storm was so fierce, no snow so deep, no cold so intense as to interfere with the inflexible rule of daily attendance at school. . . . When the weather was unfavorable, it was our custom as well as that of other children to take a little basket of luncheon and remain through the noon recess. As "Marm" depended upon her after dinner nap, our amusements were necessarily much restricted. When we grew too noisy, we were checked with the admonition, "Let your victuals stop your mouth." The old dame must have looked forward to Saturday with delightful anticipation. At the close of the morning session she was not only relieved of all care of the children till the following Monday, but was at liberty to pass the rest of the day with her son and his family. In winter she donned her scarlet cloth cloak with its numerous little capes, being kept from these weekly visits only by sickness or very severe weather.

In the room adjoining the schoolroom a bucket of water always stood on a table and near it a large pewter vessel in size and shape somewhat resembling a beer-mug. When we were very good, we were allowed to hand water around to the children, passing the pewter mug from one to another without refilling till the supply was exhausted. This was a much coveted office, but like other positions of honor and trust, it had its drawbacks. When my turn came, I remember that the weight of the mug frequently caused cramps in my small hands. Then the kind old dame would call me to her side and carefully wrap them in the red flannel nightgown which she thought had a peculiar virtue from its color. She also laid me on the bed in her little spare dark bedroom for the daily nap, an indulgence which did not seriously interfere with my education since only reading, spelling and sewing over and over were taught.

Our tuition cost the moderate sum of eight cents a week. . . . This modest charge did not include the fuel, for the following item was added to an autumn bill still in my possession: "If she comes this winter, one dollar for fire-money."

ROLE MODEL. *Jane Addams, co-founder with Ellen Gates Starr of the Hull-House settlement in Chicago, and later to be a joint winner of the Nobel Peace Prize, was born in 1860 in Cedarville, Illinois, where her father was a mill owner.*

The house at the end of the village in which I was born, and which was my home until I moved to Hull-House, in my earliest childhood had opposite to it—only across the road and then across a little stretch of greensward—two mills belonging to my father; one flour mill, to which the various grains were brought by the neighboring farmers, and one sawmill, in which the logs of the native timber were sawed into lumber. The latter offered the great excitement of sitting on a log while it slowly approached the buzzing saw which was cutting it into slabs, and of getting off just in time to escape a sudden and gory death. But the flouring mill was much more beloved. It was full of dusky, floury places which we adored, of empty bins in which we might play house; it had a basement with piles of bran and shorts which were almost as good as sand to play in, whenever the miller let us wet the edges of the pile with water brought in his sprinkling pot from the mill-race.

In addition to these fascinations was the association of the mill with my father's activities, for doubtless at that time I centered upon him all that careful imitation which a little girl ordinarily gives to her mother's ways and habits. My mother had died when I was a baby and my father's second marriage did not occur until my eighth year.

I had a consuming ambition to possess a miller's thumb, and would sit contentedly for a long time rubbing between my thumb and fingers the ground wheat as it fell from between the millstones, before it was taken up on an endless chain of mysterious little buckets to be bolted into flour. I believe I have never since wanted anything more desperately than I wanted my right thumb to be flattened, as my father's had become, during his earlier years of a miller's life. Somewhat discouraged by the slow process of structural modification, I also took measures to secure on the backs of my hands the tiny purple and red spots which are always found on the hands of the miller who dresses millstones. The marks on my father's hands had grown faint, but were quite visible when looked for, and seemed to me so desirable that they must be procured at all costs. Even when playing in our house or yard, I could always tell when the millstones were being dressed, because the rumbling of the mill then stopped, and there were few pleasures I would not instantly forego, rushing at once to the mill, that I might spread out my hands near the millstones in the hope that the little hard flints flying from the miller's chisel would light upon their backs and make the longed-for marks. . . .

I was consumed by a wistful desire to apprehend the hardships of my father's earlier life in that faraway time when he had been a miller's apprentice. I knew that he still woke up punctually at three o'clock because for so many years he had taken his turn at the mill in the early morning, and if by chance I awoke at the same hour, as curiously enough I often did, I imagined him in the early dawn in my uncle's old mill reading through the entire village library, book after book, beginning with the lives of the signers of the Declaration of Independence. Copies of the same books, mostly bound in calfskin, were to be found in the library below, and I courageously resolved that I too would read them all and try to understand life as he did.

COUNTRY SCHOOL. *In this excerpt from his autobiography, Mark Twain recalls an episode from his boyhood in the 1840s.*

The country schoolhouse was three miles from my uncle's farm. It stood in a clearing in the woods and would hold about twenty-five boys and girls. We attended the school with more or less regularity once or twice a week, in summer, walking to it in the cool of the morning by the forest paths and back in the gloaming at the end of the day. All the pupils brought their dinners in baskets—corn dodger, buttermilk and other good things—and sat in the shade of the trees at noon and ate them. It is the part of my education which I look back upon with the most satisfaction. My first visit to the school was when I was seven. A strapping girl of fifteen, in the customary sunbonnet and calico dress, asked me if I "used tobacco"—meaning did I chew it. I said no. It roused her scorn. She reported me to all the crowd and said:
    "Here is a boy seven years old who can't chaw tobacco."
    By the looks and comments which this produced I realized that I was a degraded object; I was cruelly ashamed of myself. I determined to reform. But I only made myself sick; I was not able to learn to chew tobacco. I learned to smoke fairly well but that did not conciliate anybody and I remained a poor thing and characterless. I longed to be respected but I never was able to rise. Children have but little charity for one another's defects.

BUGLER BOY. *The army always had a place for boys who preferred life in the service to life at school. Just after the Battle of the Washita, in November 1868, General George Armstrong Custer encountered one of them.*

Riding in the vicinity of the hospital, I saw a little bugler boy sitting on a bundle of dressed robes near where the surgeon was dressing and caring for the wounded. His face was completely covered with blood, which was trickling down over his cheek from a wound in his forehead. At first glance I thought a pistol bullet had entered his skull, but on stopping to inquire of him the nature of his injury he informed me that an Indian had shot him in the head with a steel-pointed arrow. The arrow had struck him just above the eye and upon encountering the skull had glanced under the covering of the latter coming out near the ear, giving the appearance of having passed through the head. There the arrow remained until the bugler arrived at the hospital, when he received prompt attention. The arrow being barbed could not be withdrawn at once, but by cutting off the steel point the surgeon was able to withdraw the wooden shaft without difficulty. The little fellow bore his suffering manfully. I asked him if he saw the Indian who wounded him. Without replying at once, he shoved his hand deep down into his capacious trousers pocket and fished up nothing more nor less than the scalp of an Indian, adding in a nonchalant manner: "If anybody thinks I didn't see him, I want them to take a look at that." He had killed the Indian with his revolver after receiving the arrow wound in his head.

COUNTING COUP. *Another youthful warrior learns his trade—this time a Crow Indian, who later took the name Chief Plenty-Coups.*

One day when the chokecherries were black and the plums red on the trees, my grandfather rode through the village, calling twenty of us older boys by name. The buffalo-runners had been out since daybreak, and we guessed what was before us. "Get on your horses and follow me," said my grandfather, riding out on the plains.

We rode fast. Nothing was in sight until Grandfather led us over a hill. There we saw a circle of horsemen about one hundred yards across, and in its center a huge buffalo bull. We knew he had been wounded and tormented until he was very dangerous, and when we saw him there defying the men on horseback we began to dread the ordeal that was at hand.

The circle parted as we rode through it, and the bull, angered by the stir we made, charged and sent us flying. The men were laughing at us when we returned, and this made me feel very small. They had again surrounded the bull, and I now saw an arrow sticking deep in his side. Only its feathers were sticking out of a wound that dripped blood on the ground.

"Get down from your horses, young men," said my grandfather. "A cool head, with quick feet, may strike this bull on the root of his tail with a bow. Be lively, and take care of yourselves. The young man who strikes, and is himself not hurt, may count coup."

I was first off my horse. Watching the bull, I slipped out of shirt and leggings, letting them fall where I stood. Naked, with only my bow in my right hand, I stepped away from my clothes, feeling that I might never see them again. I was not quite nine years old.

The bull saw me, a human being afoot! He seemed to know that now he might kill, and he began to paw the ground and bellow as I walked carefully toward him.

Suddenly he stopped pawing, and his voice was still. He came to meet me, his eyes green with anger and pain. I saw blood dripping from his side, not red blood now, but mixed with yellow.

I stopped walking and stood still. This seemed to puzzle the bull, and he too stopped in his tracks. We looked at each other, the sun hot on my naked back. Heat from the plains danced on the bull's horns and head; his sides were panting, and his mouth was bloody.

I knew that the men were watching me. I could feel their eyes on my back. I must go on. One step, two steps. The grass was soft and thick under my feet. Three steps. "I am a Crow. I have the heart of a grizzly bear," I said to myself. Three more steps. And then he charged!

A cheer went up out of a cloud of dust. I had struck the bull on the root of his tail! But I was in even greater danger than before.

Two other boys were after the bull now, but in spite of them he turned and came at me. To run was foolish. I stood still, waiting. The bull stopped very near me and bellowed, blowing bloody froth from his nose. The other boys, seeing my danger, did not move. The bull was not more than four bows' lengths from me, and I could feel my heart beating like a war-drum.

I stepped to my right. Instantly he charged—but I had dodged back to my left, across his way, and I struck him when he passed. This time I ran among the horsemen, with a lump of bloody froth on my breast. I had had enough.

PRIVATE SCHOOL. *As the offspring of one of New England's leading families, Richard Henry Dana, who was born in 1815 and was later to achieve fame as author of* Two Years Before the Mast, *was privileged to attend an elite school.*

The first man's school I went to was that of the Rev. Samuel Barrett, afterwards a Unitarian clergyman in Boston, at Cambridgeport. I was then seven years old, & with him began the Latin grammar. My recollections of this school are far from being pleasant. I am told there are great improvements in the art of school-keeping & that school houses & school going are much more attractive than formerly. Certainly from my own experience there was abundant room for improvement.

This school house was a long low dark room, with wooden benches well cut up, walls nearly black, & a close hot atmosphere, for it was winter & there was a tight sheet iron stove with a long pipe to warm the room. I had been told that the master was very severe, & I knew that flogging was the punishment for every offence. All these things, added to the dismal & repulsive appearance of the room, made my entrance one of gloomy forebodings. The master was a thin, dark complexioned, dark haired & dark eyed man, with a very austere look, & by the side of the door stood a chest in which I knew was kept the long pine ferrule with which all punishment was inflicted. Every misdemeanour,

Sketches of College Life by J.N. Mead

THE FRESHMAN

Lithograph by Tappan and Bradford from a sketch by John N. Mead,
circa 1850.

a bad recitation from carelessness or willfulness, laughing, playing, leaving seats without leave, was noted down, & for every note some punishment was to be inflicted. It was very rarely that a note was forgiven, & some punishment, if it were but one or two blows of the ferrule upon the hand, must follow every misdemeanour. The punishing was done at the close of school, & if a boy had a note early in the day there was the anticipation of the punishment before him the rest of the school hours. When the time came for dismissing school, the books were put away, & the names of all the delinquents called over, the chest unlocked & the long pine ferrule produced. How often did our hearts sicken at the sight of that chest & that ferrule! The boys were then called out, one at a time, & the blows given upon the flat of their hands, from two or four up to one or two dozen, according to the nature of the offence & the size of the boys. A few of the older boys never cried, but only changed colour violently as the blows fell: but the other boys always cried & some lustily & with good reason. . . .

Our master had a mode of punishment rather peculiar to himself; that of pulling the ears of the boys, & dragging them about by their ears. He sometimes dragged boys a good part of the way across the school room, & over the benches in this manner. One of the scholars, John Allston, nephew of Mr. Washington Allston, had an ear so sore that he could not sleep on that side of his head for several nights. This mode of punishment however came to a stop with me. I had been standing up in my class reciting, when a boy made me laugh, a thing I was very prone to do in school. The master rebuked me, but the command and the necessity of preserving my sobriety only made the temptation to laugh stronger, & I laughed again. The master then pulled my ears pretty severely. This sobered me for a time, but the mischievous boy made up the same face again, & my natural propensity to laugh added perhaps to a little desire not to seem intimidated set me going again. This provoked the master & he seized me by the ear & dragged me across the room to my seat. I sat for some time feeling no little pain, but the mischievous boy would not leave me alone & I laughed again. This time the master seized me & dragged me by one ear over the bench & back again. I sat in some pain through school hours, & when we were dismissed the other boys saw that my ear was bloody & that the skin behind, where the ear joined the head, was torn. I was taken home by a procession of boys, & afterwards taken by my father before a committee of the school proprietors. The whole resulted in a vote of the committee requesting the master not to pull boys' ears for the future. Accordingly the ferrule resumed its full sway.

School in Antebellum Savannah. *From* Reminiscences of My Life in Camp with the 33rd United States Colored Troops *by Susie King*

Taylor. After the Civil War, Taylor was a schoolteacher for a while, before moving to Boston where she worked as a companion and nurse.

I was born under the slave law in Georgia, in 1848, and was brought up by my grandmother in Savannah. There were three of us with her, my younger sister and brother. My brother and I being the eldest, we were sent to a friend of my grandmother, Mrs. Woodhouse, a widow, to learn to read and write. She was a free woman and lived on Bay Lane, between Habersham and Price streets, about half a mile from my house. We went every day about nine o'clock, with our books wrapped in paper to prevent the police or white persons from seeing them. We went in, one at a time, through the gate, into the yard to the L kitchen, which was the schoolroom. She had twenty-five or thirty children whom she taught, assisted by her daughter, Mary Jane. The neighbors would see us going in sometimes, but they supposed we were there learning trades, as it was the custom to give children a trade of some kind. After school we left the same way we entered, one by one, when we would go to a square, about a block from the school, and wait for each other. We would gather laurel leaves and pop them on our hands, on our way home. I remained at her school for two years or more, when I was sent to a Mrs. Mary Beasley, where I continued until May, 1860, when she told my grandmother she had taught me all she knew, and grandmother had better get some one else who could teach me more, so I stopped my studies for a while.

I had a white playmate about this time, named Katie O'Connor, who lived on the next corner of the street from my house, and who attended a convent. One day she told me, if I would promise not to tell her father, she would give me some lessons. On my promise not to do so, and getting her mother's consent, she gave me lessons about four months, every evening. At the end of this time she was put into the convent permanently, and I have never seen her since.

A month after this, James Blouis, our landlord's son, was attending the High School, and was very fond of grandmother, so she asked him to give me a few lessons, which he did until the middle of 1861, when the Savannah Volunteer Guards, to which he and his brother belonged, were ordered to the front under General Barton. In the first battle of Manassas, his brother Eugene was killed, and James deserted over to the Union side.

About this time I had been reading so much about the "Yankees" I was very anxious to see them. The whites would tell their colored people not to go to the Yankees, for they would harness them to carts and make them pull the carts around, in place of horses. I asked grandmother, one day, if this was true. She replied, "Certainly not!" that the white people did not want slaves to go over to the Yankees, and told them these things to frighten them. . . .

I wanted to see these wonderful "Yankees" so much, as I heard my parents say the Yankee was going to set all the slaves free. Oh, how those people prayed for freedom! I remember, one night, my grandmother went out into the suburbs of the city to a church meeting, and they were fervently singing this old hymn,—

> "Yes, we shall all be free,
> Yes, we shall all be free,
> Yes, we shall all be free,
> When the Lord shall appear,"—

when the police came in and arrested all who were there, saying they were planning freedom, and sang "the Lord," in place of "Yankee," to blind any one who might be listening. . . .

On April 1, 1862, about the time the Union soldiers were firing on Fort Pulaski, I was sent out into the country to my mother. I remember what a roar and din the guns made. They jarred the earth for miles. The fort was at last taken by them. Two days after the taking of Fort Pulaski, my uncle took his family of seven and myself to St. Catherine Island. We landed under the protection of the Union fleet, and remained there two weeks, when about thirty of us were taken aboard the gunboat P _____, to be transferred to St. Simon's Island, and at last, to my unbounded joy, I saw the "Yankee."

After we were all settled aboard and started on our journey, Captain Whitmore, commanding the boat, asked me where I was from. I told him Savannah, Ga. He asked if I could read; I said, "Yes!" "Can you write?" he next asked. "Yes, I can do that also," I replied, and as if he had some doubts of my answers he handed me a book and a pencil and told me to write my name and where I was from. I did this; when he wanted to know if I could sew. On hearing I could, he asked me to hem some napkins for him. He was surprised at my accomplishments (for they were such in those days), for he said he did not know there were any negroes in the South able to read or write.

ROSE AND SPOOKENDYKE. *Rose Wilder Lane, daughter of Laura Ingalls Wilder, recalls her school days in Mansfield, Missouri. They began in 1894, long before Rose's mother ("Mama Bess") started writing the "Little House" books. The family had recently left Dakota and were now trying their luck on a small, uncleared farm a few miles out of town.*

When I was a little girl in the Ozarks I used to start every year to school. I had a donkey. He was a stubborn, fat little beast who liked to slump his ears and neck and shoulders suddenly when going down hill, and tumble me off over his head. I think he did it for the fun of looking at me in solemn sad forgiveness when I got up. I used to bridle him myself, and strap on the little home-made saddle. At such moments he drew in enormous breaths and held them, and I, who had been fed Black Beauty in my earlier impressionable youth, shrank at the idea of pulling the girths tight, so the saddle used to slide off sidewise as soon as I was on it. . . .

I carried a small tin lunch pail with an apple in it and several slices of brown bread spread with bacon fat, as we were too poor to have butter. We had not yet been able to afford a cow, or even a calf that would grow into one, as heifer calves cost seven or eight dollars. Besides, we had to sell the hay to pay the interest on the mortgage. However, I used to plan that when the apple orchard came into bearing—the trees were then six months old—we would have butter and Mama Bess could have a new dress.

Mama Bess often put surprises in the lunch pail. Sometimes the apple was cut in two without cutting the skin in any way—which is very surprising when you peel the apple and find it in halves already, but simple to do when you know how. Or sometimes there was a raw carrot—I loved raw carrots. Or sometimes—but not often, because sugar cost so much—there was a saucer pie. On such occasions she always told me there was a surprise and it was a point of honor not to open the pail till noon, in order to have all morning the delicious anticipation of the unknown.

So we went over the hills to school, the donkey, the lunch pail and I. First down the hill from the house, Fido following as far as the pasture gate, where he remained looking wistfully after us—and where with joyful barks he always met us on our return.

The school-house . . . was a square red-brick building in a grassless yard, one half for boys, one half for girls to play in at recess. Each side had a wall-less wooden shed to tie the horses under. The horses did not like my dear donkey, whose name was Spookendyke. Spookendyke used to kick them; whenever I heard loud squealings from the yard I used to raise my hand and ask politely please might I be excused to speak to Spookendyke?

There were four rooms in the school-house, two downstairs and two upstairs. I was in the Third Reader, with the Fourth and Fifth Readers in the north room upstairs. All the desks were the same size and my feet ached from dangling. I was a poor girl from the country so I always had to sit with one of the horrid, snuffling, unwashed, barefooted mountain girls. I wanted to sit with one of the town girls—and they all turned up their noses at me. They wore wonderful dresses— red serge trimmed with satin and velvet— . . . and they chewed gum and curled their hair and were always simply throwing nickles away on candy and new tablets.

The school-room was perfectly square, and all of the wall that was not blackboard or window was that shade of green that landlords paint the walls of cheap kitchens. It made a strange feeling in my insides. I told Mama Bess that the walls made me sick. She said I imagined it and must not be silly; besides, I would not be looking at the walls if I were studying like a good girl. I did not study much; the books were so silly. The grammar was all full of things like this:

"Exercise in verbs. Insert words in following sentences:

"'The dog _____ at the cat.'

"'The horse _____ the wagon.'"

I used to sit and look at the Professor. He . . . had long whiskers and was bald. He told us that the whiskers were useful because with them he did not have to wear a tie. I never knew whether this was serious, or a joke. . . . When he was not teaching school he was auctioneer and made jokes professionally. When there was more than one sale a week we had a holiday in addition to Saturday. He got a dollar and his dinner wherever he auctioneered; for miles around, whenever a farmer sold out to move far west to Kansas, he called in Professor Kay to auctioneer. . . .

In those days the Professor used to sit before us, tipped back in his chair, watching us study, ready to catch us if we whispered. He did not have any desk; he kept his chewing tobacco in his pants pocket. In one hand he held a long cane—it was intended to represent authority but he used it mostly to scratch his back. He could run it almost out of sight between his soiled white shirt and his skin, and scratch and scratch with it. Then he would straighten up and call a class.

We all lined up with our toes on a crack in front of his chair, he took one of our books and asked us questions out of it. For spelling there was "Head" and "Foot" to the line. When one of us missed a word it passed to the next, and if he could spell it he moved up one place. Because I was such a good speller I always had to start at the foot of the class. I could move up only when others missed a word, but usually I got to the head before the recitation was over. This did not add to my popularity, but it was my one chance to feel superior to the town girls. They might laugh at my clothes but they couldn't laugh at my spelling. However, they didn't care about spelling.

In one corner of the school-room was the library. It was a bookcase, a bottom part where the erasers and boxes of chalk were kept, and above it three shelves behind glass doors. Two of the shelves were almost full of books, "donated" to the school. At recess I used to get one out and read it and forget my clothes and the green walls and everything. At noon I took my lunch pail away from where the others were eating, so they would not become cruelly aware that there was no butter on my brown bread, and while I surreptitiously ate it I read.

At night I took a book home, and after supper Papa would pop a big pan of popcorn and Mama Bess would read aloud while he and I ate it. She sat beside the table with the lamp on it. Her hair was combed back smoothly and braided in a heavy braid and the lamplight glistened on it. . . . At one end of the table was the stove. I sat on the rag carpet beside it and ate popcorn from my lap. Fido watched every kernel eagerly and I gave him every third one. . . . It was the cosy, comfortable hour for all of us. We had had supper, the room was warm, we were alone together, the horses fed and sleeping in the barn, nothing to worry or hurt us till tomorrow and Mama Bess was reading. That was best of all.

INDIAN SCHOOL. *The author of this piece, Ah-nen-la-de-ni, a Mohawk, was born in Gouverneur Village, in upper New York State, in 1879 and spent his early years on a reservation that fronted on the St. Lawrence River.*

There were four Indian day schools on the reservation, all taught by young white women. I sometimes went to one of these, but learned practically nothing. The teachers did not understand our language, and we knew nothing of theirs, so much progress was not possible.

Our lessons consisted of learning to repeat all the English words in the books that were given us. Thus, after a time, some of us, myself included, became able to pronounce all the words in the Fifth and Sixth readers, and took great pride in the exercise. But we did not know what any of the words meant.

Our arithmetic stopped at simple numeration, and the only other exercise we had was in writing, which, with us, resolved itself into a contest of speed without regard to the form of letters.

When I was thirteen a great change occurred, for the honey-tongued agent of a new Government contract Indian school appeared on the reservation, drumming up boys and girls for his institution. He made a great impression by going from house to house and describing, through an interpreter, all the glories and luxuries of the new place, the good food and teaching, the fine uniforms, the playground and its sports and toys.

All that a wild Indian boy had to do, according to the agent, was attend this school for a year or two, and he was sure to emerge therefrom with all the knowledge and skill of the white man.

My father was away from the reservation at the time of the agent's arrival, but mother and grandmother heard him with growing wonder and interest, as I did myself, and we all finally decided that I ought to go to this wonderful school and become a great man—perhaps at last a chief of our tribe. Mother said that it was good for Indians to be educated, as white men were "so tricky with papers."

I had, up to this time, been leading a very happy life, helping with the planting, trapping, fishing, basket making, and playing all the games of my tribe—which is famous at lacrosse—but the desire to travel and see new things and the hope of finding an easy way to much knowledge in the wonderful school outweighed my regard for my home and its joys, and so I was one of the twelve boys who in 1892 left our reservation to go to the Government contract school for Indians.

The journey to Philadelphia was enjoyable and interesting. It was my first ride on the "great steel horse," as the Indians called the railway train, but my frame of mind changed as soon as my new home was reached.

The first thing that happened to me and to all other freshly caught young redskins when we arrived at the institution was a bath of a particularly disconcerting sort. We were used to baths of the swimming variety, for on the reservation we boys spent a good deal of our time in the water, but this first bath at the institution was different. For one

A reading lesson from the blackboard at the Carlisle Indian School,
a boarding school in Pennsylvania for Indian children whose parents had been
moved to reservations. Photograph by Frances Benjamin Johnson, Carlisle,
Pennsylvania, circa 1900.

thing, it was accompanied by plenty of soap and very hot water, and for another thing, it was preceded by a haircut that is better described as a crop. . . . After the astonishing bath the newcomer was freshly clothed from head to foot, while the raiment in which he came from the reservation was burned. . . .

After my bath and reclothing and after having had my name taken down in the records I was assigned to a dormitory, and began my regular school life, much to my dissatisfaction. The recording of my name was accompanied by a change which, though it might seem trifling to the teachers, was very important to me. My name among my own people was "Ah-nen-la-de-ni," which in English means "Turning crowd" or "Turns the crowd," but my family had had the name "La France" bestowed on them by the French some generations before my birth, and at the institution my Indian name was discarded, and I was informed that I was henceforth to be known as Daniel La France.

It made me feel as if I had lost myself. I had been proud of myself and my possibilities as "Turns the crowd," for in spite of their civilized surroundings the Indians of our reservation in my time still looked back to the old warlike days when the Mohawks were great people; but Daniel La France was to me a stranger and a nobody with no possibilities. It seemed as if my prospect of a chiefship had vanished. I was very homesick for a long time.

The dormitory to which I was assigned had twenty beds in it, and was under a captain, who was one of the advanced scholars. It was his duty to teach and enforce the rules of the place in this room, and to report to the white authorities all breaches of discipline. Out in the school yard there was the same sort of supervision.

After the almost complete freedom of reservation life the cramped quarters and the dull routine of the school were maddening to all us strangers. There were endless rules for us to study and abide by, and hardest of all was the rule against speaking to each other in our own language. We must speak English or remain silent, and those who knew no English were forced to be dumb or else break the rules in secret. This last we did quite frequently, and were punished, when detected, by being made to stand in the "public hall" for a long time or to march about the yard while the other boys were at play.

The system when I first went to this school contemplated every Indian boy learning a trade as well as getting a grammar school education. Accordingly we went to school in the morning and to work in the afternoon, or the other way about.

There were shoemakers, blacksmiths, tinsmiths, farmers, printers, all sorts of mechanics among us. I was set to learn the tailoring trade, and stuck at it for two and a half years, making such progress that I was about to be taught cutting when I began to cough, and it was said that outdoor work would be better for me. Accordingly I went, during the vacation of 1895, up into Bucks County, Pa., and worked on a farm with benefit to my health, though I was not a very successful farmer— the methods of the people who employed me were quite different from those of our reservation.

After I had finished with the grammar school I got a situation in the office of a lawyer while still residing in the institution. I also took a course of stenography and typewriting at the Philadelphia Young Men's Christian Association. So practically I was only a boarder at the Institute during the latter part of my eight years' stay there.

Nevertheless, I was valuable to the authorities there for certain purposes, and when I wanted to leave and go to Carlisle school, which I had heard was very good, I could not obtain permission.

The reason why I and others like me were kept at the school was that we served as show scholars—as results of the system and evidences of the good work the Institute was doing.

When I first went to the school the superintendent was a clergyman, honest and well meaning, and during the first five years thereafter while he remained in charge the general administration was honest; but when he went away the school entered upon a period of changing administrations and general demoralization. New superintendents succeeded each other at short intervals, and some of them were violent and cruel, while all seemed to us boys more or less dishonest. Boys who had been inmates of the school for eight years were shown to visitors as results of two years' tuition, and shoes and other articles bought in Philadelphia stores were hung up on the walls at public exhibition or concert and exhibited as the work of us boys. I was good for various show purposes. I could sing and play a musical instrument, and I wrote essays which were thought to be very good. The authorities also were fond of displaying me as one who had come to the school a few years before unable to speak a word of English.

Over the superintendent of the Institute there was a Board of Lady Managers with a Lady Directress, and these visited us occasionally, but there was no use laying any complaint before them. They were arbitrary and almost unapproachable. Matters went from bad to worse, and when the Spanish-American War broke out, my employer, the lawyer, resolved to go to it in the Red Cross service, and offered to take me with him. I greatly desired to go, but was not allowed.

After the young lawyer had gone away, I heard of the opportunities there were for young men who could become good nurses, and of the place where such training could be secured. I desired to go there and presented this ambition to the superintendent, who at first encouraged me to the extent of giving a fair recommendation. But when the matter was laid before the Head Directress in the shape of an application for admission ready to be sent by me to the authorities of the Nurses' Training School, she flatly refused it consideration without giving any good reason for so doing.

She, however, made the mistake of returning the application to me, and it was amended later and sent to the Training School in Manhattan. It went out through a secret channel, as all the regular mail of the institution's inmates, whether outgoing or incoming, was opened and examined in the office of the superintendent.

A few days before the 4th of July, 1899, the answer to my application arrived in the form of notice to report at the school for the entrance examination. This communication found me in the school jail. . . .

I had been charged with throwing a nightgown out of the dormitory window, and truly it was my nightgown that was found in the school yard, for it had my number upon it. But I never threw it out of the window. I believe that one of the official underlings did that in order to found upon it a charge against me, for the school authorities had discovered that I and other boys of the institution had gone to members of the Indian Rights Association and had made complaint of conditions in the school, and that an investigation was coming. They, therefore, desired to disgrace and punish me as one of the leaders of those who were exposing them.

I heard about the letter from the Training School, and was very anxious to get away, but my liberation in time to attend that entrance examination seemed impossible. The days passed, and when the 4th of July arrived I was still in the school jail, which was the rear part of a stable.

At one o'clock my meal of bread and water was brought to me by the guard detailed to look after my safe keeping. After he had delivered this to me he went outside, leaving the door open, but standing there. The only window of that stable was very small, very high on the wall and protected by iron bars—but here was the door left open.

I fled, and singularly enough the guard had his back turned and was contemplating nature with great assiduity. As soon as I got out of the inclosure I dashed after and caught a trolley car, and a few hours later I was in New York.

That was the last I saw of the Institute and it soon afterward went out of existence, but I heard that as a result of the demand for an investigation the Superintendent of Indian Schools had descended on it upon a given day and found everything beautiful—for her visit had been announced. But she returned again the next day, when it was supposed that she had left the city, and then things were not beautiful at all, and much that we had told about was proven. . . .

I passed the entrance examination easily and was admitted to the Training School on probation. The Institute people wrote and wrote after me, but could not get me back or cause the Training School to turn me out, and they soon had their own troubles to attend to. The school was closed in 1900 as the Government cut off all appropriations.

LIFE AT HARVARD. *In 1639, Nathaniel Eaton, the first head of Harvard College, was charged with beating his assistant with a cudgel "big enough to have killed a horse," whipping his students "twenty and thirty stripes at a time" and giving them "nothing but porridge and pudding, and that very homely." As to this last charge, he "put it off to his wife," who took the blame.*

I must confess, that I have denied them cheese, when they have sent for it, and it have been in the house; for which I shall humbly beg pardon of them, and own the shame and confess my sin. And for such provoking words, which my servants have given, I cannot own them, but am sorry any such should be given in my house. And for bad fish, that they had it brought to table, I am sorry there was that cause of offence given them. I acknowledge my sin it. And for their mackerel, brought to them with their guts in them, and goat's dung in their hasty pudding, it's utterly unknown to me; but I am much ashamed it should be in the family, and not prevented by myself or servants, and I humbly acknowledge my negligence in it. . . .

Forty years later, when Jasper Danckaerts, a member of the Dutch Evangelical sect known as Labadists, visited Cambridge, things seem to have improved, at least from the students' point of view.

We reached Cambridge about eight o'clock. It is not a large village, and the houses stand very much apart. The college building is the most conspicuous among them. We went to it, expecting to see something unusual, as it is the only college, or would-be academy of the Protestants in all America, but we found ourselves mistaken. In approaching the house we neither heard nor saw anything mentionable; but, going to the other side of the building, we heard noise enough in an upper room to lead my comrade to say, "I believe they are engaged in disputation." We entered and went up stairs, when a person met us, and requested us to walk in, which we did. We found there eight or ten young fellows, sitting around, smoking tobacco, with the smoke of which the room was so full, that you could hardly see; and the whole house smelt so strong of it that when I was going up stairs I said, "It certainly must be also a tavern."

We excused ourselves, that we could speak English only a little, but understood Dutch or French well, which they did not. However, we

A 1790 view of Harvard. Several of the college buildings were used as barracks by Washington's troops in the early part of the Revolutionary War. Etching from *Massachusetts Magazine.*

spoke as well as we could. We inquired how many professors there were, and they replied not one, that there was not enough money to support one. We asked how many students there were. They said at first, thirty, and then came down to twenty; I afterwards understood there are probably not ten. They knew hardly a word of Latin, not one of them, so that my comrade could not converse with them. They took us to the library where there was nothing particular. We looked over it a little. They presented us with a glass of wine. This is all we ascertained there. The minister of the place goes there morning and evening to make prayer, and has charge over them; besides him, the students are under tutors or masters. Our visit was soon over, and we left them.

THE ACADEMIC YEAR. *As experienced by Joseph Cleaver, Jr., at Delaware College in Newark, Delaware, close to the border with slave-owning Maryland. The Fugitive Slave Law had been passed in 1850.*

Aug. 31, 1853. Entering day at Delaware College. I set my room in order a little but found I was late for an assembly.

Sept. 1. Classes in the morning after prayers and breakfast which I did not like much and after dinner I had no classes so I set to housekeeping and felt more at home with my things about me but they look strange in a new place. We are talking of buying a shelf for our books.

We look a lot better than most of the rooms where the boys have just opened their portmantos on a chair or on the floor and many have no books at all.

2. One of the boys came up before study hour and is sick for home and especially because the rain keeps us all in and it is cold and damp and dark in the College. I sounded very old and wise and made light of his feeling but it did not do him any good and when he was gone I had not been done any good either.

4. Morning prayers were very dull or over my head, and too long but I was . . . I was interrupted there and I cannot remember what I was going to say.

9. I put a great deal of time on my declamation which will be my first appearance before the Athenaean Literary Society and I want it to be good. They fired a cannon of some sort in the hall tonight and it shook all the building so that it was a long time before anyone settled. The old boys say there was a lot of it last spring meant to call attention to one end of the College when hall police is not wanted at the other end. But some do it just for sport and everyone knows the five or six who are the bottom of most of it. . . .

10. I declaimed at Athenaean Literary Society and did better than I feared. I am up with Cacy, Chamberlin and Clymer to debate next week the affirmative of the question of abolishing the capital punishment.

16. A bench gave way at prayers and made a great clatter while President Graham was speaking.

19. Slept through bells, prayers, breakfast and a part of class. Turner says I shall be called up to explain why I was out all night and though I know it is in jest I keep going over with my mind what I shall say and I almost begin to doubt my own story or my power to prove it to anybody.

20. Serenading which is against the rules but good sport or was until we got ourselves showered with cold water.

21. We learned today that we are misadvised about our serenades so that we would go to the dangerous places, and it is the mystery that we have not been reported to the college. We went out again tonight but with more care and better success for we were asked in to milk and cookies.

Oct. 2. I called at Mr. Curtis's house in the afternoon and though I think I took them by surprise I was made welcome and they asked me to stay to supper and I wished I might but I did not and I wondered all the way back to College why I did not.

7. Out for a walk before bed time. I fell into an open ditch which I never saw before though it was heavily grass-grown. Wet myself through and for a minute I thought I had drowned myself.

10. Ashmead takes a bath every night and the boys on the hall burned paper in the hall and cried "Fire!" when he was covered with lather and carried his clothes away so that he ran almost to the front door that way and met Professor Boswell.

21. Set out my boots for cleaning last night and I have back a pair that are not mine and I do not think that any boy in the College ever war them.

22. I was called in Society to substitute in debate affirmative on the question "Would it be advantagious for a young man to acquire a classical education if he did not intend to pursue a profession?" My side always loses.

Nov. 5. I am with Cacy to debate the affirmative of "It is probable that the Federal Union will dissolve in 2000 years." It seemed a good question when we wrote it down but it seems silly now when I think of debating it.

10. I was unprepared in Mathematics and tried to pretend. He let me hang myself and then laughed with the rest at my embarrassment.

15. We almost froze at the telescope where some of us had outs until very late. I saw no more with the telescope than without it.

16. Butternutting.

19. Too many butternuts. I was elected Treasurer of the Athenaean Literary Society.

23. They say Thatcher has been excused prayers and that has started a lot of speculation on ways to be excused.

25. I gave a little girl a kiss who was crying in the street but she cried louder and put her arms around my neck and I had a chore drying her tears and finding her way home. Now I am the but of a lot of wit bearing on young ladies.

26. I still hear about kissing strange young ladies on the street.

29. I saw my little girl of the tearful kiss and waved to her and she waved to me.

Dec. 1. There was a Nigger boy at the College this morning making his way to Wilmington and the North and asking for shelter until night but Rev. Graham would not let him stay and said the college must not break the law even when the law seems wrong and after he had said that to the boys he went away and did not ask what was done with him. So we put him in the second floor lumber room until night and when he got cold Savin took him in and the boys in his room gave him a coat and went out collecting. I gave the boots that came to me for mine and Turner calls me "Nigger lover" but would have given too I think if he had had anything to give. He left during study hour. There is a strange suppressed excitement and it is a kind of sober quiet too.

3. I was called to debate the justice of taking America from the Indians but the Nigger boy has upset my thoughts about justice.

5. DuHamel heard in Wilmington of a nigger boy being taken which sounds like our boy but not certain and did not dare ask details. Most of our boys are very sorry to hear of it and we hoped it is not the boy we helped.

13. Roe walks in his sleep and he fell down the upper stairs. We were talking of the future and how God might have created a kind of man whose memory would work to the future and the past be unknowable.

15. Playing pitch in the hall. We were reprimanded for the noise and explained that we did it to keep warm which I think did not convince him.

19. The hall is full of potato smoke which I left roasting and forgot.

Feb. 1, 1854. Roe went to sleep at study last night and overset his lamp which exploded and set him afire but Emanuel put it out with a blanket. Turner says Roe is the sort of a boy who would get drowned in a clearing up shower.

10. We bought a lock for our coal box and put it on and when T. went out to it after supper he could not open it and we had to break it open. . . .

14. We made a Valentine for Ashmead as if it was from a young lady and he blushed and stammered and opened himself to a great deal of wit.

17. We have borrowed coal and when we broke open the lid this morning we found it all gone. There is much stealing on the second floor and some people who have lost nothing are suspected.

20. I traded my pocket compas for a blue leather writing case.

21. I bought ink and saw at Mr. Bunker's a gold pen with well attached.

24. Spring weather—it is very hard to stay in and study. I did not.

26. Reed showed me his likeness taken at the new shop and I mean to have one.

27. My cold is very bad. Some of the boys have been suspecting Cathcart of the stealing without any direct cause but last night his coat was taken and now he is going without one. Vindication may not be worth so much. But he has more friends than he had two days ago.

March 3. I have lost a day and I cannot remember anything about it. I am not even sure which day it was. I have worked on my composition but I did not write what is on my mind and I cannot write what is not.

18. Carlile and Row had a fire in their room this morning from starting their stove with fluid.

20. My mind must have been wandering. It wanders when I read and then I discover that I have only been reading words and have not understood it and when I read it over I do not remember even the words.

April 28. I dreamed my Mother came down a steep hill to me and had in a bucket two silver spoons and potato skins.

May 1. There were little children selling May-day baskets at the stile for a penny. I bought one for Miss M. but I did not have the courage to drop it in the daylight and now it has withered.

6. I slept badly and was waked by the night train up, wailing in the distance, and before I could go back to sleep by an even worse bawling of the down train.

8. After supper Baird who has been cultivating Churchman's friendship took him to see the creek road and when they were far out met a gang of unrecognized ruffians who admired C's clothes so much that they took them off one by one and when they had them all got him to say he was cold and built a fire for him and burned his clothes. Then they lost interest and wandered off with Baird whom they said they hated to leave alone in the woods with a wild man and he dared not follow naked but came into hall near morning by a low window which was left open red with mosquito bites and scratches, white with rage and blue with cold.

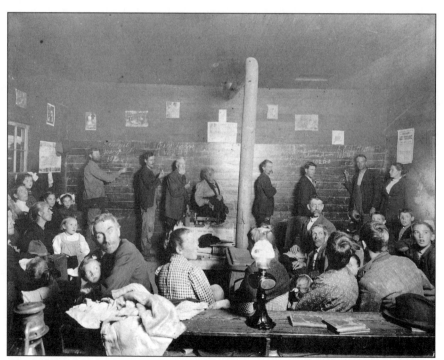

A one-room school for scholars of all ages, from *The Pictorial History of Immigration,* circa 1900.

13. There has been a lot of stealing of door handles in our hall and when I went to bed I found a cold nest of them at my feet.

15. There has been much knotting of bed clothes in our hall.

17. There was a Gypsy in town telling fortunes who cursed me because I would not be told but told others so much that was true that if she had not cursed me I would have asked her who stole from our box.

21. Our Gypsy is back in town for stealing. The skeptical are asking why she did not foresee the result of her theft.

27. I am set to debate the affirmative of "Which affords the greater pleasure sight or hearing?" Even if it were not a silly and futile subject for discussion there is still a question as to which is the affirmative aspect.

June 3. The debate was as I expected and we lost.

14. I am pleased with a musical box that I saw at Mr. Evan's store but I have not money enough to buy it or anybody to give it to.

30. Mr. Hossinger's white bull is at the top of the college stairs and will not go down. Mr. Hossinger says whoever borrowed his bull must return him in as good condition as he took him and he will not come for him so the door has been locked and all passage is by the lower door.

July 1. The bull (and they say Mr. Hossinger) very troublesome in the night; he was still on those stairs this morning where they fed and watered him. He was taken away during Prayers so we did not see him go.

Sweetly by thy side reclining—
All of joy and peace are mine,
Hand in hand—so gently twining
Thou art mine and I am thine.

Strong N.Y.

Where the bending branches shading,
From the rays of summer heat—
This true heart with love unfading
Vows of love—shall oft repeat.

A nineteenth-century lithograph by Strong, issued as a broadside.

CHAPTER

3

PAIRING

"A VERY EXTRAORDINARY METHOD of courtship...is
sometimes practised amongst the lower people of this
province, and is called Tarrying," wrote Andrew Burnaby, a
well-born English clergyman reporting back home in the middle years
of the eighteenth century on the quaint ways of the colonials. Tarrying,
or bundling as it was more generally known, was not the only "extraordinary method" used by Americans of that or other periods in the age-
old business of flirting, courting, getting engaged, getting married,
staying married, having a family, and, sometimes, separating. What
would a proper Englishman have thought of the slave ritual of jumping
over a broomstick, or of paying the justice of the peace with a sack of
potatoes, or of a Texas cowboy using his six-shooter to impress fifteen-
year-old Miss Bulah, or—worst of all—of a Yankee farm girl taking it
upon herself to pop the question?

On the other hand, England was after all the Mother Country, so
there was much in the American way of doing these things that an
Englishman would have found familiar. He would surely have sympathized with the Virginia gentleman who was always in the right when
he quarreled with his wife (but kept his diary in a secret code) or with
the bigamist who ran off into the wilds rather than face the wrath of
his various wives; he would have enjoyed tales of "lustful strumpets"
who were caught in the act and would have admired the persistence
with which a young Sioux wooed the girl he loved; and he would surely have approved of the code of behavior that obliged a young suitor
in antebellum Baton Rouge to go through the dreaded ritual of "asking Pa." And what Englishwoman would not have sympathized with
Fanny Kemble as she tells of two marriages: her own to the slave-owning Pierce Butler, and that of Psyche and Joe, two slaves on the Butler
Island plantation?

To tell these and other stories, this chapter is divided into two parts: Getting Together and then Married Life.

GETTING TOGETHER

PRIVATE PRAYER. *An extract from the journal of John Winthrop, governor of the Massachusetts Bay Colony, for the year 1638. Underhill was eventually forced to leave Massachusetts, charged with adultery and aiding the Antinomians, a religious sect.*

The next Lord's day, the same Captain Underhill, having been privately dealt with upon suspicion of incontinency with a neighbour's wife, and not hearkening to it, was publickly questioned, and put under admonition. The matter was, for that the woman being young, and beautiful, and withal of a jovial spirit and behaviour, he did daily frequent her house, and was divers times found there alone with her, the door being locked on the inside. He confessed it was ill, because it had an appearance of evil in it; but his excuse was, that the woman was in great trouble of mind, and sore temptations, and that he resorted to her to comfort her; and that when the door was found locked upon them, they were in private prayer together. But this practice was clearly condemned also by the elders, affirming, that it had not been of good report for any of them to have done the like, and that they ought, in such case, to have called in some brother or sister, and not to have locked the door, &c.

THE LADIES OF BOSTON. *Dr. Alexander Hamilton, a Scottish-born physician who settled in Maryland, visits Boston in 1744 and reports on what he saw there. Hamilton was aged thirty-two at the time, and a bachelor.*

Friday, August 10. We went on board of Mr. Peach's schooner in the harbour where we drank some Bristo' bottled syder. From thence we went to Close Street to visit Mrs. Blackater, where we saw the two young ladys, her daughters. They are both pritty ladys, gay and airy. They appear generally att home in a loose deshabille which, in a manner, half hides and half displays their charms, notwithstanding which they are clean and neat. Their fine complexion and shapes are good, but they both squint and look two ways with their eyes. When they go abroad [outdoors] they dress in a theatricall manner and seem to study the art of catching. There passed some flashes of wit and vivacity of expression in the conversation, heightened no doubt by the influencing smiles of the young ladys. The old lady, after having understood something of my history, gave me a kind invitation to come and practise physick in Boston and proffered me her business and that of the friends she could make, expressing a great regard for her countrymen, and particularly for physitians of that nation who, she said, had the best character of any. She entertained us much with the history of a brother of hers, one Philips, Governour of St. Martin's, a small Dutch settlement, and had got seven or eight copies of his picture done in graving hung up in her room. Peach passed her a compliment and said the pictures were exceeding like, for he knew her brother; but he told us afterwards that they were only words of course, for there was no more likeness betwixt the man and his picture than betwixt a horse and a cow. This old woman is rich, and her daughters are reputed fortunes. They are both beautys, and were it not for the squinting part, they would be of the first rate.

Saturday, August 11. I went this morning with Mr. Peach and break-fasted upon chocolate att the house of one Monsieur Bodineau, a Frenchman, living in School Street. This house was well furnished with women of all sorts and sizes. There were old and young, tall and short, fat and lean, ugly and pritty dames to be seen here. Among the rest was a girl of small stature, no beauty, but there was life and sense in her conversation; her witt was mixed with judgement and sollidity; her thoughts were quick, lively, and well expressed. She was, in fine, a proper mixture of the French mercury and English phlegm.

I went to Change att 12 o'clock and dined with Mr. Arbuthnott. I had a tune on the spinett from his daughter after dinner, who is a prit-ty, agreeable lady and sings well. I told her that she playd the best spinett that I had heard since I came to America. The old man, who is a blunt, honest fellow, asked me if I could pay her no other compli-ment but that, which dashed me a little, but I soon replied that the young lady was every way so deserving and accomplished that nothing that was spoke in her commendation could in a strick sense be called a compliment. I breathed a little after this speech, there being some-thing romantick in it and, considdering human nature in the propper light, could not be true. The young lady blushed; the old man was pleased and picked his teeth, and I was conscious that I had talked nonsense.

Monday, August 13. I made a tour thro the town in the forenoon with Mr. Hughes and, att a certain lady's house, saw a white monkey. It was one of those that are brought from the Muscetto shore and seemed a very strange creature. It was about a foot long in its body and, in visage, exceeding like an old man, there being no hair upon its face except a little white, downy beard. It laugh'd and grinned like any Christian (as people say), and was exceeding fond of his mistress, bussing her and handling her bubbies just like an old rake. One might well envy the brute, for the lady was very handsome; so that it would have been no disagreeable thing for a man to have been in this monkey's place. It is strange to see how fond these brutes are of women, and, on the other hand, how much the female monkeys affect men. The progress of nature is surprizing in many such instances.

BUNDLING. *This custom, which was also known as tarrying, seems to have been confined to New England—perhaps because of the cold winters there. A board down the middle of the bed and multiple petticoats were added precautions. Andrew Burnaby, an English clergyman visiting Massachusetts in the middle of the eighteenth century, tells how it worked.*

A very extraordinary method of courtship, which is sometimes practised amongst the lower people of this province, and is called Tarrying. . . . When a man is enamoured of a young woman, and wishes to marry her, he proposes the affair to her parents, (without whose consent no marriage in this colony can take place); if they have no

"Saint Valentine's Day," a woodcut composite from *Harper's Weekly*, 1861.

objection, they allow him to tarry with her one night, in order to make his court to her. At their usual time the old couple retire to bed, leaving the young ones to settle matters as they can; who, after having sate up as long as they think proper, get into bed together also, but without pulling off their undergarments, in order to prevent scandal. If the parties agree, it is all very well; the banns are published, and they are married without delay. If not, they part, and possibly never see each other again; unless, which is an accident that seldom happens, the forsaken fair-one prove pregnant, and then the man is obliged to marry her, under pain of excommunication.

BENJAMIN FRANKLIN AND THE PASSION OF YOUTH. *In his autobiography, Franklin tells what happened when, having bought the house in Philadelphia that contained his printing business, he rented part of it to the Godfrey family, who did the cooking and housekeeping. This was in the late 1720s.*

I had hitherto continu'd to board with Godfrey, who lived in Part of my House with his Wife & Children, & had one Side of the Shop for his Glazier's Business, tho' he work'd little, being always absorb'd in his Mathematics. Mrs Godfrey projected a Match for me with a relation's Daughter, took Opportunities of bringing us often together, till a serious Courtship on my Part ensu'd, the Girl being in herself very deserving. The old Folks encourag'd me by continual Invitations to Supper, & by leaving us together, till at length it was time to explain. Mrs Godfrey manag'd our little Treaty. I let her know that I expected as much Money with their Daughter as would pay off my Remaining Debt for the Printinghouse, which I believe was not then above a Hundred Pounds. She brought me Word that they had no such Sum to spare. I said they might mortgage their House in the Loan Office. The Answer to this after some Days was, that they did not approve the Match; that on Inquiry of Bradford they had been inform'd the Printing Business was not a profitable one, the Types would soon be worn out & more wanted, that S. Keimer & D. Harry had fail'd one after the other, and I should probably soon follow them; and therefore I was forbidden the House, & the Daughter shut up. Whether this was a real Change of Sentiment, or only Artifice, on a Supposition of our being too far engag'd in Affection to retract, & therefore that we should steal a Marriage, which would leave them at Liberty to give or withhold whatever they pleas'd, I know not: But I suspected the latter, resented it, and went no more. Mrs Godfrey brought me afterwards some more favorable Accounts of their Disposition, & would have drawn me on again: but I declared absolutely my Resolution to have nothing more to do with that Family. This was resented by the

Godfreys, we differ'd, and they removed, leaving me the whole House, and I resolved to take no more Inmates. But this Affair having turn'd my Thoughts to Marriage, I look'd round me, and made Overtures of Acquaintance in other Places; but soon found that the Business of a Printer being generally thought a poor one, I was not to expect Money with a Wife unless with such a one, as I should not otherwise think agreeable. In the mean time, that hard-to-be-govern'd Passion of Youth, had hurried me frequently into Intrigues with low Women that fell in my Way, which were attended with some Expense & great Inconvenience, besides a continual Risk to my Health by a Distemper which of all Things I dreaded, tho' by great good Luck I escaped it.

SPARKING IN VIRGINIA. *Philip Vickers Fithian had just graduated from the College of New Jersey (later to become Princeton University), where he studied to become a Presbyterian minister, when he took a one-year post with one of Virginia's "first families" as tutor to the children of Colonel and Mrs. Carter. These extracts from his journal begin just after he has spent the day with the Carters and others at a party on board a ship moored in the James River.*

Tuesday, August 2, 1774. About Sunset we left the Ship, & went all to Hobbs's Hole, where a *Ball* was agreed on—This is a small Village, with only a few Stores, & Shops, it is on a beautiful River, & has I am told commonly six, eight, & ten Ships loading before it the Crews of which enliven the Town—Mr Ritche, Merchant; he has great influence over the People, he has great Wealth; which in these scurvy Times gives Sanction to Power; nay it seems to give countenance to Tyranny—The Ball Room—25 Ladies—40 Gentlemen—The Room very long, well-finished, airy & cool, & well-seated—two Fidlers—Mr *Ritche* stalk'd about the Room—He was Director, & appointed a sturdy two fisted Gentleman to open the Ball with Mrs *Tayloe*. He danced midling tho'. There were about six or eight married Ladies—At last Miss *Ritche* danced a Minuet—She is a tall slim Girl, dances nimble & graceful—She was Ben Carters partner—Poor Girl She has had the third Day Ague for twelve months past, and has it yet. She appeared in a blue Silk Gown; her Hair was done up neat, without powder, it is very Black & set her to good Advantage—Soon after her danced Miss *Dolly Edmundson*—A Short pretty Stump of a Girl; She danced well, sung a Song with great applause, seemed to enter into the Spirit of the entertainment—A young Spark seemed to be fond of her; She seemed to be fond of him; they were both fond; & the Company saw it—He was Mr Ritche's Clerk, a limber, well dress'd, pretty-handsome Chap he was— The insinuating Rogue waited on her home, in close Hugg too, the Moment he left the Ball-Room—Miss *Aphia Fantleroy* danced next, the best Dancer of the whole absolutely—And the finest Girl—Her head tho' was powdered white as Snow, & crap'd [curled] in the newest Taste—She is the Copy of the goddess of Modesty—Very handsome; she seemed to be loved by all her Acquaintances, and admir'd by every Stranger—Miss *McCall*—Miss *Ford*—Miss *Brokenberry*—Two of the younger Miss *Ritche's*—Miss *Wade*—They danced till half after two—We got to Bed by three after a Day spent in constant Violent exercise, & drinking an unusual Quantity of Liquor; for my part with Fatigue, Heat, Liquor, Noise, Want of sleep, And the exertion of my Animal spirits, I was almost brought to believe several times that I felt a Fever fixing upon me.

Wednesday 3. We were call'd up to Breakfast at half after eight—We all look'd dull, pale, & haggard!—From our Beds to Breakfast—Here we must drink hot Coffee on our parching Stomachs!—But the Company was enlivening—Three of the Miss Tayloe's—Three Miss Ritche's—And Miss *Fantleroy*. . . . After Breakfast the young Ladies favoured us with several Tunes on the Harpsichord—They all play & most of them in good Taste. . . .

Saturday 27. The morning spent in setting coppies, Sums &c, for the School—After Breakfast, I spent a couple of Hours in the Dancing-Room—Mr Lee in our Room raved against the Scotch—He swore that if his Sister should marry a Scotchman, he would never speak with her again; & that if he ever Shall have a Daughter, if She marries a Scotchman he shoots her dead at once!

Monday September 5. There is wonderful *To do*, this morning among the Housekeeper & children, at the great house. They assert that a Man or a Spirit came into the Nursery about one o-Clock this morning—That if it was indeed a Spirit the Cause of his appearance is wholly unknown; but if it was Flesh & blood they are pretty confident that the design was either to rob the House, or commit fornication with Sukey, (a plump, sleek, likely Negro Girl about sixteen)—That the doors & windows were well secured, but that by some secret manner, unknown to all, the *Thing* opened the Cellar door, went through the Cellar, & up the narrow dark Stairs (which are used only on necessary occasions, as when the great Stair way is washing or on some such account)—That it left the said Cellar door standing open, & besides unbar'd, & threw open the East Window in the little Room, in order, as they wisely supposed, to have, if it should be hurried, a ready passage out—That it had previously put a small wedge in the Lock of the Nursery Door, where several of the young Ladies, & the said Sukey sleep, so that when they were going to Bed they could not Lock nor bolt the door, but this they all believed was done in mischief by the children, & went thereupon to bed, without suspicion of harm, with the door open—That Sukey some time in the Night discovered Something lying by her Side which she knew to be a Man by his having

Breeches—That She was greatly surprised, & cry'd out suddenly to the others that a Man was among them, & that the Man *tickled* her, & said *whish, whish*—That on this She left the Bed & run & squeased herself in by the side of Miss Sally the House-keeper, but that by this time the Whole Room was awake & alarmed—That when the thing knew there was a discovery it stamped several times on the floor, shook the Bedstead by the side of which it lay, rattled the Door several Times & went down Stairs walking very heavy for one barefoot—That on its leaving the Room the Housekeeper went to Ben Carters Chamber, & that he rose & they all went down & found the Doors & window as I have mentioned—All this with many other material accidents is circulating through the family to Day; some conclude it was a Ghost because it would not speak—But, more probably it was one of the warm-blooded, well fed young Negroes, trying for the company of buxom Sukey—The Colonel however, at Breakfast gave out that if any one be caught in the House, after the family are at Rest, on any Pretence what ever, that Person he will cause to be hanged!—This Afternoon Nelson the Lad who waits in our School, was in the woods about half a mile off, where he met with & kill'd a *Rattle-Snake* having six Rattles—He cut off the head, & brought Home the remainder of the Body, which we have skin'd & stuff'd.

Teusday 6. The day fine—It is whispered to Day that B . . . is the Ghost that walk'd in the Nursery the other night, but I think the report is false, and arises from calumny.

Thursday 8. Cloudy & cool. I rise now by half after six—I found it necessary to flogg *Bob* & *Harry* on account of lying in bed, after I come into School.

Sunday 11. Ben rode out yesterday after Dinner and returned this morning; but came on foot, I begin to suspect him of being actually engaged in what several alledge against him—But I will keep off so long as I possibly can, so unwelcome, & so Base a thought of its Reality. . . . Towards evening, I took a book in my hand, & strolled down the Pasture quite to the Bank of the River—Miss *Stanhope, Priss, Nancy, Fanny* & *Betsy Carter* were just passing by—They walked to the *Mill;* there they entered a Boat, & for exercise & amusement were rowed down the River quite to the granary, & then went to angling—I walked to them, & together we all marched Home to *Coffee.*

VENUS AND MARS. *Nicholas Cresswell was twenty-four when he left Derbyshire in 1776 to seek his fortune in America; but as a patriotic Englishman he could hardly have chosen a worse time to come. Suspected (rightly) of loyalism, he was arrested, then released on parole. He made his way to New York, then the headquarters of the British army. Because he was on parole, he could not enlist, and so decided to return home.*

Monday, July 7th, 1777. This morning we had orders to get our water on board with everything ready for sea and proceed to Hell-Gate to-morrow, the place appointed for the fleet rendezvous. About 4 o'clock Furneval came on board and insisted upon me going with him to spend the evening along with some gentlemen of the Navy and Army, at the Hull Tavern, where we stayed till about 12 o'clock. I thought it was too late to go on board. Went to my old lodgings in Queen Street. As I went down St. John's Street I heard something floundering in the Ditch. I stopped and by the light of the moon could perceive something like a human being stirred the mud a little. I plunged in and found it to be a man, whom I hauled to the shore quite insensible. I pulled the dirt out of his mouth with my fingers and in a little time I could perceive him make a noise. I then went to the next sentry, who happened to be a Hessian. I told him the situation of the man below in the Street, but he did not understand English.

After we had sputtered at one another for some time, the Sergeant of the Guard came who could speak English. He very civilly called a light and went with me to the man who by this time could speak, and told us that he had been insulted by a Girl of the Town and had been imprudent enough to treat her rather indelicately. One of her bullies had cut him in several places in the head, knocked him down and dragged him into the ditch. He desired that we would help him to his lodgings in Queen Street, which the Hessian Sergeant and I did. The bruises he had received and the muddy stinking water he had swallowed made him very ill. I went as soon as we had got him to bed and called Doctor Smith to him who immediately let him blood. He appears to be a genteel, well-behaved man, returned me thanks in the most polite terms for saving his life. I am happy that I have been an instrument of preserving it.

Wednesday, July 9th. Drunk tea at Mrs. Bennett's with Major L's Lady and several other ladies. After Tea I waited upon Mrs. L to her lodgings. She insisted upon me staying to sup and spend the evening with her and I did not need much solicitation to spend an evening with a handsome and polite young lady. After supper and a cheerful glass of good wine we entered into a very agreeable *tête-à-tête* and then O! Matrimony, matrimony, thou coverest more female frailties than charity does sins! Nicholas, if ever thou sinned religiously in thy life, it has been this time. This kind, affable, and most obliging lady in public was most rigidly religious. At Mrs. Bennett's she had treated the character of a poor lady in the neighbourhood, who had made a slip and unfortunately been caught in the fact, in a most barbarous and cruel manner. She ran over the Scriptures from Genesis to Revelations. In that strain she continued till after supper and then I soon found she was made of warm flesh and blood. . . .

On Board the Brig, Thursday, July 10th. This morning returned to the Ship. Ruminating upon my last night's adventure most of this day, it will not bear reflection. . . .

Friday, July 11th. A note, or rather billet-doux from Mrs. L. I am determined to go. It would be ungrateful to refuse so kind an offer. My Shipmates begin to smell a Rat, I am rated by them confoundedly, but let them go on. While I fare well at no expense to myself I care not. Should like her better if she were not so religious.

THE IRISH APPROACH. *Fredrika Bremer, a high-minded, good-humored, middle-aged Swedish spinster whom Nathaniel Hawthorne declared "worthy of being the maiden aunt of the whole known human race," was a well-established novelist when she visited this country between 1849 and 1851. Here, in a letter to her sister, she tells of an incident while staying with some friends at Harpers Ferry, Virginia.*

One evening, when somewhat late I was returning home over the hills, I saw, sitting on a style which I had to pass, a man in a blue artisan blouse, with his brow resting on his hand, in which he held a pocket-handkerchief. As I came nearer, he removed his hand and looked at me, and I saw an Irish nose in a good lively countenance, which seemed to be that of a man about thirty years of age.

"It's very warm!" said he, speaking English.

"Yes," said I, passing, "and you have worked hard, have you not?"

"Yes, my hands are quite spoiled!" and with that he exhibited a pair of coarse black hands.

I asked a little about his circumstances. He was an Irishman, named Jim, and had come hither to seek for work, which he had found at the manufactory, and by which he could earn twenty dollars a month. But still, he said, he loved the Old Country best, and he meant to return to it as soon as he could get together a thousand dollars.

I inquired if he were married.

No! he had thought it best to remain unmarried. And then he inquired if I were married.

I replied no; and added that, like him, I thought it best to remain unmarried, after which I bade him a friendly good-by.

But he rose up, and, following me, said,

"And you are wandering about here so alone, Miss! Don't you think it wearisome to go wandering about by yourself?"

"No, Jim," said I; "I like to go by myself."

"Oh, but you would feel yourself so much better off," said he; "you would find yourself so much happier, if you had a young man to go about with you, and take care of you!"

"But I find myself very well as I am, Jim," said I.

"Oh, but you'd find yourself much, much better off, if you had a young man, I assure you, a young man who was fond of you, and would go with you every where. It makes the greatest difference in the world to a lady, I do assure you!"

"But, Jim, I am an old lady now, and a young man would not trouble himself about me."

"You are not too old to be married, Miss," said he; "and then you are good-looking, Miss, you are very good-looking, Ma'am! and a nice young man would be very glad to have you, to go about every where with you."

"But, Jim, perhaps he would not like to go where I should like to go, and then how should we get on together?"

"Oh, yes, he would like, Ma'am, I assure you he would like it! And perhaps you have a thousand dollars on which you would maintain him, Ma'am."

"But, Jim, I should not like to have a husband who would merely have me for the sake of my dollars."

"You're right there, Miss, very right. But you would be so very much happier with a nice young man who would take care of you," &c.

"Look here, Jim," said I, finally; "up there, above the clouds, is a great big Gentleman who takes care of me, and if I have him, there is no need of any one else."

The thought struck my warm-hearted Irishman, who exclaimed,

"There you are right, Miss! Yes, He is the husband, after all! And if you have Him, you need not be afraid of any thing!"

"Nor am I afraid, Jim. But now," said I, " go ahead, for the path is too narrow for two."

And we separated. What now do you think of your proposed brother-in-law?

FARMER'S COURTSHIP. *From a lecture delivered in February, 1859, to the Farmer's Club of North Reading, Massachusetts, by Asa G. Sheldon. Born in 1788 near Boston, Sheldon was a man of parts, ready to turn his hand to any trade: farmer, teamster, stone-worker, inventor, railroad builder—and public speaker.*

Mr. President, allow me to relate an anecdote, which may be of service to some of the rising generation. It will show the young ladies how to reject one man and accept another. The heroine of this anecdote was a respectable farmer's daughter. A young man of her acquaintance called on her one evening, and made proposals of marriage. She told him that she wished until the next evening to decide. The following afternoon she told her father that she wanted the horse to go about

"Country Love," a stereo photograph by R. Y. Young, 1897.

two miles. At the appointed time the horse was saddled, and she mounted and rode off. On arriving at the place where she intended to stop, she saw that the great barn doors were open, and the old gentleman was pitching off a load of hay which stood on the barn floor. She rode up and inquired of him, "Where is your son Samuel?" "He is up on the mow, taking away the hay," was his answer. "I want to speak with him," said she. Sam then jumped from the mow on to the load of hay, by the side of his father. "You need not come any further," said she, "I can say what I wish here; I have nothing private." She then told him that she had received proposals of marriage from a certain young man. "But," she said, "I have never seen any one I love as I do you, and the last time we stood side by side and read in the old schoolhouse, I made up my mind that I never would give my heart and hand to any one until I knew *you* would not accept them. Now," said she, "I want to know whether you will marry me or not." The old gentleman, unable to keep silent any longer, called out, "take her Sam, take her, she'll make you a good one." The young people exchanged a few words, when the old farmer, in joy cried out, "it's a bargain, and I'm a happy witness. God bless you, my children." The next evening, when the young man came for his answer, she told him his offer was an honorable one, and she thanked him for it; that she should always respect him, and speak well of him to her female acquaintances; but duty required her to give a negative answer.

Now, this was a real farmers' courtship, and if there were more like it, there would be fewer unhappy marriages.

TWO WORLDS. *In January 1843, Richard Henry Dana, successful author of* Two Years Before the Mast, *and socially well-connected lawyer, was visiting New York for a case. In his private diary, he records what he did after spending the early part of the evening visiting such friends and acquaintances as Julia Ward Howe, the daughters of Chief Justice John Jay, and William Cullen Bryant and his family.*

Passing down Broadway, the name of Anthony street, struck me, & I had a sudden desire to see that sink of iniquity & filth, the "Five Points." Following Anthony street down, I came upon the neighborhood. It was about half past ten, & the night was cloudy. The buildings were ruinous for the most part, as well as I could judge, & the streets & sidewalks muddy & ill lighted. Several of [the] houses had wooden shutters well closed & in almost [each] such case I found by stopping & listening, that there were many voices in the rooms & sometimes the sound of music & dancing. On the opposite side of [the] way I saw a door opened suddenly & a woman thrust into the street with great resistance & most foul language on her part. She seemed to be very drunk & threatened the life of one woman who was in the house, calling upon them to turn her out too, & saying "I'll watch for you." Her oaths were dreadful, & her drunken screeches & curses were so loud that they could be heard several squares off. As I passed on I still heard them behind me. Next there passed me a man holding up under his arm a woman who was so drunk that she could not walk alone & was muttering senseless words to herself. Men & women were passing on each side of the street, sometimes in numbers together, & once or twice a company of half a dozen mere girls ran rapidly, laughed & talking loud, from one house into another. These I gradually found were dancing houses. Grog shops, oyster cellars & close, obscure & suspicious looking places of every description abounded.

Passing out of Anthony street, at the corner of one next to it, a girl who was going into a small shop with a shawl drawn over her head stopped & spoke to me. She asked me where I was going. I stopped & answered that I was only walking about a little, to look round. She said "I am only doing the same," & came down from the doorstep towards me. I hastened my pace & passed on. Turning round, I found she had followed me a few steps & then gone back to the shop.

The night was not cold, & some women were sitting in the door-ways or standing on the sidewalks. From them I received many invitations to walk in & see them, just to sit down a minute, &c., followed usually by laughter & jeers when they saw me pass on without noticing them. At one door, removed from sight & in an obscure place, where no one seemed in sight, two women were sitting, one apparently old, probably the "mother" of the house, & the other rather young, as well as I could judge from her voice & face. They invited me to walk in & just say a word to them. I had a strong inclination to see the interior of such a house as they must live in, & finding that the room was lighted & seeing no men there & no signs of noise or company, I stopped in almost before I knew what I was doing. The room had but little furniture, a sanded floor, one lamp, & a small bar on which were a few glasses, a decanter & behind the bar were two half barrels. The old woman did not speak, but kept her seat in the door way. The younger one, after letting me look round a moment, asked me in a whisper & a very insinuating air, putting on as winning a smile as she could raise, & with the affectation of a simple childish way, to "just step into the bed room: it was only the next room." Here I had a strong desire to see the whole of the establishment, yet some fear of treachery or fouled play. I had more than $50 in my pocket, a gold watch, gold pencil case, gold double eye glass, & other things of value & being well dressed, I might be looked upon as an object for plunder. I had, too, no weapon; not even a cane. When adventure is uppermost, however, we seldom weigh chances. The house I perceived was very small & it being comparatively early & people passing in the street I had little fear, & went in. The bed room was very small, being a mere closet, with one bed & one chair in it, the door through which we came & a window. There was no light in it, but it was dimly lighted by a single pane of glass over the door through which the light came from the adjoining room, in which we had been. The bed stead was a wretched truck, & the bed was of straw, judging from the sound it made when the woman sat upon it. Taking for granted that I wished to use her for the purposes of her calling she asked me how much I would give. I said "What do you ask?" She hesitated a moment, & then answered hesitatingly, & evidently ready to lower her price if necessary, "half a dollar?" I was astonished at the mere pittance for which she would sell her wretched, worn out, prostituted body. I can hardly tell the disgust & pity I felt. I told her at once that I had no object but curiosity in coming into the house, yet gave her the money from fear lest, getting nothing, she might make a difficulty or try to have me plundered. She took the money & thanked me, but expressed no surprise at my curiosity or strangeness. Perhaps they are used to having the visits of persons like myself from abroad & who wish to see the insides of such places. I thought of asking her how

"How a wine-room syren learned the extent of a loud
young man's wealth—a suit of clothes that was not so good
as it looked," reads the caption below this illustration from
The National Police Gazette, September 25, 1880.

she came into such a place & trying to drop a word of warning as to
her horrible end; but it was getting late, I had no more time to waste,
& I felt a little uneasy at my situation. The thought crossed my mind, if
anything should happen to me, if a row should take place in the
neighborhood, a descent made by the police & I taken up among others, or I should meet injury or an accident which should render me
helpless, I could ill acccount for my being found in such a place. I
therefore left the room, & passing through the front room, & by the

old woman who still sat at the door, was at once in the street. Looking round I saw the girl speak to the old woman & heard them laugh. My outside coat had been buttoned tight all the time I was in the house, yet I instinctively felt in my pockets & about my person to see if all my property [was] safe.

From these dark, filthy, violent & degraded regions, I passed into Broadway, where were lighted carriages with footmen, numerous well dressed passers by, cheerful light coming from behind curtained parlor windows, where were happy, affectionate & virtuous people connected by the ties of blood & friendship & enjoying the charities & honors of life. What mighty differences, what awful separations, wide as that of the great gulf & lasting for eternity, do what seem to be the merest chances place between human beings, of the same flesh & blood.

LOVE ON THE TRAIL. *Interviewed in her old age in the 1930s, Mary Patton Taylor, the daughter of pioneers who followed the Oregon Trail, recalls family lore about her parents' marriage.*

Father and mother's married life began with a romance crossing the plains. Right away mother and father cottoned to one another, but grandfather had other plans. There was another young fellow in their train—they come with a big wagon train of sixty wagons in '48—that grandfather liked better'n Tom Patton, and that was a young man named Trullinger. When Tom Patton asked for mother, he was told to git out. He got all right, but mother was just as stiff as grandfather. She said, "If I marry anybody, it's Tom Patton," and when she said that, with her backbone up, I guess grandfather decided he might as well give in. Anyway, they were married.

Mother always said they had an awful good time crossing the plains. When they come in '48 there wasn't any Indian trouble or anything, and at night they used to have a lot of fun. All they danced then was square dances, and after the camp was settled down for the night the young folks would turn to and dance. Grandfather was religious and awful strict. He didn't believe in dancing, so mother'd go to bed as demure as you please, and as soon as she was sure grandfather was asleep she'd slip out and dance as big as any of them.

When my folks got to Oregon they settled in the Waldo Hills. They settled on their claim just three days after they arrived. My grandparents got here in September, and in November father and mother was married. The only thing mother had to start housekeeping with was a plate. She paid fifty cents for it, and she earned the fifty cents sewing

A MOUNTAIN TRIP

Women were a rare—and very welcome—sight in mining camp. "Mountaineers celebrating the announcement of a betrothal," from *Old Black's Sketch-book; or Tales of California Life*, 1856.

three days for a woman in the Waldo Hills. Father wasn't much better off than mother. He wasn't twenty-one years old, and so he couldn't take a claim. And he didn't have any money, because all he made crossing the plains was his food and bed and fifteen dollars that he got for driving grandfather's oxen. But he wanted to get married, and, when he got there, he went to work for a man named Nicholas Shrum right away. He split rails for Shrum, and all he got was 37½¢ a hundred. Can you beat that? Just as soon as father had $2.25 he thought, Maybe that's enough to pay the preacher. When father and mother was married, father paid over the $2.25. He must have looked kind of poor about it, for right away Elder Simpson asked him how much money he had left, and father said that was all, and then Elder Simpson handed it back to him, telling him he needed it most. But father was gritty. He said, "If my girl's worth marrying, I'm willing to spend all I have to get her." And he made Elder Simpson keep the $2.25.

COWBOY'S COURTSHIP. *Charles Siringo, who described himself as "An old stove up cow puncher who has spent nearly twenty years on the Great*

Western Cattle Ranges" published his autobiography, A Texas Cow Boy, *in 1885. Here he tells of one of his adventures.*

From the "Oaks" I went to Roswell on the Reo Pecos, a distance of one hundred and twenty-five miles, by the route I took. There I struck company, a jovial old soul by the name of "Ash" Upson, who was just starting to the Texas Pacific Railroad, two hundred miles down the river, to meet Pat Garrett, who had written to come there after him, in a buggy.

We arrived at Pecos Station, on the T.P.R.R., one afternoon about three o'clock. And it being a terribly lonesome place, we, after leaving our horses and things in care of an old wolf hunter who promised to see that the horses were well fed, boarded the west bound passenger train for Toyah, a distance of twenty-two miles.

We put up at the Alverado House, in Toyah. It was kept by a man named Newell, who had a pretty little fifteen-year old daughter, whose sparkling eyes were too much for me; to use a western phrase, she broke me all up on the first round.

After supper Ash went out to take in the town, while I remained in the office exchanging glances with Miss Bulah.

It was New Year's eve and Mr. and Mrs. Newell were making preparations for a ball to be given New Year's night.

Toyah was then one of those terrible wicked infant towns, it being only a few months old and contained over a dozen saloons and gambling halls.

About midnight Ash got through taking in the town and came back to the hotel. He was three sheets in the wind, but swore he hadn't drank anything but "Tom and Jerry."

The next morning the town was full of railroaders, they having come in to spend New Years. A grand shooting match for turkeys was advertised to come off at ten o'clock, and everybody, railroaders and all, were cleaning up their pistols, when Ash and I got up, we having slept till about nine o'clock.

Miss Bulah made a remark, in my presence, that she wished someone would win a fat turkey and give it to her. Now was my time to make a "mash," so I assured her that I would bring in a dozen or two and lay them at her feet.

When the shooting commenced I was on hand and secured the ticket which was marked number eleven. The tickets were sold at twenty-five cents apiece, and if you killed the bird, you were entitled to a free shot until you missed.

Mr. Miller, the Justice, was running the business for what money there was in it. He had sent to Dallas, six hundred miles east, after the turkeys, which had cost him three dollars apiece. Hence he had to regulate the distance and everything so that there would be considerable missing done.

Everything being ready, he placed the turkey in an iron box, with nothing but its head visible and then set the box thirty-five yards from the line. The shooting to be done with pistols "off hand."

Ten shots were fired and still Mr. Turkey was casting shy glances towards the large crowd of several hundred men. Mr. Miller wore a pleasant smile, when he shouted number eleven.

I stepped forward trembling like an aspen leaf, for fear I would miss and thereby fail to win Miss Bulah's admiration. I was afraid, should the bullet miss its mark, that the few dozen birds would be all killed before my time would come around again, there being so many men waiting for a shot. At last I cut loose and off went the turkey's head, also Mr. Miller's happy smile. You see, he lacked "two bits" of getting cost for the bird.

Another one was put up, and off went his head. This was too much for Mr. Miller, two birds already gone and only two dollars and "six bits" in the pot. He finally after humming and hawing awhile, said:

"Gentlemen, I don't like to weaken this early in the game, but you all know I have got a large family to support and consequently I will have to rule this young man out of the ring. He's too slick with a pistol to have around a game of this kind anyway."

I hated to quit of course, but it was best, for I might have missed the very next time, and as it was Bulah would think I would have carried out my promise if I had been allowed to keep on.

BUXBY THE WOLF. *A "model letter" from a how-to book published in 1887 under the title* The Whole Art of Correct and Elegant Letter-Writing. *It purports to be "From an aged lady in the country to her niece in New York, cautioning her against keeping company with gentlemen of bad reputation."*

Dear Niece,

The sincere affection which I now have for your indulgent father, and ever had for your virtuous mother when she was alive, together with a tender regard for your future happiness and welfare, have prevailed on me to write you what I have heard concerning your too unguarded conduct, and the too great freedom you manifest when in the company of a certain Mr. Buxby. You have been seen with him at the theater, at Niblo's, at the Museum, as well as promenading Broadway!

Do not imagine, niece, that I write this from a principle of ill-humor; it is on purpose to save you from ruin; for let me tell you, your familiarity with him gives me no small concern, as his character is extremely bad, and as he has acted in the most ungenerous manner to two or three estimable young ladies of my acquaintance, who entertained too favorable an opinion of his honor.

It is possible, my dear girl, as you have no great fortune to expect, and as he has an uncle from whom he expects a considerable estate, that you may be tempted to imagine his addresses an offer to your advantage; but that is a matter beyond question; for I have heard that he is deeply in debt, and also that he is privately engaged to a rich old widow in the Jerseys. In short, he is a perfect libertine, and is ever boasting of the frailty of our sex, and adducing proofs to sustain himself.

Let me prevail upon you, my dear niece, to avoid his company as you would that of a madman; for, notwithstanding, I still hope you are strictly virtuous, yet your good name may be irreparably lost by such open acts of imprudence. I have no other motive but an unaffected zeal for your interest; and I flatter myself you will not be offended with the liberty taken, by

Your sincere friend, and affectionate aunt

Mrs. Clara Upton.

A SIOUX COURTSHIP. *Black Elk, an aged Sioux (Lakota) chief who was interviewed in 1932, recalls how a friend of his youth won the girl he loved.*

This young man I am telling about was called High Horse, and there was a girl in the village who looked so beautiful to him that he was just sick all over from thinking about her so much, and he was getting sicker all the time. The girl was very shy, and her parents thought a great deal of her because they were not young any more and this was the only child they had. So they watched her all day long, and they fixed it so that she would be safe at night too when they were asleep. They thought so much of her that they had made a rawhide bed for her to sleep in, and after they knew that High Horse was sneaking around after her, they took rawhide thongs and tied the girl in bed at night so that nobody could steal her when they were asleep. . . .

Well, after High Horse had been sneaking around a good while and hiding and waiting for the girl and getting sicker all the time, he finally caught her alone and made her talk to him. Then he found out that she liked him maybe a little. Of course this did not make him feel well. It made him sicker than ever, but now he felt as brave as a bison bull, and so he went right to her father and said he loved the girl so much that he would give two good horses for her—one of them young and the other one not so very old.

But the old man just waved his hand, meaning for High Horse to go away and quit talking foolishness like that.

High Horse was feeling sicker than ever about it; but there was another young fellow who said he would loan High Horse two ponies

"The Wedding Party," photograph by Edward S. Curtis. From *The North American Indian.*

and when he got some more horses, why, he could just give them back for the ones he had borrowed.

Then High Horse went back to the old man and said he would give four horses for the girl—two of them young and the other two not hardly old at all. But the old man just waved his hand and would not say anything.

So High Horse sneaked around until he could talk to the girl again, and he asked her to run away with him. He told her he thought he would just fall over and die if she did not. But she said she would not do that; she wanted to be bought like a fine woman. You see she thought a great deal of herself too.

That made High Horse feel so very sick that he could not eat a bite, and he went around with his head hanging down as though he might just fall down and die any time.

Red Deer was another young fellow, and he and High Horse were great comrades, always doing things together. Red Deer saw how High Horse was acting, and he said: "Cousin, what is the matter? Are you sick in your belly? You look as though you were going to die."

Then High Horse told Red Deer how it was, and said he thought he could not stay alive much longer if he could not marry the girl pretty quick.

Red Deer thought awhile about it, and then he said: "Cousin, I have a plan, and if you are man enough to do as I tell you, then everything will be all right. She will not run away with you; her old man will not take four horses; and four horses are all you can get. You must steal her and run away with her. Then afterwhile you can come back and the old man cannot do anything because she will be your woman. Probably she wants you to steal her anyway."

So they planned what High Horse had to do, and he said he loved the girl so much that he was man enough to do anything Red Deer or anybody else could think up.

So this is what they did.

That night late they sneaked up to the girl's tepee and waited until it sounded inside as though the old man and the old woman and the girl were sound asleep. Then High Horse crawled under the tepee with a knife. He had to cut the rawhide thongs first, and then Red Deer, who was pulling up the stakes around that side of the tepee, was going to help drag the girl outside and gag her. After that, High Horse could put her across his pony in front of him and hurry out of there and be happy all the rest of his life.

When High Horse had crawled inside, he felt so nervous that he could hear his heart drumming, and it seemed so loud he felt sure it would waken the old folks. But it did not, and afterwhile he began cutting the thongs. Every time he cut one it made a pop and nearly scared him to death. But he was getting along all right and all the thongs were cut down as far as the girl's thighs, when he became so nervous that his knife slipped and stuck the girl. She gave a big, loud yell. Then the old folks jumped up and yelled too. By this time High Horse was outside, and he and Red Deer were running away like antelope. The old man and some other people chased the young men but they got away in the dark and nobody knew who it was.

Well, if you ever wanted a beautiful girl you will know how sick High Horse was now. It was very bad the way he felt, and it looked as though he would starve even if he did not drop over dead sometime.

Red Deer kept thinking about this, and after a few days he went to High Horse and said: "Cousin, take courage! I have another plan, and I am sure, if you are man enough, we can steal her this time." And High Horse said: "I am man enough to do anything anybody can think up, if I can only get that girl."

So this is what they did.

They went away from the village alone, and Red Deer made High Horse strip naked. Then he painted High Horse solid white all over, and after that he painted black stripes all over the white and put black rings around High Horse's eyes. High Horse looked terrible. He looked so terrible that when Red Deer was through painting and took a good look at what he had done, he said it scared even him a little.

"Now," Red Deer said, "if you get caught again, everybody will be so scared they will think you are a bad spirit and be afraid to chase you."

So, when the night was getting old and everybody was sound asleep, they sneaked back to the girl's tepee. High Horse crawled in with his knife, as before, and Red Deer waited outside, ready to drag the girl out and gag her when High Horse had all the thongs cut.

High Horse crept up by the girl's bed and began cutting at the thongs. But he kept thinking, "If they see me they will shoot me because I look so terrible." The girl was restless and kept squirming around in bed, and when a thong was cut, it popped. So High Horse worked very slowly and carefully.

But he must have made some noise, for suddenly the old woman awoke and said to her old man: "Old Man, wake up! There is somebody in this tepee!" But the old man was sleepy and didn't want to be bothered. He said: "Of course there is somebody in this tepee. Go to sleep and don't bother me." Then he snored some more.

But High Horse was so scared by now that he lay very still and as flat to the ground as he could. Now, you see, he had not been sleeping very well for a long time because he was so sick about the girl. And while he was lying there waiting for the old woman to snore, he just forgot everything, even how beautiful the girl was. Red Deer who was lying outside ready to do his part, wondered and wondered what had happened in there, but he did not dare call out to High Horse.

Afterwhile the day began to break and Red Deer had to leave with the two ponies he had staked there for his comrade and girl, or somebody would see him.

So he left.

Now when it was getting light in the tepee, the girl awoke and the first thing she saw was a terrible animal, all white with black stripes on it, lying asleep beside her bed. So she screamed, and then the old woman screamed and the old man yelled. High Horse jumped up, scared almost to death, and he nearly knocked the tepee down getting out of there.

People were coming running from all over the village with guns and bows and axes, and everybody was yelling.

By now High Horse was running so fast that he hardly touched the ground at all, and he looked so terrible that the people fled from him and let him run. Some braves wanted to shoot at him, but the others said he might be some sacred being and it would bring bad trouble to kill him.

High Horse made for the river that was near, and in among the brush he found a hollow tree and dived into it. Afterwhile some braves came there and he could hear them saying that it was some bad spirit that had come out of the water and gone back in again.

That morning the people were ordered to break camp and move away from there. So they did, while High Horse was hiding in his hollow tree.

Now Red Deer had been watching all this from his own tepee and trying to look as though he were as much surprised and scared as all the others. So when the camp moved, he sneaked back to where he had seen his comrade disappear. When he was down there in the brush, he called, and High Horse answered, because he knew his friend's voice. They washed off the paint from High Horse and sat down on the river bank to talk about their troubles.

High Horse said he never would go back to the village as long as he lived and he did not care what happened to him now. He said he was going to go on the war-path all by himself. Red Deer said: "No, cousin, you are not going on the war-path alone, because I am going with you."

So Red Deer got everything ready, and at night they started out on the war-path all alone. After several days they came to a Crow camp just about sundown, and when it was dark they sneaked up to where the Crow horses were grazing, killed the horse guard, who was not thinking about enemies because he thought all the Lakotas were far away, and drove off about a hundred horses.

They got a big start because all the Crow horses stampeded and it was morning before the Crow warriors could catch any horses to ride. Red Deer and High Horse fled with their herd three days and nights before they reached the village of their people. Then they drove the whole herd right into the village and up in front of the girl's tepee. The old man was there, and High Horse called out to him and asked if he thought maybe that would be enough horses for his girl. The old man did not wave him away that time. It was not the horses that he wanted. What he wanted was a son who was a real man and good for something.

So High Horse got his girl after all, and I think he deserved her.

"**ASKING PA.**" *Baton Rouge, summer, 1860. Cast of characters: Sarah Morgan, a Southern belle, aged eighteen and the narrator; Howell Carter, aged sixteen, a relative by marriage; William Elder Pinkney, a midshipman at the U.S. Naval Academy and in love with Miriam Morgan, Sarah's older sister; Judge Morgan, patriarch and Pa. The four young people are returning in a carriage to Baton Rouge from New Orleans. Sarah and Howell are up front, William and Miriam in the back.*

The moon rose on us while we were yet four miles away from home, before the flush of sunset had died away; but the other two who had sung with us the whole way, grew very silent, and no word or sound reached us two seated in front, except an occasional sigh from the backseat, which sounded like . . . Vesuvius on the eve of an irruption—and they were redoubled, as though put out at compound interest, for every mile we drew nearer home. But *we* laughed, and sat full in the moonlight, singing together, and making Time, and the horses feet, fly.

We landed at Gibbes' house, for mother had moved there while this was being repaired. Neither she or father were home, but we made the bare walls ring with the sound of our voices, until they came in, so glad to see us home again. . . . The young midshipman's spirits were falling below zero; during supper, though I tried my best to enliven him, I only implanted pins and needles in his sensitive heart, and got only the most desperate, heart rending ghost of an occasional smile.

After supper, all walking on the pavement in the moonlight, poor Will came to Howell, and said he must speak to me . . . informed me he was going to ask father—no matter what! I argued, entreated; said father had the gout, please wait for a more auspicious moment, *do* now! but to no purpose. He *would* go right off, only—only—he didn't mind telling me that he was *awfully* afraid! and his heart—was beating like—like—just feel it! And to my infinite astonishment, with one jerk, he

POPPING THE QUESTION.

He may hesitate, but she seems to know what is coming and has dressed for the occasion. Lithograph by Sarony and Major, 1846.

placed my hand on the organ aforesaid, before I could protest. . . . If it had been in the dark, and I, unaware of my locality, I should always have believed that I had stumbled over a mouse trap containing half a dozen freshly caught inmates, each of which was endeavoring to make off in opposite directions, bearing all the others together with the trap. It was laughable—only I was too—I cant say what—to laugh. . . .

The next thing I knew, Howell and I were walking alone on the pavement; it seems to me the moon was brighter in 1860 than it has been since. Passing the parlor windows which were always wide open in summer, I beheld the prettiest tableau I ever yet have seen. Seated in the centre of the room, under the chandelier, sat father, with the crutch he was at that time obliged to use leaning against the arm of his large rocking chair. He was alone in the room reading. Through the open parlor door came two figures, hand in hand. The one nearest us was a tall, strongly made young man, who looked as firm and honest as any one who has made up his mind to a desperate venture, could look; there was actually something noble in the manly air he assumed, as he walked towards father (who had dropped his book now) grasping the front of his coat with his left hand. The other was a girl. . . . Her eyes cast down on the floor, quiet and calm as a marble statue, and yet there was that in her air, that told of a heart beating wildly under that handsome, still face.

Still hand in hand, they stopped in front of father, who was evidently waiting, though perfectly calm, to hear more. The young man's lips moved; I caught the first word, "Judge," and the proud manly look, with the head thrown back, and yet the air of humility, told the rest. I read, from his looks the story of his love, his hopes, his fears, as plainly as though I stood by him. Father looked up to answer, and Miriam sprang to his side and put her arms around his neck, and I heard her say "Yes, father." Her young, girlish face lying on his bluish grey hair, her beautiful arms clasped around his neck, the tears sparkling on her cheek; he talking so ernestly to the young man who now stood alone, with his arms folded over his breast, formed the most touching picture I had ever seen.

I felt it sacrilege to stay, though the whole had scarcely occupied a minute, so Howell and I passed on, with only this comment which I made silently to myself "It must be *awful* to 'ask pa!'"

TWO SLAVE WEDDINGS. *In the 1930s the Federal Writers' Project gathered the multivolume* Slave Narratives, *a compilation of interviews with men and women who had been born into slavery and were by then well into their seventies and eighties. These interviews were written down rather than recorded, and the writers did what they could to reproduce their subjects' tone and speech patterns.*

Tempie Durham and the Broomstick. When I growed up, I married Exter Durham. He belonged to Marse Snipes Durham, who had de plantation 'cross de county line, in Orange County. We had a big weddin'. We was married on de front po'ch of de big house. Marse George killed a shoat, an' Mis' Betsy had Georgianna, de cook, to bake a big weddin' cake, all iced up white as snow wid a bride an' groom standin' in de middle holdin' han's. De table was set out in de yard under de trees, an' you ain't never seed de like of eats. All de niggers come to de feas', an' Marse George had a dram for everybody. Dat was some weddin'. I had on a white dress, white shoes, an' long white gloves dat come to my elbows, an' Mis' Betsy done made me a weddin' veil out of a white net window curtain. When she played de weddin' ma'ch on de piano, me an' Exter ma'ched down de walk an' up on de po'ch to de alter Mis' Betsy done fixed.

Uncle Edmond Kirby married us. He was de nigger preacher dat preached at de plantation church. After Uncle Edmond said de las' words over me an' Exter, Marse George got to have his little fun. He say, "Come on, Exter, you an' Tempie got to jump over de broomstick backwards. You got to do dat to see which one gwine be boss of your househol'." Everybody come stan' roun' to watch. De one dat jump over it backwards an' never touch de handle gwine boss de house, an' if bofe of dem jump over widout touchin' it, dey ain't gwine be no bossin'; dey jus' gwine be 'genial.

I jumped fus', an' you ought to seed me. I sailed right over dat broomstick, same as a cricket. But when Exter jump, he done had a big dram an' his feets was so big an' clumsy dat dey got all tangled up in dat broom, an' he fell headlong. Marse George, he laugh an' laugh, an' tole Exter he gwine be bossed till he skeered to speak less'n I tole him to speak.

After de weddin', we went down to de cabin Mis' Betsy done all dressed up, but Exter couldn' stay no longer den dat night, 'cause he belonged to Marse Snipes Durham an' he had to go back home. He lef' de nex' day for his plantation, but he come back every Saturday night an' stay till Sunday night. We had eleven chillun. Nine was bawn befo' Surrender an' two after we was set free. I was worth a heap to Marse George, 'kaze I had so many chillun.

Rose and Rufus. I's born in Bell County, right here in Texas, and am owned by Massa William Black. He owns Mammy and Pappy, too. Massa Black has a big plantation, but he has more niggers than he need for work on that place, 'cause he am a nigger trader. He trade and buy and sell all the time.

Massa Black am awful cruel, and he whip the colored folks and works 'em hard and feed 'em poorly. We-uns have for rations the corn

At this southern "grand ball," the bride and groom celebrate the "jolly wind-up of the happy day." Sketch by W. I. Sheppard from *Happy Home* magazine, 1874.

meal and milk and 'lasses and some beans and peas and meat once a week. We-uns have to work in the field every day from daylight till dark, and on Sunday we-uns do us washing. . . .

I has the correct memorandum of when the war start. Massa Black sold we-uns right then. Mammy and Pappy powerful glad to git sold, and they and I is put on the block with 'bout ten other niggers. When we-uns git to the trading block, there lots of white folks there what come to look us over. One man shows the interest in Pappy. Him named Hawkins. He talk to Pappy, and Pappy talk to him and say, "Them my woman and childs. Please buy all of us and have mercy on we-uns." Massa Hawkins say, "That gal am a likely-looking nigger; she am portly and strong. But three am more than I wants, I guesses."

The sale start, and 'fore long Pappy am put on the block. Massa Hawkins wins the bid for Pappy, and when Mammy am put on the block, he wins the bid for her. Then there am three or four other niggers sold before my time comes. Then Massa Black calls me to the block, and the auction man say, "What am I offer for this portly, strong young wench. She's never been 'bused and will make the good breeder."

I wants to hear Massa Hawkins bid, but him say nothing. Two other men am bidding 'gainst each other, and I sure has the worriment. There am tears coming down my cheeks 'cause I's being sold to some man that would make separation from my mammy. One man bids $500, and the auction man ask, "Do I hear more? She am gwine at $500." Then someone say "$525," and the auction man say, "She am sold for $525 to Massa Hawkins." Am I glad and 'cited! Why, I's quivering all over.

Massa Hawkins takes we-uns to his place, and it am a nice plantation. Lots better than Massa Black's. There is 'bout fifty niggers what is growed and lots of children. The first thing Massa do when we-uns gits home am give we-uns rations and a cabin. . . . There am twelve cabins all made from logs and a table and some benches and bunks for sleeping and a fireplace for cooking and the heat. There am no floor, just the ground.

Massa Hawkins am good to he niggers and not force 'em work too hard. There am as much difference 'tween him and Old Massa Black in the way of treatment as 'twixt the Lord and the devil. Massa Hawkins 'lows he niggers have reasonable parties and go fishing, but we-uns am never tooken to church and has no books for larning. There am no education for the niggers.

There am one thing Massa Hawkins does to me what I can't shunt from my mind. I knows he don't do it for meanness, but I always holds it 'gainst him. What he done am force me to live with that nigger, Rufus, 'gainst my wants.

After I been at he place 'bout a year, the massa come to me and say, "You gwine live with Rufus in that cabin over yonder. Go fix it for living." I's 'bout sixteen year old and has no larning, and I's just ignomus child. I's thought that him mean for me to tend the cabin for Rufus and some other niggers. Well, that am start the pestigation for me.

I's took charge of the cabin after work am done and fixes supper. Now, I don't like that Rufus, 'cause he a bully. He am big and 'cause he so, he think everybody do what him say. We-uns has supper, then I goes here and there talking, till I's ready for sleep, and then I gits in the bunk. After I's in, that nigger come and crawl in the bunk with me 'fore I knows it. I says, "What you means, you fool nigger?" He say for me to hush the mouth. "This am my bunk, too," he say.

"You's teched in the head. Git out," I's told him, and I puts the feet 'gainst him and give him a shove, and out he go on the floor 'fore he knows what I's doing. That nigger jump up and he mad. He look like the wild bear. He starts for the bunk, and I jumps quick for the poker. It am 'bout three feet long, and when he comes at me I lets him have it over the head. Did that nigger stop in he tracks? I's say he did. He looks at me steady for a minute, and you could tell he thinking hard. Then he go and set on the bench and say, "Just wait. You thinks it am smart, but you am foolish in the head. They's gwine larn you something."

"Hush your big mouth and stay 'way from this nigger, that all I wants," I say, and just sets and hold that poker in the hand. He just sets, looking like the bull. There we-uns sets and sets for 'bout an hour, and then he go out, and I bars the door.

The next day I goes to the missy and tells her what Rufus wants, and Missy say that am the massa's wishes. She say, "You am the portly gal, and Rufus am the portly man. The massa wants you-uns for to bring forth portly children."

I's thinking 'bout what the missy say, but say to myself, "I's not gwine live with that Rufus." That night when him come in the cabin, I grabs the poker and sits on the bench and says, "Git 'way from me, nigger, 'fore I bust your brains out and stomp on them." He say nothing and git out.

The next day the massa call me and tell me, "Woman, I's pay big money for you, and I's done that for the cause I wants you to raise me childrens. I's put you to live with Rufus for that purpose. Now, if you doesn't want whipping at the stake, you do what I wants."

I thinks 'bout Massa buying me offen the block and saving me from being separated from my folks and 'bout being whipped at the stake. There it am. What am I's to do? So I 'cides to do as the massa wish, and so I yields.

When we-uns am given freedom, Massa Hawkins tells us we can stay and work for wages or share-crop the land. Some stays and some goes. My folks and me stays. We works the land on share for three years, then moved to other land near by. I stays with my folks till they dies.

I never marries, 'cause one 'sperience am 'nough for this nigger. After what I does for the massa, I's never wants no truck with any man. The Lord forgive this colored woman, but he have to 'scuse me and look for some others for to 'plenish the earth.

PIONEER WEDDING. *The author of this piece, Jessie Hill Rowland, lived in Kansas when it was still frontier country.*

My father, being one of the early pioneers and a justice of the peace, was called upon many times to report 'Wilt thou, Mary?' and 'Wilt thou, John?' . . .

On one of those occasions my father was asked to preside at a wedding ten miles away from our home and my mother received an invitation to accompany him. Upon arriving at their destination they were ushered down six steps into a dugout, where the mother of the bride was preparing a wedding feast. There was but one room and the furniture consisted of two chairs, one with only two rounds to the back and bottomless. A bed made of scantlings, a board table, a short bench, a stove and a motto hung over the door, 'God Bless Our Home.'

There was no floor, and a sheet had been stretched across one corner of the room. The bride and groom were stationed behind this, evidently under the impression it would not be proper to appear until time for the ceremony. . . .

Mrs. Brown, we will call her, was grinding something in a coffee mill but arose to receive her guests with all the dignity of the first lady of the land. She placed one chair for my mother and one for my father; seating herself upon the bench, she continued turning the coffee grinder. Soon after some of the neighbors came in and at the appointed time the bride and groom emerged arm in arm from behind the temporary curtain and stepping forward to where my father was sitting, all became quiet and he pronounced the words that made them one.

Soon after all sat down to the wedding supper. The sheet that hung across the corner of the room was taken down and spread over the table for a cloth. Mrs. Brown's efforts at the coffee mill had turned out some delicious coffee, made of dried carrots. There were seven different kinds of sauce, all made out of wild plums put up in seven different ways. The rest of the menu was quite simple and consisted of plain bread and butter, and fried pork. The table was shoved close to the bed and three sat on that side while three sat on the bench. The chairs were occupied and two or three kegs finished out the number of seats.

After supper the bridegroom took my father to one side and asked him to accept some potatoes in payment for performing the ceremony. He readily consented and returned home.

A WORD OF WARNING. *Sylvester Graham, advocate of cold showers, hard mattresses, and unsifted whole wheat flour (whence the Graham cracker) and "Public Lecturer on the Science of Human Life," gave the following advice in his book* Lecture to Young Men, *first published in 1834.*

The mere fact that a man is married to one woman, and is perfectly continent to her, will by no means prevent the evils which flow from sexual excess, if his commerce with her exceeds the bounds of that connubial chastity which is founded on the real wants of the system. Beyond all question, an immeasurable amount of evil results to the human family from sexual excess within the precincts of wedlock. Langor, lassitude, muscular relaxation, general debility and heaviness, depression of spirits, loss of appetite, indigestion, faintness and sinking at the pit of the stomach, increased susceptibilities of the skin and lungs to all atmospheric changes, feebleness of circulation, chilliness, head-ache, melancholy, hypochondria, hysterics, feebleness of all the senses, impaired vision, loss of sight, weakness of the lungs, nervous cough, pulmonary consumption, disorders of the liver and kidneys, urinary difficulties, disorders of the genital organs, weakness of the

brain, loss of memory, epilepsy, insanity, apoplexy,—and extreme feebleness and early death of offspring,—are among the too common
evils which are caused by sexual excesses between husband and wife.

MARRIED LIFE

A PURITAN TO HIS WIFE. *On March 28, 1630, while on board the*
Arbella, *which was delayed by contrary winds at Cowes, the future governor of*
Massachusetts, John Winthrop, wrote this letter to his wife, Margaret, who was
in Groton, Suffolk.

And now (my sweet soule) I must once againe take my last farewell
of thee in old England, it goeth verye neere to my heart to leave thee,
but I know to whom I have committed thee, even to him, who loves
thee much better than any husband can, who hath taken account of
the haires of thy head, and putts all thy teares in his bottle, who can,
and (if it be for his glorye) will bringe us togither againe with peace
and comfort, oh how it refresheth my heart to thinke that I shall yet
againe see thy sweet face in the lande of the livinge: that lovely countenance, that I have so much delighted in, and beheld with so great
contente! I have hetherto been so taken up with businesse, as I could
seldome looke backe to my former happinesse, but now when I shalbe
at some leysure, I shall not avoid the remembrance of thee, nor the
greife for thy absence: thou hast thy share with me, but I hope, the
course we have agreed upon wilbe some ease to us both, mundayes
and frydayes at 5: of the clocke at night, we shall meet in spiritt till we
meet in person, yet if all these hopes should faile, blessed be our God,
that we are assured, we shall meet one day, if not as husband and wife,
yet in a better condition, let that staye and comfort thy heart, neither
can the sea drowne thy husband, nor enemyes destroye, nor any adver-
sity deprive thee of thy husband or children. therefore I will onely take
thee now and my sweet children in mine armes, and kisse and
embrace you all, and so leave you with my God. farewell farewell. I
blesse you all in the name of the Lord Jesus. . . .

Thine wheresoever
Jo: Winthrop.

A BIGAMIST. *From a letter written by Governor Thomas Dudley in*
Massachusetts to "The right honourable, my very good lady, the Lady Bridget,
Countess of Lincoln" in England, March 12, 1631.

We were lately informed that one Mr. Gardiner, who arrived here a
month before us (and who passed here for a knight by the name of Sir

Christopher Gardiner all this while), was no knight, but instead thereof, had two wives, now living in a house at London, one of which came about September last from Paris in France (where her husband had left her four years before) to London, where she had heard her husband had married a second wife, and whom by enquiry she found out, and they both condoling each other's estate wrote both their letters to the Governour . . . his first wife desiring his return and conversion; his second his destruction for his foul abuse, and for robbing her of her estate of a part whereof she sent an inventory hither comprising therein many rich jewels, much plate and costly linen. This man had in his family (and yet hath) a gentlewoman whom he called his kinswoman and whom one of his wives in her letter names Mary Grove, affirming her to be a known harlot, whose sending back into Old England she also desired together with her husband.

Shortly after this intelligence we sent to the house of the said Gardiner (which was seven miles from us) to apprehend him and his woman with a purpose to send them both to London to his wives there, but the man, who having heard some rumour from some who came in the ship that letters were come to the governour requiring justice against him, was readily prepared for flight so soon as he should see any crossing the river likely to apprehend him, which he accordingly performed; for he dwelling alone easily discerned such who were sent to take him, half a mile before they approached his house, and with his piece on his neck went his way as most men think northwards, hoping to find some English there like to himself, but likely enough it is which way soever he went, he will lose himself in the woods and be stopped with some rivers in his passing, notwithstanding his compass in his pocket, and so with hunger and cold will perish, before he find the place he seeks.

ADULTERY PUNISHED. *Article Nine of the Massachusetts "Body of Liberties," adopted in 1641, stated: "If any person committeth adultery with a married or espoused wife, the adulterer and adulteress shall surely be put to death." Here is an example of the law in action.*

At this court of assistants one James Britton, a man ill affected both to our church discipline and civil government, and one Mary Latham, a proper young woman about 18 years of age, whose father was a godly man and had brought her up well, were condemned to die for adultery, upon a law formerly made and published in print. It was thus occasioned and discovered. This woman, being rejected by a young man whom she had an affection unto, vowed she would marry the next that came to her, and accordingly, against her friends' minds, she matched with an ancient man who had neither honesty nor ability, and one whom she had no affection unto. Whereupon, soon after she was married, divers young men solicited her chastity, and drawing her into bad company, and giving her wine and other gifts, easily prevailed with her, and among others this Britton. But God smiting him with a deadly palsy and fearful horror of conscience withal, he could not keep secret, but discovered this, and other the like with other women, and was forced to acknowledge the justice of God in that having often called others fools, etc., for confessing against themselves, he was now forced to do the like. The woman dwelt now in Plimouth patent, and one of the magistrates there, hearing she was detected, etc., sent her to us. Upon her examination, she confessed he did attempt the fact, but did not commit it, and witness was produced that testified (which they both confessed) that in the evening of a day of humiliation through the country for England [because of the English civil war], a company met at Britton's and there continued drinking sack, etc., till late in the night, and then Britton and the woman were seen upon the ground together, a little from the house. It was reported also that she did frequently abuse her husband, setting a knife to his breast and threatening to kill him, calling him old rogue and cuckold, and said she would make him wear horns as big as a bull. And yet some of the magistrates thought the evidence not sufficient against her, because there were not two direct witnesses; but the jury cast her, and then she confessed the fact, and accused twelve others, whereof two were married men. Five of these were apprehended and committed, (the rest were gone,) but denying it, and there being no other witness against them than the testimony of a condemned person, there could be no proceeding against them. The woman proved very penitent, and had deep apprehension of the foulness of her sin, and at length attained to hope of pardon by the blood of Christ, and was willing to die in satisfaction to justice. The man also was very much cast down for his sins, but was loth to die, and petitioned the general court for his life, but they would not grant it, though some of the magistrates spake much for it, and questioned the letter, whether adultery was death by God's law now. This Britton had been a professor [avowed Christian] in England, but coming hither he opposed our church government, etc., and grew dissolute, losing both power and profession of godliness.

They were both executed, they both died very penitently, especially the woman, who had some comfortable hope of pardon of her sin, and gave good exhortation to all young maids to be obedient to their parents, and to take heed of evil company.

A LUSTFUL STRUMPET. *A case of adultery among the Indians, as recounted by William Wood in* New England's Prospect, *1634.*

There was one Abamoch married a wife, whom a long time he entirely loved above her deservings, for that she often in his absence entertained strangers, of which he was oftentimes informed by his neighbors. But he harboring no spark of jealousy, believed not their false informations (as he deemed them) being in a manner angry they should slander his wife, of whose constancy he was so strongly conceited. A long time did her whorish glozing and Siren-like tongue, with her subtle carriage, establish her in her husband's favor till fresh complaints caused him to cast about how to find out the truth and to prove his friends liars and his wife honest, or her a whore and his friends true. Whereupon he pretended a long journey to visit his friends, providing all accoutrements for a fortnight's journey, telling his wife it would be so long before she could expect his return, who outwardly sorrowed for his departure but inwardly rejoiced that she should enjoy the society of her old leman, whom she sent for with expedition, not suspecting her husband's plot, who lay not many miles off in the woods; who, after their dishonest revelings, when they were in their midnight sleep, approaches the wigwam, enters the door, which was neither barred nor locked, makes a light to discover what he little suspected. But finding his friends' words to be true, he takes a good bastinado in his hand, brought for the same purpose, dragging him by the hair from his usurped bed, so lamentably beating him that his battered bones and bruised flesh made him a fitter subject for some skillful surgeon than the lovely object of a lustful strumpet. Which done, he put away his wife, exposing her to the courtesy of strangers for her maintenance, that so courtesan-like had entertained a stranger into her bosom.

DIVORCE IN NEW NETHERLAND. *Isaack de Rasieres' 1628 report on the customs of the Indians living in and around New Amsterdam.*

When a man is unfaithful, the wife accuses him before the Sackima, which most frequently happens when the wife has a preference for another man. The husband being found guilty, the wife is permitted to draw off his right shoe and left stocking (which they make of deer or elk skins, which they know how to prepare very broad and soft, and wear in the winter time); she then tears off the lappet that covers his private parts, gives him a kick behind, and so drives him out of the house; and then "Adam" scampers off.

PURITAN PATERFAMILIAS. *Three groups of entries from the diary of Samuel Sewall of Boston, a leading citizen, deputy to the General Court, and member of the Governor's Council. Sewall was one of the nine judges to preside over the Salem witch trials of 1692—and the only one later to confess publicly that he had been in error. At the time of the first entry, Sewall was aged twenty-four and recently married. Mother Hull was his mother-in-law.*

April 1, 1677. About Two of the Clock at night I waked and perceived my wife ill: asked her to call Mother. She said I should goe to prayer, then she would tell me. Then I rose, lighted a Candle at Father's fire, that had been raked up from Saturday night, kindled a Fire in the chamber, and after 5 when our folks up, went and gave Mother warning. She came and bad me call the Midwife, Goodwife Weeden, which I did. But my Wives pains went away in a great measure after she was up; toward night came on again, and about a quarter of an hour after ten at night, April 2, Father and I sitting in the great Hall, heard the child cry, whereas we were afraid 'twould have been 12 before she would have been brought to Bed. Went home with the Midwife about 2 o'clock, carrying her Stool, whose parts were included in a Bagg. Met with the Watch at Mr. Rocks Brew House, who bad us stand, enquired what we were. I told the Woman's occupation, so they bad God bless our labours, and let us pass. The first Woman the Child sucked was Bridget Davenport. *April 3.* Cousin Flint came to us. She said we ought to lay scarlet on the Child's head for that it had received some harm. Nurse Hurd watches. *April 4.* Clear cold weather. Goodwife Ellis watches. *April 7.* First laboured to cause the child suck his mother, which he scarce did at all. In the afternoon my Wife set up, and he sucked the right Breast bravely, that had the best nipple. *April 8.* Sabbath day, rainy and stormy in the morning, but in the afternoon fair and sunshine, though a blustering Wind; so Eliz. Weeden, the Midwife, brought the Infant to the third Church when Sermon was about half done in the afternoon, Mr. Thatcher preaching. After Sermon and Prayer, Mr. Thacher prayed for Capt. Scottow's Cousin and it, then I named him John, and Mr. Thacher baptized him into the name of the Father, Son, and H. Ghost. *April 9,* morn. Hot and gloomy with scattered Clouds: about 11 clock there fell a considerable Storm of Hail, after that it thundered a pretty while. [*Note*] The Child sucked his Mothers left Brest well as she laid in the Bed, notwithstanding the shortness of the Nipple.

Nov. 21, 1694. My wife is brought to bed of a Daughter between 9. and 10. of the Clock in the morn. Mr. Torrey prayd with Mother and me in the Kitchen of the new house for that mercy; Mother desiring Him, saying that my wife was in great and more than ordinary Extremity, so that she was not able to endure the Chamber: I went also to acquaint Mr. Willard, and as I came back, I met Mrs. Perce, who wish'd me joy of my Daughter, as came in at the Gate. Mr. Torrey was prevail'd with to go into Chamber and Return Thanks to God. Women din'd with rost Beef and minc'd Pyes, good Cheese and Tarts. Grows to a very great Storm.

Jany 2, 1701/2. My Wife had some thoughts the Time of her Travail might be come, before she went to bed: but it went over. Between 4 and 5 m. I go to prayer, Rise, make a Fire, call Mrs. Ellis, Hawkins. Mary Hawkins calls Midwife Greenlef. I go to Mr. Willard and desire him to call God. The Women call me into chamber, and I pray there. *Jany 2.* My Wife is well brought to Bed of a Daughter just about two p.m., a very cold day: Was got into Bed without a fainting Fit. Sabbath-day night my wife is very ill and something delirious. Pulse swift and high. I call Mr. Oakes about Two aclock or before. Grows a little better. *Jany 6.* Nurse Hill watch'd last night. Wife had a comfortable night.

What through my wife's many Illnesses, more than ordinary, her fall upon the stairs about 5 weeks before; from which time she kept her chamber; her thoughtfullness between whiles whether she were with child or no; her Fears what the issue would be, and the misgiving of our Unbelieving hearts, GOD hath been wonderfully Merciful to us in her comfortable Delivery; which I desire to have Recorded.

Note. This is the Thirteenth Child that I have offered up to God in Baptisme. . . . I have named this little Daughter Judith, in remembrance of her honoured and beloved Grandmother Mrs. *Judith Hull.* And it may be my dear wife may now leave off bearing.

MARRIAGE À LA MODE. *A year and a half in the married life of the Virginia aristocrat William Byrd II, thirty-five years old, member of the Governor's Council, and master of an estate of some 26,000 acres. Westover, the Byrd mansion, was on the James River, not far from Williamsburg, at that time the capital of Virginia. These extracts are from Byrd's diary, which—for good reason—he wrote in a secret code.*

February 8, 1709. I rose at 5 o'clock this morning and read a chapter in Hebrew and 200 verses in Homer's *Odyssey.* I ate milk for breakfast. I said my prayers. Jenny and Eugene [servants] were whipped. I danced my dance [gymnastic exercises]. I read law in the morning and Italian in the afternoon. I ate tough chicken for dinner. In the evening I walked about the plantation. I said my prayers. I had good thoughts, good health, and good humor this day, thanks be to God Almighty. *February 22.* I threatened Anaka [servant] with a whipping if she did not confess the intrigue between Daniel and Nurse, but she prevented by a confession. I chided Nurse severely about it, but she denied, with an impudent face, protesting that Daniel only lay on the bed for the sake of the child. I ate nothing but beef for dinner.

March 31. I rose at 6 o'clock and read a chapter in Hebrew and 200 verses in Homer's *Odyssey*. I ate nothing but boiled beef for dinner. My wife was out of humor for nothing. However I endeavored to please her again, having consideration for a woman's weakness. I played at billiards with the ladies. I read Italian. In the evening we walked about the plantation.

April 7. I rose before 6 o'clock and read two chapters in Hebrew and 250 verses in Homer's *Odyssey*. I settled my accounts and read Italian. I reproached my wife with ordering the old beef to be kept and the fresh beef used first, contrary to good management, on which she was pleased to be very angry and this put me out of humor. I went away presently after dinner to look after my people. When I returned I read more Italian and then my wife came and begged my pardon and we were friends again. *April 8.* My wife and I had another foolish quarrel about my saying she listened at the top of the stairs, which I suspected, in jest. However, I bore it with patience and she came soon after and begged my pardon. I settled my accounts and read some Dutch. Just before dinner Mr. Custis came and dined with us. I did not keep to my rule of eating but the one dish. We played at billiards and walked about the plantation. *April 9.* My wife and I had another scold about mending my shoes but it was soon over by her submission. In the evening we took a walk about the plantation. *April 17.* I rose at 5 o'clock and read a chapter in Hebrew and 150 verses in Homer. Anaka was whipped yesterday for stealing the rum and filling the bottle up with water. I went to church, where were abundance of people. *April 18.* I rose at 3 o'clock and after committing my family to the divine protection, I went in the boat to Mr. Harvey's, where I got by break of day. From thence I proceeded to Williamsburg, where I got about 10 o'clock. I went to court. When the court rose I went to dinner with the Council, where I ate nothing but boiled beef. Then we went to the President's where we played at cards till 10 o'clock. I won 25 shillings. *April 26.* We went to the Council where it was agreed to open the Indian trade. About 4 o'clock we went to dinner. Mr. Will Randolph and I went to Colonel Bray's, where we found abundance of ladies and gentlemen dancing. We did not dance but got some kisses among them. About 11 o'clock we returned home. *April 29.* About noon my spouse arrived and left all things well at home this morning, thanks be to God. We dined at Mr. Bland's. About 10 o'clock we went to bed, where I lay in my wife's arms. I had good health, good thoughts, and good humor, thanks be to God Almighty.

May 1. I rose about 6 o'clock. My wife was a little indisposed and out of humor. I ate bread and butter for breakfast. We went to church over the creek and Mr. Taylor preached a good sermon. After dinner we were forced to keep house because of the rain. In the evening we talked about religion and my wife and her sister had a fierce dispute about the infallibility of the Bible. *May 7.* We rose at break of day and were on horseback before sunrise to return home, after taking leave of our friends. My wife had a pain in her belly which made me afraid she would miscarry. However we made shift to get her home and after some rest she recovered.

June 2. I was out of humor with my wife for trusting Anaka with rum to steal when she was so given to drinking, but it was soon over. In the afternoon we played at billiards, and I translated some Greek into Latin and into English. In the evening we rode out to take the air. *June 14.* I rose at 5 o'clock and read a chapter in Hebrew and some Greek in Josephus. I said my prayers and ate chocolate for breakfast. We heard guns this morning, by which we understood that the fleet was come in. I ate bacon and chicken for dinner. I heard guns from Swinyard's and sent my boat for my letters. In the evening the boat returned and brought some letters for me from England, with an invoice of things sent for by my wife which are enough to make a man mad. It put me out of humor very much. I neglected to say my prayers, for which God forgive me.

July 12. I ate pig for dinner and ate too much. I took a nap and was out of order over it. My wife was very melancholy, but I comforted her as well as I could and was troubled to see her so. I played at billiards with the Doctor and lost.

August 24. My wife complained all day very much of her belly, but to no purpose. *August 27.* I had like to have whipped my maid Anaka for her laziness but I forgave her. I read a little geometry. I denied my man G-r-l to go to a horse race because there was nothing but swearing and drinking there. I ate roast mutton for dinner. In the afternoon I played at piquet with my own wife and made her out of humor by cheating her.

September 3. My wife was indisposed again but not to much purpose. I ate roast chicken for dinner. In the afternoon I beat Jenny for throwing water on the couch. *September 5.* My wife was much out of order and had frequent returns of her pains. In the evening I took a walk about the plantation and when I returned I found my wife very bad. I sent for Mrs. Hamlin and my cousin Harrison about 9 o'clock and I said my prayers heartily for my wife's happy delivery. I went to bed about 10 o'clock and left the women full of expectation with my wife. *September 6.* About one o'clock this morning my wife was happily delivered of a son, thanks be to God Almighty. I was awake in a blink and rose and my cousin Harrison met me on the stairs and told me it was a boy. We drank some French wine and went to bed again and rose at 7 o'clock. *September 28.* About 11 o'clock Mr. Anderson came and soon after Mr. Harrison, his wife, and daughter. About 12 o'clock our son was christened and his name was Parke. God grant him grace to be a good man. The two captains of the men-of-war were godfathers. When this was over we played at cards again till dinner. *September 30.* I rose at 8 o'clock because my cold was bad. I said my prayers shortly and ate milk for breakfast. I gave my wife a flourish this morning. About 12 o'clock I rode to Mr. Anderson's where I ate some roast beef.

October 6. I rose at 6 o'clock and said my prayers and ate milk for breakfast. Then I proceeded to Williamsburg, where I found all well. I went to the capitol where I sent for the wench to clean my room and when I came I kissed her and felt her, for which God forgive me. Then I went to see the President [of the council], whom I found indisposed in his ears. I dined with him on beef. Then we went to his house and played at piquet where Mr. Clayton came to us. We had much to do to get a bottle of French wine. About 10 o'clock I went to my lodgings. I had good health but wicked thoughts, God forgive me. *October 27.* We went to court and sat till 4 o'clock. In the evening we played at cards and I won £5. We drank some of Will Robinson's cider till we were very merry and then went to the coffeehouse and pulled poor Colonel Churchill out of bed. I went home about one o'clock in the morning. *October 29.* Went to court where we sat till about 3 o'clock and then I learned that my sister Custis was at Mr. Bland's. I went to her and there was also Mrs. Chiswell. Here I stayed till 8 o'clock and then walked home. *October 31.* We sat in court till about 4 o'clock and then I rode to Green Springs to meet my wife. I found her there and had the pleasure to learn that all was well at home, thanks be to God. There was likewise Mrs. Chiswell. We danced and were merry till about 10 o'clock.

November 2. In the evening I went to Dr. Barret's where my wife came this afternoon. Here I found Mrs. Chiswell, my sister Custis, and other ladies. We sat and talked till about 11 o'clock and then retired to our chambers. I played with Mrs. Chiswell and kissed her on the bed till she was angry and my wife also was uneasy about it, and cried as soon as the company was gone. I neglected to say my prayers, which I should not have done, because I ought to beg pardon for the lust I had for another man's wife.

December 1. I rose at 4 o'clock and read two chapters in Hebrew. Eugene was whipped for pissing in bed and Jenny for concealing it. About 11 o'clock came Captain Stith and his wife, not on a visit but Mrs. Stith came to desire me justify her to Mrs. Harrison that she had not told me that Mrs. Harrison was delivered of two children before her time. I wrote to Mrs. Harrison to assure her that Mrs. Stith had never told me any such thing. But my wife could not deny but she had told that Mrs. Stith told her so. *December 2.* My wife was very much vexed with the conversation she had yesterday with Mrs. Stith. *December 3.* Eugene pissed abed again for which I made him drink a pint of piss. About 12 o'clock I went to court where I found little good company. I ate a venison pasty for dinner. *December 13.* Last night I gave my wife a flourish and this morning I quarreled with her about her neglect of the family. *December 16.* My wife had a great pain in her belly and so took a purge which worked very well. Eugene was whipped for doing nothing yesterday. I settled several accounts. I ate roast mutton for dinner. My wife was better after her physic, which worked 12 times. In the afternoon I played at piquet with my wife to divert her. *December 28.* It continued very cold with a strong wind. About 10 o'clock I ate some chocolate with the rest of the company. Then we played at billiards and I lost. In the afternoon we played again at billiards till we lost one of the balls. Then we walked about the plantation and took a slide on the ice. In the evening we played at cards till about 10 o'clock.

January 3, 1710. I gave my wife a flourish and then rose at 7 o'clock. News was brought that the distemper was at Captain Stith's where he had ten negroes sick of it. God of his excessive goodness deliver from it! My wife was very sick. I ate hashed turkey. My son began to breed teeth which disordered him. In the afternoon I took a walk about the plantation and when I came home I gave a vomit to six of my people by way of prevention. God send it may succeed.

February 20. My maid Anaka was taken sick yesterday but I gave her a vomit that worked very much and she was better this day. Then I had her sweated and bled which gave her some ease. However her fever continued violently. We rode to Colonel Hill's where we were kindly received. We played at cricket and I sprained my backside. When we came away I was forced to get on my horse by a chair. We found my wife not very well. In the evening we played at piquet. *February 23.* My maid Anaka was better, thank God. The Captain's bitch killed a lamb yesterday, for which we put her into a house with a ram that beat her violently to break her of that bad custom. *February 26.* In the afternoon we saw a good battle between a stallion and Robin about the mare, but at last the stallion had the advantage and covered the mare three times. The Captain's bitch killed another lamb for which she was beat very much. We took another walk about the plantation. My maid Anaka was very well again, thank God. My wife was out of humor with us for going to see so filthy a sight as the horse to cover the mare. In the evening we drank a bottle of wine and were very merry till 9 o'clock.

March 20. My wife was indisposed and took a sweat and so did Nurse and it did them both service. I was amicable with my wife in her sickness.

May 12. It was very hot this day, and the first day of summer. In the afternoon I read a sermon in Tillotson. Then my wife and I took a walk about the plantation; when we returned we found our son very sick of a fever and he began to break out terribly. We gave him some treacle water. I said my prayers and had good health, good thoughts, and indifferent good humor, thanks be to God Almighty. *May 17.* I rose at 5 o'clock. My son was a little worse, which made me send for Mr. Anderson. He advised some oil of juniper which did him good. *May 21.* The child continued indisposed. I read two sermons in Tillotson, which edified me very much. I ate roast shoat for dinner. I was out of humor with my wife for forcing Evie [their daughter] to eat against her will. In the afternoon we went in the coach to Mrs. Harrison's. In the evening we walked home and found Evie in a great fever. I remembered both my children in my prayers. *May 23.* My daughter was very ill, but the boy had lost his fever, thank God. In the afternoon Evie had a sweat that worked pretty well but not long enough, for which I was out of humor with my wife. I read some Italian and some news and then took a walk about the plantation. When I returned I had a great quarrel with my wife, in which she was to blame altogether; however I made the first step to a reconciliation to [which] she with much difficulty consented. *May 24.* I sent for my cousin Harrison to let Evie blood who was ill. When she came she took away about four ounces. We put on blisters and gave her a glyster which worked very well. Her blood was extremely thick, which is common in distemper of this constitution. About 12 o'clock she began to sweat of herself, which we prompted by tincture of saffron and sage and snake-root. This made her sweat extremely, in which she continued little or more all night. *May 25.* Evie was much better, thank God Almighty, and had lost her fever. The boy was better likewise but was restless. I never was more incommoded with heat in my whole life. *May 26.* I rose at 5 o'clock. Evie was better but the boy was worse, with a cold and fever for which we gave him a sweat which worked very well. *May 27.* Evie took a purge which worked but a little and my son had a little fever. *May 28.* I rose at 6 o'clock and read two chapters in Hebrew. I said my prayers and ate bread and butter for breakfast. The boy was still ill of his fever. We went to church and heard a sermon and received the Sacrament. *May 29.* The boy continued very ill of the fever. I read some Italian. I ate roast mutton for dinner. My belly ached exceedingly and continued so till the evening and gave me many stools. I took a long walk about the plantation. My boy appeared to be a little better this evening, blessed be God for it. *May 31.* The child had a fever still. In the afternoon I played at billiards with my wife and was exceedingly griped in my belly. I ate as many cherries as I could get for it, but they did no good.

June 2. The child was worse and his nurse was very ill. I gave her a vomit which worked very well. *June 3.* I rose at 6 o'clock and as soon as I came out news was brought that the child was very ill. We went out and found him just ready to die and he died about 8 o'clock in the morning. God gives and God takes away; blessed be the name of God. Mrs. Harrison and Mr. Anderson and his wife and some other company came to see us in our affliction. My wife was much afflicted but I submitted to His judgment better, notwithstanding I was very sensible of my loss, but God's will be done. Mr. Anderson and his wife dined here. I ate roast mutton. In the afternoon I was griped in my belly very much but it grew better towards the night. In the afternoon it rained and was fair again in the evening. My poor wife and I walked in the garden. *June 4.* I rose at 6 o'clock and read nothing because I took a physic which did not work. I had no more than two stools but was a little griped. I was so indisposed that I could not settle to anything. My wife had several fits of tears for our dear son but kept within the bounds of submission. I ate hashed mutton for dinner. In the afternoon we walked a little abroad but it was so hot we soon returned. Jimmy brought a coffin from Falling Creek made of walnut tree. *June 5.* My gripes continued still, and made me uneasy. My wife continued very melancholy, notwithstanding I comforted her as well as I could. I took a glyster in the evening which worked a little. Then we walked in the garden. *June 6.* I rose at 6 o'clock and prepared to receive company for the funeral. I said my prayers and ate cake and water gruel for breakfast. About 10 o'clock Colonel Hill, Mr. Anderson and his wife came. Half an hour after my sister Duke came and about 11 came my cousin Harrison with her son and daughter. We gave them burnt claret and cake. About 2 o'clock we went with the corpse to the churchyard and as soon as the service was begun it rained very hard so that we were forced to leave the parson and go into the church porch but Mr. Anderson stayed till the service was finished. *June 7.* My wife continued to be exceedingly afflicted for the loss of her child, notwithstanding I comforted her as well as I could. I ate calf's head for dinner. In the afternoon my gripes returned again and made me uneasy. I drank several strong things for them but they did no good. *June 11.* It continued to rain so that we could not go to church. My wife was still disconsolate. I was better, thank God. I ate roast veal for dinner. In the afternoon I read a sermon of Tillotson's. *June 14.* I rose at 5 o'clock. I said my prayers and ate milk for breakfast. My wife began to be comforted, thank God, and I lost my gripes. *June 17.* I rose at 5 o'clock and drank some milk hot from the cow. Colonel Hill sent his man with a basket of apricots, of which my wife ate twelve immediately and I ate eight which however did not make my gripes return. In the afternoon I caused L-s-n to be whipped for beating his wife and Jenny was whipped for being his whore. In the evening the sloop came from Appomattox with tobacco. *June 25.* I rose at 6 o'clock and found myself a little hot and therefore I took a vomit of infused ipecac, which worked but moderately. I could not go to church nor would my wife leave me. I ate poached eggs for dinner. In the afternoon I found myself a little better and my wife and I took a walk. *June 26.* I rose about 6 o'clock and took a purge which worked very extremely. I had eight stools and my fundament was swelled with a sharp humor and very sore. I drank some water gruel. They began to reap this day. I ate some boiled chicken for dinner. In the afternoon I took a nap which refreshed me a little. The violence of the purge gave me the piles extremely. *June 28.* I lay abed till 10 o'clock and read some letters. My wife anointed my bum with hot linseed oil which had done it some good. However it was not easy yet. I ate fish for dinner. I went to bed early and had my breech anointed. *June 30.* I rose at 7 o'clock and read some Greek. I ate milk for breakfast. My bum was better, thank God, and I was well again. In the afternoon the sloop came from Appomattox with tobacco. I ate some bread and butter for supper. In the evening I said a short prayer and had good health, good thoughts, and good humor, thank God. I gave my wife a flourish.

July 8. It rained gently all day. I sent away the sloop to Falling Creek. I ate roast pork for dinner. I unpacked several things in the afternoon and then gave my wife a flourish and then read in the *Tatler.* Two negroes of mine brought five of the cows that strayed away from hence and told me all was well above. *July 9.* About 11 o'clock we went to church and had a good sermon. In the afternoon my wife and I had a terrible quarrel about the things she had come in [ordered from England] but at length she submitted because she was in the wrong. For my part I kept my temper very well. In the evening I took a walk about the plantation. *July 25.* I said no prayers this morning but ate milk and apples for breakfast. Then I went to the store and sent 15 hogsheads more of tobacco on board Captain Burbydge. I ate dry beef for dinner. My wife was out of humor this evening for nothing, which I bore very well and was willing to be reconciled. *July 30.* I rose at 5 o'clock. I said my prayers and ate boiled milk for breakfast. I danced my dance. I read a sermon in Dr. Tillotson and then took a little [nap]. I ate fish for dinner. In the afternoon my wife and I had a little quarrel which I reconciled with a flourish. Then she read a sermon in Dr. Tillotson to me. It is to be observed that the flourish was performed on the billiard table. I read a little Latin. In the evening we took a walk about the plantation. I neglected to say my prayers but had good health, good thoughts, and good humor, thanks be to God.

TWO MARRIAGES. *In January 1839, Fanny Kemble and her husband, Pierce Butler, were visiting his family's rice and indigo plantation on Butler*

Island, Georgia, shortly after their wedding. Kemble, a great beauty and one of England's leading actresses, had married the handsome Pierce Butler without realizing that his wealth came from owning slaves. Her reaction comes in this letter to her New England friend, Elizabeth Sedgwick. Kemble's habit of referring to her husband as "Mr. Butler" was normal for the period.

My dearest Elizabeth,

A rather longer interval than usual has elapsed since I last wrote to you, but I must beg you to excuse it. I have had more than a usual amount of small daily occupations to fill my time; and, as a mere enumeration of these would not be very interesting to you, I will tell you a story which has just formed an admirable illustration for my observation of all the miseries of which this accursed system of slavery is the cause, even under the best and most human administration of its laws and usages.

We have, as a sort of under nursemaid and assistant of my dear Margery [a white woman], . . . a young [slave] woman named Psyche, but commonly called Sack. . . . She cannot be much over twenty, has a very pretty figure, a graceful, gentle deportment, and a face which, but for its color (she is a dingy mulatto), would be pretty, and is extremely pleasing, from the perfect sweetness of its expression; she is always serious, not to say sad and silent, and has always an air of melancholy and timidity, that has frequently struck me very much, and would have made me think some special anxiety or sorrow must occasion it, but that God knows the whole condition of these wretched people naturally produces such a deportment, and there is no necessity to seek for special or peculiar causes to account for it. . . .

The other day Margery asked me if I knew to whom Psyche belonged, as the poor woman had inquired of her with much hesitation and anguish if she could tell her who owned her and her children. She has two nice little children under six years old, whom she keeps as clean and tidy, and who are sad and as silent as herself. My astonishment at this question was, as you will readily believe, not small, and I forthwith sought out Psyche for an explanation. She was thrown into extreme perturbation at finding that her question had been referred to me, and it was some time before I could sufficiently reassure her to be able to comprehend, in the midst of her reiterated entreaties for pardon, and hopes that she had not offended me, that she did not know herself who owned her. She was, at one time, the property of Mr. King, the former overseer, of whom I have already spoken to you, who has just been paying Mr. Butler a visit. He, like several of his predecessors in the management, has contrived to make a fortune

An old couple eating in rural Virginia. Photograph by Frances Benjamin Johnson, 1890s.

upon it . . . and has purchased a plantation of his own in Alabama, I believe, or one of the Southwestern states. Whether she still belonged to Mr. King or not she did not know, and entreated me, if she did, to endeavor to persuade Mr. Butler to buy her.

Now you must know that this poor woman is the wife of one of Mr. Butler's slaves, a fine, intelligent, active, excellent young man, whose whole family are among some of the very best specimens of character and capacity on the estate. I was so astonished at the (to me) extraordinary state of things revealed by poor Sack's petition, that I could only tell her that I had supposed all the Negroes on the plantation were Mr. Butler's property, but that I would certainly inquire, and find out for her, if I could, to whom she belonged, and if I could, endeavor to get Mr. Butler to purchase her, if she really was not his.

Now, Elizabeth, just conceive for one moment the state of mind of this woman, believing herself to belong to a man who in a few days was going down to one of those abhorred and dreaded Southwestern states, and who would then compel her, with her poor little children, to leave her husband and the only home she had ever known, and all the ties of affection, relationship, and association of her former life, to follow him thither, in all human probability never again to behold any living creature that she had seen before; and this was so completely a matter of course that it was not even thought necessary to apprise her positively of the fact, and the only thing that interposed between her and this most miserable fate was the faint hope that Mr. Butler *might have* purchased her and her children. . . .

I did not see Mr. Butler until the evening; but, in the meantime, meeting Mr. O_____, the overseer, with whom, as I believe I have already told you, we are living here, I asked him about Psyche, and who was her proprietor, when, to my infinite surprise, he told me that *he* had bought her and her children from Mr. King, who had offered them to him, saying that they would be rather troublesome to him than otherwise down where he was going. "And so," said Mr. O_____, "as I had no objection to investing a little money that way, I bought them."

With a heart much lightened, I flew to tell poor Psyche the news, so that, at any rate, she might be relieved from the dread of any immediate separation from her husband. You can imagine better than I can tell you what her sensations were; but she still renewed her prayer that I would, if possible, induce Mr. Butler to purchase her, and I promised to do so.

Early the next morning while I was still dressing, I was suddenly startled by hearing voices in loud tones in Mr. Butler's dressing room, which adjoins my bedroom, and the noise increasing until there was an absolute cry of despair uttered by some man. I could restrain myself no longer, but opened the door of communication and saw Joe, the young man, poor Psyche's husband, raving almost in a state of frenzy, and in a voice broken with sobs and almost inarticulate with passion, reiterating his determination never to leave this plantation, never to go to Alabama, never to leave his old father and mother, his poor wife and children, and dashing his hat, which he was wringing like a cloth in his hands, upon the ground, he declared he would kill himself if he was compelled to follow Mr. King. I glanced from the poor wretch to Mr. Butler, who was standing, leaning against a table with his arms folded, occasionally uttering a few words of counsel to his slave to be quiet and not fret, and not make a fuss about what there was no help for. I retreated immediately from the horrid scene, breathless with surprise and dismay, and stood for some time in my own room, with my heart and temples throbbing to such a degree that I could hardly support myself.

As soon as I recovered myself I again sought Mr. O_____, and inquired of him if he knew the cause of poor Joe's distress. He then told me that Mr. Butler, who is highly pleased with Mr. King's past administration of his property, wished, on his departure for his newly acquired slave plantation, to give him some token of his satisfaction,

A slave father is sold away from his family. A wood engraving
from *The Child's Anti-Slavery Book*, 1860.

and *had made him a present* of the man Joe, who had just received the
intelligence that he was to go down to Alabama with his new owner the
next day, leaving father, mother, wife, and children behind. . . .

When I saw Mr. Butler after this most wretched story became
known to me in all its details, I appealed to him, for his own soul's
sake, not to commit so great a cruelty. Poor Joe's agony while remon-
strating with his master was hardly greater than mine while arguing
with him upon this bitter piece of inhumanity—how I cried, and how
I adjured, and how all my sense of justice, and of mercy, and of pity for
the poor wretch, and of wretchedness at finding myself implicated in
such a state of things, broke in torrents of words from my lips and
tears from my eyes! God knows such a sorrow at seeing anyone I
belonged to commit such an act was indeed a new and terrible experience to me, and it seemed to me that I was imploring Mr. Butler to
save himself more than to spare these wretches. He gave me no answer
whatever, and I have since thought that the intemperate vehemence of
my entreaties and expostulations perhaps deserved that he should
leave me as he did without one single word of reply; and miserable
enough I remained.

Toward evening, as I was sitting alone, my children having gone to bed, Mr. O_____ came into the room. I had but one subject in my mind; I had not been able to eat for it. I could hardly sit still for the nervous distress which every thought of these poor people filled me with. As he sat down looking over some accounts, I said to him: "Have you seen Joe this afternoon, Mr. O_____?" (I give you our conversation as it took place.)

"Yes, ma'am; he is a great deal happier than he was this morning."

"Why, how is that?" asked I, eagerly.

"Oh, he is not going to Alabama. Mr. King heard that he had kicked up a fuss about it" (being in despair at being torn from one's wife and children is called *kicking up a fuss;* this is a sample of overseer appreciation of human feelings), "and said that if the fellow wasn't willing to go with him, he did not wish to be bothered with any niggers down there who were to be troublesome, so he might stay behind."

"And does Psyche know this?"

"Yes, ma'am, I suppose so."

I drew a long breath; and whereas my needle had stumbled through the stuff I was sewing for an hour before, as if my fingers could not guide it, the regularity and rapidity of its evolutions were now quite edifying. The man was for the present safe, and I remained silently pondering his deliverance and the whole proceeding, and the conduct of everyone engaged in it, and, above all, Mr. Butler's share in the transaction, and I think, for the first time, almost a sense of horrible personal responsibility and implication took hold of my mind, and I felt the weight of an unimagined guilt upon my conscience; and yet, God knows, this feeling of self-condemnation is very gratuitous on my part, since when I married Mr. Butler I knew nothing of these dreadful possessions of his, and even if I had I should have been much puzzled to have formed any idea of the state of things in which I now find myself plunged, together with those whose well-doing is as vital to me almost as my own.

With these agreeable reflections I went to bed. Mr. Butler said not a word to me upon the subject of these poor people all the next day, and in the meantime I became very impatient of this reserve on his part, because I was dying to prefer my request that he would purchase Psyche and her children, and so prevent any future separation between her and her husband, as I supposed he would not again attempt to make a present of Joe, at least to anyone who did not wish to be *bothered* with his wife and children.

In the evening I was again with Mr. O_____ alone in the strange, bare, wooden-walled sort of shanty which is our sitting room, and revolving in my mind the means of rescuing Psyche from her miserable suspense, a long chain of all my possessions, in the shape of bracelets, necklaces, brooches, earrings, etc., wound in glittering procession through my brain, with many hypothetical calculations of the value of each separate ornament, and the very doubtful probability of the amount of the whole being equal to the price of this poor creature and her children; and then the great power and privilege I had foregone of earning money by my own labor occurred to me, and I think, for the first time in my life, my past profession assumed an aspect that arrested my thoughts most seriously. For the last four years of my life that preceded my marriage I literally coined money, and never until this moment, I think, did I reflect on the great means of good, to myself and others, that I so gladly agreed to give up forever for a maintenance by the unpaid labor of slaves—people toiling not only unpaid, but under the bitter conditions the bare contemplation of which was then wringing my heart. You will not wonder that when, in the midst of such cogitations, I suddenly accosted Mr. O_____, it was to this effect: "Mr. O_____, I have a particular favor to beg of you. Promise me that you will never sell Psyche and her children without first letting me know of your intention to do so, and giving me the option of buying them."

Mr. O_____ is a remarkably deliberate man, and squints, so that when he has taken a little time in directing his eyes to you, you are still unpleasantly unaware of any result in which you are concerned; he laid down a book he was reading and directed his head and one of his eyes toward me and answered: "Dear me, ma'am, I am very sorry—I have sold them."

My work fell down on the ground, and my mouth opened wide, but I could utter no sound, I was so dismayed and surprised; and he deliberately proceeded: "I didn't know, ma'am, you see, at all, that you entertained any idea of making an investment of that nature; for I'm sure, if I had, I would willingly have sold the woman to you; but I sold her and her children this morning to Mr. Butler."

My dear Elizabeth, though Mr. Butler had resented my unmeasured upbraidings, you see they had not been without some good effect, and though he had, perhaps justly, punished my violent outbreak of indignation about the miserable scene I witnessed by not telling me of his humane purpose, he had bought these poor creatures, and so, I trust, secured them from any such misery in future. I jumped up and left Mr. O_____ still speaking, and ran to find Mr. Butler, to thank him for what he had done, and with that will now bid you good-by. Think, Elizabeth, how it fares with slaves on plantations where there is no crazy English-woman to weep, and entreat, and implore, and upbraid for them, and no master willing to listen to such appeals.

MINISTER'S WIFE. *One of the stories told by Ida B. Wells in her book* A Red Record. *To avoid accusations of partiality, the author relied largely on accounts from white newspapers, in this case the* Cleveland Gazette *of January 16, 1892.*

Mrs. J. C. Underwood, the wife of a minister of Elyria, Ohio, accused an Afro-American of rape. She told her husband that during his absence in 1888, stumping the state for the Prohibition Party, the man came to the kitchen door, forced his way into the house and insulted her. She tried to drive him out with a heavy poker, but he overpowered and chloroformed her, and when she revived her clothing was torn and she was in a horrible condition. She did not know the man, but could identify him. She subsequently pointed out William Offett, a married man, who was arrested, and, being in Ohio, was granted a trial [i.e., he was not lynched].

The prisoner vehemently denied the charge of rape, but confessed he went to Mrs. Underwood's residence at her invitation and was criminally intimate with her at her request. This availed him nothing against the sworn testimony of a minister's wife, a lady of the highest respectability. He was found guilty, and entered the penitentiary, December 14, 1888, for fifteen years. Sometime afterwards the woman's remorse led her to confess to her husband that the man was innocent. These are her words: "I met Offett at the postoffice. It was raining. He was polite to me, and as I had several bundles in my arms he offered to carry them home for me, which he did. He had a strange fascination for me, and I invited him to call on me. He called, bringing chestnuts and candy for the children. By this means we got them to leave us alone in the room. Then I sat on his lap. He made a proposal to me and I readily consented. Why I did so I do not know, but that I did is true. He visited me several times after that and each time I was indiscreet. I did not care after the first time. In fact I could not have resisted, and had no desire to resist."

When asked by her husband why she told him she had been outraged, she said: "I had several reasons for telling you. One was the neighbors saw the fellow here, another was, I was afraid I had contracted a loathsome disease, and still another was that I feared I might give birth to a Negro baby. I hoped to save my reputation by telling you a deliberate lie." Her husband, horrified by the confession, had Offett, who had already served four years, released, and secured a divorce.

ALL FOR THE CAUSE. *Six months after leaving Rochester (and her husband, to whom—despite his impotence—she had been married twice) nineteen-year-old Emma Goldman found employment as a garment worker in New York* *and a cause to which to devote herself. Emma, who had been born in Kovno, Lithuania, had come to this country in 1885.*

The people mentioned in this extract from her autobiography, Living My Life, *are as follows:*

Alexander Berkman (Sasha), a youthful and dedicated anarchist who was later to spend fourteen years in prison for attempting to assassinate Henry Clay Frick during the Homestead Strike.

Johann Most, "the man of magic tongue and powerful pen," who had been expelled from Germany and imprisoned in England, and who was now editor of the anarchist German-language newspaper, Die Freiheit (Freedom), *"shooting forth flames of ridicule, scorn and defiance."*

Fedya, an artist with a "sensitive mouth" and "dreamy expression."

Anna and Helen Minkin, "Russian Jewish working girls."

"The Chicago Martyrs," eight anarchists accused of responsibility for the Haymarket bombing in Chicago in 1886, in which seven policemen were killed and scores injured. Of the accused, three were imprisoned, one committed suicide, and four were hanged.

The 11th of November was approaching, the anniversary of the Chicago martyrdoms. Sasha and I were busy with preparations for the great event of so much significance to us. Cooper Union had been secured for the commemoration. The meeting was to be held jointly by anarchists and socialists, with the co-operation of advanced labor organizations. . . .

Our own little group, consisting of Anna, Helen, Fedya, Sasha and I, decided on a contribution—a large laurel-wreath with broad black and red satin ribbons. At first we wanted to buy eight wreaths, but we were too poor, since only Sasha and I were working. . . .

We found the historic hall densely packed, but with our wreath held high over our heads we finally managed to get through. Even the platform was crowded. I was bewildered until I saw Most standing next to a man and a woman; his presence made me feel at ease. His two companions were distinguished-looking people; the man radiated friendliness, but the woman, clad in a tight-fitting black velvet dress with a long train, her pale face framed in a mass of copper hair, seemed cold and aloof. She evidently belonged to another world.

Presently Sasha said, "The man near Most is Sergey Sevitch, the famous Russian revolutionist, now editor-in-chief of the socialist daily *Die Volkszeitung*; the woman is his wife, the former Helene von Donniges." "Not the one Ferdinand Lassalle loved—the one he lost his life for?" I asked. "Yes, the same; she has remained an aristocrat. She really doesn't belong among us. But Shevitch is splendid. . . . "

Soon the meeting began. Shevitch and Alexander Jonas, his co-editor on the *Volkszeitung*, . . . were impressive speakers. The rest left me cold. Then Most ascended the platform, and everything else seemed blotted out. I was caught in the storm of his eloquence, tossed about, my very soul contracting and expanding in the rise and fall of his voice. It was no longer a speech, it was thunder interspersed with flashes of lightning. It was a wild, passionate cry against the terrible thing that had happened in Chicago—a fierce call to battle against the enemy, a call to individual acts, to vengeance.

The meeting was at an end. Sasha and I filed out with the rest. I could not speak; we walked in silence. When we reached the house where I lived, my whole body began to shake in a fever. An overpowering yearning possessed me, an unutterable desire to give myself to Sasha, to find relief in his arms from the fearful tension of the evening.

My narrow bed now held two human bodies, closely pressed together. My room was no longer dark; a soft, soothing light seemed to come from somewhere. As in a dream I heard sweet endearing words breathed into my ear, like the soft, beautiful Russian lullabies of my childhood. I became drowsy, my thoughts in confusion. The meeting . . . Shevitch . . . the cold face of Helene von Donniges . . . Johann Most . . . the force and wonder of his speech, his call to extermination . . .

I was roused from my drowsiness as if by an electric current. I felt a trembling, shy hand tenderly glide over me. Hungrily I reached for it, for my lover. We were engulfed in a wild embrace. . . . I felt terrific pain, like the cut of a sharp knife. But it was numbed by my passion, breaking through all that had been suppressed, unconscious, and dormant.

The morning still found me eagerly reaching out, hungrily seeking. My beloved lay at my side, asleep in blissful exhaustion. I sat up, my head resting on my hand. Long I watched the face of the boy who had so attracted and repelled me at the same time, who could be so hard and whose touch was yet so tender. Deep love for him welled up in my heart—a feeling of certainty that our lives were linked for all time. I pressed my lips to his thick hair and then I, too, fell asleep.

The people from whom I rented my room slept on the other side of the wall. Their nearness always disturbed me, and now in Sasha's presence it gave me a feeling of being seen. He also had no privacy where he lived. I suggested that we find a small apartment, and he consented joyfully. When we told Fedya of our plan, he asked to be taken in. The fourth of our little commune was Helen Minkin. . . .

From the very first we agreed to share everything, to live like real comrades. Helen continued to work in the corset factory, and I divided my time between sewing silk waists and keeping house. Fedya devoted himself to painting. The expense of his oils, canvases, and brushes often consumed more than we could afford, but it never occurred to any of us to complain. From time to time he would sell a picture to some dealer for fifteen or twenty-five dollars, whereupon he would bring an armful of flowers or some present for me. Sasha would upbraid him for it: the idea of spending money for such things, when the movement needed it so badly, was intolerable to him. His anger had no effect on Fedya. He would laugh it off, call him a fanatic, and say he had no sense of beauty.

One morning Fedya asked me to pose for him. I experienced no sense of shame at standing naked before him. He worked away for a time, and neither of us talked. Then he began to fidget about and finally said he would have to stop: he could not concentrate, the mood was gone. I went back behind the screen to dress. I had not quite finished when I heard violent weeping. I rushed forward and found Fedya stretched on the sofa, his head buried in the pillow, sobbing. As I bent over him, he sat up and broke loose in a torrent—said he loved me, that he had from the very beginning, though he had tried to keep in the background for Sasha's sake; he had struggled fiercely against his feeling for me, but he knew now that it was no use. He would have to move out.

I sat by him, holding his hand in mine and stroking his soft wavy hair. Fedya had always drawn me to him by his thoughtful attention, his sensitive response, and his love of beauty. Now I felt something stronger stirring within me. Could it be love for Fedya, I wondered. Could one love two persons at the same time? . . . Sasha had left something untouched in me, something Fedya could perhaps waken to life. Yes, it must be possible to love more than one! . . .

I asked Fedya what he thought of love for two or even for more persons at once. He looked up in surprise and said he did not know, he had never loved anyone before. His love for me had absorbed him to the exclusion of anyone else. He knew he could not care for another woman while he loved me. And he was certain Sasha would never want to share me; his sense of possession was too strong.

Later in the day I had to meet Most. He had spoken to me about a short lecture tour he was planning for me, but though I did not take it seriously, he had asked me to come to see him about it.

The *Freiheit* office was crowded. Most suggested a near-by saloon, which he knew to be quiet in the early afternoon. We went there. He began to explain his plan for my tour; I was to visit Rochester, Buffalo, and Cleveland. It threw me into a panic. "It is impossible!" I protested; "I don't know a thing about lecturing." He waved my objections aside, declaring that everybody felt that way in the beginning. He was determined to make a public speaker of me, and I would simply have to

An organ-grinder and his wife, New York City.
Photograph by Elizabeth Alice Austen, 1897.

begin. He had already chosen the subject for me and he would help me prepare it. I was to speak on the futility of the struggle for the eight-hour workday, now again much discussed in labor ranks. . . .

When I got home, away from Most's presence, I again experienced the sinking feeling that had come upon me when I had first tried to speak in public. I still had three weeks in which to read up, but I was sure I could never go through with it.

How great was my astonishment when Sasha and Helen Minkin grew enthusiastic about Most's plan! It was a marvellous opportunity, they said. What if I would have to work hard to prepare my talk? It would be the making of me as a popular lecturer, the first woman speaker in the German anarchist movement in America! Sasha was especially insistent: I must set aside every consideration, I must think only of how useful I would become to the Cause. Fedya was dubious.

The day of my departure for Rochester arrived. I met Most for a last talk; I came in a depressed mood, but a glass of wine and Most's spirit soon lifted the weight. . . .

He took me to the Grand Central in a cab. On the way he moved close to me. He yearned to take me in his arms and asked if he might. I nodded, and he held me pressed to him. Conflicting thoughts and emotions possessed me; the speeches I was going to make, Sasha, Fedya, my passion for the one, my budding love for the other. But I yielded to Most's trembling embrace, his kisses covering my mouth as of one famished with thirst. I let him drink; I could have denied him nothing. He loved me, he said; he had never known such longing for any woman before. . . . My whole being had awakened him to a new meaning in life. I was his *Blondkopf*, his "blue eyes;" he wanted me to be his own, his helpmate, his voice.

I lay back with my eyes closed. I was too overpowered to speak, too limp to move. Something mysterious stirred me, something entirely unlike the urge towards Sasha or the sensitive response to Fedya. It was

Eating pie in front of a log cabin in Boise, Idaho.
Turn-of-the-century photograph by Otto M. Jones.

different from these. It was infinite tenderness for the great man-child at my side. As he sat there, he suggested a rugged tree bent by winds and storm, making one supreme last effort to stretch itself towards the sun. "All for the Cause," Sasha had so often said. The fighter next to me had already given all for the Cause. But who had given all for him? He was hungry for affection, for understanding. I would give him both.

A scene from a New York sweatshop. From a composite illustration, "The Female Slaves of New York," published in *Frank Leslie's Illustrated Newspaper*, November, 1888.

CHAPTER
4

WORKING

FROM SUNUP TO SUNDOWN—and well after sundown when gas and electricity made artificial lighting cheap—six days a week, and in harvest time seven; willingly, with the prospect of a fortune to be made in trapping furs or finding gold; unwillingly, as indentured servants or slaves driven on by the slave driver's whip; indoors in factories and sweatshops and kitchens and trading posts, or outdoors on farms and cattle trails, most Americans have spent most of their waking time engaged in work.

This has been so from the first. People have worked because it was believed to be divinely ordained, the result of Adam's sin ("In the sweat of thy face shalt thou eat bread, till thou return unto the ground"); because "Idleness is the parent of every vice," as Dr. Benjamin Rush said, and not to work was shameful—it was to be a lubber, a sluggard; because it was the law—servants who refused to do their master's bidding could be sentenced to a whipping; but mostly because unless everyone in the family worked, and worked hard, they could not survive. The three dollars a week earned by a child of eight by stripping feathers in a slum workshop in New York was as vital as the dollar a week plus board earned by the twelve-year-old Lucy Larcom in one of the Lowell mills or the seventeen hours of unpaid daily labor put in by an Illinois farmer's wife. For them, as for the first settlers at Jamestown, it was as Captain John Smith said, "He that doth not work shall not eat."

INDENTURED SERVANTS. *People unable to afford the cost of transportation to the colonies often indentured themselves to work for a master for a fixed period; when their time was up they were free to go or to negotiate their own terms. Governor John Winthrop of Massachusetts here records one instance of how the system worked.*

1645. The wars in England kept servants from coming to us, so as those we had could not be hired, when their times were out, but upon unreasonable terms, and we found it very difficult to pay their wages to their content, (for money was very scarce). I may upon this occasion report a passage between one of Rowley and his servant. The master, being forced to sell a pair of his oxen to pay his servant his wages, told his servant he could keep him no longer, not knowing how to pay him the next year. The servant answered, he would serve him for more of his cattle. But how shall I do (saith the master) when all my cattle are gone? The servant replied, you shall then serve me, and so you may have your cattle again.

TROUBLEMAKERS. *From the proceedings of the Provincial Court, Calvert County, Maryland, March 1663.*

To the honorable the Governor and Council of Maryland:

The humble petition of Richard Preston showeth:

That your petitioner's servants did, upon the 5th day of the last week, called Thursday, peremptorily and positively refuse to go and do their ordinary labor upon the account (as they then alleged) that if they had not flesh, they could not work. Your suppliant's answer then was to them, that if they would not go to work unless they had flesh, I could not help it; for I had not flesh then to give them (your suppliant's business calling him that day abroad). And at night returning home, found that his said servants had not been at work upon the account of not having that day some meat, although until that time they have not wanted for the most part, since the crop of tobacco was in, to have meat three times in the week and at least twice, they having other provision by them at all times to dress and eat when they will. And they continuing still in that obstinate rebellious condition, although I have instead of flesh for the present provided sugar, fish, oil, and vinegar for them, am constrained to address myself to this court, that according to equity and their demerits they may receive such censure as shall be judged equal for such perverse servants, lest a worse evil by their example should ensue by encouraging other servants to do the like.

To the honorable the Governor and Council:

The humble Petition of John Smith, Richard Gibbs, Samuel Coplen, Samuel Styles, etc., servants to Mr. Richard Preston, showeth:

That Mr. Preston doth not allow your petitioners sufficient provisions for the enablement to our work, but straitens us so far that we are brought so weak we are not able to perform the employments he puts us upon. We desire but so much as is sufficient, but he will allow us nothing but beans and bread. These premises seriously considered, your petitioners humbly address themselves unto your honors to relieve our wants and provide that our master may afford us such sustenance as may enable us to go through with our labors for the future.

Upon these petitions of Mr. Richard Preston and his servants, and upon examination of the said servants present in court: the court, taking the same into serious consideration, ordered that these servants now petitioning, viz., John Smith, Richard Gibbs, Samuel Coplen, Samuel Styles, Henry Gorslett, and Thomas Broxam, be forthwith whipped with 30 lashes each. Then the court further ordered that two of the mildest (not so refractory as the others) should be pardoned and that those two so pardoned should inflict the censure or punishment on their other companions. And thereupon the said servants, kneeling on their knees, asking and craving forgiveness of their master and the court for their former misdemeanor and promising all compliance and obedience hereafter, their penalty is remitted or suspended at present. But they are to be of good behavior towards their said master ever hereafter (upon their promise of amendment as aforesaid). And so to be certified from court to court.

SLUGGARDS. *The aristocratic Virginian William Byrd II, on his back-country neighbors to the south, in 1728.*

Surely there is no place in the World where the Inhabitants live with less Labour than in North Carolina. It approaches nearer to the Description of Lubberland than any other, by the great felicity of the Climate, the easiness of raising Provisions, and the Slothfulness of the People. Indian Corn is of so great increase, that a little pains will Subsist a very large Family with Bread, and then they may have meat without any pains at all, by the Help of the Low Grounds, and the great Variety of Mast [nuts, suitable for hogs] that grows on the Highland. The Men, for their Parts, just like the Indians, impose all the Work upon the poor Women. They make their Wives rise out of their Beds early in the Morning, at the same time that they lye and Snore, till the Sun has run one third of his course, and disperst all the unwholesome Damps. Then, after Stretching and Yawning for half an Hour, they light their Pipes, and, under the Protection of a cloud of Smoak, venture out into the open Air; tho', if it happens to be never so little cold, they quickly return Shivering into the Chimney corner. When the weather is mild, they stand leaning with both their arms upon the corn-field fence, and gravely consider whether they had best go and take a Small Heat at the Hough [hoe]: but generally find reasons to put it off till another time.

RUNAWAYS. *A notice for two indentured servants that appeared in* Dunlap's Maryland Gazette, *September 12, 1775.*

RAN AWAY last night from the subscribers [the undersigned], an English servant man named John Scott, a square well made fellow, about five feet four inches high, a good complexion, something sunburnt, wears his own brown straight hair; took with him a blue cloth coat with a red plush cape, a good scarlet knit jacket with calimanco back, old buckskin breeches, a pair of double channelled pumps capped at each toe, but may change his cloaths, as he stole a very good dark claret coloured coat with yellow buttons; he is a very artful scoundrel. Also a white woman, something taller than the fellow, of a very dark complexion, a ring-worm on her upper lip, a small scar on one cheek; she has left behind a mulatto bastard, for having which she is bound to appear next in court; It is probable they will pass for man and wife. TWENTY SHILLINGS Reward for each if taken in the county, and FORTY SHILLINGS each if taken fifty miles from home, will be paid by

WILLIAM BORDLEY, and
WOOLMAN GIBSON the 3rd.

SENTRY DUTY. *During the campaign of 1776, Private Joseph Plumb Martin was with the Revolutionary Army on the northern end of Manhattan Island, where the British and American lines were very close to each other.*

A simple affair happened, while I was upon guard at a time while we were here, which made considerable disturbance amongst the guard and caused me some extra hours of fatigue at the time. As I was the cause of it at first, I will relate it. The guard consisted of nearly two hundred men, commanded by a field officer. We kept a long chain of sentinels placed almost within speaking distance of each other, and being in close neighborhood with the enemy we were necessitated to be pretty alert. I was upon my post as sentinel about the middle of the night. Thinking we had overgone the time in which we ought to have been relieved, I stepped a little off my spot towards one of the next sentries, it being quite dark, and asked him in a low voice how long he had been on sentry. He started as if attacked by the enemy and roared out, "Who comes there?" I saw I had alarmed him and stole back to my spot as quick as possible. He still kept up his cry, "Who comes there?", and receiving no answer, he discharged his piece, which alarmed the whole guard, who immediately formed and prepared for action and sent off a non-commissioned officer and file of men to ascertain the cause of alarm.

They came first to the man who had fired and asked him what was the matter. He said that someone had made an abrupt advance upon his premises and demanded, "How comes you on, sentry?" They next came to me, inquiring what I had seen. I told them that I had not seen or heard anything to alarm me but what the other sentinel had caused. The men returned to the guard, and we were soon relieved, which was all I had wanted.

Upon our return to the guard I found, as was to be expected, that the alarm was the subject of general conversation among them. They were confident that a spy or something worse had been amongst us and consequently greater vigilance was necessary. We were accordingly kept the rest of the night under arms, and I cursed my indiscretion for causing the disturbance, as I could get no more rest during the night. I could have set all to rights by speaking a word, but it would not do for me to betray my own secret. But it was diverting to me to see how much the story gained by being carried about, both among the guard and after its arrival in the camp.

PHILADELPHIA DOCTOR. *In his* Account of the Bilious Yellow Fever of 1793, *Dr. Benjamin Rush tells of his experiences during the epidemic, which killed over four thousand people. A former member of the Second Continental Congress and a signer of the Declaration of Independence, Rush had also served as surgeon general in the Continental Army.*

Some time before the fever made its appearance, my wife and children went into the state of New-Jersey, where they had long been in the habit of spending the summer months. My family, about the 25th of August, consisted of my mother, sister, who was on a visit to me, a black servant man, and a mulatto boy. I had five pupils, viz. Warner Washington and Edward Fisher, of Virginia; John Alston, of South-Carolina, and John Redman Coxe (grandson to Dr. Redman) and John Stall, both of this city. They all crowded round me upon the sudden increase of business, and with one heart devoted themselves to my service, and to the cause of humanity.

The credit which the new mode of treating the disease acquired, in all parts of the city, produced an immense influx of patients to me from all quarters. My pupils were constantly employed; at first in putting up purging powders, but, after a while, only in bleeding and visiting the sick.

Between the 8th and 15th of September I visited and prescribed for between a hundred and a hundred and twenty patients a day. Several of my pupils visited a fourth or fifth part of that number. For a while we refused no calls. In the short intervals of business, which I spent at my meals, my house was filled with patients, chiefly the poor, waiting for advice. For many weeks I seldom ate without prescribing for numbers as I sat at my table. To assist me at these hours, as well as in the night, Mr. Stall, Mr. Fisher, and Mr. Coxe accepted of rooms in my house, and became members of my family. Their labours now had no remission.

Immediately after I adopted the antiphlogistic mode of treating the disease, I altered my manner of living. I left off drinking wine and malt liquors. The good effects of the disuse of these liquors helped to confirm me in the theory I had adopted of the disease. A troublesome headache, which I had occasionally felt, and which excited a constant apprehension that I was taking the fever, now suddenly left me. I likewise, at this time, left off eating solid animal food, and lived wholly, but sparingly, upon weak broth, potatoes, raisins, coffee, and bread and butter.

From my constant exposure to the sources of the disease, my body became highly impregnated with miasmata. My eyes were yellow, and sometimes a yellowness was perceptible in my face. My pulse was preternaturally quick, and I had profuse sweats every night. These sweats were so offensive, as to oblige me to draw the bed-clothes close to my neck, to defend myself from their smell. They lost their foetor entirely, upon my leaving off the use of broth, and living entirely upon milk and vegetables. But my nights were rendered disagreeable, not only by these sweats, but by the want of my usual sleep, produced in part by the frequent knocking at my door, and in part by anxiety of mind, and the stimulus of the miasmata upon my system. I went to bed in conformity to habit only, for it ceased to afford me rest or refreshment. When it was evening I wished for morning; and when it was morning, the prospect of the labours of the day, at which I often shuddered, caused me to wish for the return of the evening. The degrees of my anxiety may be easily conceived when I add, that I had at one time upwards of thirty heads of families under my care; among these were Mr. Joseph Coates, the father of eight, and Mr. Benjamin Scull and Mr. John Morell, both fathers of ten children. They were all in imminent danger; but it pleased God to make me the instrument of saving each of their lives.

Every moment in the intervals of my visits to the sick was employed in prescribing, in my own house, for the poor, or in sending answers to messages from my patients; time was now too precious to be spent in counting the number of persons who called upon me for advice. From circumstances I believe it was frequently 150, and seldom less than 50 in a day, for five or six weeks. The evening did not bring with it the least relaxation from my labours. I received letters every day from the country, and from distant parts of the union, containing inquiries into the mode of treating the disease, and after the health and lives of persons who had remained in the city. The business of every evening was to answer these letters, also to write to my family. These employments, by affording a fresh current to my thoughts, kept me from dwelling on the gloomy scenes of the day. After these duties were performed, I copied into my note book all the observations I had collected during the day, and which I had marked with a pencil in my pocket-book in sick rooms, or in my carrriage. To these constant labours of body and mind were added distresses from a variety of causes. Having found myself unable to comply with the numerous applications that were made to me, I was obliged to refuse many every day. My sister counted forty-seven in one forenoon before eleven o'clock. Many of them left my door with tears, but they did not feel more distress than I did from refusing to follow them. Sympathy, when it vents itself in acts of humanity, affords pleasure, and contributes to health; but the reflux of pity, like anger, gives pain, and disorders the body. In riding through the streets, I was often forced to resist the intreaties of parents imploring a visit to their children, or of children to their parents. I recollect, and even *yet* with pain, that I tore myself at one time from five persons in Moravian alley, who attempted to stop me, by suddenly whipping my horse, and driving my chair as speedily as possible beyond the reach of their cries.

But I had other afflictions besides the distress which arose from the abortive sympathy which I have described. On the 11th of September, my ingenious pupil, Mr. Washington, fell a victim to his humanity. He had taken lodgings in the country, where he sickened with the disease. Having been almost uniformly successful in curing others, he made light of his fever, and concealed the knowledge of his danger from me, until the day before he died. On the 18th of September Mr. Stall sickened in my house. A delirium attended his fever from the first hour it affected him. He refused, and even resisted force when used to compel him to take medicine. He died on the 23d of September. Scarce had I recovered from the shock of the death of this amiable youth, when I was called to weep for a third pupil, Mr. Alston, who died in my neighbourhood the next day. He had worn himself down, before his sickness, by uncommon exertions in visiting, bleeding, and even sitting up with sick people. At this time Mr. Fisher was ill in my house. On the 26th of the month, at 12 o'clock, Mr. Coxe, my only assistant, was seized with the fever, and went to his grandfather's. I followed him with a look, which I feared would be the last in my house. At two o'clock my sister, who had complained for several days, yielded to the disease, and retired to her bed. My mother followed her, much indisposed, early in the evening. My black servant man had been confined with the fever for several days, and had on that day, for the first time quitted his bed. My little mulatto boy, of eleven years old, was the only person in my family who was able to afford me the least assistance. At eight o'clock in the evening I finished the business of the day. A solemn stillness at that time pervaded the streets. In vain did I strive to forget my melancholy situation by answering letters and putting up medicines, to be distributed next day among my patients. My faithful black man crept to my door, and at my request sat down by the fire, but he added, by his silence and dullness, to the gloom, which suddenly overpowered every faculty of my mind.

On the first day of October, at two o'clock in the afternoon, my sister died. I got into my carriage within an hour after she expired, and spent the afternoon in visiting patients. According as a sense of duty, or as grief has predominated in my mind, I have approved, and disapproved, of this act, ever since. She had borne a share in my labours. She had been my nurse in sickness, and my casuist in my choice of duties. My whole heart reposed itself in her friendship. Upon being invited to a friend's house in the country, when the disease made its appearance in the city, she declined accepting the invitation, and gave as a reason for so doing, that I might probably require her services in case of my taking the disease, and that, if she were sure of dying, she would remain with me, provided that, by her death, she could save my life. From this time I declined in health and strength. All motion became painful to me. My appetite began to fail. My night sweats continued. My short and imperfect sleep was disturbed by distressing or frightful dreams. The scenes of them were derived altogether from sick rooms and grave-yards. I concealed my sorrows as much as possible from my patients; but when alone, the retrospect of what was past, and the prospect of what was before me, the termination of which was invisible, often filled my soul with the most poignant anguish.

I have said before, that I early left off drinking wine; but I used it in another way. I carried a little of it in a vial in my pocket, and when I felt myself fainty, after coming out of a sick room, or after a long ride, I kept about a table spoonful of it in my mouth for half a minute, or longer, without swallowing it. So weak and excitable was my system, that this small quantity of wine refreshed and invigorated me as much as half a pint would have done at any other time. The only difference was, that the vigour I derived from the wine in the former, was of shorter duration than when taken in the latter way.

For the first two weeks after I visited patients in the yellow fever, I carried a rag wetted with vinegar, and smelled it occasionally in sick rooms: but after I saw and felt the signs of the universal presence of the miasmata in my system, I laid aside this and all other precautions. I rested myself on the bed-side of my patients, and I drank milk and ate fruit in their sick-rooms. Besides being saturated with miasmata, I had another security against being infected in sick rooms, and that was, I went into scarcely a house which was more infected than my own. Many of the poor people, who called upon me for advice, were bled by my pupils in my shop, and in the yard which was between it and the street. From the want of a sufficient number of bowls to receive their blood, it was sometimes suffered to flow and putrefy upon the ground. From this source, streams of miasmata were constantly poured into my house, and conveyed into my body by the air, during every hour of the day and night.

On the 9th of October, I visited a considerable number of patients, and, as the day was warm, I lessened the quantity of my clothing. Towards evening I was seized with a pain in the back, which obliged me to go to bed at eight o'clock. About twelve I awoke with a chilly fit. A violent fever, with acute pains in different parts of my body, followed it. At one o'clock I called for Mr. Fisher, who slept in the next room. He came instantly, with my affectionate black man, to my relief. I saw my danger painted in Mr. Fisher's countenance. He bled me plentifully, and gave me a dose of the mercurial medicine. This was immediately rejected. He gave me a second dose, which likewise acted as an emetic, and discharged a large quantity of bile from my stomach. The remaining part of the night was passed under an apprehension that my labours were near an end. I could hardly expect to survive so violent attack of the fever, broken down, as I was, by labour, sickness, and grief. My wife and seven children, whom the great and distressing events that were passing in our city had jostled out of my mind for six or seven weeks, now resumed their former place in my affections. My wife had stipulated, in consenting to remain in the country, to come to my assistance in case of my sickness; but I took measures which, without alarming her, proved effectual in preventing it. My house was enveloped in foul air, and the probability of my death made her life doubly necessary to my family. In the morning the medicine operated kindly and my fever abated. In the afternoon it returned, attended with a great inclination to sleep. Mr. Fisher bled me again, which removed the sleepiness. The next day the fever left me, but in so weak a state, that I awoke two successive nights with a faintness which threatened the extinction of my life. It was removed each time by taking a little aliment. My convalescence was extremely slow. I returned, in a very gradual manner, to my former habits of diet. The smell of animal food, the first time I saw it at my table, forced me to leave the room. During the month of November, and all the winter months, I was harassed with a cough, and a fever somewhat of the hectic kind. The early warmth of the spring removed those complaints, and restored me, through Divine Goodness to my usual state of health.

The Peddler has "all kinds of cotton that are all the better for bein' turned—for the inside gets fresh as t'other's wearin' out," John Bernard. Illustration from *Harper's Weekly,* June 20, 1868.

YANKEE PEDDLER. *In his book* Retrospectives of America 1797–1811, *the English-born actor John Bernard writes about another kind of performer. (Moravians were members of a Pennsylvania Dutch religious sect, noted for their pious ways.)*

Suppose a village in one of the rich Virginian or Carolinian valleys. . . . About sunset labor has ceased and the inhabitants are leaning or lying out of their doors, the cows are wandering home, the children are playing about, and the "niggers" are laughing loud in the distant sugarhouse. In this sweet hour of calm all hearts are disposed to indulge in Christian emotions. Look at the group and you'd take them for a colony of Moravians, with all enemies pardoned and all cares forgotten; when suddenly a pedestrian is seen wending down the hill, his legs, in the slanting sunbeams, sending their shadows half a mile before him. By his length of staff he might be taken for a pilgrim, but the sprawl of his walk awakens anything but sacred associations. Gradually his hull looms into distinctness, they perceive he is a long-backed man, with a crouching head and loaded shoulders; suspicions are excited; and at length one who may have suffered more than the rest . . . exclaims, "I'll be shot if it ain't a Yankee! . . . "

As the enemy advances at a swinging pace among them, his keen gray eye rolling round in selection of a victim, they remember the strange man who first found out their quiet hiding-place, and the wonder and contempt this curious species of fellow-creature at first excited—a fellow who would neither drink, bet, nor talk politics, but kept prying into holes and corners to prove the extent of their needs, and who ultimately walked away with all the silver of the settlement. Whatever may have been their former experiences, one of the number is a doomed man. If he doesn't want a clock which ticks loud enough to scare away the rats, or a razor so keen that if you but strop it overnight and put it under your pillow you'll wake up clean shaved in the morning, yet—"Sure alive, missis wants a new cap," and he's got a small stock, "jest such as the squires' wives wear at the camp-meetin's;" or, "The young gals need some gowns," and he has "all kinds of cotton that are all the better for bein' turned—for the inside gets fresh as t'other's wearin' out."

The "Down-Easter's" system of attacking a stubborn antagonist displays great generalship. He begins by resting his pack upon the half-hatch of the door; its numerous contents presently require a field of display; nowhere so fitting as on the counter within, if it be a shop; he begs leave but to show them; "Look at them, mister, they won't sting you." The outworks once carried, his shot (caps and combs, "hanky-chers," etc.) fly about in all directions and take deadly effect on some of the family. By a singular fatality everything that is tried on seems to be made expressly for the wearer; she never looked so well in anything before. And equally strange is the discovery that, up to that moment, they had been living without a solitary convenience. Every one but the father perceives the necessity of Sally having a pair of shoes, Enoch a jack-knife, and the parlor a timepiece. From the shop Jonathan fights his way into the backroom, and . . . when the campaign is over in one house he proceeds to another, and so on to all in succession, till he arrives at the tavern, where he usually succeeds in trading the landlord out of bed and breakfast.

TRADING WITH THE INDIANS. *The Lewis and Clark Expedition, begun in 1803, had reached Fort Clatsop, at the mouth of the Columbia River, when Meriwether Lewis made this entry.*

January 9th 1806.
The persons who usually visit the entrance of this river for the purpose of traffic or hunting I believe are either English or Americans; the Indians inform us that they speak the same language with ourselves, and give us proofs of their varacity by repeating many words of English, as musquit, powder, shot, nife, file, damned rascal, sun of a

bitch &c. whether these traders are from Nootka sound, from some other late establishement on this coast, or immediately from the U'States or Great Brittain, I am at a loss to determine, nor can the Indians inform us. . . .

This traffic on the part of the whites consists in vending guns, (principally old british or American musquits) powder, balls and shot, Copper and brass kettles, brass teakettles and coffee pots, blankets from two to three point, scarlet and blue Cloth (coarse), plates and strips and sheet copper and brass, large brass wire, knives, beads and tobacco, with fishinghooks buttons and some other small articles; also a considerable quantity of Sailor's cloaths, as hats coats, trowsers and shirts. for these they receive in return from the natives, dressed and undressed Elk-skins, skins of the sea Otter, common Otter, beaver, common fox, spuck, and tiger cat; also dryed and pounded sammon in baskets, and a kind of buisquit, which the natives make of roots called by them shappelell. The natives are extravegantly fond of the most common cheap blue and white beads, of moderate size, or such that from 50. to 70. will weigh one penneyweight. the blue is usually prefered to the white; these beads constitute the principal circulating medium with all the indian tribes on this river; for these beads they will dispose any article they possess.

FIREWOOD. *Asa Sheldon, who was to write the story of his life in* Yankee Drover, *finds there is no such thing as "a mean business." This was in 1812.*

Capt. Joseph Bond had just given his business of baking into the hands of his sons Joseph and William. To increase their manufactures, they were at a loss how to procure fagots, which were then used exclusively for oven heating.

I told them there would be no trouble if they would pay enough for them. "It is such mean business, nobody will make them," they said.

"It will not be a mean business if you will pay a fair price for them."

"Who will make them, if we will pay well for it?"

"I will," said I.

"I should laugh to see you making fagots."

"I should laugh to see you paying me the money for it," said I.

The bargain was concluded between us, that I should make all I could in five days, anywhere in Wilmington [Massachusetts] where they could go with a team, and they would draw them and pay 1-1/2 cents per bundle. At work I went, and in five days made 1000 bundles, for which they paid me $15. In less than a fortnight after, many respectable citizens, together with the minister, his two sons and the deacon, employed themselves in making fagots for the Bonds. And from that day to this it has never been considered mean business.

Many a laboring man has earned a few dollars, who could not get it in any other way. Besides the benefit arising from the fagots themselves, it has been the cause of clearing many acres of swamp or lowland, which proves the best land for cultivation we have in Wilmington.

FARM WORKERS. *William Cobbett, an English farmer and radical politician who lived on Long Island from 1818 to 1819, gives a favorable report.*

It is, too, of importance to know, *what sort* of labourers these Americans are; for, though a labourer is a labourer, still there is some difference in them; and, these Americans are *the best that I ever saw*. They mow *four acres* of *oats, wheat, rye*, or *barley* in a day, and, with a cradle, lay it so smooth in the swarths, that it is tied up in sheaves with the greatest neatness and ease. They mow *two acres and a half of grass* in a day, and they do the work well. . . .

The causes of these performances, so far beyond those in England, is first, the men are *tall* and well built; they are *bony* rather than *fleshy*; and they *live*, as to food, as well as man can live. And, secondly, they have been *educated* to do much in a day. The farmer here generally is at the *head* of his "*boys*," as they, in the kind language of the country, are called. Here is the best of examples. My old and beloved friend, Mr.

VENERATE THE PLOUGH

"Besides the great quantity of work performed by the American labourer, his skill, the versatility of his talent, is a great thing. . . . In short, a good labourer here, can do anything that is to be done upon a farm," William Cobbett, 1819. Illustrated detail from *Columbian Magazine*, October, 1786.

JAMES PAUL, used, at the age of nearly *sixty* to go at *the head of his mowers*, though his fine farm was his own, and though he might, in other respects, be called a rich man; and, I have heard, that Mr. ELIAS HICKS, the famous Quaker Preacher, who lives about nine miles from this spot, has this year, at *seventy* years of age, cradled down four acres of rye in a day. I wish some of the *preachers* of other descriptions, especially our fat parsons in England, would think a little of this, and would betake themselves to "work with their hands the things which be good, that they may have to give to him who needeth," and not go on any longer gormandizing and swilling upon the labour of those who need.

Besides the great quantity of work performed by the American labourer, his *skill,* the *versatility* of his talent, is a great thing. Every man can use an *ax,* a *saw,* and a *hammer.* Scarcely one who cannot do any job at rough carpentering, and mend a plough or a waggon. Very few indeed, who cannot kill and dress pigs and sheep, and many of them Oxen and Calves. Every farmer is a *neat* butcher; a butcher for *market;* and, of course, "the boys" must learn. This is a great convenience. It makes you so independent as to a main part of the means of housekeeping. All are *ploughmen.* In short, a good labourer here, can do *anything* that is to be done upon a farm.

BUDDING ARTIST. *James Guild, born in 1797, having tried his hand at being a peddler, tinker, and profile-cutter, decides to take up portrait painting. This is from his diary.*

Now I went to canadagua [in New York]. Here I went into a painters shop, one who painted likenesses, and my profiles looked so mean when I saw them I asked him what he would show me one day for, how to distinguish the coulers & he said $5, and I consented to it and began to paint. He showed me one day and then I went to Bloomfield and took a picture of Mr goodwins painting for a sample on my way. I put up at a tavern and told a Young Lady if she would wash my shirt, I would draw her likeness. Now then I was to exert my skill in painting. I opperated once on her but it looked so like a rech I throwed it away and tried again. The poor Girl sat niped up so prim and look so smileing it makes me smile when I think of while I was daubing on paint on a piece of paper, it could not be caled painting, for it looked more like a strangle cat than it did like her. However I told her it looked like her and she believed it, but I cut her profile and she had a profile if not a likeness.

Then I traveled on and stoped at every house and inquired if they wanted any profile likeness taken, and if I could not get but a trifle, I would paint for the sake of learning. In about 3 day I was quite a painter for I had one dollar for painting, and when I came to bloomfield I thought I was quite capable of the task. Here I painted this that and the other. After I had got through and ready for a start, one Miss Narvin sent in to have me come in and see her, for she wanted their little childrens likeness taken, and I went in and shewd her some painting while she caled to her husband to come and see them. He came out and sat down in a chair. Com, Says Miss Marvin, wont you have our childrens likenesses taken? The reply was no, get out of my house in a minute, or I will horse whip you, you dam profiters and pedlers, you ought to have a good whipping by every one that sees you. Get out of my house you rasckal. I replied in a soft tone, why now, uncle, you wont hurt me, will you? I shant go untill I have my pictures that your wife has got. They gave them to me and I says now, sir, I will go with pleasur, but I want to take a little spell with you. I know you are a man who would have acquaintanc very well and you wont hurt me. I am one of the best natured fellows you ever see. Now, uncle, you have one of the finest situations, (her I was interupted). Get out of enclosure, you rascal, or I will horse whip you and you shall leave the town in one hour or I will horse whip you all the way out. Stop, says he, give me your name, Ill warn you out of town. Show me your authority to demand my name and you shall have it, and not without authority. I'll let you know my authority. With that he caught me by the color and with great threats declares a horse whipping while I was very calm and many pleasant observations which made him the more angry. He puled me along by the collar and riseing on the second step to enter the house while I was on the first.

Now was a good opportunity for me. I flew my hand round and caught him I no not where and droped on my back and with my foot pitched him over my head and the first that struck was his face on a sharp board purposed for a goos pen and I gess he carrys the mark untill this day. Now sir if you will come here I will serve you the same sauce again, only touch me with your little finger and I will make you my footstool. After a few minutes of bustle he recovered and to enter a complaint for hurting him. So a woman that belonged in the first tavern told me if I wanted to get a way, she would tell me where to go, so she pointed the way through a barnyard and into a footpath which in the end prove the same.

YOUNGEST SON. *Joseph Hollingworth, a skilled textile worker and youngest member of a family that recently emigrated from England, writes to complain.*

South Leicester Nov^br 7th 1829 Saturday evening.

Dear Aunt, and Uncle.

I write this letter INCOGNITO, I therfore desire you to keep it to your selves. I shall state a few of my grieveances in a brief manner. I should have told you somthing of it when you was here, but I thought it best not to trouble you then; besides I had no oppertunity. You well know how things went on in our Family in England, with regard to me, that I was always the BAD LAD, &c. Were I to enumerate all the evils that has been practised against me in this country, I might fill sheets upon sheets; but I forbear. Let a few suffice. You know how James and I was clothed when we left England; he had 3 or 4 good suits, & I only one, besides my old clothes, which was wore out when I got here. I had to take one of James's old coats, which has been my every-day coat ever scince; and which I have got on this present moment. I did not have any new cloths till last June, (Hat Boots & satinet trousers excepted,) and might not have had any to this day; but I told them plain terms, that if they did not get me some I would look out for myself. Last winter, I had to work a good deal of overtime at Nights; had I refused the whole Family might have lost their work: so I calculated to have the overtime wages for myself. It amounted to nearly five Dollars. I have succeeded in getting 2 dol^{rs}. ONLY! which is all the pocket money I have had in this country! I might have overlooked all these circumstances, at least a little longer, had not one, transpired, of a diabolical nature. We have a new Family Bible, and I thought to make it a practice, every Night, to read the lessons; as set aparte in the callender. I did so, 3 or 4 nights when Lo, and Behold! last Tuesday night, when I got redy to read my lesson, James had locked up the Bible, which he called his; and refused to let me have it, because it was too good to be used! (Turn over)

> In days of old, the word of God,
> By Monks, and Friars, was read o'er;
> But now, a selfish PEDDY-NOD,
> Has lock'd it up within his Draw'r.

This is too much for me, to have the Family Bible locked up; in a Land of Liberty and Freedom. Nor can I bear all their frumps and scornings, to be called a selfish Devil when I ask for the money which I earned when they sleeped in their beds; and ever and anon, to be told, that it is not my own Coat that I wear. I say, I can not bear it. I will not bear it. It is too much for mortal man.

> I am no Cat, I am no Dog,
> I am no Ox, I am no Hog,
> I am not either Sheep or Cow,
> Or any beast, that I should bow
> To their proud wills, or haughty minds;
> Which are as various as the winds:
> But I'm a mortal man by birth,
> Am born to live upon the earth;

O'er other men I want no sway,
But want my rights as well as they.

But after all, I do not wish to abcond clandestinely; far, very, from my idea, to become a tramp. I wish to live among relations and friends. Will you acquiesce in a plan that I have formed, and give me a little assistance in changing my situation. My plan is this, that you, on the receipt of this letter, procure me some work at Poughkeepsie (any kind of work that I can do, I shall not be exact at first) and then write to my Father, to request him to let me come, without giving him any knowlege, or even insinuiating, that you have had a letter from me. By this means I should leave them in a friendly manner, and they would find me money for the Journey. If you will thus assist me in time of tribulation, you will lay me under the greatest obligations possible; but should you refuse me; then write to me immediately, that I may know to use some other plan. For I am determined to break the bands of opression this once, let what will be the consequence. Whatever way you determin to do, I hope you will make no delay; for I shall wait with unceasing anxiety, till I see the result of this letter. I Still Remain,

Dear Aunt and Uncle;
Your Affectionate Nephew,
Joseph Hollingworth

MILL GIRL. *Recently widowed, Lucy Larcom's mother decided to leave Beverly, Massachusetts, and make a living by running one of the boardinghouses for young women at the Lowell mills. This was in 1832, when Lucy was eleven.*

Most of my mother's boarders were from New Hampshire and Vermont, and there was a fresh, breezy sociability about them which made them seem almost like a different race of beings from any we children had hitherto known.

We helped a little about the housework, before and after school, making beds, trimming lamps, and washing dishes. The heaviest work was done by a strong Irish girl, my mother always attending to the cooking herself. She was, however, a better caterer than the circumstances required or permitted. She liked to make nice things for the table, and, having been accustomed to an abundant supply, could never learn to economize. At a dollar and a quarter a week for board, (the price allowed for mill-girls by the corporations) great care in expenditure was necessary. It was not in my mother's nature closely to calculate costs, and in this way there came to be a continually increasing leak in the family purse. The older members of the family did everything they could, but it was not enough. I heard it said one day, in a distressed tone, "The children will have to leave school and go into the mill."

There were many pros and cons between my mother and sisters before this was positively decided. The mill-agent did not want to take us two little girls, but consented on condition we should be sure to attend school the full number of months prescribed each year. I, the younger one, was then between eleven and twelve years old.

I listened to all that was said about it, very much fearing that I should not be permitted to do the coveted work. For the feeling had already frequently come to me, that I was the one too many in the overcrowded family nest. Once, before we left our old home, I had heard a neighbor condoling with my mother because there were so many of us, and her emphatic reply had been a great relief to my mind:—

"There isn't one more than I want. I could not spare a single one of my children."

But her difficulties were increasing, and I thought it would be a pleasure to feel that I was not a trouble or burden or expense to any-body. So I went to my first day's work in the mill with a light heart. The novelty of it made it seem easy, and it really was not hard, just to change the bobbins on the spinning-frames every three quarters of an hour or so, with half a dozen other little girls who were doing the same thing. When I came back at night, the family began to pity me for my long, tiresome day's work, but I laughed and said,—

"Why, it is nothing but fun. It is just like play."

And for a little while it was only a new amusement; I liked it better than going to school and "making believe" I was learning when I was not. And there was a great deal of play mixed with it. We were not occupied more than half the time. The intervals were spent frolicking around among the spinning-frames, teasing and talking to the older girls, or entertaining ourselves with games and stories in a corner, or exploring, with the overseer's permission, the mysteries of the card-ing-room, the dressing-room, and the weaving-room. . . . In a room below us we were sometimes allowed to peer in through a sort of blind door at the great waterwheel that carried the works of the whole mill. It was so huge that we could only watch a few of its spokes at a time, and part of its dripping rim, moving with a slow, measured strength through the darkness that shut it in.

When I took my next three months at the grammar school, every-thing there was changed, and I too was changed. The teachers were kind, and thorough in their instruction; and my mind seemed to have been ploughed up during that year of work, so that knowledge took root in it easily. It was a great delight to me to study, and at the end of the three months the master told me that I was prepared for the high school.

But alas! I could not go. The little money I could earn—one dollar a week, besides the price of my board—was needed in the family, and I must return to the mill. It was a severe disappointment to me, though I did not say so at home. . . . I went back to my work, but now without enthusiasm. I had looked through an open door that I was not willing to see shut upon me.

We were children still, whether at school or at work, and Nature still held us close to her motherly heart. Nature came very close to the mill-gates, too, in those days. There was green grass all around them; violets and wild geraniums grew by the canals; and long stretches of open land between the corporation buildings and the street made the town seem country-like. The slope behind our mills . . . was a green lawn; and in front of some of them the overseers had gay flower-gardens. We passed in to our work through a splendor of dahlias and hollyhocks.

At home I was among children of my own age, for some cousins and other acquaintances had come to live and work with us. We had our evening frolics and entertainments together, and we always made the most of our brief holiday hours.

A family of bright girls, near neighbors of ours, proposed that we should join with them, and form a little society for writing and discussion, to meet fortnightly at their house. We met,—I think I was the youngest of the group—prepared a Constitution and By-Laws, and named ourselves "The Improvement Circle." If I remember rightly, my sister was our first president. The older ones talked and wrote on many subjects quite above me. I was shrinkingly bashful, as half-grown girls usually are, but I wrote my little essays and read them, and listened to the rest, and enjoyed it all exceedingly. Out of this little "Improvement Circle" grew the larger one whence issued the "Lowell Offering," a year or two later.

At this time I had learned to do a spinner's work, and I obtained permission to tend some frames that stood directly in front of the river-windows, with only them and the wall behind me, extending half the length of the mill—and one young woman beside me, at the farther end of the row. She was a sober, mature person, who scarcely thought it worth her while to speak often to a child like me; and I was, when with strangers, rather a reserved girl; so I kept myself occupied with the river, my work, and my thoughts. And the river and my thoughts flowed on together, the happiest of companions. Like a loitering pilgrim, it sparkled up to me in recognition as it glided along, and bore away my little frets and fatigues on its bosom. When the work "went well," I sat in the window-seat, and let my fancies fly whither they would,—downward to the sea, or upward to the hills that hid the mountain-cradle of the Merrimack.

The printed regulations forbade us to bring books into the mill, so I made my window-seat into a small library of poetry, pasting its side all over with newspaper clippings. In those days we had only weekly papers, and they had always a "poet's corner," where standard writers were well represented, with anonymous ones also. I was not, of course, much of a critic. I chose my verses for their sentiment, and because I wanted to commit them to memory; sometimes it was a long poem, sometimes a hymn, sometimes only a stray verse.

I was just beginning, in my questionings as to the meaning of life, to get glimpses of its true definition from the poets,—that it is love, service, the sacrifice of self for others' good. The lesson was slowly learned, but every hint of it went to my heart.

A very familiar extract from Carlos Wilcox, almost the only quotation made nowadays from his poems, was often on my sister Emilie's lips, whose heart seemed always to be saying to itself:—
"Pour blessings round thee like a shower of gold!"

Some of the girls could not believe that the Bible was meant to be counted among forbidden books. We all thought that the Scriptures had a right to go wherever we went. . . . The overseer, caring more for law than gospel, confiscated all he found. He had his desk full of Bibles. It sounded oddly to hear him say to the most religious girl in the room, when he took hers away, "I did think you had more conscience than to bring that book here. . . . "

The last window in the row behind me was filled with flourishing house-plants—fragrant-leaved geraniums, the overseer's pets. They gave that corner a bowery look; the perfume and freshness tempted me there often. Standing before that window, I could look across the room and see girls moving backwards and forwards among the spinning-frames, sometimes stooping, sometimes reaching up their arms, as their work required, with easy and not ungraceful movements. On the whole, it was far from being a disagreeable place to stay in. The girls were bright-looking and neat, and everything was kept clean and shining.

My grandfather came to see my mother once at about this time and visited the mills. When he had entered our room, and looked around for a moment, he took off his hat and made a low bow to the girls, first toward the right, and then toward the left. We were familiar with his courteous habits, partly due to his French descent; but we had never seen anybody bow to a room full of mill girls in that polite way, and some one of the family afterwards asked him why he did so. He looked a little surprised at the question, but answered promptly and with dignity, "I always take off my hat to ladies."

LOADING HIDES. *Among the many duties Richard Henry Dana had to perform as an ordinary seaman was loading and unloading cargoes as his ship traded along the California coast. This was in the 1830s, when California was still part of Mexico, and docks were so rare that his ship had to moor well out from the shore. This account comes from his book* Two Years Before the Mast.

Occasionally we landed a few goods, which were taken away by Indians in large, clumsy ox-carts, with the bow of the yoke on the ox's neck instead of under it, and with small solid wheels. A few hides were brought down, which we carried off in the California style. This we had now got pretty well accustomed to, and hardened to also; for it does require a little hardening, even to the toughest.

The hides are brought down dry, or they will not be received. When they are taken from the animal, they have holes cut in the ends, and are staked out, and thus dried in the sun without shrinking. They are then doubled once, lengthwise, with the hair side usually in, and sent down upon mules or in carts, and piled above high-water mark; and then we take them upon our heads, one at a time, or two, if they are small, and wade out with them and throw them into the boat, which as there are no wharves, we usually kept anchored by a small kedge, or keeleg, just outside of the surf. We all provided ourselves with thick Scotch caps, which would be soft to the head, and at the same time protect it; for we soon learned that, however it might look or feel at first, the "head-work" was the only system for California. For besides that the seas, breaking high, often obliged us to carry the hides so, in order to keep them dry, we found that, as they were very large and heavy, and nearly as stiff as boards, it was the only way that we could carry them with any convenience to ourselves.

The great art is in getting them on the head. We had to take them from the ground, and as they were often very heavy, and as wide as the arms could stretch, and were easily taken by the wind, we used to have some trouble with them. I have often been laughed at myself, and joined in laughing at others, pitching ourselves down in the sand in trying to swing a large hide upon our heads, or nearly blown over with one in a little gust of wind. The captain made it harder for us, by telling us that it was "California fashion" to carry two on the head at a time; and as he insisted upon it, and we did not wish to be outdone by other vessels, we carried two for the first few months; but after falling in with a few other "hide droghers," and finding that they carried only one at a time, we "knocked off" the extra one, and thus made our duty somewhat easier.

After our heads had become used to the weight, and we had learned the true California style of *tossing a hide*, we could carry off two or three hundred in a short time, without much trouble; but it was always wet work, and, if the beach was stony, bad for our feet; for we, of course, went barefooted on this duty, as no shoes could stand such constant wetting with salt water. And after this we had a pull of three miles, with a loaded boat, which often took a couple of hours.

JOURNALIST. *By 1845, Richard Henry Dana had gone from being an ordinary seaman to a successful lawyer and lecturer. In his diary he records an encounter that took place in Philadelphia, where he was to deliver a lecture before the Mercantile Library Association.*

December 9. Tuesday. I went to the U.S. Hotel, ordered a fire in my room, & after dinner sat down to read over my lecture. While reading, heard a loud knock at my door. Had hardly answered it before it burst open & in tumbled a short, fat, greasy looking man, with a soiled neck-cloth, & wet black hair, quite out of breath & breathing like a porpoise.

"Mr. Dana—I presume. Mr. R. H. Dana Jr., from Boston?" "Yes, Sir." "You lecture to-night, before the Merc. Lib." "Yes, Sir, I hope to." "Well, Sir, I am Mr.___of the___ ___. You may know the paper, if you don't know me." I told him I knew the paper by reputation. He then apologised, said he was out of breath, was large, & tired, & took a chair. He then told me that it was their custom to give a notice of the lecture in the paper of the next morning, that if they employed a reporter, they could not get it set up in season,—& in short that he would be much obliged to me if I would give him a sketch of my lecture for the press.

I asked him if it was usual to do this. He assured me that it was, & was considered perfectly proper. Without more ado, he moved his chair up to the table, took off his great coat, & India rubbers, drew from his pocket a roll of fools cap paper which he put on the table, took from another pocket an ink-stand & quills & proceeded to make a pen. He then desired me to give him the heads of the lecture, & planting himself, ready for action, said "American Loyalty! Well! Go on, Sir, if you please."

I told him what my first point was. "I shall put it in the third person," said he, & began repeating aloud, as he wrote—"The lecturer opened by a happy allusion"—"now go on, if you please, Sir," & took down my first point. "Done!" said he, & looked up for some more. I then gave him the second head. Still muttering in the same undertone,—"The orator next forcibly & clearly defined & illustrated . . . " he took down my second point. The next paragraphs he varied by "Mr. Dana proceeded," or "Mr.D. then eloquently &c.," & so on to the end.

"Now," said he, "a lecturer usually has some favorite sentences, some pet forms of expression, or the like, some passage more high wrought than the rest. Suppose you give me some of these. Select 'em for yourself."

Here was a ridiculous position. I had some thought of breaking off with him, & telling him I did not quite like the manner of proceeding, but he was good natured & seemed to depend upon it, & it was a difficult thing to do. I told him I had some sentences which had been applauded in other places, & which I rather relied upon to hit the humor of the audience. "That's it," said he, "that's what I want. Now, Sir, go on if you please, Sir." I then picked out two passages which he copied verbatim, introduced with phrases of "poetical," "graphical," & the like, & one of them he prefaced by saying—"as nearly as we could catch his words," & then copied from my manuscript.

As he was counting over his pages I observed that the first was numbered two. I told him he had made a mistake. "No, Sir," said he, "I'm right. The first page *has been set up.*" He then felt in his pockets & produced a crumbled sheet, & said "Here it is, Sir. I thought I would read it to you," & then he went through a paragraph in which it stated that last evening—Mr. Dana &c.—large audience,—elite of the city,—marked approbation,—frequent applause—glowing with patriotism, gems of poetical effect, &c. &c. "I have said 'notwithstanding the bad walking,' for I don't think it will rain" (here he looked out of the window), "but it's safe to say the walking was bad."

I asked what he would do if that was not true. Perhaps the audience would be thin, or I might fail, or get no applause. "Oh, never fear," said he, "it will be all right. We'll take care of that, Sir. That's our lookout" &c. &c.

Here he jumped up, thanked me for my kindness & hurried off.

APPRENTICE CAULKER. *Before escaping to freedom in the North, where he was to become a leading abolitionist, newspaper editor, and public lecturer, Frederick Douglass was put to learn a trade in the dockyards of Baltimore. This episode from the* Narrative of the Life of Frederick Douglass, *took place in 1835, when Douglass was eighteen.*

In a few weeks after I went to Baltimore, Master Hugh hired me to Mr. William Gardner, an extensive ship-builder, on Fell's Point. I was put there to learn how to calk. It, however, proved a very unfavorable place for the accomplishment of this object. Mr. Gardner was engaged that spring in building two large man-of-war brigs, professedly for the Mexican government. The vessels were to be launched in the July of that year, and in failure thereof, Mr. Gardner was to lose a considerable sum; so that when I entered, all was hurry. There was no time to learn anything. Every man had to do that which he knew how to do.

In entering the ship-yard, my orders from Mr. Gardner were to do whatever the carpenters commanded me to do. This was placing me at the beck and call of about seventy-five men. I was to regard all these as masters. Their word was to be my law. My situation was a most trying one. At times I needed a dozen pair of hands. I was called a dozen ways in the space of a single minute. Three or four voices would strike my ear at the same moment. It was—"Fred, come help me to cant this timber here."—"Fred, come carry this timber yonder."—"Fred, bring that roller here."—"Fred, go get a fresh can of water."—"Fred, come help saw off the end of this timber."—"Fred, go quick, and get the crowbar."—"Fred, hold on the end of this fall."—"Fred, go to the blacksmith's shop, and get a new punch."—"Hurra, Fred! run and bring me a cold chisel."—"I say, Fred, bear a hand, and get up a fire as quick as lightning under that steam-box." "Halloo, nigger! come, turn this grindstone."—"Come, come! move, move! and *bowse* this timber forward."—"I say, darky, blast your eyes, why don't you heat up some pitch?"—"Halloo! halloo! halloo!" (Three voices at the same time.) "Come here!—Go there!—Hold on where you are! Damn you, if you move, I'll knock your brains out!"

This was my school for eight months; and I might have remained there longer, but for a most horrid fight I had with four of the white apprentices, in which my left eye was nearly knocked out, and I was horribly mangled in other respects. The facts in the case were these: Until a very little while after I went there, white and black ship-carpenters worked side by side, and no one seemed to see any impropriety in it. All hands seemed to be very well satisfied. Many of the black carpenters were freemen. Things seemed to be going on very well. All at once, the white carpenters knocked off, and said they would not work with free colored workmen. Their reason for this, as alleged, was, that if free colored carpenters were encouraged, they would soon take the trade into their own hands, and poor white men would be thrown out of employment. They therefore felt called upon at once to put a stop to it. And, taking advantage of Mr. Gardner's necessities, they broke off, swearing they would work no longer, unless he would discharge his black carpenters.

Now, though this did not extend to me in form, it did reach me in fact. My fellow-apprentices very soon began to feel it degrading to them to work with me. They began to put on airs, and talk about the "niggers" taking the country, saying we all ought to be killed; and, being encouraged by the journeymen, they commenced making my condition as hard as they could, by hectoring me around, and sometimes striking me. I, of course, . . . struck back again, regardless of consequences; and while I kept them from combining, I succeeded very well; for I could whip the whole of them, taking them separately. They, however, at length combined, and came upon me, armed with sticks, stones, and heavy handspikes. One came in front with a half brick. There was one at each side of me, and one behind me. While I was attending to those in front, and on either side, the one behind ran up with the handspike, and struck me a heavy blow upon the head. It stunned me. I fell, and with this they all ran upon me, and fell to beating me with their fists. I let them lay on for a while, gathering strength. In an instant, I gave a sudden surge, and rose to my hands and knees. Just as I did that, one of their number gave me, with his heavy boot, a powerful kick in the left eye. My eyeball seemed to have burst. When they saw my eye closed, and badly swollen, they left me. With this I seized the handspike, and, for a time pursued them. But here the carpenters interfered, and I thought I might as well give it up. It was impossible to stand my hand against so many.

All this took place in sight of not less than fifty white ship-carpenters, and not one interposed a friendly word; but some cried, "Kill the damned nigger! Kill him! Kill him! He struck a white person." I found my only chance for life was in flight. I succeeded in getting away without an additional blow and barely so; for to strike a white man is death by Lynch law,—and that was the law in Mr. Gardner's ship-yard; nor is there much of any other out of Mr. Gardner's ship-yard.

TAVERN KEEPER. *T. S. Arthur, author of the 1854 temperance classic* Ten Nights in a Bar-room, *tells an instructive tale.*

I have known some women to set up grog-shops; but they were women of bad principles and worse hearts. I remember one case, where a woman, with a sober, church-going husband, opened a dram-shop. The husband opposed, remonstrated, begged, threatened—but all to no purpose. The wife, by working for the clothing stores, had earned and saved about three hundred dollars. The love of money, in the slow process of accumulation, had been awakened; and, in administering to the depraved appetites of men who loved drink and neglected their families, she saw a quicker mode of acquiring the gold she coveted. And so the dram shop was opened. And what was the result? The husband quit going to church. He had no heart for that; for, even on the Sabbath day, the fiery stream was stayed not in his house. Next he began to tipple. Soon alas! the subtle poison so pervaded his system that morbid desire came; and then he moved along quick-footed in the way of ruin. In less than three years, I think, from the time the grog shop was opened by his wife, he was in a drunkard's grave. A year or two more, and the pit that was digged for others by the hands of the wife, she fell into hersef. After breathing an atmosphere poisoned by the fumes of liquor, the love of tasting it was gradually formed, and she, too, in the end, became a slave to Demon Drink. She died at last, poor as a beggar in the street. Ah! this liquor-selling is the way to ruin; and they who open the gates, as well as those who enter the downward path, alike go to destruction.

LIGHTHOUSE KEEPER. *Between 1849 and 1855, Henry David Thoreau made several visits to Cape Cod, during one of which he stayed at the Highland Light, near Truro.*

The Highland Light-house, where we were staying, is a substantial-looking building of brick, painted white, and surmounted by an iron cap. Attached to it is the dwelling of the keeper, one story high, also of brick, and built by government. As we were going to spend the night in a light-house, we wished to make the most of so novel an experience, and therefore told our host that we would like to accompany him when he went to light up.

At rather early candle-light he lighted a small Japan lamp, allowing it to smoke rather more than we like on ordinary occasions, and told us to follow him. He led the way first through his bedroom, which was placed nearest to the light-house, and then through a long, narrow, covered passage-way, between whitewashed walls like a prison entry, into the lower part of the light-house, where many great butts of oil were arranged around; thence we ascended by a winding and open iron stairway, with a steadily increasing scent of oil and lamp-smoke, to a trap-door in an iron floor, and through this into the lantern. It was a neat building, with everything in apple-pie order, and no danger of anything rusting there for want of oil. The light consisted of fifteen argand lamps, placed within smooth concave reflectors twenty-one inches in diameter, and arranged in two horizontal circles one above the other, facing every way excepting directly down the Cape. These were surrounded, at a distance of two or three feet, by large plate-glass windows, which defied the storms, with iron sashes, on which rested the iron cap. All the iron work, except the floor, was painted white. And thus the light-house was completed.

We walked slowly round in that narrow space as the keeper lighted each lamp in succession, conversing with him at the same moment that many a sailor on the deep witnessed the lighting of the Highland Light. His duty was to fill and trim and light his lamps, and keep bright the reflectors. He filled them every morning and trimmed them commonly once in the course of the night. . . .

Formerly, when this light-house had windows with small and thin panes, a severe storm would sometimes break the glass, and then they were obliged to put up a wooden shutter in haste to save their lights and reflectors,—and sometimes in tempests, when the mariner stood most in need of their guidance, they had thus nearly converted the light-house into a dark lantern, which emitted only a few feeble rays, and those commonly on the land or lee side. He spoke of the anxiety and sense of responsibility which he felt in cold and stormy nights in the winter; when he knew that many a poor fellow was depending on him, and his lamps burned dimly, the oil being chilled. Sometimes he was obliged to warm the oil in a kettle in his house at midnight, and fill his lamps over again.—for he could not have a fire in the light house, it produced such a sweat on the windows.

Our host said that the frost, too, on the windows caused him much trouble, and in sultry summer nights the moths covered them and dimmed his lights; sometimes even small birds flew against the thick plate glass, and were found on the ground beneath in the morning with their necks broken. In the spring of 1855 he found nineteen small yellowbirds, perhaps goldfinches or myrtle-birds, thus lying dead around the light-house; and sometimes in the fall he had seen where a golden plover had struck the glass in the night. . . . Thus he struggled, by every method, to keep his light shining before men.

COTTON PLANTATION. *Frederick Law Olmsted, one of the chief designers of New York's Central Park and Brooklyn's Prospect Park, was also a prolific author whose best-known book,* The Cotton Kingdom, *was based on his extensive travels in the South in the 1850s. Here he is visiting a large and profitable plantation on a tributary of the Mississippi.*

Each overseer regulated the hours of work on his own plantation. I saw the negroes at work before sunrise and after sunset. At about eight o'clock they were allowed to stop for breakfast, and again about noon, to dine. The length of these rests was at the discretion of the overseer or drivers, usually, I should say, from half an hour to an hour. There was no rule.

The number of hands directed by each overseer was considerably over one hundred. The manager thought it would be better economy to have a white man over every fifty hands, but the difficulty of obtaining trustworthy overseers prevented it. Three of those he then had were the best he had ever known. He described the great majority as being passionate, careless, inefficient men, generally intemperate, and totally unfitted for the duties of the position. The best overseers, ordinarily, are young men, the sons of small planters, who take up the business temporarily, as a means of acquiring a little capital with which to purchase negroes for themselves.

"The Cotton Gin," an 1869 wood engraving from *Harper's Weekly*.
The first gin was invented by Eli Whitney in 1793.

The ploughs at work, both with single and double mule teams, were generally held by women, and very well held, too. I watched with some interest for any indication that their sex unfitted them for the occupation. Twenty of them were ploughing together, with double teams and heavy ploughs. They were superintended by a negro man who carried a whip, which he frequently cracked at them, permitting no dawdling or delay at the turning; and they twitched their ploughs around on the head-land, jerking their reins, and yelling to their mules, with apparent ease, energy, and rapidity. Throughout the Southwest the negroes, as a rule, appeared to be worked much harder than in the Eastern and Northern Slave States. I do not think they accomplish as much in the same time as agricultural labourers at the North usually do, but they certainly labour much harder, and more unremittingly. They are constantly and steadily driven up to their work, and the stupid, plodding, machine-like manner in which they labour, is painful to witness. This was especially the case with the hoe-gangs. One of them numbered nearly two hundred hands (for the force of two plantations was working together), moving across the field in parallel lines, with a considerable degree of precision. I repeatedly rode through the lines at a canter, without producing the smallest

change or interruption in the dogged action of the labourers, or causing one of them, so far as I could see, to lift an eye from the ground. I
had noticed the same thing with smaller numbers before, but here,
considering that I was a stranger, and that strangers could but very
rarely visit the plantation, it amazed me very much. I think it told a
more painful story than any I had ever heard, of the cruelty of slavery.
It was emphasized by a tall and powerful negro who walked to and fro
in the rear of the line, frequently cracking his whip, and calling out in
the surliest manner, to one and another, "Shove your hoe, there!
shove your hoe!" But I never saw him strike any one with the whip.

The whip was evidently in constant use, however. There were no
rules on the subject, that I learned; the overseers and drivers punished
the negroes whenever they deemed it necessary, and in such manner,
and with such severity, as they thought fit. "If you don't work faster," or
"If you don't work better," or "If you don't recollect what I tell you, I
will have you flogged," I often heard. I said to one of the overseers, "It
must be disagreeable to have to punish them as much as you do?" "Yes,
it would be to those who are not used to it—but it's my business, and I
think nothing of it. Why, sir, I wouldn't mind killing a nigger more
than I would a dog." I asked if he had ever killed a negro? "Not quite
that," he said, but overseers were often obliged to. Some negroes are
determined never to let a white man whip them, and will resist you,
when you attempt it; of course you must kill them in that case. Once a
negro, whom he was about to whip in the field, struck at his head with
a hoe. He parried the blow with his whip, and, drawing a pistol, tried
to shoot him; but the pistol missing fire, he rushed in and knocked
him down with the butt of it. At another time, a negro whom he was
punishing insulted and threatened him. He went to the house for his
gun, and as he was returning, the negro, thinking he would be afraid
of spoiling so valuable a piece of property by firing, broke for the
woods. He fired at once, and put six buck-shot into his hips. He always
carried a bowie-knife, and not a pistol unless he anticipated some
unusual act of insubordination. He always kept a pair of pistols ready
loaded over the mantel-piece, however, in case they should be needed.
It was only when he first came upon a plantation that he ever had
much trouble. A great many overseers were unfit for their business,
and too easy and slack with the negroes. When he succeeded such a
man, he had hard work for a time to break the negroes in; but it did
not take long to teach them their place. His conversation on the subject was exactly like what I have heard said, again and again, by
Northern shipmasters and officers, with regard to seamen.

I happened to see the severest corporeal punishment of a negro
that I witnessed at the South while visiting this estate. . . . The manner
of the overseer who inflicted the punishment, and his subsequent

conversation with me about it, indicated that it was by no means unusual in severity.

I had accidentally encountered him, and he was showing me his plantation. In going from one side of it to the other, we had twice crossed a deep gully, at the bottom of which was a thick covert of brushwood. We were crossing it a third time, and had nearly passed through the brush, when the overseer suddenly stopped his horse exclaiming, "What's that? Hallo! who are you, there?"

It was a girl lying at full length on the ground at the bottom of the gully, evidently intending to hide herself from us in the bushes.

"Who are you, there?"

"Sam's Sall, sir."

"What are you skulking there for?"

The girl half rose, but gave no answer.

"Have you been here all day?"

"No, sir."

"How did you get here?"

The girl made no reply.

"Where have you been all day?"

The answer was unintelligible.

After some further questioning, she said her father accidentally locked her in, when he went out in the morning.

"How did you manage to get out?"

"Pushed a plank off, sir, and crawled out."

The overseer was silent for a moment, looking at the girl, and then said, "That won't do; come out here." The girl arose at once, and walked towards him. She was about eighteen years of age. A bunch of keys hung at her waist, which the overseer espied, and he said, "Your father locked you in; but you have got the keys." After a little hesitation, she replied that these were the keys of some other locks; her father had the door-key.

Whether her story was true or false, could have been ascertained in two minutes by riding on to the gang with which her father was at work, but the overseer had made up his mind.

"That won't do," said he; "get down." The girl knelt on the ground; he got off his horse, and holding him with his left hand, struck her thirty or forty blows across the shoulder with his tough, flexible, "raw-hide" whip (a terrible instrument for the purpose). They were well laid on, at arm's length, but with no appearance of angry excitement on the part of the overseer. At every stroke the girl winced and exclaimed, "Yes, sir!" or "Ah, sir!" or "Please, sir!" not groaning or screaming. At length he stopped and said, "Now tell me the truth." The girl repeated the same story. "You have not got enough yet," said he; "pull up your clothes—lie down." The girl without any hesitation, without a word or look of remonstrance or entreaty, drew closely all her garments under her shoulders, and lay down upon the ground with her face toward the overseer, who continued to flog her with the raw-hide, across her naked loins and thighs, with as much strength as before. She now shrunk away from him, not rising, but writhing, grovelling, and screaming, "Oh, don't, sir! oh, please stop, master! please, sir! please, sir! oh, that's enough, master! oh, Lord! oh, master, master! oh, God, master, do stop! oh, God, master! oh, God, master!"

A young gentleman of fifteen was with us; he had ridden in front, and now turning on his horse, looked back with an expression only of impatience at the delay. It was the first time I had ever seen a woman flogged. I had seen a man cudgelled and beaten, in the heat of passion, before, but never flogged with a hundredth part of the severity used in this case. I glanced again at the perfectly passionless but rather grim business-like face of the overseer, and again at the young gentleman, who had turned away; if not indifferent he had evidently not the faintest sympathy with my emotion. Only my horse chafed. I gave him rein and spur and we plunged into the bushes and scrambled fiercely up the steep acclivity. The screaming yells and the whip strokes had ceased when I reached the top of the bank. Choking, sobbing, spasmodic groans only were heard. I rode on to where the road, coming diagonally up the ravine, ran out upon the cotton-field. My young companion met me there, and immediately afterward the overseer. He laughed as he joined us, and said:

"She meant to cheat me out of a day's work, and she has done it, too."

"Did you succeed in getting another story from her?" I asked, as soon as I could trust myself to speak.

"No; she stuck to it."

"Was it not perhaps true?"

"Oh no, sir; she slipped out of the gang when they were going to work, and she's been dodging about all day, going from one place to another as she saw me coming."

"I suppose they often slip off so."

"No, sir; I never had one do so before—not like this; they often run away to the woods, and are gone some time, but I never had a dodge-off like this before."

"Was it necessary to punish her so severely?"

"Oh yes, sir," (laughing again). "If I hadn't, she would have done the same thing again to-morrow, and half the people on the plantation would have followed her example. Oh, you've no idea how lazy these niggers are; you Northern people don't know anything about it. They'd never do any work at all if they were not afraid of being whipped."

STOREKEEPER. *Isaac Meyer, born in 1825 in Prussia, arrived in California in 1857. After a short stay in San Francisco he opened a store in a small town, which he does not name but calls "a lonely place of thirteen houses," before eventually moving to Los Angeles.*

Before moving into the city, an incident happened some time in June, 1858. A man by the name of Stark, who came to this section of the state with the first thrashing machine from Missouri, came into my store and demanded liquor. He was too full to give him any more, because he must cross a stream called the Santa Ana River, to reach his lodging house, and this sometimes was very dangerous. So I refused him, whereupon he drew a big horse pistol revolver and pointed it at my head and threatened to kill me by blowing my brains out if I did not comply with his request.

I had nothing left but my bravery, so I responded: "Shoot, if I deserve to be shot." I was very well acquainted with him and was determined not to let him have any more liquor, but I knew there was no use to try to reason with him. I tore up my shirt and showed my courage and said: "Blaize away!" So he started to cry and said: "I cannot shoot so brave a little man." Then he threw his revolver through the open door. This came pretty near to killing my landlord's sister, who was sitting a few paces from where it fell and accidentally discharged. Fortunately, it did not hit her, but she had a narrow escape and saved my life.

The landlord happened to be the justice of the peace and also very well acquainted with the man. However, he [Stark] was scared, because he came the next day and begged on his knees for forgivness and asked us not to prosecute, so we let him off and forgave him. But all of my misfortunes did not end just yet.

One month later, which was in August of the same year, my landlord's father-in-law got on a big spree and came into my store and ran me out of my store into the middle of the street and made an attack on me. His own daughter had to interfere and tried to protect me from his onslaught, ferocious, deathly attack, but he threatened to rip her open if she did not desist. Nobody knew the cause. All the inhabitence of the town, which consisted of eleven houses, came together and tried to interfere and find the cause of so ferocious an attack, to prevent it, but without avail.

He said he would kill anybody who interfered, as I had killed his son, Nicholas de Colema. He was told it was not true, but he insisted to kill me. He ran me around in the rear of my store. It was only a small open space, and on such occasions the people had a style in such a small town. They formed a ring, and there we were in the middle, he after me with a great, big, long knife, a very powerful man, strong like a lion, and me with nothing for protection but heaven and God.

I was trying to avoid the ferocious deathblow, but I became desperate and impatient of the danger that I was in and started to holler at the top of my voice: "If this is a theater between life and death, give me a little more room so I can defend and save my life, if possible." Among strangers, nothing was left me but to defend my life as dearly as I possibly could, but I had presence of mind, notwithstanding the dangerous condition I was in.

The soil was very sandy, to my good fortune, so I thought of a simple scheme and watching my chance as he was raving like a wild lion. But I had determined not to perish in such a way. I stooped down and grabbed two handfuls of fine quicksand, and as quick as lightening, I threw it in his eyes. That settled the whole difficulty.

All were happy at my miraculous escape and clapped hands while he, my assassin, rubbed his eyes. I made for my store and saved my life. His friends and relatives closed in on him, overpowered him, and took him home to his house and stood guard over him and watched him until he fell asleep.

In the meantime, my partner returned from a visit to his cousin, who lived three miles from us on a ranch. While we were narrating of this singular, dangerous occurence, he advised me to go to town, Los Angeles, for a good rest from everything, for a few days, until the excitement subsided. The same night I went to Los Angeles, which was thirteen miles from my place of business, and stayed there for three days, sick from excitement.

GOVERNESS. *Before finding success as a writer, Louisa May Alcott had a hard time making ends meet, as she describes in this 1858 letter. (In another letter, she calls her charge, Alice Lovering, "A demonic little girl who don't digest her food & does rave & tear & scold & screech like an insane cherubim.")*

To the Alcott Family

Boston Sunday evening

Dear People

You will laugh when you hear what I have been doing. Laugh, but hear, unless you prefer to cry, & hear.

Last week was a busy, anxious time, & my courage most gave out, for every one was so busy, & cared so little whether I got work or jumped into the river that I thought seriously of doing the latter. In fact did go over the Mill Dam & look at the water. But it seemed so mean to turn & run away before the battle was over that I went home, set my teeth & vowed I'd *make* things work in spite of the world, the flesh & the devil.

Lovering sent no answer about Alice, & nothing else could I find. I waited till Friday, then rushed out & clamored for work. Called on Mrs Lovering, she was out. Tore across the Common to Mrs Reed. She had no sewing but would remember me if she had. Asked Mr. Sargent, had nothing for me to do. Then I said "Damn!" & after a tempestuous night got up, went straight to Mr Parker's & demanded him. You may judge what desperate earnest I was in to go to people I knew so little. Mr. P. was out also Miss L. But Mrs P. was in. . . . I dont know what she thought of me for I was muddy & shabby, pale & red-eyed, grim one minute & choky the next. Altogether a nice young person to come bouncing in & demanding work like a reckless highway woman.

I told her in a few words that we were poor, I *must* support myself, & was willing to do anything honest; sew, teach write, house work, nurse, &c.

She was very kind, said she would confer with Theodore & Hannah; & I came away feeling better, for, though she gave me no work a little sympathy was worth its weight in gold just then, & no one else offered me a bit.

To day went to church, heard a sermon on "Good is set against evil." Tried to apply it, but did n't do it very well. At noon Hannah H. called & offered me a place as seamstress at the Reform School Winchester. Sew 10 hours a day, making & mending for 30 girls. Pay small at first, but it is a beginning & honest work.

Miss H. evidently thought I wouldn't take it for she said "Mrs P. told me of your visit, was it in earnest or only a passing idea?" "I was in desperate earnest, & shall be glad of any thing, no matter how hard or humble," said I in my tragic way. "May I depend on you, & do you like sewing?" "You may depend on me if my health holds out with the 10 hours work. As for liking, it was not what I *want* but what I can *get* that I must take & be grateful for." She seemed satisfied, gave me a ticket, said, "Try it a week," & told me to go on Monday.

So I shall go & try my best, though it will be hard to sit patching & darning day after day with a dozen stories bubbling in my brain & "knocking proudly on the lid demanding to be taken out & sold." Knocking about is good for me I suppose. I get so much of it, I shall grow mellow & fit to eat in the fullness of time, though I think peacefully growing on the parent tree with plenty of sun an easier way.

Monday eve

Now what *do* you think? Last eve when my mind was all made up to go out to W[inchester] in comes a note from Lovering saying that on talking it over they concluded to have me come & governess Alice for the winter.

I skipped for joy, & dear Molly said "Stay here & sew for me & that will pay your board, you help so much in many ways & make it so lively." I agreed at once, & there I am. Allyluyer! I went & told Hannah H and she was glad & said, "I knew it was n't the thing for you & only offered it as a little test of your earnestness, meaning to get you something better in time." Mr. P. said "The girl has got true grit," & "we were all pleased with you." So that is right, & the ten hours will dwindle to four, with walking, playing & lessons to vary the time.

It has been a hard week but it is all right now, & I guess the text will prove true in the end, for my despair found me friends, & duty was made easier when I had accepted the hardest. Amen.

I begin tomorrow & am in fine spirits again. "Here we go up up up—And here we go down down downy" is a good song for me.

With love your tragic comic

Lu

FUR TRAPPER. *In 1859, shortly after his father had been murdered in Kansas for publicly expressing his antislavery opinions, William Cody (soon to reinvent himself as Buffalo Bill but still only a teenager) set out to restore the family fortune.*

During my stay in and about Fort Laramie I had seen much of the Indian traders, and accompanied them on a number of expeditions. Their business was to sell to the Indians various things they needed, chiefly guns and ammunition, and to take in return the current Indian coin, which consisted of furs. . . . I felt that I should be able to embark in the fur business on my own account—not as a trader but as a trapper.

With my friend Dave Harrington as a companion I set out. Harrington was older than I, and had trapped before in the Rockies. I was sure that with my knowledge of the Plains and his of the ways of the fur-bearing animals, we should form an excellent partnership, as in truth we did.

We bought a yoke of oxen, a wagon-sheet, wagon, traps of all sorts, and strychnine with which to poison wolves. Also we laid in a supply of grub—no luxuries, but coffee, flour, bacon and everything that we actually needed to sustain life.

We headed west, and about two hundred miles from home we struck Prairie Creek, where we found abundant signs of beaver, mink, otter and other fur-bearing animals. No Indians had troubled us, and we felt safe in establishing headquarters here and beginning work. The first task was to build a dugout in a hillside, which we roofed with brush, long grass, and finally dirt, making everything snug and cozy. A little fireplace in the wall served as both furnace and kitchen. Outside we built a corral for the oxen, which completed our camp.

Our trapping was successful from the start, and we were sure that prosperity was at last in sight. We set our steel traps along the "runs" used by the animals, taking great care to hide our tracks, and give the game no indication of the presence of an enemy. The pelts began to pile up in our shack. Most of the day we were busy at the traps, or skinning and salting the hides, and at night we would sit by our little fire and swap experiences till we fell asleep. Always there was the wail of the coyotes and the cries of other animals without, but as long as we saw no Indians we were not worried.

One night, just as we were dozing off, we heard a tremendous commotion in the corral. Harrington grabbed his gun and hurried out. He was just in time to see a big bear throw one of our oxen and proceed with the work of butchering him.

He fired, and the bear, slightly wounded, left the ox and turned his attention to his assailant. He was leaping at my partner, growling savagely, when I, gun in hand, rounded the corner of the shack. I took the best aim I could get in the dark, and the bear, which was within a few feet of my friend, rolled over dead.

Making sure that he was past harming us we turned our attention to the poor bull, but he was too far gone to recover, and another bullet put him out of his misery.

We were now left without a team, and two hundred miles from home. But wealth in the shape of pelts was accumulating about us, and we determined to stick it out till spring. Then one of us could go to the nearest settlement for a teammate for our remaining steer, while the other stayed in charge of the camp.

This plan had to be carried out far sooner than we expected. A few days later we espied a herd of elk, which meant plentiful and excellent meat. We at once started in pursuit. Creeping stealthily along toward them, keeping out of sight, and awaiting an opportunity to get a good shot, I slipped on a stone in the creek bed.

"Snap!" went something and looking down I saw my foot hanging useless. I had broken my leg just above the ankle, and my present career as a fur-trapper had ended.

I was very miserable when Harrington came up. I urged him to shoot me as he had the ox, but he laughingly replied that that would hardly do.

"I'll bring you out all right!" he said. "I owe you a life anyway for saving me from that bear. I learned a little something about surgery when I was in Illinois, and I guess I can fix you up."

He got me back to camp after a long and painful hour, and with a wagon-bow, which he made into a splint, set the fracture. But our

"Most of the day we were busy at the traps, or skinning and salting the hides, and at night we would sit by our little fire and swap experiences till we fell asleep. Always there was the wail of the coyotes and the cries of other animals without, but as long as we saw no Indians we were not worried. . . . The Plains teach men and boys fortitude," William Cody (Buffalo Bill), 1859. "The American Trapper," wood engraving in *Appleton's Journal*, April, 1871.

enterprise was at an end. Help would have to be found now, and before spring. One man and a cripple could never get through the winter.

It was determined that Harrington must go for this needful assistance just as soon as possible. He placed me on our little bunk, with plenty of blankets to cover me. All our provisions he put within my reach. A cup was lashed to a long sapling, and Harrington made a hole in the side of the dugout so that I could reach this cup out to a snow-bank for my water supply. Lastly he cut a great pile of wood and heaped it near the fire. Without leaving the bunk I could thus do a little cooking, keep the fire up, and eat and sleep. . . .

The nearest settlement was a hundred and twenty-five miles distant. Harrington figured that he could make the round trip in twenty days. My supplies were ample to last that long. I urged him to start as soon as possible, that he might the sooner return with a new yoke of oxen. Then I could be hauled out to where medical attendance was to be had.

I watched him start off afoot, and my heart was heavy. But soon I stopped thinking of my pain and began to find ways and means to cure my loneliness. We had brought with us a number of books, and these I read through most of my waking hours. But the days grew longer and longer, for all that. Every morning when I woke I cut a notch in a long stick. . . . I had cut twelve of these notches when one morning I was awakened from a sound sleep by the touch of a hand on my shoulder.

Instantly concluding that Harrington had returned, I was about to cry out in delight when I caught a glimpse of a war-bonnet, surmounting the ugly, painted face of a Sioux brave. The brilliant colors that had been smeared on his visage told me more forcibly than words could have done that his tribe was on the warpath. It was a decidedly unpleasant discovery for me.

While he was asking me in the Sioux language what I was doing there, and how many more were in the party, other braves began crowding through the door till the little dugout was packed as full of Sioux warriors as it could hold. Outside I could hear the stamping of horses and the voices of more warriors. I made up my mind it was all over but the scalping.

And then a stately old brave worked his way through the crowd and came toward my bunk. It was plain from the deference accorded him by the others that he was a chief. And as soon as I set eyes on him I recognized him as old Rain-in-the-Face, whom I had often seen and talked with at Fort Laramie, and whose children taught me the Sioux language as we played about the wagonbeds together. . . .

I showed the chief my broken leg, and asked him if he did not remember me. He replied that he did. I asked him if he intended to kill the boy who had been his children's playmate. He consulted with his warriors, who had begun busily to loot the cabin. After a long parley the old man told me that my life would be spared, but my gun and pistol and all my provisions would be regarded as the spoils of the war.

Vainly I pointed out that he might as well kill me as leave me without food or the means to defend myself against wolves. He said that his young men had granted a great deal in consenting to spare my life. As for food, he pointed to the carcass of a deer that hung from the wall.

The next morning they mounted their ponies and galloped away. I was glad enough to see them go. . . . But, even with the Indians gone, I was in a desperate situation. As they had taken all my matches I had to keep the fire going continuously. This meant that I could not sleep long at a time, and the lack of rest soon began to tell on me. I would cut slices from the deer carcass with my knife, and holding it over the fire with a long stick, cook it, eating it without salt. Coffee I must do without altogether.

The second day after the departure of the Indians a great snow fell. The drifts blocked the doorway and covered the windows. It lay to a depth of several feet on the roof over my head. My woodpile was covered by the snow that drifted in and it was with great difficulty that I could get enough wood to keep my little fire going. And on that fire depended my life. Worse than all these troubles was the knowledge that the heavy snow would be sure to delay Harrington.

I would lie there, day after day, a prey to all sorts of dark imaginings. I fancied him killed by Indians on the trail, or snowbound and starving on the Plains. Each morning my notches on my calendar stick were made. Gradually their number grew till at last the twentieth was duly cut. But no Harrington came.

The wolves, smelling meat within, had begun to gather round in increasing numbers. They made the night hideous with their howlings, and pawed and scratched and dug at the snow by the doorway, determined to come in and make a meal of everything the dugout contained, myself included.

How I endured it I do not know. But the Plains teach men and boys fortitude. . . .

It was on the twenty-ninth day, as marked on my stick, when I had about given up hope, that I heard a cheerful voice shouting "Whoa!" and joyfully recognized it as the voice of Harrington. A criminal on the scaffold with the noose about his neck and the trap sagging underneath his feet could not have welcomed a pardon more eagerly than I welcomed my deliverance out of this torture-chamber.

MINING ON THE HUMBOLDT. *Mark Twain, in* Roughing It, *describes how he tried to strike it rich on the Humboldt River in Nevada.*

We went out "prospecting" with Mr. Ballou. We climbed the mountainsides, and clambered among sagebrush, rocks, and snow til we were ready to drop with exhaustion, but found no silver—nor yet any gold. Day after day we did this. Now and then we came upon holes burrowed a few feet into the declivities and apparently abandoned;

and now and then we found one or two listless men still burrowing. But there was no appearance of silver. . . .

Day after day we toiled, and climbed and searched, and we younger partners grew sicker and still sicker of the promiseless toil. At last we halted under a beetling rampart of rock which projected from the earth high upon the mountain. Mr. Ballou broke off some fragments with a hammer, and examined them long and attentively with a small eyeglass; threw them away and broke off more; said this rock was quartz, and quartz was the sort of rock that contained silver. *Contained* it! I had thought that at least it would be caked on the outside of it, like a kind of veneering. He still broke off pieces and critically examined them, now and then wetting the piece with his tongue and applying the glass. At last he exclaimed:

"We've got it!"

A group of mule drivers at the entrance of a coal mine in Scranton, Pennsylvania, circa 1900. Photograph by Keystone View Company.

We were full of anxiety in a moment. The rock was clean and white, where it was broken, and across it ran a ragged thread of blue. He said that that little thread had silver in it, mixed with base metals, such as lead and antimony, and other rubbish, and that there was a speck or two of gold visible. After a great deal of effort we managed to discern some little fine yellow specks, and judged that a couple of tons of them massed together might make a gold dollar, possibly. We were not jubilant, but Mr. Ballou said there were worse ledges in the world than that. He saved what he called the "richest" piece of the rock, in order to determine its value by the process called the "fire assay." Then we named the mine "Monarch of the Mountains" (modesty of nomenclature is not a prominent feature in the mines), and Mr. Ballou wrote out and stuck up the following "notice," preserving a copy to be entered upon the books in the mining recorder's office in the town.

NOTICE
We the undersigned claim three claims, of three hundred feet each (and one for discovery), on this silver-bearing quartz lead or lode, extending north and south from this notice, with all its dips, spurs, and angles, variations and sinuosities, together with fifty feet of ground on either side for working the same.

We put our names to it and tried to feel that our fortunes were made. But when we talked the matter over with Mr. Ballou, we felt depressed and dubious. He said that this surface quartz was not all there was to our mine; but that the wall or ledge of Rock called the "Monarch of the Mountains" extended down hundreds and hundreds of feet into the earth . . . and that down in the great depths of the ledge was its richness, and the deeper it went the richer it grew. Therefore, instead of working here on the surface, we must either bore down into the rock with a shaft till we came to where it was rich— say a hundred feet or so—or else we must go down into the valley and bore a long tunnel into the mountainside and tap the ledge far under the earth.

We decided to sink a shaft. So, for a week we climbed the mountain, laden with picks, drills, gads, crowbars, shovels, cans of blasting powder and coils of fuse, and strove with might and main. At first the rock was broken and loose and we dug it up with picks and threw it out with shovels, and the hole progressed very well. But the rock became more compact, presently, and gads and crowbars came into play. But shortly nothing could make an impression but blasting powder. That was the weariest work! One of us held the iron drill in its place and another would strike with an eight-pound sledge—it was like driving nails on a large scale. In the course of an hour or two the drill would reach a depth of two or three feet, making a hole a couple of inches in diameter. We would put in a charge of powder, insert half a yard of fuse, pour in sand and gravel and ram it down, then light the fuse and run. When the explosion came and the rocks and smoke shot into the air, we would go back and find about a bushel of that hard rebellious quartz jolted out. Nothing more. One week of this satisfied me. I resigned. Claget and Oliphant followed. Our shaft was only twelve feet deep. We decided that a tunnel was the thing we wanted.

So we went down the mountainside and worked a week; at the end of which time we had blasted a tunnel about deep enough to hide a hogshead in, and judged that about nine hundred feet more of it would reach the ledge. I resigned again, and the other boys only held out one day longer.

Meantime the camp was filling up with people, and there was a constantly growing excitement about our Humboldt mines. We fell victims to the epidemic and strained every nerve to acquire more "feet." We prospected and took up new claims, put "notices" on them and gave them grandiloquent names. We traded some of our "feet" for "feet" in other people's claims. In a little while we owned largely in the "Gray Eagle," the "Columbiana," the "Branch Mint," the "Maria Jane," the "Universe," the "Root-Hog-or-Die," the "Samson and Delilah," the "Treasure Trove," the "Golconda," the "Sultana," the "Boomerang," the "Great Republic," the "Grand Mogul," and fifty other "mines" that had never been molested by a shovel or scratched with a pick. We had not less than thirty thousand "feet" apiece in the "richest mines on earth" as the frenzied cant phrase had it—and were in debt to the butcher. . . . Every man you met had his new mine to boast of, and his "specimens" ready; and if the opportunity offered, he would infallibly back you into a corner and offer as a favor to *you*, not to *him*, to part with just a few feet in the "Golden Age," or the "Sarah Jane," or some other unknown stack of croppings. . . . And you were never to reveal that he had made you the offer at such a ruinous price, for it was only out of friendship for you that he was willing to make the sacrifice. Then he would fish a piece of rock out of his pocket, and after looking mysteriously around as if he feared he might be waylaid and robbed if caught with such wealth in his possession, he would dab the rock against his tongue, clap an eyeglass to it, and exclaim:

"Look at that! Right there in that red dirt! See it? See the specks of gold? And the streak of silver? That's from the 'Uncle Abe.' There's a hundred thousand tons like that in sight! Right in sight, mind you!

And when we get down on it and the ledge comes in solid, it will be the richest thing in the world! Look at the assay! I don't want you to believe *me*—look at the assay!"

Then he would get out a greasy sheet of paper which showed that the portion of rock assayed had given evidence of containing silver and gold in the proportion of so many hundreds or thousands of dollars to the ton. I little knew, then, that the custom was to hunt out the *richest* piece of rock and get it assayed! Very often, that piece, the size of a filbert, was the only fragment in a ton that had a particle of metal in it—and yet the assay made it pretend to represent the average value of the ton of rubbish it came from!

On such a system of assaying as that, the Humboldt world had gone crazy. On the authority of such assays its newspaper correspondents were frothing about rock worth four and seven thousand dollars a ton!

We never touched our tunnel or our shaft again. Why? Because we judged that we had learned the *real* secret of success in silver mining— which was, *not* to mine the silver ourselves by the sweat of our brows and the labor of our hands, but to *sell* the ledges to the dull slaves of toil and let them do the mining!

TOWN MARSHAL. *By 1868 the Kansas-Pacific Railroad had reached Hays City, "a wild and woolly town" whose "Main Street was almost a solid row of saloons, dance halls, restaurants, barber shops and houses of prostitution kept by such notorious characters as 'Calamity Jane,' 'Lousy Liz,' 'Stink-Foot Mag,' and 'Steamboat.'" To maintain law and order, the town's vigilance committee had hired "Wild Bill" Hickok to serve as marshal. In* My Life on the Frontier, *Miguel Otero recalls watching him in action.*

I was an eye-witness to Wild Bill's encounter with Bill Mulvey, and shall relate the details as they linger in my mind:

I was standing near Wild Bill on Main Street, when someone began "shooting up the town" at the eastern end of the street. It was Bill Mulvey, a notorious murderer from Missouri, known as a handy man with a gun. He had just enough red liquor in him to be mean and he seemed to derive great amusement from shooting holes into the mirrors, as well as the bottles of liquor behind the bars, of the saloons in that section of the street. As was usually the case with such fellows, he was looking for trouble, and when someone told him that Wild Bill was the town marshal and therefore it behooved him to behave himself, Mulvey swore that he would find Wild Bill and shoot him on sight. He further averred that the marshal was the very man he was looking for and that he had come to the "damn' town" for the express purpose of killing him.

The tenor of these remarks was somehow made known to Wild Bill. But hardly had the news reached him than Mulvey appeared on the scene, tearing toward us on his iron-grey horse, rifle in hand, full cocked. When Wild Bill saw Mulvey he walked out to meet him, apparently waving his hand to some fellows behind Mulvey and calling to them: "Don't shoot him in the back; he is drunk."

Mulvey stopped his horse and, wheeling the animal about, drew a bead on his rifle in the direction of the imaginary man he thought Wild Bill was addressing. But before he realized the ruse that had been played upon him, Wild Bill had aimed his six-shooter and fired—just once. Mulvey dropped from his horse—dead, the bullet having penetrated his temple and then passed through his head.

FARMER'S WIFE. *The anonymous wife of an Illinois farmer, married for thirteen years, who said of herself "I am not a practical woman," describes her life in the late nineteenth century.*

No man can run a farm without some one to help him, and in this case I have always been called upon and expected to help to do anything that a man would be expected to do; I began this when we were first married, when there were few household duties and no reasonable excuse for refusing to help.

I was reared on a farm, was healthy and strong, was ambitious, and the work was not disagreeable, and having no children for the first six years of married life, the habit of going whenever asked to became firmly fixed, and he had no thought of hiring a man to help him, since I could do anything for which he needed help.

I was always religiously inclined; brought up to attend Sunday school, not in a haphazard way, but to attend every Sunday all the year round, and when I was twelve years old I was appointed teacher to a Sunday school class, a position I proudly held until I was married at eighteen years of age.

I was an apt student at school and before I was eighteen I had earned a teacher's certificate of the second grade and would gladly have remained in school a few more years, but I had, unwittingly, agreed to marry the man who is now my husband, and though I begged to be released, his will was so much stronger that I was unable to free myself without wounding a loving heart, and could not find it in my nature to do so.

I always had a passion for reading; during girlhood it was along educational lines; in young womanhood it was for love stories, which remained ungratified because my father thought it was sinful to read stories of any kind, and especially love stories. Later, when I was married,

Not until 1920 did the rural population fall below half the nation's total. Here, a woman wearing her Sunday best milks a cow outside a barn. Photograph circa 1900.

I borrowed everything I could find in the line of novels and stories and read them by stealth still, for my husband thought it was a willful waste of time to read anything and that it showed a lack of love for him if I would rather read than talk to him when I had a few moments of leisure, and, in order to avoid giving offense and still gratify my desire, I would only read when he was not at the house. . . .

In reading miscellaneously I got glimpses now and then of the great poets and authors, which aroused a great desire for a thorough perusal of them all; but up till the present time I have not been permitted to satisfy this desire. As the years have rolled on there has been more work and less leisure until it is only by the greatest effort that I may read current news.

My work is so varied that it would be difficult, indeed, to describe a typical day's work.

Any bright morning in the latter part of May I am out of bed at four o'clock; next, after I have dressed and combed my hair, I start a fire in the kitchen stove, and while the stove is getting hot I go to the flower garden and gather a choice, half-blown rose and a spray of bride's wreath, and arrange them in my hair, and sweep the floors and then cook breakfast.

While the other members of the family are eating breakfast I strain away the morning's milk (for my husband milks the cows while I get breakfast), and fill my husband's dinner-pail, for he will go to work on our other farm for the day.

By this time it is half-past five o'clock, my husband is gone to his work, and the stock loudly pleading to be turned out into the pastures. The younger cattle, a half-dozen steers, are left in the pasture at night, and I now drive the two cows a half-quarter mile and turn them in with the others, come back, and then there's a horse in the barn that belongs in a field where there is no water, which I take to a spring quite a distance from the barn; bring it back and turn it into a field with the sheep, a dozen in number, which are housed at night.

The young calves are then turned out into the warm sunshine, and the stock hogs, which are kept in a pen, are clamoring for feed, and I carry a pailful of swill to them, and hasten to the house and turn out the chickens and put out feed and water for them, and it is, perhaps, 6.30 a.m.

I have not eaten breakfast yet, but that can wait; I make the beds next and straighten things up in the living room, for I dislike to have the early morning caller find my house topsy-turvy. When this is done I go to the kitchen, which also serves as a dining room, and uncover the table, and take a mouthful of food occasionally as I pass to and fro at my work until my appetite is appeased.

By the time the work is done in the kitchen it is about 7.15 a.m., and the cool morning hours have flown, and no hoeing done in the garden yet, and the children's toilet has to be attended to and churning has to be done.

Finally the children are washed and the churning done, and it is eight o'clock, and the sun getting hot, but no matter, weeds die quickly when cut down in the heat of the day, and I use the hoe to a good advantage until the dinner hour, which is 11.30 a.m. We come in, and I comb my hair, and put fresh flowers in it, and eat a cold dinner, put out feed and water for the chickens; set a hen, perhaps, sweep the floors again; sit down and rest, and read a few moments, and it is nearly one o'clock, and I sweep the door yard while I am waiting for the clock to strike the hour.

I make and sow a flower bed, dig around some shrubbery, and go back to the garden to hoe until time to do the chores at night, but ere long some hogs come up to the back gate, through the wheat field, and when I go to see what is wrong I find that the cows have torn the fence down, and they, too, are in the wheat field.

With much difficulty I get them back into their own domain and repair the fence. I hoe in the garden till four o'clock; then I go into the house and get supper, and prepare something for the dinner pail tomorrow; when supper is all ready it is set aside, and I pull a few hundred plants of tomato, sweet potato or cabbage for transplanting, set them in a cool, moist place where they will not wilt, and I then go after the horse, water him, and put him in the barn; call the sheep and house them, and go after the cows and milk them, feed the hogs, put down hay for the horses, and put oats and corn in their troughs, and set those plants and come in and fasten up the chickens, and it is dark. By this time it is 8 o'clock p.m.; my husband has come home, and we are eating supper; when we are through eating I make the beds ready, and the children and their father go to bed, and I wash the dishes and get things in shape to get breakfast quickly next morning.

It is now about 9 o'clock p.m., and after a short prayer I retire for the night.

As a matter of course, there's hardly two days together which require the same routine, yet every day is as fully occupied in some way or other as this one, with varying tasks as the seasons change.

I have never had a vacation, but if I should be allowed one I should certainly be pleased to spend it in an art gallery.

SANDHOG. *Frank Harris was fifteen and virtually penniless when he stepped off the boat from Ireland in 1870. Luckily for him, he soon found room and board with the Mulligans, a blue-collar family in New York.*

Mike had a day off, so he came home for dinner at noon and he had great news. They wanted men to work under water in the iron caissons of Brooklyn Bridge and they were giving from five to ten dollars a day.

"Five dollars," cried Mrs. Mulligan. "It must be dangerous or unhealthy or somethin'—sure, you'd never put the child to work like that."

Mike excused himself, but the danger, if danger there was, appealed to me almost as much as the big pay: my only fear was that they'd think me too small or too young. I had told Mrs. Mulligan I was sixteen, for I didn't want to be treated as a child. . . .

Next morning Mike took me to Brooklyn Bridge soon after five o'clock to see the contractor; he wanted to engage Mike at once but shook his head over me. "Give me a trial," I pleaded; "you'll see I'll make good." After a pause, "O.K.," he said; "four shifts have gone down already underhanded: you may try."

In the bare shed where we got ready, the men told me no one could do the work for long without getting the "bends"; the "bends" were a sort of convulsive fit that twisted one's body like a knot and often made you an invalid for life. They soon explained the whole procedure to me. We worked, it appeared, in a huge bell-shaped caisson of iron that went to the bottom of the river and was pumped full of compressed air to keep the water from entering it from below: the top of the caisson is a room called the "material chamber," into which the stuff dug out of the river passes up and is carted away. On the side of the caisson is another room, called the "air-lock," into which we were to go to be "compressed." As the compressed air is admitted, the blood keeps absorbing the gasses of the air till the tension of the gasses in the blood becomes equal to that in the air: When this equilibrium has been reached, men can work in the caisson for hours without serious discomfort, if sufficient pure air is constantly pumped in. It was the foul air that did the harm, it appeared. "If they'd pump in good air, it would be O.K.; but that would cost a little time and trouble, and men's lives are cheaper." I saw that the men wanted to warn me, thinking I was too young, and accordingly I pretended to take little heed.

When we went into the "air-lock" and they turned on one air-lock after another of compressed air, the men put their hands to their ears and I soon imitated them, for the pain was very acute. Indeed, the drums of the ears are often driven in and burst if the compressed air is brought in too quickly. I found that the best way of meeting the pressure was to keep swallowing air and forcing it up into the middle ear, where it acted as an air-pad on the innerside of the drum. . . .

When the air was fully compressed, the door of the air-lock opened at a touch and we all went down to work with pick and shovel on the gravelly bottom. My headache soon became acute. The six of us were working naked to the waist in a small iron chamber with a temperature of about 80° Fahrenheit: in five minutes the sweat was pouring from us, and all the while we were standing in icy water that was only kept from rising by the terrific air pressure. No wonder the headaches were blinding. The men didn't work for more than ten minutes at a time, but I plugged on steadily, resolved to prove myself and get constant employment; only one man, a Swede named Anderson, worked at all as hard.

The amount done each week was estimated, he told me, by an inspector. Anderson was known to the contractor and received half a wage extra as head of our gang. He assured me I could stay as long as I liked, but he advised me to leave at the end of a month: it was too unhealthy: above all, I mustn't drink and should spend all my spare time in the open. He was kindness itself to me, as indeed were all the others. After two hours' work down below we went up into the air-lock room to get gradually "decompressed," the pressure of air in our veins having to be brought down gradually to the usual air pressure. The men began to put on their clothes and passed round a bottle of schnapps; but though I was soon as cold as a wet rat and felt depressed and weak to boot, I would not touch the liquor. In the shed above I took a cupful of hot cocoa with Anderson, which stopped the shivering, and I was soon able to face the afternoon's ordeal.

For three or four days things went fairly well with me, but on the fifth day or sixth we came on a spring of water, or "gusher," and were wet to the waist before the air pressure could be increased to cope with it. As a consequence, a dreadful pain shot through both my ears: I put my hands to them tight and sat still for little while. Fortunately, the shift was almost over and Anderson came with me to the horse-car. "You'd better knock off," he said. "I've known 'em go deaf from it."

Mrs. Mulligan saw at once something was wrong and made me try her household remedy—a roasted onion cut in two and clapped tight on each ear with a flannel bandage. It acted like magic: in ten minutes I was free of pain; then she poured in a little warm sweet oil and in an hour I was walking in the park as usual. Still, the fear of deafness was on me and I was very glad when Anderson told me he had complained to the boss and we were to get an extra thousand feet of pure air. It would make a great difference, Anderson said, and he was right, but the improvement was not sufficient.

One day, just as the "decompression" of an hour and a half was ending, an Italian named Manfredi fell down and writhed about, knocking his face on the floor till the blood spurted from his nose and mouth. When we got him into the shed, his legs were twisted like plaited hair. The surgeon had him taken to the hospital. I made up my mind that a month would be enough for me.

COWBOY. *From* Up the Trail in '79, *by Baylis John Fletcher, then aged twenty. The trail here is the Chisholm Trail.*

On the morning of April 11, a supreme moment for us, we started up the trail to Cheyenne, Wyoming. To gather the cattle in the pasture into one great herd took up the forenoon. In the afternoon we made only about five miles, bedding our cattle that night just south of Victoria, near the Guadalupe River. On the following morning we forded the river, which was low.

When we were passing through the streets of Victoria, a lady, fearful that the cattle would break down her fence and ruin her roses, ran out to the pickets and, waving her bonnet frantically at the cattle, stampeded those in front. With a dull roar, they charged back upon the rear of the herd, and but for the discreet management of boss Arnett, heavy damage to city property would have resulted.

"Give way at all street crossings and let the cattle have room," he shouted as he galloped about, giving orders to save the City of Roses from a disaster.

We complied quickly and soon had half a dozen residence blocks surrounded by excited and infuriated cattle. Soon they became so confused that the stampede was ended. We gave their fears time to subside, then drove them quietly out of the city without doing any serious damage.

We proceeded to the north and, in a few days, reached the mouth of Peach Creek, north of Cuero. . . . Here water was procured in the Guadalupe River, and we stopped on its banks to rest our cattle and eat dinner. While grazing the cattle along the bank of the river, we discovered a big alligator idly floating on the water's surface. All hands were attracted by the strange sight and began shouting at the big saurian, who protected himself by sinking out of sight in the turbid waters.

After dinner Joe Felder took off his boots and washed his feet in the river. Then he sat on the root of a big tree facing the stream and fell asleep. Manuel García, our cook, with that levity characteristic of the Mexican, conceived a practical joke. Throwing a log so that it fell into the river just in front of the sleeping Joe, he shouted, "Alligator!" In a quick effort to rise, Joe slipped into the river, going entirely under and rising by the side of the floating log, which he mistook for the alligator. He screamed for help, and stake ropes were thrown him, which he seized frantically, to be drawn out, as he thought, from the jaws of death. His disgust was profound when he discovered that he was escaping only from a rotten log.

On the following night we bedded our cattle in a short, wide lane between high rail fences a few miles east of Gonzales. This was a thickly settled region, timbered with a variety of oaks, and the surface was covered with gravel. My shift at guard duty was the last in the night, and at about two a.m., Sam Allen, Carteman García, and I were called to go on herd. Allen and I were stationed at the east end of the lane, while the Mexican guarded the other end. The night was frosty, and as the cattle seemed to be sleeping soundly, Sam and I dismounted and built a fire of dry branches by which to warm. At first we would warm by turns and ride time about. But everything was so still that we became careless and both dismounted at the fire, where we began to spin yarns. As the bright fire lit up the scene, it was beautiful to behold. Two thousand cattle rested quietly, lying down and chewing their cuds.

Suddenly there was a loud and ominous roar, while a cloud of dust obscured our vision.

The end of the trail: a herd of Texas longhorns being driven through
Dodge City. From *Frank Leslie's Illustrated Newspaper,* July 1878.

"Stampede!" shouted Sam as he let loose his bridle reins and
sprang behind an oak, which he hugged with both hands. I did not
have time to turn Happy Jack loose but threw my arms around Allen
on the side of the tree opposite the herd. We were none too quick, for
now the horns of the stampeding bovines were raking the bark from
the opposite side of the oak as they rushed madly past us. It was a
moment of supreme terror, but only a moment. In less time than it
takes to relate it, the cattle had passed us and, mounting Happy Jack, I
was in full pursuit.

I soon overtook the cattle, pressed on past them, and turned their
leaders back. They now formed a circle, where they milled in one
great wheel, revolving with almost lightning velocity. By holding them
in this mill, I soon had them confused, and they began to bellow to
one another. I had learned that these were welcome sounds in a stampede. As soon as the bellowing becomes general, the run begins to
subside. Of course, such a revolving wheel cannot be stopped suddenly. The momentum they have acquired makes it necessary to slow
down the cattle gradually, or else the ones that stopped first would be
trampled to death.

I now heard a voice shouting, "Stay with them, Fletcher." In a
moment I was joined by Mr. Snyder, riding one of the wagon horses
bareback and with a blind bridle. "Where is Sam?" he asked. But I did
not know.

We soon had the cattle quiet, and as it now was about dawn, we drove them back to the bed ground. I learned from Mr. Snyder that something had frightened the cattle in about the middle of the lane where we had bedded them and that I was holding only a part of the herd, the remainder having run out of the other end of the lane past García. After getting the fragments of our herd together, we strung them out in a thin line, and as they passed a certain point, the cattle were counted. It was found that we were about one hundred head short. . . .

While we were discussing the feasibility of recovering the lost cattle, four hard-looking citizens rode up and said, "Had a stampede last night, did you?" We answered in the affirmative. Then the strangers offered their services to help put the cattle back in the herd. Their offer was to bring in all they could for one dollar per head. Mr. Snyder then offered them fifty cents per head, to which they readily agreed. It seemed plain to us that these accommodating gentry had stampeded our herd for this revenue.

CHILD LABOR. *Helen Campbell was a city missionary and philanthropist whose book* Darkness and Daylight *or* Lights and Shadows of New York Life *did much to make the public aware of conditions in the city's slums of the 1890s.*

In one night-school eighty of them [girls] registered as "nurses." Being interpreted, this means that they take care of the baby at home while the mother goes out to "day's work." It is astonishing to see the real motherliness of the little things, who lug about the baby with devotion; and if they feed it on strange diet they are but following in the footsteps of the mothers, who regard the baby at six months old as the sharer of whatever the family bill of fare has to offer. The small German child is early to take his portion of lager; . . . the Irish children have tea or coffee and even a sup of the "craytur. . . . "

I have seen a six-year-old girl scrubbing the floor of the one room in which lived a widowed mother and three children.

"She's a widdy washerwoman," said the dot, a creature with big blue eyes and a thin eager little face. "Yes, ma'am, she's a widdy washerwoman, an' I keep house. That's the baby there, an' he's good all the time, savin' whin his teeth is too big for him. It's teeth that's hard on babies, but I mind him good an' he thinks more o' me than he does of mother. See how beautiful he sucks at the pork."

The small housekeeper pointed with pride to the bed, where the tiny baby lay, a strip of fat pork in his mouth.

"He's weakly like, an' mother gives him the pork to set him up. An' he takes his sup o' tay beautiful too. Whin the summer comes we'll get

"'It's hard on 'em,' one of the women said. 'We work till ten and sometimes later.'" Illustration and text from Helen Campbell's *Darkness and Daylight*, 1891.

to have him go to the Children's Home at Bath, maybe, or down to Coney Island or somewhere. I might be a 'Fresh Air' child meself, but I have to keep house you know, an' so mother can't let me go."

This is one phase of child-labor, and the most natural and innocent one, though it is a heavy burden to lay on small shoulders, and premature age and debility are its inevitable results. Far truer is this of the long hours in shop or manufactory. A child of eight—one of a dozen in a shop on Walker Street—stripped feathers, and had for a year earned three dollars a week. In this case the father was dead and the mother sick, and the little thing went home to do such cooking as she could. Like many a worker, she had already learned to take strong tea and to believe that it gave her strength. She was dwarfed in growth from confinement in the air of the workshop, from lack of proper food and no play, and thousands of these little feather-strippers are in like case.

In another workshop in the same neighborhood, children of from eight to ten, and one much younger, cut the feathers from cock-tails.

The hours were from eight to six, and so for ten hours daily they bent over the work, which included cutting from the stem, steaming, curling, and packing.

Eight thousand children make envelopes at three and a half cents a thousand. They gum, separate, and sort. The hours are the same, but the rooms are generally lighter and better ventilated than the feather workers' surroundings. Many more burnish china, for, strange as it may seem, the most delicate ware is entrusted to children of ten or twelve. The burnishing instrument is held close against the breast, and this is a fruitful source of sickness, since the constant pressure brings with it various stomach and other troubles, dyspepsia being the chief.

"The Flypaper and Match Seller," Chicago, 1891.
Photograph by Krausz.

Paper collars employ a host. The youngest bend over them, for even a child of five can do this. One child of twelve counts and boxes twenty thousand a day, and one who pastes the lining on the Button-holes does five thousand a day. Over ten thousand children make paper boxes. Even in the making of gold-leaf a good many are employed, though chiefly young girls of fifteen and upwards. It is one of the most exhausting of the trades, as no air can be admitted, and the atmosphere is stifling.

Feathers, flowers, and tobacco employ the greatest number. A child of six can strip tobacco or cut feathers. In one great firm, employing over a thousand men, women, and children, a woman of eighty and her grandchild of four sit side by side and strip the leaves. . . . With the exception of match-making and one or two other industries there is hardly a trade so deadly in its effects. There are many operations which children are competent to carry on, and the phases of work done at home in the tenement-houses often employ the entire family.

In a report of the State Bureau of Labor it is stated that in one room less than twelve by fourteen feet, whose duplicate can be found at many points, a family of seven worked. Three of these, all girls, were under ten years of age. Tobacco lay in piles on the floor and under the long table at one end where cigars were rolled. Two of the children sat on the floor, stripping the leaves, and another sat on a small stool. A girl of twenty sat near them, and all had sores on lips, cheeks, and hands. Some four thousand women are engaged in this industry, and an equal number of unregistered young children share it with them. As in sewing, a number of women often club together and use one room, and in such cases their babies crawl about in the filth on the wet floors, playing with the damp tobacco and breathing the poison with which the room is saturated.

Skin diseases of many sorts develop in the children who work in this way, and for the women and girls nervous and hysterical complaints are common, the direct result of poisoning by nicotine. . . .

Twine-factories are clean and well ventilated, but they are often as disastrous in their effects. The twisting-room is filled with long spindles, innocent-looking enough, but taking a finger along with the flax as silently and suddenly as the thread forms. . . .

One [child] explained how it happened in her case.

"You see you mustn't talk or look off a minute. They just march right along. My sister was like me. She forgot and talked, and just that minute her finger was off, and she didn't even cry till she picked it up. My little finger always did stick out, and I was trying to twist fast like the girl next to me, and somehow it caught in the flax. I tried to jerk away, but it wasn't any use. It was off just the same as hers, and it took a great while before I could come back. I'm sort of afraid of them, for any minute your whole hand might go and you'd hardly know till it was done."

In a small room on Hester Street a woman at work on overalls—for the making of which she received one dollar a dozen—said:—

"I couldn't do as well if it wasn't for Jinny and Mame there. Mame has learned to sew on buttons first-rate, and Jinny is doing almost as well. I'm alone to-day, but most days three of us sew together here, and Jinny keeps right along. We'll do better yet when Mame gets a bit older."

As she spoke the door opened and a woman with an enormous bundle of overalls entered and sat down on the nearest chair with a gasp.

"Them stairs is killin'," she said. "It's lucky I've not to climb 'em often."

Something crept forward as the bundle slid to the floor, and busied itself with the string that bound it.

"Here you, Jinny," said the woman, "don't you be foolin'. What do you want anyhow?"

The something shook back a mat of thick hair and rose to its feet,—a tiny child who in size seemed scarcely three, but whose countenance indicated the experience of three hundred.

"It's the string I want," the small voice said. "Me and Mame was goin' to play with it."

"There's small time for play," said the mother; "there'll be two pair more in a minute or two, an' you are to see how Mame does one an' do it good, too, or I'll find out why not."

Mame had come forward and stood holding to the one thin garment which but partly covered Jinny's little bones. She, too, looked out from a wild thatch of black hair, and with the same expression of deep experience, the pallid, hungry little faces lighting suddenly as some cheap cakes were produced. Both of them sat down on the floor and ate their portion silently.

"Mame's seven, and Jinny's goin' on six," said the mother, "but Jinny's the smartest. She could sew on buttons when she wasn't much over four. I had five, but the Lord took 'em all but these two. I couldn't get on if it wasn't for Mame."

Mame looked up, but said no word, and, as I left the room, settled herself with her back against the wall, Jinny at her side, laying the coveted string near at hand for use if any minute for play arrived.

CRUSADER. *Carry Nation, author of* The Use and Need of the Life of Carry A. Nation, *who signed her autograph "Your Loving Home Defender," tells how she resorted to direct action to save the people of Kansas.*

At the time these dives were open, contrary to the statutes of our state, the officers were really in league with this lawless element. I was heavily burdened and could see "the wicked walking on every side, and the vilest men exalted." (Ps.12:8) I was ridiculed, was called "meddler," "crazy," was pointed to as a fanatic. I spent much time in tears, prayer and fasting. I would fast days at a time. One day I was so sad: I opened the Bible with a prayer for light, and saw these words: "Arise, shine, for thy light is come and the glory of the Lord is risen upon thee." (Isa. 60:1.) These words gave me unbounded delight.

I ran to my sister and said: "There is to be a change in my life."

As Jail Evangelist for the W.C.T.U. [the Women's Christian Temperance Union] in Medicine Lodge, I would ask the men in prison, young and old, why are you here? The answer was, it was "drink," "drink." I said, why do you get drunk in Kansas where we have no saloons? They told me that they got their drink in Kiowa. This town was in Barber county, a county right on the border with Oklahoma. I went to Mr. Sam Griffen, the County Attorney, time after time, telling him of these men being in jail from drink. He would put the matter off and seem very much annoyed because I asked him to do what he swore he would do, for he was oath bound to get out a warrant and put this in the hands of the sheriff who was oath bound to arrest these dive-keepers and put them in jail, and the place or dive was to be publicly abated or destroyed. Mr. Griffen was determined that these dive-keepers should not be arrested. I even went down to Kiowa myself and went into these places and came back asking this County Attorney to take my evidence and he would not do it. Then I wrote to Mr. A. A. Godard of Topeka, the State's Attorney, whose duty it was to see that all the County Attorneys did their duties. I saw he did not intend to do anything, then I went to William Stanley the Governor at Topeka. I told him of the prisoners in jail in our county from the sale of liquor in the dives of Kiowa, told him of the broken families and trouble of all kinds in the county, told him of two murders that had been committed in the county, one alone costing the tax payers $8,000.00, told him of the broken hearted women and the worse than fatherless children as the result. I found out that he would not do his duty. I had gone from the lowest to the chief-executive of the state, and after appealing to the governor in vain I found that I could go to no other authority on earth.

Now I saw that Kansas was in the power of the bitter foe to the constitution, and that they had accomplished what the whiskey men and their tools, the Republican party and politicians had schemed and worked for. When two thirds of the voters of Kansas said at the ballot box—about 1880, I think it was—"We will not have a saloon in our state," this was made constitutional by the two-thirds majority. Nothing could change this or take it out of the constitution except by having the amendment resubmitted and two-thirds of the people voting to bring the saloons back.

Every representative to Congress at Topeka was in favor of re-submission without an exception. Money was sent into Kansas by the thousands from brewers and distillers to be used by politicians for the purpose of bringing about re-submission. Kansas was the storm center. If the liquor men could bring back saloons into Kansas then a great blow would be struck against prohibition in all the states. This would discourage the people all over. Their great word was, "you can't," "prohibition will not prohibit." I do not belong to the "can't" family. When I was born my father wrote my name Carry A. Moore, then later it was Nation, which is more still. C.A.N. are the initials of my name, then C.(see) A. Nation! And all together Carry A. Nation! This is no accident but Providence. This does not mean that I will carry a nation, but that the roused heart and conscience will, as I am the roused heart and conscience of the people. There are just two crowds, God's crowd and the Devil's crowd. One gains the battle by can, and the other loses it by can't. . . .

When I found I could effect nothing through the officials, I was sad, indeed. I saw that Kansas homes, hearts and souls were to be sacrificed. I had lost all the hopes of my young life through drink, I saw the terrible butchery that would follow. I felt that I had rather die than see the saloons come back into Kansas. I felt desperate. I took this to God daily, feeling that he only could rescue. On the 5th of June, 1899, before retiring, I threw myself face downward at the foot of my bed at my home in Medicine Lodge. I poured out my grief and agony to God, in about this strain: "Oh Lord you see the treason in Kansas, they are going to break the mothers' hearts, they are going to send the boys to drunkards' graves and a drunkard's hell. I have exhausted all my means, Oh Lord, you have plenty of ways. You have used the base things and the weak things, use me to save Kansas. I have but one life to give you. If I had a thousand, I would give them all, please show me something to do."

The next morning I was awakened by a voice which seemed to be speaking in my heart, these words, "Go to Kiowa," and my hands were lifted and thrown down and the words, "I'll stand by you." The words, "Go to Kiowa," were spoken in a murmuring, musical tone, low and soft, but, "I'll stand by you," was very clear, positive and emphatic. I was impressed with a great inspiration, the interpretation was very plain, it was this: "Take something in your hands, and throw at these places in Kiowa and smash them." I was very much relieved and overjoyed and was determined to be "obedient to the heavenly vision." (Acts 26:19.) I told no one what I had heard or what I intended to do.

JUST BEFORE I LEFT WICHITA JAIL A PHOTOGRAPHER CAME TO MY CELL AND ASKED TO TAKE MY PICTURE. HERE IT IS IN THE POSITION OF KNEELING, READING MY BIBLE, WHICH WAS MY USUAL ATTITUDE.

Carry Nation in Wichita Jail. From *Carry A. Nation*, published in 1904.

When no one was looking I would walk out in the yard and pick up brick bats and rocks, would hide them under my kitchen apron, would take them in my room, would wrap them up in newspapers one by one. I did this until I got quite a pile.

At half past three that day I was ready to start, hitched up the buggy by myself, drove out of the stable, rode down a hill and over a bridge that was just outside the limits of Medicine Lodge. I saw in the middle of the road perhaps a dozen or so creatures in the forms of men leaning towards the buggy as if against a rope which prevented them from coming nearer. Their faces were those of demons and the gestures of their hands as if they would tear me up. I did not know what to do, but I lifted my hands, and my eyes to God, saying: "Oh! Lord, help me, help me." When I looked down these diabolical creatures were not in front of the buggy, but they were off to the right fleeing as if they were terrified.

I got to Kiowa at half past eight, stayed all night. Next morning I had my horse hitched and drove to the first dive kept by a Mr. Dobson, whose brother was then sheriff of the county. I stacked up these smashers on my left arm, all I could hold. They looked like packages wrapped in paper. I stood before the counter and said: "Mr. Dobson, I told you last spring to close this place, you did not do it, now I have come down with another remonstrance, get out of the way, I do not want to strike you, but I am going to break this place up." I threw as hard, and as fast as I could, smashing mirrors and bottles and glasses and it was astonishing how quickly this was done. These men seemed terrified, threw up their hands and backed up in the corner. My strength was that of a giant. I felt invincible. God was certainly by me.

I will tell you a very strange thing. As the stones were flying . . . I saw Mr. McKinley, the President, sitting in an old fashion arm chair and as the stones would strike I saw them hit the chair and the chair fell to pieces, and I saw Mr. McKinley fall over. I did not understand this until very recently, now I know that the smashing in Kansas was intended to strike the head of this nation the hardest blow, for every saloon I smashed in Kansas had a license from the head of this government which made the head of the government more responsible than the dive-keeper. I broke up three of these dives that day, broke the windows on the outside to prove that the man who rents his house is a partner also with the man who sells. The party who licenses and the paper that advertises, all have a hand in this and are *particeps criminis*. I smashed five saloons with rocks, before I ever took a hatchet.

In the last place, kept by Lewis, there was quite a young man behind the bar. I said to him: "Young man, come from behind that bar, your mother did not raise you for such a place." I threw a brick at the mirror, which was a very heavy one, and it did not break, but the brick fell and broke everything in its way. I began to look around for something that would break it. I was standing by a billiard table on which there was one ball. I said: "Thank God," and picked it up, threw it, and it made a hole in the mirror.

By this time, the streets were crowded with people; most of them seemed to look puzzled. There was one boy about fifteen years old who seemed perfectly wild with joy, and he jumped, skipped and yelled with delight. I have since thought of that as being a significant sign. For to smash saloons will save the boy.

I stood in the middle of the street and spoke in this way: "I have destroyed three of your places of business, and if I have broken a statute of Kansas, put me in jail; if I am not a law-breaker your mayor and councilmen are. You must arrest one of us, for if I am not a criminal, they are."

One of the councilmen, who was a butcher, said: "Don't you think we can attend to our business?"

"Yes," I said, "You can, but you won't. As Jail Evangelist of Medicine Lodge, I know you have manufactured many criminals and this county is burdened down with taxes to prosecute the results of these dives. Two murders have been committed in the last five years in this county, one in a dive I have just destroyed. You are a butcher of hogs and cattle, but they are butchering men, women and children, positively contrary to the laws of God and man, and the mayor and councilmen are more to blame than the jointist. And now if I have done wrong in any particular, arrest me."

When I was through with my speech I got into my buggy and said: "I'll go home."

"Inuit housing," Alaska. Photograph by Edward S. Curtis, 1899.

HOUSING

'Mid pleasures and palaces though we may roam
Be it ever so humble, there's no place like home

WITH THESE NOSTALGIC OPENING LINES, written while he was in semi-exile in England in 1823, John Howard Payne struck a chord that continues to resonate in the nation's psyche. "Home, Sweet Home," as its refrain goes, is more than just a popular song. With its stately measures and lofty phrasing it is almost a hymn, an anthem raised to the ideal of Home as a place of modest comfort, safe refuge, and warm domesticity available to everyone.

As ideals go, this is fairly recent. For much of America's history it was generally accepted that most people would live without complaint in whatever shelter they could manage, using whatever materials were at hand, whether adobe or buffalo hides or roughly hewn logs or canvas tents or sods of turf. Progress was erratic, and by the end of the last century huge numbers of people were living in misery in overcrowded tenements and slums or in ramshackle rural housing. Still, the ideal of Home, though remote for many, and at times sentimentalized to the point of absurdity, did at least provide a standard that helped to make these harsh realities unacceptable. For reformers like Jacob Riis and Helen Campbell, it was enough to expose the squalor of slum life; their readers could supply for themselves the picture of how things ought to be.

Other but lesser household ideals—sanitation, security, convenience—have also been put into practice. Fires are relatively less destructive today; most people have indoor plumbing; garbage may still pile up in the streets, but it is usually bagged; mattresses are no longer filled with straw and fleas; chairs are soft; housework is still boring, but it is no longer the endless drudgery it once was; and cats and dogs, who once had to justify their presence indoors by catching mice and rats, are now free to lie around all day, objects of affection and attention, and indeed to many people symbolizing the very idea of Home.

This chapter first covers dwelling places and then moves on to a section on household matters.

DWELLING PLACES

ADOBE HOUSES. *Pedro de Castañeda, chronicler of Francisco Vázquez de Coronado's 1540 expedition to Cibola, describes the Pueblo Indian villages of what is now New Mexico.*

They all work together to build the villages, the women being engaged in making the mixture and the walls, while the men bring the wood and put it in place. They have no lime, but they make a mixture of ashes, coals, and dirt which is almost as good as mortar, for when the house is to have four stories, they do not make the walls more than half a yard thick. They gather a great pile of twigs of thyme and sedge grass and set it afire, and when it is half coals and ashes they throw a quantity of dirt and water on it and mix it all together. They make round balls of this, which they use instead of stones after they are dry, fixing them with the same mixture, which comes to be like a stiff clay. . . .

The young men live in the *estufas* [kivas], which are in the yards of the village. They are underground, square or round, with pine pillars. Some were seen with twelve pillars and with four in the center as large as two men could stretch around. They usually had three or four pillars. The floor was made of large, smooth stones, like the baths which they have in Europe. They have a hearth made like the binnacle or compass box of a ship, in which they burn a handful of thyme at a time to keep up the heat, and they can stay in there just as in a bath. The top was on a level with the ground. Some that were seen were large enough for a game of ball. . . . It is forbidden for women to sleep in the *estufas,* or to enter these for any purpose except to give their husbands or sons something to eat.

The villages are free from nuisances, because they go outside to excrete, and they pass their water into clay vessels, which they empty at a distance from the village. They keep the separate houses where they prepare the food for eating and where they grind the meal, very clean. This is a separate room or closet, where they have a trough with three stones fixed in stiff clay. Three women go in here, each one having a stone, with which one of them breaks the corn, the next grinds it, and the third grinds it again. They take off their shoes, do up their hair, shake their clothes, and cover their heads before they enter the door. A man sits at the door playing on a fife while they grind, moving the stones to the music and singing together.

WIGWAM. *Before finally deciding on Plymouth as their new home, the Pilgrims, who had made their first landfall in 1620 at Provincetown, set out to explore Cape Cod. In a journal of the Pilgrims at Plymouth,* Mourt's Relation, *Edward Winslow and William Bradford describe what they found.*

Whilst we were thus ranging and searching, two of the sailors, which were newly come on the shore, by chance espied two houses which had been lately dwelt in, but the people were gone. They, having their pieces and hearing nobody, entered the houses and took out some things, and durst not stay but came again and told us. So some seven or eight of us went with them, and found how we had gone within a flight shot of them before. The houses were made with long young sapling trees, bended and both ends stuck into the ground. They were made round, like unto an arbor, and covered down to the floor with thick and well wrought mats, and the door was not over a yard high, made of a mat to open. The chimney was a wide open hole in the top, for which they had a mat to cover it close when they pleased. One might stand and go upright in them. In the midst of them were four little trunches [short wooden posts] knocked into the ground, and small sticks laid over, on which they hung their pots, and what they had to seethe. . . .

The houses were double matted, for as they were matted without, so were they within, with newer and fairer mats. In the houses we found wooden bowls, trays and dishes, earthen pots, handbaskets made of crabshells wrought together, also an English pail or bucket; it wanted a bail, but it had two iron ears. There was also baskets of sundry sorts, bigger and some lesser, finer and some coarser; some were curiously wrought with black and white in pretty works, and sundry other of their household stuff. We found also two or three deer's heads, one whereof had been newly killed, for it was still fresh. There was also a company of deer's feet stuck up in the houses, harts' horns, and eagles' claws, and sundry such like things, there was also two or three baskets full of parched acorns, pieces of fish, and a piece of a broiled herring. We found also a little silk grass, and a little tobacco seed, with some other seeds which we knew not. Without was sundry bundles of flags [wild iris], and sedge, bulrushes and other stuff to make mats. There was thrust into a hollow tree two or three pieces of venison, but we thought it fitter for the dogs than for us.

Secoton: an engraving by Theodore de Bry, after a painting by John White, from Thomas Harriot's *Briefe and True Report of the New Found Land of Virginia*, published in 1588. "This people . . . voyde of all covetousness, lyve cherfullye and at their harts ease."

Some of the best things we took away with us, and left the houses standing still as they were.

MOVABLE HOUSES. *The first English–Indian phrase book,* A Key into the Language of America, *was prepared by Roger Williams and issued in 1643. The book, designed to help both missionary and trader, included observations on Indian beliefs and customs as well as useful phrases.*

Nqussútam: *I remove house.*

Which they doe upon these occasions: From thick warme vallies, where they winter, they remove a little neerer to their Summer fields; when 'tis warme Spring, then they remove to their fields where they plant Corne.

In middle of Summer, because of the abundance of Fleas, which the dust of the house breeds, they will flie and remove on a sudden from one part of their field to a fresh place: And sometimes having fields a mile or two, or many miles asunder, when the worke of one field is over, they remove house to the other: If death fall in amongst them, they presently remove to a fresh place: If an enemie approach, they remove into a Thicket, or Swampe, unlesse they have some Fort to remove unto.

Sometimes they remove to a hunting house in the end of the yeere, and forsake it not until Snow lie thick, and then will travel home, men, women and children, thorow the snow, thirtie, yea, fiftie or sixtie miles; but their great remove is from their Summer fields to warme and thicke woodie bottomes where they winter: They are quicke; in halfe a day, yea, sometimes a few houres warning to be gone and the house up elsewhere; especially, if they have stakes readie pitcht for their *Mats.*

I once in travell lodged at a house, which in my returne I hoped to have lodged againe there the next night, but the house was gone in that interim, and I was glad to lodge under a tree.

The men make the poles or stakes, but the women make and set up, take downe, order, and carry the *Mats* and houshold stuffe.

CELLARS. *A description by Cornelis van Tienhoven, secretary of the province of New Netherland, in a 1650 report. Tienhoven, a supporter of Peter Stuyvesant, was said by his enemies to have "run about the same as an Indian, with a little covering and a small patch in front, from lust after the prostitutes to whom he has always been mightily inclined."*

Those in New Netherland and especially in New England, who have no means to build farm houses at first according to their wishes, dig a square pit in the ground, cellar fashion, six or seven feet deep [and] as long and as broad as they think proper. [They] case the earth inside with wood all around the wall, and line the wood with the bark of trees or something else, to prevent the caving in of the earth. [They] floor this cellar with plank and wainscot it overhead for a ceiling; raise a roof of spars, clear up, and cover the spars with bark or green sods—so that they can live dry and warm in these houses with their entire families for two, three, and four years, it being understood that partitions are run through those cellars which are adapted to the size of the family.

FRONTIER HOUSING. *In 1682 a printing press in Cambridge published the country's first best-seller, a short book with a long title:* The Soveraignty and Goodness of God . . . being a Narrative of the Captivity and Restauration of Mrs. Mary Rowlandson . . . Written by Her Own Hand for Her private Use, and now made Publick at the earnest Desire of some Friends. *Mrs. Rowlandson, who with two of her children was eventually ransomed, was the wife of the minister at what was then the frontier settlement of Lancaster, Massachusetts. Their stoutly built house has an important role in the opening scene of her book.*

On the tenth of February, 1675, came the Indians in great numbers upon Lancaster. Their first coming was about sun-rising. Hearing the noise of some guns, we looked out: several houses were burning, and the smoke ascending to heaven. There were five persons taken in one house; the father, the mother, and a suckling child they knocked on the head; the other two they took and carried away alive. There were two others, who being out of their garrison upon some occasion, were set upon; one was knocked on the head, the other escaped. Another there was, who, running along, was shot and wounded, and fell down; he begged of them his life, promising them money, (as they told me) but they would not hearken to him, but knocked him in the head, and stripped him naked, and split open his bowels. Another, seeing many of the Indians about his barn, ventured and went out, but was quickly shot down. There were three others belonging to the same garrison who were killed; the Indians getting up upon the roof of the barn, had advantage to shoot down upon them over their fortification. Thus these murderous wretches went on burning and destroying before them.

At length they came and beset our own house, and quickly it was the dolefulest day that ever mine eyes saw. The house stood upon the edge of a hill; some of the Indians got behind the hill, others into the barn, and others behind any thing that would shelter them; from all which places they shot against the house, so that the bullets seemed to fly like hail; and quickly they wounded one man among us, then another, and then a third. About two hours (according to my observation in that amazing time) they had been about the house before they prevailed to fire it (which they did with flax and hemp which they brought out of the barn, there being no defence about the house, only two flankers at two opposite corners, and one of them not finished). They fired it once, but one ventured out and quenched it, but they quickly fired it again, and that took. Now is the dreadful hour come, that I have often heard of (in time of war, as was the case with others) but now mine eyes see it. Some in our house were fighting for their lives, others wallowing in their blood, the house on fire over our heads, and the bloody heathen ready to knock us on the head if we stirred out. Now might we hear mothers and children crying out for themselves, and one another, *Lord, what shall we do?* Then I took my children (and one of my sisters hers) to go forth and leave the house: but as soon as we came to the door, and appeared, the Indians shot so thick, that the bullets rattled against the house, as if one had taken an handful of stones and threw them, so that we were fain to give back. We had six stout dogs belonging to our garrison, but none of them would stir, though another time, if an Indian had come to the door, they were ready to fly upon him and tear him down. The Lord hereby would make us the more to acknowledge his hand, and to see that our help is always in him. But out we must go, the fire increasing, and coming along behind us, roaring, and the Indians gaping before us with their guns, spears, and hatchets, to devour us. No sooner were we out of the house, but my brother-in-law (being before wounded, in defending the house, in or near the throat) fell down dead, whereat the Indians scornfully shouted, and hallooed, and were presently upon him, stripping off his clothes. The bullets flying thick, one went through my side, and the same (as would seem) through the bowels and hand of my dear child in my arms. One of my elder sister's children, named William, had then his leg broken, which the Indians perceiving, they knocked him on the head. Thus were we butchered by those merciless heathens, standing amazed, with the blood running down to our heels.

ALBANY, NEW YORK. *A report by Dr. Alexander Hamilton, a Maryland physician, who visited the city in 1744, when most of its approximately four thousand inhabitants were Dutch or of Dutch descent.*

The Dutch here keep their houses very neat and clean, both without and within. Their chamber floors are generally laid with rough plank which, in time, by constant rubbing and scrubbing becomes as smooth as if it had been plained. Their chambers and rooms are large and handsom. They have their beds generally in alcoves so that you may go thro all the rooms of a great house and see never a bed. They affect pictures much, particularly scripture history, with which they adorn their rooms. They set out their cabinets and bouffetts much with china. Their kitchens are likewise very clean, and there they hang earthen or delft plates and dishes all round the walls in manner of pictures, having a hole drilled thro the edge of the plate or dish and a loop of ribbon put into it to hang it by. But notwithstanding all this nicety and cleanliness in their houses, they are in their persons slovenly and dirty. They live here very frugally and plain, for the chief merit among them seems to be riches, which they spare no pains or trouble to acquire, but are a civil and hospitable people in their way but, att best, rustick and unpolished.

They live in their houses in Albany as if it were prisons, all their doors and windows being perpetually shut. But the reason for this may be the little desire they have for conversation and society, their whole thoughts being turned upon profit and gain which necessarily makes them live retired and frugall. . . . Their women in generall, both old and young, are the hardest favoured ever I beheld. Their old women wear a comicall head dress, large pendants, short petticoats, and they stare upon one like witches. They generally eat to their morning's tea raw hung beef sliced down in thin chips in the manner of parmezan cheese. Their winter here is excessive cold so as to freeze their cattle stiff in one night in the stables.

The young men here call their sweethearts luffees, and a young fellow of 18 is reckoned a simpleton if he has not a luffee; but their women are so homely that a man must never have seen any other luffees else they will never entrap him.

PROSPEROUS FARMS. *William Cobbett, an English radical who spent several years living in this country, comments favorably on the farms of Pennsylvania.*

This is a fine part of America. *Big Barns,* and modest dwelling houses. Barns of *stone,* a *hundred feet* long and *forty wide,* with two floors, and raised roads to go into them, so that the waggons go into the *first floor up-stairs.* Below are stables, stalls, pens, and all sorts of conveniences. Up-stairs are rooms for threshed corn and grain; for tackle, for meal, for all sorts of things. In the front (South) of the barn is the cattle yard. These are very fine buildings. And, then, all about them looks so comfortable, and gives such manifest proofs of ease, plenty and happiness! Such is the country of WILLIAM PENN's settling!

It is a curious thing to observe the *farm-houses* in this country. They consist, almost without exception, of a considerably large and a very neat house, with sash windows, and of a *small house,* which seems to have been *tacked on* to the large one; and, the proportion they bear to each other, in point of dimensions, is, as nearly as possible, the proportion of size between a *Cow* and *her Calf,* the latter a month old. But, as to the *cause,* the process has been the opposite of this instance of the works of nature, for, it is *the large house which has grown out of the small one.* The father, or grandfather, while he was toiling for his children, lived in the small house, constructed chiefly by himself, and consisting of rude materials. The means, accumulated in the small house, enabled a son to rear the large one; and, though, when *pride* enters

View from Bushongo Tavern, near Yorktown, Virginia. Engraving by Trenchard in
Columbian Magazine, July 1788.

the door, the small house is sometimes demolished, few sons in
America have the folly or want of feeling to commit such acts of filial
ingratitude, and of real self-abasement. For, what inheritance so valuable and so honourable can a son enjoy as the proofs of his father's
industry and virtue? The progress of wealth and ease and enjoyment,
evinced by this regular increase of the size of the farmers' dwellings, is
a spectacle, at once pleasing, in a very high degree, in itself; and, in
the same degree, it speaks the praise of the system of government,
under which it has taken place.

LOG HOUSE. *While doing research for* Democracy in America, *Alexis de
Tocqueville traveled extensively around the country in the years 1831 and 1832.
In his journal he tells of a night spent with a pioneer family in the backwoods.*

The bell which the pioneers hang round the necks of their cattle, in
order to find them again in the woods, announced from afar our
approach to a clearing; and we soon afterwards heard the stroke of
the axe, hewing down the trees of the forest. As we came nearer, traces
of destruction marked the presence of civilized man: the road was
strewn with cut boughs; trunks of trees, half consumed by fire, or
mutilated by the axe, were still standing in our way. We proceeded till

we reached a wood in which all the trees seemed to have been suddenly struck dead; in the middle of summer their boughs were as leafless as in winter; and upon closer examination we found that a deep circle had been cut through the bark, which by stopping the circulation of the sap, soon kills the tree. We were told that this is commonly the first thing a pioneer does, as he cannot, in the first year, cut down all the trees that cover his new domain; he sows Indian corn under their branches, and puts the trees to death in order to prevent them from injuring his crop.

Beyond this field, at present imperfectly traced out, . . . we suddenly came upon the cabin of its owner, situated in the center of a plot of ground more carefully cultivated than the rest, but where man was still waging unequal warfare with the forest. There the trees were cut down, but not uprooted, and the trunks still encumbered the ground which they so recently shaded. Around these dry blocks, wheat, oak seedlings, and plants of every kind grow and intertwine in all the luxuriance of wild, untutored nature. Amid this vigorous and varied vegetation stands the house of the pioneer, or, as they call it, the *log house*. Like the ground about it, this rustic dwelling bore marks of recent and

"The Pioneer's Home." A highly romanticized view of pioneer life, as depicted in one of Currier & Ives' immensely popular lithographs, published in 1867.

hasty labor: its length seemed not to exceed thirty feet, its height fifteen; the walls as well as the roof were formed of rough trunks of trees, between which a little moss and clay had been inserted to keep out the cold and rain.

As night was coming on, we determined to ask the master of the log house for a lodging. At the sound of our footsteps the children who were playing among the scattered branches sprang up, and ran towards the house, as if they were frightened at the sight of man; while two large dogs, half wild, with ears erect and outstretched nose, came growling out of their hut to cover the retreat of their young masters. The pioneer himself appeared at the door of his dwelling; he looked at us with a rapid and inquisitive glance, made a sign to the dogs to go into the house, and set them the example, without betraying either curiosity or apprehension at our arrival.

We entered the log house: the inside is quite unlike that of the cottages of the peasantry of Europe; it contains more that is superfluous, less that is necessary. A single window with a muslin curtain; on a hearth of trodden clay an immense fire, which lights the whole interior; above the hearth, a good rifle, a deerskin, and plumes of eagles' feathers; on the right hand of the chimney, a map of the United States, raised and shaken by the wind through the crannies in the wall; near the map, on a shelf formed of a roughly hewn plank, a few volumes of books: a Bible, the first six books of Milton, and two of Shakespeare's plays; along the wall, trunks instead of closets; in the center of the room, a rude table, with legs of green wood with the bark still on them, looking as if they grew out of the ground on which they stood; but on this table a teapot of British china, silver spoons, cracked teacups, and some newspapers.

The master of this dwelling has the angular features and lank limbs peculiar to the native of New England. It is evident that he was not born in the solitude in which we have found him. . . . He belongs to that restless, calculating, and adventurous race of men who . . . endure the life of savages for a time in order to conquer and civilize the backwoods.

When the pioneer perceived that we were crossing his threshold, he came to meet us and shake hands, as is their custom; but his face was quite unmoved. He opened the conversation by inquiring what was going on in the world; and when his curiosity was satisfied, he held his peace. . . . When we questioned him in our turn, he gave us all the information we asked; he then attended sedulously, but without eagerness, to our wants. . . .

By the side of the hearth sits a woman with a baby on her lap; she nods to us without disturbing herself. Like the pioneer, this woman is in the prime of life; her appearance seems superior to her condition, and her apparel even betrays a lingering taste for dress; but her delicate limbs appear shrunken, her features are drawn in, her eye is mild and melancholy; her whole physiognomy bears marks of religious resignation.

Her children cluster about her, full of health, turbulence, and energy: they are true children of the wilderness. Their mother watches them from time to time with mingled melancholy and joy: to look at their strength and her languor, one might imagine that the life she has given them has exhausted her own. . . .

The house inhabited by these emigrants has no internal partition or loft. In the one chamber of which it consists the whole family is gathered for the night. The dwelling is itself a little world, an ark of civilization amid an ocean of foliage: a hundred steps beyond it the primeval forest spreads its shades, and solitude resumes its sway.

REBUILDING NEW YORK. *Philip Hone, one-time mayor of New York, reports on changes in his city. May Day was customarily the day renters renewed their leases or moved.*

1839 May 1.—May day is fine, pleasant weather, much to the comfort of jaded wives and fretting husbands. There is a great deal of moving in the streets out of Broadway, in the upper part of the city, but less, I think, than usual amongst the tenants of good houses. But the pulling down of houses and stores in the lower parts is awful. Brickbats, rafters and slates are showering down in every direction. There is no safety on the sidewalks, and the head must be saved at the expense of soiling the boots. In Wall Street, besides the great Exchange, which occupies with huge blocks of granite a few acres of the highway of merchants, there is the beautiful new Bank of the United States opposite, still obstructing the walk. Besides which, four banks—the City, Manhattan, Merchants', and Union—are in progress of destruction; it looks like the ruins occasioned by an earthquake. The house on the corner of Broadway is undergoing alteration, which usurps the sidewalk. My poor, dear house, 235 Broadway, is coming down forthwith, and in a few weeks the home of my happy days will be incontinently swept from the earth. Farther up, at the corner of Chambers Street, a row of low buildings has been removed to make way for one of those mighty edifices called hotels,—eating, drinking, and lodging above and gay shops below; and so all the way up; the spirit of pulling down and building up is abroad. The whole of New York is rebuilt about once in ten years.

BOOM TOWN. *San Francisco in the early days of the Gold Rush, described first by Bayard Taylor, a reporter for the* New York Tribune, *who has just arrived there by ship.*

September, 1849.—We obtained a room with two beds at twenty-five dollars per week, meals being in addition twenty dollars per week. I asked the landlord whether he could send a porter for our trunks. "There is none belonging to the house," said he; "every man is his own porter here." I returned to the Parker House, shouldered a heavy trunk, took a valise in my hand and carried them to my quarters in the teeth of the wind. Our room was in a sort of garret over the only story of the hotel; two cots, evidently of California manufacture and covered only with a pair of blankets, two chairs, a rough table, and a small looking glass constituted the furniture. There was not space enough between the bed and the bare rafters overhead to sit upright, and I gave myself a severe blow in rising the next morning without the proper heed. Through a small roof window of dim glass I could see the opposite shore of the bay, then partly hidden by the evening fogs. The wind whistled around the eaves and rattled the tiles with a cold, gusty sound that would have imparted a dreary character to the place, had I been in a mood to listen.

Many of the passengers began speculation at the moment of landing. The most ingenious and successful operation was made by a gentleman of New York who took out fifteen hundred copies of the *Tribune* and other papers, which he disposed of in two hours at one dollar apiece! Hearing of this, I bethought me of about a dozen papers which I had used to fill up crevices in packing my valise. There was a newspaper merchant at the corner of the City Hotel, and to him I proposed the sale of them, asking him to name a price. "I shall want to make a good profit on the retail price," said he, "and can't give more than ten dollars for the lot." I was satisfied with the wholesale price, which was a gain of just four thousand per cent!

Born in Poland in 1828, Morris Shloss was twenty-one when—after rounding Cape Horn—he arrived in San Francisco, at the same time as Bayard Taylor.

[I] arrived in San Francisco, September 25, 1849, landing at the foot of Broadway Street with my baggage.

I brought with me a wagon packed in a large box and, at the landing, a man asked me what was in the box. I told him, a wagon, and he asked the price of it. I answered $125, and he offered me $100, which rather surprised me, as the man had not seen the contents of the box. I accepted his offer, and he paid me in gold dust. I had only paid $15 for this wagon in New York, so I thought this was rather a good beginning for me.

The man was very careful in opening the box not to break the lid, and then, taking out the wagon, he said to me: "Stranger, you may keep the wagon, for I only want the box" (for which I had paid $3).

"That case is what I want," he said. "I am a cobbler, and in the daytime it will be my shop, and at night, my residence." That box measured seven feet by four feet.

POOR WHITES. *In the 1850s Frederick Law Olmsted traveled widely in the cotton-growing regions of the South, gathering material for his book* The Cotton Kingdom. *Here he is in Mississippi, looking for a night's lodging.*

The next house at which I arrived was one of the commonest sort of cabins. I had passed twenty like it during the day, and I thought I would take the opportunity to get an interior knowledge of them. The fact that a horse and waggon were kept, and that a considerable area of land in the rear of the cabin was planted with cotton, showed that the family were by no means of the lowest class; yet, as they were not able even to hire a slave, they may be considered to represent very favourably, I believe, the condition of the poor whites of the plantation districts. . . .

It was raining and nearly nine o'clock. The door of the cabin was open, and I rode up and conversed with the occupant as he stood within. He said that he was not in the habit of taking in travelers, and his wife was about sick, but if I was a mind to put up with common fare, he didn't care. Grateful, I dismounted and took the seat he had vacated by the fire, while he led away my horse to an open shed in the rear—his own horse ranging at large, when not in use, during the summer.

The house was all comprised in a single room, twenty-eight by twenty-five feet in area, and open to the roof above. There was a large fireplace at one end and a door on each side—no windows at all. Two bedsteads, a spinning-wheel, a packing-case, which served as a bureau, a cupboard, made of rough hewn slabs, two or three deer-skin seated chairs, a Connecticut clock, and a large poster of Jayne's patent medicines, constituted all the visible furniture, either useful or ornamental in purpose. A little girl, immediately, without having had any directions to do so, got a frying-pan and a chunk of bacon from the cupboard, and cutting slices from the latter, set it frying for my supper. The woman of the house sat sulkily in a chair tilted back and leaning against the logs, spitting occasionally at the fire, but took no notice of me, barely nodding when I saluted her. A baby lay crying on the floor. I quieted it and amused it with my watch till the little girl, having made "coffee" and put a piece of corn-bread on the table with the bacon, took charge of it.

I hoped the woman was not very ill.

"Got the headache right bad," she answered. "Have the headache a heap, I do. Knew I should have it to-night. Been cuttin' brush in the cotton this afternoon. Knew't would bring on my headache. Told him so when I begun."

As soon as I had finished my supper and fed Jude [his horse], the little girl put the fragments and the dishes in the cupboard, shoved the table into a corner, and dragged a quantity of quilts from one of the bedsteads, which she spread upon the floor, and presently crawled among them out of sight for the night. The woman picked up the child—which, though still a suckling, she said was twenty-two months old—and nursed it, retaking her old position. The man sat with me by the fire, his back towards her. The baby having fallen asleep was laid away somewhere, and the woman dragged off another lot of quilts from the beds, spreading them upon the floor. Then taking a deep tin pan, she filled it with alternate layers of corn-cobs and hot embers from the fire. This she placed upon a large block, which was evidently used habitually for the purpose, in the centre of the cabin. A furious smoke arose from it, and we soon began to cough. "Most *too* much smoke," observed the man. "Hope 'twill drive out all the gnats, then," replied the woman. (There is a very minute flying insect here, the bite of which is excessively sharp.)

The woman suddenly dropped off her outer garment and stepped from the midst of its folds, in her petticoat; then, taking the baby from the place where she had deposited it, lay down and covered herself with the quilts upon the floor. The man told me that I could take the bed which remained on one of the bedsteads, and kicking off his shoes only, rolled himself into a blanket by the side of his wife. I ventured to take off my cravat and stockings, as well as my boots, but almost immediately put my stockings on again, drawing their tops over my pantaloons. The advantage of this arrangement was that, although my face, eyes, ears, neck, and hands, were immediately attacked, the vermin did not reach my legs for two or three hours. Just after the clock struck two, I distinctly heard the man and the woman, and the girl and the dog scratching, and the horse out in the shed stamping and gnawing himself. Soon afterward the man exclaimed, "Good God Almighty-mighty! mighty! mighty!" and jumping up pulled off one of his stockings, shook it, scratched his foot vehemently, put on the stocking, and lay down again with a groan. The two doors were open, and through the logs and the openings in the roof, I saw the clouds divide and the moon and stars reveal themselves. The woman, after having been nearly smothered by the smoke from the pan which she had originally placed close to her own pillow, rose and placed it on the sill of the windward door, where it burned feebly and smoked lustily, like an altar to the Lares, all night. Fortunately the cabin was so open that it gave us little annoyance, while it seemed to answer the purpose of keeping all flying insects at a distance.

When, on rising in the morning, I said that I would like to wash my face, water was given me for the purpose in an earthen pie-dish. Just as breakfast, which was of exactly the same materials as my supper, was ready, rain began to fall, presently in such a smart shower as to put the fire out and compel us to move the table under the least leaky part of the roof.

At breakfast occurred the following conversation:—

"Are there many niggers in New York?"

"Very few."

"How do you get your work done?"

"There are many Irish and German people constantly coming there who are glad to get work to do. . . . A great many American-born work for wages, too. . . ."

"I wish there warn't no niggers here. They are a great cuss to this country, I expect. But 'twouldn't do to free 'em; that wouldn't do nohow!"

"Are there many people here who think slavery a curse to the country?"

"Oh, yes, a great many. I reckon the majority would be right glad if we could get rid of the niggers. But it wouldn't never do to free 'em and leave 'em here. I don't know anybody, hardly, in favour of that. Make 'em free and leave 'em here and they's steal everything we made. Nobody couldn't live here then."

These views of slavery seem to be universal among people of this class. They were repeated to me at least a dozen times.

"Where I used to live [Alabama], I remember when I was a boy—must ha' been about twenty years ago—folks was dreadful frightened about the niggers. I remember they built pens in the woods where they could hide, and Christmas time they went and got into the pens, 'fraid the niggers was rising."

"I remember the same time where we was in South Carolina," said his wife; "we had all our things put up in bags, so we could tote 'em, if we heered they was comin' our way."

My horse and dog were as well cared for as possible, and a "snack" of bacon and corn-bread was offered me for noon, which has been unusual in Mississippi. When I asked what I should pay, the man hesitated and said he reckoned what I had had, wasn't worth much of anything; he was sorry he could not have accommodated me better. I offered him a dollar, for which he thanked me warmly. It is the first instance of hesitation in charging for a lodging which I have met with from a stranger at the South.

OGLALA CAMP. *In 1864, while on her way to Idaho with an emigrant train, Fanny Kelly—nineteen years old and recently married—was captured by a band of Oglala Sioux. After being held prisoner for several months, she was released and wrote a best-selling account of her experiences*—Narrative of My Captivity Among the Sioux Indians.

Nothing can be more simple in its arrangement than an Indian camp when journeying, and especially when on the war path. The camping ground, when practicable, is near a stream of water, and adjacent to timber. After reaching the spot selected, the ponies are unloaded by the squaws, and turned loose to graze. The tents, or "tipis," are put up, and wood and water brought for cooking purposes. All drudgery of this kind is performed by the squaws, an Indian brave scorning as degrading all kinds of labor not incident to the chase or the war path.

An Indian tipi is composed of several dressed skins, usually of the buffalo, sewed together and stretched over a number of poles, the larger ones containing as many as twenty of these poles, which are fifteen to twenty feet long. They are of yellow pine, stripped of bark, and are used as "travois" in traveling. Three poles are tied together near the top or small ends, and raised to an upright position, the bottoms being spread out as far as the fastening at the top will permit. Other

Brule Sioux camp near Pine Ridge, Dakota Territory, photographed by
J. C. H. Grabill in 1891, the year of the Wounded Knee massacre.

poles are laid into the crotch thus formed at the top, and spread out in a circular line with the three first put up. This comprises the frame work, and when in the position described is ready to receive the covering, which is raised to the top by means of a rawhide rope, when, a squaw seizing each lower corner, it is rapidly brought around, and the edges fastened together with wooden pins, a squaw getting down on all fours, forming a perch upon which the tallest squaw of the family mounts and inserts the pins as high as she can reach. A square opening in the tent serves for a door, and is entered in a stooping posture. A piece of hide hangs loosely over this opening, and is kept in position by a heavy piece of wood fastened at the bottom. . . . The outer edge of the tent contains the beds of the family, which are composed of buffalo robes and blankets. These are snugly rolled up during the day, and do service as seats.

When it becomes necessary to move a village, . . . a crier goes through the camp, shouting, "Egalakapo! Egalakapo!" when all the squaws drop whatever work they may be engaged in, and in an instant are busy as bees, taking down tipis, bringing in the ponies and dogs, and loading them; and in less than fifteen minutes the cavalcade is on the march.

ORPHANAGE AND ASYLUM. *In a letter to her family back home in Concord, Massachusetts, Louisa May Alcott tells how she spent Christmas Day, 1875. The institutions were on Randall's Island, New York, reached by ferry. "Mrs. G." was Abigail Hopper Gibbons, a Quaker philanthropist. They were accompanied by her husband and a newspaper reporter.*

We drove in an old ramshackle hack to the chapel, whither a boy had raced before us, crying joyfully to all he met, "She's come! Miss G.— she's come!" And all faces beamed, as well they might, since for thirty years she has gone to make set after set of little forlornities happy on this day.

The chapel was full. On one side, in front, girls in blue gowns and white pinafores; on the other, small chaps in pinafores likewise; and behind them, bigger boys in gray suits with cropped heads, and larger girls with ribbons in their hair and pink calico gowns. They sang alternately; the girls gave "Juanita" very well, the little chaps a pretty song about poor children asking a "little white angel" to leave the gates of heaven ajar, so they could peep in, if no more. Quite pathetic, coming from poor babies who had no home but this. . . .

Then we drove to the hospital, and there the heart-ache began, for me at least, so sad it was to see these poor babies, born of want and sin, suffering every sort of deformity, disease, and pain. Cripples half blind, scarred with scrofula, burns, and abuse,—it was simply awful and indescribable!

As we went in, I with a great box of dolls and the young reporter with a bigger box of candy, a general cry of delight greeted us. Some children tried to run, half-blind ones stretched out their groping hands, little ones crawled, and big ones grinned, while several poor babies sat up in their bed, beckoning us to "come quick."

One poor mite, so eaten up with sores that its whole face was painted with some white salve,—its head covered with an oilskin cap; one eye gone, and the other half filmed over; hands bandaged, and ears bleeding,—could only moan and move its feet till I put a gay red dolly in one hand and a pink candy in the other; then the dim eye brightened, the hoarse voice said feebly, "Tanky, lady!" and I left it contentedly sucking the sweetie, and *trying* to *see* its dear new toy. It can't see another Christmas, and I like to think I helped make this one happy, even for a minute.

It was pleasant to watch the young reporter trot round with the candybox, and come up to me all interest to say, "One girl hasn't got a doll, ma'am, and looks *so* disappointed."

After the hospital, we went to the idiot house; and there I had a chance to see faces and figures that will haunt me a long time. A hundred or so of half-grown boys and girls ranged down a long hall, a table of toys in the middle, and an empty one for Mrs. G.'s gifts. A cheer broke out as the little lady hurried in waving her handkerchief and a handful of gay bead necklaces, and "Oh! Ohs!" followed the appearance of the doll-lady and the candy man.

A pile of gay pictures was a new idea, and Mrs. G. told me to hold up some bright ones and see if the poor innocents would understand and enjoy them. I held up one of two kittens lapping spilt milk, and the girls began to mew and say "Cat! ah, pretty." Then a fine horse, and the boys bounced on their benches with pleasure; while a ship in full sail produced a cheer of rapture from them all. . . .

All wanted dolls, even boys of nineteen; for all were children in mind. But the girls had them, and young women of eighteen cuddled their babies and were happy. The boys chose from the toy-table, and it was pathetic to see great fellows pick out a squeaking dog without even the wit to pinch it when it was theirs. One dwarf of thirty-five chose a little Noah's ark, and brooded over it in silent bliss.

At four, we left and came home, Mrs. G. giving a box of toys and sweeties on board the boat for the children of the men who run it. So leaving a stream of blessings and pleasures behind her, the dear old lady drove away, simply saying, "There now, I shall feel better for the next year!" Well she may; bless her!

COWBOYS AND SETTLERS. *This story was told by an anonymous contributor to Solomon D. Butcher's* Pioneer History of Custer County, Nebraska.

Early in the fall of 1884 a few settlers located homesteads in the northeast corner of the Brighton Ranch Company's pasture, on Ash creek. This pasture was about fifteen miles square, and extended several miles south of the Loup river almost to Broken Bow, and was inclosed with a wire fence. The land being government land, and subject to entry, these settlers served notice on the ranch company to remove their fence from about their claims within thirty days. The company paid no atttention to this request, and at the expiration of the time the settlers made a raid on the fence and appropriated the posts to make roofs for their sod houses. Roofs in those days were made by laying a large log, called a ridge log, lengthwise of the building at the top. The fence posts were then laid up to form the rafters, to which brush was fastened, the whole being covered with one or two layers of prairie sod, coated with several inches of yellow clay procured from the canyons, which turned the water effectually.

In a short time after the appropriation of these posts the foreman of the ranch had the settlers arrested and taken to Broken Bow for trial. The sheriff had no sooner departed with the prisoners than the second foreman of the ranch rigged up two large wagons, drawn by

Sod house and family, Nebraska, 1887. Photograph by S. D. Butcher.

four mules each, and proceeded to the houses of the settlers, accompanied by a number of the cowboys. They drove up to a house, took a team and large chain, hitched onto the projecting end of the ridge log, and in about three seconds the neat little home was a shapeless mass of sod, hay, brush and posts mixed up in almost inextricable confusion. The ranchmen then culled their posts from the wreck and loaded them into the wagons, when they went to the next house and repeated the operation, leaving the occupants to pick their few household goods out of the ruins at their leisure. The boys were having great fun at the expense of the settlers, cracking jokes and making merry as the work of destruction went on. After destroying several houses in this manner they proceeded to the claim of a Mr. King, and Mrs. King, seeing them approaching, met them with a shotgun and dared them to come on. Had it been Mr. King, the invitation would possibly have been accepted, but the cowboys were too gallant to enter into a quarrel with a lady, and withdrew without molesting her.

In the meantime a boy of the settlement had been despatched to Broken Bow on the fastest pony that could be procured, to secure help, and quite a posse of men from the town started for the scene of action. The foreman of the ranch, who was in Broken Bow at the time as complaining witness against the settlers, heard of this and sent one of his cowboys in haste to warn the second foreman of the impending invasion. This messenger arrived at the settlement in advance of the citizens and gave the alarm. The housewreckers were thoroughly scared, and turning the heads of their mule teams towards the South Loup, applied the whip freely. As the mules began to run over the rough prairie the posts began to fall off the wagons, and as the teams began to show signs of weariness the cowboys began to heave off more posts to lighten the load as they bumped along, leaving a trail behind them like that of a railroad construction gang. Arriving at the ranch, they turned out their mules, secured their Winchesters and made a break for the hills on the south side of the river to await developments. When the posse of rescuers arrived at the little settlement and found the invaders gone, they did not follow them, but returned to Broken Bow. The cowboys remained in the hills two days, watching for the approach of the enemy in vain.

The ranch company failed to make any case against the settlers, it being shown that the ranch pasture was government land and that the claims were lawfully held by the homesteaders, who had a perfect right to remove the fence which inclosed their property. The prisoners were accordingly released and were not again molested. The second foreman of the ranch was subsequently arrested for tearing down the houses of the settlers, tried at Broken Bow, found guilty, fined $25 and costs and confined one day in the county jail.

An advertisement from *The Manufacturer and Builder*, 1872.

LIFE IN THE STOCKADE. *The anonymous narrator of the following story was born during the Civil War on a Georgia plantation.*

When I reached twenty-one the Captain told me I was a free man but urged me to stay with him. He said he would treat me right, and pay me as much as anybody else would. The Captain's son and I were about the same age, and the Captain said that, as he had owned my mother and uncle during slavery, and as his son didn't want me to leave them (since I had been with them so long), he wanted me to stay with the old family. And I stayed. I signed a contract—that is, I made my mark—for one year. The Captain was to give me $3.50 a week, and furnish me a little house on the plantation—a one-room log cabin similar to those used by his other laborers.

During that year I married Mandy. For several years Mandy had been the house-servant for the Captain, his wife, his son and his three daughters, and they all seemed to think a good deal of her. As an evidence of their regard they gave us a suite of furniture, which cost about $25, and we set up housekeeping in one of the Captain's two-room shanties. I thought I was the biggest man in Georgia. Mandy still kept her place in the "Big House" after our marriage. We did so well for the first year that I renewed my contract for the second year, and for the third, fourth and fifth year I did the same thing. Before the end of the fifth year the Captain had died, and his son, who had married some two or three years before, took charge of the plantation. Also, for two or three years this son had been serving at Atlanta in some big office to which he had been elected. I think it was in the Legislature or something of that sort—anyhow, all the people called him Senator. At the end of the fifth year the Senator suggested that I sign up a contract for ten years; then, he said, we wouldn't have to fix up papers every year. I asked my wife about it; she consented; and so I made a ten-year contract.

Not long afterward the Senator had a long, low shanty built on his place. A great big chimney, with a wide, open fireplace, was built at one end of it, and on each side of the house, running lengthwise, there was a row of frames or stalls just large enough to hold a single mattress. The places for these mattresses were fixed one above the other; so that there was a double row of these stalls or pens on each side. They looked . . . like stalls for horses. Since then I have seen cabooses similarly arranged as sleeping quarters for railroad laborers. Nobody seemed to know what the Senator was fixing for. All doubts were put aside one bright day in April when about forty able-bodied negroes, bound in iron chains, and some of them handcuffed, were brought out to the Senator's farm in three big wagons. They were quartered in the long, low shanty, and it was afterward called the stockade. This was the beginning of the Senator's convict camp. These men were prisoners who had been leased by the Senator from the State of Georgia at about $200 each per year, the State agreeing to pay for guards and physicians, for necessary inspections, for inquests, all rewards for escaped convicts, the cost of litigation, and all other incidental camp expenses. When I saw these men in shackles, and the guards with their guns, I was scared nearly to death. I felt like running away, but I didn't know where to go. And if there had been any place to go, I would have had to leave my wife and child behind. We free laborers held a meeting. We all wanted to quit. We sent a man to tell the Senator about it. Word came back that we were all under contract for ten years and that the Senator would hold us to the letter of the contract, or put us in chains and lock us up—the same as the other prisoners. It was made plain to us by some white people we talked to that in the contracts we had signed we had all agreed to be locked up in a stockade at night or at any other time that our employer saw fit; further, we learned that we could not lawfully break our contract for any reason and go and hire ourselves to somebody else without the consent of our employer; and, more than that, if we got mad and ran away, we could be run down by bloodhounds, arrested without process of law, and be returned to our employer, who according to the contract, might beat us or administer any other kind of punishment that he thought proper. In other words, we had sold ourselves into slavery—and what could we do about it? The white folks had all the courts, all the guns, all the hounds, all the railroads, all the telegraph wires, all the newspapers, all the money, and nearly all the land—and we had only our ignorance, our poverty and our empty hands. We decided that the best thing to do was to shut our mouths, say nothing, and go back to work. And most of us worked side by side with those convicts during the remainder of the ten years.

At the close of the ten-year period, . . . just when we thought that our bondage was at an end, we found that it had really just begun. Two or three years before, after the Senator had started his camp, he had established a large store, which was called the commissary. All of us free laborers were compelled to buy our supplies—food, clothing, etc.—from that store. We never used any money in our dealings with the commissary, only tickets or orders, and we had a general settlement once a year, in October. In this store we were charged all sorts of high prices for goods, because every year we would come out in debt to our employer. If not that, we seldom had more than $5 or $10 coming to us—and that for a whole year's work. Well, at the close of the tenth year, when we kicked and meant to leave the Senator, he said to some of us with a smile (and I never will forget that smile—I can see it now):

"Boys, I'm sorry you're going to leave me. I hope you will do well in your new places—so well that you will be able to pay me the little balances which most of you owe me."

Word was sent out for all of us to meet him at the commissary at 2 o'clock. There he told us that, after we had signed what he called a written acknowledgment of our debts, we might go and look for new places. The store-keeper took us one by one and read to us statements of our accounts. According to the books there was no man of us who owed the Senator less than $100; some of us were put down for as much as $200. I owed $165, according to the bookkeeper. These debts were not accumulated during one year, but ran back for three and four years, so we were told—in spite of the fact that we understood that we had had a full settlement at the end of each year. But no one of us would have dared to dispute a white man's word— oh, no; not in those days. Besides, we fellows didn't care anything about the amounts—we were after getting away; and we had been told that we might go, if we signed the acknowledgments. We would have signed anything, just to get away. So we stepped up, we did, and made our marks. That same night we were rounded up by a constable and ten or twelve white men, who aided him, and we were locked up, every one of us, in one of the Senator's stockades. The next morning it was explained to us by the two guards appointed to watch us that, in the papers we had signed the day before, we had not only made acknowledgment of our indebtedness, but that we had also agreed to work for the Senator until the debts were paid by hard labor. And from that day forward we were treated just like convicts. We had made ourselves lifetime slaves, or peons, as the laws called us. . . .

I lived in that camp, as a peon, for nearly three years. My wife fared better than I did, as did the wives of some of the other negroes, because the white men about the camp used these unfortunate creatures as their mistresses. When I was first put in the stockade my wife was still kept for a while in the "Big House," but my little boy, who was only nine years old, was given away to a negro family across the river in South Carolina, and I never saw or heard of him after that. When I left the camp my wife had had two children by one of the white bosses, and she was living in fairly good shape in a little house off to herself. . . .

The stockades in which we slept were, I believe, the filthiest places in the world. . . . No sheets were used, only dark-colored blankets. Most of the men slept every night in the clothing that they had worked in all day. Some of the worst characters were made to sleep in chains. The doors were locked and barred each night, and tallow candles were the only lights allowed. Really the stockades were but little more than cow sheds, horse stables or hog pens. Strange to say, not a great number of these people died while I was there, though a great many came away maimed and bruised and, in some cases, disabled for life.

When I had served as a peon for nearly three years, . . . one of the bosses came to me and said that my time was up. He happened to be the one who was said to be living with my wife. He gave me a new suit of overalls, which cost about seventy-five cents, took me in a buggy and carried me across the Broad River into South Carolina, set me down and told me to "git." I didn't have a cent of money. . . . I begged my way to Columbia. In two or three days I ran across a man looking for laborers to carry to Birmingham, and I joined his gang. I have been here in the Birmingham district since they released me, and I reckon I'll die either in a coal mine or an iron furnace. It don't make much difference which. Either is better than a Georgia peon camp. And a Georgia peon camp is hell itself!

A DUG-OUT. *Charles Siringo, author of* A Texas Cow Boy, *first published in 1885, recounts the trouble he had in providing himself with lodging.*

After sending mother twenty dollars by registered mail and laying in a supply of corn, provisions, ammunition, etc., I pulled back to Eagle Chief, to make war with wild animals—especially those that their hides would bring me in some money, such as gray wolves, coyotes, wild cats, buffaloes and bears. I left Kiowa with just three dollars in money.

The next morning after arriving in camp I took my stuff and moved down the river about a mile to where I had already selected a spot for my winter quarters. I worked like a turk all day long building me a house out of dry poles—covered with grass. In the north end I built a "sod" chimney and in the south end, left an opening for a door. When finished it lacked about two feet of being high enough for me to stand up straight.

It was almost dark and snowing terribly when I got it finished and a fire burning in the low, Jim Crow fire-place. I then fed Whisky-peat [his horse] some corn and stepped out a few yards after an armful of good solid wood for morning. On getting about half an armful of wood gathered I heard something crackling and looking over my shoulder discovered my mansion in flames. I got there in time to save nearly everything in the shape of bedding, etc. Some of the grub, being next to the fireplace, was lost. I slept at Johnson's camp that night.

The next morning I went about two miles down the river and located another camp. This time I built a dug-out right on the bank of the stream, in a thick bunch of timber.

I made the dug-out in a curious shape; started in at the edge of the steep bank and dug a place six feet long, three deep and three wide, leaving the end next to the creek open for a door. I then commenced at the further end and dug another place same size in an opposite direction, which formed an "L." I then dug still another place, same size, straight out from the river which made the whole concern almost in the shape of a "Z." In the end furthest from the stream I made a fire-place by digging the earth away—in the shape of a regular fire-place. And then to make a chimney I dug a round hole, with the aid of a butcher knife, straight up as far as I could reach; then commencing at the top and connecting the two holes. The next thing was to make it "draw," and I did that by cutting and piling sods of dirt around the hole, until about two feet above the level.

I then proceeded to build a roof over my 3 x 18 mansion. To do that I cut green poles four feet long and laid them across the top, two or three inches apart. Then a layer of grass and finally, to finish it off, a foot of solid earth. She was then ready for business. My idea in making it so crooked was, to keep the Indians, should any happen along at night, from seeing my fire. After getting established in my new quarters I put out quite a number of wolf baits and next morning in going to look at them found several dead wolves besides scores of skunks, etc. But they were frozen too stiff to skin, therefore I left them until a warmer day.

The next morning on crawling out to feed my horse I discovered it snowing terribly, accompanied with a piercing cold norther. I crawled back into my hole after making Whisky-peat as comfortable as possible and remained there until late in the evening, when suddenly disturbed by a horny visitor.

It was three or four o'clock in the evening, while humped up before a blazing fire, thinking of days gone by, that all at once, before I had time to think, a large red steer came tumbling down head first, just missing me by a few inches. In traveling ahead of the storm the whole Johnson herd had passed right over me, but luckily only one broke through.

Talk about your ticklish places! That was truly one of them; a steer jammed in between me and daylight, and a hot fire roasting me by inches.

I tried to get up through the roof—it being only a foot above my head—but failed. Finally the old steer made a terrible struggle, just about the time I was fixing to turn my wicked soul over to the Lord, and I got a glimpse of daylight under his flanks. I made a dive for it and by tight squeezing I saved my life.

After getting out and shaking myself I made a vow that I would leave that God-forsaken country in less than twenty-four hours; and I did so.

LIFE AT THE BOTTOM. *The social reformer and writer Helen Campbell visits the cheapest of cheap lodging houses in the New York slums of the 1890s, a time when the density of population in several of the city's wards exceeded 200,000 to the square mile, and in the notorious tenth ward was 334,000.*

Shed lodging-houses of the lowest order are found in the rear of the great Bend in Mulberry Street. To gain access to them one must pass through narrow, foul-smelling alleys, reeking with accumulated filth, or through long, dirty hallways of tenement-houses. These passageways lead to the rear of the street buildings and open into back yards surrounded by crowded and filthy tenements, where life at its worst exists. Here, among rookeries swarming with low and ignorant Italians, street-venders, rag-pickers, and the most dangerous scum of Mulberry Street and its vicinity, are old sheds made of rotten boards through the cracks of which winds moan and snow and rain find easy access. Indescribable filth abounds within these lodging sheds; vermin hold undisputed possession and swarm on walls and floor.

"Early Morning in a Shed-Lodging House," from Helen Campbell's *Darkness and Daylight*, 1891. "Here dissolute persons of both sexes and all ages and nationalities sleep promiscuously by night and sally forth by day often to commit fresh crimes."

The shed usually incloses but a single room on the ground floor. A broken skylight in the roof admits the only light of the day. There is no furniture of any description save a bench about eighteen inches wide running around the four sides of the room and fastened to its walls. Occasionally a low platform—made of uneven and the roughest of planks—is provided for the use of those who can afford to pay the extra price demanded. Sometimes a small space in one corner is partially inclosed by boards reaching half-way to the ceiling; the luxury of such a "reserved room," furnished with a filthy husk mattress, may be had for five cents a night. For the rest, the bench, and the bare and uneven floor with perhaps a sprinkling of saw-dust, are the only places left, the usual charge being three cents a night for the privilege of a spot on either. The dirty rags on the lodgers' backs are the only bed and covering they have. The bench is a coveted place and is quickly filled. A tallow candle, or more often a smoking kerosene lamp, furnishes a feeble light by night. The air is thick with tobacco smoke from a dozen or more black clay pipes. Some of the miserable inmates sit up all night and are designated as "sitters"; others stand or move about uneasily; all catch such sleep as the din of frequent quarrels and fights and the noisome stench will permit. Here, criminals who shun the light of day, and women of the lowest and most degraded type, of all ages and nationalities, congregate at night, and sleep promiscuously. Dissolute persons of both sexes skulk and loaf in these rooms by day, and so do thieves and burglars who meet here to make new plans and sally forth at night to commit fresh crimes. Old scrub women, without homes or friends, who wearily tramp all day looking for a chance to scrub floors of offices or public buildings, often take shelter for the night in these dens. Street girls, young in years, but most of them old in sin, in some of whose faces still linger traces of former good looks, are often driven by storms or dire distress to spend a night in these horrible lodging sheds. Not unfrequently homeless children creep in unobserved and cuddle down to sleep in a corner. On a cold or stormy night in winter these rooms are filled to their utmost capacity.

The Bandits' Roost, a back alley in the tenements off Mulberry Street, New York, photographed by Jacob Riis in 1890. The property, "notorious for years as the vilest and worst to be found" was owned by "an honored family, one of the 'oldest and best,'" in the city.

CLEANING THE STREETS OF CHICAGO. *Jane Addams, who with Ellen Gates Starr founded the Hull-House settlement house in 1889, takes on City Hall.*

One of the striking features of our neighborhood twenty years ago, and one to which we never became reconciled, was the presence of huge wooden garbage boxes fastened to the street pavement in which the undisturbed refuse accumulated day by day. The system of garbage collecting was inadequate throughout the city but it became the greatest menace in a ward such as ours, where the normal amount of waste was much increased by the decayed fruit and vegetables discarded by the Italian and Greek fruit peddlers, and by the residuum left over from the piles of filthy rags which were fished out of the city dumps and brought to the homes of the rag pickers for further sorting and washing.

The children of our neighborhood twenty years ago played their games in and around these huge garbage boxes. They were the first objects that the toddling child learned to climb; their bulk afforded a barricade and their contents provided missiles in all the battles of the older boys, and finally they became the seats upon which absorbed lovers held enchanted converse.

During our first three years on Halsted Street, we had established a small incinerator at Hull-House and we had many times reported the untoward conditions of the ward to the city hall. We had also arranged many talks for the immigrants, pointing out that although a woman may sweep her own doorway in her native village and allow the refuse to innocently decay in the open air and sunshine, in a crowded city quarter, if the garbage is not properly collected and destroyed, a tenement-house mother may see her children sicken and die, and that the immigrants must therefore not only keep their own houses clean, but must also help the authorities to keep the city clean.

Possibly our efforts slightly modified the worst conditions, but they still remained intolerable, and the fourth summer . . . we began a systematic investigation of the city system of garbage collection, both as to its efficiency in other wards and its possible connection with the death rate in the various wards of the city.

The Hull-House Woman's Club had been organized the year before by the resident kindergartner who had first inaugurated a mothers' meeting. The members came together, however, in quite a new way that summer when we discussed with them the high death rate so persistent in our ward. After several meetings devoted to the subject, despite the fact that the death rate rose highest in the congested foreign colonies and not in the streets in which most of the Irish American club women lived, twelve of their number undertook in connection with the residents, to carefully investigate the condition of the alleys. During August and September the substantiated reports of violations of the law sent in from Hull-House to the health department were one thousand and thirty-seven. For the club woman who had finished a long day's work of washing or ironing followed by the cooking of a hot supper, it would have been much easier to sit on her doorstep during a summer evening than to go up and down ill-kept alleys and get into trouble with her neighbors over the condition of their garbage boxes. It required both civic enterprise and moral conviction to be willing to do this three evenings a week during the hottest and most uncomfortable months of the year. Nevertheless, a certain number of women persisted, as did the residents, and three city inspectors in succession were transferred from the ward because of unsatisfactory services. Still the death rate remained high and the condition seemed little improved throughout the next winter. In sheer desperation, the following spring when the city contracts were awarded for the removal of garbage, with the backing of two well-known business men, I put in a bid for the garbage removal of the nineteenth ward. My paper was thrown out on a technicality but the incident induced the mayor to appoint me the garbage inspector of the ward.

The salary was a thousand dollars a year, and the loss of that political "plum" made a great stir among the politicians. The position was no sinecure whether regarded from the point of view of getting up at six in the morning to see that the men were early at work; or of following the loaded wagons, uneasily dropping their contents at intervals, to their dreary destination at the dump; or of insisting that the contractor must increase the number of his wagons from nine to thirteen and from thirteen to seventeen, although he assured me that he lost money on every one and that the former inspector had let him off with seven; or of taking careless landlords into court because they would not provide the proper garbage receptacles; or of arresting the tenant who tried to make the garbage wagons carry away the contents of his stable.

With the two or three residents who nobly stood by, we set up six of those doleful incinerators which are supposed to burn garbage with the fuel collected in the alley itself. The one factory in town which could utilize old tin cans was a window weight factory, and we deluged that with ten times as many tin cans as it could use—much less would pay for. We made desperate attempts to have the dead animals removed by the contractor who was paid most liberally by the city for that purpose but who, we slowly discovered, always made the police ambulances do the work, delivering the carcasses upon freight cars for shipment to a soap factory in Indiana where they were sold for a good price although the contractor himself was the largest stockholder in the concern.

Perhaps our greatest achievement was the discovery of a pavement eighteen inches under the surface in a narrow street, although after it was found we triumphantly discovered a record of its existence in the city archives. The Italians living on the street were much interested but displayed little astonishment, perhaps because they were accustomed to see buried cities exhumed.

HOUSEHOLD MATTERS

STEAM BATH. *In "Short Historical and Journal-Notes of Various Voyages Performed in the Four Quarters of the Globe," 1655, David de Vries includes this report on the Indians living near New Amsterdam.*

When they wish to cleanse themselves of their foulness, they go in the autumn, when it begins to grow cold, and make, away off, near a running brook, a small oven, large enough for three or four men to lie in it. In making it they first take twigs of trees, and then cover them tight with clay, so that smoke cannot escape. This being done, they take a parcel of stones, which they heat in a fire, and then put in the oven, and when they think that it is sufficiently hot, they take the stones out again, and go and lie in it, men and women, boys and girls, and come out so perspiring, that every hair has a drop of sweat on it. In this state they plunge into the cold water; saying that it is healthy, but I let its healthfulness pass; they then become entirely clean, and are more attractive than before.

MAN'S BEST FRIEND. *From the journal of John Winthrop, governor of Massachusetts, 1644.*

One Dalkin and his wife dwelling near Meadford coming from Cambridge, where they had spent their Sabbath, and being to pass over the river at a ford, the tide not being fallen enough, the husband adventured over, and finding it too deep, persuaded his wife to stay a while; but it raining very sore, she would needs adventure over, and was carried away with the stream past her depth. Her husband not daring to go help her, cried out, and thereupon his dog, being at his house near by came forth, and seeing something in the water, swam to her, and she caught hold on the dog's tail, so he drew her to the shore and saved her life.

NEIGHBORS. *From the court records of New Amsterdam.*

Oct. 5, 1654: Wolfert Webber was summoned to Court by the Worshipful Magistrates on the complaint of some Neighbours in consequence of damage he inflicted attacking with dogs and beating certain pigs which went on his land. Wolfert Webber demands the name of Complainant. William Beekman states it to be on the complaint handed to him of Mde. Verleth and Stillen's wife, because their hogs were unwarrantably attacked and injured by Webber and his dogs, so that he considered it proper to acquaint the court. Webber said he was so annoyed by the hogs on his land, whereby all his seed was destroyed that he divers times drove them home, but he did not injure them in the least; on the contrary, he was at various times insulted and threatened with a beating by Mde. Verleth. The Worshipful Court admonished Webber to keep himself clear of complaint, and to institute his action should he suffer wrong.

June 28, 1655: Wolfert Webber plaintiff v/s Judith Verleth appeared in court, complaining of violence force and abuse committed against him by defendant and her sister, Sarah, last week in his house; striking him in his own house and flinging stones at him; requesting that said defendant be ordered to let him remain in peace in his own house.

Judith Verleth denied that she ever gave plaintiff any trouble; complains that he berated her for a whore and strumpet, and threatened in his own house to strike her with the whip, as he daily does his wife; that he assaulted her, bruising and dragging her arm, and kicked her sister so that her hip is blue. Parties were ordered to prove their complaints and statements on both sides by the next Court day, and further to leave each other unmolested. Webber was fined 12 stivers on account of fulminating lies, etc., in presence of the Court.

EXPLOSION. *Samuel Sewall, who kept a diary for over fifty years (1674–1729), records a catastrophe at Salem. Sewall was a judge of the Superior Court at the time, and later became chief justice.*

Tuesday, June 28. 1698. Court at Salem, Major Brown praesident; were remov'd to the Ship Tavern and candles lighted; a cry of Fire was made. A Girl drawing Rum in a litle Warehouse of Mr. Lyndon's, or looking after a cask that leak'd, the candle fired it, which took the cask and broke it up with a Report, so catch'd Cotton and fired Mr. Willoughbys house in the Garret of which was a Barrel of Powder, that taking fire blew off the Roof and very much dispersed the flaming partickles; much of which was thrown on Major Brown's house over the way, the wind carrying it thither so that and his warehouse were quickly burnt down, and much Money and Goods lost with the Buildings. Five houses in all burnt, Mr. Hirst's for one. This is the first considerable Fire that ever was in Salem. It seems the stroke makes a deep impression on Major Brown. Has lost 3 or four Thousand pounds.

PET. *Peter Kalm, a Swedish naturalist trained by Linnaeus, visited this country from 1748 to 1751 to observe flora and fauna.*

Some persons in Philadelphia have tamed beavers, so that they go fishing with them, and they always come back to their masters. Major Roderfort, in New York, related that he had a tame beaver over half a year in his house, where he went about loose, like a dog. The Major gave him bread, and sometimes fish, which he liked very much. He got as much water as he wanted in a bowl. All the rags and soft things he found he dragged into a corner where he used to sleep, and made a bed of them. The cat in the house, having kittens, took possession of his bed, and he did not hinder her. When the cat went out, the beaver often took a kitten between his forepaws and held it to his breast to warm it, and doted upon it; as soon as the cat returned he gave her the kitten again. Sometimes he grumbled but never did any harm or attempted to bite.

HOUSEWIFE. *Extracts from Lydia Maria Child's bestseller,* The American Frugal Housewife, *published first in 1828 and in its twelfth edition by 1833. The book is "Dedicated to those who are not ashamed of economy."*

If you would avoid waste in your family, attend to the following rules, and do not despise them because they appear so unimportant: 'many a little makes a mickle.'

Look frequently to the pails, to see that nothing is thrown to the pigs which should have been in the grease-pot. Look to the grease-pot, and see that nothing is there which might have served to nourish your own family, or a poorer one.

See that the beef and pork are always *under* brine; and that the brine is sweet and clean.

Attend to all the mending in the house, once a week, if possible. Never put out sewing. If it be impossible to do it in your own family, hire some one into the house, and work with them.

Make your own bread and cake. Some people think it is just as cheap to buy of the baker and confectioner; but it is not half as cheap. True, it is more convenient; and therefore the rich are justifiable in employing them; but those who are under the necessity of being economical, should make convenience a secondary object. In the first place, confectioners make their cake richer than people of moderate income can afford to make it; in the next place, your domestic, or yourself, may just as well employ your own time, as to pay them for theirs.

An ox's gall will set any color,—silk, cotton, or woollen. I have seen the colors of calico, which faded at one washing, fixed by it. When one lives near a slaughter-house, it is worth while to buy cheap, fading

"The Kitchen; Prang's Aids for Object Teaching."
Lithograph by L. Prang & Company, 1874.

goods, and set them in this way. The gall can be bought for a few cents. Get out all the liquid, and cork it up in a large phial. One large spoonful of this in a gallon of warm water is sufficient.

A warming-pan full of coals, or a shovel of coals, held over varnished furniture, will take out white spots. Care should be taken not to hold the coals near enough to scorch; and the place should be rubbed with flannel while warm.

An ounce of quicksilver, beat up with the white of two eggs, and put on with a feather, is the cleanest and surest bed-bug poison. What is left should be thrown away: it is dangerous to have it about the house.

Lamps will have a less disagreeable smell if you dip your wick-yarn in strong hot vinegar, and dry it.

If feather-beds smell badly, or become heavy, . . . empty them, and wash the feathers thoroughly in a tub of suds; spread them in your garret to dry, and they will be as light and as good as new.

New England rum, constantly used to wash the hair, keeps it very clean, and free from disease, and promotes its growth a great deal more than Macassar oil. Brandy is very strengthening to the roots of the hair; but has a hot drying tendency, which New England rum has not.

After old coats, pantaloons, &c. have been cut up for boys, and are no longer capable of being converted into garments, cut them into strips, and employ the leisure moments of children, or domestics, in sewing and braiding them for door-mats.

Cream of tartar, rubbed upon soiled white kid gloves, cleanses them very much.

If you have a greater quantity of cheeses in the house than is likely to be soon used, cover them carefully with paper, fastened on with flour paste, so as to exclude the air. In this way they may be kept free from insects for years. They should be kept in a dry, cool place.

When mattresses get hard and bunchy, rip them, take the hair out, pull it thoroughly by hand, let it lie a day or two to air, wash the tick, lay it in as light and even as possible, and catch it down, as before. Thus prepared they will be as good as new.

In winter, always set the handle of your pump as high as possible, before you go to bed. Except in very rigid weather, this keeps the handle from freezing. When there is reason to apprehend extreme cold, do not forget to throw a rug or horse-blanket over your pump; a frozen pump is a comfortless preparation for a winter's breakfast. . . .

Always have your tinder-box and lantern ready for use, in case of sudden alarm.

PIANO LEGS. *Captain Frederick Marryat, an officer of the Royal Navy and author of popular sea yarns, observes some examples of American refinement during a visit in the 1830s.*

When at Niagara Falls I was escorting a young lady with whom I was on friendly terms. She had been standing on a piece of rock, the better to view the scene, when she slipped down, and was evidently hurt by the fall; she had, in fact, grazed her shin. As she limped a little in walking home, I said, "Did you hurt your leg much?" She turned from me, evidently much shocked, or much offended; and not being aware that I had committed any very heinous offence, I begged to know what was the reason of her displeasure. After some hesitation she said that, as she knew me well, she would tell me that the word *leg* was never mentioned before ladies. I apologized for my want of refinement, which was attributable to having been accustomed only to *English* society; and added, that as such articles must occasionally be referred to, even in the most polite circles in America, perhaps she would inform me by what name I might mention them without shocking the company. Her reply was that the word *limb* was used; "Nay," continued she, "I am not so particular as some people are, for I know those who always say limb of a table, or limb of a pianoforte."

There the conversation dropped; but a few months afterwards I was obliged to acknowledge that the young lady was correct when she asserted that some people were more particular than even she was.

I was requested by a lady to escort her to a seminary for young ladies, and on being ushered into the reception-room, conceive my astonishment at beholding a square pianoforte with four *limbs*. However, that the ladies who visited their daughters might feel in its full force the extreme delicacy of the mistress of the establishment, and her care to preserve in their utmost purity the ideas of the young ladies under her charge, she had dressed all these four limbs in modest little trousers, with frills at the bottom of them!

FIRE. *The twenty-year-old George Templeton Strong, already an inveterate diarist, records a blaze in New York in 1840, a time when ships still docked at the slips in lower Manhattan.*

January 27. This has been an igneous evening. When I left the office at half-past seven, there was a fire in Broad Street, or rather in Water near Broad. . . . I didn't stay to see the end of the combustion, for there were so many "soap locks" and "round rimmers" [street toughs] and other amiable persons there congregated, and so much hustling and swearing and rowdying going forward, that I concluded to clear out—and walked off for a ramble uptown. Got a little way up when I saw that another fire which had broken out an hour or so before in South Street was making quite a show and the temptation was irresistible so I made for the scene of action, the corner of Dover Street. I couldn't get in front of the fire and was unable to make out whether two or three stores were burning, but it was quite a showy affair: the fire reflected on the snow and lighted up the masts and rigging of the ships, the groups of firemen on the docks with their engine and lamps, the crowd and bustle in front of the buildings, the raging fire, and just above it the cupola of Thomas H. Smith's big store blazing away and half-hidden by the eddying smoke—altogether made quite a display. Thomas H.'s store I think must have been saved; I didn't stay to see the finale, being rather tired of wet feet and obstreperous rowdies. . . .

At three o'clock [this morning] I was waked by a furious alarm of fire which seemed so near and so terrible that I roused the old gentleman and we bundled on our clothes and made streaks. On reaching Wall Street we saw it wasn't there, but the cinders were showering down . . . and the fire shown as brightly on top of the Exchange and other elevated buildings as if it were only one block off. It *was* the Thomas H. Smith store, probably the finest and largest, twice over, in the city, and I never saw such a scene as Peck Slip presented: the store extending from South to Front Streets was burning like a volcano, one body of fire from top to bottom. It was crammed with hemp, cotton, and tea, and the fire was so intense it was impossible to come near it. There were only two engines and perhaps a couple of hundred men. Several other stores had caught and were burning fiercely; in fact the whole block was on fire. . . .

January 28. The loss last night is estimated at about $1,500,000. Everything from Smith's store to Dover Street on South and Front Streets has gone *in fumo.* Went down to the scene of action with George Anthon; they were demolishing walls, etc., and I noticed in pulling down a five-story brick front, entirely supported by side walls, that a rope passed in at the fourth story window and out at the third so as to form a noose, when pulled, though the wall shook and tottered and cracked in every direction, actually *tore* through the wall intermediate the windows, as if it had been made of wet paper, bringing out just bricks enough to come through—a pretty specimen certainly of modern masonry. Smith's store still burning fiercely. Two whole cargoes of tea in it just from Canton, and I noticed the melted lead of the chests streaming down from the piles of ignited matter that are piled within the ruins. It is most fortunate that there was no wind when this fire took place. Had there been any, half the city might have been used up, for the firemen were exhausted and totally inefficient. As it is, the shipping seems to have escaped by miracle; they were mostly frozen in and couldn't be hauled out of the docks.

VOLUNTEER FIREMAN. *Thomas Knox, a nineteenth-century New York journalist, interviews a former member of the city's old volunteer fire department.*

The volunteer firemen were recruited from all kinds of trades and occupations. It was an invariable rule with them to answer every fire alarm at whatever hour it was sounded, no matter what they were doing at the time.

"One time," said an old fire-laddie, "Barnum, the showman, was giving a play called 'Moll Pitcher, or the Battle of Monmouth,' at this old museum at the corner of Broadway and Ann Street. There were Red-coats and Continentals in uniform, and no end of Indians with feathers and war paint and tomahawks in the battle scene, and a lot of us that ran with an engine a little way down Ann Street had hired out for 'supes' to make up the 'armies' that went on the stage.

"Well, one day, just as we were all dressed in our stage costumes and it was almost time for us to march on the stage for the great battle, the fire-bell rang out a signal for a fire in our district. We didn't stop for anything, but went yelling down the stairs and out into the street just as we were—the most motley crowd of firemen that ever turned out at a fire. We met the engine coming up Ann Street, grabbed the rope, and went on to the fire with the rest of the boys. How the small boys did scamper out of the way, and how folks did stare at us, especially at the Indians in war paint and feathers, and the Red-coats in their gay uniforms; but we kept at our work and put out the fire and then went back to the Museum, though by that time the play was over.

Barnum was awful mad at first, as his battle scene was all broken up, but next morning the story was in the papers and he got such a good advertisement out of the affair for nothing, that he was all serene again by the time of the afternoon performance."

FEATHER BED. *In a 1930s Federal Writers' Project interview, "Aunt" Cheney Cross of Alabama recalls the arrival of the Yankees near the end of the Civil War, when she was a young house slave.*

I's setting there in the loomroom, and Mr. Thad Watt's little gal, Louise, she's standing at the window. She say: "O-o-h! Nannie! Just look down yonder!" "Baby, what is that?" I says. "Them's the Yankees coming!" "God help us!" I says, and before I can catch my breath, the place is covered. You couldn't stir 'em up with a stick. Feets sounded like muttering thunder. Them bayonets stick up like they just setting on the mouth of they guns. They swords hanging on they sides, singing a tune whilst they walk. A chicken better not pass by. Iffen he do, off come his head!

When they pass on by me, they pretty nigh shook me outa my skin. "Where's the mens?" they say and shake me up. "Where's the arms?" They shake me til my eyeballs loosen up. "Where's the silver?" Lord! Was my teeths drapping out? They didn't give me time to catch my breath. All the time, Miss Mary just look 'em in the eye and say nothing!

They took them Enfield rifles, half as long as that door, and bust in the smokehouse window. They jack me up offen my feet and drag me up the ladder and say: "Git that meat out." I kept on throwing out Miss Mary's hams and sausages till they holler, "Stop." I come backing down that ladder like a squirrel, and I ain't stop backing till I reach Miss Mary.

Yes, Lord! Them Yankees loaded up a wagon full of meat and took the whole barrel of 'lasses! Taking that 'lasses kilt us children! Our mainest 'musement was making 'lasses candy. Then us cakewalk round it. Now that was all gone. Look like them soldiers had to sharpen they swords on everything in sight. The big crepe mullen bush by the parlor window was blooming so pink and pretty, and they just stood there and whack off them blooms like folks' heads drapping on the ground.

I seed the sergeant when he run his bayonet clean through Miss Mary's bestest feather bed and rip it slam up! With that, a wind blowed up and took them feathers every whichaway for Sunday. You couldn't see where you's at. The sergeant, he just throwed his head back and laugh fit to kill hisself. Then first thing next, he done suck a feather down his windpipe. Lord, honey, that white man sure struggled. Them soldiers throwed water in his face. They shook him and beat him and roll him over, and all the time he's getting limberer and bluerer. Then they jack him up by his feets and stand him on his head. Then they pump him up and down. Then they shook him till he spit. Then he come to.

They didn't cut no more mattresses. And they didn't cut nothing much up in the parlor, 'cause that's where the lieutenant and the sergeant slept. But when they left the next day, the whole place was strewed with mutilation.

THE EARTH CLOSET. *As described by George E. Waring, Jr., of Newport, Rhode Island, in Catharine Beecher's* The American Woman's Home, *1869.*

Mr. Waring was formerly Agricultural Engineer of the New York Central Park, and has given much attention to sanitary and agricultural engineering, having published several valuable works bearing in the same general direction. He is now consulting director of "The Earth-Closet Company," Hartford, Ct., which manufactures the apparatus and all things appertaining to it—any part which might be needed to complete a home-built structure. But with generous and no less judicious freedom, they are endeavoring to extend the knowledge of this wholesome and economical process of domestic sanitary engineering as widely as possible.

The following information and statements are appropriated bodily, either directly or with mere modifications for brevity, from the little pamphlet of Mr. Waring.

The earth-closet is the invention of the Rev. Henry Moule, of Fordington Vicarage, Dorsetshire, England.

It is based on the power of clay, and the decomposed organic matter found in the soil, to absorb and retain all offensive odors and all fertilizing matters; and it consists, essentially, of a mechanical contrivance (attached to the ordinary seat) for measuring out and discharging into the vault or pan below a sufficient quantity of sifted dry earth to entirely cover the solid ordure and to absorb the urine.

The discharge of earth is effected by an ordinary pull-up similar to that used in the water-closet, or (in the self-acting apparatus) by the rising of the seat when the weight of the person is removed. The vault or pan under the seat is so arranged that the accumulation may be removed at pleasure.

From the moment when the earth is discharged, and the evacuation is covered, all offensive exhalation entirely ceases. Under certain circumstances, there may be, at times, a slight odor as of guano mixed with earth; but this is so trifling and so local, that a commode arranged on this plan may, without the least annoyance, be kept in use in any room.

The ACCIDENT in LOMBARD-STREET PHILAD.ᵃ 1787

A Philadelphia street scene. Illustration by Charles Wilson Peale, 1787.
The girl has just dropped her pie "And laughing Sweeps collect around/
The pye that's scatter'd on the ground."

This statement is made as the result of personal experience. Mr. Waring says:

"I have in constant use in a room in my house an earth-closet commode; and even when the pan is entirely full, with the accumulation of a week's use, visitors examining it invariably say, with some surprise, 'You don't mean that this particular one has been used!'"

URBAN PASTORALE. *Until well into the twentieth century, the country was never far from the town. In this 1879 sketch celebrating the coming of spring to Philadelphia, Walt Whitman shows just how close the two could be.*

Winter relaxing its hold, has already allow'd us a foretaste of spring. As I write, yesterday afternoon's softness and brightness, (after the morning fog, which gave it a better setting, by contrast,) show'd Chestnut street—say between Broad and Fourth—to more advantage in its various asides, and all its stores, and gay-dress'd crowds generally, than for three months past. I took a walk there between one and two. Doubtless, there were plenty of hard-up folks along the pavements, but nine-tenths of the myriad-moving human panorama to all appearance seem'd flush, well-fed, and fully-provided. At all events it was good to be on Chestnut street yesterday. The peddlers on the sidewalk—("sleeve-buttons, three for five cents")—the handsome little fellow with canary-bird whistles—the cane men, toy men, toothpick men—the old woman squatted in a heap on the cold stone flags, with her basket of matches, pins and tape—the young negro mother, sitting, begging, with her two little coffee-color'd twins on her lap—the beauty of the cramm'd conservatory of rare flowers, flaunting reds, yellows, snowy lilies, incredible orchids, at the Baldwin mansion near Twelfth street—the show of fine poultry, beef, fish, at the restaurants—the china stores, with glass and statuettes—the luscious tropical fruits—the street cars plodding along, with their tintinnabulating bells—the fat, cab-looking, rapidly driven one-horse vehicles of the post-office, squeez'd full of coming or going letter-carriers, so healthy and handsome and manly-looking, in their gray uniforms—the costly books, pictures, curiosities, in the windows—the gigantic policemen at most of the corners—will all be readily remember'd and recognized as features of this principal avenue of Philadelphia.

A few days ago one of the six-story clothing stores along here had the space inside its plate-glass show-window partition'd into a little corral, and litter'd deeply with rich clover and hay, (I could smell the odor outside,) on which reposed two magnificent fat sheep, full-sized

A woman peeling peaches by the smokehouse door.
Photograph by F. M. Steele, circa 1900.

but young—the handsomest creatures of the kind I ever saw. I stopp'd long and long, with the crowd, to view them—one lying down chewing the cud, and one standing up, looking out, with dense-fringed patient eyes. Their wool, of clear tawny color, with streaks of glistening black—altogether a queer sight amidst that crowded promenade of dandies, dollars and drygoods.

A Hopi girl grinds corn, circa 1909.

CHAPTER
6

EATING

THE PLEASURES OF HUNTING —for those who like to hunt—are many: the thrill of the chase, the satisfaction of returning home with whatever has been killed, and, not least, the infinitely repeatable pleasure of talking about past exploits. In an age when winter evenings were spent around the fireside with little entertainment other than talk, a well-told tale was always welcome; and because for the early settlers and pioneers, hunting was not a sport but an important source of food, hunters' stories were probably listened to with more respect and attention than is the case today.

Tastes in food have changed greatly since then. Few people now eat bear's meat or dogs or cormorants, or dyspepsia bread or election cake. Means of buying and selling have also changed; open-air markets are largely gone, as is the kind of country fair where people would stock up for the coming season. Methods of preparing food are also different: No one now has to cook on a fire made of buffalo chips, or start that fire by rubbing two sticks together, or preserve meat by hanging thin strips out to dry in the wind and sun or by pickling it in brine, nor do we follow seventeenth-century instructions on how to "boyle a Mallard curiously."

There have been hard times, certainly: the "starving time" at Jamestown, when people were "constrayned to eate Doggs, Catts, Ratts, Snakes, Toadstooles, horse hides and what-nott"; shortages and impossibly high prices; and blizzards and other disasters. But there have been plenty of high times too, for this has always been a land of plenty: a place where, as at the first Thanksgiving, there has usually been good cause to celebrate abundance; a land even of superabundance, as exemplified in the instructions for a Gilded Age dinner party with which the chapter closes.

But to begin with, here is a kind of gastronomical tour, showing how food was obtained and prepared in different parts of the country at various times, starting with the early settlers in Jamestown.

OBTAINING, PREPARING, AND COOKING FOOD

JAMESTOWN AND JOHN SMITH. *In 1608, Captain John Smith, "Governour of Virginia," ventured up the Potomac to check out reports of "a Glistening Mettal" but returned empty-handed.*

The mine we found 9 or 10 myles up in the country from the river, but it proved of no value. Some Otters, Beavers, Martins, Luswarts, and sables we found and, in divers places, that abundance of fish lying so thicke with their heads above the water, as for want of nets (our barge driving amongst them) we attempted to catch them with a frying pan; but we found it a bad instrument to catch fish with. Neither better fish, more plenty or variety, had any of us ever seene in any place, swimming in the water, then in the bay of Chesapeack, but there not to be caught with frying-pans.

Next, in his General Historie of Virginia, *published in London in 1626, Smith describes the Indians' more successful methods of hunting and fishing.*

The men bestow their time in fishing, hunting, wars, and such man-like exercises, scorning to be seen in any woman-like exercise, which is the cause that the women be very painful [hardworking] and the men often idle. The women and children do the rest of the work. They make mats, baskets, pots, mortars, pound their corn, make their bread, prepare their victuals, plant their corn, gather their corn, bear all kinds of burdens, and such like.

Their fire they kindle presently by chafing a dry pointed stick in a hole of a little square piece of wood, that firing itself will so fire moss, leaves, or any such like dry thing that will quickly burn.

For fishing, hunting, and wars they use much their bow and arrow. They bring their bows to the form of ours by the scraping of a shell. Their arrows are made, some of straight young sprigs, which they head with bone some two or three inches long. These they use to shoot at squirrels on trees. Another sort of arrows they use made of reeds. These are pierced with wood, headed with splinters of crystal or some sharp stone, the spurs of a turkey, or the bill of some bird. For his knife he hath the splinter of a reed to cut his feathers in form. With this knife also he will joint a deer or any beast, shape his shoes, buskins, mantles, etc. To make the notch of his arrow he hath the

"Neither better fish, more plenty or variety, had any of us ever seene in any place, swimming in the water, then in the bay of Chesapeack," wrote John Smith. "Their manner of fishing in Virginia," engraving by Theodore de Bry from Thomas Harriot's *Briefe and True Report of the New Found Land of Virginia*, 1590.

tooth of a beaver set in a stick, wherewith he grateth it by degrees. His arrow head he quickly maketh with a little bone, which he ever weareth at his bracer, of any splint of a stone or glass in the form of a heart, and these they glue to the end of their arrows. With the sinews of deer and the tops of deer horns boiled to a jelly, they make a glue that will not dissolve in cold water.

Their fishing is much in boats. These they make of one tree by burning and scratching away the coals with stones and shells, till they have made it in form of a trough. Some of them are an ell deep and forty or fifty foot in length, and some will bear forty men, but the most ordinary are smaller and will bear ten, twenty, or thirty, according to their bigness. Instead of oars, they use paddles and sticks, with which they will row faster than our barges.

Betwixt their hands and thighs their women use to spin the barks of trees, deer sinews, or a kind of grass they call pemmenaw; of these they make a thread very even and readily. This thread serveth for many uses, as about their housing, apparel, as also they make nets for fishing. . . .

Their hooks are either a bone grated as they notch their arrows, in the form of a crooked pin or fishhook, or of the splinter of a bone tied to the cleft of a little stick, and with the end of the line they tie on the bait.

They use also long arrows tied on a line, wherewith they shoot at fish in the rivers. But they of Accomac use staves like unto javelins headed with bone. With these they dart fish swimming in the water. They have also many artificial weirs in which they get abundance of fish.

In their hunting and fishing they take extreme pains; yet it being their ordinary exercise from their infancy, they esteem it a pleasure and are very proud to be expert therein. And by their continual ranging and travel they know all the advantages and places most frequented with deer, beasts, fish, fowl, roots, and berries. At their huntings they leave their habitations and reduce themselves into companies, as the Tartars do, and go to the most desert [open] places with their families, where they spend their time in hunting and fowling up towards the mountains, by the heads of their rivers, where there is plenty of game. For betwixt the rivers the grounds are so narrow that little cometh here which they devour not. . . .

Their hunting houses are like unto arbors covered with mats. These their women bear after them, with corn, acorns, mortars, and all bag and baggage they use. When they come to the place of exercise, every man doth his best to show his dexterity, for by their excelling in those qualities they get their wives. Forty yards will they shoot level or very near the mark, and one hundred and twenty is their best at random.

At their huntings in the deserts they are commonly two or three hundred together. Having found the deer, they environ them with many fires, and betwixt the fires they place themselves. And some take their stands in the midsts. The deer being thus feared by the fires and their voices, they chase them so long within that circle that many times they kill six, eight, ten, or fifteen at a hunting. They use also to drive them into some narrow point of land when they find that advantage, and so force them into the river, where with their boats they have ambuscados to kill them. When they have shot a deer by land, they follow him like bloodhounds by the blood and strain, and oftentimes so take them. Hares, partridges, turkeys, or eggs, fat or lean, young or old, they devour all they can catch in their power.

NEW ENGLAND. *Just off the* Mayflower *in 1620, a party of Pilgrims led by Captain Miles Standish explores Cape Cod.*

We went on further and found new stubble, of which they had gotten corn this year, and many walnut trees full of nuts, and great store of strawberries, and some vines. Passing thus a field or two, which were not great, we came to another which had also been new gotten, and there we found where a house had been, and four or five old planks laid together; also we found a great kettle which had been some ship's kettle and brought out of Europe. There was also a heap of sand, made like the former—but it was newly done, we might see how they had paddled it with their hands—which we digged up, and in it we found a little old basket full of fair Indian corn, and digged further and found a fine great new basket full of very fair corn of this year, with some thirty-six goodly ears of corn, some yellow, and some red, and others mixed with blue, which was a very goodly sight. The basket was round, and narrow at the top; it held about three or four bushels, which was as much as two of us could lift up from the ground, and was very handsomely and cunningly made. But whilst we were busy about these things, we set our men sentinel in a round ring, all but two or three which digged up the corn. We were in suspense what to do with it and the kettle, and at length, after much consultation, we concluded to take the kettle and as much of the corn as we could carry away with us; and when our shallop came, if we could find any of the people, and come to parley with them, we would give them the kettle again, and satisfy them for their corn. So we took all the ears, and put a good deal of the loose corn in the kettle for two men to bring away on a staff; besides, they that could put any into their pockets filled the same. The rest we buried again, for we were so laden with armor that we could carry no more.

Isaack de Rasieres, visiting Plymouth from New Amsterdam in 1627, finds the Pilgrims well supplied with fish, both to eat and use as fertilizer.

The bay is very full of fish, of cod, so that the governor before named [William Bradford] has told me that when the people have a desire for fish they send out two or three persons in a sloop, whom they remunerate for their trouble, and who bring them in three or four hours' time as much fish as the whole community require for a whole day—and they muster about fifty families.

At the south side of the town there flows down a small river of fresh water, very rapid, but shallow, which takes its rise from several lakes in the land above, and there empties into the sea; where in April and the beginning of May, there come so many shad from the sea which want to ascend that river, that it is quite surprising. This river the English have shut in with planks, and in the middle with a little door, which slides up and down, and at the sides with trellice work, through which the water has its course, but which they can also close with slides.

At the mouth they have constructed it with planks, like an eel-pot, with wings, where in the middle is also a sliding door, and with trellice work at the sides, so that between the two there is a square pool, into which the fish aforesaid come swimming in such shoals, in order to get up above, where they deposit their spawn, that at one tide there are 10,000 to 12,000 fish in it, which they shut off in the rear at the ebb, and close up the trellices above, so that no more water comes in; then the water runs out through the lower trellices, and they draw out the fish with baskets, each according to the land he cultivates, and carry them to it, depositing in each hill three or four fishes, and in these they plant their maize, which grows as luxuriantly therein as though it were the best manure in the world. And if they do not lay this fish therein, the maize will not grow, so that such is the nature of the soil.

A tale of a Narragansett deer hunt, from A Key into the Language of America, *by Roger Williams, published in 1643. By then, Williams, who questioned the right of the English settlers to expropriate Indian land, had been banished from Massachusetts and had settled in Providence.*

When a Deere is caught by the leg in the Trap, sometimes there it lies a day together before the Indian come, and so lies a prey to the ranging Wolfe, and other wild Beasts (most commonly the Wolfe) who seaseth upon the Deere and robs the Indian (at his first devouring) of neere halfe his prey, and if the Indian come not the sooner, hee makes a second greedie Meale, and leaves him nothing but the bones, and the torne Deere-skins, especially if he call some of his greedy Companions to his bloody banquet.

Upon this the *Indian* makes a falling trap called *Sunnúckhig* (with a great weight of stones) and so sometimes knocks the Wolfe on the head, with a gainefull Revenge, especially if it bee a blacke Wolfe, whose Skins they greatly prize.

I remember how a poore Deere was long hunted and chased by a Wolfe, at last (as their manner is) after the chase of ten, it may be more miles running, the stout Wolfe tired out the nimble Deere, and seasing upon it, kill'd: In the act of devouring his prey, two *English*

Swine, big with Pig, past by, assaulted the Wolfe, drove him from his prey, and devoured so much of that poore Deere, as they both surfeted and dyed that night.

The Wolfe is an Embleme of a fierce bloodsucking persecutor.

The Swine of a covetous rooting worldling. Both make a prey of the Lord Jesus in his Poor servants.

An Indian dish of many ingredients as described by the seventeenth-century colonist Daniel Gookin in Historical Collections of the Indians in New England.

Their food is generally boiled maize, or Indian corn, mixed with kidney-beans, or sometimes without. Also they frequently boil in this pottage fish and flesh of all sorts, either new taken or dried, as shads, eels, alewives or a kind of herring, or any other sort of fish. . . . These they cut in pieces, bones and all, and boil them in the aforesaid pottage. I have wondered many times that they were not in danger of being choked with fish bones; but they are so dexterous to separate the bones from the fish in their eating thereof, that they are in no hazard. Also they boil in this furmenty all sorts of flesh, they take in hunting; as venison, beaver, bears flesh, moose, otters, rackoons, or any kind that they take in hunting; cutting this flesh in small pieces, and boiling it as aforesaid. Also they mix with the said pottage several sorts of roots; as Jerusalem artichokes, and ground nuts, and other roots, and pompions, and squashes, and also several sorts of nuts or masts, as oak-acorns, chestnuts, walnuts; these husked and dried, and powdered, they thicken their pottage therewith.

In his book An Account of Two Voyages to New England, *published in London in 1674, John Josselyn tells how the Indians went about catching cormorants—also known in those days as "shapes" or "sharkes."*

The Cormorant. Though I cannot commend them to our curious palats, the *Indian* will eat them when they are fley'd, they take them prettily, they roost in the night upon some Rock that lyes out in the Sea, thither the *Indian* goes in his Birch-*Canow* when the moon shines clear, and when he is come almost to it, he lets his *Canow* drive on of it self, when he is come under the Rock he shoves his Boat along till he comes just under the *Cormorants* watchman, the rest being asleep, and so soundly do sleep that they will snore like so many Piggs; the *Indian* thrusts up his hand of a sudden, grasping the watchman so hard round about his neck that he cannot cry out; as soon as he hath him in his *Canow* fast, he clambreth to the top of the Rock, where walking softly he takes them up as he pleaseth, still wringing off their heads; when he hath slain as many as his *Canow* can carry, he gives a shout which awakens the surviving *Cormorants*, who are gone in an instant.

COLONIAL RECIPES. The Housewife's Skill in Cookery, *by Gervase Markham, was first published in England in 1630. These recipes are from the eleventh edition, which appeared in 1683.*

Puddings. White pudding. Take a pint of the best, thickest, and sweetest Creame, boyl it, than whilst it is hot, put thereunto a good quantity of great sweet Oatmeal Grots very sweet and clean pickt and formerly steept in milk twelve hours at least. Let it soak in this Creame another night. Then put thereto at least eight yolkes of Egges, a little Pepper, Cloves, Mace, Saffron, Currants, Dates, Sugar, Salt, and a great store of Swines Suet, or for want thereof great store of Beef Suet. Then fill it up in the formes [linen bags] according unto the order of good Housewiferie. Boyl them on a soft and gentle fire, and as they swell, prick them with a great Pin, or small awl, to keep them that they burst not. When you serve them to the Table, which must not be untill they be a day old, first boyl them a little, then take them out and toast them brown before the fire. Trim the edge of the dish with either Salt or Sugar.

Roste Meats. In the generall knowledge thereof are to be observed these few rules. First, the clean keeping and scouring of the spits and cob-irons; then the spitting and broaching of meat which must be done so strongly and firmly that the meat may by no means turn about the spit yet ever to observe that the spit do not go through any principal part of the meat, but such as is of least account.

Then to know the best bastings for meat, which is sweet Butter, sweet Oyl, Barrel butter, or fine rendred up seam [lard] with Cinamon, Cloves, and Mace. There be some that will baste onely with Water and Salt and nothing else, yet it is but opinion and that must be the worlds Master alwayes.

If you will Roast any Venison, after you have washt it and clensed all the blood from it, you shall stick it with cloves all over on the outside. If it be leane, you shall lard it either with mutton lard or pork lard, but mutton is the best. Then spit it and rost it by a soaking fire. Take vinegar, bread crumms, and some of the gravy which comes from the venison and boyl them well in a dish. Season it with suger, cinamon, ginger and salt. Serve the venison forth upon the sawce when it is rosted enough.

To boyl a Mallard curiously. Take the Mallard when it is fair dressed, washed, and trust, and put it on a spit and roast it till you get the gravy out of it. Then take it from the spit and boyl it. Take the best of the broth into a pipkin, and the gravy which you saved, with a peece of sweet butter, and Currants, Vinegar, Pepper, and grated bread. Thus boyl all these together, and when the Mallard is boyled sufficiently, lay it on a dish with sippets and the broth upon it and so serve it forth.

A Minc't Pie. Take a Legge of Mutton and cut the best of the flesh from the bone and parboyl it well. Then put to it three pound of the best Mutton suet and shred it very small, then spread it abroad and season it with Salt, Cloves, and Mace. Then put in good store of Currants, great Raisins, and Prunes clean washt and pickt, a few Dates sliced, and some Orange-pills sliced. Then being all mixt together, put into a coffin [pastry shell] or into divers coffins and so bake them. When they are served up, open the lids and strow store of Suger on the Top of the meat and upon the lid. And in this sort, you may also bake Beef or Veal.

IN THE WOODS. *Paul Dudley, attorney general and later chief justice of Massachusetts, and a talented natural scientist, submits his report on how to find honey to the Royal Society in London in 1720.*

The hunter in a clear sun-shiny day, takes a plate or trencher, with a little Sugar, Honey or Molosses spread on it, and when got into the Woods, sets it down on a Rock or Stump in the Woods: this the Bees soon scent and find out; for 'tis generally supposed a Bee will scent Honey or Wax above a Mile's distance. The Hunter secures in a Box or other Conveniency, one or more of the Bees as they fill themselves, and after a little time, lets one of them go, observing very carefully the Course the Bee steers; for after he rises in the Air, he flies directly, or upon a streight Course to the Tree where the Hive is.

In order to do this, the Hunter carries with him his Pocket Compass, his Rule, and other Implements, with a Sheet of paper, and sets down the Course, suppose it be West; by this he is sure the Tree must be somewhere in a West Line from where he is, but wants to know the exact Distance from his Station; in order to determine that, he makes an off-set either South or North (we'll suppose North) an hundred Perch or Rod, (if it be more, it will still be more exact, because the Angle will not be so acute) then he takes out another Bee and lets him go, observing his Course also very carefully, for he being loaded will, as the first, (after he is mounted a convenient height) fly directly to the Hive; this second Course, (as I must call it) the Hunter finds to be South, 54 Degrees West; then there remains nothing but to find out where the two Courses intersect. . . .

An ingenious Man of my Acquaintance the last Year took two or three of his Neighbours that knew nothing of the matter, and after he had taken his Bees, set the Courses the first and second Bee steered, made the off-set, and taken the Distance from the two Stations to the Intersection, he gave orders to cut down such a Tree, pointing to it; the Labourers smiled, and were confident there was no Honey there, for they could not perceive the Tree to be hollow, or to have any hole for the Bees to enter by, and would have disswaded the Gentleman from felling the Tree, but he insisted on it, and offered to lay them any Wager that the Hive was there, and so it proved to the great surprize of the Country-men.

I cannot dismiss this Subject, without acquainting you, that all the Bees we have in our Gardens, or in our Woods, and which now are in great numbers, are the produce of such as were brought in Hives from *England* near a hundred Years ago, and not the natural produce of this part of *America*; for the first Planters of *New England* never observed a Bee in the Woods, until many Years after the Country was settled; but that which proves it beyond question is, that the *Aborigines* (the *Indians*) have no word in their Language for a Bee, as they have for all Animals whatsoever proper to, or aboriginally of the Country, and therefore for many Years called a Bee by the name of *English Man's Fly.*

Some passages from William Byrd's "History of the Dividing Line Betwixt Virginia and North Carolina." Byrd was in charge of the surveying party and wrote his account in 1729.

Our men kill'd a very fat Buck and Several Turkeys. These two kinds of Meat boil'd together, with the addition of a little Rice or French Barley, made excellent Soupe, and, what happens rarely in Other good things, it never cloy'd, no more than an Engaging Wife wou'd do, by being a Constant Dish.

Our Indian was very Superstitious in this Matter, and told us, with a face full of concern, that if we continued to boil Venison and Turkey together, we Shou'd for the future kill nothing, because the Spirit that presided over the Woods would drive all the Game out of our Sight. But we had the Happiness to find this an Idle Superstition, and tho' his Argument could not convince us, yet our repeated Experience at last, with much ado, convinc'd Him.

Because I am persuaded that very usefull Matters may be found out by Searching this great Wilderness, especially the upper parts of it about the Mountains, I conceive it will help to engage able men in that good work, if I recommend a wholesome kind of Food, of very small Weight and very great Nourishment, that will secure them from Starving, in case they shou'd be so unlucky as to meet with no Game. . . .

The Portable Provisions I would furnish our Foresters withal are Glue-Broth and rockahomini: one contains the Essence of Bread, the other of Meat.

The best way of making Glue-Broth is after the following method: Take a Leg of Beef, Veal, Venison, or any other Young Meat, because Old Meat will not so easily Jelly. Pare off all the fat, in which there is no Nutriment, and of the Lean make a very strong Broth, after the usual Manner, by boiling the meat to Rags till all the Goodness be out. After Skimming off what fat remains, pour the Broth into a wide Stew-Pan, well tinn'd, & let it simmer over a gentle, even Fire, till it come to a thick Jelly. Then take it off and set it over Boiling Water, which is an Evener Heat, and not so apt to burn the Broth to the Vessel. Over that let it evaporate, stirring it very often till it be reduc'd, when cold, into a Solid Substance like Glue. Then cut it into small Pieces, laying them Single in the Cold, that they may dry the Sooner. When the Pieces are perfectly dry, put them into a Cannister, and they will be good, if kept Dry, a whole East India Voyage.

This Glue is so Strong, that two or three Drams, dissolv'd in boiling Water with a little Salt, will make half a pint of good Broth, & if you shou'd be faint with fasting or Fatigue, let a small piece of this Glue melt in your Mouth, and you will find yourself surprisingly refreshed.

One Pound of this cookery wou'd keep a man in good heart above a Month, and is not only Nourishing, but likewise very wholesome. Particularly it is good against Fluxes, which Woodsmen are very liable to, by lying too near the moist ground, and guzzling too much cold Water. But as it will be only us'd now and then, in times of Scarcity, when Game is wanting, two Pounds of it will be enough for a Journey of Six Months.

But this Broth will be still more heartening if you thicken every mess with half a Spoonful of Rockahominy, which is nothing but Indian Corn parched without burning, and reduced to Powder. The Fire drives out all the Watery Parts of the Corn, leaving the Strength of it behind, and this being very dry, becomes much lighter for carriage and less liable to be Spoilt by the Moist Air.

Thus half a Dozen Pounds of this Sprightful Bread will sustain a Man for as many Months, provided he husband it well.

Our Indian kill'd a Bear, of two years old, that was feasting on these Grapes. He was very fat, as they generally are in that season of the year. In the fall, the Flesh of this Animal has a high Relish, different from that of other Creatures, tho' inclining nearest to that of Pork, or rather of Wild Boar.

A true Woodsman prefers this Sort of meat to that of the fattest Venison, not only for the *Hautgout* but also because the Fat of it is well tasted, and never rises in the stomach. Another proof of the goodness of this meat is, that it is less apt to corrupt than any other we are acquainted with. As agreeable as such rich Diet was to the men, yet we who were not accustom'd to it, tasted it at first with some sort of Squeamishness, that Animal being of the Dog-kind; tho' a little Use soon reconcil'd us to the American Venison. And that its being of the Dog kind might give us the less disgust, we had the Example of the Ancient and polite People, the Chinese, who reckon Dog's Flesh too good for any under the Quality of a mandarin.

The Beast is in truth a very clean Feeder, living, while the Season lasts, upon Acorns, Chestnuts and Chinkapins, Wild-Honey and Wild-Grapes. They are naturally not carniverous, unless Hunger constrains them to it, after the Mast is all gone, and the Products of the Woods quite exhausted.

And now, for the good of mankind, and for the better Peopling an Infant colony, which has no want but that of Inhabitants, I will venture to publish a Secret of Importance, which our Indian disclos'd to me. I askt him the reason why few or none of his Countrywomen were barren: To which curious Question he answered, with a Broad grin upon his Face, they had an infallible SECRET for that. Upon my being importunate to know what the secret might be, he informed me that, if any Indian woman did not prove with child at a decent time after Marriage, the Husband, to save his Reputation with the women, forthwith entered into a Bear-dyet for Six Weeks, which in that time makes him so vigorous that he grows exceedingly impertinent to his poor wife and 'tis great odds but he makes her a Mother in Nine Months.

And thus I am able to say, besides, for the Reputation of the Bear Dyet, that all the Marryed men of our Company were joyful Fathers within forty weeks after they got Home, and most of the Single men had children sworn to them within the same time, our chaplain always excepted, who, with much ado, made a shift to cast out that importunate kind of Devil, by Dint of Fasting and Prayer.

HUNTER'S TALES. *William Bartram, whose writings influenced Coleridge and Wordsworth, was a naturalist who traveled widely in Carolina, Georgia, and Florida in the 1770s. This episode took place in Florida.*

My companion, the trader, being desirous of crossing the river to the opposite shore, in hopes of getting a turkey, I chose to accompany him, as it offered a good opportunity to observe the natural productions of those rich swamps and islands of the river. Having crossed the river, which is here five or six hundred yards wide, we entered a narrow channel, which after a serpentine course, for some miles, rejoins the main river again, above; forming a large fertile island, of rich low land. We landed on this island, and soon saw a fine roebuck, at some distance from us, who appeared leader of a company of deer, that were feeding near him, on the verge of a green meadow. My companion parting from me, in pursuit of the deer, one way, and I, observing a flock of turkeys at some distance, on the other, directed my steps towards them, and with great caution, got near them; when singling out a large cock, and being just on the point of firing, I observed several young cocks were affrighted, and in their language, warned the rest to be on their guard, against an enemy, whom I plainly perceived was industriously making his subtile approaches towards them, behind the fallen trunk of a tree, about twenty yards from me. This cunning fellow hunter, was a large fat wild cat [lynx]. He saw me, and at times seemed to watch my motions, as if determined to seize the delicious prey before me. Upon which I changed my object, and levelled my piece at him. At that instant, my companion, at a distance, also discharged his piece at the deer, the report of which alarmed the flock of turkeys, and my fellow hunter, the cat, sprang over the log and trotted off. The trader also missed his deer: thus we foiled each other.

John Tanner, captured by Shawnee Indians in 1789 at the age of nine, and adopted into the tribe, was under the tutelage of Pe-shau-ba, a warrior. Wa-me-gon-a-biew was a youth four years older than Tanner. The tribe moved about a good deal in the area of Minnesota, Dakota, and Ontario.

About this place elks were numberous, and it was now the rutting season. I remember one day, Pe-shau-ba sent me with the two young women, to bring some meat from an elk he had killed at some distance. The women, finding that the elk was large and fat, determined on remaining to dry the meat before they carried it home. I took a load of meat, and started for home by myself. I had my gun with me, and perceiving there were plenty of elk, I loaded it, and concealing myself in a small thicket of bushes, began to imitate the call of the female elk; presently a large buck came bounding so directly towards the spot where I was, and with such violence, that becoming alarmed for my own safety, I dropped my load and fled; he seeing me, turned and ran in an opposite direction. Remembering that the Indians would ridicule me for such conduct, I determined to make another attempt, and not suffer any apprehension for my own safety to be the cause of another failure. So hiding myself again, in a somewhat more carefully chosen place, I repeated my call from time to time, till at length another buck came up, and him I killed. In this manner, great part of the day had been consumed, and I now perceived it was time to hasten home with my load.

The old woman becoming uneasy at my long absence, sent Wa-me-gon-a-biew to look for me. He discovered me as I was coming out of a piece of woods into a large prairie. He had on a black capot [cloak], which, when he saw me, he turned over his head in such a manner as to make himself resemble a bear. At first I took it to be a common black bear, and sought a chance to shoot him; but it so happened that he was in such a situation as enabled him to see me, and I knew he would certainly have turned and fled from me had it been a black bear. As he continued to advance directly towards me, I concluded it must be a grizly bear, so I turned and began to run from him; the more swiftly I ran, the more closely he seemed to follow. Though much frightened, I remembered Pe-shau-ba's advice, never to fire upon one of these animals unless trees were near into which I could escape; also, in case of being pursued by one, never to fire until he came very close to me. Three times I turned, and raised my piece to fire, but thinking him still too far off, turned and ran again. Fear must have blinded my eyes, or I should have seen that it was not a bear. At length, getting between him and the lodge, I ran with such speed as to outstrip him, when I heard a voice behind me, which I knew to be that of Wa-me-gon-a-biew. I looked in vain for the bear, and he soon convinced me that I owed all my terror to the disguise which he had effected, with the aid only of an old black coat. This affair being related to the old people when we came home, they reproved Wa-me-gon-a-biew; his mother telling him, that if I had shot him in that disguise, I should have done right, and according to the custom of the Indians she could have found no fault with me for so doing.

IN KENTUCKY. *In 1813, while in the Green River country of Kentucky, John James Audubon finds himself lost in the woods as night falls.*

A little doubtful as to my course, I proceeded slowly and cautiously by the friendly light of the moon. The air seemed unusually keen; and the wind in the treetops made me think of halting to camp for the night. The strange adventures of Daniel Boone in these very woods, and his extraordinary walk to save those at Fort Massacre from scalping, kept passing through my mind.

Now and then a Racoon or Opossum, rustling the fallen leaves, made me pause for a moment. In short, I was thinking of many things, both dismal and pleasing, until the glimmer of a distant fire broke upon my reveries. As I drew nearer I could see figures moving to and fro like spectres. Pretty soon I heard bursts of laughter, shouts and songs of merrymaking. I thought I was stumbling across a camp meeting, at first, but soon saw that the mirth came from a band of sugar-makers.

Every man, woman and child stared as I passed them, but all were friendly. Without much ceremony I walked up to the fire where two or three old women and their husbands were attending to the kettles. . . . I was heartily welcomed with a serving of good pone bread, a plate of molasses and some sweet potatoes.

Fatigued by my long ramble, I lay down under the lee of the smoke and fell sound asleep.

Frost lay heavy in the morning, but the campers, cheerful and invigorated, prepared for work. The place was pleasing and had been cleared of underbrush. Several brooklets meandered among the tall straight maples that seemed as if planted in rows. The sun began to melt the frozen dews. Some feathered songsters joined in the chorus of the woodsmen's daughters. As often as a burst of laughter echoed through the woods an Owl or Wild Turkey responded with a sound that was very welcome to the young men of the party. With large ladles, the sugar-makers began to stir the thickening juice of the maple. They collected pails of sap from the trees. Some hacked cuts in the trees then bored a hole with an auger, for a piece of hollow cane to drain off the sap into the pails. Half a dozen men felled a fine yellow poplar, sawed its big trunk into many pieces, and split them to make troughs to go beneath the cane-corks.

Ten gallons of sap are needed to produce one pound of fine sugar. But an inferior, lumpy cake-sugar is obtained in greater quantity. Towards the close of the season the juice will no longer grain by boiling and only produces syrup. I have seen maple sugar so good that it resembled candy some months after it was manufactured. Well do I remember the time when it was an article of commerce through Kentucky. Around 1810 or so it brought from 6-1/2¢ to 12-1/2¢ per pound, according to quality, over my own counter.

Vast flocks of passenger pigeons—now extinct—were once common. Here, John James Audubon tells how in 1813 he joined a crowd of farmers and other hunters on the banks of the Green River, Kentucky, awaiting their arrival.

As the time of the arrival of the passenger pigeons approached, their foes anxiously prepared to receive them. Some persons were ready with iron pots containing sulphur, others with torches of pine knots; many had poles, and the rest, guns. . . . Everything was ready and all eyes were fixed on the clear sky which could be glimpsed amid the tall tree-tops. . . .

Suddenly a general cry burst forth, 'Here they come!' The noise they made, even though still distant, reminded me of a hard gale at sea, passing through the rigging of a close-reefed vessel. As the birds arrived and passed over me, I felt a current of air that surprised me. Thousands of the pigeons were soon knocked down by the polemen, whilst more continued to pour in. The fires were lighted, then a magnificent, wonderful, almost terrifying sight presented itself. The pigeons, arriving by the thousands, alighted everywhere, one above another, until solid masses were formed on the branches all around. Here and there the perches gave way with a crack under the weight, and fell to the ground, destroying hundreds of birds beneath, and forcing down the dense groups of them with which every stick was loaded. The scene was one of uproar and confusion. I found it quite

Passenger Pigeons, by John James Audubon.
From *Birds of America*, published in England
between 1827 and 1838.

useless to speak or even to shout, to those persons nearest to me. Even the gun reports were seldom heard, and I was made aware of the firing only by seeing the shooters reloading. . . . The pigeons were constantly coming, and it was past midnight before I noticed any decrease in the number of those arriving. The uproar continued the whole night. . . .

Towards the approach of day, the noise somewhat subsided. Long before I could distinguish them plainly, the pigeons began to move off in a direction quite different from the one in which they flew when they arrived in the evening before. By sunrise all that were able to fly had disappeared. The howling of the wolves now reached our ears, and the foxes, the lynxes, cougars, bears, opossums and polecats were sneaking off. Eagles and hawks, accompanied by a crowd of vultures, took their place and enjoyed their share of the spoils. Then the authors of all this devastation began to move among the dead, the dying and the mangled, picking up the pigeons and piling them in heaps. When each man had as many as he could possibly dispose of, the hogs were let loose to feed on the remainder.

ON THE PLAINS. *Two entries from the journal of Meriwether Lewis. The Lewis and Clark Expedition is now in present-day Montana, traveling along the Missouri River and just west of the junction with the Judith River, so named by William Clark in honor of his future bride, Judy Hancock.*

May 29, 1805. Today we passed on the Starboard side the remains of a vast many mangled carcases of Buffalow which had been driven over a precipice of 120 feet by the Indians and perished; the water appeared to have washed away a part of this immence pile of slaughter and still their remained the fragments of at least a hundred carcases   they created a most horrid stench.   in this manner the Indians of the Missouri distroy vast herds of buffaloe at a stroke;   for this purpose one of the most active and fleet young men is scelected and disguised in a robe of buffaloe skin, having also the skin of the buffaloe's head with the years and horns fastened on his head in form of a cap, thus caparisoned he places himself at a convenient distance between a herd of buffaloe and a precipice proper for the purpose, which happens in many places on this river for miles together; the other indians now surround the herd on the back and flanks and at a signal agreed on all shew themselves at the same time moving forward towards the buffaloe;   the disguised indian or decoy has taken care to place himself sufficiently nigh the buffaloe to be noticed by them when they take to flight and runing before them they follow him in full speede to the precipice, the cattle behind driving those in front over and seeing them go do not look or hesitate about following untill the whole are precipitated down the precepice forming one common mass of dead and

An American having struck a Bear but not killed him, escapes into a Tree.

An illustration from the journal kept by Sergeant Patrick Gass, a member of the
Lewis and Clark expedition, published in 1810.

mangled carcases: the decoy in the mean time has taken care to
secure himself in some cranney or crivice of the clift which he had previously prepared for that purpose. the part of the decoy I am informed is
extreamly dangerous, if they are not very fleet runners the buffaloe tread
them under foot and crush them to death, and sometimes drive them
over the precipice also, where they perish in common with the buffaloe.

 Friday, June 14th, 1805. . . . I decended the hill and directed my
course to the bend of the Missouri near which there was a herd of at
least a thousand buffaloe; here I thought it would be well to kill a buffaloe and leave him untill my return from the river. . . .
 I scelected a fat buffaloe and shot him very well, through the lungs;
while I was gazeing attentively on the poor anamal discharging blood in
streams from his mouth and nostrils, expecting him to fall every instant,
and having entirely forgotten to reload my rifle, a large white, or reather
brown bear, had perceived and crept on me within 20 steps before I discovered him;   in the first moment I drew up my gun to shoot, but
at the same instant recolected that she was not loaded and that he was
too near for me to hope to perform this opperation before he reached
me, as he was then briskly advancing on me; it was an open level plain,
not a bush within miles nor a tree within less than three hundred yards
of me; the river bank was sloping and not more than three feet above
the level of the water; in short there was no place by means of which I
could conceal myself from this monster untill I could charge my
rifle;   in this situation I thought of retreating in a brisk walk as fast

as he was advancing untill I could reach a tree about 300 yards below me, but I had no sooner terned myself about but he pitched at me, open mouthed and full speed,   I ran about 80 yards and found he gained on me fast, I then run into the water   the idea struk me to get into the water to such debth that I could stand and he would be obliged to swim, and that I could in that situation defend myself with my espontoon [staff with sharp metal point]; accordingly I ran haistily into the water about waist deep, and faced about and presented the point of my espontoon,   at this instant he arrived at the edge of the water within about 20 feet of me; the moment I put myself in this attitude of defence he sudonly wheeled about as if frightened, declined to combat on such unequal grounds, and retreated with quite as great precipitation as he had just before pursued me.

As soon as I saw him run in that manner I returned to the shore and charged my gun, which I had still retained in my hand throughout this curious adventure. I saw him run through the level open plain about three miles, till he disappeared in the woods on medecine river; during the whole of this distance he ran at full speed, sometimes appearing to look behind him as if he expected pursuit. I now began to reflect on this novil occurence and indeavoured to account for this sudden retreat of the bear. I at first thought that perhaps he had not smelt me bofore he arrived at the waters edge, so near me, but I then reflected that he had pursued me for about 80 or 90 yards before I took the water and on examination saw the grownd toarn with his tallons immediately on the impression of my steps; and the cause of his allarm still remains with me misterious and unaccountable. so it was and I felt myself not a little gratifyed that he had declined the combat. my gun reloaded I felt confidence once more in my strength.

A master carpenter, Reuben Cole Shaw was twenty-three when he decided to leave Boston and seek his fortune in the California gold mines. Although he did not find it, he did eventually settle down to become a prosperous farmer in Indiana, where he wrote his memoirs, Across the Plains in Forty-Nine, *from which these two extracts are taken.*

On reaching the Platte, the General informed us that for three hundred miles along the river we should not find a particle of timber, and that the cooking would have to be done over a fire made from buffalo chips (the dried excrement of the buffalo), which, when used in the trapper's fireplace, proved a very satisfactory fuel.

For the benefit of the reader, I will briefly explain the manner in which the fireplace, or oven, of the trapper was constructed, when using buffalo chips as fuel along the Platte.

While waiting to strike it rich in the California gold mines, two prospectors whip up a basic meal. Wood engraving published in *Harper's Weekly*, October 3, 1857.

Selecting a spot a short distance from the steep river bank, a hole about six inches in diameter and eight to twelve inches deep was excavated. An air tunnel was then formed by forcing a ramrod horizontally from the river bank to the bottom of the cavity, giving the oven the required draught. In making a fire (after gathering a quantity of dry chips, which were found in abundance), a wisp of dry grass was lighted and placed at the bottom of the oven, opposite the air tunnel, feeding the flame with finely pulverized dry chips, which readily ignited. Then after filling the fireplace with broken chips and placing around the oven two or three small rocks on which to rest cooking utensils, we had a combination which at first gave us a grand surprise, as but little smoke and only slight odor emitted from the fire, and we found, after having eaten our first meal cooked in this manner, that the prejudice previously entertained against buffalo chips as fuel had vanished into thin air.

Here we saw the Indian squaws boiling meat in baskets. In my younger days I had heard of this being done, and was at a loss to know how a basket could be made to hold water, but when I saw their filthy method of cooking had filled all the open spaces between the ribs of the basket with dirt, the mystery was explained. Their baskets for cooking purposes were about six or eight inches deep, sixteen to twenty inches in diameter, and almost the exact shape of a large wooden bowl. In front of each lodge a few rocks were arranged, forming a small fireplace, in which fire was burning, while in and around the fire were quite a number of round, smooth stones, about the size of base-balls. The heated stones, which were handled with two sticks the thickness of a lead pencil and about a foot long, were being taken from the fire by the squaws and placed in the boiling baskets, and the sputtering which followed seemed to be highly satisfactory to the operators. One of the old squaws, noticing our interest in the matter, handed me the sticks and motioned for me to go to work. I accepted the challenge, and, after several trials, succeeded in taking a stone from the fire, dropping it in the boiling water with a splash and burning my hands quite severely. I made no attempt to repeat the experiment, while the old squaw laughed at my dismal failure.

Some extracts from Randolph Marcy's 1859 book The Prairie Traveler, A Handbook for Overland Expeditions. *Marcy was a captain in the U.S. Army and spent much of his service in the West.*

Supplies for a march should be put up in the most secure, compact, and portable shape.

Bacon should be packed in strong sacks of a hundred pounds to each; or, in very hot climates, put in boxes and surrounded with bran, which in a great measure prevents the fat from melting away.

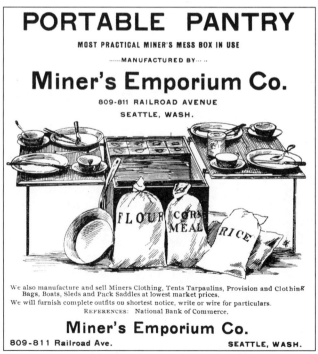

Progress comes to the mines: an 1897 advertisement for a portable pantry that also provided fold-out tables.

Flour should be packed in stout double canvas sacks well sewed, a hundred pounds in each sack.

Butter may be preserved by boiling it thoroughly, and skimming off the scum as it rises to the top until it is quite clear like oil. It is then placed in tin canisters and soldered up. This mode of preserving butter has been adopted in the hot climate of southern Texas, and it is found to keep sweet for a great length of time, and its flavor is but little impaired by the process.

Sugar may be well secured in India-rubber or gutta-percha sacks, or so placed in the wagon as not to risk getting wet.

Desiccated or dried vegetables are almost equal to the fresh, and are put up in such a compact and portable form as easily to be transported over the plains. They have been extensively used in the Crimean war, and by our own army in Utah, and have been very generally approved. They are prepared by cutting the fresh vegetables into thin slices and subjecting them to a very powerful press, which removes the juice and leaves a solid cake, which after having been thoroughly dried in an oven, becomes almost as hard as a rock. A small piece of this, about half the size of a man's hand, when boiled, swells up so as to fill a vegetable dish, and is sufficient for four men. It is believed that the antiscorbutic properties of vegetables are not

A group of cowboys gather by a river to eat the meal brought by the chuckwagon.
Photograph by W. D. Harper, Denver, circa 1900.

impaired by desiccation, and they will keep for years if not exposed to dampness. Canned vegetables are very good for campaigning, but are not so portable as when put up in the other form.

Pemmican, which constitutes almost the entire diet of the Fur Company's men in the Northwest, is prepared as follows: The buffalo meat is cut into thin flakes, and hung up to dry in the sun or before a slow fire; it is then pounded between two stones and reduced to a powder; this powder is placed in a bag of the animal's hide, with the hair on the outside; melted grease is then poured into it, and the bag sewn up. It can be eaten raw, and many prefer it so. Mixed with a little flour and boiled, it is a very wholesome and exceedingly nutritious food, and will keep fresh for a long time.

When the deer are lying down in the smooth prairie, unless the grass is tall, it is difficult to get near them, as they are generally looking around, and become alarmed at the least noise.

The Indians are in the habit of using a small instrument which imitates the bleat of the young fawn, with which they lure the doe within range of their rifles. The young fawn gives out no scent upon its track until it is sufficiently grown to make good running, and instinct teaches the mother that this wise provision of nature to preserve the helpless little quadruped from the ravages of wolves, panthers, and other carnivorous beasts, will be defeated if she remains with it, as her tracks can not be concealed. She therefore hides her fawn in the grass, where it is almost impossible to see it, even when very near it, goes off to some neighboring thicket within call, and makes her bed alone. The Indian pot-hunter, who is but little scrupulous as to the means he employs in accomplishing his ends, sounds the bleat along near the places where he thinks the game is lying, and the unsuspicious doe, who imagines that her offspring is in distress, rushes with headlong impetuosity toward the sound, and often goes within a few yards of the hunter to receive her death-wound.

I once undertook to experiment with the instrument myself, and made my first essay in attempting to call up an antelope which I discovered in the distance. I succeeded admirably in luring the wary victim within shooting range, had raised upon my knees, and was just in the act of pulling trigger, when a rustling in the grass on my left drew my attention in that direction, where, much to my surprise, I beheld a huge panther within about twenty yards, bounding with gigantic strides directly toward me. I turned my rifle, and in an instant, much to my relief and gratification, its contents were lodged in the heart of the beast.

THE WEST COAST. *Joaquin Miller, who lived with the Modoc Indians in the Mount Shasta region of California between 1856 and 1860, tells how the Pit River got its name.*

We crossed the McCloud, and our course lay through a saddle in the mountains to Pit River; so called from the blind pits dug out like a jug by the Indians in places where their enemies or game are likely to pass. These pits are dangerous traps; they are ten or fifteen feet deep, small at the mouth, but made to diverge in descent, so that it is impossible for anything to escape that once falls into their capacious maws. To add to their horror, at the bottom, elk and deer antlers that have been ground sharp at the points are set up so as to pierce any unfortunate man or beast they may chance to swallow up. They are dug by the squaws, and the earth taken from them is carried in baskets and thrown into the river. They are covered in the most cunning manner; even footprints in an old beaten trail are made above the treacherous pits, and no depression, no broken earth, nothing at all indicates their presence except the talismanic stones or the broken twigs and other signs of a sort of rude freemasonry which only the members of a tribe can understand.

MARKETS. *Three markets—one in South Carolina, one in Massachusetts, and one in Illinois. First, the Charleston Market of the 1830s, as witnessed by the Maryland-born Mrs. Anna Royall, one of the country's first professional travel writers and unkindly described by John Quincy Adams as "a virago errant."*

There is more West India fruit in Charleston market, perhaps, in one day, than can be found in the northern markets in six months, and some that is never seen there, much of which I was unable to learn the names, the sellers being averse to converse with you, unless they think you are going to purchase. Besides every species of orange is to be seen, in astonishing quantities, even to the wild orange, which grows in the neighborhood; this is about the size of an egg, supposing it to be round, they are of a deep yellow, and sour as a lemon. Lemons in cart loads, and the *banana*; this is in taste, substance and color, like our *pawpaus*, but not in shape: it is long, perhaps four inches, and crooked like a long-necked squash; it has a sweetish, insipid taste, and grows in clusters upon a small twig, to the amount of a peck, and are brought into market hanging upon the stalk. Besides these, there were a great variety of fruits, and all the nuts of the globe, the names of which I could not learn.

This was in the month of March, and I saw all kinds of vegetables, excepting green beans; peas, cabbages, onions, turnips, and every other species of garden vegetable, were in great profusion, and very neat: the meat was thin and poor, it would be condemned in our market. Butter

The watermelon market in Charleston in 1866; southern chivalry
required men to carry the shopping baskets. Wood engraving from
Frank Leslie's Illustrated Newspaper, December 15, 1866.

is neither plenty nor good; fowls are only tolerable; fish is pretty good,
I think bass mostly, they are fresh and neat. But I did not dream that
such a variety of sweet potatoes, peas (dried) and beans existed on the
globe, as I saw in Charleston market.

The stalls are different from ours, which are between, or outside of
the pillars—these are inside under the cover, and are boxed up with a
species of railing and raised from the floor, and have a gate opening
from the outside: these stalls are filled with vegetables, and negro
women to sell them. The negro goes in and shuts herself up, and is
seated, and hands the articles over. These stalls are on both sides, and
the whole is very neat.

But the *Buzzards*, they are all through the market as gentle as dogs.
They were the only polite gentlemen I saw, and made me very many
handsome bows; and one who strikes one of these pays a fine of $5. It
is laughable to see how assiduous they inspect the meat and fish market, and how quietly and soberly they walk about the houses; and the
chimnies are covered with them. They seem fond of smoke: they
breed over Ashley River, near the town. They are a great advantage to
the citizens in removing all kinds of filth and carrion: the moment a
cow, horse, or any animal dies, hundreds of these Buzzards light on it,
and in a few minutes it disappears (even before it is known by the
owner that the animal is dead) except the bones, which are stript

clean, not a vestige of flesh or sinew is left. They are not so large as the Buzzard in our country and are properly called carrion Crows.

Nathaniel Hawthorne goes to market in Massachusetts to sell a calf.

Sept. 27, 1841. A Ride to Brighton yesterday morning, it being the day of the weekly cattle fair. William Allen and myself went in a wagon, carrying a calf, to be sold at the fair. The calf had not had his breakfast, as his mother had preceded him to Brighton; and he kept expressing his hunger and discomfort by loud, sonorous baa-s, especially when we passed any cattle in the fields or on the road. The cows, grazing within hearing expressed great interest, and some of them came galloping to the roadside to behold the calf. Little children, also, on their way to school, stopt to laugh and point at poor little Bossie. He was a prettily behaved urchin, and kept thrusting his hairy muzzle between William and myself, apparently wishing to be stroked and patted. It was an ugly thought, that his confidence in human nature, and Nature in general, was to be so ill rewarded as by cutting his throat, and selling him in quarters. . . .

Market day in Jacksonville, Illinois, as witnessed in the 1850s by William Henry Milburn, a Methodist Episcopal clergyman and author of Ten Years of Preacher Life.

In the centre of the town was the public square. . . . The sides of the square were lined with the shanties in which was transacted the business of the place. The occupants of these lowly shops, in which was sold all manner of merchandise—from the ribbon that trimmed the bonnet of the rustic belle, to the plough which broke up her father's acres—were styled merchants, and the occupation of bartering molasses and calico, for beeswax, butter and eggs, was denominated the mercantile. At frequent intervals were located "groceries," most commonly called "doggeries," where spirits were sold by "the small" i.e. the glass. In the centre of the square stood the court and market houses, the one brick, the other frame. The market was two stories high, the lower story devoted to the sale of meats, and the upper to a newspaper and lawyers' offices, the gallery at the side serving as a rostrum for stump orators.

Saturday was a great day, when from many miles around the old and young, male and female, came with every product of the land, by every means of conveyance, to trade. Homespun dames and damsels, making the circuit of the square inquiring at every door: "D'ye buy eggs and butter yer?" and sometimes responding indignantly, as I heard a maiden once when told that eggs were bringing only three cents a dozen: "What, do ye s'pose our hens are gwine to strain theirselves a laying eggs at three cents a dozen? Lay 'em yourself, and see how you'd like the price."

It was a lively scene on a market day; and its crowds of prairie wagons, long, low uncovered boxes placed on wheels, in which the articles sold and bought, to which the generic name of plunder was applied, were conveyed to and from the town; while groups of saddled horses, pawing the earth and neighing their neighborly recognitions to each other, stood fastened at the posts. Here you might descry a piratical cow, boarding a wagon by adroitly raising her fore legs into it, smelling around, while the trading owner was absent, for fruits and vegetables, or even devouring his purchased stock of sugar; and there sweeping along at full gallop, some half drunken jockey, showing off the points of his steed, and with stentorian voice offering to bet any man ten dollars that it was the best piece of horse flesh on the ground. Groups are gathered in front of all the "doggeries," at the street corners, and at the doors of the court-house, discussing politics, or other urgent questions of the time; differences of opinion, stimulated by bald-face whisky, often bringing these conferences to a pugilistic termination. Meanwhile the older ladies, arrayed in dark linsey-woolsey dresses— the lower front adorned by blue check aprons—their heads covered with sun-bonnets, and their feet with yarn stockings and brogan shoes or moccasins, having brought the interesting and complicated operations of trading to a close, stand idly about with folded arms, regaling themselves with fumes of tobacco, inhaled from a corncob or sweet potato pipe. The exercises of the day were usually varied by political speeches, a sheriff's sale, a half dozen free fights, and thrice as many horse swaps. Just before sundown the traders departed, and the town was left to its inhabitants.

IN THE KITCHEN. *From "Common Cooking" by Lydia Maria Child, who also wrote romantic novels and juvenile books and edited abolitionist newspapers and pamphlets. "Common Cooking" was published as part of* The American Frugal Housewife, *which first appeared in 1829 and went through twenty editions in seven years.*

It is necessary to be very careful of fresh meat in the summer season. The moment it is brought into the house, it should be carefully covered from the flies, and put in the coldest place in the cellar. If it consist of pieces, they should be spread out separate from each other, on a large dish, and covered. If you are not to cook it soon, it is well to sprinkle salt on it. The kidney, and fat flabby parts, should be raised up above the lean, by a skewer, or stick, and a little salt strewn in. If you have to keep it over night, it should be looked to the last thing when you go to bed; and if there is danger, it should be scalded.

Calf's Head. Calf's head should be cleansed with very great care; particularly the lights. The head, the heart, and the lights should boil full two hours; the liver should be boiled only one hour. It is better to leave the wind-pipe on, for if it hangs out of the pot while the head is cooking, all the froth will escape through it. The brains, after being thoroughly washed, should be put in a little bag; with one pounded cracker, or as much crumbled bread, seasoned with sifted sage, and tied up and boiled one hour. After the brains are boiled, they should be well broken up with a knife, and peppered, salted, and buttered. They should be put upon the table in a bowl by themselves.

Roast Pig. Strew fine salt over it an hour before it is put down. It should not be cut entirely open; fill it up plump with thick slices of buttered bread, salt, sweet-marjoram and sage. Spit it with the head next the point of the spit; take off the joints of the leg, and boil them with the liver, with a little whole pepper, allspice, and salt, for gravy sauce. The upper part of the legs must be braced down with skewers. Shake on flour. Put a little water in the dripping-pan, and stir it often. When the eyes drop out, the pig is half done. When it is nearly done, baste it with butter. Cut off the head, split it open between the eyes. Take out the brains, and chop them fine with the liver and some sweet-marjoram and sage; put this into melted butter, and when it has boiled a few minutes, add it to the gravy in the dripping-pan. When your pig is cut open, lay it with the back to the edge of the dish; half a head to be placed at each end.

Rennet Pudding. If your husband brings home company when you are unprepared, rennet pudding may be made at five minutes' notice; provided you keep a piece of calf's rennet ready prepared soaking in a bottle of wine. One glass of this wine to a quart of milk will make a sort of cold custard. Sweetened with white sugar, and spiced with nutmeg, it is very good.

Election Cake. Old-fashioned election cake is made of four pounds of flour; three quarters of a pound of butter; four eggs; one pound of sugar; one pound of currants, or raisins if you choose; half a pint of good yeast; wet it with milk as soft as it can be and be moulded on a board. Set to rise over night in winter; in warm weather, three hours is usually enough for it to rise. A loaf, the size of common flour bread, should bake three quarters of an hour.

Pancakes. Pancakes should be made of half a pint of milk, three great spoonfuls of sugar, one or two eggs, a tea-spoonful of dissolved pearlash, spiced with cinnamon, or cloves, a little salt, rose-water, or lemon-brandy, just as you happen to have it. Flour should be stirred in till the spoon moves round with difficulty. If they are thin, they are apt to soak fat. Have the fat in your skillet boiling hot, and drop them in with a spoon. Let them cook till thoroughly brown. . . . Flip makes very rich pancakes. In this case, nothing is done but to sweeten your mug of beer with molasses; put in one glass of New England rum; heat it till it foams, by putting in a hot poker; and stir it up with flour as thick as other pancakes.

Dyspepsia Bread. The American Farmer publishes the following receipt for making bread, which has proved highly salutary to persons afflicted with that complaint, viz:—three quarts unbolted wheat meal; one quart soft water, warm, but not hot; one gill of fresh yeast; one gill of molasses, or not, as may suit the taste; one tea-spoonful of saleratus. This will make two loaves, and should remain in the oven at least one hour; and when taken out, placed where they will cool gradually. Dyspepsia crackers can be made with unbolted flour, water and saleratus.

Coffee. As substitutes for coffee, some use dry brown bread crusts, and roast them; others soak rye grain in rum, and roast it; others roast peas in the same way as coffee. None of these are very good; and peas so used are considered unhealthy. Where there is a large family of apprentices and workmen, and coffee is very dear, it may be worth while to use the substitutes, or to mix them half and half with coffee; but, after all, the best economy is to go without.

A bit of fish-skin as big as a ninepence, thrown into coffee while it is boiling, tends to make it clear. If you use it just as it comes from the salt-fish, it will be apt to give an unpleasant taste to the coffee: it should be washed clean as a bit of cloth, and hung up till perfectly dry. The white of eggs, and even egg shells are good to settle coffee. Rind of salt pork is excellent.

Some people think coffee is richer and clearer for having a bit of sweet butter, or a whole egg, dropped in and stirred, just before it is done roasting, and ground up, shell and all, with the coffee.

HIGH TIMES AND HARD TIMES

A FAMOUS DINNER. *The first Thanksgiving, as described in a letter back to England by Edward Winslow, one of the Pilgrims, in 1621.*

Our harvest being gotten in, our governor sent four men on fowling, that so we might after a special manner rejoice together after we had gathered the fruit of our labors. They four in one day killed as much fowl as, with a little help beside, served the company almost a week. At which time, amongst other recreations, we exercised our arms, and many of the Indians coming amongst us, and among the rest their greatest king Massasoit, with some ninety men, whom for three days we entertained and feasted, and they went out and killed five deer, which they brought to the plantation and bestowed on our governor, and upon the captain and others. And although it be not always so plentiful as it was at this time with us, yet by the goodness of God, we are so far from want that we often wish you partakers of our plenty.

STARVING TIME IN EARLY JAMESTOWN. *From* The Tragical Relation of the Virginia Assembly, *written in 1624.*

The allowance in those tymes for a man was only eight ounces of meale and half a pinte of pease for a daye, the one and the other mouldy, rotten, full of Cobwebs and Maggotts loathsome to man and not fytt for beasts, which forced many to flee for reliefe to the Savage Enemy, . . . and others were forced by famine to filch for their bellies, of whom one for steelinge of 2 or 3 pints of oatemeale had a bodkinge [knife] thrust through his tongue and was tyed with a chaine to a tree untill he starved. If a man through his sicknes had not been able to worke, he had noe allowance at all, and soe consequently perished. Many through these extremities, being weery of life, digged holes in the earth and there hidd themselves till they famished. Soe lamentable was our scarsitie that we were constrayned to eate Doggs, Catts, ratts, Snakes, Toadstooles, horse hides and what nott, one man out of the mysery that he endured, killinge his wiefe powdered [salted] her upp to eate her, for which he was burned. Many besides fedd on the Corps of dead men, and one who had gotten unsatiable, out of custome to that foode could not be restrayned, untill such tyme as he was executed for it.

GOURMET FOOD. *Advertisement from the* Boston Gazette, *September 19, 1752.*

John Ingram the Original Flower of Mustard Maker, from Lisbon, now living at the House of Mrs. Townsend, near Oliver's Dock, Boston, Prepares Flower of Mustard to such Perfection, by a Method unknown to any Person but himself, that it retains its Strength, Flavour and Colour Seven Years; being mix'd with hot or cold water, in a Minute's Time it makes the strongest Mustard ever eat, not in the least Bitter, yet of a delicate and delightful Flavour, and gives a most surprising grateful Taste to Beef, Pork, Lamb, Fish, Sallad, or other Sauces. It is approved of by divers eminent Physicians as the only Remedy in the Universe in all nervous Disorders, sweetens all the Juices, and rectifies the whole Mass of Blood to Admiration. If close stopt it will keep its Strength and Virtue Seven years in any Climate. Merchants and Captains of Ships shall have good Allowance to sell again.

ON PAROLE. *After the Hessian general Baron von Riedesel surrendered at Saratoga in 1777, the baroness and her children were released on parole to make their way to New York.*

One day we came to a pretty little place, but our supply wagon not having been able to follow us, we could not endure our hunger longer. Observing a quantity of butcher's meat in the house in which we put up, I begged the hostess to let me have some. "I have," answered she, "several different kinds. There is beef, veal, and mutton." My mouth already watered at the prospect. "Let me have some," I said, "I will pay you well for it." Snapping her fingers almost under my very nose, she replied, "You shall not have a morsel of it. Why have you come out of your land to kill us, and waste our goods and possessions? Now you are our prisoners; it is, therefore, our turn to torment you." "See," rejoined I, "these poor children, they are almost dead with hunger." She remained inflexible. But when, finally, my three and a half year old little daughter, Caroline, came up to her, seized her by the hand, and said to her in English, "Good woman, I am very hungry!" she could not longer withstand her: she took her in a room and gave her an egg. "No," said the good little child, "I have still two sisters." At this the woman was touched, and gave her three eggs, saying, "I am just as angry as ever, but I cannot withstand the child." She then became more gentle, and offered me bread and milk. I made tea for ourselves. The woman eyed us longingly, for the Americans love it very much; but they had resolved to drink it no longer, as the famous duty on the tea had occasioned the war. I offered her a cup, and poured out for her a saucer of tea. This mollified her completely, and she begged me to follow her into the kitchen, where I found the husband gnawing at a pig's tail, while his wife, to my great satisfaction, brought out of the cellar a basket of potatoes. When she came back he reached out to her his tit-bit. She ate some of it, and gave it back to him in a little while, when he again began to feast upon it. I saw this singular mutual entertainment with amazement and disgust; but he believed that hunger made me begrudge it him, and he reached out to me the already thoroughly gnawed tail. What should I do? Throw it away, and not only injure his feelings, but lose my loved basket of potatoes! I accordingly took it, pretended to eat it, and quietly threw it into the fire. We had now made our entire peace with them. They gave me my potatoes, and I made a good supper off them, with excellent butter.

SOUTHERN COMFORT. *In a letter to his sister Betty back in New England in 1833, Henry Barnard rejoices in the hospitality he is enjoying in Virginia.*

For the last week I have had a succession of feasts. I accompanied Mrs. Campbell who is one of the most devoted mothers and well educated women I ever met with and her daughter Miss Betty, a beautiful sprightly accomplished girl, to Shirley, the seat of the Carter family. Mrs. Carter is of a high and wealthy family, and is one of the plainest most unassuming women, you will meet with any where. Now, that you may understand how we lived there, and how one of these large establishments was carried on, I will describe a single day there. . . .

When you wake in the morning, you are surprised to find that a servant has been in, and without disturbing you, built up a large fire—taken out your clothes and brushed them, and done the same with your boots—brought in hot water to shave, and indeed stands ready to do your bidding—as soon as you are dressed, you walk down into the dining room—At eight o'clock you take your seat at the breakfast table of rich mahogany—each plate standing separate on its own little cloth—Mr. Carter will sit at one end of the table and Mrs. Carter at the other—Mrs. C. will send you by two little black boys, as fine a cup of coffee as you ever tasted, or a cup of tea—it is fashionable here to drink a cup of tea after coffee—Mr. Carter has a fine cold ham before him of the real Virginia flavor—this is all the meat you will get in the morning, but the servant will bring you hot muffins and corn batter cakes every 2 minutes—you will find on the table also, loaf wheat bread, hot and cold—corn bread—

After breakfast visitors consult their pleasure—if they wish to ride, horses are ready at their command—read, there are books enough in the Library,—write, fire and writing materials are ready in his room—The Master and Mistress of the House are not expected to entertain visitors till an hour or two before dinner, which is usually at 3. If company has been invited to the dinner they will begin to come about 1—Ladies in carriage and gentlemen horseback—After making their toilet, the company amuse themselves in the parlor—about a half hour before dinner, the gentlemen are invited out to take grog. When dinner is ready . . . Mr. Carter politely takes a Lady by the hand and leads the way into the dining room, and is followed by the rest, each lady led by a gentleman. Mrs. C. is at one end of the table with a large dish of rich soup, and Mr. C. at the other, with a saddle of fine mutton, scattered round the table, you may choose for yourself, ham—beef—turkey—ducks—eggs with greens—etc—etc—for vegetables, potatoes, beets—hominy—This last you will find always at dinner, it is made of their white corn and beans and is a very fine dish—after you have dined, there circulates a bottle of sparkling champagne. After that off passes the things, and the *upper* table cloth, and upon that is placed the dessert, consisting of fine plum pudding, tarts, etc, etc,—after this comes ice cream, West India preserves—peaches preserved in brandy, etc,—When you have eaten this, off goes the second table cloth, and then upon the bare mahogany table is set the figs, raisins, and almonds, and before Mr. Carter is set 2 or 3 bottles of wine—Madeira, Port, and a sweet wine for the Ladies—he fills his glass, and pushes them on, after the glasses are all filled, the gentlemen pledge their services to the Ladies, and down goes the wine, after the first and second glass the ladies retire, and the gentlemen begin to circulate the bottle briskly. You are at liberty however to follow the Ladies as soon as you please, who after music and a little chit chat prepare for their ride home.

A TOLERABLE GOOD DINNER. *From the diary of William Johnson, a prosperous free black living in antebellum Natchez. His friend McCary— "Mc"—was also a free black.*

1836, November 11. Thare were to Day Several of us went into the Swamp a Duck hunting. We went way Down to the Cypress Buyio. Our game was as follows. Mc got One Duck, one squerrill, 1 wood cock, 1 King Fisher, 1 Pelican—Mr Minet Killed 1 Duck & wounded a Brant, so he told me—and I Killed 6 Ducks, 1 squerrel, 1 Loon, 1 wood Cock, 1 King Fisher,   Mr Hanchet get 3 Ducks, 1 squerril Mr Harrison get 2 Ducks, 1 squerril. Maj Miller came to Natchez—I forgot to mention that when we were a coming Home that Mr Minet got thrown twice by that Little Sorril mare of mine, the way that he was first trowned was by McCarys Shooting off his gun behind the Horses. Mr Hanchet was thrown at the Same time—Mc and myself had a tolerable good Dinner—We had as follows—Mc had two Bottles of Medoc Clarlet, 1 Bottle of Champagne wine, Buiscuit Egg Bread, P. pork, 1 Broiled Chicken and Beef Stake, I had a piece of good Bacon, wheat Bread, Oysters in Flitters, one large Bottle of Anneset, one Dozen Orenges, 1 small Bottle of Muscat wine. Minet Brought a pint of whiskey or Brandy, I cant know which, but he Drank it up himself—Mc had a Bottle of Brandy & honey.

BREAKFAST. *In 1848, E. Gould Buffum left the army, which he had joined as a volunteer for the war with Mexico, and headed for the recently discovered California gold mines. Here he recalls how he and his companions went to Culoma to buy provisions and get a meal.*

We reached the mill about nine o'clock in the morning, a little too late to get a breakfast at one of the stores, where sometimes the proprietor was sufficiently generous to accommodate a traveler with a meal for the moderate price of five dollars. The only resource was to lay a cloth on the storekeeper's counter, and make a breakfast on crackers, cheese, and sardines. In order not to make a rush upon the trade, we divided ourselves into three parties, each going to a different store. Mac and myself went together, and made a breakfast from the following items;—one box of sardines, one pound of sea-biscuit, one pound of butter, a half-pound of cheese, and two bottles of ale. We ate and drank with great gusto, and when we had concluded our repast called for the bill. It was such a curiosity in the annals of a retail grocery business, that I preserved it, and here are the items. . . .

One box of sardines	$16.00
One pound of hard bread	$ 2.00
One pound of butter	$ 6.00
A half-pound of cheese	$ 3.00
Two bottles of ale	$16.00
Total.	$43.00

A pretty expensive breakfast, thought we!

DAKOTA TREAT. *Francis Parkman was a twenty-three-year-old Harvard graduate when he set out on a journey west to study Indian life and improve his health. The result was* The Oregon Trail, *published in 1849, from which comes this account of a dinner party. Reynal and Raymond were guides.*

As I left the lodge next morning, I was saluted by howling and yelping all around the village, and half its canine population rushed forth to the attack. Being as cowardly as they were clamorous, they kept jumping about me at a distance of a few yards, only one little cur about ten inches long having spirit enough to make a direct assault. He dashed violently at the leather tassel which in Dakota fashion was trailing behind the heel of my moccasin, and kept his hold, growling and snarling all the while, though every step I made almost jerked him over on his back. As I knew that the eyes of the whole village were on the watch to see if I showed any sign of fear, I walked forward without looking to the right or left, surrounded wherever I went by this magical circle of dogs. When I came to Reynal's lodge I sat down by it, on which the dogs dispersed growling to their respective quarters. Only one large white one remained, running about before me and showing his teeth. I called him, but he only growled the more. I looked at him well. He was fat and sleek; just such a dog as I wanted. "My friend," thought I, "you shall pay for this. I will have you eaten this very morning!"

I intended that day to give the Indians a feast, by way of conveying a favorable impression of my character and dignity; and a white dog is the dish which the customs of the Dakota prescribe for all occasions of formality and importance. I consulted Reynal; he soon discovered that an old woman in the next lodge was the owner of the white dog. I took a gaudy cotton handkerchief and, laying it on the ground, arranged some vermilion, beads, and other trinkets upon it. Then the old squaw was summoned. I pointed to the dog and to the handkerchief. She gave a scream of delight, snatched up the prize, and vanished with it into her lodge. For a few more trifles I engaged the services of two other squaws, each of whom took the white dog by one of his paws, and led him away behind the lodges. Having killed him, they threw him into a fire to singe; then chopped him up and put him into two large kettles to boil. Meanwhile I told Raymond to fry in buffalo fat what little flour we had left, and also to make a kettle of tea as an additional luxury.

The Big Crow's squaw was briskly at work sweeping out the lodge for the approaching festivity. I confided to my host himself the task of inviting the guests, thinking that I might thereby shift from my own shoulders the odium of neglect and oversight.

When feasting is in question, one hour of the day serves an Indian as well as another. My entertainment came off at about eleven o'clock. At that hour Reynal and Raymond walked across the area of the village, to the admiration of the inhabitants, carrying the two kettles of dog meat slung on a pole between them. These they placed in the center of the lodge, and then went back for the bread and tea. Meanwhile I had put on a pair of brilliant moccasins, and substituted for my old buckskin frock a coat which I had brought with me in view of such public occasions. I also made careful use of the razor, an operation which no man will neglect who desires to gain the good opinion of Indians. Thus attired, I seated myself between Reynal and Raymond at the head of the lodge. Only a few minutes elapsed before all the guests had come in and were seated on the ground, wedged together in a close circle. Each brought with him a wooden bowl to hold his share of the repast. When all were assembled, two of the officials called "soldiers" by the white men came forward with ladles made of the horn of the Rocky Mountain sheep, and began to distribute the feast, assigning a double share to the old men and chiefs. The dog vanished with astonishing celerity, and each guest turned his dish bottom upward to show that all was gone. Then the bread was distributed in its turn, and finally the tea. As the soldiers poured it out into the same wooden bowls that had served for the substantial part of the meal, I thought it had a particularly curious and uninviting color.

"Oh," said Reynal, "there was not tea enough, so I stirred some soot in the kettle to make it look strong."

Fortunately an Indian's palate is not very discriminating. The tea was well sweetened, and that was all they cared for.

NEW YEAR'S DAY DINNER. *From a letter home written by Abigail Malick, member of a pioneering family in Oregon Territory, in 1852.*

Now I suppose you Would Wish to know What We had for Dinner. . . . Well We had Rosted Ducks and Fat Chickens And Rosted pig and Sausages And green Apl pie And Mince pies and Custard pies And Cakes of difrent kindes Inglish goosburyes And Plums Blue And green Gages And Siberian crab Apples And oregon Apples. . . . Like wise Buter And Sturson pikles and Beet pickles And Sauce and Bread and Mashed potatoes and Oister pie And Coffe And Tea to be shore.

Now I Must tel you What other preserves that I have. I have peaches And citrons And Sweet Aples, Crab Aples Jelley And Tomatoes And Mince And pairs and Aple Butter. And now I will Tel you of the Rest of My Winter Suplies. I have A plentey of Butter And Milk and a Thousand pounds of Salman and Plentey Cabage And Turnips And A Bout A Hundred and Fiftey Bushel of potatoes And plentey of dried fruits—Aples and Black Buryes the Best that I evr saw. . . . I never Saw Sutch Black Buryes and Ras Bryes As There Is in this Countrey in All My Life Time. . . . O yes I Have plentey Shougar Laid in For Winter This Year Two, And Salt.

BLIZZARD. *Laura Ingalls Wilder on life in De Smet, South Dakota, during the winter of 1880–81.*

De Smet was built as the railroad went thru, out in the midst of the great Dakota prairies far ahead of the farming settlements, and the first winter of its existence it was isolated from the rest of the world from December 1 until May 10 by the fearful blizzards that piled the snow 40 feet deep on the railroad tracks. The trains could not get thru. It was at the risk of life that anyone went even a mile from shelter, for the storms came up so quickly and were so fierce it was literally impossible to see the hand before the face and men have frozen to death within a few feet of shelter because they did not know they were near safety.

The small supply of provisions in town soon gave out. The last sack of flour sold for $50 and the last of the sugar at $1 a pound. There was some wheat on hand, brought in the fall before for seed in the spring, and two young men dared to drive 15 miles to where a solitary settler had also laid in his supply of seed wheat. They brought it in on sleds. There were no mills in town or country so this wheat was all ground in the homes in coffee mills. Everybody ground wheat, even the children taking their turns, and the resultant whole wheat flour made good bread. It was also a healthful food and there was not a case of sickness in town that winter.

It may be that the generous supply of fresh air had something to do with the general good health. Air is certainly fresh when the thermometer registers all the way from 15 to 40 degrees below zero with the wind moving at blizzard speed. In the main street of the town, snow drifts in one night were piled as high as the second stories of the houses and packed hard enough to drive over and the next night the wind might sweep the spot bare. As the houses were new and unfinished, so that the snow would blow in and drift across us as we slept, fresh air was not a luxury. The houses were not overheated in daytime either, for the fuel gave out early in the winter and all there was left with which to cook and keep warm was the long prairie hay. A handful of hay was twisted into a rope, then doubled and allowed to twist back on itself, and the two ends came together in a knot, making what we called "a stick of hay."

It was a busy job to keep a supply of these "sticks" ahead of a hungry stove when the storm winds were blowing, but everyone took his turn good naturedly. There is something in living close to the great elemental forces of nature that causes people to rise above small annoyances and discomforts.

A train got thru May 10 and stopped at the station. All the men in town were down at the tracks to meet it, eager for supplies, for even the wheat had come to short rations. They found that what had been sent into the hungry town was a trainload of machinery. Luckily, there were also two emigrant cars well supplied with provisions, which were taken out and divided among the people. Our days of grinding wheat in coffee mills were over.

PRISON FARE. *From* The Road, *by Jack London. The author, then aged eighteen, has just been sentenced to prison for vagrancy; this was in 1894, in upper New York.*

For two days I toiled in the prison-yard. It was heavy work, and, in spite of the fact that I malingered at every opportunity, I was played out. This was because of the food. No man could work hard on such food. Bread and water, that was all that was given us. Once a week we were supposed to get meat; but this meat did not always go around, and since all nutriment had first been boiled out of it in the making of soup, it didn't matter whether one got a taste of it once a week or not.

Furthermore, there was one vital defect in the bread-and-water diet. While we got plenty of water, we did not get enough of the bread.

HARD TIMES IN NEW YORK.—THE SOUP-HOUSE NO. 110 CENTRE STREET, ONE OF THE NUMBER INSTITUTED BY COMMODORE JAMES GORDON BENNETT, AND SUPERINTENDED BY L. DELMONICO.

Hard times in New York—the Soup House, 1874. Wood engraving from
Frank Leslie's Illustrated Newspaper.

A ration of bread was about the size of one's two fists, and three rations a day were given to each prisoner. There was one good thing, I must say, about the water—it was hot. In the morning it was called "coffee," at noon it was dignified as "soup," and at night it masqueraded as "tea." But it was the same old water all the time. The prisoners called it "water bewitched." In the morning it was black water, the color being due to boiling it with burnt breadcrusts. At noon it was served minus the color, with salt and a drop of grease added. At night it was served with a purplish-auburn hue that defied all speculation; it was darn poor tea, but it was dandy hot water.

After two days of work in the yard I was taken out of my cell and made a trusty, a "hall-man." At morning and night we served the bread to the prisoners in their cells; but at twelve o'clock a different method was used. The convicts marched in from work in a long line. As they entered the door of our hall, they broke the lock-step and took their hands down from the shoulders of their linemates. Just inside the door were piled trays of bread, and here also stood the First Hall-man and two ordinary hall-men. I was one of the two. Our task was to hold the trays of bread as the line of convicts filed past. As soon as the tray, say, that I was holding was emptied, the other hall-man took my place with a full tray. And when his was emptied, I took his place with a full tray. Thus the line tramped steadily by, each man reaching with his right hand and taking one ration of bread from the extended tray.

The task of the First Hall-man was different. He used a club. He stood beside the tray and watched. The hungry wretches could never get over the delusion that sometime they could manage to get two rations of bread out of the tray. But in my experience that sometime never came. The club of the First Hall-man had a way of flashing out—quick as the stroke of a tiger's claw—to the hand that dared ambitiously. The First Hall-man was a good judge of distance, and he had smashed so many hands with that club that he had become infallible. He never missed. . . .

At times, while all these men lay hungry in their cells, I have seen a hundred or so extra rations of bread hidden away in the cells of the hall-men. It would seem absurd, our retaining this bread. But it was one of our grafts. . . . We peddled the bread. Once a week, the men who worked in the yard received a five-cent plug of chewing tobacco. This chewing tobacco was the coin of the realm. Two or three rations of bread for a plug was the way we exchanged, and they traded, not because they loved tobacco less, but because they loved bread more.

Here was a hungry man without any tobacco. Maybe he was a profligate and had used it all up on himself. Very good; he had a pair of suspenders. I exchanged a half a dozen rations of bread for it—or a dozen rations if the suspenders were very good. Now I never wore suspenders, but that didn't matter. Around the corner lodged a long-timer, doing ten years for manslaughter. He wore suspenders, and he wanted a pair. I could trade them to him for some of his meat. Meat was what I wanted. Or perhaps he had a tattered, paper-covered novel. That was treasure-trove. I could read it and then trade it off to the bakers for cake, or to the cooks for meat and vegetables, or to the firemen for decent coffee, or to some one or other for the newspaper that occasionally filtered in, heaven alone knows how. The cooks, bakers, and firemen were prisoners like myself, and they lodged in our hall in the first row of cells over us.

In short, a full-grown system of barter obtained in the Erie County Pen. There was even money in circulation. This money was sometimes smuggled in by the short-timers, more frequently came from the barber-shop graft, where the newcomers were mulcted, but most of all flowed from the cells of the long-timers—though how they got it I don't know.

But that money was made in the Pen I had direct evidence, for I was cell-mate quite a time with the Third Hall-Man. He had over sixteen dollars. He used to count his money every night after nine o'clock, when we were locked in. Also, he used to tell me each night what he would do to me if I gave away on him to the other hall-men. You see, he was afraid of being robbed, and danger threatened him from three different directions. There were the guards. A couple of them might jump upon him, give him a good beating for alleged insubordination, and throw him into the "solitaire" (the dungeon); and in the mix-up that sixteen dollars of his would take wings. Then again, the First Hall-man could have taken it all away from him by threatening to dismiss him and fire him back to hard labor in the prison-yard. And yet again, there were the ten of us who were ordinary hall-men. If we got an inkling of his wealth, there was a large liability, some quiet day, of the whole bunch of us getting him into a corner and dragging him down. Oh, we were wolves, believe me—just like the fellows who do business in Wall Street.

He had good reason to be afraid of us, and so had I to be afraid of him. He was a huge, illiterate brute, an ex-Chesapeake-Bay-oyster-pirate, an "ex-con" who had done five years in Sing Sing, and a general all-around stupidly carnivorous beast. He used to trap sparrows that flew into our hall through the open bars. When he made a capture, he hurried away with it into his cell, where I have seen him crunching bones and spitting out feathers as he bolted it raw. Oh, no, I never gave away on him to the other hall-men. This is the first time I have mentioned his sixteen dollars.

THE GILDED AGE. *A few tips on how to serve dinner from Ward McAllister, author of* Society As I Have Found It, *and the man who coined the term "The Four Hundred" (the number of people who constituted "true" New York society). His book was published in 1890.*

And now, leaving the fish, we come to the *pièce de résistance* of the dinner, called the *relevé.* No Frenchman will ever willingly cook a ladies' dinner and give anything coarser or heavier than a *filet de bœuf.* He will do it, if he has to, of course, but he will think you a barbarian if you order him to do it. I eschew the mushroom and confine myself to the truffle in the treatment of the *filet.* I oftentimes have a *filet à la moelle de bœuf,* or *à la jardinière.* In the fall of the year, turkey *poules à la Bordelaise, à la Toulouse,* or a saddle of Southdown mutton or lamb, are a good substitute. Let me here say that the American turkey, as found on Newport Island, all its feathers being jet black and its diet grasshoppers, is exceptionally fine.

Now for the *entrées.* In a dinner of twelve or fourteen, one or two hot *entrées* and one cold is sufficient. If you use the truffle with the *filet,* making a black sauce, you must follow it with a white sauce, as a *riz de veau à la Toulouse,* or a *suprême de volaille;* then a *chaud-froid,* say of *pâté de foie gras en Bellevue,* which simply means *pâté de foie gras* incased in jelly. Then a hot vegetable, as artichokes, sauce *Barigoule,* or *Italienne,* or asparagus, sauce *Hollandaise.* Then your *sorbet,* known in France as *la surprise,* as it is an ice, and produces on the mind the effect that the dinner is finished, when the grandest dish of the dinner makes its appearance in the shape of the roast canvasbacks, woodcock, snipe, or truffled capons, with salad.

A Russian salad is a pleasing novelty at times, and is more attractive if it comes in the shape of a *Macédoine de légumes.* Camembert cheese, with a biscuit, with which you serve your Burgundy, your old Port, or your Johannisberg, the only place in the dinner where you can introduce this latter wine. A genuine Johannisberg, I may say here, by way of parenthesis, is rare in this country, for if obtained at the Chateau, it is comparatively a dry wine; if it is, as I have often seen it, still lusciously sweet after having been here twenty years or more, you may be sure it is not a genuine Chateau wine.

The French always give a hot pudding, as pudding *suédoise,* or a *croûte au Madère,* or *ananas,* but I always omit this dish to shorten the dinner. . . .

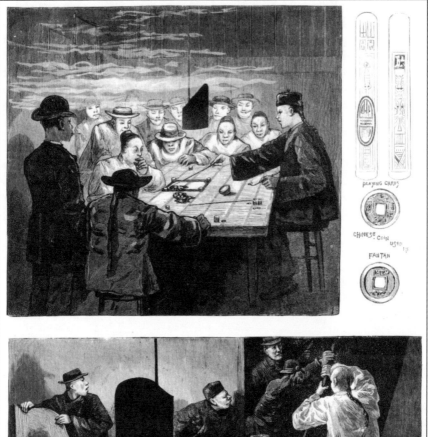

A game of Fan-tan: The dealer removes coins from the pile four at a time;
the gamblers bet on how many are left at the end; the police interrupt.
From *Frank Leslie's Illustrated Newspaper*, December 1887.

CHAPTER

7

PLAYING

I N   E A R L Y   T I M E S ,   W H E N   P E O P L E   had to work six full days a week and then keep the seventh holy, they were spared at least some of today's anxieties. There was no problem of what to do on Saturday night, because that was when the Sabbath began. No one argued about where to spend the family vacation, because people didn't have vacations.

To be sure, there were holidays: New Year's, the Fourth of July, election days, Christmas. But these were hardly enough to satisfy the natural human desire to enjoy life, and as the country grew and money became more plentiful and people became less in thrall to puritanical killjoys, the number and variety of sports, shows, games, and other diversions gradually increased. The theater, once banned as sinful in itself and as a haunt for "low women," grew in popularity, even if—or perhaps because—many of the shows were of the minstrel or melodrama type. Quilting and corn-husking bees turned chores into parties. Novel-reading ceased to be regarded as a waste of time, and an author such as Charles Dickens was treated as a celebrity. The East had genteel parlor games and fancy dress balls, and the West buffalo hunts and shoot-'em-up saloons. By the end of the last century, with the arrival of Edison's kinetoscope, there was something for just about everyone and entertainment was well on its way to becoming a major industry.

This chapter falls into three parts: holidays, starting with New Year's and ending with Christmas; a review of some sports, games, and shows; and "The Pursuit of Pleasure"—accounts of some notable good times.

HOLIDAYS

NEW YEAR'S DAY AND MAY DAY IN NEW AMSTERDAM. *Governor Peter Stuyvesant lays down the law in December 1655. The high-handed and irascible Stuyvesant, director general from 1647 to 1664, was described by one of his enemies as a man who "railed frequently at the Councillors for this thing and the other with ugly words which would better suit the fish-market than the Council chamber."*

Whereas experience has manifested and shown us, that on New Year's and May days much drunkenness and other irregularities are committed besides other sorrowful accidents such as woundings frequently arising therefrom, by Firing, May planting, and Carousing, in addition to the unnecessary waste of powder, to prevent which for the future, the Director General and Council expressly forbid that from now henceforward there shall be, within this Province of New Netherland on New Years or May Days, any Firing of Guns, or any Planting of May Poles, or any beating of Drums, or any treating with Brandy, wine or Beer; and all such and greater dangers and mischiefs to prevent, a fine of twelve guilders shall be imposed for the first offence; double for the second, and an arbitrary Correction for the third—to wit one third for the poor, and one third for the Officer and one third for the Informer.

FANDANGO. *Twenty-three-year-old James Pattie, along with a party of beaver-trappers and traders, has arrived in southern New Mexico, at the village of Perdido, after a difficult and dangerous trek overland from St. Louis. His "Indian friends" were Navajos. This account is taken from* Personal Narrative of James O. Pattie of Kentucky.

On New Year's eve, January 1st, 1827, the Spaniards of the place gave a fandango, or Spanish ball. All our company were invited to it, and went. We appeared before the Alcaide, clad not unlike our Indian friends; that is to say, we were dressed in deer skin, with leggins, moccasins and hunting shirts, all of this article, with the addition of the customary Indian article of dress around the loins, and this was of red cloth, not an article of which had been washed since we left the Copper Mines. It may be imagined that we did not cut a particular dandy-like figure, among people, many of whom were rich, and would be considered well dressed any where. Notwithstanding this, it is a strong proof of their politeness, that we were civilly treated by the ladies, and had the pleasure of dancing with the handsomest and richest of them. When the ball broke up, it seemed to be expected of us, that we should each escort a lady home, in whose company we passed the night, and we none of us brought charges of severity against our fair companions.

The fandango room was about forty by eighteen or twenty feet, with a brick floor raised four or five feet above the earth. That part of the room in which the ladies sat, was carpetted with carpetting on the benches, for them to sit on. Simple benches were provided for the accommodation of the gentlemen. Four men sang to the music of a violin and guitar. All that chose to dance stood up on the floor, and at the striking up of a certain note of the music, they all commenced clapping their hands. The ladies then advanced, one by one, and stood facing their partners. The dance then changed to a waltz, each man taking his lady rather unceremoniously, and they began to whirl round, keeping true, however, to the music, and increasing the swiftness of their whirling. Many of the movements and figures seemed very easy, though we found they required practise, for we must certainly have made a most laughable appearance in their eyes, in attempting to practise them. Be that as it may, we cut capers with the nimblest, and what we could not say, we managed by squeezes of the hand, and little signs of that sort, and passed the time to a charm.

ELECTION DAY IN KENTUCKY, 1830. *One year before Alexis de Tocqueville arrived in this country to study democracy in America, George Prentice, writing for a New England newspaper, reports on how the system worked in the Bluegrass State.*

An election in Kentucky lasts three days, and during that period whisky and apple toddy flow through our cities and villages like the Euphrates through ancient Babylon. I must do Lexington the justice to say that matters were conducted here with tolerable propriety; but in Frankfort, a place which I had the curiosity to visit on the last day of the election, Jacksonism and drunkenness stalked triumphant—"an unclean pair of lubberly giants."

A number of runners, each with a whisky bottle poking its long neck from his pocket, were busily employed bribing voters, and each party kept half a dozen bullies under pay, genuine specimens of Kentucky alligatorism, to flog every poor fellow who should attempt to vote illegally. A half a hundred of mortar would scarcely fill up the chinks of the skulls that were broken on that occasion. I barely escaped myself. One of the runners came up to me, and slapping me on the shoulder with his right hand, and a whisky bottle with his left, asked me if I was a voter. "No," said I. "Ah, never mind," quoth the fellow, pulling a corn cob out of the neck of the bottle, and shaking it up to the best advantage, "jest take a swig at the cretur and toss in a vote

for old Hickory's boys—I'll fight for you, damme!" Here was a temptation, to be sure; but after looking alternately at the bottle and the bullies who were standing ready with their sledge-hammer fists to knock
down all interlopers, my fears prevailed and I lost my whisky.

Shortly after this I witnessed a fight that would have done honor to
Mendoza and Big Ben. A great ruffian-looking scoundrel, with arms
like a pair of cables knotted at the ends, and a round black head that
looked like a forty-pound cannon shot, swaggered up to the polls and
threw in his bit of paper, and was walking off in triumph.

"Stop, friend," exclaimed one of the Salt River Roarers, stepping
deliberately up to him, "are you a voter?" "Yes, by—," replied he of the
Bullet Head. "That's a lie," rejoined the Roarer, "and you must just
prepare yourself to go home an old man, for I'll be damned if I don't
knock you into the middle of your ninety-ninth year." "Ay, ay," replied
the other, "come on, then; I'll ride you to hell, whipped up with the
sea sarpint!"

They had now reached an open space, and the Salt River bully,
shaking his fist a moment by way of a feint, dropped his chin suddenly
upon his bosom and pitched headforemost toward the stomach of his
antagonist with the whole force of his gigantic frame. Bullet Head,
however, was on his guard, and, dodging aside with the quickness of
lightning to avoid the shock, gave the assailant a blow that sent him
staggering against a whisky table, where he fell to the ground amid the
crash of bottles, mugs, and tumblers. Nothing daunted by this temporary discomfiture, the bully gathered himself up, and with a single
muttered curse renewed his place in front of his foe.

Several blows were now given on both sides with tremendous
effect, and in a few moments the Salt River boy, watching his opportunity, repeated the maneuver in which he had first been foiled. This
time he was successful. His head was planted directly in his antagonist's stomach, who fell backward with such force that I had no expectation of his ever rising again.

"Is the scoundrel done for?" inquired the temporary victor, walking up and looking down on his prostrate foe. Bullet Head spoke not,
but with the bound of a wildcat leaped to his feet and grappled with
his enemy. It was a trial of strength, and the combatants tugged and
strained and foamed at the mouth, and twined like serpents around
each other's bodies, till at length the strength of the Bullet Head prevailed and his opponent lay struggling beneath him.

"Gouge him!" "Gouge him!" exclaimed a dozen voices, and the
topmost combatant seized his victim by the hair and was preparing to
follow the advice that was thus shouted in his ear, when the prostrate
man, roused by desperation and exerting a strength that seemed
superhuman, caught his assailant by the throat with a grasp like that of

fate. For a few moments the struggle seemed to cease, and then the face of the throttled man turned black, his tongue fell out of his mouth, and he rolled to the ground as senseless as a dead man.

I turned away a confirmed believer in the doctrine of total depravity.

JULY 4, 1837. *The celebrations in New York as witnessed by a visiting Englishman, Captain Frederick Marryat, famous in his day as the author of nautical tales and* The Children of the New Forest.

The commemoration commenced, if the day did not, on the evening of the 3rd, by the municipal police going round and pasting up placards, informing the citizens of New York that all persons letting off fireworks would be taken into custody, which notice was immediately followed up by the little boys proving their independence of the authorities, by letting off squibs, crackers, and bombs—and cannons, made out of shin bones, which flew in the face of every passenger, in the exact ratio that the little boys flew in the face of the authorities. This continued the whole night, and thus was ushered in the great and glorious day, illumined by a bright and glaring sun (as if bespoken on purpose by the mayor and corporation), with the thermometer at 90° in the shade. The first sight which met the eye after sunrise was the

"The Fourth of July in the country," a drawing after Thomas Worth, from *Harper's Weekly*, July 11, 1868. The orator is in full patriotic flow, but few in the crowd seem to be listening.

precipitate escape, from a city visited with the plague of gunpowder, of respectable or timorous people in coaches, carriages, wagons, and every variety of vehicle. "My kingdom for a horse!" was the general cry of all those who could not stand fire.

In the meanwhile, the whole atmosphere was filled with independence. Such was the quantity of American flags which were hoisted on board of the vessels, hung out of windows, or carried about by little boys, that you saw more stars at noonday than ever could be counted on the brightest night. On each side of the whole length of Broadway were ranged booths and stands, similar to those at an English fair, and on which were displayed small plates of oysters, with a fork stuck in the board opposite to each plate; clams sweltering in the hot sun; pineapples, boiled hams, pies, puddings, barley-sugar, and many other indescribables. But what was most remarkable, Broadway being three miles long, and the booths lining each side of it, in every booth there was a roast pig, large or small, as the centre attraction. Six miles of roast pig! and that in New York City alone; and roast pig in every other city, town, hamlet, and village in the Union. What association can there be between roast pig and independence?

Let it not be supposed that there was any deficiency in the very necessary articles of potation on this auspicious day: no! the booths were loaded with porter, ale, cider, mead, brandy, wine, ginger-beer, pop, soda-water, whiskey, rum, punch, gin slings, cocktails, mint juleps, besides many other compounds, to name which nothing but the luxuriance of American-English could invent a word. . . .

Martial music sounded from a dozen quarters at once; and as you turned your head, you tacked to the first bars of a march from one band, the concluding bars of Yankee Doodle from another. At last the troops of militia and volunteers, who had been gathering in the park and other squares, made their appearance, well dressed and well equipped, and, in honour of the day, marching as independently as they well could. I did not see them go through many maneuvres, but there was one which they appeared to excel in, and that was grounding arms and eating pies.

I found that the current went toward Castle Garden, and away I went with it. There the troops were all collected on the green, shaded by the trees, and the effect was very beautiful. The artillery and infantry were drawn up in a line pointing to the water. The officers in their regimental dresses and long white feathers, generals and aides-de-camp, colonels, commandants, majors, all galloping up and down in front of the line—white horses and long tails appearing the most fashionable and correct. The crowds assembled were, as American crowds usually are, quiet and well behaved. I recognized many of my literary friends turned into generals, and flourishing their swords instead of their pens.

The scene was very animating; the shipping at the wharfs were loaded with star-spangled banners; steamers, paddling in every direction, were covered with flags; the whole beautiful Sound was alive with boats and sailing vessels, all flaunting with pennants and streamers. . . .

Then the troops marched up into town again, and so did I follow them as I used to do the reviews in England, when a boy. All creation appeared to be independent on this day; some of the horses particularly so, for they would not keep "in no line not no how." Some preferred going sideways like crabs, others went backwards, some would not go at all, others went a great deal too fast, and not a few parted company with their riders, whom they kicked off just to show their independence; but let them go which way they would, they could not avoid the squibs and crackers. And the women were in the same predicament: they might dance right, or dance left, it was only out of the frying-pan into the fire, for it was pop, pop; bang; fiz, pop, bang so that you literally trod upon gunpowder.

When the troops marched up Broadway, louder even than the music were to be heard the screams of delight from the children at the crowded windows on each side. "Ma! ma! there's pa!" "Oh! there's John." "Look at uncle on his big horse."

The troops did not march in very good order, because, independently of their not knowing how, there was a great deal of independence to contend with. At one time an omnibus and four would drive in and cut off the general and his staff from his division; at another, a cart would roll in and insist upon following close upon the band of music; so that it was a mixed procession—generals, omnibus and four, music, cartloads of bricks, troops, omnibus and pair, artillery, hackney-coach, etc. etc. Notwithstanding all this, they at last arrived at the City Hall, when those who were old enough heard the Declaration of Independence read for the sixty-first time. . . .

I was invited to dine with the mayor and corporation at the City Hall. We sat down in the Hall of Justice, and certainly, great justice was done to the dinner. . . . The crackers popped outside, and the champagne popped in. The celerity of the Americans at a public dinner is very commendable; they speak only now and then; and the toasts follow so fast that you have just time to empty your glass before you are requested to fill again. Thus the arranged toasts went off rapidly, and after them, anyone might withdraw. I waited till the thirteenth toast, the last on the paper, to wit, the ladies of America; and, having previously, in a speech from the recorder, bolted Bunker's Hill and New Orleans, I thought I might as well bolt myself, as I wished to see the fireworks, which were to be very splendid.

Unless you are an amateur, there is no occasion to go to the various places of public amusement where the fireworks are let off, for they are sent up everywhere in such quantities that you hardly know which way to turn your eyes. It is, however, advisable to go into some place of safety, for the little boys and the big boys have all got their supply of rockets, which they fire off in the streets—some running horizontally up the pavement, and sticking into the back of a passenger, and others mounting slantingdicularly and Paul-Prying into the bedroom windows on the third floor or attics, just to see how things are going on *there*. Look in any point of the compass, and you will see a shower of rockets in the sky: turn from New York to Jersey City, from Jersey City to Brooklyn, and shower is answered by shower on either side of the water. Hoboken repeats the signal; and thus it is carried on to the east, the west, the north, and the south, from Rhode Island to the Missouri, from the Canada frontier to the Gulf of Mexico. At the various gardens the combinations were very beautiful, and exceeded anything that I had witnessed in London or Paris. What with sea-serpents, giant rockets scaling heaven, Bengal lights, Chinese fires, Italian suns, fairy bowers, crowns of Jupiter, exeranthemums, Tartar temples, Vesta's diadems, magic circles, morning glories, stars of Columbia, and temples of liberty, all America was in a blaze.

JULY 4 IN OREGON. *Nettie Spencer was in her seventies when, in a 1938 Federal Writers' interview, she looked back to her girlhood in Oregon in the 1870s.*

There wasn't much social life on the farm, and I didn't pay any attention to it until I was older and moved into Salem and Corvallis. The churches didn't have any young people's organizations and they were dead serious with everything. Sermons lasted for hours and you could smell the hellfire in them. We never had church suppers or the like until way past my time. The only social thing about the church was the camp meetings. That was where most of the courting was done. When a boy would get old enough for a wife, the father would let him use the horse and buggy for a trip to the camp meeting to get him a wife.

Most of these people came to church on foot over the muddy roads. The ones who came by wagon used a hay-rack, and the mother and father sat in a chair at the front while the children were churned about in the straw strewn in the wagon bed. After a long meeting was out, neighbors had a grand hand-shaking party, and then families often invited other families to dinner.

The big event of the year was the Fourth of July. Everyone in the countryside got together on that day for the only time in the year. The new babies were shown off, and the new brides who would be exhibiting babies next year. Everyone would load their wagons with all the food they could haul and come to town early in the morning. On our first big Fourth at Corvallis, mother made two hundred gooseberry pies. There would be floats in the morning and the one that got the girl's eye was the Goddess of Liberty. She was supposed to be the most wholesome and prettiest girl in the countryside—if she wasn't, she had friends who thought she was. She rode on a hay-rack and wore a white gown. Sometimes the driver wore an Uncle Sam hat and striped pants. All along the side of the hay-rack were little girls who represented the states of the union. The smallest was always Rhode Island. Following the float would be the Oregon Agricultural College cadets, and some kind of a band.

Just before lunch some senator or lawyer would speak. These speeches always had one pattern. First, the speaker would challenge England to a fight and berate the King and say that he was a skunk. This was known as twisting the lion's tail. Then the next theme was that anyone could find freedom and liberty on our shores. The speaker would invite those who were heavy laden in other lands to come to us and find peace. The speeches were pretty firey and by that time the men who drank got into fights and called each other Englishmen. In the afternoon we had what we call the "plug uglies"—funny floats and clowns who took off on the political subjects of the day. There would be some music and then the families would start gathering together to go home. There were cows waiting to be milked and the stock to be fed and so there was no night life.

CHRISTMAS IN EDENTON, NORTH CAROLINA. *Harriet Jacobs, who wrote the autobiographical* Incidents in the Life of a Slave Girl *after her escape to freedom in 1845, recalls a festival that had its origins in West Africa.*

Every child rises early on Christmas morning to see the Johnkannaus. Without them, Christmas would be shorn of its greatest attraction. They consist of companies of slaves from the plantations, generally of the lower class. Two athletic men, in calico wrappers, have a net thrown over them, covered with all manner of bright-colored stripes. Cows' tails are fastened to their backs, and their heads are decorated with horns. A box, covered with sheepskin, is called the gumbo box. A dozen beat on this, while others strike triangles and jawbones, to which bands of dancers keep time. For a month previous they are composing songs, which are sung on this occasion. These companies, of a hundred each, turn out early in the morning, and are allowed to go round till twelve o'clock, begging for contributions. Not a door is left unvisited where there is the least chance of obtaining a penny or a glass of rum. They do not drink while they are out, but carry the rum home in jugs, to have a carousal. These Christmas donations frequently amount to twenty or thirty dollars. It is seldom that any white man

"Winter Holidays in the Southern States. Plantation frolic on Christmas Eve."
Wood engraving from *Frank Leslie's Illustrated Newspaper,* December 1857.

or child refuses to give them a trifle. If he does, they regale his ears
with the following song:—

> "Poor massa, so dey say;
> Down in de heel, so dey say;
> Got no money, so dey say;
> Not one shillin, so dey say;
> God A'mighty bress you, so dey say."

CHRISTMAS IN KANSAS. *Ida Lindgren writes to her mother back in Sweden.*
Gustaf is her husband, Magnus her brother, and Johanna is Magnus's wife. The
Lindgrens have five children. The entire group emigrated from Sweden in 1870.

5 January 1871, Manhattan, Kansas

Dear, beloved Mamma,

It is Twelfth Night today and only now have I had the first peaceful
moment during the Christmas season to write; I had meant to write just
at Christmas but didn't have time. But today I am all alone in the house
with little Anna and Ida, and so I can, I hope, be left in peace, at least
for a while. Mamma's last letter I got a few days after my birthday; thank
you for it, dear Mamma, and a thousand thanks for your unfailing love!

It was so cold, so cold, the week before Christmas, that we never felt the likes of it in Sweden. We have a thermometer with us from Sweden which cannot show anything lower than minus twenty-five degrees, but it was below that; we don't know how many degrees, but Gustaf's watch, which was in his vest pocket in among his clothes, stopped one night from the cold; there you can see that it was cold. When Gustaf warmed it up again in the morning, it started to go again; it was terrible.

We kept the fire going the whole day through and sat around the fireplace, and still we could see our breath when we talked. We piled everything we could think of on top of us at night and I sat up until midnight to tend the fire and then Gustaf got up at three and built the fire up again, and still we were so cold we thought we would get the chills, and Ida and Anna had frost on both their faces and hands, poor dears! Yes, it was hard those days and we thought we would become ill, but, thank God, no one has been sick yet, and now it is not so cold any more. . . .

I must tell you about our Christmas! On "Little Christmas Eve," Sylvan (he had been in Chicago but came here to celebrate Christmas with us) and Tekla Littorin (she is employed four miles on the other side of Manhattan) arrived, then we all went over to Magnus and his family for Christmas Eve. They had everything so fine and cozy, three rooms downstairs and the attic all in order, and a Christmas tree of green cedar with candles and bonbons and apples on it, and the coffee table set, so it was really Christmas-like, and because of that I could not tear my thoughts away from you and from my old home and the tears kept welling up! Magnus played and we were to sing, but it didn't go too well. Then we had a few Christmas presents, the finest was a rocking chair which Magnus and his family gave us. From Gustaf I got two serving dishes, since we had none before, from Olga a rolling pin for cookies and three dozen clothespins to hang up wet clothes with when you do laundry, from Hugo a pair of woolen mittens, from Littorin a knitting bag, from Hedenskog material for a little sofa which we have made for the children to sleep on, from Carlson a pair of fire tongs.

I gave Magnus and the family a sofa cover, which I sewed last summer to exhibit, and a couple of pictures of Gustaf Vasa which we had with us. Hugo gave them a pair of drinking glasses and Olga gave Magnus a pipe pouch and Johanna clothespins like those I got. Helge had himself sewn a little lamp mat for them. I gave Gustaf a pair of real coarse, strong gloves for working, and Olga, Hugo, and Helge had gotten together to buy him a hat. Olga and Hugo had earned the money themselves that they used for Christmas presents.

After we had eaten our rice pudding and Christmas cookies, we sang a few hymns and "Hosianna," and then we broke up, though we all slept there, all the bachelors in the attic, Magnus and family in the kitchen, Gustaf, the younger children, and myself in the bedroom, and Olga, Tekla, and their hired girl in the parlor. We stayed until the morning after the second day of Christmas and then we went home.

SHOWS, GAMES, AND SPORTS

INDIAN GAMES. *A Puritan view, as expressed by Roger Williams in* A Key into the Language of America, *first published in 1643.*

Their *Games* (like the *English*) are of two sorts; private and publike:

Private, and sometimes publike; A *Game* like unto the *English* Cards; yet, in stead of Cards they play with strong *Rushes*.

Secondly, they have a kinde of Dice which are Plumb [lead] stones painted, which they cast in a Tray, with a mighty noyse and sweating: Their publique *Games* are solemnized with the meeting of hundreds; sometimes thousands, and consist of many vanities, none of which I durst ever be present at, that I might not countenance and partake of their folly, after I once saw the evill of them.

The chiefe Gamesters amongst them much desire to make their Gods side with them in their Games (as our *English* Gamesters so farre also acknowledge God) therefore I have seene them keepe as a precious stone a piece of Thunderbolt, which is like unto a Chrystall, which they dig out of the ground under some tree Thunder-smitten, and from this stone they have an opinion of successe, and I have not heard any of these prove losers, which I conceive may be *Satans* policie, and Gods holy Justice to harden them for their not rising higher from the Thunderbolt, to the God that send or shoots it.

Puttuckquapuonck—A Playing Arbour. This Arbour or Play-house is made of long poles set in the earth, foure square, sixteen or twentie foot high, on which they hang great store of their stringed money, have great stakings, towne against towne, and two chosen out of the rest by course to play the *Game* at this kinde of Dice in the midst of all their Abettors, with great shouting and solemnity: beside, they have great meetings of foot-ball playing, onely in Summer, towne against towne, upon some broad sandy shoare, free from stones, or upon some soft heathie plot, because of their naked feet, at which they have great stakings, but seldome quarrell.

OTHELLO BY ANY OTHER NAME. *Until well into the eighteenth century, playgoing was widely condemned as frivolous and immoral, forcing acting companies to resort to devices such as this 1761 playbill.*

KING'S ARMS TAVERN, NEWPORT, RHODE ISLAND.
ON MONDAY, JUNE 10, AT THE PUBLIC ROOM OF THE ABOVE
INN, WILL BE DELIVERED A SERIES OF
MORAL DIALOGUES,
IN FIVE PARTS,
DEPICTING THE EVIL EFFECTS OF JEALOUSY
AND OTHER BAD PASSIONS,
AND PROVING THAT HAPPINESS CAN ONLY SPRING FROM
THE PURSUIT OF VIRTUE

MR. DOUGLAS will represent a noble and magnanimous Moor named Othello, who loves a young lady named Desdemona, and after he has married her, harbors (as in too many cases) the dreadful passion of jealousy.

> Of jealousy, our being's bane,
> Mark the small cause, and the most dreadful pain.

MR. ALLYN will depict the character of a specious villain, in the regiment of Othello, who is so base as to hate his commander on mere suspicion, and to impose on his best friend. Of such characters, it is to be feared, there are thousands in the world, and the one in question may present to us a salutary warning.

> The man that wrongs his master and his friend,
> What can he come to but a shameful end?

MR. HALLAM will delineate a young and thoughtless officer, who is traduced by Mr. Allyn, and, getting drunk, loses his situation and his general's esteem. All young men whatsoever, take example from Cassio.

> The ill effects of drinking would you see?
> Be warned, and keep from evil company.

MR. MORRIS will represent an old gentleman, the father of Desdemona, who is not cruel or covetous, but is foolish enough to dislike the noble Moor, his son-in-law, because his face is not white, forgetting that we all spring from one root. Such prejudices are very numerous and very wrong.

> Fathers beware what sense and love ye lack,
> 'Tis crime, not color, makes the being black.

MR. QUALCH will depict a fool, who wishes to become a knave, and trusting to one, gets killed by him. Such is the friendship of rogues—take heed.

> When fools would knaves become, how often you'll
> Perceive the knave not wiser than the fool.

MRS. MORRIS will represent a young and virtuous wife, who being wrongfully suspected, gets smothered (in an adjoining room) by her husband.

> Reader, attend; and e'er thou goest hence
> Let fall a tear to hapless innocence.

MRS. DOUGLAS will be her faithful attendant, who will hold out a good example to all servants, male and female, and to all people in subjection.

> Obedience and gratitude
> Are things as rare as they are good.

Various other dialogues, too numerous to mention here, will be delivered at night, all adapted to the improvement of the mind and manners. The whole will be repeated on Wednesday and Saturday. Tickets six shillings each, to be had within. Commencement at 7, conclusion at half-past 10, in order that every spectator may go home at a sober hour, and reflect upon what he has seen before he retires to rest.

> God save the king,
> And long may he sway
> East, North, and South,
> And fair America.

RARE PIG. *As recorded by Dr. Benjamin Rush of Philadelphia in his commonplace book for 1797.*

July 14. Went to see a "learned pig." He was a year old, was about 1/2 a foot high, and had cost the owner 1000 Dollars. He distinguished all the letters in the alphabet on cards and picked them up with his mouth, he spelled every word that was told him by bringing the letters of which those words were composed and laying them at his owner's feet. He did several small sums in addition, subtraction, and multiplication, he distinguished colors, and lastly he told the name of the card taken out of a pack, by taking up with his mouth the corresponding card from a pack on the floor.

A DELIGHTFUL SPORT. *John James Audubon on a popular Kentucky pastime of the early nineteenth century.*

Barking off Squirrels is delightful sport, and in my opinion requires a greater degree of accuracy than any other. I first witnessed this manner of procuring squirrels near Frankfort. The performer was the celebrated Daniel Boone. We walked out together along the Kentucky River until we reached flat land thickly covered with black walnuts, oaks and hickories. Because the nuts were generally good that year,

"Horse Racing of the Sioux Indians." Illustration by Karl Bodmer, circa 1840.

Squirrels were gamboling on every tree around us. The stout, hale, athletic Boone, in homespun hunting skirt, moccasined but bare-legged, carried a long heavy rifle. As he loaded it, he said he hoped it would prove as efficient as it had on other occasions, because he felt proud to show me his skill. He wiped it, measured powder, patched the ball with six-hundred-thread linen, and sent the charge home with a hickory rod. We moved not a step, for the Squirrels were so numerous that it was unnecessary to go after them. Boone pointed to one crouched on a branch about fifty paces off, watching us. He bade me mark the spot well, and gradually raised his rifle until the *bead* or sight was in line with the spot. A whiplike report reverberated through the woods and along the hills. Judge of my surprise when I saw that the ball had hit the piece of bark just beneath the Squirrel and shivered it into splinters. The concussion killed the animal and sent it whirling through the air as if it had been blown up by a powder-magazine explosion. Since that first interview with our veteran Boone, I have seen many others perform the feat.

STAG HUNT. *From* Retrospectives of America *by John Bernard, an English actor who lived here from 1787 to 1811.*

A friend of mine near Richmond, who had a pack of hounds, invited me to go out with him at the next meeting, proffering the use of a thoroughbred quadruped. I accepted the kindness, but more with a view of discovering what the sport consisted of than from any abstract love of it. . . .

One cool and cloudy morning I trotted with my friend to the scene of action, where I met a host of acquaintances, all of whom entertained the idea that I was a superior rider, . . . Our salutations were soon over, and we proceeded to hostilities by skulking into a dark wood, while I perceived that every eye was fixed upon me in evident expectation of something extraordinary. In a few minutes the hounds opened, a young red-deer went off, and, from the spirit of my horse and the thick array of branches, I was in some danger of following his example. Luckily, however, the game took to a field, and there, with the inspiration of the general yelling, I certainly did master two or three hedges and ditches in a style that surprised myself, and riveted my friends in their delusion. In a short time I got separated from the rest, and found myself again in that Tartarean wood where, every stump threatening a case for a surgeon, a calculating trot was the utmost I could accomplish. . . . All sound of the chase had now died away, and I found myself alone in a strange country without the slightest means of obtaining a clew to the track of my companions. In this dilemma I threw the reins on my steed's neck . . . and, at an easy canter, he carried me some miles across country without my perceiving road, house, or human being. At length, beginning to suspect his judgment, I reined up, when the cry of the hounds came suddenly upon us in the direction we were going. My Bucephalus needed neither voice nor spur to renew his best pace—bogs and brakes glided past me with fearful rapidity—and, lo! at a bound he brought me into an area where the deer had been run to bay on the edge of a deep stream, in which all the horses were splashing and snorting. I was actually *the first in at the death!* The compliments and congratulations which I now received on all sides for my extraordinary riding would take pages to enumerate. I must have crossed rocks and swamps which they had been compelled to skirt; in fact, I had done more than any hunter in Virginia had ever achieved before me. As I was not in a humor to quarrel with this reputation, I affected to refer all the merit to my horse; but, as we jogged home to dinner, I could not help settling into the conviction, how much more, after all, a man's fame in this world depends upon accident than on ability!

FOOTBALL. *Laura Russell, in her privately printed memoir,* Laura Russell Remembers, *looks back on her childhood in Plymouth, Massachusetts, in the 1830s.*

There was one boys' sport in which our brother occasionally condescended to allow us to join. This was football, but we had to pay dearly for the privilege of getting up early in the winter mornings and shivering in the back yard while he had the lion's share of the fun. There was no such thing as an Indian rubber football; the bladder of an ox or a pig was blown up inside of a case of leather or bed ticking or sometimes was used with no case at all. The bladder was kept in pickle when not in use, and in its collapsed state was put into the case and inflated through a piece of pipe stem. The delightful part assigned to one of us was to hold the slippery evil-smelling string till our brother should notify us by a sharp kick that the moment had arrived when the bladder and the case together were fully blown up, and the knot must be drawn tight. He, being of a nautical turn of mind, preferred to call it "taut." The wet, slimy twine would often slip through our numb fingers in which case we were sure to get a sharp reprimand for our clumsiness. Now and then we took a turn at the pipe stem, but being only girls, this was an indulgence rarely allowed us. Though we nearly cracked our cheeks, we were always contemptuously told that we didn't blow half hard enough. When this part of the preparation had been successfully accomplished and the case was laced up and firmly tied, our brother would kick it about the yard while we stood at a safe distance blue with cold, half hoping, half fearing, that at some time it would come near us. Occasionally it did, but he came too, and our unprotected ankles and feet shod with ankleties had a very poor chance against his thick long-legged winter boots and superior skill. I am sure we got a great many more kicks than we gave. We tried to think we enjoyed it, but at this distance of time, it does not strike me as attractive amusement.

CHILDREN'S GAMES. *In 1826, the New England author Lydia Maria Child founded the* Juvenile Miscellany, *the first American monthly magazine for children. Seven years later she published* The Girl's Own Book, *a work that combines entertainment with instruction and "contains nothing to corrupt or mislead."*

HIDE AND GO SEEK!

One goes out of the room, while the others hide a thimble, pocket handkerchief, or something of that sort. When they are ready, they call "Whoop!" and she enters. If she moves toward the place, they cry, "You burn!" "Now you burn more!" If she goes very near, they say, "Oh! you are almost blazing!" If she moves from the object, they say, "How cold she grows!" If the article is found, the one who hid it must take the next turn to seek for it.

BLIND MAN'S BUFF

This ancient game is so well known that it needs but a brief notice. One of the company is blinded, and runs round to catch the others, who all try to keep out of his grasp, at the same time that they go as near him as they can. If he catches one, and cannot tell who it is, he must let her go, and try again. Sometimes a forfeit is paid in this case; but all the varieties of blind man's buff are usually played without forfeits. One fairly caught and known, must take the blind man's place.

DOLLS

The dressing of dolls is a useful as well as a pleasant employment for little girls. If they are careful about small gowns, caps, and spencers, it will tend to make them ingenious about their own dresses, when they are older. I once knew a little girl who had twelve dolls; some of them were given her; but the greater part she herself made from rags, and her elder sister painted their lips and eyes. She took it into her head that she would dress the dolls in the costumes of different nations. No one assisted; but, by looking in a book called Manners and Customs, she dressed them all with great taste and propriety. There was the Laplander, wrapped up in furs; the African, with jewels in her nose and on her arm; the Indian, tattooed, with her hair tied tight upon the top of her head; the French lady, all bows and flounces; and the Turk in spangled robes, with turban and feather. I assure you they were an extremely pretty sight. The best thing of all was that the sewing was done with the most perfect neatness. When little girls are alone, dolls may serve for company. They can be scolded, and advised, and kissed, and taught to read, and sung to sleep—and anything else the fancy of the owner may devise.

SNOW-BALLING

I like this exercise, because it is played in the open air. Endurance of cold is a very good thing: it makes the constitution hardy. But rudeness and violence must never be allowed in this, or any other game: little girls should never forget that they are miniature ladies.

DANCING

Many people object to dancing, because they consider it a waste of time; but I believe it is only wrong when too much time is given to it, to the neglect of more important duties. Children must have exercise; and dancing is healthy, innocent, and elegant. Those who learn to dance when very young, acquire an ease of motion that can be gained in no other way; at a very early age, the joints bend easily; and if a habit of moving gracefully is then acquired, it is never lost. Little girls should practise their steps at home every day; it will serve for exercise and amusement, and tend greatly to their improvement. Great care should be taken to turn the feet outward; nothing is more awkward, either in walking or dancing, than feet that turn inward; by taking a little pains, the instep will habitually curve outward the moment the foot is raised from the floor. The arms should never remain crooked, so as to give the elbows a sharp, inelegant appearance. Care should be taken to carry the shoulders back, and the head erect; a dancer who stoops, or runs her chin out, is a pitiful sight. Here I would tell those who are round-shouldered, or carry their heads too much forward, of an excellent way to cure these bad habits: walk an hour, or more, every day, with a large heavy book balanced on your head, without any assistance from your hands. The lower orders of Egyptian women are remarkable for walking majestically and gracefully; and it is because they constantly go down to the Nile, to bring up heavy burdens of water upon their heads.

PUZZLES, RIDDLES, CHARADES

The observing reader will perceive that there are several species of puzzles, distinct from each other, and known by marks peculiar to them. Puzzles and enigmas are general terms, applied to those which come under no particular class. A Conundrum is founded on a comparison between two things resembling each other in sound, but not in sense; thus:—Why is a nail driven into timber, like a very old man? Ans. because it is *in firm* (infirm). A Riddle describes the various powers and qualities of an object in the most puzzling way possible; thus an andiron is said to stand upon three feet, to run upon none, to bear heavy burdens, to dwell in a warm climate, &c. A riddle can be translated into another language, but charades, anagrams, &c. cannot be. A Charade is made of a word divided into syllables, and each syllable described separately, thus: My first marks time, my second spends it, and my whole tells it. Watch-man.

A Rebus is composed of *initials*, instead of syllables, thus: The first letter of a weight, the beginning of what little girls will be, and the first letter of a musical instrument, make a very unmusical bird. Ounce, woman, lute—O-w-l.

A Logogriph is where the letters of any particular word are used to make other words, by being differently arranged. There is no need of using all the letters each time, and they may be used over and over again; but care must be taken to employ no letter that is not in the original word. Thus in the word *pillory,* may be found *pill, rill, lip, oil, roll, lily,* &c.

An Anagram is somewhat similar to a logogriph, but the letters are not used twice over. A phrase is taken, and the letters must all be used in another phrase made, by transposing the letters—thus in the word *potentates,* you may find just the same letters that make *ten tea-pots.* Observe no letter is added, none left out, and none used twice.

A Pun is like a conundrum: indeed, a conundrum is nothing but a pun, put in the form of a question. When a gentleman said of Mr. Hook, "Hook and I are often together," he made a very good pun. *(Hook and eye.)*

MINSTREL SHOW. *The first shows featuring white singers and comedians in blackface were staged around 1828 in Louisville, Kentucky, by T. D. Rice, who originated the so-called "Jim Crow" routine. Here Mark Twain recalls a visit by one of the touring companies.*

I remember the first negro musical show I ever saw. It must have been in the early forties. It was a new institution. In our village of Hannibal we had not heard of it before and it burst upon us as a glad and stunning surprise.

The show remained a week and gave a performance every night. Church members did not attend these performances, but all the worldlings flocked to them and were enchanted. Church members did not attend shows out there in those days. The minstrels appeared with coal-black hands and faces and their clothing was a loud and extravagant burlesque of the clothing worn by the plantation slave of the time; not that the rags of the poor slave were burlesqued, for that would not have been possible; burlesque could have added nothing in the way of extravagance to the sorrowful accumulation of rags and patches which constituted his costume; it was the form and color of his dress that was burlesqued. Standing collars were in fashion in that day and the minstrel appeared in a collar which engulfed and hid half of his head and projected so far forward that he could hardly see sideways over its points. His coat was sometimes made of curtain calico with a swallowtail that hung nearly to his heels and had buttons as big as a blacking box. His shoes were rusty and clumsy and cumbersome and five or six sizes too large for him. . . .

There was one member of the minstrel troupe of those early days who was not extravagantly dressed and did not use the negro dialect. He was clothed in the faultless evening costume of the white society gentleman and used a stilted, courtly, artificial and painfully grammatical form of speech, which the innocent villagers took for the real thing as exhibited in high and citified society, and they vastly admired it and envied the man who could frame it on the spot without reflection and deliver it in this easy and fluent and artistic fashion. "Bones" sat at one end of the row of minstrels, "Banjo" sat at the other end, and the dainty gentleman just described sat in the middle. This middleman was the spokesman of the show. The neatness and elegance of his dress, the studied courtliness of his manners and speech and the shapeliness of his undoctored features made him a contrast to the rest of the troupe and particularly to "Bones" and "Banjo."

"Bones" and "Banjo" were the prime jokers and whatever funniness was to be gotten out of paint and exaggerated clothing they utilized to the limit. Their lips were thickened and lengthened with bright red paint to such a degree that their mouths resembled slices cut in a ripe watermelon.

The original ground plan of the minstrel show was maintained without change for a good many years. There was no curtain to the stage in the beginning; while the audience waited they had nothing to look at except the row of empty chairs back of the footlights; presently the minstrels filed in and were received with a wholehearted welcome; they took their seats, each with his musical instrument in his hand; then the aristocrat in the middle began with a remark like this:

"I hope, gentlemen, I have the pleasure of seeing you in your accustomed excellent health and that everything has proceeded prosperously with you since last we had the good fortune to meet."

"Bones" would reply for himself and go on and tell about something in the nature of peculiarly good fortune that had lately fallen to his share; but in the midst of it he would be interrupted by "Banjo," who would throw doubt upon his statement of the matter; then a delightful jangle of assertion and contradiction would break out between the two; the quarrel would gather emphasis, the voices would grow louder and louder and more and more energetic and vindictive, and the two would rise and approach each other, shaking fists and instruments and threatening bloodshed, the courtly middleman meantime imploring them to preserve the peace and observe the proprieties—but all in vain, of course. Sometimes the quarrel would last five minutes, the two contestants shouting deadly threats in each other's faces with their noses not six inches apart, the house shrieking with laughter all the while at this happy and accurate imitation of the usual and familiar negro quarrel, then finally the pair of malignants would gradually back away from each other, each making impressive threats as to what was going to happen the "next time" each should have the misfortune to cross the other's path; then they would sink into their chairs and growl back and forth at each other across the front of the line until the house had had time to recover from its convulsions and hysterics and quiet down.

The aristocrat in the middle of the row would now make a remark which was surreptitiously intended to remind one of the end men of an experience of his of a humorous nature and fetch it out of him—which it always did. It was usually an experience of a stale and moldy sort and as old as America. One of these things, which always delighted the audience of those days until the minstrels wore it threadbare, was "Bones's" account of the perils which he had once endured during a storm at sea. The storm lasted so long that in the course of time all the provisions were consumed. Then the middleman would inquire anxiously how the people managed to survive.

"Bones" would reply, "We lived on eggs."

"You lived on eggs! Where did you get eggs?"

"Every day, when the storm was so bad, the Captain laid *to*."

During the first five years that joke convulsed the house, but after that the population of the United States had heard it so many times that they respected it no longer and always received it in a deep and reproachful and indignant silence, along with others of its caliber which had achieved disfavor by long service.

The minstrel troupes had good voices and both their solos and their choruses were a delight to me as long as the negro show continued in existence. In the beginning the songs were rudely comic, such as "Buffalo Gals," "Camptown Races," "Old Dan Tucker," and so on; but a little later sentimental songs were introduced, such as "The Blue Juniata," "Sweet Ellen Bayne," "Nelly Bly," "A Life on the Ocean Wave," "The Larboard Watch," etc.

The minstrel show was born in the early forties and it had a prosperous career for about thirty-five years; then it degenerated into a variety show and was nearly all variety show with a negro act or two thrown in incidentally. The real negro show has been stone dead for thirty years. To my mind it was a thoroughly delightful thing and a most competent laughter-compeller and I am sorry it is gone.

CELEBRITY-WATCHING. *Famous as the author of* The Pickwick Papers *and* Nicholas Nickleby, *the young Charles Dickens visited this country in 1842 and found his celebrity a burden.*

I can do nothing that I want to do, go nowhere where I want to go, and see nothing that I want to see. If I turn into the street, I am followed by a multitude. If I stay at home, the house becomes, with callers, like a fair. If I visit a public institution, with only one friend, the directors come down incontinently, waylay me in the yard, and address me in a long speech. I go to a party in the evening, and am so enclosed and hemmed about by people, stand where I will, that I am exhausted for want of air. I dine out, and have to talk about everything and everybody. I go to church for quiet, and there is a violent rush to the neighbourhood of the pew I sit in, and the clergyman preaches *at* me. I take my seat in a railroad car, and the very conductor won't leave me alone. I get out at a station, and can't drink a glass of water, without having a hundred people looking down my throat when I open my mouth to swallow. Conceive what all this is! Then by every post, letters on letters arrive, all about nothing, and all demanding an immediate answer. This man is offended because I won't live in his house; and that man is thoroughly disgusted because I won't go out more than four times in one evening. I have no rest or peace, and am in a perpetual worry.

AN AVID READER. *Thirty years after Dickens visited this country, his friend and biographer, John Forster, quotes a letter from an American correspondent.*

"Like all Americans who read," writes an American gentleman, "and that takes in nearly all our people, I am an admirer and student of Dickens. . . . Its perusal" (that of my second volume) "has recalled an incident which may interest you. Twelve or thirteen years ago I crossed the Sierra Nevada mountains as a government surveyor under a famous frontiersman and civil engineer—Colonel Lander. We were too early by a month, and became snow-bound just on the very summit. Under these circumstances it was necessary to abandon the wagons for a time, and drive the stock [mules] down the mountains to the valleys where there was a pasturage and running water. This was a long and difficult task, occupying several days. On the second day, in a spot where we expected to find nothing more human than a grizzly bear or an elk, we found a little hut, built of pine boughs and a few rough boards clumsily hewn out of small trees with an axe. The hut was covered with snow many feet deep, excepting only the hole in the roof which served for a chimney, and a small pit-like place in front to permit egress. The occupant came forth to hail us and solicit whisky and tobacco. He was dressed in a suit made entirely of flour-sacks, and was curiously labelled on various parts of his person *Best Family Flour. Extra.* His head was covered by a wolf's skin drawn from the brute's head—with the ears standing erect in a fierce alert manner. He was a most extraordinary object, and told us he had not seen a human being in four months. He lived on bear and elk meat and flour, laid in during his short summer. Emigrants in the season paid him a kind of ferry-toll. I asked him how he passed his time, and he went to a barrel and produced *Nicholas Nickleby* and *Pickwick*. I found he knew them almost by heart.

MELODRAMA. *George Templeton Strong takes his son, Johnny, then aged seven, to the theater. Lucknow is a town in India where British troops were besieged during the Indian Mutiny.*

1858. March 24. Was at the Broadway Theatre this afternoon with Johnny and little Lucy Derby to see the grand *Relief of Lucknow* performance, with the real elephant and all the horses; not legitimate drama exactly, but the intensity of its commonplace and the extravagance of its clap-trap made it comical. Johnny was moved even to tears by the grand concluding scene where the "Demon of Cawnpore" (Nona Sahib, to wit), having ordered all the other English prisoners to be instantly put to death with frightful torments, invites Colonel Somebody to renounce the service of the English Dogs and enter his. "Do it, or your wife and daughter shall perish before your eyes." Colonel smites his forehead and undergoes a tremendous mental struggle. Wife bids him not hesitate. Colonel, encouraged and fortified, says: "Noblest of women, I will now shew myself worthy to be thy husband. Inhuman Monster, I defy thee." Inhuman Monster sends for elephant. "The child shall be the first." Child asks her mamma, with touching simplicity, "whether that man ever says his prayers." Enter elephant. The dumb slave in charge of that pachyderm, having been aided with cold water and human sympathy by the touchingly simple child while confined and pinioned as a spy (in Act 1), pleads in most moving pantomime for the preservation of that innocent. Demon of Cawnpore shrieks infuriated: "She shall die. I have said it. Bismillah." Elephant, subtly instigated by dumb slave, instead of trampling on interesting infant picks her up with his trunk, gives her a cockhorsical see-sawing ride in the air, and exits with her to a place of safety. Baffled miscreant says: "Ho! My guards!" Heroic wife of colonel becomes suddenly excited and listens and says "Dinna ye hear it?" and so forth. Demon in human form, with a vague presentiment of something wrong, strides uneasily about his *musnud.* Row and fusillade. Enter British soldiers with lavish expenditure of real powder; enter Sepoys on their side who tumble down and are prodded by victorious Britons. Single combat of gallant colonel with Demon of Cawnpore, and grand final *tableau.*

All this was to John R. Strong a new revelation of profound dramatic power. His face worked and his eyes filled, and he was ashamed, and got up an apocryphal story of sick headache. But the sick headache had vanished when we reached home, and he was full of chatter and enquiry about the marvels he had witnessed.

CUSTER HUNTS A BUFFALO. *From* My Life on the Plains, *published in 1874, two years before the Battle of the Little Bighorn.*

When leaving our camp that morning I felt satisfied that the Indians, having travelled at least a portion of the night, were then many miles in advance of us, and there was neither danger nor probability of encountering any of them near the column. We were then in a magnificent game country, buffaloes, antelope, and smaller game being in abundance on all sides of us. Although an ardent sportsman, I had never hunted the buffalo up to this time, consequently was exceedingly desirous of tasting its excitement. I had several fine English greyhounds, whose speed I was anxious to test with that of the antelope, said to be—which I believe—the fleetest of animals. I was mounted on a fine large thoroughbred horse. Taking with me but one man, the chief bugler, and calling my dogs around me, I galloped ahead of the column as soon as it was daylight, for the purpose of having a chase after some antelope which could be seen grazing nearly two miles distant.

That such a course was rashly imprudent I am ready to admit. A stirring gallop of a few minutes brought me near enough to the antelope, of which there were a dozen or more, to enable the dogs to catch sight of them. Then the chase began, the antelope running in a direction which took us away from the command. By availing myself of the turns in the course, I was able to keep well in view of the exciting chase until it was evident that the antelope were in no danger of being caught by the dogs, which latter had become blown from want of proper exercise. I succeeded in calling them off, and was about to set out on my return to the column. The horse of the chief bugler, being a common-bred animal, failed early in the race and his rider wisely concluded to regain the command, so that I was alone. How far I had travelled from the troops I was trying to determine, when I discovered a large, dark-looking animal grazing nearly a mile distant. As yet I had never seen a wild buffalo, but I at once recognized this as not only a buffalo, but a very large one.

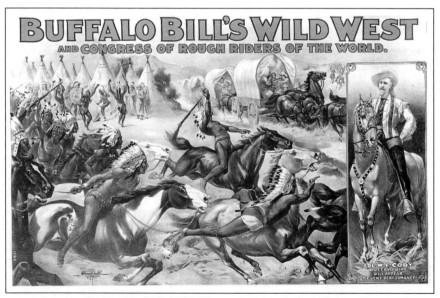

A poster for Buffalo Bill's Wild West, promising "wily dusky warriors . . .
giving their weird war-dances and picturesque style of horsemanship."
Lithograph by Courier Lithograph Company, 1898.

Here was my opportunity. A ravine near by would enable me to approach unseen until almost within pistol range of my game. Calling my dogs to follow me, I slowly pursued the course of the ravine, giving my horse opportunity to gather himself for the second run. When I emerged from the ravine I was still several hundred yards from the buffalo, which almost instantly discovered me and set off as fast as his legs could carry him. Had my horse been fresh the race would have been a short one, but the preceding long run had not been without effect. How long or how fast we flew in pursuit, the intense excitement of the chase prevented me from knowing. I only knew that even the greyhounds were left behind, until finally my good steed placed himself and me close alongside the game. It may be because this was the first I had seen, but surely of the hundreds of thousands of buffaloes which I have since seen, none have corresponded with him in size and lofty grandeur. My horse was above the average size, yet the buffalo towered even above him. I had carried my revolver in my hand from the moment the race began. Repeatedly could I have placed the muzzle against the shaggy body of the huge beast, by whose side I fairly yelled with wild excitement and delight, yet each time would I withdraw the weapon, as if to prolong the enjoyment of the race.

It was a race for life or death, yet how different the award from what could be imagined. Still we sped over the springy turf, the high breeding and mettle of my horse being plainly visible over that of the huge beast that struggled by his side. Mile after mile was traversed in this way, until the rate and distance began to tell perceptibly on the bison, whose protruding tongue and labored breathing plainly betrayed his distress. Determined to end the chase and bring down my game, I again placed the muzzle of the revolver close to the body of the buffalo, when, as if divining my intention, and feeling his inability to escape by flight, he suddenly determined to fight and at once wheeled, as only a buffalo can, to gore my horse. So sudden was this movement, and so sudden was the corresponding veering of my horse to avoid the attack, that to retain my control over him I hastily brought up my pistol hand to the assistance of the other. Unfortunately as I did so my finger, in the excitement of the occasion, pressed the trigger, discharged the pistol, and sent the fatal ball into the very brain of the noble animal I rode. Running at full speed he fell dead in the course of his leap. Quick as thought I disengaged myself from the stirrups and found myself whirling through the air over and beyond the head of my horse. My only thought, as I was describing this trajectory, and my first thought on reaching *terra firma*, was: "What will the buffalo do with me?" Although at first inclined to rush upon me, my strange procedure seemed to astonish him. Either that or pity for the utter helplessness of my condition inclined him to alter his course and leave me alone to my own bitter reflections.

In a moment the danger into which I had unluckily brought myself stood out in bold relief before me. Under ordinary circumstances the death of my horse would have been serious enough. I was strongly attached to him; had ridden him in battle during a portion of the late war; yet now his death, except in its consequences, was scarcely thought of. Here I was, alone in the heart of the Indian country, with warlike Indians known to be in the vicinity. I was not familiar with the country. How far I had travelled, or in what direction from the column, I was at a loss to know. In the excitement of the chase I had lost all reckoning. Indians were liable to pounce upon me at any moment. My command would not note my absence probably for hours. Two of my dogs overtook me, and with mute glances first at the dead steed, then at me, seemed to inquire the cause of this strange condition of affairs. Their instinct appeared to tell them that we were in misfortune.

While I was deliberating what to do, the dogs became uneasy, whined piteously, and seemed eager to leave the spot. In this desire I sympathized with them, but whither should I go? I observed that their eyes were generally turned in one particular direction; this I accepted as my cue, and with one parting look at my horse, and grasping a revolver in each hand, I set out on my uncertain journey. As long as the body of my horse was visible above the horizon I kept referring to it as my guiding point, and in this way contrived to preserve my direction. This resource soon failed me, and I then had recourse to weeds, buffalo skulls, or any two objects I could find on my line of march. Constantly my eyes kept scanning the horizon, each moment expecting, and with reason too, to find myself discovered by Indians.

I had travelled in this manner what seemed to me about three or four miles, when far ahead in the distance I saw a column of dust rising. A hasty examination soon convinced me that the dust was produced by one of three causes: white men, Indians, or buffaloes. Two to one in my favor at any rate. Selecting a ravine where I could crawl away undiscovered should the approaching body prove to be Indians, I called my dogs to my side and concealed myself as well as I could to await developments. The object of my anxious solicitude was still several miles distant. Whatever it was, it was approaching in my direction, as was plainly discernible from the increasing columns of dust. Fortunately I had my field-glass slung across my shoulder, and if Indians I could discover them before they could possibly discover me. Soon I was able to see the heads of mounted men running in irregular order. This discovery shut out the probability of their being buffaloes, and simplified the question to white men or Indians. Never during the war did I scan an enemy's battery or approaching column with half the anxious care with which I watched the party then approaching me. For a long time nothing satisfactory could be determined, until my eye caught sight of an object which, high above the heads of the approaching riders, told me in unmistakable terms that friends were approaching. It was the cavalry guidon, and never was the sight of stars and stripes more welcome. My comrades were greatly surprised to find me seated on the ground alone and without my horse. A few words explained all. A detachment of my men, following my direction, found my horse and returned with the saddle and other equipments. Another horse, and Richard was himself again, plus a little valuable experience and minus a valuable horse.

THE PURSUIT OF PLEASURE

POCAHONTAS THROWS A PARTY. *Writing of himself in the third person, Captain John Smith tells how he and four others went to visit Powhatan and were entertained by his daughter in his absence.*

Powhatan being thirty miles off, was presently sent for. In the meantime Pocahontas and her women entertained Captain Smith in this manner.

In a fair plain field they made a fire, before which he was placed sitting upon a mat. Suddenly amongst the woods was heard such a hideous noise and shrieking that the English betook themselves to their arms and seized on two or three old men by them, supposing Powhatan with all his power was come to surprise them. But presently Pocahontas came, willing him to kill her if any hurt was intended; and the beholders, which were men, women, and children satisfied the captain there was no such matter.

Then presently they were presented with this antic. Thirty young women came naked out of the woods, only covered behind and before with a few green leaves, their bodies all painted, some of one color, some of another, but all differing. Their leader had a fair pair of buck's horns on her head, and an otter's skin at her girdle, and another at her arm, a quiver of arrows at her back, a bow and arrows in her hand. The next had in her hand a sword, another a club, another a pot-stick; all horned alike. The rest every one with their several devices.

These fiends with most hellish shouts and cries, rushing from among the trees, cast themselves in a ring about the fire, singing and dancing with most excellent ill variety, oft falling into their infernal passions, and solemnly again to sing and dance. Having spent an hour in this mascarado, as they entered in like manner they departed.

Having reaccommodated themselves, they solemnly invited him to their lodgings, where he was no sooner within the house but all these nymphs more tormented him than ever, with crowding, pressing, and hanging about him, most tediously crying, "Love you not me? Love you not me?"

This salutation ended, the feast was set, consisting of all the savage dainties they could devise; some attending, others singing and dancing about them. Which mirth being ended, with firebrands instead of torches they conducted him to his lodging.

NOT IN NEW ENGLAND. *From* An Arrow Against Profane and Promiscuous Dancing *by the Reverend Increase Mather, Boston, 1684.*

Concerning the Controversy about *Dancing,* the Question is not, whether all *Dancing* be in it self sinful. It is granted, that *Pyrrhical* or *Polemical Saltation:* i.e. when men vault in their Armour, to shew their strength and activity, may be of use. Nor is the question, whether a sober and grave *Dancing* of Men with Men, or of Women with Women, be not allowable; we make no doubt of that, where it may be done without offence, in due season, and with moderation. The Prince of Philosophers has observed truly, that *Dancing* or *Leaping* is a natural expression of joy: So that there is no more Sin in it, than in laughter, or any outward expression of inward Rejoycing.

But our question is concerning *Gynecandrical Dancing* or that which is commonly called *Mixt* or *Promiscuous Dancing, viz* of Men and Women (be they elder or younger persons) together: Now this we affirm to be utterly unlawful, and that it cannot be tollerated in such a place as *New-England,* without great Sin. . . . We cannot find one Orthodox and Judicious Divine, that writeth on the Commandments, but mentions *Promiscuous Dancing,* as a breach of the seventh Commandment, as being an occasion, and an incentive to that which is evil in the sight of God. . . . It is sad, that when in times of Reformation, Children have been taught in their Catechism, that such *Dancing* is against the Commandment of God, that now in *New-England* they should practically be learned the contrary. The unchast Touches and Gesticulations used by *Dancers* have a palpable tendency to that which is evil.

VIRGINIA REELS. *Philip Vickers Fithian had just graduated from Nassau Hall (later Princeton), where he had studied to become a Presbyterian minister, when he was invited to spend a year with one of Virginia's first families as tutor to the children of Colonel and Mrs. Carter of Nomini Hall. While there he kept a diary.*

December 1773. Thursday 16. I had the pleasure of walking to Day at twelve o-Clock with Mrs Carter; She shewed me her stock of *Fowls & Mutton* for the winter; She observed, with great truth, that to live in the Country, and take no pleasure at all in Groves, Fields, or Meadows; nor in Cattle, Horses, & domestic Poultry, would be a manner of life too tedious to endure.

Fryday 17. I dismissed the children this morning til' monday on account of Mr Christian's *Dance*, which, as it goes through his Scholars in Rotation, happens to be here to Day—and I myself also am unwell, so as not to go out;—Mrs Carter sent me over Coffee for Breakfast; & soon after some Spirits of *Hartshorn* for my Head—At twelve she sent the waiting Man to know if I was better, & what I would choose for Dinner. I thank'd her, & desired that She would give herself no trouble; She was careful, however, from her undistinguished kindness, to send me before Dinner some hot *Barley Broth,—Ben Carter* before Noon introduced into my Room, Mr *Billy Booth*, a young Gentleman of Fortune, who is one of Mr Christians pupils—The two Master Fantleroys came in also to see me . . . Towards Evening I grew Better, & walked down, with a number of young Fellows to the River; after our return I was strongly solicited by the young Gentlemen to go in and dance. I declined it, however, and went to my Room not without Wishes that it had been a part of my Education to learn what I think is an innocent and an ornamental, and most certainly, in this province is a necessary qualification for a person to appear even decent in Company!—

Mrs *Carter* in the Evening, sent me for Supper, a Bowl of hot Green Tea, & several *Tarts.* I expected that they would have danced til late in the Night, but intirely contrary to my Expectation, the Company were separated to their respective apartments before half after nine o'*Clock.*

Saturday 18. Rose by Seven, Sent for Mr Carters Barber and was drest for Breakfast—We went in to Breakfast at ten. . . . There were present of Grown persons Mr & Mrs *Carter*, Mrs *Lee*, & Miss *Jenny Corbin*; young Misses about Eleven: & Seven young Fellows, including myself;—After Breakfast, we all retired into the Dancing-Room, & after the Scholars had their Lesson singly round Mr Christian, very politely, requested me to step a *Minuet*; I excused myself however, but signified my peculiar pleasure in the Accuracy of their performance— There were several Minuets danced with great ease and propriety; after which the whole company Joined in country-dances, and it was indeed beautiful to admiration, to see such a number of young persons, set off by dress to the best Advantage, moving easily, to the sound of well performed Music, and with perfect regularity, tho' apparently in the utmost Disorder—The Dance continued til two, we dined at half after three—soon after Dinner we repaired to the Dancing-Room again; I observe in the course of the lessons, that Mr Christian is punctual, and rigid in his discipline, so strict indeed that he struck two of the young Misses for a fault in the course of their performance, even in the presence of the Mother of one of them! And he rebuked one of the young Fellows so highly as to tell him he must alter his manner, which he had observed through the Course of the Dance, to be insolent, and wanton, or absent himself from the School—I thought this was a sharp reproof, to a young Gentleman of seventeen, before a large number of Ladies!—When it grew too dark to dance, the young Gentlemen walked over to my Room, we conversed til half after six; Nothing is now to be heard of in conversation, but the *Balls*, the *Fox-hunts*, the fine *entertainments*, and the *good fellowship*, which are to be exhibited at the approaching *Christmas*. . . .

When the candles were lighted we all repaired, for the last time, into the dancing Room; first each couple danced a Minuet; then all joined as before in the country Dances, those continued till half after Seven when Mr Christian retired; and at the proposal of several, (with Mr Carters approbation) we played *Button*, to get Pauns for Redemption; here I could join with them, and indeed it was carried on with sprightliness, and Decency; in the course of redeeming my Pauns, I had several Kisses of the Ladies!—Early in the Evening cam colonel Philip Lee, in a travelling Chariot from Williamsburg—Half after eight we were rung in to Supper; The room looked luminous and splendid; four very large candles burning on the table where we supp'd, three others in different parts of the Room; a gay, sociable Assembly, & four well instructed waiters!—So soon as we rose from supper, the Company form'd into a semicircle round the fire, & Mr Lee, by the voice of the Company was chosen *Pope*, and Mr Carter, Mr Christian, Mrs Carter, Mrs Lee, and the rest of the company were appointed Friars, in the Play call'd "break the Popes neck"—Here we had great Diversion in the respective Judgments upon offenders, but we were all dismiss'd by ten, and retired to our several Rooms.

A MEMORABLE ADVENTURE. *Nicholas Cresswell arrived from England in 1774 to seek his fortune in what were still the colonies. At the start of these extracts from his diary he finds himself in the frontier regions of western Pennsylvania doing some desultory trading in partnership with the more experienced Mr. Anderson.*

Friday, August 25th, 1775. Very heavy rain all day. Lost our horses, but an Indian brought them to us in the evening for which we gave him a pair of leggings. Breakfasted, dined and supped on Plums and Wild Cherries. Here are wild Plums in great abundance, about the size of our common white plums in England, some Red, others White and very well flavoured. The Cherries are small and black, very sweet, and grow in Bunches like Currants.

Saturday, August 26th. Set out early this morning, travelled very hard till noon, when we passed through the largest Plum Tree Thicket I ever saw. I believe it was a mile long, nothing but the Plum and Cherry Trees. Killed a Rattlesnake. Just as the Sun went down we stopped to get our Supper on some Dewberries (a small berry something like a Gooseberry). Mr. Anderson had gone before me and said he would ride on about two miles to a small run where he intended to camp, as soon as I had got sufficient. I mounted my Horse and followed him till I came to a place where the road forked. I took the path that I supposed he had gone and rode till it began to be dark, when I imagined myself to be wrong, and there was not a possibility of me finding my way back in the night. Determined to stay where I was till morning, I had no sooner alighted from my horse, but I discovered the glimmering of a fire about four hundred yards from me. This rejoiced me exceedingly, supposing it was Mr. Anderson. When I got there, to my great disappointment and surprise found three Indian women and a little boy. I believe they were as much surprised as I was. None of them could speak English and I could not speak Indian. I alighted and marked the path I had come and that I had left, on the ground with the end of my stick, made a small channel in the earth which I poured full of water, laid some fire by the side of it, and then laid myself down by the side of the fire, repeating the name of Anderson which I soon understood they knew.

The youngest Girl immediately unsaddled my Horse, unstrapped the Belt, Hoppled him, and turned him out, then spread my blankets at the fire and made signs for me to sit down. The Oldest made me a little hash of dried Venison and Bear's Oil, which eat very well, but neither Bread nor Salt. After supper they made signs I must go to sleep. Then they held a consultation for some time which made me very uneasy, the two eldest women and the boy laid down on the opposite side of the fire and some distance away. The youngest (she had taken so much pains with my horse) came and placed herself very near me. I began to think she had some amorous design upon me. In about half an hour she began to creep nearer me and pulled my Blanket. I found what she wanted and lifted it up. She was young, handsome, and healthy. Fine regular features and fine eyes, had she not painted them with Red before she came to bed.

Sunday, August 27th. This morning my Bedfellow went into the woods and caught her horse and mine, saddled them, put my Blanket on the saddle, and prepared everything ready, seemingly with a great deal of good nature. Absolutely refused my assistance. The old Woman got me some dried venison for Breakfast. When I took my leave returned the thanks as well as I could by signs. My Bedfellow was my guide and conducted me through the woods, where there were no signs of a road or without my knowing with certainty whither I was going. She often mentioned John Anderson and talked a great deal in Indian. I attempted to speak Indian, which diverted her exceedingly. In about an hour she brought me to Mr. Anderson's camp, who had been very uneasy at my absence and employed an Indian to seek me. I gave my Dulcinea a match coat [cloak of coarse wool], with which she seemed very well pleased. Proceeded on our journey and about noon got to an Indian Town called Wale-hack-tap-poke, or the Town with a good Spring, on the Banks of the Muskingham and inhabited by Dellawar Indians. Christianized under the Moravian Sect, it is a pretty town consisting of about sixty houses, and is built of logs and covered with Clapboards. It is regularly laid out in three spacious streets which meet in the centre, where there is a large meeting house built of logs sixty foot square covered with Shingles, Glass in the windows and a Bell, a good plank with two rows of forms. Adorned with some few pieces of Scripture painting, but very indifferently executed. All about the meeting house is kept very clean.

In the evening went to the meeting. But never was I more astonished in my life. I expected to have seen nothing but anarchy and confusion, as I have been taught to look upon these beings with contempt. Instead of that, here is the greatest regularity, order, and decorum, I ever saw in any place of Worship, in my life. With that solemnity of behaviour and modest, religious deportment would do honour to the first religious society on earth, and put a bigot or enthusiast out of countenance. The parson was a Dutchman, but preached in English. He had an Indian interpreter, who explained it to the Indians by sentences. They sung in the Indian language. The men sit on one row of forms and the women on the other with the children in the front. Each sex comes in and goes out of their own side of the house. The old men sit on each side the parson. Treated with Tea, Coffee, and Boiled Bacon at supper. The Sugar they make themselves out of the sap of a certain tree. Lodged at Whiteman's house, married to an Indian woman.

Monday, August 28th. Met several Indians coming from a Feast dressed and painted in the grandest manner. Lodged at White-Eye's Town only three houses in it. Kindly treated at a Dutch Blacksmith's, who lives with an Indian Squaw. Got a very hearty supper of a sort of Dumplings made of Indian Meal and dried Huckleberries which serves instead of currants. Dirty people, find it impossible to keep myself free from lice. Very disagreeable companions.

Tuesday, August 29th. Left White-Eye's town. Saw the bones of one Mr. Cammel, a White man, that had been killed by the Indians. Got to

Co-a-shoking about noon. It is at the forks of the Muskingham. The Indians have removed from Newcomer Town to this place. King Newcomer lives here. Sold part of my goods here to good advantage. Crossed a branch of Muskingham and went to Old Hundy, this is a scattering Indian settlement. Lodged at a Mohawk Indian's house, who offered me his Sister and Mr. Anderson his Daughter to sleep with us, which we were obliged to accept.

Wednesday, August 30th. My bedfellow very fond of me this morning and wants to go with me. Find I must often meet with such encounters as these if I do not take a Squaw to myself. She is young and sprightly, tolerably handsome, and can speak a little English. Agreed to take her. She saddled her horse and went with us to New Hundy about 3 miles off, where she had several relations who made me very welcome to such as they had. From there to Coashoskis, where we lodged in my Squaw's Brother's, made me a compliment of a young wolf but I could not take it with me.

Thursday, August 31st. At Coashoskis. Mr. Anderson could not find his horse. Sold all my goods for Furs. In the afternoon rambled about the Town, smoking Tobacco with the Indians and did everything in my power to make myself agreeable to them. Went to see the King. He lives in a poor house, and he is as poor in dress as any of them, no emblem of Royalty or Majesty about him. He is an old man, treated me very kindly, called me his good friend, and hoped I would be kind to my Squaw. Gave me a small string of Wampum as a token of friendship. My Squaw uneasy to see me write so much.

Friday, September 1st. At Coashoskin. Mr. Anderson found his horse. Saw an Indian Dance in which I bore a part. Painted by my Squaw in the most elegant manner. Divested of all my clothes, except my Calico short breech-clout, leggings, and Mockesons. A fire was made which we danced round with little order, whooping and hallooing in a most frightful manner. I was but a novice at the diversion and by endeavouring to act as they did made them a great deal of sport and ingratiated me much in their esteem. This is the most violent exercise to the adepts in the art I ever saw. No regular figure, but violent distortion of features, writhing and twisting the body in the most uncouth and antic postures imaginable. Their music is an old Keg with one head knocked out and covered with a skin and beat with sticks which regulates their times. The men have strings of Deer's hoofs tied round their ankles and knees, and gourds with shot or pebblestones in them in their hands which they continually rattle. The women have Morris bells or Thimbles with holes in the bottom and strung upon a leather thong tied round their ankles, knees and waists. The jingling of these Bells and Thimbles, the rattling of the Deer's hoofs and gourds, beating of the drum and kettle, with the horrid yells of the Indians, render it the most unharmonious concert, that human idea can possibly conceive. It is a favourite diversion, in which I am informed they spend a great part of their time in Winter. Saw an Indian Conjuror dressed in a Coat of Bearskin with a Visor mask made of wood, frightful enough to scare the Devil. The Indians believe in conjuration and Witchcraft. Left the Town, went about two miles. Camped by the side of a run. A young Indian boy, son of one Baubee a Frenchman, came after us and insists on going with us to Fort Pitt. Find myself very unwell this evening, pains in my head and back. Nancy [his Indian companion] seems very uneasy about my welfare. Afraid of the Ague.

Saturday, September 2nd. Very sick. Nancy is gone to fetch an old Indian woman to cure me as she says, therefore I must lay by my pen.

Sunday, September 3rd. Last night, Nancy brought an Indian Squaw which called me her Nilum. i.e. Nephew, as Mr. Anderson told me, and behaved very kindly to me. She put her hand on my head for some time, then took a small brown root out of her pocket and with her knife chopped part of it small, then mixed it with water which she gave me to drink, or rather swallow, being about a spoonful, but this I evaded by keeping it in my mouth till I found an opportunity to spit it out. She then took some in her mouth and chewed it and spit on the top of my head, rubbing my head well at the same time. Then she unbuttoned my shirt collar and spat another mouthful down my back. This was uncomfortable but I bore it with patience. She lent me her Matchcoat and told me to go to sleep. Nancy was ordered not to give me any water till morning, however, I prevailed on the good-natured creature to let me take a vomit that Mr. Anderson had with him as soon as the old woman was gone, which has cured me, tho' the old woman believes that her nostrum did it. Obliged to stay here this day, somebody has stolen one of Mr. A's horses.

Monday, September 4th. Saw an Indian scalp. Heard an Indian play upon a Tin Violin and make tolerable good music. Went to Kanaughtonhead, walked all the way, my horse loaded with skins. Camped close by the Town. Nancy's kindness to be remembered.

Tuesday, September 5th. Drank Tea with Captain White-Eyes and Captain Wingenund at an Indian house in Town. This Tea is made of the tops of Ginsing, and I think it very much like Bohea Tea. The leaves are put into a tin canister made water tight and boiled till it is dry, by this means the juices do not evaporate. N. did not choose to go into the town, but employed herself in making me a pair of Mockesons.

Wednesday, September 6th. Mr. Anderson bought several cows there which he intends to take to Fort Pitt. Camped within two miles of Walehacktappoke.

Thursday, September 7th. Got to Walehacktappoke to breakfast. N. refused to go into the Town, knowing that the Moravians will not allow anyone to cohabit with Indians in their town. Saw an Indian child baptized, eight Godfathers and four Godmothers, could not understand the ceremony as it was performed in Indian.

Sunday, September 10th. Rambled till noon when we found ourselves at Bouquet's old Fort now demolished. Went to an Indian Camp, where Mr. Anderson met with an old wife of his, who would go with him, which he agreed to. We have each of us a Girl. It is an odd way of travelling, but we are obliged to submit to it.

Monday, September 11th. Mr. Anderson and I with our Ladies proceeded, and left the people to bring the skins and cattle which he had purchased. Travelled over a great deal of bad land. About sundown Mr. A. called out, "A Panther." I looked about and saw it set in a tree about twenty yards from me. Fired at it on horseback and shot it through the neck. It is of a Brown colour and shaped like a cat, but much larger. It measured five foot nine inches from Nose end to Tail end. Camped and skinned the Panther. This exploit has raised me in N. esteem exceedingly, tho' I claim no merit from it, being merely accidental.

Tuesday, Sept. 12th. Our Squaws are very necessary, fetching our horses to the Camp and saddling them, making our fire at night and cooking our victuals, and every other thing they think will please us.

Fort Pitt—Thursday, September 14th. Got to Fort Pitt about noon. Left our Girls amongst the Indians that are coming to the Treaty.

Saturday, September 16th. N. finished my Leggings and Mockeysons, very neat ones.

Sunday, September 17th. Here are members of Congress to treat with the Indians, Delegates from the Conventions of Virginia and Pensylvania for the purpose, and Commissioners from the Convention of Virginia to settle the accounts of the last campaign against the Indians. All Colonels, Majors, or Captains and very big with their own importance. Confound them altogether.

Thursday, September 28th. My peltry arrived this day, which I sold to Mr. Anderson, but find I shall be a loser upon the whole. Determined to leave the town on Monday.

Saturday, September 30th. N. very uneasy, she weeps plentifully. I am unhappy that this honest creature has taken such a fancy to me.

Sunday, October 1st. Took leave of most of my acquaintances in town. Mr. Douglas gave me an Indian Tobacco pouch made of a Mink Skin adorned with porcupine quills. He is desirous of keeping a correspondence with me, which in all probability will be for the interest of us both. I have conceived a great regard for the Indians and really feel a most sensible regret in parting from them, however contemptible opinion others may entertain of these honest poor creatures. If we take an impartial view of an Indian's general conduct with all the disadvantages they labour under, at the same time divest ourselves of prejudice, I believe every honest man's sentiments would be in favour of them.

Monday, October 2nd. Settled my affairs with Mr. John Anderson, who has behaved more like a Father than a common acquaintance. Made him a compliment of my silver buckles and agreed to keep up a correspondence. Parting with N. was the most affecting thing I have ever experienced since I left home. The poor creature wept most plentifully. However base it may appear to conscientious people, it is absolutely necessary to take a temporary wife if they have to travel amongst the Indians. Left Fort Pitt. Dined at widow Myers.

HUSKING BEE. *As recalled by the father of the novelist William Dean Howells, William Cooper Howells, who grew up on a farm in Ohio early in the nineteenth century.*

When the season for gathering the corn came the farmers went through the fields and pulled off the ears and husks together, throwing them upon the ground in heaps, whence they were hauled into the barnyard and there piled up in a neat pile of convenient length, according to the crop, and say four or five feet high, rising to a sharp peak from a base of about six feet. Care was taken to make this pile of equal width and height from end to end, so that it would be easily and fairly divided in the middle by a rail laid upon it.

When the husking party had assembled they were all called out into line, and two fellows, mostly ambitious boys, were chosen captains. These then chose their men, each calling out one of the crowd alternately, till all were chosen. Then the heap was divided, by two judicious chaps walking solemnly along the ridge of the heap of corn, and deciding where the dividing rail was to be laid, and, as this had to be done by starlight or moonlight at best, it took considerable deliberation, as the comparative solidity of the ends of the heap and the evenness of it had to be taken into account. This done, the captains placed a good steady man at each side of the rail, who made it a point to work through and cut the heap in two as soon as possible; and then the two parties fell to husking, all standing with the heap in front of them, and throwing the husked corn on to a clear place over the heap, and the husks behind them. From the time they began till the corn was all husked at one end, there would be steady work, each man husking all the corn he could, never stopping except to take a pull at the stone jug of inspiration that passed occasionally along the lines; weak lovers of the stuff were sometimes overcome, though it was held to be a disgraceful thing to take too much. The captains would go up and down their lines and rally their men as if in a battle, and the whole was an exciting affair.

As soon as one party got done, they raised a shout, and hoisting their captain on their shoulders, carried him over to the other side with general cheering. Then would come a little bantering talk and explanation why the defeated party lost, and all would turn to and husk up the remnants of the heap. All hands would then join to carry the husks into the fodder-house. The shout at hoisting the captain was the signal for bringing the supper on the table, and the huskers and the supper met soon after. These gatherings often embraced forty or fifty men. If the farmhouse was small it would be crowded, and the supper would be managed by repeated sittings at the table. At a large house there was less crowding and more fun, and if, as was often the case, some occasion had been given for an assemblage of the girls of the neighborhood, and particularly if the man that played the fiddle should attend, after the older men had gone, there was very apt to be a good time. There was a tradition that the boys who accidentally husked a red ear and saved it would be entitled to a kiss from somebody. But I never knew it to be necessary to produce a red ear to secure a kiss where there was a disposition to give or take one.

MRS. BREVOORT'S BAL COSTUMÉ. *The diarist Philip Hone and his family attend a fancy-dress ball given by the wealthy Mr. and Mrs. Brevoort in New York.*

1840. February 25. This long-anticipated affair came off last evening, and I believe the expectations of all were realized. The mansion of our entertainers, Mr. and Mrs. Brevoort, is better calculated for such a display than any other in the city, and everything which host and hostess could do in preparing and arranging, in receiving their guests, and making them feel a full warrant and assurance of welcome, was done to the topmost round of elegant hospitality. Mrs. B., in particular, by her kind and courteous deportment, threw a charm over the splendid pageant which would have been incomplete without it.

My family contributed a large number of actors in the gay scene. I went as Cardinal Wolsey, in a grand robe of new scarlet merino, with an exceedingly well-contrived cap of the same material: a cape of real ermine, which I borrowed from Mrs. Thomas W. Ludlow, gold chain and cross, scarlet stockings, etc.; Mary and Catherine, as Night and Day; Margaret, Annot Lyle in the "Legend of Montrose;" John, as Washington Irving's royal poet; Schermerhorn, as Gessler, the

Austrian governor who helped to make William Tell immortal; Robert, a Highlander; and our sweet neighbour, Eliza Russell, as Lalla Rookh.

Never before has New York witnessed a fancy ball so splendidly gotten up, in better taste, or more successfully carried through. We went at ten o'clock, at which time the numerous apartments, brilliantly lighted, were tolerably well filled with characters. The notice on the cards of the invitation, *"Costume à la rigueur,"* had virtually closed the door to all others, and with the exception of some eight or ten gentlemen who, in plain dress, with a red ribbon at the button-hole, officiated as managers, every one appeared as some one else; the dresses being generally new, some of them superbly ornamented with gold, silver, and jewelry; others marked by classical elegance, or appropriately designating distinguished characters of ancient and modern history and the drama; and others again most familiarly grotesque and ridiculous. The *coup d'oeil* dazzled the eyes and bewildered the imagination.

Soon after our party arrived the five rooms on the first floor (including the library) were completely filled. I should think there were about five hundred ladies and gentlemen; many a beautiful "point device," which had cost the fair or gallant wearer infinite pains in the selection and adaptation, was doomed to pass unnoticed in the crowd; and many who went there hoping each to be the star of the evening, found themselves eclipsed by some superior luminary, or at best forming a unit in the milky way. Some surprise was expressed at seeing in the crowd a man in the habit of a knight in armour,—a Mr. Attree, reporter and one of the editors of an infamous penny paper called the "Herald." Bennett, the principal editor, called upon Mr. Brevoort to obtain permission for this person to be present to report in his paper an account of the ball. He consented, as I believe I should have done under the same circumstances, as by doing so a sort of obligation was imposed upon him to refrain from abusing the house, the people of the house, and their guests, which would have been done in the case of a denial. But this is a hard alternative; to submit to this kind of surveillance is getting to be intolerable, and nothing but the force of public opinion will correct the insolence.

RUSTIC IDYLL. *A quilting bee, as conjured up by Daniel R. Hundley in* Social Relations in our Southern States, *published in 1860, just before the Civil War.*

There is, indeed, nothing to compare to a country quilting for the simple and unaffected happiness which it affords all parties. The old women and old men sit demurely beside the blazing kitchen fire, and frighten one another with long-winded ghost stories; thus leaving the young folks all to themselves in the "big room," wherein is also the quilt-frame, which is either suspended at the corners by ropes attached to the ceiling, or else rests on the tops of four chairs. Around this assemble the young men and the young maidens, robust with honest toil and honestly ruby-cheeked with genuine good health. The former know nothing of your *dolce far niente* or dyspepsia, and the latter are not troubled with crinoline or consumption, but all are merry as larks and happy as it is possible for men and women to be in this lower world. No debts, nor duns, nor panics, nor poverty, nor wealth disturbs their thoughts or mars the joyousness of the hour. Serene as a summer's day, and cloudless as the skies in June, the moments hurry by, as they ply their nimble needles and sing their simple songs, or whisper their tales of love, heedless of the great world and all the thoughtless worldlings who live only to win the smiles of "our best society." Meanwhile the children play hide and seek, in-doors and out, whooping, laughing, and chatting like so many magpies; and, in the snug chimney-corner, Old Bose, the faithful watch-dog, stretches himself out to his full length and dozes comfortably in the genial warmth of the fire, in his dreams chasing after imaginary hares, or baying the moon.

THE WILD WEST: A VISIT TO DODGE CITY. *Andy Adams, author of* The Log of a Cowboy, *recalls a memorable stopover while on the trail in 1882.*

On reaching Dodge, we rode up to the Wright House, where Flood [the foreman] met us and directed our cavalcade across the railroad to a livery stable, the proprietor of which was a friend of Lovell's [Don Lovell, owner of the cattle]. We unsaddled and turned our horses into a large corral, and while we were in the office of the livery, surrendering our artillery, Flood came in and handed each of us twenty-five dollars in gold, warning us that when that was gone no more would be advanced. On receipt of the money, we scattered like partridges before a gunner. Within an hour or two, we began to return to the stable by ones and twos, and were stowing into our saddle pockets our purchases, which ran from needles and thread to .45 cartridges, every mother's son reflecting the art of the barber, while John Officer had his blond mustaches blackened, waxed, and curled like a French dancing master. "If some of you boys will hold him," said Moss Strayhorn, commenting on Officer's appearance, "I'd like to take a good smell of him, just to see if he took oil up there where the end of his neck's haired over." As Officer already had several drinks comfortably stowed away under his belt, and stood up strong six feet two, none of us volunteered.

"Hurdy-gurdy girls singing bacchanalian songs" in Virginia City, Nevada, in Gold Rush days. Wood engraving from *Harper's New Monthly Magazine*, June 1865.

After packing away our plunder, we sauntered around town, drinking moderately, and visiting the various saloons and gambling houses. I clung to my bunkie, The Rebel [Paul Priest's nickname], during the rounds, for I had learned to like him, and had confidence he would lead me into no indiscretions. At the Long Branch, we found Quince Forrest [the deputy foreman] and Wyatt Roundtree playing the faro bank, the former keeping cases. They never recognized us, but were answering a great many questions, asked by the dealer and lookout, regarding the possible volume of the cattle drive that year. Down at another gambling house, The Rebel met Ben Thompson, a faro dealer not on duty and an old cavalry comrade, and the two cronied around for over an hour like long lost brothers, pledging anew their friendship over several social glasses, in which I was always included. There was no telling how long this reunion would have lasted, but happily for my sake, Lovell—who had been asleep all the morning—started out to round us up for dinner with him at the Wright House, which was at that day a famous hostelry, patronized almost exclusively by the Texas cowmen and cattle buyers.

We made the rounds of the gambling houses, looking for our crowd. We ran across three of the boys piking at a monte game, who came with us reluctantly; then, guided by Lovell, we started for the Long Branch, where we felt certain we would find Forrest and Roundtree, if they had any money left. Forrest was broke, which made him ready to come, and Roundtree, though quite a winner, out of deference to our employer's wishes, cashed in and joined us. Old man Don could hardly do enough for us; and before we could reach the Wright House, had lined us up against three different bars; and while I had confidence in my navigable capacity, I found they were coming just a little too fast and free, seeing I had scarcely drunk anything in three months but branch water. As we lined up at the Wright House bar for the final before dinner, The Rebel, who was standing next to me, entered a waiver and took a cigar, which I understood to be a hint, and I did likewise.

We had a splendid dinner. Our outfit, with McNulta, occupied a ten-chair table, while on the opposite side of the room was another large table, occupied principally by drovers who were waiting for their herds to arrive. Among those at the latter table, whom I now remember, was "Uncle" Henry Stevens, . . . "Lum" Slaughter, . . . "Dun" Houston, and last but not least, Colonel "Shanghai" Pierce.

After dinner, all the boys, with the exception of Priest and myself, returned to the gambling houses as though anxious to work overtime. Before leaving the hotel, Forrest effected the loan of ten from Roundtree, and the two returned to the Long Branch, while the others as eagerly sought out a monte game.

Along early in the evening, Flood advised us boys to return to the herd with him, but all the crowd wanted to stay in town and see the sights. Lovell interceded in our behalf, and promised to see that we left town in good time to be in camp before the herd was ready to move the next morning. On this assurance, Flood saddled up and started for the Saw Log, having ample time to make the ride before dark. By this time most of the boys had worn off the wire edge for gambling and were comparing notes. Three of them were broke, but Quince Forrest had turned the tables and was over a clean hundred winner for the day. Those who had no money fortunately had good credit with those of us who had, for there was yet much to be seen, and in Dodge in '82 it took money to see the elephant. There were several variety theatres, a number of dance halls, and other resorts which, like the wicked, flourish best under darkness.

After supper, just about dusk, we went over to the stable, caught our horses, saddled them, and tied them up for the night. We fully expected to leave town by ten o'clock, for it was a good twelve mile ride to the Saw Log. In making the rounds of the variety theatres and dance halls, we hung together. Lovell excused himself early in the evening, and at parting we assured him that the outfit would leave for camp before midnight. We were enjoying ourselves immensely over at the Lone Star dance hall, when an incident occurred in which we entirely neglected the good advice of McNulta, and had the sensation of hearing lead whistle and cry around our ears before we got away from town.

Quince Forrest was spending his winnings as well as drinking freely, and at the end of a quadrille gave vent to his hilarity in an old-fashioned Comanche yell. The bouncer of the dance hall of course had his eye on our crowd, and at the end of a change, took Quince to task. He was a surly brute, and instead of couching his request in appropriate language, threatened to throw him out of the house. Forrest stood like one absent-minded and took the abuse, for physically he was no match for the bouncer, who was armed, moreover, and wore an officer's star. I was dancing in the same set with a red-headed, freckled-faced girl, who clutched my arm and wished to know if my friend was armed. I assured her that he was not, or we would have had notice of it before the bouncer's invective was ended. At the conclusion of the dance, Quince and The Rebel passed out, giving the rest of us the word to remain as though nothing was wrong. In the course of half an hour, Priest returned and asked us to take our leave one at a time without attracting any attention, and meet at the stable. I remained until the last, and noticed The Rebel and the bouncer taking a drink together at the bar,—the former apparently in a most amiable mood. We passed out together shortly afterward, and found the other boys mounted and awaiting our return, it being now about midnight. It took but a moment to secure our guns, and once in the saddle, we rode through the town in the direction of the herd. On the outskirts of the town, we halted. "I'm going back to that dance hall," said Forrest, " and have one round at least with that whore-herder. No man who walks this old earth can insult me, as he did, not if he has a hundred stars on him. If any of you don't want to go along, ride right on to camp, but I'd like to have you all go. And when I take his measure, it will be the signal to the rest of you to put out the lights. All that's going, come on."

There were no dissenters to the programme. I saw at a glance that my bunkie was heart and soul in the play, and took my cue and kept my mouth shut. We circled round the town to a vacant lot within a block of the rear of the dance hall. Honeyman was left to hold the horses; then, taking off our belts and hanging them on the pommels of our saddles, we secreted our six-shooters inside the waistbands of our trousers.

The hall was still crowded with the revelers when we entered, a few at a time, Forrest and Priest being the last to arrive. Forrest had

"Barroom Dancing," by John Lewis Krimmel, 1820.

changed hats with The Rebel, who always wore a black one, and as the bouncer circulated around, Quince stepped squarely in front of him. There was no waste of words, but a gun-barrel flashed in the lamp-light, and the bouncer, struck with the six-shooter, fell like a beef. Before the bewildered spectators could raise a hand, five six-shooters were turned into the ceiling. The lights went out at the first fire, and amidst the rush of men and the screaming of women, we reached the outside, and within a minute were in our saddles. All would have gone well had we returned by the same route and avoided the town; but after crossing the railroad track, anger and pride having not been properly satisfied, we must ride through the town.

On entering the main street, leading north and opposite the bridge on the river, somebody of our party in the rear turned his gun loose into the air. The Rebel and I were riding in the lead, and at the clattering of hoofs and shooting behind us, our horses started on the run, the shooting by this time having become general. At the second street crossing, I noticed a rope of fire belching from a Winchester in the doorway of a store building. There was no doubt in my mind but we were the object of the manipulator of that carbine, and as we reached the next cross street, a man kneeling in the shadow of a build-ing opened fire on us with a six-shooter. Priest reined in his horse, and not having wasted cartridges in the open-air shooting, returned the compliment until he emptied his gun. By this time every officer in the town was throwing lead after us, some of which cried a little too close for comfort. When there was no longer any shooting on our flanks, we turned into a cross street and soon left the lead behind us. At the outskirts of the town we slowed up our horses and took it leisurely. . . .

The next morning, . . . when McCann started to get breakfast, he hung his coat on the end of the wagon rod, while he went for a bucket of water. During his absence, John Officer was noticed slipping something into his coat pocket, and after breakfast when our cook went to his coat for his tobacco, he unearthed a lady's cambric handkerchief, nicely embroidered, and a silver mounted garter. He looked at the articles a moment, and, grasping the situation at a glance, ran his eye over the outfit for the culprit. But there was not a word or a smile. He walked over and threw the articles into the fire, remarking, "Good whiskey and bad women will be the ruin of you varmints yet."

"The Snow-Shoe Dance," from George Catlin's *North American Indian Portfolio*. These Chippewa or Ojibwa Indians, gathered near Fort Snelling, Minnesota, are captured by Catlin singing and giving thanks for the first snowfall.

CHAPTER

8

PRAYING

RELIGIONS IN THIS COUNTRY have run the gamut from A to Z—from Anabaptism to Zen Buddhism. In between, all the mainstream religions have made their appearance; and—reflecting the American genius for improvisation—so too have hundreds of sects, many of them little more than the small followings of eccentric but charismatic leaders.

Obviously, some of these religious movements have influenced more people and made more lasting impressions than others. Puritanism, for example, has had a profound influence that is still felt; and Shakerism is significant as an example of the utopian communities that have come and gone over the centuries. Both these movements are covered in this chapter. Also included are pieces about slave religion, anti-Catholicism, Spiritualism, Judaism, and finally—under the heading "Spreading the Word"—several examples of the missionary zeal with which members of most religions have set out to share with others the good news that has been revealed to them.

THE VARIETIES OF RELIGIOUS LIFE

NEW ENGLAND PURITANISM AND WITCHCRAFT. *Though often embroiled in controversies about abstruse theological issues, the Puritans lived by a number of simple, bedrock beliefs. Among these was the conviction that just as they looked up to God for guidance in all things, so he looked down with particular interest and favor on his "Saints." Many were the occasions when the Hand of God was revealed conferring benefits, or the Finger seen pointing the way. And if the Hand sometimes held "the Rod of Correction," even that was but another proof of God's fatherly concern.*

What wonder then that a people so virtuous, so favored, who kept holy the Sabbath day and were punctilious in observing all the other Commandments, should have aroused the envy and hatred of Satan and his Powers of the Air?

The following examples of Puritans believing themselves to be under God's special Providence are drawn from the diaries and journals of William Bradford, John Winthrop, and Edward Johnson. The first section on witchcraft is by the Reverend Cotton Mather, the second is by Robert Calef.

William Bradford of Plymouth, 1623.

I may not here omit how, notwithstand all their great pains and industry, and the great hopes of a large crop, the Lord seemed to blast, and take away the same, and to threaten further and more sore famine unto them by a great drought which continued from the third week in May, till about the middle of July, without any rain and with great heat for the most part, insomuch as the corn began to wither away though it was set with fish, the moisture whereof helped it much. Yet at length it began to languish sore, and some of the drier grounds were parched like withered hay, part whereof was never recovered. Upon which they set apart a solemn day of humiliation, to seek the Lord by humble and fervent prayer, in this great distress. And He was pleased to give them a gracious and speedy answer, both to their own and the Indians' admiration [amazement] that lived amongst them. For all the morning, and greatest part of the day, it was clear weather and very hot, and not a cloud or any sign of rain to be seen; yet toward evening it began to overcast, and shortly after to rain with such sweet and gentle showers as gave them cause of rejoicing and blessing God. It came without either wind or thunder or any violence, and by degrees in that abundance as that

Late seventeenth-century gravestone for the Reverend Nathaniel Rogers in Ipswich, Massachusetts.

the earth was thoroughly wet and soaked therewith. Which did so apparently revive and quicken the decayed corn and other fruits, as was wonderful to see, and made the Indians astonished to behold. And afterwards the Lord sent them such seasonable showers, with interchange of fair warm weather as, through His blessing, caused a fruitful and liberal harvest, to their no small comfort and rejoicing. For which mercy, in time convenient, they also set apart a day of thanksgiving.

John Winthrop of Boston, 1623.

Two little girls of the governor's family were sitting under a great heap of logs, plucking of birds, and the wind driving the feathers into the house, the governor's wife caused them to remove away. They were no sooner gone, but the whole heap of logs fell down in the place, and had crushed them to death, if the Lord, in his special providence, had not delivered them.

Edward Johnson, author of Wonder-Working Providence of Sion's Saviour in New England.

To end this yeare 1639, the Lord was pleased to send a very sharp winter, and more especially in strong storms of weekly snows, with very bitter blasts: And here the Reader may take notice of the sad hand of the Lord against two persons, who were taken in a storme of snow, as they were passing from Boston to Roxbury, it being much about a mile distant, and a very plaine way. One of Roxbury sending to Boston his servant maid for a Barber-Chirurgion, to draw his tooth, they lost their way in their passage between, and were not found till many dayes after, and then the maid was found in one place, and the man in another, both of them frozen to death; in which sad accident, this was taken into consideration by divers people, that this Barber was more than ordinary laborious to draw men to those sinfull Errors, that were formerly so frequent, and now newly overthrowne by the blessing of the Lord, upon the endeavour of his faithfull servants (with the word of truth). He having a fit opportunity, by reason of his trade, so soone as any were set downe in his chaire, he would commonly be cutting of their haire and the truth together; notwithstanding some report better of the man, the example is for the living, the dead is judged of the Lord alone.

John Winthrop, 1640.

Mr. Pelham's house in Cambridge took fire in the dead of the night by the chimney. A neighbor's wife hearing some noise among her hens, persuaded her husband to arise, which, being very cold, he was loth to do, yet through her great importunity he did, and so espied the fire, and came running in his shirt, and had much to do to awake any body, but he got them up at last, and so saved all. The fire being ready to lay hold upon the stairs, they had all been burnt in their chambers, if God had not by his special providence sent help at that very instant.

John Winthrop, 1641.

A godly woman of the church of Boston, dwelling sometimes in London, brought with her a parcel of very fine linen of great value, which she set her heart too much upon, and had been at charge to have it all newly washed, and curiously folded and pressed, and so left it in the press in her parlor over night. She had a negro maid went into the room very late, and let fall some snuff of the candle upon the linen, so as by the morning all the linen was burned to tinder, and the boards underneath, and some stools and a part of the wainscot burned, and never perceived by any in the house, though some lodged in the chamber over head, and no ceiling between. But it pleased God that the loss of this linen did her much good, both in taking off her heart from worldly comforts, and in preparing her for a far greater affliction by the untimely death of her husband, who was slain not long after at Isle of Providence.

John Winthrop, 1643.

One John Cook, an honest young man, being in his master's absence to salute a ship, in the vanity of his mind thought to make the gun give a great report, and accordingly said to some, that he would make her speak. Overcharging her, she brake all into small pieces and scattered round about some men a flight shot off. Himself was killed, but no hurt found about him, but only one hand cut off and beaten a good distance from the place where he stood. And there appeared a special providence of God in it, for although there were many people up and down, yet none was hurt, nor was any near the gun when she was fired, whereas usually they gather thither on such occasions.

John Winthrop, 1643.

There arose a sudden gust at N.W. so violent for half an hour, as it blew down multitudes of trees. It lifted up their meeting house at Newbury, the people being in it. It darkened the air with dust, yet through God's great mercy it did no hurt, but only killed one Indian with the fall of a tree.

John Winthrop, 1646.

One Smith of Watertown had a son about five years old, who fell into the river near the mill gate, and was carried by the stream under the wheel, and taken up on the other side, without any harm. One of the boards of the wheel was fallen off, and it seems (by special providence) he was carried through under that gap, for otherwise if an eel pass through, it is cut asunder. The miller perceived his wheel to check on the sudden, which made him look out, and so he found the child sitting up to the waist in the shallow water beneath the mill.

Edward Johnson, 1649.

Also the Lord was pleased to awaken us with an Army of caterpillers, that had he not suddainly rebuked them, they had surely destroyed the husbandmans hope; where they fell upon trees, they left them like winter-wasting cold, bare and naked; and although they fell on fields very rarely, yet in some places they made as clear a riddance, as the harvest mans hand, and uncovered the gay green Medow ground, but indeed the Lord did by some plats shew us what he could have done with the whole, and in many places cast them into the highwayes, that the Cartwheels in their passage were painted green with running over the great swarms of them.

Also the Lord was pleased to command the wind and Seas to give us a jog on the elbow, by sinking the very chief of our shipping in the deep, and splitting them in shivers against the shores; a very goodly Ship called the *Seaforce* was cast away, and many New England people put to hard shifts for their lives, and some drowned, as the godly and dearly beloved servant of Christ, Mr. Thomas Coitmire, a very able Seaman, and also a good Scholar, who had spent both his labour and estate for the helping on of this Wilderness-work: as also another ship set forth by the Merchants of New-haven, of which the godly Mr. Lamberton went Master, neither ship, persons, nor goods ever heard of.

John Winthrop of Boston, 1649. The Sabbath was supposed to begin on Saturday evening.

This puts me in mind of another child very strangely drowned a little before winter. The parents were also members of the church of Boston. The father had undertaken to maintain the mill-dam, and being at work upon it, (with some help he had hired,) in the afternoon of the last day of the week, night came upon them before they had finished what they intended, and his conscience began to put him in mind of the Lord's day, and he was troubled, yet went on and wrought an hour within night. The next day, after evening exercise, and after they had supped, the mother put two children to bed in the room where themselves did lie, and they went out to visit a neighbor. When they returned, they continued about an hour in the room, and missed not the child, but then the mother going to the bed, and not finding her youngest child, (a daughter about five years of age,) after much search she found it drowned in a well in her cellar; which was very observable, as by a special hand of God, that the child should go out of that room into another in the dark, and then fall down at a trap door, or go down the stairs, and so into the well in the farther end of the cellar, the top of the well and the water being even with the ground. But the father, freely in the open congregation, did acknowledge it the righteous hand of God for his profaning his holy day against the checks of his own conscience.

Witchcraft—the official view; excerpts from Wonders of the Invisible World *by the Reverend Cotton Mather. The Salem witchcraft trials began in June 1692; Mather published his book justifying them soon afterward. In it, he first explains why New England was the scene of such an outbreak and how the infernal system worked, and then moves on to the trials themselves.*

The *New-Englanders* are a People of God settled in those which were once the *Devil's* Territories; and it may easily be supposed that the Devil was exceedingly disturbed, when he perceived such a People here accomplishing the Promise of old made unto our Blessed Jesus, *That He should have the Utmost parts of the Earth for his Possession.* There was not a greater Uproar among the *Ephesians,* when the Gospel was first brought among them, than there was among *The Powers of the Air* (after whom those *Ephesians* walked) when first the *Silver Trumpets* of the gospel here made the *Joyful Sound.* The Devil thus Irritated, immediately try'd all sorts of Methods to overturn this poor Plantation, and . . . I believe, that never were more *Satanical Devices* used for the Unsetling of any People under the Sun, than what have been Employ'd for the Extirpation of the *Vine* which God has here *Planted.* . . .

But, all those Attempts of Hell have hitherto been Abortive. . . . Wherefore the Devil is now making one Attempt more upon us; an Attempt more Difficult, more Surprizing, more snarl'd with unintelligible Circumstances than any that we have hitherto Encountered; an Attempt so *Critical,* that if we get well through, we shall soon enjoy *Halcyon Days* with all the *Vultures* of hell *Trodden under our Feet.* . . .

We have been advised by some Credible Christians yet alive, that a Malefactor, accused of *Witchcraft* as well as *Murder,* and Executed in this place more than Forty Years ago, did then give Notice of, *An Horrible* PLOT *against the Country by* WITCHCRAFT *then laid, which if it were not seasonably discovered, would probably Blow up, and pull down all the Churches in the Country.* And we have now with Horror seen the *Discovery* of such a

Witchcraft! An Army of *Devils* is horribly broke in upon the place which is the *Center*, and after a sort, the *First-born* of our *English* Settlements: and the Houses of the Good People there are fill'd with the doleful Shrieks of their Children and Servants, Tormented by Invisible Hands, with Tortures altogether preternatural.

The *Devil* Exhibiting himself ordinarily as a small *Black man*, has decoy'd a fearful knot of proud, froward, ignorant, envious and malicious creatures, to list themselves in his horrid Service, by entering their Names in a *Book* by him tendered unto them. These *Witches*, whereof above a Score have now Confessed . . . have met in Hellish *Randezvouzes*, wherein the Confessors do say, they have had their Diabolical Sacraments, imitating the *Baptism* and the *Supper* of our Lord. In these hellish meetings, these Monsters have associated themselves to do no less a thing than, *To destroy the Kingdom of our Lord Jesus Christ, in these parts of the World*; and in order thereunto, First they each of them have their *Spectres*, or Devils, commmission'd by them, & representing of them, to be the Engines of their Malice. By these wicked *Spectres*, they seize poor people about the Country, with various and bloudy Torments. . . . The people thus afflicted, are miserably scratched and bitten, so that the Marks are most visible to all the World, but the causes utterly invisible; and the same Invisible Furies do most visibly stick Pins into the bodies of the afflicted, and *scale* them, and hideously distort, and disjoint all their members, besides a thousand other sorts of Plagues beyond these of any natural diseases which they give unto them. Yea, they sometimes drag the poor people out of their chambers, and carry them over Trees and Hills, for divers miles together.

A large part of the persons tortured by these Diabolical *Spectres* are horribly tempted by them, sometimes with fair promises, and sometimes with hard threatnings, but always with felt miseries, to sign the *Devils Law* in a Spectral Book laid before them; which two or three of these poor Sufferers, being by their tiresome sufferings overcome to do, they have immediately been released from all their miseries, and they appear'd in *Spectre* then to Torture those that were before their Fellow-Sufferers.

The Tryal of Bridget Bishop, Alias Oliver, at the Court of Oyer and Terminer, Held at Salem, June 2, 1692.

She was indicted for Bewitching of several Persons in the Neighourhood, the Indictment being drawn up, according to the *Form* in such Cases usual. And pleading, *Not Guilty*, there were brought in several persons, who had long undergone many kinds of Miseries, which were preternaturally inflicted, and generally ascribed unto an *horrible Witchcraft.* There was little occasion to prove the *Witchcraft,* it being evident and notorious to all beholders. Now to fix the *Witchcraft* on the Prisoner at the Bar, the first thing used, was the Testimony of the *Bewitched*; whereof several testifi'd, That the *Shape* of the Prisoner did oftentimes very grievously Pinch them, Choak them, Bite them, and Afflict them; urging them to write their Names in a *Book,* which the said Spectre called, *Ours.* One of them did further testifie, that it was the *Shape* of the Prisoner, with another, which one day took her from her Wheel, and carried her to the Riverside, threatned there to Drown her, if she did not Sign to the *Book* mentioned: which yet she refused. Others of them did also testifie, that the said *Shape* did in her Threats brag to them that she had been the Death of sundry Persons, then by her named; that she had *Ridden* a Man then likewise named. Another testifi'd, the Apparition of *Ghosts* unto the Spectre of *Bishop,* crying out, *You Murdered us!* About the Truth whereof, there was in the Matter of Fact but too much suspicion.

It was testifi'd, That at the Examination of the Prisoner before the Magistrates, the Bewitched were extreamly tortured. If she did but cast her Eyes on them, they were presently struck down; and this in such a manner as there could be no Collusion in the Business. But upon the Touch of her Hand upon them, when they lay in their Swoons, they would immediately Revive; and not upon the Touch of any ones else.

One *Deliverance Hobbs,* who had confessed her being a Witch, was now tormented by the Spectres for her Confession. And she now testifi'd, That this *Bishop* tempted her to Sign the *Book* again, and to deny what she had confess'd. She affirm'd, That it was the Shape of this Prisoner, which whipped her with Iron Rods to compel her thereunto. And she affirmed, that this *Bishop* was at a General Meeting of the Witches, in a Field at *Salem*-Village, and there partook of a Diabolical Sacrament in Bread and Wine then administred.

To render it further unquestionable that the Prisoner at the Bar was the Person truly charged in THIS *Witchcraft,* there were produced many Evidences of OTHER *Witchcrafts,* by her perpetrated. For Instance, *John Cook* Testifi'd, That about five or six Years ago, one Morning, about Sun-Rise, he was in his Chamber assaulted by the *Shape* of this Prisoner: which look'd on him, grinn'd at him, and very much hurt him with a Blow on the side of the Head: and that on the same day, about Noon, the same *Shape* walked in the Room where he was, and an Apple strangely flew out of his Hand, into the Lap of his Mother, six or eight Foot from him.

John Bly and his Wife testifi'd, That he bought a Sow of *Edward Bishop,* the Husband of the Prisoner; and was to pay the Price agreed unto another person. This Prisoner being angry that she was thus hindred from fingring the Mony, quarrell'd with *Bly*. Soon after which, the Sow was taken with strange Fits; Jumping, Leaping, and Knocking her Head against the Fence; she seem'd Blind and Deaf, and would neither Eat nor be Suck'd. Whereupon a Neighbour said she believed the Creature was *Over-looked*; and sundry other Circumstances concurred, which made the Deponents believe that *Bishop* had bewitched it.

John Louder testify'd, That upon some little Controversy with *Bishop* about her Fowls, going well to Bed, he did awake in the Night by Moonlight, and did see clearly the likeness of this Woman grievously oppressing him; in which miserable condition she held him, unable to help himself, till near Day. He told *Bishop* of this; but she deny'd it, and threatned him very much. Quickly after this, being at home on a Lords day, with the doors shut about him, he saw a black Pig approach him; at which, he going to kick, it vanished away. Immediately after, sitting down, he saw a black Thing jump in at the Window, and come and stand before him. The Body was like that of a Monkey, the Feet like a Cocks, but the Face much like a Mans. He being so extreamly affrighted, that he could not speak; this Monster spoke to him, and said, *I am a Messenger sent unto you, for I understand that you are in some Trouble of Mind, and if you will be ruled by me, you shall want for nothing in this world.* Whereupon he endeavoured to clap his Hands upon it; but he could feel no substance; and it jumped out of the Window again; but immediately came in by the Porch, tho' the Doors were shut, and said, *You had better take my Counsel!* He then struck at it with a Stick, but struck only the Ground-sel, and broke the Stick: and it vanished away. He presently went out at the Back-door, and spied this *Bishop*, in her Orchard, going toward her House; but he had not power to set one foot forward unto her. Whereupon, returning into the House, he was immediately accosted by the Monster he had seen before; which Goblin was now going to fly at him; whereat he cry'd out, *The whole armour of God be between me and you!* So it sprang back, and flew over the Apple-tree; shaking many Apples off the Tree in its flying over. At its leap, it flung Dirt with its Feet against the Stomack of the Man; whereon he was then struck Dumb, and so continued for three Days together. Upon the producing of this Testimony, *Bishop* deny'd that she knew this Deponent: Yet their two Orchards joined; and they had often had their little Quarrels for some years together.

William Stacy testify'd, That receiving Mony of this *Bishop*, for work done by him; he was gone but a matter of three Rods from her, and looking for his Mony, found it unaccountably gone from him. Some time after, *Bishop* asked him, whether his Father would grind her Grist for her? He demanded why? She reply'd, *Because Folks count me a Witch.*

He answered, *No question but he will grind it for you*. Being then gone about six Rods from her, with a small Load in his Cart, suddenly the Off-wheel stump'd, and sunk down into a hole, upon plain Ground; so that the Deponent was forced to get help for the recovering of the Wheel: But stepping back to look for the hole, which might give him this Disaster, there was none at all to be found. Some time after, he was waked in the Night; but it seem'd as light as day; and he perfectly saw the shape of this *Bishop* in the Room, troubling of him; but upon her going out, all was dark again. He charg'd *Bishop* afterwards with it, and she deny'd it not; but was very angry. Quickly after, this Deponent having been threatned by *Bishop*, as he was in a dark Night going to the Barn, he was very suddenly taken or lifted from the Ground, and thrown against a Stone-wall: After that, he was again hoisted up and thrown down a Bank, at the end of his House. . . .

Many other Pranks of this *Bishop's* this Deponent was ready to testify. He also testify'd, That he verily believ'd the said *Bishop* was the Instrument of his Daughter *Priscilla's* Death; of which suspicion, pregnant Reasons were assigned.

To crown all, *John Bly* and *William Bly* testify'd, That being employ'd by *Bridget Bishop*, to help to take down the Cellar-wall of the old house wherein she formerly lived they did in holes of the said old Wall, find several *Poppets*, made up of Rags and Hogs-bristles, with headless Pins in them, the Points being outward; whereof she could give no account unto the Court, that was reasonable or tolerable. . . . Besides this, a Jury of Women found a preternatural Teat upon her Body: But upon a second search, within 3 or 4 hours, there was no such thing to be seen. There was also an Account of other People whom this Woman had Afflicted; and there might have been many more, if they had been enquired for; but there was no need of them.

There was one very strange thing more, with which the Court was newly entertained. As this Woman was under a Guard, passing by the great and spacious Meeting-house of *Salem*, she gave a look towards the House: And immediately a *Dæmon* invisibly entring the Meeting-house, tore down a part of it; so that tho' there was no Person to be seen there, yet the People, at the noise, running in, found a Board, which was strongly fastned with several Nails, transported unto another quarter of the House.

A more skeptical account of witchcraft in excerpts from More Wonders of the Invisible World *by the Boston merchant Robert Calef, which was published in 1700, a few years after the Salem trials. "This vile volume," as Cotton Mather called it, was publicly burned in Harvard Yard.*

The 30th of June, the court according to adjournment again sat, five more were tried, viz Sarah Good and Rebecca Nurse, of Salem Village; Susanna Martin, of Amsbury; Elizabeth How of Ipswitch; and Sarah Wildes of Topsfield: these were all condemned that session and were all executed on the 19th of July.

At the trial of Sarah Good, one of the afflicted fell in a fit; and after coming out of it she cried out of the prisoner, for stabbing her in the breast with a knife, and that she had broken the knife in stabbing her; accordingly a piece of the blade of a knife was found about her. Immediately information being given to the court, a young man was called, who produced a haft and part of the blade, which the court having viewed and compared, saw it to be the same; and upon inquiry the young man affirmed, that yesterday he happened to break that knife, and that he cast away the upper part. This afflicted person being then present, the young man was dismissed, and she was bidden by the court not to tell lies.

At the trial of Rebecca Nurse, it was remarkable that the jury brought in their verdict not guilty; immediately all the accusers in the court, and suddenly after all the afflicted out of court, made a hideous outcry, to the amazement not only of the spectators, but the court also seemed strangely surprised: one of the judges exprest himself not satisfied; another of them, as he was going off the bench, said they would have her indicted anew. The chief judge said he would not impose upon the jury; but intimated as if they had not well considered one expression of the prisoner when she was upon trial, viz. that when one Hobbs, who had confessed herself to be a witch, was brought into the court to witness against her, the prisoner, turning her head to her, said, *What do you bring her? She is one of us*, or to that effect; this, together with the clamours of the accusers, induced the jury to go out again, after their verdict, not guilty. But not agreeing, they came into the court; and she being then at the bar, her words were repeated to her, in order to have her explanation of them; and she making no reply to them, they found the bill, and brought her in guilty; these words being the inducement to it, as the foreman has signified in writing, as follows:

July 4, 1692. I, Thomas Fisk, the subscriber hereof, being one of them that were of the jury last week at Salem court, upon the trial of Rebecca Nurse, &c. being desired by some of the relations to give a reason why the jury brought her in guilty, after her verdict not guilty; I do hereby give my reasons to be as follows, viz. When the verdict was, not guilty, the honoured court was pleased to object against it, saying to them, that they think they let slip the words which the prisoner at the bar

spake against herself, which were spoken in reply to goodwife Hobbs and her daughter, who had been faulty in setting their hands to the devil's book, as they had confessed formerly; the words were, *What, do these persons give in evidence again me now? they used to come among us.* After the honoured court had manifested their dissatisfaction of the verdict, several of the jury declared themselves desirous to go out again, and thereupon the court gave leave; but when we came to consider of the case, I could not tell how to take her words as an evidence against her, till she had a further opportunity to put her sense upon them, if she would take it; and then, going into court, I mentioned the words aforesaid, which by one of the court were affirmed to have been spoken by her, she being then at the bar, but made no reply, nor interpretation of them; whereupon these words were to me a principal evidence against her.
                                                                THOMAS FISK.

When goodwife Nurse was informed what use was made of these words, she put in this following declaration into the court:

These presents do humbly shew to the honoured court and jury, that I being informed that the jury brought me in guilty, upon my saying that goodwife Hobbs and her daughter were of our company; but I intended no otherways, than as they were prisoners with us, and therefore did then, and yet do, judge them not legal evidence against their fellow prisoners. And I being something hard of hearing, and full of grief, none informing me how the court took up my words, and therefore had no opportunity to declare what I intended, when I said they were of our company.   REBECCA NURSE.

After her condemnation she was by one of the ministers of Salem excommunicated; yet the governor saw cause to grant a reprieve; which when known (and some say immediately upon granting) the accusers renewed their dismal outcries against her, insomuch that the governor was by some Salem gentlemen prevailed with to recall the reprieve, and she was executed with the rest.

The testimonials of her christian behaviour, both in the course of her life and at her death, and her extraordinary care in educating her children, and setting them good examples, &c. under the hands of so many, are so numerous, that for brevity they are here omitted.

August 5, the court again sitting, six more were tried on the same account, viz. mr. George Burroughs, sometime minister of Wells, John Proctor, and Elizabeth Proctor his wife, with John Willard, of Salem Village, George Jacobs senior, of Salem, and

Martha Carrier, of Andover; these were all brought in guilty, and condemned; and were all executed, *August 19,* except Proctor's wife, who pleaded pregnancy.

Mr. Burroughs was carried in a cart with the others, through the streets of Salem to execution. When he was upon the ladder, he made a speech for the clearing of his innocency, with such solemn and serious expressions, as were to the admiration of all present: his prayer (which he concluded by repeating the Lord's prayer) was so well worded, and uttered with such composedness, and such (at least seeming) fervency of spirit, as was very affecting, and drew tears from many, so that it seemed to some that the spectators would hinder the execution. The accusers said the black man stood and dictated to him. As soon as he was turned off, mr. Cotton Mather, being mounted upon a horse, addressed himself to the people, partly to declare that he [Burroughs] was no ordained minister, and partly to possess the people of his guilt, saying that the devil has often been transformed into an angel of light; and this somewhat appeased the people, and the executions went on. When he was cut down, he was dragged by the halter to a hole, or grave, between the rocks, about two feet deep, his shirt and breeches being pulled off, and an old pair of trowsers of one executed put on his lower parts; he was so put in, together with Willard and Carrier, that one of his hands and his chin, and a foot of one of them, were left uncovered.

John Proctor and his wife being in prison, the sheriff came to his house and seized all the goods, provisions and cattle that he could come at, and sold some of the cattle at half price, and killed others, and put them up for the West-Indies; threw out the beer out of a barrel, and carried away the barrel; emptied a pot of broth, and took away the pot, and left nothing in the house for the support of the children. No part of the said goods are known to be returned. Proctor earnestly requested mr. Noyes to pray with and for him; but it was wholly denied, because he would not own himself to be a witch.

During his imprisonment he sent the following letter in behalf of himself and others.

> Salem Prison, July 23, 1692
>
> Here are five persons who have lately confessed themselves to be witches, and do accuse some of us of being along with them at a sacrament, since we were committed into close prison, which we know to be lies. Two of the five are (Carrier's sons) young men who would not confess any thing till they tied them neck and heels, till the blood was ready to come out of their noses; and it is

credibly believed and reported this was the occasion of making them confess what they never did, by reason they said one had been a witch a month, and another five weeks, and that their mother had made them so, who has been confined here this nine weeks. My son William Proctor, when he was examined, because he would not confess that he was guilty, when he was innocent, they tied him neck and heels till the blood gushed out at his nose, and would have kept him so twenty-four hours, if one, more merciful than the rest, had not taken pity on him, and caused him to be unbound. These actions are very like the popish cruelties. They have already undone us in our estates, and that will not serve their turns without our innocent blood.

He pleaded very hard at execution for a little respite of time, saying that he was not fit to die; but it was not granted.

September 9, six more were tried, and received sentence of death, viz. Martha Cory, of Salem Village; Mary Easty, of Topsfield; Alice Parker and Ann Pudeater, of Salem; Dorcas Hoar, of Beverly, and Mary Bradberry, of Salisbury. Sept. 16, Giles Cory was prest to death.

Giles Cory pleaded not guilty to his indictment, but would not put himself on trial by the jury (they having cleared none upon trial) and knowing there would be the same witnesses against him, rather chose to undergo what death they would put him to. In pressing, his tongue being prest out of his mouth, the sheriff with his cane forced it in again when he was dying. He was the first in New-England that was ever prest to death.

The cart, going to the hill with these eight to execution, was for some time at a set; the afflicted and others said that the devil hindered it, &c.

Martha Cory, wife to Giles Cory, protesting her innocency, concluded her life with an eminent prayer upon the ladder.

Wardwell, having formerly confessed himself guilty, and after denied it, was soon brought upon his trial; his former confession and spectre testimony was all that appeared against him. At execution, while he was speaking to the people, protesting his innocency, the executioner being at the same time smoking tobacco, the smoke coming in his face interrupted his discourse; those accusers said that the devil did hinder him with smoke.

Some, that had been of several juries, have given forth a paper, signed with their own hands, in these words:

We, whose names are under written, being in the year 1692 called to serve as jurors in court at Salem on trial of many, who were by some suspected guilty of doing acts of witchcraft upon the bodies of sundry persons:

We confess that we ourselves were not capable to understand, nor able to withstand, the mysterious delusions of the powers of darkness, and prince of the air; but were, for want of knowledge in ourselves, and better information from others, prevailed with to take up with such evidence against the accused, as, on further consideration and better information, we justly fear was insufficient for the touching the lives of any, (*Deut. xvii.* 6) whereby we fear we have been instrumental, with others, though ignorantly and unwittingly, to bring upon ourselves and this people of the Lord the guilt of innocent blood; which sin the Lord saith, in scripture, he would not pardon, (2 *Kings, xxiv.* 4) that is, we suppose, in regard of his temporal judgments. We do therefore hereby signify to all in general (and to the surviving sufferers in special) our deep sense of, and sorrow for, our errors, in acting on such evidence to the condemning of any person; and do hereby declare, that we justly fear that we were sadly deluded and mistaken; for which we are much disquieted and distressed in our minds; and do therefore humbly beg forgiveness, first of God for Christ's sake, for this our error; and pray that God would not impute the guilt of it to ourselves, nor others; and we also pray that we may be considered candidly, and aright, by the living sufferers, as being then under the power of a strong and general delusion, utterly unacquainted with, and not experienced in, matters of that nature.

We do heartily ask forgiveness of you all, whom we have justly offended; and do declare, according to our present minds, we would none of us do such things again on such grounds for the whole world; praying you to accept of this in way of satisfaction for our offence, and that you would bless the inheritance of the Lord, that he may be entreated for the land.

Foreman,	*Thomas Fisk,*	*Th. Pearly,* sen.
	William Fisk,	*John Peabody,*
	John Bacheler,	*Thomas Perkins,*
	Thomas Fisk, jun.	*Samuel Sayer,*
	John Dane,	*Andrew Eliot,*
	Joseph Evelith,	*Henry Herrick,* sen.

THE SHAKERS. *Also known as the United Society of Believers in Christ's Second Appearing; the Children of Truth; or the Millennial Church, the Shaker movement was founded by Ann Lee. Born in Manchester, England, in 1736, Lee grew up with little education and worked as a cook and in a factory. Influenced by some friends, she joined a local group of Shaking Quakers, who claimed to speak in tongues, prophesy, and heal the sick; they also interrupted Church of England services with singing, dancing, and angry tirades, and for this Ann Lee was put in jail. While there she had several visions; one of them, concerning Adam and Eve, revealed to her that sex was sinful; another vision told her to go to America, which she did in 1774, settling with a small band of followers at Watervliet, near Albany, New York. From there she led missions throughout New England, and these settlements continued after her death in 1784. The Shakers reached their high point in the years 1830–50, when they had some six thousand members in twenty communities throughout New England and in Indiana, Kentucky, and Ohio. They revered Ann Lee—"Mother Ann"—and looked forward to the Second Coming, when the Messiah was to be a woman. In the meantime, they farmed, made furniture, grew seeds, and attracted the attention of curious travelers, Charles Dickens among them. Because strict celibacy was a basic rule, the sect could grow only by gaining new converts, and when the Shakers stopped doing this, the movement died. The account that follows is by an anonymous author who lived at the Watervliet community for four months in 1842–43.*

Daily Routine.

The hours of rising were five o'clock in the summer, and half-past five in the winter. The family all rose at the toll of the bell, and in less than ten minutes vacated the bedrooms. The sisters then distributed themselves throughout the rooms, and made up all the beds, putting everything in the most perfect order before breakfast. The brothers proceeded to their various employments, and made a commencement for the day. The cows were milked, and the horses were fed. At seven o'clock the bell rang for breakfast, but it was ten minutes after when we went to the tables. The brothers and sisters assembled each by themselves, in rooms appointed for the purpose; and at the sound of a small bell the doors of these rooms opened, and a procession of the family was formed in the hall, each individual being in his or her proper place, as they would be at table. The brothers came first, followed by the sisters, and the whole marched in solemn silence to the dining room. The brothers and sisters took separate tables, on opposite sides of the room. All stood up until each one had arrived at his or her proper place, and then at a signal from the Elder at the head of the table, they all knelt down for about two minutes, and at another signal they all arose and commenced eating their breakfast. Each individual

A visitor, seated to the left, watches the Shakers "worship God with
all their might in the dance." Dickens also visited and commented
on their "grim" looks. Line drawing, 1830s.

helped himself; which was easily done, as the tables were so arranged
that between every four persons there was a supply of every article
intended for the meal. At the conclusion they all arose and marched
away from the tables in the same manner as they marched to them;
and during the time of marching, eating and re-marching, not one
word was spoken, but the most perfect silence was preserved.

After breakfast all proceeded immediately to their respective
employments, and continued industriously occupied until ten minutes to twelve o'clock, when the bell announced dinner. Farmers then
left the field and mechanics their shops, all washed their hands, and
formed procession again, and marched to dinner in the same way as
to breakfast. Immediately after dinner they went to work again, (having no hour for resting), and continued steady at it until the bell
announced supper. At supper the same routine was gone through as
at the other meals, and all except the farmers went to work again. The
farmers were supposed to be doing what were called 'chores,' which
appeared to mean any little odd jobs in and about the stables and
barns. At eight o'clock all work was ended for the day, and the family
went to what they called a 'union meeting.' This meeting generally
continued one hour, and then at about nine o'clock, all retired to bed.

The routine I have described was continually going on; and it was
their boast that they were then the same in their habits and manners

as they were sixty years before. The furniture of the dwellings was of the same old-fashioned kind that the early Dutch settlers used; and every thing about them and their dwellings, I was taught, was originally designed in heaven, and the designs transmitted to them by angels. The plan of their buildings, the style of their furniture, the pattern of their coats and pants, and the cut of their hair, is all regulated according to communications received from heaven by Mother Ann.

The Dancing Meetings.

At half past seven p.m. on the dancing days, all the members retired to their separate rooms, where they sat in solemn silence, just gazing at the stove, until the silver tones of the small tea-bell gave the signal for them to assemble in the large hall. Thither they proceeded in perfect order and solemn silence. Each had on thin dancing shoes; and on entering the door of the hall they walked on tip-toe, and took up their positions as follows: the brothers formed a rank on the right, and the sisters on the left, facing each other, about five feet apart. After all were in their proper places the chief Elder stepped into the center of the space, and gave an exhortation for about five minutes, concluding with an invitation to them all to 'go forth, old men, young men and maidens, and worship God with all their might in the dance.' Accordingly they 'went forth,' the men stripping off their coats and remaining in their shirt-sleeves. First they formed a procession and marched around the room in double-quick time, while four brothers and sisters stood in the center singing for them. After marching in this manner until they got a little warm, they commenced dancing, and continued it until they were pretty well tired. During the dance the sisters kept on one side, and the brothers on the other, and not a word was spoken by any of them. After they appeared to have had enough of this exercise, the Elder gave the signal to stop, when immediately each one took his or her place in an oblong circle formed around the room, and all waited to see if anyone had received a 'gift,' that is, an inspiration to do something odd. Then two of the sisters would commence whirling round like a top, with their eyes shut; and continued this motion for about fifteen minutes; when they suddenly stopped and resumed their places, as steady as if they had never stirred. . . .

On some occasions when a sister had stopped her whirling, she would say, 'I have a communication to make;' when the head Eldress would step to her side and receive the communication, and then make known the nature of it to the company. The first message I heard was as follows: 'Mother Ann has sent two angels to inform us that a tribe of Indians has been round here two days, and want the brothers and sisters to take them in. They are outside the building there, looking in at the windows.' I shall never forget how I looked round at the windows, expecting to see the yellow faces, when this announcement was made; but I believe some of the old folks who eyed me, bit their lips and smiled. It caused no alarm to the rest, but the first Elder exhorted the brothers 'to take in the poor spirits and assist them to get salvation.' He afterward repeated more of what the angels had said, viz., 'that the Indians were a savage tribe who had all died before Columbus discovered America, and had been wandering about ever since. Mother Ann wanted them to be received into the meeting to-morrow night.' After this we dispersed to our separate bed-rooms. . . .

The next dancing night we again assembled in the same manner as before, and went through the marching and dancing as usual; after which the hall doors were opened, and the Elder invited the Indians to come in. The doors were soon shut again, and one of the sisters (the same who received the original communication) informed us that she saw Indians all around and among the brothers and sisters. The Elder then urged upon the members the duty of 'taking them in.' Whereupon eight or nine sisters became possessed of the spirits of Indian squaws, and about six of the brethren became Indians. Then ensued a regular pow-wow, with whooping and yelling and strange antics, such as would require a Dickens to describe. The sisters and brothers squatted on the floor together, Indian fashion, and the Elders and Eldresses endeavored to keep them asunder, telling the men they must be separated from the squaws, and otherwise instructing them in the rules of Shakerism. Some of the Indians then wanted some 'succotash,' which was soon brought them from the kitchen in two wooden dishes, and placed on the floor; when they commenced eating it with their fingers. These performances continued till about ten o'clock; then the chief Elder requested the Indians to go away, telling them they would find someone waiting to conduct them to the Shakers in the heavenly world. At this announcement the possessed men and women became themselves again, and all retired to rest.

Spiritual Presents.

At one of the meetings, after a due amount of marching and dancing, by which all the members had got pretty well excited, two or three sisters commenced whirling, which they continued to do for some time, and then stopped suddenly and revealed to us that Mother Ann was present at the meeting, and that she had brought a dozen baskets of spiritual fruit for her children; upon which the Elder invited all to go forth to the baskets in the center of the floor, and help themselves. Accordingly they all stepped forth and went through the various motions of taking fruit and eating it. You will wonder if I helped myself to the fruit, like the rest. No; I had not faith enough to see the baskets or the fruit; and you may think, perhaps, that I laughed at the scene; but in truth, I was so affected by the general gravity and the solemn faces I saw around me, that it was impossible for me to laugh.

A Revival in Hades.

During my whole stay with the Shakers a revival was going on among the spirits of the invisible world. Information of it was first received by one of the families in Ohio, through a heavenly messenger. The news of the revival soon spread from Ohio to the families in New York and New England. It was caused as follows: George Washington and most of the Revolutionary fathers, had, by some means, got converted, and were sent out on a mission to preach the gospel to the spirits who were wandering in darkness. Many of the wild Indian tribes were sent by them to the different Shaker Communities, to receive instruction in the gospel. One of the tribes came to Watervliet and was 'taken in,' as I have described.

At one of the Sunday meetings, when the several families were met for worship, one of the brothers declared himself possessed of the spirit of George Washington; and made a speech informing us that Napoleon and all his Generals were present at our meeting, together with many of his own officers, who fought with him in the Revolution. These, as well as many more distinguished personages, were all Shakers in the other world, and had been sent to give information relative to the revival now going on. In a few minutes, each of the persons present at the meeting fell to representing some one of the great personages alluded to.

This revival commenced when I first went there; and during the four months I remained, much of the members' time was spent in such performances. It appeared to me, that whenever any of the brethren or sisters wanted to have some fun, they got possessed of spirits, and would go to cutting up capers; all of which were tolerated even during the hours of labor, because whatever they chose to do, was attributed to the spirits.

SLAVE RELIGION. *Among the many arguments once used to justify slavery, there was one that held that bringing people from the "Dark Continent" of Africa to Christian America was actually doing them a favor. Only here could their souls be saved.*

Oddly enough, this view was most famously expressed by someone who had herself been brought to this country as a slave—Phillis Wheatley, who in 1773, when she was nineteen, published the poem "On Being Brought from Africa to America":

> *'Twas Mercy Brought me from my* Pagan *Land,*
> *Taught my benighted soul to understand*
> *That there's a God . . .*

No doubt Wheatley's view of things was influenced by the fact that she was virtually adopted by the prosperous Boston family who bought her. Other slaves, as we shall see after two more examples of owners' opinions, felt very differently.

An extract from a law passed in Virginia in September 1667.

Whereas some doubts have risen whether children that are slaves by birth, and by the charity and piety of their owners made partakers of the blessed sacrament of baptism, should by the virtue of their baptism be made free, *it is enacted and declared by this Grand Assembly, and the authority thereof,* that the conferring of baptism does not alter the condition of the person as to his bondage or freedom; that divers masters, freed from this doubt, may more carefully endeavor the propagation of Christianity by permitting children, though slaves, or those of greater growth if capable, to be admitted to that sacrament.

Extracts from a catechism for slaves that appeared in the Southern Episcopalian, *published in Charleston, South Carolina, in April 1854.*

Q. Who keeps the snakes and all bad things from hurting you?
A. God does.
Q. Who gave you a master and a mistress?
A. God gave them to me.
Q. Who says that you must obey them?
A. God says that I must.
Q. What book tells you these things?
A. The Bible.
Q. How does God do all his work?
A. He always does it right.
Q. Does God love to work?
A. Yes, God is always at work.
Q. Did Adam and Eve have to work?
A. Yes, they had to keep the garden.
Q. Was it hard to keep that garden?
A. No, it was very easy.
Q. What makes you lazy?
A. My wicked heart.
Q. How do you know your heart is wicked?
A. I feel it every day.
Q. Who teaches you so many wicked things?
A. The Devil.
Q. Must you let the Devil teach you?
A. No, I must not.

Reminiscences from former slaves, collected by the Federal Writers' Project (part of the W.P.A.) during the New Deal.

The Reverend Anderson Edwards. I's been preaching the Gospel and farming, since slavery time. I jined the chu'ch eighty-three years ago, when I was a slave of Master Gaud. Till freedom, I had to preach what they told me to. Master made me preach to the other niggers that the Good Book say that if niggers obey their master, they would go to Heaven. I knew there was something better for them, but I darsen't tell them so, 'lest I done it on the sly. That I did lots. I told the niggers—but not so Master could hear it—that if they keep praying, the Lord would hear their prayers and set them free.

Rachel Reed. I was a 'ligious chile, in dem days, and I'm 'ligious now, too, but colored folks jes' naturally had more 'ligion back dere, 'fore de War. I kin remember when my ma used to put us chillun outside de cabin in de quarters, and den she would shut de doors, and shut de windows tight, and sit a tub of water in de middle of de floor, and kneel down, and pray dat de yoke of bondage be removed from de nigger's neck. All de niggers done dat. Dey did. Ma allus said de sound of dey voices went down into de tub of water and de white folks couldn't hear dem prayin'.

"Meeting in the African Church, Cincinnati, Ohio." Those who wish to be saved begin to come forward. From the *Illustrated News*, April 1830.

Alice Sewell. Dey did 'low us to go to church on Sunday, about two miles down de public road, and dey hired a white preacher to preach to us. He never did tell us nothing but be good servants, pick up Old Marse' and Old Mis' things about de place, and don't steal no chickens or pigs, and don't lie 'bout nothing. Den, dey baptize you and call dat, "You got religion." Never did say nothing 'bout a slave dying and going to Heaven. When we die, dey bury us next day, and you is just like any of de other cattle dying on de place. Dat's all 'tis to it and all 'tis of you. You is jest dead. Dat's all.

July Halfen. Marse Carter had a house gal by de name uf Frances, an' she had to wait on de white folks all day long, an' when night wud come, he made her slip out 'mongst de slaves an' see what dey wus doin' an' talkin' 'bout.

My mammy wus livin' wid' 'nudder man, named Joe, an' one night Joe an' my mammy an' some more slaves wus down on deir knees prayin' fur de good Lord to sot dem free, an' Frances wus slippin' round de corner uf de house an' heard what dey wus sayin'. An' she goes back to de house an' tells de old marse, an' he sont de oberseer down dar an' brung ebery one uf dem to de stake, an' tied dem, an' whupped dem so hard dat blood come from some uf dem's backs.

CATHOLICS. *Welcomed only in Maryland, which had been founded by the Catholic George Calvert—and even there soon denied full civil liberties— Catholics had a hard time of it in this country until massive immigration from Ireland, Italy, and Poland gave them the numbers that command respect. Until then the English view of them had largely prevailed: Catholics were mostly Frenchmen or Spaniards, traditional enemies; if English, they were probably traitors like Guy Fawkes, who plotted to blow up Parliament—king, lords, and commons all at once. Their beliefs, enforced by the Inquisition, were regarded as absurd, their ceremonies as idolatrous, and they themselves as blindly obedient to an unscrupulous clergy. The pope frequently was characterized as the Scarlet Whore, the Triple Tyrant, or, more simply, the Anti-Christ. Here are five examples of the kind of rough treatment and bad press Catholics received.*

The Dutch pastor Johannes Megalopensis writes to his superiors in Amsterdam about the Jesuit priest, Father Jogues, who was later to be designated one of the Martyrs of North America and, in 1930, canonized a saint.

In a preceding letter of September 24, 1658, mention was made of a Jesuit who came to this place, Manhattans, overland, from Canada. I shall now explain the matter more fully, for your better understanding of it. It happened in the year 1642, when I was minister in the colony of Rensselaerswyck, that our Indians in the neighborhood, who are generally called Maquaas, but who call themselves Kajingehaga, were at war with the Canadian or French Indians, who are called by our Indians Adyranthaka. Among the prisoners whom our Indians had taken from the French, was this Jesuit, whom they according to their custom had handled severely. When he was brought to us, his left thumb and several fingers on both hands had been cut off, either wholly or in part, and the nails of the remaining fingers had been chewed off. As this Jesuit had been held in captivity by them for some time, they consented that he should go among the Dutch, but only when accompanied by some of them. At last the Indians resolved to burn him. Concerning this he came to me with grievous complaint. We advised him that next time the Indians were asleep, he should run away and come to us, and we would protect and secure him, and send him by ship to France. This was done. After concealing him and entertaining him for six weeks, we sent him to the Manhattans and thence to England and France, as he was a Frenchman, born at Paris.

Afterward this same Jesuit came again from France to Canada. As our Indians had made peace with the French, he again left Canada, and took up his residence among the Mohawks. He indulged in the largest expectations of converting them to popery, but the Mohawks with their hatchets put him to a violent death. They then brought and presented to me his missal and breviary together with his underclothing, shirts and coat. When I said to them that I would not have thought that they would have killed this Frenchman, they answered, that the Jesuits did not consider the fact, that their people (the French) were always planning to kill the Dutch.

Extracts from The Laws of New England to the Year 1700. *Other colonies, New York among them, had similar laws.*

Jesuits. No Jesuit or Priest to abide in the Jurisdiction.

Whoever can't clear himself from Suspicion to the Court of Assistants, to be banish'd, not to return on Pain of Death, unless by Shipwreck, or in Company with any upon Business, with whom they are to return.

Whatever Priest residing there, did not depart before November 1700, he was to be imprisoned for Life, and to die if he broke Prison.

Whoever conceal'd such, to be Pillory'd, or pay 200 pounds, half to the Informer.

Any Justice may commit one suspected, in order to a Trial, and he may be seiz'd by any, without Warrant.

If a Priest is driven on the Coast, he must go to one of the Council, observe his Orders and depart as soon as possible.

From the trial in July 1741 of John Ury, a schoolteacher recently arrived in New York and accused of masterminding a plot to raise a rebellion among the black slaves, burn the city, and massacre its white inhabitants—a conspiracy that came to be known as "The Great Negro Plot." Ury, who was also suspected of being a Catholic priest in the service of the Spanish, then at war with the English, served as his own lawyer. The trial took place in the colony's Supreme Court. Mr. Smith was counsel for the king, i.e., the prosecutor.

Mr. Smith summed up the evidence for the king, and addressing himself to the court and jury, proceeded as followeth.

Though this work of darkness, in the contrivance of a horrible plot, to burn and destroy this city, has manifested itself in many blazing effects, to the terror and amazement of us all; yet the secret springs of this mischief lay long concealed: this destructive scene has opened by slow degrees: but now, gentlemen, we have at length great reason to conclude, that it took its rise from a foreign influence; and that it originally depended upon causes that we ourselves little thought of, and which, perhaps, very few of the inferior and subordinate agents were intimately acquainted with.

The monstrous wickedness of this plot would probably among strangers impeach its credit; but if it be considered as the contrivance of the public enemy, and the inhuman dictate of a bloody religion, the wonder ceases.

What more cruel and unnatural can be conceived, than what Rome has contrived; yea what more savage and barbarous, than what popery has attempted, and sometimes executed, for the extirpation of that which the papists call heresy? We need not go so far from home as the vallies of Piedmont, nor rake into the ashes of the ancient Waldenses and Albigenses, for tragical instances of popish cruelty. We need not remind you of the massacre at Paris, nor the later desolations in France, nor mention the horrible slaughters of the duke d'Alva, in the Low Countries. We need not recount the many millions of lives, that in remote countries, and different ages, have been sacrificed to the Roman idol; nor measure out to you that ocean of foreign blood with which the scarlet whore hath made herself perpetually drunk.

No, gentlemen, the histories of our native country will give us a formidable idea of popery; and inform us of the detestable principles of that religion. . . . which, in order to promote its interests, never boggles at the vilest means, can sanctify the most execrable villainies; and to encourage its votaries, will canonize for saints a Guy Faux and others, some of the greatest monsters of iniquity that ever trod upon the face of the earth!

Gentlemen, if the evidence you have heard is sufficient to produce a general conviction that the late fires in this city, and the murderous design against its inhabitants, are the effects of a Spanish and popish plot, then the mystery of this iniquity, which has so much puzzled us, is unveiled, and our admiration [wonder] ceases: all the mischiefs we have suffered or been threatened with, are but a sprout from that evil root, a small stream from that overflowing fountain of destruction, that has often deluged the earth with slaughter and blood, and spread ruin and desolation far and wide.

We need not wonder to see a popish priest at this bar, as a prime incendiary; nor think it strange that an Englishman of that religion and character should be concerned in so detestable a design. What can be expected from those that profess a religion that is at war with God and man; not only with the truths of the Holy Scriptures, but also with common sense and reason; and is destructive of all the kind and tender sensations of human nature? When a man, contrary to the evidence of his senses, can believe the absurd doctrine of transubstantiation; can give up his reason to a blind obedience and an implicit faith; can be persuaded to believe that the most unnatural crimes, such as treason and murder, when done in obedience to the pope, or for the service of the holy church, by rooting out what they call heresy, will merit heaven: I say, when a man has imbibed such principles as these, he can easily divest himself of every thing that is human but his shape; he is capable of any villainy, even as bad as that which is charged on the prisoner at the bar.

From Awful Disclosures of the Hotel Dieu Nunnery of Montreal, *by Maria Monk, published in 1836. Despite evidence that Maria was an escapee from a lunatic asylum in upper New York, large numbers of readers swallowed her best-selling story of innocent, blue-eyed young women forced to take the veil and then submit to "criminal intercourse" with lustful priests who entered the fortress-like nunnery by a secret underground passageway.*

I must now come to one deed, in which I had some part, and which I look back upon with greater horror and pain, than any occurrences in the Convent. . . . One day, the Superior sent for me and several other nuns, to receive her commands at a particular room. We found the Bishop and some priests with her; and speaking in an unusual tone of fierceness and authority, she said, "Go to the room for the Examination of Conscience, and drag Saint Francis [a young nun] up-stairs." Nothing more was necessary than this unusual command with the tone and manner which accompanied it, to excite in me most gloomy anticipations. . . . What terrified me was, first, the Superior's angry manner; second, the expression she used, being a French term, whose peculiar use I had learnt in the Convent, and whose meaning is rather softened when translated into *drag*; third, the place to which we were directed to take the interesting young nun, and the persons assembled there as I supposed to condemn her. My fears were such, concerning the fate that awaited her, and my horror at the idea that she was in some way to be sacrificed, that I would have given any thing to be allowed to stay where I was. But I feared the consequences of disobeying the Superior, and proceeded with the rest towards the room for the examination of conscience.

The room to which we were to proceed from that, was in the second story, and the place of many a scene of a shameful nature. It is sufficient for me to say, after what I have said in other parts of this book, that things had there occurred which made me regard the place with the greatest disgust. Saint Francis had appeared melancholy for some time. I well knew that she had cause, for she had been repeatedly subject to trials which I need not name—our common lot. When we reached the room where we had been bidden to seek her, I entered the door, my companions standing behind me, as the place was so small as hardly to hold five persons at a time. The young nun was standing alone, near the middle of the room; she was probably about twenty, with light hair, blue eyes, and a very fair complexion. I spoke to her in a compassionate voice, but at the same time with such a decided manner, that she comprehended my full meaning—

"Saint Francis, we are sent for you."

Several others spoke kindly to her, but two addressed her very harshly. The poor creature turned round with a look of meekness, and without expressing any unwillingness or fear, without even speaking a word, resigned herself to our hands. The tears came into my eyes. I had not a moment's doubt that she considered her fate as sealed, and was already beyond the fear of death. She was conducted, or rather hurried to the staircase, which was near by, and then seized by her limbs and clothes, and in fact almost dragged upstairs, in the sense the Superior had intended. I laid my own hands upon her—I took hold of her too,—more gently indeed than some of the rest; yet I encouraged and assisted them in carrying her. I could not avoid it. My refusal would not have saved her; nor prevented her being carried up; it would only have exposed me to some severe punishment, as I believed some of my companions would have seized the first opportunity to complain of me.

All the way up the staircase, Saint Francis spoke not a word, nor made the slightest resistance. When we entered with her the room to which she was ordered, my heart sunk within me. The Bishop, the Lady Superior, and five priests, viz. Bonin, Richards, Savage, and two others, I now ascertained, were assembled for her trial, on some charge of great importance.

When we had brought our prisoner before them, Father Richards began to question her, and she made ready but calm replies. I cannot pretend to give a connected account of what ensued: my feelings were wrought up to such a pitch, that I knew not what I did, nor what to do. . . . I am inclined to the belief, that Father Richards wished to shield the poor prisoner from the severity of her fate, by drawing from her expressions that might bear a favourable construction. He asked her, among other things, if she was not sorry for what she had been overheard to say (for she had been betrayed by one of the nuns), and if she would not prefer confinement in the cells, to the punishment which was threatened her. But the Bishop soon interrupted him, and it was easy to perceive that he considered her fate as sealed, and was determined she should not escape. In reply to some of the questions put to her, she was silent; to others I heard her voice reply that she did not repent of words she had uttered, though they had been reported by some of the nuns who had heard them; that she still wished to escape from the Convent; and that she had firmly resolved to resist every attempt to compel her to the commission of crimes which she detested. She added, that she would rather die than cause the murder of harmless babes.

"That is enough, finish her!" said the Bishop.

Two nuns instantly fell upon the young woman, and in obedience to directions, given by the Superior, prepared to execute her sentence.

She still maintained all the calmness and submission of a lamb. Some of those who took part in this transaction, I believe, were as unwilling as myself; but of others I can safely say, that I believe they delighted in it. Their conduct certainly exhibited a most blood-thirsty spirit. But, above all others present, and above all human fiends I ever saw, I think Saint Hypolite was the most diabolical. She engaged in the horrible task with all alacrity, and assumed from choice the most revolting parts to be performed. She seized a gag, forced it into the mouth of the poor nun, and when it was fixed between her extended jaws, so as to keep them open at their greatest possible distance, took hold of the straps fastened at each end of the stick, crossed them behind the helpless head of the victim, and drew them tight through the loop prepared as a fastening.

The bed which had always stood in one part of the room, still remained there; though the screen, which had usually been placed before it, and was made of thick muslin, with only a crevice through which a person behind might look out, had been folded up on its hinges in the form of a W, and placed in a corner. On the bed the prisoner was laid with her face upward, and then bound with cords, so that she could not move. In an instant another bed was thrown upon her. One of the priests, named Bonin, sprung like a fury first upon it, and stamped upon it, with all his force. He was speedily followed by the nuns, until there were as many upon the bed as could find room, and all did what they could, not only to smother, but to bruise her. Some stood up and jumped upon the poor girl with their feet, some with their knees, and others in different ways seemed to seek how they might best beat the breath out of her body, and mangle it without coming in direct contact with it, or seeing the effects of their violence.

After the lapse of fifteen or twenty minutes, and when it was presumed that the sufferer had been smothered, and crushed to death, Father Bonin and the nuns ceased to trample upon her, and stepped from the bed. All was motionless and silent beneath it.

They then began to laugh at such inhuman thoughts as occurred to some of them, rallying each other in the most unfeeling manner, and ridiculing me for the feelings which I in vain endeavoured to conceal. They alluded to the resignation of our murdered companion, and one of them tauntingly said, "She would have made a good Catholic martyr." After spending some moments in such conversation, one of them asked if the corpse should be removed. The Superior said it had better remain a little while. After waiting a short time longer, the feather-bed was taken off, the cords unloosed, and the body taken by the nuns and dragged down stairs. I was informed that it was taken into the cellar, and thrown unceremoniously into the hole which I have already described, covered with a great quantity of lime, and afterward sprinkled with a liquid, of the properties and name of which I am ignorant. This liquid I have seen poured into the hole from large bottles, after the necks were broken off, and have heard that it is used in France to prevent the effluvia rising from cemeteries.

I was informed immediately after receiving the veil, that infants were occasionally murdered in the Convent. I was one day in the nuns' private sick-room, when I had an opportunity, unsought for, of witnessing deeds of such a nature. It was, perhaps, a month after the death of Saint Francis. Two little twin babes, the children of Sainte Catherine, were brought to a priest, who was in the room, for baptism. I was present while the ceremony was performed, with the Superior and several of the old nuns, whose names I never knew, they being called Ma tante, Aunt.

The priests took turns in attending to confession and catechism in the Convent, usually three months at a time, though sometimes longer periods. The priest then on duty was Father Larkin. He is a good-looking European, and has a brother who is a professor in the college. He baptized, and then put oil upon the heads of the infants, as is the custom after baptism. They were then taken, one after another, by one of the old nuns, in the presence of us all. She pressed her hand upon the mouth and nose of the first, so tight that it could not breathe, and in a few minutes, when the hand was removed, it was dead. She then took the other, and treated it in the same way. No sound was heard, and both the children were corpses. The greatest indifference was shown by all present during this operation; for all, as I well knew, were long accustomed to such scenes. The little bodies were taken into the cellar, thrown into the pit I have mentioned, and covered with a quantity of lime.

This excerpt is from a letter to his family back in Michigan sent by Walter T. Post, a twenty-six-year-old accountant and ticket agent for the Northern Pacific Railroad office in St. Paul, Minnesota. The letter is dated April 18, 1893.

I enclose a clipping from the paper in regard to the Catholics and the A.P.A. [American Protective Association]. If you will notice you will find in the papers from time to time little articles like that in different parts of the country. I have just joined the A.P.A. which is a secret society of no political party but who are sworn to vote for no Catholic to any office what ever, to employ no Catholic when a Protestant can be got, also to enter in no agreement with a Catholic to strike—we swear to denounce Roman Catholicism and the Pope. It is not even known to but few outside of the society that there is such a society in the city and members are sworn not to tell the names of any member. we work in secret, as we are not strong enough to come out openly, but expect to be strong enough to make an effect at the next municipal election. do not mention this outside of the family. The Catholics are doing their best to get control of all the offices in the city. nearly all the police force and the fire men and the heads of several city depts. are under the control of them now. a good share of the school teachers are Catholics. The fifth of next Sept. has been fixed by the Pope in his Encyclical letter as the time when all Catholics will be absolved from the oath of Alegiance to the U.S. and then they are to fall on the Protestants and will be doing God service by killing them right here in this city they are drilling and have arms and ammunition stores in the cellars of their churches, these are facts. the A.P.A. have had detectives watching them and several things have occurred to confirm their suspicions. one was a mysterious explosion in a Catholic store.

SPIRITUALISM. *By the middle of the nineteenth century, what in witchcraft days had been termed "spectral evidence" had become Spiritualism, a respectable quasi-religion—at least if judged by the social standing of some of* *its adherents. The movement is generally supposed to have begun with the "Rochester Rappings" in upper New York State, and it caught on quickly. It is true that Margaret Fox, one of the sisters who set the movement going, publicly confessed in 1888 that their performances had been a hoax, but soon afterward she disavowed her confession and went back to rapping. Thomas Low Nichols, the author of this piece, was himself a believer in Spiritualism. He was also a socialist, communitarian, vegetarian, libertarian, pacifist, and advocate of free love. He left the country in 1861 because of his opposition to what he called "military despotism," and died in France in 1901.*

About 1850, there began to appear in the newspapers accounts of strange phenomena in the Fox family, in Western New York. There were a mother and three daughters, fifteen to twenty years old; persons of moderate intelligence and decent position, getting their livelihood by their needles. The manifestations consisted of loud rappings on floors, furniture, on the walls, doors, &c.; violent opening and shutting of doors and drawers, and the movement or throwing about of furniture and smaller articles, as if the house had been possessed by the spirits of mischief.

The women, according to their own statements, were first frightened, then annoyed, and then so overwhelmed by the natural curiosity of the public, that they locked their doors. This could not last. People would be admitted, and they were compelled to gratify their desire to penetrate the mystery.

What makes the noises? What moves the furniture? were natural questions. One, bolder than the rest, asked these questions and got answers, not very intelligible at first, but they led to an understanding. Their "who?" or "what?" was answered by raps. Finally some one suggested the use of the alphabet, and the raps, by indicating letters, as they were called over, spelled out words and sentences. It was but a short time before there were in various places, hundreds of miles apart, scores and hundreds of so-called mediums, and a variety of manifestations.

I went, one evening, with a party of friends, to see one of the "Fox girls." We sat around a long dining-table in a well-lighted room in New York. I chanced to sit next the medium, a fair, plump, and pleasant lady, who was suffering from a swollen face, which her spirit-friends had neglected to cure. She conversed easily about the weather, the opera, or whatever happened to be the topic, and appeared to pay very little attention to the manifestations. While they were going on, and persons were asking questions and receiving answers, she was giving me an animated and amusing description of

Mrs. Fish and the Misses Fox, three sisters who were "the original
mediums of the mysterious noises at Rochester, Western New York."
Lithograph by Nathaniel Currier, 1852.

the early experiences of herself and her family, some of which I have
already mentioned.

The raps were loud, percussive poundings, or explosions, which
appeared to be upon or within the table. I looked upon and under it.
I listened to them carefully. I watched every person present: I am certain the raps were not made by the lady beside me. As long as there
were one, two, or three raps, she kept on talking. If there were five, she
interrupted our conversation to call over the alphabet, which she did
very rapidly until letters enough had been selected to spell out a sentence. The person interested took it down. She did not seem to mind
what it was.

The raps, I observed, varied. Each professed spirit had its own characteristic rap. Some were more loud and energetic than others. The raps which purported to come from the spirits of children were slight and infantile. The messages were, I believe, of the usual character. They seemed intended only to satisfy the inquirers of the identity of the spirits and their good wishes. They appeared to satisfy the circle of inquiring friends.

After we had risen from the table, and I was still talking with and watching carefully the medium, she said the rapping often came upon the doors, when she stood near them; and, approaching a door, but still standing at a few feet distance, I heard loud knocks as of a person striking with a heavy mallet. I opened the door, so that I could see both sides of it at once. The thumps continued. I felt the vibrations of the invisible blows, percussions, or explosions. It is very certain that the lady did not make them by any visible method, and that I cannot tell who did. I failed to detect the slightest sign of deception, collusion, machinery, sleight of hand, or anything of the sort; and, truly, the metaphysical manifestations—communications to fifteen or twenty persons, strangers to the medium and to each other, from what purported to be their departed friends, with satisfactory evidences to each of the identity of the communicating spirit—were, if possible, more difficult to account for than the physical phenomena.

HEBREW SUNDAY SCHOOL. *In 1897, Rosa Mordecai published* Recollections of the First Hebrew Sunday School. *The Zane Street Sunday School was in Philadelphia and had been founded in 1838, when the Jewish community there was quite small.*

My first distinct impression of going to the Hebrew Sunday school was some years after it was organized by my great-aunt, Miss Rebecca Gratz, and while she was still its moving spirit (some time, I think, in the early fifties). The room which the school then occupied was on Zane Street (now Filbert Street) above Seventh Street, over the Phoenix Hose Company. This was prior to the days of the paid fire department. Before mounting the stairs, I would linger, as many of the girls and all the boys did, to admire the beautifully-kept machines, with the gentlemanly loungers, who never wearied of answering our questions. The sons of our most "worthy and respected" citizens ran after the Phoenix in those days [i.e., were volunteer firemen]. But I catch a glimpse of Miss Gratz approaching, and we all scatter as she says: "Time for school, children!"

The room in which we assembled was a large one with four long windows at the end. Between the centre windows was a raised platform with a smaller one upon which stood a table and a chair. On the table was a much-worn Bible containing both the Old and the New Testaments (Rev. Isaac Leeser's valuable edition of the Hebrew Bible had not then been published), a hand-bell, Watts's Hymns, and a penny contribution box "for the poor in Jerusalem."

Here Miss Gratz presided. A stately commanding figure, always neatly dressed in plain black, with thin white collar and cuffs, close-fitting bonnet over her curled front, which time never touched with grey; giving her, even in her most advanced years, a youthful appearance. Her eyes would pierce every part of the hall and often detect mischief which escaped the notice of the teachers.

The only punishment I can recall was for the delinquent to be marched through the school and seated upon the little platform, before mentioned, under the table. Sometimes this stand would be quite full, and I was rather disposed to envy those children who had no lessons to say. But, her duties over, Miss Gratz would call them by name to stand before her for reproof, which, apparently mild, was so soul-stirring that even the most hardened sinner would quail before it. She was extremely particular to instill neatness and cleanliness. A soiled dress, crooked collar, or sticky hands never escaped her penetrating glance, and the reproof or remedy was instantaneous.

The benches held about ten children each. They were painted bright yellow, with an arm at each end; on the board across the back were beautiful medallions of mills, streams, farmhouses, etc., etc.

The instruction must have been principally oral in those primitive days. Miss Gratz always began school with the prayer, opening with "Come ye children, hearken unto me, and I will teach you the fear of the Lord." This was followed by a prayer of her composition, which she read verse by verse, and the whole school repeated after her. Then she read a chapter of the Bible, in a clear and distinct voice, without any elocution, and this could be heard and understood all over the room. The closing exercises were equally simple: a Hebrew hymn sung by the children, then one of Watts's simple verses, whose rhythm the smallest child could easily catch as all repeated: "Send me the voice that Samuel heard," etc., etc.

Many old scholars can still recall the question: "Who formed you, child, and made you live?" and the answer: "God did my life and spirit give"—the first lines of that admirable Pyke's *Catechism*, which long held its place in the Sunday school, and was, I believe, the first book printed for it. The Scripture lessons were taught from a little illustrated work published by the Christian Sunday School Union. Many a long summer's day have I spent, pasting pieces of paper over answers unsuitable for Jewish children, and many were the fruitless efforts of those children to read through, over, or under the hidden lines.

"Jewish rites and ceremonies; Ushamnu," New York City, turn of the century.

I could recall the names of many who sat on the long benches as scholars, or in the chairs as teachers, but they have all scattered, some to far distant homes, others to the eternal home. And those who are left are now all men and women, advanced in age, some of them grandfathers, some grandmothers of the present generation. Yet all still bear a grateful recollection of the Zane Street Sunday school, over the Phoenix Hose Company.

SPREADING THE WORD

WITH THE JESUITS. *Juan Mateo Manje was an officer in the Compania Volante (Flying Column) that escorted the Jesuit Father Kino on his various missions to the Pima Indians of southern Arizona. Here are two extracts from Manje's* Luz de Tierra Incognita.

February 12, 1699. After mass, we continued west over hills covered with pasture; and after five leagues, we came to a spring of crystal water which we named Santa Eulalia. Nearby we found a small settlement where we counted 60 persons, who took us to a big square *corral* with stone walls. Near this there was a smoked cave on a rocky hill.

We were told that a giant monster with the features of a woman, mouth of a pig and claws of an eagle had come from the north and made his home in this cave. (I do not know whether or not they are telling a fable.) This monster would fly around catching as many Indians as he could to eat. The Pima Indians began very carefully to gather large quantities of wood. One day the Indians invited the monster to this place and sacrificed for him two Indian prisoners they had caught from the enemies, with whom they were at war. When the monster was satiated, the Indians started a dance which lasted three days in the *corral*—built so that the monster would come in.

When the Indians who were dancing got tired and sleepy, others would take their place. When the monster became sleepy and went to his cave, the Indians followed him. When he was sound asleep, they closed the door of the cave with the wood they had gathered and set it on fire. The flames and smoke asphyxiated the monster, which died growling. Thus the Indians got rid of this terrible beast.

October 29, 1699. After having heard mass, we left this place and traveled north through a fertile land; and after going 10 leagues, we arrived at noon at the great settlement of San Javier del Bac, where the natives came out quite a distance on the road to meet us. There were 50 Indians, each one carrying a cross and chanting a song of the Christian doctrine that the fiscal Indian of the mission of Dolores had taught them before. With this show and demonstration of pleasure, they went ahead of us and gave us lodgings in the *adobe* and flat roofed houses with beams, which on another occasion they had built for us. Near this house the rest of the Indians and women of the town were formed in two rows as in the Christian towns. There were 400 men.

In a short time after we had arrived, the governor of a settlement located west, called Otcan, arrived with 270 heathen men together with their corresponding families to greet the Father Visitor. We exchanged compliments with them. Since it was early and a quiet and pleasant evening, the soldiers and I, accompanied by the Reverend Father Visitor, started afoot to a nearby hill where we could see in all directions a good portion of the extensive plains. There was no other hill besides this one. We went to the top and found all around a wall of stone with a plaque in the middle. In the center of this there was a white stone, like a sugar loaf of half a vara in height, imbedded in the ground. We guessed it might be some idol that the heathen Indians worshipped, so with great effort we pulled out the stone which was stuck in about one-third of the way, thereby exposing a large hole. At the time, we did not know what it could be. While we were coming down the hill, and before we arrived at the settlement, a great and furious hurricane developed. We could scarcely walk because of the terrific windstorm. None of the Indians had gone with us to the top of the hill; but when the furious wind arose they started to yell, saying in sort of rebellion, "*Vbiriqui cupioca,*" which meant that the House of the Wind (god) had been opened. All evening and all night the wind blew so severely that we could not sleep. It seemed the house and trees were going to fall down. In the morning we were told that the Indians went up to cover the hole. The hurricane ceased completely, and the day remained calm and serene. It seems as if it might have been a wind volcano, but the land is not subject to earthquakes the Indians told us. We rested in the settlement one and one-half days, informing them of God and His Sacred Law.

JOHN ELIOT. *Known as the Apostle to the Indians, Eliot was the first to preach to the Indians in their own language; he also translated the Bible. This episode comes from Daniel Gookin's* Historical Collections of the Indians in New England.

May 5th, 1674, according to our usual custom, Mr. Eliot and myself took our journey to Wamesit, or Pawtuckett; and arriving there that evening, Mr. Eliot preached to as many of them as could be got together, out of Matthew xxii. 1-14. the parable of the marriage of the king's son. We met at the wigwam of one called Wannalancet, about two miles from the town, near Pawtuckett falls, and bordering upon Merrimak river. This person, Wannalancet, is the eldest son of old Pasaconaway, the chiefest sachem of Pawtuckett. He is a sober and grave person, and of years, between fifty and sixty. He hath been always loving and friendly to the English. Many endeavours have been used several years to gain this sachem to embrace the christian religion; but he hath stood off from time to time, and not yielded up himself personally, though for four years past he hath been willing to hear the word of God preached, and to keep the sabbath.—A great reason that hath kept him off, I conceive, hath been the indisposition and averseness of sundry of his chief men and relations to pray to God; which he foresaw would desert him, in case he turned christian.—But at this time, May 6th, 1674, it pleased God so to influence and overcome his heart that it being proposed to him to give his answer concerning praying to God, after some deliberation and serious pause, he stood up, and made a speech to this effect:

Sirs, you have been pleased for four years last past, in your abundant love, to apply yourselves particularly unto me and my people, to exhort, press, and persuade us to pray to God. I am very thankful to you for your pains. I must acknowledge, said he, I have, all my days, used to pass in an old canoe (alluding to his frequent custom to pass in a canoe upon the river) and now you exhort me to change and leave my old canoe, and embark in a new canoe, to which I have hitherto been unwilling; but now I yield up myself to your advice, and enter into a new canoe, and do engage to pray to God hereafter.

A HELLFIRE SERMON. *Jonathan Edwards, Congregationalist pastor in Northampton, Massachusetts, was a leading preacher of the Great Awakening, a religious revival of the mid-eighteenth century. His sermons included "Why Saints in Glory will Rejoice to See the Torments of the Damned" and "Sinners in the Hands of an Angry God," of which this is a small part.*

Imagine yourself to be cast into a fiery oven, all of a glowing heat, or into the midst of a glowing brick-kiln, or of a great furnace, where your pain would be as much greater than that occasioned by accidentally touching a coal of fire, as the heat is greater. Imagine also that your body were to lie there for a quarter of an hour, full of fire, as full within and without as a bright coal of fire, all the while full of quick sense; what horror would you feel at the entrance of such a furnace! And how long would that quarter of an hour seem to you! If it were to be measured by a glass, how long would the glass seem to be running! And after you had endured it for one minute, how overbearing would it be to you to think that you had it to endure the other fourteen!

But what would be the effect on your soul, if you knew you must lie there enduring that torment to the full for twenty-four hours! And how much greater would be the effect, if you knew you must endure it for a whole year; and how vastly greater still, if you knew you must endure it for a thousand years! O then, how would your heart sink, if you thought, if you knew, that you must bear it for ever and ever! That there would be no end! That after millions of millions of ages, your torment would be no nearer to an end, than ever it would; and that you never, never should be delivered!

A BAPTIST AND A MOB. *From* A Door Opened for Equal Christian Liberty, and No Man Can Shut It *by Isaac Backus, a New Light Separate Baptist and one of the founders of Brown University.*

Mr. Richard Lee, a gifted member of one of our churches having laboured with success in Scituate, was earnestly requested by a man in Hingham, to come and hold a meeting at his house, which he consented to. The meeting was appointed to be in the evening of May 28, 1782; but as the people were assembling for worship, a large mob came up, armed with clubs and staves, and warned Lee and his friends to depart out of

Hingham immediately, or it would be much worse for them. He inquired whether they came with any authority? and finding that they did not, he, with the bible in his hand, began to exhort the people to fear God rather than man. Upon which one of them violently seized him by his arm and collar, and others also laying hold of him, halled him away out of the house, and out of the town. When he attempted to speak, and to recite passages of scripture, they repeatedly smote him on his mouth, with the palms of their hands, and also made loud noises to prevent his being heard. As one who had hold of him blundered down, another shook a club over his head, and swore that if he flung another down, he would sink Lee to hell in a moment. He then said, "I look upon this holy bible to be the very best law that ever I heard of." Upon which it was spitefully struck out of his hand, and stamped under foot, with curses and execrations too horrid to be here repeated! When the mob had got him over the town line, their captain shook a club over Lee's head, and swore, that if he ever came into that town again, he would tie him up, and whip him thirty stripes. Said our suffering brother, "that's not so much as they whipt Paul." *What! d—n you*, said one, *do you compare yourself with Paul!* A Hingham man said, Mr. Lee may go and hold a meeting at my house.— But others declared that if he did, they would burn his house down, and carry him out of town. One of the mob cast soft cow-dung in Lee's face, and then they insulted him because of that defilement, with a great deal more of abuse to men, and blasphemy against God. Two other baptist brethren were then hauled by violence out of Hingham, and they went and held a religious meeting in Scituate the same night.

A METHODIST AT WORK. *Peter Cartwright, born in Virginia in 1785, grew up in Kentucky and began his career as a Methodist circuit rider at the age of seventeen. In 1846 he ran for Congress but lost to his Whig opponent, Abraham Lincoln. Here he recalls two episodes from his early days.*

A new exercise broke out among us, called the *jerks*, which was overwhelming in its effect upon the bodies and minds of the people. No matter whether they were saints or sinners, they would be taken under a warm song or sermon, and seized with a convulsive jerking all over, which they could not by any possibility avoid, and the more they resisted the more they jerked. If they would not strive against it and pray in good earnest, the jerking would usually abate. I have seen more than five hundred persons jerking at one time in my large congregations. Most usually persons taken with the jerks, to obtain relief, as they said, would rise up and dance. Some would run, but could not get away. Some would resist; on such the jerks were generally very severe.

To see those proud young gentlemen and young ladies dressed in their silks, jewelry, and prunella, from top to toe, take the *jerks*, would

"The Jerking Exercise," a caricature of an outdoor prayer
meeting. Engraving by Lossing-Barrett, circa 1840.

often excite my risibilities. The first jerk or so, you would see their fine
bonnets, caps, and combs fly; and so sudden would be the jerking of
the head that their long loose hair would crack almost as loud as a
wagoner's whip.

At one of my appointments in 1804 there was a very large congregation turned out to hear the Kentucky boy, as they called me.
Among the rest there were two very finely-dressed, fashionable young
ladies, attended by two brothers with loaded horse-whips. Although

the house was large, it was crowded. The two young ladies, coming in late, took their seats near where I stood, and their two brothers stood in the door. I was a little unwell, and I had a phial of peppermint in my pocket. Before I commenced preaching I took out my phial and swallowed a little of the peppermint. While I was preaching, the congregation was melted into tears. The two young gentlemen moved off to the yard fence, and both the young ladies took the jerks, and they were greatly mortified about it. There was a great stir in the congregation. Some wept, some shouted, and before our meeting closed several were converted.

As I dismissed the assembly a man stepped up to me, and warned me to be on my guard, for he had heard the two brothers swear they would horsewhip me when meeting was out, for giving their sisters the jerks. "Well," said I, "I'll see to that."

I went out and said to the young men that I understood they intended to horsewhip me for giving their sisters the jerks. One replied that he did. I undertook to expostulate with him on the absurdity of the charge against me, but he swore I need not deny it; for he had seen me take out a phial, in which I carried some truck [cheap substance] that gave his sisters the jerks. As quick as thought it came into my mind how I would get clear of my whipping, and jerking out the peppermint phial, said I, "Yes; if I gave your sisters the jerks I'll give them to you." In a moment I saw he was scared. I moved toward him, he backed, I advanced, and he wheeled and ran, warning me not to come near him, or he would kill me. It raised the laugh on him, and I escaped my whipping. I had the pleasure before the year was out of seeing all four soundly converted to God, and I took them into the Church.

I journeyed on toward my home in Christian County, Kentucky. Saturday night came on, and found me in a strange region of country, and in the hills, knobs, and spurs of the Cumberland Mountains. . . . [L]ate in the evening, I hailed at a tolerably decent house, and the landlord kept entertainment. I rode up and asked for quarters. The gentleman said I could stay, but he was afraid I would not enjoy myself very much as a traveler, inasmuch as they had a party meeting there that night to have a little dance. I inquired how far it was to a decent house of entertainment on the road; he said seven miles. I told him if he would treat me civilly and feed my horse well, by his leave I would stay. He assured me I should be treated civilly. I dismounted and went in. The people collected, a large company. I saw there was not much drinking going on.

I quietly took my seat in one corner of the house, and the dance commenced. I sat quietly musing, a total stranger, and greatly desired to preach to this people. Finally, I concluded to spend the next day

(Sabbath) there, and ask the privilege to preach to them. I had hardly settled this point in my mind, when a beautiful ruddy young lady walked very gracefully up to me, dropped a handsome courtesy, and pleasantly, with winning smiles, invited me out to take a dance with her. I can hardly describe my thoughts or feelings on that occasion. However, in a moment I resolved on a desperate experiment. I rose as gracefully as I could; I will not say with some emotion, but with many emotions. The young lady moved to my right side; I grasped her right hand with my right hand, while she leaned her left arm on mine. In this position we walked on the floor. The whole company seemed pleased at this act of politeness in the young lady, shown to a stranger. The colored man, who was the fiddler, began to put his fiddle in the best order. I then spoke to the fiddler to hold a moment, and added that for several years I had not undertaken any matter of importance without first asking the blessing of God upon it, and I desired now to ask the blessing of God upon this beautiful young lady and the whole company, that had shown such an act of politeness to a total stranger.

Here I grasped the young lady's hand tightly and said, "Let us all kneel down and pray," and then instantly dropped on my knees, and commenced praying with all the power of soul and body that I could command. The young lady tried to get loose from me, but I held her tight. Presently she fell on her knees. Some of the company kneeled, some stood, some fled, some sat still, all looked curious. The fiddler ran off into the kitchen saying, "Lord a marcy, what de matter? what is dat mean?"

While I prayed some wept out aloud, and some cried for mercy. I rose from my knees and commenced an exhortation, after which I sang a hymn. The young lady who invited me on the floor lay prostrate, crying earnestly for mercy. I exhorted again, I sang and prayed nearly all night. About fifteen of that company professed religion, and our meeting lasted next day and next night, and as many more were powerfully converted. I organized a society, took thirty-two into the Church, and sent them a preacher. My landlord was appointed leader, which post he held for many years. This was the commencement of a great and glorious revival of religion in that region of country, and several of the young men converted at this Methodist preacher dance became useful ministers of Jesus Christ.

WOODLAND WORSHIP. *Frances Trollope, mother of the novelist Anthony Trollope, was an Englishwoman who spent three years living in this country, mostly in Cincinnati. She published her generally unfavorable impressions in* Domestic Manners of the Americans, *in 1832.*

The prospect of passing a night in the back woods of Indiana was by no means agreeable, but I screwed my courage to the proper pitch, and set forth determined to see with my own eyes, and hear with my own ears, what a camp-meeting really was. I had heard it said that being at a camp-meeting was like standing at the gate of heaven, and seeing it opening before you; I had heard it said, that being at a camp-meeting was like finding yourself within the gates of hell; in either case there must be something to gratify curiosity, and compensate one for the fatigue of a long rumbling ride and a sleepless night.

We reached the ground about an hour before midnight, and the approach to it was highly picturesque. The spot chosen was the verge of an unbroken forest, where a space of about twenty acres appeared to have been partially cleared for the purpose. Tents of different sizes were pitched very near together in a circle round the cleared space; behind them were ranged an exterior circle of carriages of every description, and at the back of each were fastened the horses which had drawn them thither. Through this triple circle of defence we distinguished numerous fires burning brightly within it; and still more numerous lights flickering from the trees that were left in the enclosure. The moon was in meridian splendour above our heads.

We left the carriage to the care of a servant who was to prepare a bed in it for Mrs. B. and me, and entered the inner circle. . . .

Four high frames constructed in the form of altars, were placed at the four corners of the enclosure; on these were supported layers of earth and sod, on which burned immense fires of blazing pine-wood. On one side a rude platform was erected to accommodate the preachers, fifteen of whom attended this meeting, and with very short intervals for necessary refreshment and private devotion, preached in rotation, day and night, from Tuesday to Saturday.

When we arrived, the preachers were silent; but we heard issuing from nearly every tent mingled sounds of praying, preaching, singing, and lamentation. The curtains in front of each tent were dropped, and the faint light that gleamed through the white drapery, backed as it was by the dark forest, had a beautiful and mysterious effect, that set the imagination at work; and had the sounds which vibrated around us been less discordant, harsh, and unnatural, I should have enjoyed it; but listening at the corner of a tent, which poured forth more than its proportion of clamour, in a few moments chased every feeling derived from imagination, and furnished realities that could neither be mistaken or forgotten.

Great numbers of persons were walking about the ground, who appeared like ourselves to be present only as spectators; some of these very unceremoniously contrived to raise the drapery of this tent, at one corner, so as to afford us a perfect view of the interior.

The floor was covered with straw, which round the sides was heaped in masses, that might serve as seats, but which at that moment were used to support the heads and the arms of the close-packed circle of men and women who kneeled on the floor.

Out of about thirty persons thus placed, perhaps half a dozen were men. One of these, a handsome looking youth of eighteen or twenty, kneeled just below the opening through which I looked. His arm was encircling the neck of a young girl who knelt beside him, with her hair hanging dishevelled upon her shoulders, and her features working with the most violent agitation; soon after they both fell forward on the straw, as if unable to endure in any other attitude the burning eloquence of a tall grim figure in black, who, standing erect in the centre, was uttering with incredible vehemence an oration that seemed to hover between praying and preaching; his arms hung stiff and immoveable by his side, and he looked like an ill-constructed machine, set in action by a movement so violent, as to threaten its own destruction, so jerkingly, painfully, yet rapidly, did his words tumble out; the kneeling circle ceasing not to call in every variety of tone, on the name of Jesus; accompanied with sobs, groans, and a sort of low howling inexpressibly painful to listen to.

At midnight a horn sounded through the camp, which, we were told, was to call the people from private to public worship; and we presently saw them flocking from all sides to the front of the preachers' stand. Mrs. B. and I contrived to place ourselves with our backs supported against the lower part of this structure, and we were thus enabled to witness the scene which followed without personal danger. There were about two thousand persons assembled.

One of the preachers began in a low nasal tone, and, like all other Methodist preachers, assured us of the enormous depravity of man as he comes from the hands of his Maker, and of his perfect sanctification after he had wrestled sufficiently with the Lord to get hold of him, *et caetera.* The admiration of the crowd was evinced by almost constant cries of "Amen! Amen!" "Jesus! Jesus!" "Glory! Glory!" and the like. But this comparative tranquillity did not last long: the preacher told them that "this night was the time fixed upon for anxious sinners to wrestle with the Lord;" that he and his brethren "were at hand to help them," and that such as needed their help were to come forward into "the pen."

"The pen" was the space immediately below the preachers' stand; we were therefore placed on the edge of it, and were enabled to see and hear all that took place in the very centre of this extraordinary exhibition.

The crowd fell back at the mention of the *pen*, and for some minutes there was a vacant space before us. The preachers came down for their stand and placed themselves in the midst of it, beginning to sing a hymn, calling upon the penitents to come forth. As they sung they kept turning themselves round to every part of the crowd, and, by degrees, the voices of the whole multitude joined in chorus. This was the only moment at which I perceived any thing like the solemn and beautiful effect, which I had heard ascribed to this woodland worship. It is certain that the combined voices of such a multitude, heard at dead of night from the depths of their eternal forests, the many fair young faces turned upward, and looking paler and lovelier as they met the moon-beams, the dark figures of the officials in the middle of the circle, the lurid glare thrown by the altar-fires on the woods beyond, did altogether produce a fine and solemn effect, that I shall not easily forget; but ere I had well enjoyed it, the scene changed, and sublimity gave place to horror and disgust. . . .

Above a hundred persons, nearly all females, came forward, uttering howlings and groans, so terrible that I shall never cease to shudder when I recall them. They appeared to drag each other forward, and on the word being given, "let us pray," they all fell on their knees; but this posture was soon changed for others that permitted greater scope for the convulsive movements of their limbs; and they were soon all lying on the ground in an indescribable confusion of heads and legs. They threw about their limbs with such incessant and violent motion, that I was every instant expecting some serious accident to occur.

But how am I to describe the sounds that proceeded from this strange mass of human beings? I know no words which can convey an idea of it. Hysterical sobbings, convulsive groans, shrieks and screams the most appalling, burst forth on all sides. I felt sick with horror. As if their hoarse and overstrained voices failed to make noise enough, they soon began to clap their hands violently.

Many of these wretched creatures were beautiful young females. The preachers moved about among them, at once exciting and soothing their agonies. I heard the muttered "Sister! dear sister!" I saw the insidious lips approach the cheeks of the unhappy girls; I heard the murmured confessions of the poor victims, and I watched their tormentors, breathing into their ears consolations that tinged the pale cheek with red. Had I been a man, I am sure I should have been guilty of some rash act of interference; nor do I believe that such a scene could have been acted in the presence of Englishmen without instant punishment being inflicted; not to mention the salutary discipline of the tread-mill, which, beyond all question, would, in England, have been applied to check so turbulent and so vicious a scene.

After the first wild burst that followed their prostration, the moanings, in many instances, became loudly articulate; and I then experienced a strange vibration between tragic and comic feeling. A very pretty girl, who was kneeling in the attitude of Canova's Magdalene immediately before us, amongst an immense quantity of jargon, broke out thus: "Woe! Woe to the backsliders! Hear it, hear it Jesus! When I was fifteen my mother died, and I backslided, oh Jesus, I backslided! Take me home to my mother, Jesus! Take me home to her, for I am weary! Oh John Mitchel! John Mitchel!" and after sobbing piteously behind her raised hands, she lifted her sweet face again, which was as pale as death, and said, "Shall I sit on the sunny bank of salvation with my mother? My own dear mother? Oh Jesus, take me home, take me home!"

Who could refuse a tear to this earnest wish for death in one so young and so lovely? But I saw her, ere I left the ground, with her hand fast locked, and her head supported by a man who looked very much as Don Juan might, when sent back to earth as too bad for the regions below.

MORMON SERMON. *Samuel Bowles, editor of the* Springfield *[Massachusetts]* Republican, *claimed that the following was a verbatim record of a sermon he had heard in Salt Lake City in 1865, delivered by Heber C. Kimball, first vice president of the Mormon Church.*

Ladies and gentleman, good morning. I am going to talk to you by revelation. I never study my sermons, and when I get up to speak, I never know what I am going to say only as it is revealed to me from on high; then all I say is true; could it help but be so, when God communicates to you through me? The Gentiles [non-Mormons] are our enemies; they are damned forever; they are thieves and murderers, and if they don't like what I say they can go to hell, damn them! They want to come here in large numbers and decoy our women. I have introduced some Gentiles to my wives, but I will not do it again, because if I do, I will have to take them to my houses and introduce them to Mrs. Kimball at one house, and Mrs. Kimball at another house, and so on; and they will say Mrs. Kimball such, and Mrs. Kimball such, and so on, are whores. They are taking some of our fairest daughters from us now in Salt Lake City, damn them. If I catch any of them running after my wives I will send them to hell! and ladies you must not keep their company, you sin if you do, and you will be damned and go to hell. What do you think of such people? They hunt after our fairest and prettiest women, and it is a lamentable fact that they would rather go with them damned scoundrels than stay with us. If Brother Brigham [Brigham Young] comes to me, and says he wants one of my daughters, he has a right to take her, and I have the exclusive right to give her to who I

A Mormon, his mother, his five wives and new baby.
Photograph by John P. Soule in 1885.

please, and she has no right to refuse; if she does, she will be damned forever and ever, because she belongs to me. She is part of my flesh, and no one has a right to take her unless I say so, any more than he has a right to take one of my horses or cows.

ALL-NIGHT MISSIONARY GIBBUD'S STORY. *Under this heading, the social reformer Helen Campbell quotes the following first-person account in her book* Darkness and Daylight.

I had been holding meetings in a small room in the midst of the slums of Baxter Street [in New York City], going out into the alleys, saloons, and dives of the neighborhood, and literally compelling the people to come in. I made frequent visits after dark to "Hell Gate," "Chain and Locker," and "Bottle Alley," resorts for sailors and low characters, and invited them to the meeting. The proprietors, though in a bad business, generally treated me with courtesy, though I sometimes succeeded in taking nearly all their customers away.

One summer night I started out to gather in my audience. The streets were full. . . . A "mud-gutter" band in front of one of the dance-halls was making discordant music, while children of all ages, from the babe just out of the mother's arms to the young girl in her teens, jostled each other in a rude attempt at dancing. Bare-headed colored women, in soiled calico dresses, with sleeves rolled up, stopped, before entering the brothels, to join with rough-looking sailors in a "breakdown." From a cellar-way leading to filthy underground apartments came the noise of a piano, drummed by unskilled hands, while the painted women at the door tried to induce victims to enter.

I had just come out of the place named "Hell Gate" when I saw a partially intoxicated woman supporting herself against a lamp-post, and near by stood a burly negro. The woman was tall and thin, and it was plain even then that consumption was doing its fatal work. She had no hat, no shoes; a dirty calico dress was all the clothing she had on, and that was not in condition to cover her nakedness. Her hair was matted and tangled, her face bruised and swollen; both eyes were blackened by the fist of her huge negro companion, who held her as his slave and had beaten her because she had not brought him as much

A group of street urchins gather with missionary workers in Chicago, 1877.
The boys have given themselves street names such as Butcher Kilroy, Smikes,
Rag-breeches Cadet, Madden the Butcher, Black Stove Pipe, and Red-eye.
Photograph by Shaw.

money as he wanted. I invited her to the meeting and passed on. Near the close of the service she came in; with tearful eyes she listened to the story of Jesus, and was one of the first to request prayers. After the meeting she expressed a desire for a better life, but she had no place to go, save to the dens of infamy from which she came. I decided at once to take her to the Florence Night Mission, and, accompanied by a friend who had assisted me in the meeting, we started.

We were going toward the horse-cars, and congratulating ourselves that we had gotten away unobserved, when we were confronted by the very negro from whom we sought to escape. With an oath he demanded,

"Whar you folks takin' dat gal to?"

It was a fearful moment, near midnight, a dark street, and not a soul in sight. I expected every moment that he would strike me. I was no match for him. Signaling my friend to go on with the girl, and taking the negro by the coat, I said excitedly,

"I am taking her to a Christian home—to a better life. If ever you prayed for any one, pray for her; I know you are a bad man, but you ought to be glad to help any girl away from this place. So pray for her as you have never prayed before."

All this time my friend and the woman were going down the street as fast as possible. I had talked so fast that the negro did not have a chance to say a word, and before he could recover from his astonishment I ran on. He did not attempt to follow.

Four cars were hailed before one would let us on. The drivers would slacken up, but, seeing the woman's condition, would whip up their horses and drive on. Finally, when the next driver slackened, we lifted our frail burden to the platform before he could prevent us.

Arriving at the Mission, we helped her up the steps and rang the bell; she turned to me and said, "You will be proud of me some day." I smiled then, as I thought the chances of being proud of her were slim, but how many times since, when vast audiences have been moved to tears by the pathos of her story, or spellbound by her eloquence, have I indeed been proud of her.

She was admitted to the house, giving the assumed name of Nellie Conroy. For nine years she had lived in Baxter Street slums, becoming a victim to all the vices that attend a dissipated life until at last she became an utter wreck. Everything was done for her at the Mission, and in time permanent employment was found.

Some time after, word reached the Mission that Nellie had left her place and gone back to her old haunts in Baxter Street. A card with the address of "The Florence" was left at one of her resorts, and the whole matter was forgotten, until late one night the doorbell of the Mission rooms softly rang, and the poor wretched object admitted proved to be Nellie. At the meeting the next night she was the first to come forward. When asked to pray, she lifted her pale face to heaven, and quoted, with tearful pathos, that beautiful hymn:

> The mistakes of my life have been many,
>   The sins of my heart have been more;
> And I scarce can see for weeping,
>   But I'll knock at the open door.

Then followed a touching prayer, a humble confession of sin, an earnest pleading for pardon, a quiet acceptance of Christ by faith, a tearful thanksgiving for knowledge of sins forgiven.

Her life from that time until her death—nearly two years later—was that of a faithful Christian. She gave satisfaction to her employers; she was blessed of God in her testimony at the Mission, and soon she was sought after by churches, temperance societies, and missions to tell what great things the Lord had done for her. She spoke to a large assemblage of nearly 3,000 people in the Cooper Union, New York, holding the audience spellbound with her pathetic story. She possessed a wonderful gift of language and great natural wit, that, combined with her thrilling story, made her a most interesting and entertaining speaker. She was uneducated, but she had a remarkable memory; she soon became familiar with the Bible, and many were won to Christ through her testimony. Her pale face would become flushed with a hectic glow as she spoke of the wonderful things God had done for her.

"Glory be to His great name!" she would say; "it was no common blood that washed Nellie Conroy from her sins, and no common power that reached down and took her from the slums of Baxter Street after nine years of sin and dissipation. It was nothing but the precious blood of Jesus that saved me. Where are my companions who started down life's stream with me, young, fresh, and happy? We started out to gather the roses of life, but found only the thorns. Many of them to-day sleep in nameless and dishonored graves in the Potter's Field, and their souls—oh! where are they?—while I am spared, redeemed!"

Her life was indeed a changed one; from idleness, filth, drunkenness, and sin, she was transformed into a neat, industrious, sober, godly woman. But sin had sown its seed and she must reap the harvest; she grew weaker until at last she went to the hospital to linger for months in great suffering and pain, borne with Christian resignation. Her constant testimony was—

> The love He has kindled within me
> Makes service or suffering sweet.

One day a visitor said, "Nellie, you are nearing the river." "Yes," she said, "I have already stepped in, but God's word says, 'When thou passest

An engraving from a photograph, in Helen Campbell's *Darkness and Daylight*, 1891. "With folded hands, and eyes tight shut, the little lips of these homeless ones repeat in unison the prayer that happy mothers in many a home bend to hear: 'Now I lay me down to sleep, I pray the Lord my soul to keep.'"

through the waters I will be with thee, and through the rivers they shall not overflow thee.' The promise is true; I am dry shod."

At the last she could scarcely speak; she knew her end was near, and when the 14th chapter of St. John's gospel was read to her she said, "My mansion is there, the Comforter is here; the promise is fulfilled. Sing at my funeral, 'I am going home to die no more.'"

Summoned to her bedside, the nurse bent down to hear her faintly whisper, "Jesus, precious Jesus." These were her last words, her face lit up as she seemed to catch a glimpse of the better land, and, with the name of Jesus on her lips the spirit of the once poor, despised Magdalene took its flight to the bright mansions of whose possession she had been so sure.

At her funeral many Christian workers and friends gathered to do honor to her remains. Many converts from the slums who had been won to Christ by her testimony were among the mourners, and not a few came to look on that pale face who still lived in sin and shame, but who sincerely loved one who had so often entreated them to turn and live.

Jesse James, a specialist in bank and train robberies, shortly after being shot in the back by one of his gang for the sake of the Missouri government reward, 1882.

9

ERRING

PESSIMISTS WHO BELIEVE that society is becoming increasingly lawless may well be right, but they are wrong if they think that we have declined from some Golden Age of innocence and civility. Crime of all kinds, from murder and rape to libel and petty swindles, has been with us from the very first. Optimists who see improvement in the history of the crime rate must allow for the fact that many activities once illegal now fall outside the law—working on a Sunday, kissing a woman in the streets of Boston, being a witch.

At first the usual way of dealing with criminals was to punish them with varying degrees of harshness: fines, the pillory, the whipping post, the jail cell, and the scaffold. In the absence of official authorities to enforce these measures, vigilance committees, posses, or, more commonly, individuals or mobs were only too ready to take the law into their own hands.

Sometimes the result was a kind of rough justice; often it was no justice at all; but either way it was hugely popular public entertainment. Whole families would once gather to deride the drunkard in the pillory or watch the fornicator being whipped through the streets or be edified by the execution sermon that preceded an open-air hanging on Gallows Hill. That such spectacles are nowadays almost unthinkable is surely at least one indisputable improvement!

HARSH PUNISHMENT. *Writing in 1612 about Powhatan, Captain John Smith described him as the powerful chief of a confederation of some thirty Indian tribes, "a tall, well proportioned man, with a sower look, his head somewhat gray," then went on to detail his methods of administering justice. (In a famous episode, Smith was himself saved from the "sacrificing stone" by Powhatan's daughter, Pocahontas.)*

It is strange to see with what great feare and adoration all these people doe obay this Powhatan. For at his feet, they present whatsoever he commandeth, and at the least frowne of his browe, their greatest spirits will tremble with feare: and no marvell, for he is very terrible and tyrannous in punishing such as offend him. For example, he caused certaine malefactors to be bound hand and foot, then having of many fires gathered great store of burning coles, they rake these coles round in the forme of a cockpit, and in the midst they cast the offenders to broyle to death. Sometimes he causeth the heads of them that offend him, to be laid upon the altar or sacrificing stone, and one with clubbes beates out their braines. When he would punish any notorious enimie or malefactor, he causeth him to be tied to a tree, and, with muscle shels or reeds, the executioner cutteth off his joints one after another, ever casting what they cut off into the fire; then doth he proceed with shels and reeds to case the skinne from his head and face; then doe they rip his belly, and so burne him with the tree and all.

PILLORY. *From* Proceedings of the Virginia Assembly, *1619.*

Captaine William Powell presented a pettition to the generall Assembly against one Thomas Garnett, a servant of his, not onely for extreame neglect of his business to the great loss and prejudice of the said Captaine, and for openly and impudently abusing his house, in sight both of Master and Mistress, through wantonnes with a woman servant of theirs, a widdowe, but also for falsely accusing him to the Governor both of Drunkennes and Thefte, and besides for bringing all his fellow servants to testifie on his side, wherein they justly failed him. It was thought fitt by the general assembly (the Governour himself giving sentence), that he should stand fower dayes with his eares nayled to the Pillory, viz: Wednesday, Aug. 4th, and so likewise Thursday, fryday, and Satturday next following, and every of those dayes should be publiquely whipped.

HOLDUP, 1631. *Governor William Bradford of Plymouth tells the story.*

This year their house [trading station] at Penobscot was robbed by the French, and all their goods of any worth they carried away to the value of £400 or £500 worth as they cost first penny; in beaver 300 pounds' weight, and the rest in trading goods, as coats, rugs, blanket, biscuit, etc. It was in this manner. The master of the house and part of the company with him were come with their vessel to the westward to fetch a supply of goods which was brought over for them. In the meantime comes a small French ship into the harbor, and amongst the company was a false Scot. They pretended they were newly come from the sea and knew not where they were, and that their vessel was very leaky, and desired they might haul her ashore and stop their leaks. And many French compliments they used, and congees [flowery greetings] they made; and in the end, seeing but three or four simple men that were servants, and by this Scotchman understanding that their master and the rest of the company were gone from home, they fell of commending their guns and muskets that lay upon racks by the wall side, and took them down to look on them, asking if they were charged. And when they were possessed of them, one presents a piece ready charged against the servants, and another a pistol, and bid them not stir but quietly deliver them their goods, and carries some of the men aboard and made the other help to carry away the goods. And when they had took what they pleased, they set them at liberty and went their way.

ANOTHER SCARLET LETTER. *From John Winthrop's journal for March 4, 1634.*

Robert Cole, having been oft punished for drunkenness, was now ordered to wear a red D about his neck for a year.

A SHIFTLESS MAID. *From Winthrop's journal for September 28, 1637, about two men who had been hanged in Boston for murder. The first, John Williams, hid his victim's body under a pile of stones, but "the kine, smelling the blood, made such a roaring, as the cow-keeper, looking about, found the dead body."*

The other, William Schooler, was a vintner in London, and had been a common adulterer, (as himself did confess,) and had wounded a man in a duel, for which he fled into the Low Country, and from thence he fled from his captain and came into this country, leaving his wife (a handsome, neat woman) in England. He lived with another fellow at Merrimack, and there being a poor maid at Newbury, one Mary Sholy, who had desired a guide to go with her to her master, who dwelt at Pascataquack, he inquired her out, and agreed, for fifteen shillings, to conduct her thither. But, two days after, he returned, and, being asked why he returned so soon, he answered, that he had carried her within two or three miles of the place, and then she would go no farther. Being examined for this by the magistrates at Ipswich, and no proof found against him, he was let go. But, about a year after . . . he was again examined, and divers witnesses produced about it. Whereupon he was committed, arraigned, and condemned, by due proceeding. The effect of the evidence was this:—

1. He had lived a vicious life, and now lived like an atheist.

2. He had sought out the maid, and undertook to carry her to a place where he had never been.

3. When he crossed Merrimack, he landed in a place three miles from the usual path, from whence it was scarce possible she should get into the path.

4. He said he went by Winicowett house, which he said stood on the contrary side of the way.

5. Being, as he said, within two or three miles of Swamscote, where he left her, he went not thither to tell them of her, nor staid by her that night, nor, at his return home, did tell any body of her, till he was demanded of her.

6. When he came back, he had above ten shillings in his purse, and yet he said she would give him but seven shillings, and he carried no money with him.

7. At his return, he had some blood upon his hat, and on his skirts before, which he said was with a pigeon, which he killed.

8. He had a scratch on the left side of his nose, and, being asked by a neighbor how it came, he said it was with a bramble, which could not be, it being of the breadth of a small nail; and being asked after by the magistrate, he said it was with his piece, but that could not be on the left side.

9. The body of the maid was found by an Indian, about half a year after, in the midst of thick swamp, ten miles short of the place he said he left her in, and about three miles from the place where he landed by Merrimack, (and it was after seen, by the English,) the flesh being rotted off it, and the clothes laid all on a heap by the body.

10. He said, that soon after he left her, he met with a bear and he thought that bear might kill her, yet he would not go back to save her.

11. He brake prison, and fled as far as Powder Horn Hill, and there hid himself out of the way, for fear of pursuit, and after, when he arose to go forward, he could not, but (as himself confessed) was forced to return back to prison again.

At his death he confessed he had made many lies to excuse himself, but denied that he had killed or ravished her. He was very loath to die, and had hope he should be reprieved; but the court held him worthy of death, in undertaking the charge of a shiftless maid, and leaving her (when he might have done otherwise) in such a place as he knew she must needs perish, if not preserved by means unknown.

SIN IN PLYMOUTH. *Governor William Bradford records a lurid crime that took place in 1642.*

There was a youth whose name was Thomas Granger. He was servant to an honest man of Duxbury, being about 16 or 17 years of age. (His father and mother lived at the same time at Scituate.) He was this year detected of buggery, and indicted for the same, with a mare, a cow, two goats, five sheep, two calves and a turkey. Horrible it is to mention, but the truth of the history requires it. He was first discovered by one that accidentally saw his lewd practice towards the mare. (I forbear particulars.) Being upon it examined and committed, in the end he not only confessed the fact with that beast at that time, but sundry times before and at several times with all the rest of the forenamed in his indictment. And this his free confession was not only in private to the magistrates (though at first he strived to deny it) but to sundry, both ministers and others; and afterwards, upon his indictment, to the whole Court and jury; and confirmed it at his execution. And whereas some of the sheep could not so well be known by his description of them, others with them were brought before him and he declared which were they and which were not. And accordingly he was cast by the jury and condemned, and after executed about the 8th of September, 1642. A very sad spectacle it was. For first the mare and then the cow and the rest of the lesser cattle were killed before his face, according to the law, Leviticus xx.15; and then he himself was executed. The cattle were all cast into a great and large pit that was digged of purpose for them, and no use made of any part of them.

Upon the examination of this person and also of a former that had made some sodomitical attempts upon another, it being demanded of them how they came first to the knowledge and practice of such wickedness, the one confessed he had long used it in old England; and this youth last spoken of said he was taught it by another that had heard of such things from some in England when he was there, and they kept cattle together. By which it appears how one wicked person may infect many, and what care all ought to have what servants they bring into their families.

ATTEMPTED MURDER IN CONNECTICUT. *Governor John Winthrop of Massachusetts, whose son (also called John Winthrop) was to become governor of Connecticut, narrates this 1644 story in his journal.*

At Stamford an Indian came into a poor man's house, none being at home but the wife, and a child in the cradle, and taking up a lathing hammer as if he would have bought it, the woman stooping down to take her child out of the cradle, he struck her with the sharp edge upon the side of her head, wherewith she fell down, and then he gave her two cuts more which pierced into her brains, and so left her for dead, carrying away some clothes which lay at hand. This woman after a short time came to herself and got out to a neighbor's house, and told what had been done to her, and described the Indian by his person

A Colonial court of law. A poem accompanying this 1787 woodcut begins: "How blest
is that INTERPRETER of Laws/Who rich and Poor make equal in a Cause! . . ."
From *Bickerstaff's Genuine Boston Almanack.*

and clothes, etc. Whereupon many Indians of those parts were
brought before her, and she charged one of them confidently to be
the man, whereupon he was put in prison with intent to have put
him to death, but he escaped, and the woman recovered, but lost her
senses. A good time after the Indians brought another Indian whom
they charged to have committed that fact, and he, upon examination, confessed it, and gave the reason thereof, and brought forth
some of the clothes which he had stolen. Upon this the magistrates
of New Haven, taking advice of the elders in those parts, and some
here, did put him to death. The executioner would strike off his
head with a falchion [curved sword], but he had eight blows at it
before he could effect it, and the Indian sat upright and stirred not
all the time.

SILENCER. *From John Winthrop's journal. The story concerns "A Woman of
Salem, one Oliver His Wife" and takes place in 1646.*

This woman was adjudged to be whipped for reproaching the magistrates. She stood without tying, and bare her punishment with a masculine spirit, glorying in her suffering. But after (when she came to
consider the reproach, which would stick by her, etc.) she was much
dejected about it. She had a cleft stick put on her tongue half an hour,
for reproaching the elders.

OTHER CRIMES AND PUNISHMENTS. *From naturalist John Josselyn's summary of Massachusetts laws drawn up in 1646.*

For kissing a woman in the street, though in way of civil salute, whipping or a fine.

An *English* woman suffering an *Indian* to have carnal knowledge of her, had an *Indian* cut out exactly in red cloth sewed upon her right Arm, and injoyned to wear it twelve moneths.

Scolds they gag and set them at their doors for certain hours, for all comers and goers by to gaze at.

INFANTICIDE. *From John Winthrop's journal, 1646. In his book* Demonologie, *King James I of England expressed a common belief: "In a secret murther, if the dead carkas be at any time thereafter handled by the murtherer, it will gush out of blood, as if the blood were crying to the Heaven for revenge. . . . "*

There fell out at this time a very sad occasion. A merchant of Plimouth in England, (whose father had been mayor there,) called Martin, being fallen into decay, came to Casco Bay, and after some time, having occasion to return into England, he left behind him two daughters, (very proper maidens and of modest behavior,) but took not that course for their safe bestowing in his absence, as the care and wisdom of a father should have done, so as the eldest of them, called Mary, twenty-two years of age, being in house with one Mr. Mitton, a married man of Casco, within one quarter of a year, he was taken with her, and soliciting her chastity, obtained his desire, and having divers times committed sin with her, in the space of three months, she then removed to Boston, and put herself in service to Mrs. Bourne; and finding herself to be with child, and not able to bear the shame of it, she concealed it, and though divers did suspect it, and some told her mistress their fears, yet her behavior was so modest, and so faithful she was in her service, as her mistress would not give ear to any such report, but blamed such as told her of it. But, her time being come, she was delivered of a woman child in a back room by herself upon the 13 October in the night, and the child was born alive, but she kneeled upon the head of it, till she thought it had been dead, and having laid it by, the child, being strong, recovered, and cried again. Then she took it again, and used violence to it till it was quite dead. Then she put it into her chest, and having cleansed the room, she went to bed, and arose again the next day about noon, and went about her business, and so continued till the nineteenth day, that her master and mistress went on shipboard to go for England. They being gone, and she removed to another house, a midwife in the town, having formerly suspected her, and now coming to her again, found she had been delivered of a child, which, upon examination, she confessed, but said it was still-born, and so she put it into the fire. But, search being made, it was found in her chest, and when she was brought before the jury, they caused her to touch the face of it, whereupon the blood came fresh into it. Whereupon she confessed the whole truth, and a surgeon, being called to search the body of the child, found a fracture in the skull. Before she was condemned, she confessed, that she had prostituted her body to another also, one Sears. She behaved herself very penitently while she was in prison, and at her death, 18 January, complaining much of the hardness of her heart. She confessed, that the first and second time she committed fornication, she prayed for pardon, and promised to commit it no more; and the third time she prayed to God, that if she did fall into it again, he would make her an example, and therein she justified God, as she did in the rest. Yet all the comfort God would afford her, was only trust (as she said) in his mercy through Christ. After she was turned off and had hung a space, she spake, and asked what they did mean to do. Then some stepped up, and turned the knot of the rope backward, and then she soon died.

PIRATES. *As reported first by the* Boston News-Letter, *and then by Samuel Sewall in his diary, 1704. The Reverend Cotton Mather, as well as preaching the execution sermon, had also preached a sermon, called "Faithful Warnings to Prevent Fearful Judgments," before the condemned pirates on the preceding Sunday. Major Sewall was Samuel's brother.*

GOD Save the QUEEN.

Salem, June 11. This Afternoon, Major *Sewall* brought in to this Port, the *Larrimore* Galley, and Seven Pirates, viz. *Erasmus Peterson, Charles James, John Carter, John Pitman, Francis King, Charles King, John King,* whom he with his Company Surprized and Seized at the Isles of Sholes the 10*th* Instant, *viz.,* four of them on Board the *Larrimore* Galley, and three on Shoar on *Starr* Island, being assisted by *John Hinckes* and *Thomas Phipps* Esqrs. (Two of Her Majesties Justices of New-Hampshire, who were happily there, together with the Justices, and the Captain of the place.) He also Seized 45 Ounces and Seven Penny weight of Gold of the said Pirates.

Boston, June 17. On the 13. Instant, Major *Sewall* attended with a strong guard brought to Town the above mentioned Pirates, and Gold he had Seized, and gave His Excellency a full Account of his Procedure in Seizing them. The Prisoners were committed to Gaol in order to a Tryal, and the Gold delivered to the Treasurer and Committee appointed to receive the same. The Service of Major *Sewall* and Company was very well Accepted and Rewarded by the Governour.

Boston, June 24. On Monday last, The 19. Currant, The High Court of Admiralty Sat again, when the Tryal of *John Quelch* late Commander

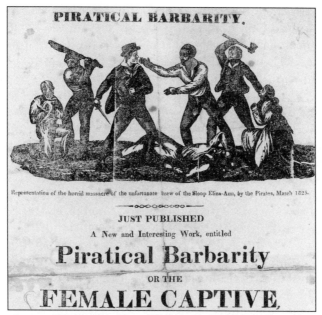

A pamphlet costing "the trifling sum of 12 1-2 cents" about
"the Unparalleled Sufferings of Miss Lucretia Parker . . .
who, after being retained a Prisoner eleven days by
the Pirates, was miraculously delivered."

of the Briganteen *Charles,* and Company for Piracy and Murder,
Committed by them upon Her Majesties *Allies* the Subjects of the King
of *Portugal,* was brought forward, and the said *Quelch* was brought to
the Bar, being charged with Nine several Articles of Piracy and Murder
whereupon he had been Arraigned and Pleaded, *Not Guilty:* The
Queen's Attorney opened the case, and the Court proceeded to the
Examination of the Evidences for Her Majesty. And the Council for
the Prisoner and the Prisoner himself being fairly heard, The Court
was cleared, and after Advisement, the Prisoner was again brought to
the Bar; & the Judgment of the Court declared. That he was guilty of
the Felony, Piracy and Murder, laid in said Articles: Accordingly
Sentence of Death was pronounced against him.

The next day being Tuesday, *John Lambert, Charles James, John Miller*
and *Christopher Scudamore,* were brought to the Bar, who pleaded Not
Guilty: And were severally tryed as Quelch was, and found guilty and
Sentenced to Dy in like manner.

Then was brought to the Bar, *William Whiting,* and *John Templeton*
being Arraigned. They pleaded *Not Guilty,* and the Witnesses proving
no matter of Fact upon them, said *Whiting* being Sick all the Voyage, &
not active, and *Templeton* a Servant about 14 years of Age, and not
charged with any action, were acquited by the Court, paying Prison

Fees. Next 15 more being brought to the Bar and Arraign'd . . . who severally pleaded Guilty, and threw themselves on the Queen's Mercy. And Sentence of Death was past upon them, in like manner as those abovenamed. 'Tis said some of them will be Executed the next Fryday, and the whole proceeding be put out in print.

From the diary of Samuel Sewall. June 30, 1704. After Dinner, about 3. p.m. I went to see the Execution. . . . Many were the people that saw upon Broughton's Hill. But when I came to see how the River was cover'd with People, I was amazed: Some say there were 100 Boats. 150 Boats and Canoes, saith Cousin Moody of York. . . . Mr. Cotton Mather came with Capt Quelch and six others for Execution from the Prison to Scarlet's Wharf, and from thence in the Boat to the place of Execution about the midway between Hudson's point and Broughton's Warehouse. Mr. Bridge was there also. When the scaffold was hoisted to a due height, the seven Malefactors went up; Mr. Mather pray'd for them standing upon the Boat. Ropes were all fasten'd to the Gallows (save King, who was Repriev'd). When the Scaffold was let sink, there was such a Screech of the Women that my wife heard it sitting in our Entry next the Orchard, and was much surprised at it; yet the wind was sou-west. Our house is a full mile from the place.

SATURDAY-NIGHT ROWDIES. *Judge Samuel Sewall, now aged sixty-one, enforces the law in Boston—in this case "An Act for the better Observation and Keeping the Lord's Day." The Sabbath was held to begin at sunset on Saturday night. The Queen was Queen Anne.*

[1714.] Seventh-Day, Feb 6. . . . My neighbor Colson knocks at our door about 9. or past to tell of the Disorders at the Tavern at the South-end in Mr. Addington's house, kept by John Wallis. He desired me that I would accompany Mr. Bromfield and Constable Howell thither. It was 35 Minutes past Nine at Night before Mr. Bromfield came; then we went. I took Æneas Salter with me. Found much Company. They refus'd to go away. Said were there to drink the Queen's Health, and they had many other Healths to drink. Call'd for more Drink: drank to me, I took notice of the Affront . . . Mr. John Netmaker drank the Queen's Health to me. I told him I drank none; upon that he ceas'd. Mr. Brinley put on his Hat to affront me. I made him take it off. I threaten'd to send some of them to prison; that did not move them. They said they could but pay their Fine, and doing that they might stay. I told them if they had not a care, they would be guilty of a Riot. Mr. Bromfield spake of raising a number of Men to Quell them, and was in some heat, ready to run into the Street. But I did not like that.

Not having Pen and Ink, I went to take their Names with my Pensil, and not knowing how to Spell their Names, they themselves of their own accord writ them. Mr. Netmaker, reproaching the Province, said they had not made one good Law.

At last I address'd myself to Mr. Banister. I told him he had been longest an Inhabitant and Freeholder, I expected he should set a good Example in departing thence. Upon this he invited them to his own House, and away they went; and we, after them, went away. The Clock in the room struck a pretty while before they departed. I went directly home, and found it 25 Minutes past Ten at Night when I entered my own House.

SLAVE LAW. *Some extracts from a South Carolina law passed in 1712.*

WHEREAS, the plantations and estates of this Province cannot be well and sufficiently managed and brought into use, without the labor and service of negroes and other slaves; and forasmuch as the said negroes and other slaves brought unto the people of this Province for that pur-pose, are of barbarous, wild, savage natures, and such as renders them

Broadside offering a reward for runaway slaves, St. Louis, Missouri, October 1847.

wholly unqualified to be governed by the laws, customs, and practices of this Province . . . it is absolutely necessary, that such other constitutions, laws and orders, should in this Province be made and enacted, for the good regulating and ordering of them, as may restrain the disorders, rapines and inhumanity, to which they are naturally prone and inclined, and may also tend to the safety and security of the people of this Province and their estates; to which purpose,

Be it enacted by the authority aforesaid, That no master, mistress, overseer, or other person whatsoever, that hath the care and charge of any negro or slave, shall give their negroes and other slaves leave, on Sundays, hollidays, or any other time, to go out of their plantations, except such negro or other slave as usually wait upon them at home or abroad, or wearing a livery; and every other negro or slave that shall be taken hereafter out of his master's plantation, without a ticket, or leave in writing, from his master or mistress, or some other person by his or her appointment, or some white person in the company of such slave, to give an account of his business, shall be whipped; and every person who shall not (when in his power,) apprehend every negro or other slave which he shall see out of his master's plantation, without leave as aforesaid, and after apprehended, shall neglect to punish him by moderate whipping, shall forfeit twenty shillings. . . .

And for the better security of all such persons that shall endeavor to take any runaway, or shall examine any slave for his ticket, passing to and from his master's plantation, it is hereby declared lawful for any white person to beat, maim or assault, and if such negro or slave cannot otherwise be taken, to kill him, who shall refuse to shew his ticket, or, by running away or resistance, shall endeavor to avoid being apprehended or taken.

EX-GOVERNOR. *Deposition in a case brought in 1725 by the newly appointed governor of North Carolina, Sir Richard Everard, against his predecessor, James Burrington.*

The deposition of Mrs. Susanna Parris, wife of Mr. Thomas Parris of Edenton and Burgess for said town, who, being of full age and sworn on the holy evangelists, sayeth:

That on Monday, the fifteenth day of this instant November, about three of the clock in the morning, as she was in bed, she heard a knocking at the outer door of the house; and her husband, inquiring who was there, was answered, "damn you, get up." But he not immediately rising, the person at the door swore he would break into the house, if the doors were not immediately opened; upon which her husband opened the door and found it was Mr. Burrington, the late

Governor, who immediately went to the door of Mr. Cockburne's room where the said Cockburne lay sick and speechless in bed. And upon Mrs. Cockburne inquiring who was there, this deponent heard Mr. Burrington answer it was a doctor come to Mr. Cockburne, which gained him admittance into the room where he lay. And upon this deponent's afterwards asking Mrs. Cockburne what his business was with her husband, she told this deponent that he had very much abused Mr. Cockburne as he lay in that condition, giving all manner of abusive language and threatening to cut off his ears. And this deponent further sayeth that after he came out of Mr. Cockburne's room she heard Mr. Burrington speaking to her husband, said "are all you country men such fools as Sir Richard Everard? He is a noodle, an ape," and several other epithets. And further said that he (the said Richard Everard meaning) was not more fit to be a governor than a hog in the woods. Soon after Mr. Burrington, directing his discourse to one James Winwright, a person that he had previously made Provost Marshal, he swore to him that before nine months he would make him Provost Marshal again; and offered to lay five thousand pounds that he the said Burrington should be Governor again by that time. And then a health was drunk by the company to Governor Burrington. And this deponent further remembers that, in the midst of his speeches and abusive language of the Governor Sir Richard, she heard him mention Judge Gale, whom he called "a perjured old rogue," and swore he should never be easy till he had cut his ears off, which sort of language about the Judge she has heard him several times repeat since Colonel Gale came last from England.

SOME PENNSYLVANIA LAWS. *As recorded by Peter Kalm, a Swedish naturalist who visited this country from 1748 to 1751.*

Law concerning liberty of conscience. Whosoever believeth in God the Father, His Son and Holy Ghost, and acknowledges the Holy Scriptures and wishes to live in peace, shall have religious freedom.

The governor alone has the right to purchase land from the Indians.

The blasphemer has to give 10£ to the poor and spend three months in the penitentiary at hard labor.

Fences must be five feet high.

A ship carrying sick people may not approach within a mile of Philadelphia or any other city. The breaking of this ordinance is punished by a fine of 100£.

If someone cashes a check on an English bank and it is returned with a protest, he must pay a fine of 20£, and restore the money.

A wooden house is moved past the jail in Philadelphia. Engraving by William Birch and Son from *The City of Philadelphia. . . as it appeared in the Year 1800.*

The produce of the land, such as wheat, rye, corn, barley, oats, pork, meat and tobacco shall in trade be valid as money, unless the contract has definitely stipulated payment in silver.

Fire in a chimney entails a fine of 40 shillings. Every house must have a water barrel and a leather bucket; failure to comply with this provision brings a fine of 10 shillings. Smoking on the street costs 1 shilling and the fine is used for purchasing leather buckets, pumps, etc. for the public welfare.

There is a bounty of three pence per dozen on blackbirds, and threepence apiece on crows. The heads should be shown to a town official.

Anyone selling rum to the Indians, secretly or otherwise, must pay a fine of 10£.

He who works on Sunday is fined 20 shillings.

An adulterer must suffer twenty-one lashes on his bare back and spend a year in prison at hard labor or pay a fine of 50£. Besides, the wife who has suffered shall have the right to divorce the guilty from bed and board. If he be guilty a second time, he shall receive the same number of lashes and seven years of hard labor in prison, or pay a fine of 100£, and a like amount for every subsequent offense. Fornication is punishable with a fine of 10£ or twenty-one lashes on his bare body at a whipping-post. If a woman gives birth to an illegitimate child and at the birth or in court accuses someone, he shall be father to the child. Anyone proven father shall support the child.

Bigamy is punished by thirty-nine lashes on the bare back, life imprisonment at hard labor, and declaration of invalidity of the second marriage.

No pigs may run loose in Philadelphia, Chester or Bristol. Offenders against this ordinance lose the pigs thus running wild.

All saloons and taverns must be licensed.

To prevent degeneration of horses, small stallions, eighteen months old or more, are forbidden to run loose.

A bounty of fifteen shillings was first paid for wolves, but this was later raised to 20 shillings. For a young wolf cub the bounty at first was 7 shillings sixpence, which was raised later to 10 shillings. An old red fox brought 2 shillings' reward, a young red fox cub, 1 shilling.

A BAD HAT. *Whether delivered from the scaffold, or—as here—written up with professional help, the confession of a condemned criminal was always a popular entertainment. "Benefit of the clergy," which Arthur mentions near the end of his confession, was a plea for clemency on the grounds that the prisoner could read— a legal relic from the Middle Ages, when generally only clerics were literate.*

The LIFE, and dying SPEECH of *ARTHUR*, a Negro Man; Who was Executed at *Worcester,* October 20th 1768. For a Rape committed on the Body of one *Deborah Metcalfe.* I Was born at *Taunton,* January 15. 1747, in the House of *Richard Godfrey,* Esq; my Mother being his Slave, where I lived fourteen Years; was learned to read and write, and was treated very kindly by my Master; but was so unhappy as often to incur the Displeasure of my Mistress, which caused me then to run away: And this was the beginning of the many notorious Crimes, of which I have been guilty. I went first to *Sandwich,* where I fell in Company with some Indians, with whom I lived two Months in a very dissolute Manner, frequently being guilty of Drunkenness and Fornication; for which Crimes I have been since famous, and by which I am now brought to this untimely Death.

At *Sandwich,* I stole a Shirt, was detected, and settled the Affair, by paying twenty Shillings. My Character being now known, I thought proper to leave the Place; and accordingly shipped my self on board a Whaling Sloop, with Capt. *Coffin,* of *Nantucket:* We were out eight Months, and then returned to *Nantucket,* from whence we sailed, where I tarried six Weeks. In which Time I broke a Store of Mr. *Roach's,* from which I stole a Quantity of Rum, a pair of Trowsers, a Jacket, and some Calicoe.—The next Day I got drunk, and by wearing the Jacket, was detected, for which Offence I was whip'd fifteen Stripes, and committed to Gaol, for the Payment of Cost &c from whence I escaped in half an Hour by breaking the Lock. Being now hardened in my Wickedness, I the next Night broke another Store in the same Place, from which I took several Articles, and then shipped myself on board a Vessel bound to *Swanzey*, where I was discovered, taken on Shoar, and whip'd sixteen Stripes; being then set at Liberty, I returned to *Taunton*, after one Year's Absence, where my Master received me kindly, whom I served three Years: In which Time I followed the Seas, sailing from *Nantucket*, and *Newport*, to divers parts of the *West-Indies*, where I whored and drank, to great Excess. Being now weary of the Seas, on the 27th of October 1764, I came again to live with my Master at *Taunton*, where I behaved well for six Weeks; at the Expiration of which Time, going to Town with some Negroes, I got intoxicated; on returning home went into an House where were several Women only, to whom I offered Indecencies, but was prevented from executing my black Designs, by the coming in of *James Williams*, Esq; upon which I left the House, but was overtaken by him, who with the Assistance of Mr. *Job Smith*, committed me to *Taunton* Gaol: On the next Day I was tried before the same Mr. *Williams*, and was whip'd thirty-nine Stripes for abusing him, uttering three profane Oaths, and threatning to fire Mr. *Smith's* House. My Master being now determined, by the Advice of his friends, to send me out of the Country, I was sold to _____ *Hill*, of *Brookfield*, with whom I lived only one Week; was then sold to my last Master, Capt. *Clarke*, of *Rutland* District, where I behaved well for two Months, and was very kindly treated by my Master and Mistress. I then unhappily commenced an Acquaintance with a young Squaw, with whom (having stole Six Shillings from one of my Master's Sons) I was advised by other Negroes, to run away, to avoid being taken up. By Advice of my Companion (who like the rest of her Sex, was of a very fruitful Invention) I had recourse to the following Expedient: I dressed in the Habit of a Squaw, and made of my own Cloaths a Pappoose; in this manner we proceeded to *Hadley* undiscover'd, where I was introduced by my Companion, to an Indian Family, where I tarried only one Night, being discover'd in the Morning by one Mr. *Shurtless*, a Person who had been sent after me; with him I went to *Springfield*, where I met my Master, who took me down to *Middletown* with a Drove of Horses where he sold me to a Dutch Gentleman, whose Name I have since forgot. The very Night after I stole from the Widow *Sherley*, (a Person who kept a public House in that Place) five Pounds; and the next Night, by getting drunk and loosing some of my Money, I was detected and put under the Custody of two Men, for Trial the next Day: From whom I escaped, and went to ... *Natick*, where I met with the Squaw, with whom I formerly made my

Tour to *Hadley*, and with her spent the Day; and returning to *Cambridge*, I met my Master, with another Man, in pursuit of me. At our Arrival there, I was sentenced by five Men (to whom the Matter was left) to receive fifteen Stripes, or pay four Dollars; and my Master was so good natur'd, or rather silly, as to pay the Money and let me go with Impunity.

My Master . . . once more took me home, where I had not been three Weeks, before another Negro of my Master's told me that the young Squaw, so often mentioned, was very desirous of seeing me. I one Night, after having stole some Rum from my Master, got pretty handsomely drunk, took one of his Horses, and made the best of my way to her usual Place of Abode; but she not being at home, the Devil put it into my Head to pay a Visit to the Widow *Deborah Metcalfe*, whom I, in a most inhumane manner, ravished: The Particulars of which are so notorious, that it is needless for me here to relate them. The next Morning the unhappy Woman came and acquainted my Master of it, who immediately tyed me, to prevent my running away, and told her (if she was desirous of prosecuting me) to get a Warrant as soon as possible; but she being unwilling to have me hanged, proposed making the Matter up for a proper Consideration, provided my Master would send me out of the Country; to which he agreed, and accordingly set off with me for *Albany:* But we were overtaken at *Glasgow*, by Mr. *Nathaniel Jennison*, who it seem'd had got a Warrant for me. On our return to *Rutland* District, we stop'd at a Tavern in *Hardwick*, where after I had warmed my self, *Jennison* was Fool enough to bid me put along, and he would overtake me; accordingly I went out of the Door, and seeing his Horse stand handily, what should I do, but mount him, and rode off as fast as I could, leaving *Jennison* to pursue me on Foot. I got home before Bed-time, and took up my Lodging in my Master's Barn for the Night, where I had a Bottle of Cherry-Rum (which I found in Mr. *Jennison's* Baggs) to refresh my self with.

On the next Day, being the 30th of March 1767, was discovered and committed to *Worcester* Gaol, where I continued 'till the 20th of April following; at which Time I broke out with the late celebrated *FRASIER*, and a young Lad, who was confined for stealing. After which, at *Worcester* we broke into a Barber's Shop, from whence we stole a Quantity of Flour, a Comb, and a Razor: We then set off for *Boston*. At *Shrewsbury*, we stole a Goose from Mr. *Samuel Jennison:* and from the Widow *Kingsley*, in the same Place, we stole a Kettle, in which we boiled the Goose, in *Westborough* Woods. At *Marlborough*, we broke into a Distill-House, from whence we stole some Cyder Brandy: In the same Town we broke into a Shoe-maker's Shop, and took each of us a pair of Shoes. We like wise broke into Mr. *Ciperon Howe's* House, in the same Place, from whence we stole some Bread, Meat and Rum. At *Sudbury*, we stole each of us a Shirt, and one pair of Stockings. At *Weston* we stole some Butter from off a Horse. At *Waltham* we broke into a House belonging to one Mr. *Fisk*, from whom we took a small Sum of Money, some Chocolate and Rum. At *Watertown* we stole a Brass Kettle from one Mrs. *White* of that Place. My Companions now left me; upon which I went to Mr. *Fish's* in *Waltham*, who knew me. And having heard of my Escape from *Worcester* Gaol, immediately secured me, and with the Assistance of another Man, brought me back again, where on the 17th of September following, I was tryed and found guilty. Upon which, by the Advice of my Counsel, I prayed for the Benefit of the Clergy; which after a Year's Consideration, the Court denied me: And accordingly I was, on the 24th of Sept. last, sentenced to be hanged, which I must confess is but too just a Reward for my many notorious Crimes.

I cannot conclude this my Narrative, without gratefully acknowledging the unwearied Pains that was taken by the Rev. Mr. *Mccarty*, to awaken me to a proper Sense of my miserable and wretched Condition, whose frequent Exhortations, and most fervent Prayers, together with those of the rest of God's People, and my own sincere Endeavours after true Repentance, will I hope prove the Means of my eternal Well-being; which I hope is still the Prayers of every Christian, to whom my unhappy Situation is known.—I earnestly desire that this Recital of my Crimes, and the ignominious Death to which my notorious Wickedness has bro't me, may prove a Warning to all Persons who shall become acquainted therewith. But in a particular Manner, I would solemnly warn those of my own Colour, as they regard their own Souls, to avoid Desertion from their Masters, Drunkenness and Lewdness; which three Crimes was the Source from which have flowed the many Evils and Miseries of my short Life: Short indeed! For I am now at the Age of 21 Years only, just going to launch into a never-ending eternity; not by a natural Death, but to the Dissolution of Soul and Body, so dreadful in itself, are added the Ignominy and Terror of that particular kind of Death, which I am now going to suffer.—I freely acknowledge I have been better treated by Mankind in general, than I deserved: Yet some Injuries I have received, which I now freely forgive. I also humbly ask Forgiveness of all whom I have injured, and desire that they would pray that I may receive the Forgiveness of God, whom I have most of all offended; and on whose Pardon and Grace depends my eternal Happiness or Misery.—

Worcester Gaol,
Oct. 18, 1768.

Arthur.

MAKING AMENDS. *While attending a council called by Governor Cass at St. Mary's on the Miami River in Ohio in 1819, John Tanner—who as a boy had been kidnapped by the Shawnee and then sold to an Ojibwa family—fell sick with the fever and ague. Then this happened.*

A young man of the Ottawwaws, whom Be-nais-sa had given me to cook for me and assist about me in my sickness, went across the creek to a camp of the Po-ta-wa-to-mies who had recently arrived and were drinking. At midnight he was brought into the lodge drunk, and one of the men who came with him, said to me, as he pushed him in, "Take care of your young man. He has been doing mischief." I immediately called Be-nais-sa to kindle a fire, when we saw, by the light of it, the young man standing with his knife in his hand, and that, together with his arm and great part of his body covered with blood. The Indians could not make him lie down, but when I told him to, he obeyed immediately and I forbade them to make any inquiries about what he had done, or take any notice of his bloody knife. In the morning, having slept soundly, he was perfectly unconscious of all that had passed. He said he believed that he had been very drunk, and as he was now hungry, he must hurry and get ready something to eat. He was astonished and confounded when I told him he had killed a man. He remembered only that in his drunkenness he had began to cry for his father, who had been killed on that spot several years before by white men. He expressed much concern, and went immediately to see the man he had stabbed, who was not yet dead. We learned from the Po-ta-wa-to-mies that he had found the young man sleeping, or lying in a state of insensibility from intoxication, and had stabbed him without any words having been exchanged, and apparently without knowing who he was. The relations of the wounded man said nothing to him, but the interpreter of Gov. Cass reproved him very sharply.

It was evident to all that the young man he had wounded could not recover; indeed, he was now manifestly near his end. When our companion returned, we had made up a considerable present, one giving a blanket, one a piece of strouding, some one thing, and some another. With these he immediately returned, and placing them on the ground beside the wounded man, he said to the relatives who were standing about, "My friends, I have, as you see, killed this, your brother; but I knew not what I did. I had no ill will against him, and when, a few days since, he came to our camp, I was glad to see him. But drunkenness made me a fool, and my life is justly forfeited to you. I am poor, and among strangers, but some of those who came from my own country with me, would gladly bring me back to my parents. They have, therefore, sent me with this small present. My life is in your hands, and my present is before you, take which ever you choose. My friends will have no cause to complain." He then sat down beside the wounded man, and stooping his head, hid his eyes with his hands, and waited for them to strike. But the mother of the man he had wounded, an old woman, came a little forward and said, "For myself and my children, I can answer, that we wish not to take your life; but I cannot promise to protect you from the resentment of my husband, who is now absent; nevertheless, I will accept your present, and whatever influence I may have with him, I shall not fail to use it in your behalf. I know that it was not from design, or on account of any previous hatred that you have done this, and why should your mother be made to cry as well as myself?" She took the presents, and the whole affair being reported to Gov. Cass, he was satisfied with the course that had been taken.

On the following day the wounded man died, and some of our party assisted the young man who had killed him in making his grave. When this was completed, the governor gave the dead man a valuable present of blankets, cloth, etc. to be buried with him, according to the Indian custom, and these were brought and heaped up on the brink of the grave. But the old woman, instead of having them buried, proposed to the young men to play for them. As the articles were somewhat numerous, various games were used, as shooting at the mark, leaping, wrestling, etc. but the handsomest piece of cloth was reserved as the prize for the swiftest in the foot race, and was won by the young man himself who had killed the other. The old woman immediately afterwards called him to her, and said, "Young man, he who was my son, was very dear to me, and I fear I shall cry much and often for him. I would be glad if you would consent to be my son in his stead, to love me and take care of me as he did. . . . "

The young man, who was grateful to her for the anxiety she showed to save his life, immediately consented to this arrangement, and entered heartily upon it.

LIFE IN ANTEBELLUM NATCHEZ. *From the diary of William Johnson, a "free Negro" and prosperous owner of the town's leading barber shop and of several slaves. Johnson was born in 1809.*

November 24, 1835. A Bear belonging to Mr Phiffs Killed a Little Yellow Child Down at Mr Parkers Hotel. They had to shoot him Dead to Loose him— . . . Mr Pulling and Milne has a sort of a fight about the moving of some coal. Mr P. threw a Hatchet at Mr M. and it mist him. Mr M attempted to get a gun Down to shoot.

June 4, 1836. Old La Vine and a Little Frenchman by the name of Surie has a Street fight, the one with a shovell, the other with a stick. Surie made La Viene back clear Back from Mr Murchersons store to his own. It was very Laughable.

November 28, 1836. To Day we had Bloody work for a while in the streets up at Throckmortons Corner. Last night up at Mrs Rowans Bourding House several gentlemen were in conversation about a Duel that was fought in South Carolina. When Mr Charles Stewart stated that those Gentlement that fought actually fought with Bullits, Mr Dahlgreen Said they must have fought with paper Bullits—Mr C. Stewart then Said if any man would say that they fought with paper Bullits that he is a Damned Lyar and a Dd Scoundrel & a Dmd Coward—this was at the Supper Table

Mr Dalhgreen Jumped up and Slaped Mr C. Stewarts Cheek one very hard Slapp. They were then parted so young Stewart told him that they would settle it in the morning—So this morning young Stewart took a Stand up at Carpenters Drug Store for the purpose of making the attackt upon Dahlgreen as he would be going to the Bank—Dr Hubbard at the Request of his Brother went up to Carpenters with young Stewart to see him Out in the affair

Elick Stewart said that he would not take any part in the affair and he took a stand over on Sorias Corner—and as Dalhgreen past the Door Stewart stepped up to him and told him that now was the time to Settle therr Dispute and at the Same time Struck Mr Dalhgreen with his stick; Mr D then Struck him Back with an umberralla—Stewart Struck him with the Stick again—Mr D. then steped Back and Drew a Pistol and Fired at Mr S. and missed him—Mr S. then Drew and Fired and the Ball Lodged under the arm in the Left Side of Mr Dalhgreen; Mr D. then steped in at Throckmortons Store.

S. steped in at the Door but finding that D. had another Pistol he steped Back and stood in the caseing of the Door.

D. then advanced on him, shot Him on Left Side of the face on the Temple or uper hinge of the Jaw Bone and the instant the Ball took Effect he Droped on his Knees and Fell over on the pavement as Dead, so Dead that he Barely Breathed.

At the instant he fell Mr Elick Stewart ran up and struck D. with his fist. D. then advanced on him with an Empty Pistol and in doing so Dr Hubbard shoved Him Back, E. S. Drew a Bouye Knife and commenced cuting at him—Mr D. had no weapon at this time and was fighting with his naked hands and Mr E.S. with the Knife—It was one of the gamest fights that we have Ever had in Our City before—E.S. cut him twice over the Head and cut his Little finger nearly off and split his hand pretty Bad.

CHEATING THE GALLOWS. *John Colt, a New York businessman, has been convicted of the murder of Samuel Adams, whose dismembered body was found in a box on board a ship about to sail for New Orleans. Colt's guilt was clear— a witness, looking through a keyhole, had seen him wiping blood off the floor of*

his office—and the governor has refused a stay of execution. Dr. Henry Anthon
was a clergyman and friend of George Templeton Strong, who tells the rest of the
story in his diary for November 1842.

Henry Anthon was with him today and is firmly convinced of his innocence. But it's clear that his sympathies have been most powerfully
wrought upon. The sheriff asked him today to ask Colt at what hour
tomorrow he would be executed; he could not do it himself, he said.
Dr. Anthon did so, and Colt flung himself on the bed and rocked
there in agony for a moment or two, and then named "sunset."

From eight o'clock this morning the Tombs were literally
besieged by a mob, blocking up every street around it, all assembled
not with the hope of getting admission, but to gaze eagerly at the
walls that contained the miserable prisoner and to catch what
rumors they could of what was going on within them. All over the
city a like feeling seemed to prevail. The approaching act of justice
seemed to be a weight on people's minds, to be constantly present
to them, and painfully so, though very little sympathy, if any, was
expressed for him and a reprieve would have raised a storm of
indignation. . . .

Dr. Anthon was at the prison all the morning. He married Colt to
his mistress Caroline Henshaw, and Colt was as he has been since
Monday, deeply penitent to all appearance. . . . At two o'clock the
Doctor went into his cell; the execution was to take place at four. Colt
himself prayed most fervently and poor Dr. Anthon went into the next
vacant cell and counted the minutes till four o'clock. . . . At five minutes to four, the sheriff and Westervelt made their appearance; the
procession was formed (Colt had requested after Dr. Anthon left him
to be left alone till the hour arrived). They opened the door, and
there lay Colt on his bed with one hand holding a dirk which he had
driven into his heart and had the resolution to *twist* as he did it, to
make the wound more sure.

By a strange coincidence, the great cupola of the Tombs caught
fire at this moment somehow or other, the alarm was given, the cupola, made of wood, was soon in a blaze, and the row among the mob
outside reached its height. They knew nothing of the suicide and
thought it was an attempt at a rescue—and it looked very like it, to be
sure. . . .

As to the suicide, when the rowdies heard of it of course they did-
n't believe it—it was all a trick to secure Colt's escape—and I suppose
that there'll be a prevalent tradition among the vagabonds of the city
for a long time to come that Colt's alive and all sorts of rumors of his
being in this place and that.

JUSTICE IN THE GOLD MINES. *Louise Clappe, wife of a young doctor in Indian Bar on the north fork of the Feather River, California, writes to her sister back East in a letter dated December 14, 1851.*

Last fall, two men were arrested by their partners, on suspicion of having stolen from them eighteen hundred dollars in gold dust. The evidence was not sufficient to convict them, and they were acquitted. They were tried before a meeting of the miners—as at that time the law did not even *pretend* to wave its scepter over this place.

The prosecutors still believed them guilty, and fancied that the gold was hidden in a "coyote hole," near the camp from which it had been taken. They therefore watched the place narrowly while the suspected men remained on the Bar. They made no discoveries, however; and soon after the trial, the acquitted persons left the mountains for Marysville.

A few weeks ago, one of these men returned, and has spent most of the time since his arrival in loafing about the different bar-rooms upon the river. He is said to have been constantly intoxicated. As soon as the losers of the gold heard of his return, they bethought themselves of the "coyote hole," and placed about its entrance some brushwood and stones, in such a manner that no one could go into it without disturbing the arrangement of them. In the meanwhile the thief settled at Rich Bar, and pretended that he was in search of some gravel ground for mining purposes.

A few mornings ago, he returned to his boarding place—which he had left some hour earlier—with a spade in his hand, and as he laid it down, carelessly observed that he had "been out prospecting." The losers of the gold went, immediately after breakfast, as they had been in the habit of doing, to see if all was right at the "coyote hole." On this fatal day, they saw that the entrance had been disturbed, and going in, they found upon the ground, a money belt which had apparently just been cut open. Armed with this evidence of guilt, they confronted the suspected person and sternly accused him of having the gold in his possession. Singularly enough, he did not attempt a denial, but said that if they would not bring him to a trial, (which of course they promised) he would give it up immediately. He then informed them that they would find it beneath the blankets of his *bunk,*—as those queer shelves on which miners sleep, ranged one above another, somewhat like the berths of the ship, are generally called. There, sure enough, were six hundred dollars of the missing money, and the unfortunate wretch declared that his partner had taken the remainder to the States.

By this time the exciting news had spread all over the Bar. A meeting of the miners was immediately convened, the unhappy man taken into custody, a jury chosen, and a judge, lawyer, etc., appointed.

Whether the men, who had just regained a portion of their missing property, made any objections to the proceedings which followed, I know not; if they had done so, however, it would have made no difference, as the *people* had taken the matter entirely out of their hands.

At one o'clock, so rapidly was the trial conducted, the judge charged the jury, and gently insinuated that they could do no less than to bring in with their verdict of guilty, a sentence of *death!* Perhaps you know that when a trial is conducted without the majesty of the law, the jury are compelled to decide, not only upon the guilt of the prisoner, but the mode of his punishment also. After a few minutes' absence, the twelve men who had consented to burden their souls with a responsibility so fearful, returned, and the foreman handed to the judge a paper, from which he read the will of the *people,* as follows: "That William Brown, convicted of stealing, etc., should in *one hour* from that time, be hung by the neck until he was dead."

By the persuasions of some men more mildly disposed, they granted him a respite of *three hours,* to prepare for his sudden entrance into eternity. He employed the time in writing in his native language (he is a Swede) to some friends in Stockholm; God help them when that fatal post shall arrive; for no doubt *he,* also, although a criminal, was fondly garnered in many a loving heart.

He had exhibited during the trial, the utmost recklessness and *nonchalance,* had drank many times in the course of the day, and when the rope was placed about his neck, was evidently much intoxicated. All at once, however, he seemed startled into a consciousness of the awful reality of his position, and requested a few moments for prayer.

The execution was conducted by the jury, and was performed by throwing the cord, one end of which was attached to the neck of the prisoner, across the limb of a tree standing outside of the Rich Bar grave-yard; when all, who felt disposed to engage in so revolting a task, lifted the poor wretch from the ground, in the most awkward manner possible. The whole affair, indeed, was a piece of cruel butchery, though *that* was not intentional, but arose from the ignorance of those who made the preparations. In truth, life was only crushed out of him, by hauling the writhing body up and down several times in succession, by the rope which was wound round a large bough. . . . Almost everybody was surprised at the severity of the sentence; and many, with their hands on the cord, did not believe even *then,* that it would be carried into effect, but thought that at the last moment, the jury would release the prisoner and substitute a milder punishment.

It is said that the crowd, generally, seemed to feel the solemnity of the occasion; but many of the drunkards, who form a large part of the community on these Bars, laughed and shouted, as if it were a spectacle got up for their particular amusement. A disgusting specimen of intoxicated humanity, struck with one of those luminous ideas peculiar to his class, staggered up to the victim, who was praying at the moment, and crowding a dirty rag into his almost unconscious hand, in a voice broken by a drunken hiccough, tearfully implored him to take his "hankercher," and if he were *innocent* (the man had not denied his guilt since first accused), to drop it as soon as he was drawn up into the air, but if *guilty*, not to let it fall on any account.

The body of the criminal was allowed to hang for some hours after the execution. It had commenced storming in the earlier part of the evening; and when those, whose business it was to inter the remains, arrived at the spot, they found them enwrapped in a soft, white shroud of feathery snow-flakes.

MARTIAL LAW IN BOSTON. *After making a name for himself as the author of* Two Years Before the Mast, *Richard Henry Dana settled into a successful career as a lawyer. His best-known case, in 1854, was his defense of Anthony Burns, an escaped slave who was being reclaimed by his Virginia owner under the notorious Fugitive Slave Act.*

June 2. FRIDAY. This was a day of intense excitement and deep feeling in the city, in the State and throughout New England, & indeed a great part of the Union. The hearts of millions of persons were beating high with hope, or indignation, or doubt. The Mayor of Boston, who is a poor shoat, a physician of a timid, conceited, scatter-brain character, raised by accident to a Mayoralty, has vacillated about for several days, & at last has done what a weak man always does, he has gone too far. He has ordered out the entire military force of the city, from 1500 to 1800 men, & undertaken to place full discretionary power in the hands of General Edmands. These troops & the three companies of regulars fill the streets & squares from the Court House to the end of the wharf where the Revenue Cutter lies, & in which it is understood that Burns, if remanded, will be taken to Virginia.

The decision was short. . . . Convicted on an *ex parte* record, against the actual evidence, and on his own admissions made at the moment of arrest to his alleged Master! A tyrannical statute and a weak judge!

The decision was a grievous disappointment to us all, and chiefly to the poor prisoner. He looked the image of despair.

The Court Room was ordered to be cleared at once of all but the prisoner & the "guard." I remained with the prisoner, & so did Mr. Grimes, the preacher. . . . Mr. Grimes talked constantly with the prisoner & kept up his spirits as he best could. He told him he thought that it was only a point of honor with the Government and the slaveholders to take him to Virginia, and that he would be bought as soon as he arrived there. This cheered him.

At about 11 o'clock, Burns was led back to his room. . . . Mr. Grimes and I walked to & fro in front of the Court House for an hour or so, the entire Square being cleared of the people, & filled with troops. Every window was filled, & beyond the lines drawn by the police was an immense crowd. Whenever a body of troops passed to or fro, they were hissed & hooted by the people, with some attempts at applause from their favorers. Nearly all the shops in Court and State streets were closed & hung in black, & a huge coffin was suspended across State Street, and flags Union down [as a sign of distress]. A brass field piece, belonging to the Fourth Artillery was ostentatiously loaded in sight of all the people & carried by the men of that corps in rear of the hollow Square in which Burns was placed. Some 1500 or 1800 men of the Volunteer Militia were under arms, all with their guns loaded & capped, & the officers with revolvers. These men were stationed at different posts in all the streets and lanes that lead into Court or State streets, from the Court House to Long Wharf. The police forced the people back to a certain line, generally at the foot or middle of the lanes & streets leading into the main streets, & whenever there was a passage, there, a few paces behind the police, was a body of troops, from 20 or 30 to 50 or 100d, according to the sise & importance of the passage.

The Mayor having given General Edmands discretionary orders to preserve peace & enforce the laws, General Edmands gave orders to each commander of a post to fire on the people whenever they passed the line marked by the police in a manner he should consider turbulent and disorderly. So, from nine o'clock in the morning until towards night, the city was really under Martial law.

Mr. Grimes & I remained in the Court House until the vile procession moved. Notwithstanding their numbers & the enormous military protection, the Marshal's company were very much disturbed & excited. They were exceedingly apprehensive of some unknown and unforeseen violence.

The "guard" at length filed out and formed a hollow square. Each man was armed with a short Roman sword and one revolver hanging in his belt. In this square marched Burns with the Marshal. The United States troops and the squadron of Boston light horse preceded and followed the square, with the field-piece. As the procession moved down, it was met with a perfect howl of Shame! Shame! and hisses.

THE KLAN AT WORK. *Some examples of Ku Klux Klan activities as recalled by Ben Johnson, of Durham, South Carolina, when interviewed at the age of eighty-five for the Federal Writers' Project's* Slave Narratives. *The period is just after the Civil War.*

I never will forgit when they hung Cy Guy. They hung him for a scandalous insult to a white woman, and they comed after him a hundred strong.

They tries him there in the woods, and they scratches Cy's arm to git some blood, and with that blood they writes that he shall hang 'tween the heavens and the earth till he am dead, dead, dead, and that any nigger what takes down the body shall be hunged too.

TWO MEMBERS OF THE KU-KLUX KLAN IN THEIR DISGUISES.

Members of the recently formed "Invisible Empire of the South"—
probably Confederate veterans—in an 1863 woodcut.

Well, sir, the next morning there he hung, right over the road, and the sentence hanging over his head. Nobody'd bother with that body for four days, and there it hung, swinging in the wind, but the fourth day the sheriff comes and takes it down.

There was Ed and Cindy, who 'fore the war belonged to Mr. Lynch, and after the war he told 'em to move. He gives 'em a month, and they ain't gone, so the Ku Kluxes gits 'em.

It was on a cold night when they comed and drugged the niggers outen bed. They carried 'em down in the woods and whup them, then they throws 'em in the pond, their bodies breaking the ice. Ed come out and come to our house, but Cindy ain't been seed since.

Sam Allen in Caswell County was told to move, and after a month the hundred Ku Klux come a-toting his casket, and they tells him that his time has come and iffen he wants to tell his wife goodbye and say his prayers hurry up.

They set the coffin on two chairs, and Sam kisses his old woman who am a-crying, then he kneels down side of his bed with his head on the pillow and his arms throwed out in front of him.

He sets there for a minute and when he riz he had a long knife in his hand. 'Fore he could be grabbed he done kill two of the Ku Kluxes with the knife, and he done gone outen the door. They ain't catch him neither, and the next night when they comed back, 'termined to git him, they shot another nigger by accident. . . .

I know one time Miss Hendon inherits a thousand dollars from her pappy's 'state, and that night she goes with her sweetheart to the gate, and on her way back to the house she gits knocked in the head with a axe. She screams, and her two nigger servants, Jim and Sam, runs and saves her, but she am robbed.

Then she tells the folkses that Jim and Sam am the guilty parties, but her little sister swears that they ain't, so they gits out of it.

After that they finds out that it am five mens—Atwater, Edwards, Andrews, Davis, and Markham. The preacher comes down to where they am hanging to preach their funeral, and he stands there while lightning plays round the dead men's heads and the wind blows the trees, and he preaches such a sermon as I ain't never heard before.

Bob Boylan falls in love with another woman, so he burns his wife and four young-uns up in their house.

The Ku Kluxes gits him, of course, and they hangs him high on the old red oak on the Hillsboro road. After they hunged him, his lawyer says to us boys, "Bury him good, boys, just as good as you'd bury me iffen I was dead."

I shook hands with Bob 'fore they hunged him, and I helped to bury him too, and we bury him nice, and we all hopes that he done gone to glory.

DANGEROUS TIMES IN SANTA FE. *As reported by the* New Mexican, *a weekly newspaper, in 1864.*

JANUARY 2, 1864:
SHAMEFUL.

We have heard of what we hope never will again occur in Santa Fe. It is, that at a fandango, a few evenings since, two of the females became insulted and enraged at each other, and that American men present endeavored to inflame the ill will and violence of the two women, the one against the other, and that a ring was formed and knives placed in the hands of each, for a desperate fight.

We hope no American will so far forget the dignity of human nature—his name and race, as to be found encouraging, again, such an exhibition of passion and violence between two females who, but

"Terrific Combat in a Church near Ft. Scott, Kansas"—
an illustration from the November 8, 1879 *National
Police Gazette*, a publication that specialized in spicy
"true crime" stories.

for being animated and excited by spectators, would restrain within decent bounds their personal animosities.

JANUARY 31, 1864:

Reliable information has been received in town, that Col. Carson, with a portion of his command, has passed through the Cañon de Chelle, making war upon the Navajoes, in the places of their safest residences, retreats and fastnesses. In his route, his command killed twenty three Indians and took one hundred and fifty prisoners. The passing of the Cañon, with a military body, has been several times, as we are informed, attempted by other commanders, such as Gen. Sumner and Col. Miles, and perhaps Gen. Canby. It may be that some command succeeded, but we are not now, so informed. The success of Col. Carson, will distinguish him and those with him. They deserve, and will receive the gratitude of the people, for every Indian they have killed or made captive. Go on, gallant Kit, says New Mexico, and "wipe out" the hostile Indians.

TEXAS RANGERS. *John King Fisher, who at the age of twenty-six boasted that he had killed a man for each year of his life, is brought to justice by a party of Rangers commanded by Captain Leander McNelly. The story is told by Napoleon Augustus Jennings, himself a Ranger and later a newspaperman.*

It was May 25, 1876 when we arrived at Laredo, and we camped near the town for three days. Then we continued our journey on toward the Nueces River, where we camped not far from the place where I had helped Peterson lay out homestead sections, over a year before. Here we remained for a few days to rest our horses, and then began our work of running desperadoes to earth—the work which has since made western Texas a law-abiding, safe country in which to live.

At the camp near the Nueces River, we learned first about the desperado, King Fisher, and his notorious gang of horse thieves, cattle thieves, and murderers. Fisher lived on Pendencia Creek, near the Nueces, in Dimmit County. He had a little ranch there, and about forty or fifty of his followers were nearly always with him. These men, too lazy or too vicious to work for themselves, preyed upon the substance of the toiling settlers. They stole the ranchmen's horses and cattle and robbed their corn cribs, and they did not stop at murder to further their ends. Captain McNelly (I was then his field secretary) wrote, in a letter to the Adjutant General, from this part of Texas:

> On my arrival here, I found the people greatly terrified, and on the eve of deserting their homes and property to save their lives—the homes which for years they had defended against

Indians and invading Mexicans alternately, and never once thought of leaving. Some of the oldest and best citizens told me that, in all of their frontier experience, they had never suffered so much as from these American robbers. For weeks past they have not dared to leave their homes for fear of being waylaid and murdered.

Every house in this part of the county has been repeatedly fired into by armed men, from fifteen to twenty in number at a time. The ranchmen's horses and cattle have been driven from their range, and even from pens at the houses, until the people are left almost destitute of means of support. If anyone had the temerity to protest against being robbed, he was told that he had just so many days to live if he did not leave the county. Some of those who had the courage to remain have been foully murdered.

The fourth morning after arriving in camp, we started for Pendencia, to arrest King Fisher and those of his gang who should happen to be with him. The Captain had received information from some of the less timid ranchmen that Fisher was at his ranch, making ready, they thought, to go on another raid and gather cattle to drive north. These men said that Fisher had about thirty men with him at that time at his place. His house was at Carrizo Springs.

McNelly divided the troop into two squads when we started, and we proceeded in the direction of Fisher's stronghold, the two squads being about two miles apart and traveling in parallel lines. Scouts were sent out about a mile in advance and told to ride half a mile apart and arrest all the men they saw. In this way, a number of men were picked up and turned over to the main troop for safekeeping. We wanted to take Fisher and his gang by surprise, and we did not propose to be thwarted by his friends apprising him of our coming. We went very rapidly over unused roads and trails, and succeeded in arriving at a point in the chaparral about a quarter of a mile from Fisher's house without being seen by any of his men.

Both squads came together at this place, but Captain McNelly divided us again and sent part of the troop through the chaparral, around to the other side of the house. Then, at a prearranged moment, all of us dashed for the house at full speed, six-shooters in hand. A fence was in our way, but the horses went over it like hunters after the hounds, and before Fisher and his men perceived us we were within a hundred yards of the place.

Most of the desperadoes were playing poker under the shed-like extension in front of the ranch house. They jumped up and started for the house proper to secure their arms, but before half of them

"Fierce Bandits at Bay—Two Desperadoes Tackled By Detectives in Hotel Dining-Room at Minden, Nevada." From *National Police Gazette*, 1882.

succeeded in getting inside the door, we were around them and our six-shooters were cocked and pointed at their heads.

"You'll have to surrender or be killed!" cried McNelly to Fisher, who stood halfway out of the door, with the lieutenant of his band, one Burd Obenchain, but known to his companions as Frank Porter.

Fisher did not move, but Porter half raised his Winchester, and coolly looked along the line of Rangers.

"Drop that gun!" yelled McNelly. "Drop it, I say, or I'll kill you."

Porter looked McNelly squarely in the eyes, half raised his rifle again, and then slowly dropped it to his side, and with a sigh leaned it against the side of the house.

"I reckon there's too many of yer to tackle," he said, calmly. "I only wisht I'd a-seen yer sooner."

The other men gave up without a struggle. They were badly frightened at first, for they thought we were members of a vigilance committee, come to deal out swift justice to them and hang them by lynch law. They were agreeably disappointed when they discovered we were the Rangers, officers of the law of Texas.

There were only nine of the desperadoes at the house at the time, but a precious gang of outlaws and cutthroats they were. Here are their names: J.K. Fisher, known as "King" Fisher; Burd Obenchain, alias Frank Porter, wanted for murder and cattle-stealing, as desperate a ruffian as ever the Texas border knew; Warren Allen, who shot a Negro in a barroom at Fort Clark for drinking at the same bar with him, and then deliberately turned and finished his own drink and ordered another; Bill Templeton, horse thief; Will Wainwright, Jim Honeycutt, Wes Bruton, Al Roberts, and Bill Bruton. All of them were "wanted" for numberless crimes.

A few weeks before we arrested them, King Fisher and Frank Porter, by themselves, stole a herd of cattle from six Mexican *vaqueros* who were driving the herd for its owner, near Eagle Pass. Fisher and Porter rode around the herd and killed every one of the six Mexicans. The *vaqueros* were all buried together, and I saw the place where they were buried. It was known as "Frank Porter's Graveyard."

Fisher was about twenty-five years old at that time, and the most perfect specimen of a frontier dandy and desperado that I ever saw. He was tall, beautifully proportioned, and exceedingly handsome. He wore the finest clothing procurable, but all of it was the picturesque, border, dime novel kind. His broad-brimmed white Mexican *sombrero* was profusely ornamented with gold and silver lace and had a golden snake for a band. His fine buckskin Mexican short jacket was heavily embroidered with gold. His shirt was of the finest and thinnest linen and was worn open at the throat, with a silk handkerchief knotted loosely about the collar. A brilliant crimson silk sash was wound about his waist, and his legs were hidden by a wonderful pair of *chaparejos,* or "chaps," as the cowboys called them—leather breeches to protect the legs while riding through the brush. These *chaparejos* were made of the skin of a royal Bengal tiger and ornamented down the seams with gold and buckskin fringe. The tiger's skin had been procured by Fisher at a circus in northern Texas. He and some of his fellows had literally captured the circus, killed the tiger and skinned it, just because the desperado chief fancied he'd like to have a pair of tiger skin "chaps." His boots were of the finest high heeled variety, the kind all cowboys loved to wear. Hanging from his cartridge-filled belt were two ivory-handled, silver-plated six-shooters. His spurs were of silver and ornamented with little silver bells.

He was an expert revolver shot, and could handle his six-shooters as well with his left hand as with his right. He was a fine rider, and rode the best horses he could steal in Texas or Mexico. Among the desperadoes, the stolen horses were known as "wet stock"—that is, horses which had been stolen in Mexico and swum across the Rio Grande to Texas, or *vice versa.*

We took the men with us at once to Eagle Pass and put them in jail there. We tied the feet of the prisoners to their stirrups and then tied the stirrups together under the horses' bellies. We also tied the desperadoes' hands to the pommels of their saddles and led their horses. Before we started, Captain McNelly told us, in the hearing of the prisoners and of Fisher's wife—a pretty girl, with wonderfully fine, bold black eyes—that if any of our prisoners attempted to escape or if an attempt was made to rescue them, we were to kill them without warning or mercy. That is, or was, known on the frontier as *la ley de fuga,* the shooting of escaping or resisting prisoners. It was well understood among the outlaws, and was a great protection to the officers who were compelled to escort prisoners over long distances through the sparsely settled country. The knowledge of this condition of the border prevented members of a desperado gang from attempting to rescue prisoners, for such an attempt meant instant death to the captives.

VIGILANTES IN KANSAS. *Laura Ingalls Wilder, looking back to the 1870s, tells a story that she felt would not be suitable for the usual readers of her "Little House" books.*

There were some stories I wanted to tell but would not be responsible for putting in a book for children, even though I knew them as a child.

There was the story of the Bender family that belonged in the third volume, *Little House on the Prairie.* The Benders lived half way between it and Independence, Kansas. We stopped there, on our way in to the Little House, while Pa watered the horses and brought us all a drink from the well near the door of the house. I saw Kate Bender standing in the doorway. We did not go in because we could not afford to stop at a tavern.

On his trip to Independence to sell his furs, Pa stopped again for water, but did not go in for the same reason as before.

There were Kate Bender and two men, her brothers, in the family and their tavern was the only place for travelers to stop on the road south from Independence. People disappeared on that road. Leaving Independence and going south they were never heard of again. It was thought they were killed by Indians but no bodies were ever found.

Then it was noticed that the Bender's garden was always freshly plowed but never planted. People wondered. And then a man came from the east looking for his brother, who was missing.

He made up a party in Independence and they followed the road south, but when they came to the Bender place there was no one there. There were signs of hurried departure and they searched the place.

The front room was divided by a calico curtain against which the dining table stood. On the curtain back of the table were stains about as high as the head of a man when seated. Behind the curtain was a trap door in the floor and beside it lay a heavy hammer.

In the cellar underneath was the body of a man whose head had been crushed by the hammer. It appeared that he had been seated at the table back to the curtain and had been struck from behind it. A grave was partly dug in the garden with a shovel close by. The posse searched the garden and dug up human bones and bodies. One body was that of a little girl who had been buried alive with her murdered parents. The garden was truly a grave-yard kept plowed so it would show no signs. The night of the day the bodies were found a neighbor rode up to our house and talked earnestly with Pa. Pa took his rifle down from its place over the door and said to Ma, "The vigilantes are called out." Then he saddled a horse and rode away with the neighbor.

It was late the next day when he came back and he never told us where he had been.

For several years there was more or less a hunt for the Benders and reports that they had been seen here or there. At such times Pa always said in a strange tone of finality, "They will never be found." They never were found and later I formed my own conclusions why.

You will agree it is not a fit story for a children's book.

MAIL FRAUD. *In his book* Frauds Exposed, *published in 1880, Anthony Comstock quotes a classic example.*

BULLION GOLD AND SILVER MINING COMPANY,
FERRIS GOLD MINING DISTRICT, CARBON COUNTY, WYOMING.
ISAAC LUDLAM, *President.*   G. H. HILDRETH, *Secretary.*
JOHN McCASEY, *Superintendent of the Mines.*

NEW YORK OFFICE, 176 Broadway, New York.

Perhaps no event could be more opportune, considering the deranged condition of labor and the depression of business through-out the country, than the discovery of the rich gold mines of the Ferris Gold and Silver Mining Districts of Wyoming. It embraces a broad extent of country, and its wonderful richness exceeds anything hither-to discovered on this continent, from which all classes may, for generations to come, draw support.

Meet who you will, ask who you may, and there is but one answer. The Ferris Gold and Silver Mining District surpasses them all. It is the richest gold mining country in the world. For miles away, up in the height of those tremendous elevations of mountain ranges, glisten rich veins of gold quartz, that run in golden ribbons at close intervals across their breasts. Here are mines in this district that will take centuries to exhaust, and so numerous that it will take years of prospecting to locate them all judiciously. Here the field for prospectors is rich and extensive.

A MOUNTAIN OF GOLD AND SILVER ORE.

It seems as though the Bullion mine is a mountain of rich gold quartz, which, when properly worked, would go far toward paying off the national debt, as will be seen by official tests made August 12th,

1876, viz.:—Bullion mine first grade ore, $1,060 gold, and $30 silver, per ton; second grade ore, $56 per ton, gold, and $4 per ton, silver. The climate is lovely in summer and moderate in winter, stock being able to get their own living the year round. Now, when we consider the high grade of ore in this company's mine, what are we to expect when it is known that even $20 ore will pay immense dividends.

GREAT ADVANTAGES.

The Ferris Mining District being only 35 miles from the Union Pacific R.R., free from Indians, can be worked the year round. There is close by an abundant supply of wood and water, and labor is only about one-half the price paid in California.

THE BULLION GOLD AND SILVER MINING CO.

The Bullion Gold and Silver Mining Company has been organized for the purpose of developing these mines, and, in order to obtain the means for the purchase of the necessary machinery, have concluded to put upon the market a limited number of the shares of the company (which shares, be it remembered, are unassessed) at such a low figure as to induce not only capitalists, but the people at large to invest in them. The owners of these mines not having capital to work them, and not willing to allow grasping men of wealth to control them, prefer to sell a few shares at one-half their par value.

THE TURNING POINT.

There is a turning point in every man's life. One chance in every man's life to make a fortune.

NOW IS YOUR TIME.

Many persons who secured shares on the Comstock Lode when first discovered found themselves in an incredible short space of time independent for life. From an investment of $50 to $100, they found themselves worth thousands and thousands of dollars in less than one year. The prospects now of the Bullion Company are even greater than those of the Comstock on the start, and persons who secure a few shares at $4 per share now, may realize even greater profits and in a short time find themselves independent for life. In 1870, the Capital Stock of the Consolidated Virginia Mine was only $50,000. Now its par value is over $63,000,000. Sixty-three millions! and yielding over two millions per month. In the Bullion Mine there are immense quantities of rich ore in sight, ready to be milled as soon as sufficient money is raised to build mills, and reduction works; and bids fair to yield even better than Consolidated Virginia.

These facts prove that a small amount invested in a good mining company, on the start, is the surest and safest method of becoming suddenly rich. With a small investment a person may any morning wake up and find himself independent for life. In one instance a boarding-house keeper—a poor woman—was obliged to take some mining stock, or nothing, in payment of a board bill. Imagine her surprise one day when she was offered $75,000 for her stock, which she had even forgotten she owned.

AGENTS WANTED, LIBERAL PAY ALLOWED.

Any person or club sending $25 will receive by return of mail, six shares, par value $60, which may soon be worth many thousands.

References as to the richness of the company's mines, furnished to all who desire, on application.

Money may be sent by Post-Office Order, registered letter, draft, or express.

Address,   ISAAC LUDLAM,
I. LUDLAM, *President.*   176 Broadway, New York.
G.H. HILDRETH, *Secretary.*

CIVIL RIGHTS. *Ida B. Wells, later to become a crusading journalist, writes of an incident in 1884 when she was a young schoolteacher and often rode on the Chesapeake and Ohio Railroad.*

I secured a school in Shelby County, Tennessee, which paid a better salary and began studying for the examination for city schoolteacher which meant an even larger increase in salary. One day while riding back to my school I took a seat in the ladies' coach of the train as usual. There were no jim crow cars then. But ever since the repeal of the Civil Rights Bill by the United States Supreme Court in 1877 there had been efforts all over the South to draw the color line on the railroads.

When the train started and the conductor came along to collect tickets, he took my ticket, then handed it back to me and told me that he couldn't take my ticket there. I thought that if he didn't want the ticket I wouldn't bother about it so went on reading. In a little while when he finished taking tickets, he came back and told me I would have to go in the other car. I refused, saying that the forward car was a smoker, and as I was in the ladies' car I proposed to stay. He tried to drag me out of the seat, but the moment he caught hold of my arm I fastened my teeth in the back of his hand.

I had braced my feet against the seat in front and was holding to the back, and as he had already been badly bitten he didn't try it again by himself. He went forward and got the baggageman and another man to help him and of course they succeeded in dragging me out. They were encouraged to do this by the attitude of the white ladies and gentlemen in the car; some of them even stood on the seats so that they could get a good view and continued applauding the conductor for his brave stand.

By this time the train had stopped at the first station. When I saw that they were determined to drag me into the smoker, which was already filled with colored people and those who were smoking, I said I would get off the train rather than go in—which I did. Strangely, I held on to my ticket all this time, and although the sleeves of my linen duster had been torn out and I had been pretty roughly handled, I had not been hurt physically.

I went back to Memphis and engaged a colored lawyer to bring suit against the railroad for me. After months of delay I found he had been bought off by the road, and as he was the only colored lawyer in town I had to get a white one. This man, Judge Greer, kept his pledge with me and the case was finally brought to trial in the circuit court. Judge Pierce, who was an ex-union soldier from Minnesota, awarded me damages of five hundred dollars. I can see to this day the headlines in the *Memphis Appeal* announcing DARKY DAMSEL GETS DAMAGES.

The railroad appealed the case to the state's supreme court, which reversed the findings of the lower court, and I had to pay the costs. Before this was done, the railroad's lawyer had tried every means in his power to get me to compromise the case, but I indignantly refused. Had I done so, I would have been a few hundred dollars to the good instead of having to pay out over two hundred dollars in court costs.

VICE-BUSTER. *Anthony Comstock, founder of and enforcer for the New York Society for the Suppression of Vice, has just been criticized by Judge Gildersleeve for spending two hours watching a sex show, long enough to qualify him as a participator in the crime. Here, Comstock tells what really happened.*

Numerous complaints came to our office against a most disgusting and obscene exhibition that was given by beastly women, to the ruin of hundreds of thoughtless young men. These exhibitions were given almost nightly. At first, I felt such a disgust and abhorrence at the descriptions I received in these complaints, that I was inclined to be cowardly and not act. My conscience, my whole being as a man cried out against this cowardice. I knew well what it would cost me. I humbly and earnestly prayed for grace to do my duty, and then I went forward. The first essential to a successful effort is legal evidence. The momentous question then arose how to get it? There was but one legal way. That was to get it legally. To do it, some one must see this exhibition in order to prove what it was, and identify the parties carrying it on. I could not send young men there; to do that would have been dastardly, after I had been informed of its character. I could not make a strong case without the most positive proof, as it is difficult to conceive of anything more horrible. For two years this place had existed and thrived in the rear of the 15th Precinct Police Station, the yards adjoining. Consequently I could not go there for help. What then? I went to the Mayor's squad and selected six of the truest and best men I knew on the Police force—some of them Christian men. We visited this den, and I saw the party who kept the house, and so doubtful was I of the truth of what I had heard, before anything else I asked if _____ exhibitions were given there? This matron replied, "Oh yes. This has been the headquarters for more than two years. There are six exhibitors, and a regular programme, and the performance lasts about an hour." She further informed us, "that some of the exhibitors were absent, but that it would make no difference, as *the same programme* was always enacted." Here then I had official and reliable information from the mouth of the proprietress of this exhibition, that *it existed,* as it had done for *more than two years* previous, and with a *regular programme.* Here then is a pit-fall for the feet of young men! Shall I close it? Here is a hell-trap for the souls of our youth! Shall I allow it to exist? Here is an exhibition given by women that beggars description— so gross that even a reference to it brings a blush.—Shall it continue? No! no! By all that is in us as men, *no!*

There was but one thing left. Close this hell-hole up at once, by all means! you say. Not so fast. The vilest have rights. Whatever an officer of the law does, he must do legally. First get the evidence, and *then* forward. After getting further light from this proprietress, we then did precisely as those frequenters of the vile exhibition formerly known as the "Black Crook," (that sent thousands of youthful souls to perdition,) did; we paid our admission fee, and went into the hall where the performance was nightly given. Here we, sworn officers of the law, remained sufficiently long to secure two things, *and no longer;* to wit:

First.—Legal evidence of an indecent exhibition.

Second.—Proofs that there was a regular programme regularly enacted.

Having obtained these, I immediately went out, and having secured the keeper of this den first (and one thing that delayed was, that she had gone over to one of her other dens of infamy, for she had two or three in this precinct), we arrested the occupants of this hell-hole. The principal was held for trial on a complaint for "keeping a disorderly house." The exhibitors, for an "indecent exhibition."

Now what of the trial . . .

The Assistant District Attorney, of course, had to *nolle prosequi* the indictment against the exhibitors, and then, although the case had closed so far as the testimony went, he asked an adjournment in the case of the principal. He then came into court the next day, and stated he had been informed that it was a conspiracy to injure the Captain of Police of that precinct. I, in open court, declared such a statement false. I had, the previous day, asked him to call some of the officers of that precinct to prove that this was a disorderly house. He said no, that the case was fully made out, and yet the judge granted a motion the next day, made by this officer, to dismiss. The motion was granted, on the ground that the Assistant District Attorney moved it, because, as he said in open court, if this woman is convicted, charges might be preferred against the captain of this precinct and he be dismissed. The court ruled it was the duty of the courts to protect the police, and the case was dismissed.

LYNCH LAW. *From an appendix to* Mob Rule in New Orleans, *by Ida B. Wells, published in 1900. During the 1890s, over fifteen hundred blacks had been lynched, mostly by shooting or hanging; others were burned to death. To avoid charges of partiality, Wells relied heavily on accounts from white-owned newspapers.*

In 1891 Ed Coy was burned to death in Texarkana, Ark. He was charged with assaulting a white woman, and after the mob had tied him securely to a tree, the men and boys amused themselves for some time sticking knives into Coy's body and slicing off pieces of flesh. When they had amused themselves sufficiently, they poured coal oil over him and the woman in the case set fire to him. It is said that fifteen thousand people stood by and saw him burned. This was on a Sunday night, and press reports told how the people looked on while the Negro burned to death.

Feb. 1st, 1893, Henry Smith was burned to death in Paris, Texas. The entire county joined in that exhibition. The district attorney himself went for the prisoner and turned him over to the mob. He was placed upon a float and drawn by four white horses through the principal streets of the city. Men, women and children stood at their doors and waved their handkerchiefs and cheered the echoes. They knew that the man was to be burned to death because the newspaper had declared for three days previous that this would be so. Excursions were run by all the railroads, and the mayor of the town gave the children a holiday so that they might see the sight.

Henry Smith was charged with having assaulted and murdered a little girl. He was an imbecile, and while he had killed the child, there was no proof that he had criminally assaulted her. He was tied to a stake on a platform which had been built ten feet high, so that everybody might see the sight. The father and brother and uncle of the little white girl

Boys and men of mixed races pose for the photographer after witnessing
the lynching of McManus, a white man, 1882.

that had been murdered were upon that platform about fifty minutes entertaining the crowd of ten thousand persons by burning the victim's flesh with red-hot irons. Their own newspapers told how they burned his eyes out and ran the red-hot iron down his throat, cooking his tongue, and how the crowd cheered with delight. At last, having declared themselves satisfied, coal oil was poured over him and he was burned to death, and the mob fought over the ashes for bones and pieces of his clothes.

Feb. 22d, 1898, at Lake City, S.C., Postmaster Baker and his infant child were burned to death by a mob that had set fire to his house. Mr. Baker's crime was that he had refused to give up the postoffice, to which he had been appointed by the National Government. The mob had tried to drive him away by persecution and intimidation. Finding that all else had failed, they went to his home in the dead of night and set fire to his house, and as the family rushed forth they were greeted by a volley of bullets. The father and his baby were shot through the open door and wounded so badly that they fell back in the fire and were burned to death. The remainder of the family, consisting of the wife and five children, escaped with their lives from the burning house, but all of them were shot, one of the number made a cripple for life.

Jan. 7th, 1898, two Indians were tied to a tree at Maud Postoffice, Indian Territory, and burned to death by a white mob. They were charged with murdering a white woman. There was no proof of their guilt except the unsupported word of the mob. Yet they were tied to a tree and slowly roasted to death. Their names were Lewis McGeesy and Hond Martin. Since that time these boys have been found to be absolutely innocent of the charge. Of course that discovery is too late to be of any benefit to them, but because they were Indians the Indian Commissioner demanded and received from the United States Government an indemnity of $13,000.

April 23d, 1899, at Palmetto, Ga., Sam Hose was burned alive in the presence of a throng, on Sunday afternoon. He was charged with killing a man named Cranford, his employer, which he admitted he did because his employer was about to shoot him. To the fact of killing the employer was added the absolutely false charge that Hose assaulted the wife. Hose was arrested and no trial was given him. According to the code of reasoning of the mob, none was needed. A white man had been killed and a white woman was said to have been assaulted. That was enough. When Hose was found he had to die.

The Atlanta Constitution, in speaking of the murder of Cranford, said that the Negro who was suspected would be burned alive. Not only this, but it offered $500 reward for his capture. After he had been apprehended, it was publicly announced that he would be burned alive. Excursion trains were run and bulletins were put up in the small towns. The Governor of Georgia was in Atlanta while excursion trains were being made up to take visitors to the burning. Many fair ladies drove out in their carriages on Sunday afternoon to witness the torture and burning of a human being. Hose's ears were cut off, then his toes and fingers, and passed round to the crowd. His eyes were put out, his tongue torn out and flesh cut in strips by knives. Finally they poured coal oil on him and burned him to death. They dragged his half-consumed trunk out of the flames, cut it open, extracted his heart and liver, and sold slices for ten cents each for souvenirs, all of which was published most promptly in the papers of Georgia and boasted over by the people of that section.

VAGRANT. *In* The Road, *his account of his experiences as a hobo, Jack London tells how he fell afoul of the law in 1894.*

I rode into Niagara Falls in a "side-door Pullman," or, in common parlance, a box-car, . . . and headed straight from the freight train to the falls. Once my eyes were filled with that wonder-vision of down-rushing water, I was lost. I could not tear myself away long enough to "batter" the "privates" (domiciles) for my supper. Even a "set-down" could not have lured me away. Night came on, a beautiful night of moonlight, and I lingered by the falls until after eleven. Then it was up to me to hunt for a place to "kip."

"Kip," "doss," "flop," "pound your ear," all mean the same thing; namely, to sleep. Somehow, I had a "hunch" that Niagara Falls was a "bad" town for hoboes, and I headed out into the country. I climbed a fence and "flopped" in a field. John Law would never find me there, I flattered myself. I lay on my back in the grass and slept like a babe. It was so balmy warm that I woke up not once all night. But with the first gray daylight my eyes opened, and I remembered the wonderful falls. I climbed the fence and started down the road to have another look at them. It was early—not more than five o'clock—and not until eight o'clock could I begin to batter for my breakfast. I could spend at least three hours by the river. Alas! I was fated never to see the river nor the falls again.

The town was asleep when I entered it. As I came along the quiet street, I saw three men coming toward me along the sidewalk. They were walking abreast. Hoboes, I decided, like myself, who had got up early. In this surmise I was not quite correct. I was only sixty-six and two-thirds per cent correct. The men on each side were hoboes all right, but the man in the middle wasn't. I directed my steps to the edge of the sidewalk in order to let the trio go by. But it didn't go by. At some word from the man in the centre, all three halted, and he of the centre addressed me.

I piped the lay on the instant. He was a "fly-cop" and the two hoboes were his prisoners. John Law was up and out after the early worm. I was a worm. Had I been richer by the experiences that were to befall me in the next several months, I should have turned and run like the very devil. He might have shot at me, but he'd have had to hit me to get me. He'd have never run after me, for two hoboes in the hand are worth more than one on the get-away. But like a dummy I stood still when he halted me. Our conversation was brief.

"What hotel are you stopping at?" he queried.

He had me. I wasn't stopping at any hotel, and, since I did not know the name of a hotel in the place, I could not claim residence in any one of them. Also, I was up too early in the morning. Everything was against me.

"I just arrived," I said.

"Well, you turn around and walk in front of me, and not too far in front. There's somebody who wants to see you."

I was "pinched." I knew who wanted to see me. With that "fly-cop" and the two hoboes at my heels, and under the direction of the former, I led the way to the city jail. There we were searched and our names registered. . . .

From the office we were led to the "Hobo" and locked in. The "Hobo" is that part of a prison where the minor offenders are confined together in a large iron cage. Since hoboes constitute the principal division of the minor offenders, the aforesaid iron cage is called the Hobo. Here we met several hoboes who had already been pinched that morning, and every little while the door was unlocked and two or three more were thrust in on us. At last, when we totalled sixteen, we were led upstairs into the court-room. And now I shall faithfully describe what took place in that court-room, for know that my patriotic American citizenship there received a shock from which it has never fully recovered.

In the court-room were the sixteen prisoners, the judge, and two bailiffs. The judge seemed to act as his own clerk. There were no witnesses. There were no citizens of Niagara Falls present to look on and see how justice was administered in their community. The judge glanced at the list of cases before him and called out a name. A hobo stood up. The judge glanced at a bailiff. "Vagrancy, your Honor," said the bailiff. "Thirty days," said his Honor. The hobo sat down, and the judge was calling another name and another hobo was rising to his feet.

The trial of that hobo had taken just about fifteen seconds. The trial of the next hobo came off with equal celerity. The bailiff said, "Vagrancy, your Honor," and his Honor said, "Thirty days." Thus it went like clockwork, fifteen seconds to a hobo—and thirty days.

They are poor dumb cattle, I thought to myself. But wait till my turn comes; I'll give his Honor a "spiel." Part way along in the performance, his Honor, moved by some whim, gave one of us an opportunity to speak. As chance would have it, this man was not a genuine hobo. He bore none of the ear-marks of the professional "stiff." Had he approached the rest of us while waiting at a water-tank for a freight, we should have unhesitatingly classified him as a "gay-cat." Gay-cat is the synonym for tenderfoot in Hobo Land. This gay-cat was well along in years—somewhere around forty-five, I should judge. His shoulders were humped a trifle, and his face was seamed by weather-beat.

For many years, according to his story, he had driven team for some firm in (if I remember rightly) Lockport, New York. The firm had ceased to prosper, and finally, in the hard times of 1893, had gone out of business. He had been kept on to the last, though toward the last his work had been very irregular. He went on and explained at length his difficulties in getting work (when so many were out of work) during the succeeding months. In the end, deciding that he would find better opportunities for work on the Lakes, he had started for Buffalo. Of course he was "broke," and there he was. That was all.

"Thirty days," said his Honor, and called another hobo's name.

Said hobo got up. "Vagrancy, your Honor," said the bailiff, and his Honor said, "Thirty days."

And so it went, fifteen seconds and thirty days to each hobo. The machine of justice was grinding smoothly. Most likely, considering how early it was in the morning, his Honor had not yet had his breakfast and was in a hurry.

But my American blood was up. Behind me were the many generations of my American ancestry. One of the kinds of liberty those ancestors of mine had fought and died for was the right of trial by jury. This was my heritage, stained sacred by their blood, and it devolved upon me to stand up for it. All right, I threatened to myself; just wait till he gets to me.

He got to me. My name . . . was called, and I stood up. The bailiff said, "Vagrancy, your Honor," and I began to talk. But the judge began talking at the same time, and he said, "Thirty days." I started to protest, but at that moment his Honor was calling the name of the next hobo on the list. His Honor paused long enough to say to me, "Shut up!" The bailiff forced me to sit down. And the next moment that next hobo had received thirty days and the succeeding hobo was just in process of getting his.

When we had all been disposed of, thirty days to each stiff, his Honor, just as he was about to dismiss us, suddenly turned to the teamster from Lockport—the one man he had allowed to talk.

"Why did you quit your job?" his Honor asked.

Now the teamster had already explained how his job had quit him, and the question took him aback.

"Your Honor," he began confusedly, "isn't that a funny question to ask?"

"Thirty days more for quitting your job," said his Honor, and the court was closed.

The ANATOMY of Man's Body, as governed by the Twelve CONSTELLATIONS.

♈ The Head and Face.

♊ Arms	♉ Neck
♌ Heart	♋ Breast
♎ Reins	♍ Bowels
♐ Thighs	♏ Secrets
♒ Legs	♑ Knees

♓ The Feet.

To know where the Sign is

First Find the Day of the Month, and against the Day you have the Sign or place of the Moon in the 6th Column. Then finding the Sign here, it shews the part of the Body it governs.

The Names and Characters of the Seven Planets

☉ Sol, ♄ Saturn, ♃ Jupiter, ♂ Mars, ♀ Venus, ☿ Mercury, ☽ Luna, ☊ Dragon's head, and ☋ tail.

The Five Aspects.

☌ Conjunction, ☍ Opposition, ✶ Sextile, △ Trine, □ Quartile.

Illustrated chart from Benjamin Franklin's *Poor Richard's Almanack* showing the influences of certain planets and stars on different parts of the body, eighteenth century.

CHAPTER
10

AILING

PROGRESS—THAT BELIEF SO DEAR to the hearts of the
Victorians that things were steadily getting better and better—
has few champions today, and probably for good reason. But
while it may be hard to detect improvement in morals or politics, who
can deny that where medicine is concerned there has been immense,
indeed almost miraculous, progress? Cholera, yellow fever, malaria,
smallpox—these have gone the way of polio and diphtheria. Surgery
is painless. So is dentistry!

Of course, many ailments remain, from those caused by accidents
through those caused by old age, but here, too, things have
improved; people who suffer from the complaints of old age can at
least console themselves with the thought that they did not die
young. And as for accidents, it has been a long time since first aid
consisted of little more than a plaster applied externally and a bottle
of brandy internally.

At any rate, the case for progress will, it is hoped, be made con-
vincing by the contents of this chapter. It is arranged alphabetically
like a home medical guide; and, as is usual with such guides, it comes
with the warning that you consult your physician before using any of
the remedies it contains.

ACCIDENTS. *Accidents will happen, and always have. Here are three: one
from John Winthrop's journal, dated September 1644; one from the diary of
Samuel Sewall, dated March 9, 1693; and one from the memoirs of the
Revolutionary War soldier Joseph Plumb Martin that occurred in 1777.*

John Winthrop. One of the deacons of Boston church, Jacob Eliot, (a
man of a very sincere heart and an humble frame of spirit,) had a
daughter of eight years of age, who being playing with other children

about a cart, the hinder end thereof fell upon the child's head, and an iron sticking out of it struck into the child's head, and drove a piece of the skull before it into the brain, so as the brains came out, and seven surgeons (some of the country, very experienced men, and others of the ships, which rode in the harbor) being called together for advice, etc., did all conclude, that it was the brains, (being about half a spoon-ful at one time, and more at other times,) and that there was no hope of the child's life, except the piece of skull could be drawn out. But one of the ruling elders of the church, an experienced and very skilful surgeon, liked not to take that course, but applied only plasters to it; and withal earnest prayers were made by the church to the Lord for it, and in six weeks it pleased God that the piece of skull consumed, and so came forth, and the child recovered perfectly; nor did it lose the senses at any time.

Samuel Sewall. Joseph [his son, aged five] puts his Grandmother and Mother in great fear by swallowing a Bullet which for a while stuck in his Throat: He had quite got it down, before I knew what the matter was. This day in the Afternoon One of Mr. Holyoke's Twins falls into the Well and is drownd, no body but a Negro being at home; was a very lovely Boy of about 4 years old. Satterday, March 11, about Sunset He is buried. When I come home from the funeral, my wife shows me the Bullet Joseph swallowed, which he voided in the Orchard. The Lord help us to praise Him for his distinguishing Favour.

Private Joseph Plumb Martin. We marched to Peekskill and rejoined our regiments sometime in the fore part of the month of August. A short time after my arrival at Peekskill, I was sent off to King's Ferry, about five miles below, to take some batteaux [flat-bottomed boats] that were there and carry [escort] them to Fort Montgomery, in the edge of the Highlands.

While upon this tour of duty, an accident happened to me which caused me much trouble and pain. After we had arrived at the fort with the boats, we tarried an hour or two to rest ourselves, after which we were ordered to take a couple of boats and return again to King's Ferry. Wishing to be the first in the boat, I ran down the wharf and jumped into it. There happened to be the butt part of an oar lying on the bottom of the boat, and my right foot, on which the whole weight of my body bore, alighted, in my leap, directly upon it, lengthwise. It rolled over and turned my foot almost up to my ankle, so much so, that my foot lay nearly in a right angle with my leg. I had then to go to the ferry, where I was landed, and having no acquaintance with any of the party, most of whom were New Yorkers, and consequently, at that time, no great friends to the Yankees, I was obliged to hop on one foot all the way, upwards of five miles, not being able in the whole distance to procure a stick to assist me, although I often hobbled to the fences on each side of the road in hopes to obtain one. It was dark when I was landed at the ferry, and it was quite late before I arrived at the camp. Some of my messmates went immediately for the surgeon, but he was at a game of backgammon and could not attend to minor affairs. However, in about an hour he arrived, bathed my foot, which was swelled like a bladder, fumbled about it for some time, when he gave it a wrench, which made me, like the old woman's dying cat, "merely yawl out."

The next day, as I was sitting under the shade before my tent, my foot lying upon a bench, swelled like a puffball, my captain passed by and must needs have a peep at it. I indulged his curiosity, upon which he said it was not set right, and taking hold of it, he gave it a twist, which put it nearly in the same condition it was at first. I had then to send for Mr. Surgeon again, but he was not to be found. There was a corporal in our company who professed to act the surgeon in such cases, and he happening at the time to be present, undertook the job and accomplished it, but it was attended with more difficulty than at the first time, and with more pain to me. It was a long time before it got well and strong again, indeed it never has been entirely so well as it was before the accident happened. I was not long confined by it, however, but was soon able to perform my duty in the army again.

AGUE. *From the notebooks of the Swedish naturalist Peter Kalm, writing in the late 1740s, two folk cures for this once common ailment.*

A woman who had suffered a long time from chills and had used several remedies for it had at the advice of an old woman placed some spider's web inside a baked apple which she ate. She repeated this process twice with no effect, but the third time she tried it she became so inconceivably ill that everyone thought she would die. She fell into such a coma that she looked dead. Finally after two or three hours she regained consciousness, her sickness left her and she recovered and became well, but it was both a severe and adventurous cure.

People who lived near the iron mines declared that they were seldom if ever visited by the fever and ague; but when they had the fever they drank the water of such springs as came from the iron districts and had a strong metallic taste; and they assured me that this remedy was infallible. Other people therefore, who did not live very far from such springs, went to them for a few days when they had the fever in order to drink the water, which commonly cured them.

AMPUTATION. *As a boy John Tanner was captured by the Shawnee and sold to an Ojibwa family, who raised him as one of their own. Here he tells of an incident that took place near Clear Water Lake in the late 1790s.*

After remaining a few days at the trading house, we all went together to join the Indians. This party consisted of three lodges, the principal man being Wah-gee-kaut, (crooked legs.) Three of the best hunters were Ka-kaik, (the small hawk,) Meh-ke-nauk, (the turtle,) and Pa-ke-kun-ne-gah-bo, (he that stands in the smoke.) This last was, at the time I speak of, a very distinguished hunter. Some time afterwards he was accidentally wounded, receiving a whole charge of shot in his elbow, by which the joint and the bones of his arm were much shattered. As the wound did not show any tendency to heal, but, on the contrary, became worse and worse, he applied to many Indians, and to all white men he saw, to cut it off for him. As all refused to do so, or to assist him in amputating it himself, he chose a time when he happened to be left alone in his lodge, and taking two knives, the edge of one of which he had hacked into a sort of saw, he with his right hand and arm cut off his left, and threw it from him as far as he could. Soon after, as he related the story himself, he fell sleep, in which situation he was found by his friends, having lost a very great quantity of blood; but he soon afterwards recovered, and notwithstanding the loss of one arm, he became again a great hunter. After this accident, he was commonly called Kosh-kin-ne-kait, (the cut off arm.)

ASYLUMS. *In August 1850, the pioneering reformer Dorothea Dix presented a memorial to the Senate and the House of Representatives, asking them to appropriate public lands "for the benefit of the indigent insane." Here are some passages from her report.*

I have myself seen *more than nine thousand idiots, epileptics, and insane, in these United States, destitute of appropriate care and protection;* and of this vast and most miserable company, sought out in *jails,* in *poor-houses,* and in *private dwellings,* there have been hundreds, nay, rather thousands, bound with galling chains, bowed beneath fetters and heavy iron balls, attached to drag-chains, lacerated with ropes, scourged with rods, and terrified beneath storms of profane execrations and cruel blows; now subject to gibes, and scorn, and torturing tricks—now abandoned to the most loathsome necessities, or subject to the vilest and most outrageous violations. These are strong terms, but language fails to convey the astounding truths. I proceed to verify this assertion.

In the eighth annual report of the Vermont hospital for 1844, is the following record, which being a repetition in fact, if not almost literal expression of my own notes, I adopt in preference:

"The sins of the drunken father . . . a thief and a woman of shame visit their lunatic father in the criminal lunatic asylum," from a series of four lithographs published in 1884.

One case was brought to the hospital four and a half years ago, of a man who had been insane more than twelve years. During the four years previous to his admission he had not worn any article of clothing, and had been caged in a cellar, without feeling the influence of a fire. A nest of straw was his only bed and covering. He was so violent that his keeper thought it necessary to cause *an iron ring to be riveted about his neck,* so that they could hold him when they changed his bed of straw. . . . Another man, insane more than thirty years, *was sold to the lowest bidder. For many years* he was *caged,* and had his feet frozen so that he lost his toes, and endured cruel sufferings which no person in a natural state could have supported. . . . Another patient, a woman 61 years of age, was taken to the hospital. She had been confined for several years in a half subterranean cage, &c., which was nothing other than a cave excavated in the side of a hill near the house, and straw thrown in for a bed; no warmth was admitted save what the changing seasons supplied. Her condition in all respects was neglected and horrible in the extreme.

Examples here, as in *every State of the Union,* might be multiplied of the insane caged and chained, confined in garrets, cellars, corn-houses, and other out-buildings, until their extremities were seized by the frost, and their sufferings augmented by extreme torturing pain.

In Massachusetts . . . in a prison which I visited often was an idiot youth. He would follow me from cell to cell with eager curiosity, and for a long time manifested no appearance of thought. Cheerful expressions, a smile, frequent small gifts, and encouragement to acquire some improved personal habits, at length seemed to light up his mind to a limited power of perception. He would claim his share in the distribution of books, though he could not read, examine them with delight, and preserve them with singular care. If I read from the Scriptures, he was reverently attentive; if I conversed, he listened earnestly, with half conscious aspect. One morning I passed more hurriedly than usual, and did not speak to him. "Me book! me book!" he exclaimed, eagerly thrusting his hand through the iron bars of the closed door of his cell. "Take this, and be careful," I said. Suddenly stooping, he seized the bread which had been brought for his breakfast, and pushing it eagerly through the bars, he exclaimed, in a more connected speech than was known before, "Here's bread, ain't you hungry?" How much might be done to develop the minds of idiots, if we but knew how to touch the instrument with a skilful hand!

In the yard of a poorhouse in the southern part of the State [Rhode Island], I was conducted by the mistress of the establishment to a small building constructed of plank; the entrance into a small cell was through a narrow passage, bare and unlighted. The cell was destitute of every description of furniture, unless a block of wood could be called such; and on this was seated a woman—clothed, silent and sad. A small aperture, opening upon a dreary view, and this but a few inches square, alone admitted light and air. The inmate was quiet, and evidently not dangerous in her propensities. In reply to my remonstrances in her behalf, the mistress said that she was directed to keep her always close; that otherwise she would run away, or pull up the flowers!

I visited every county and considerable town in the State [Pennsylvania] in the summer and autumn of 1844 . . . In N—, in the jail, two madmen in chains; no furniture or decent care. One was rolling in the dust, in the highest excitement: he had been in close confinement for fifteen years. On one occasion he became exasperated at the introduction of a drunken prisoner into his cell, who perhaps provoked him. No one knows; but the keeper, on entering, found the insane man furious, covered with the blood of the other, who was murdered and mutilated in the most shocking manner. Another insane man had been in confinement seven years, and both are to this day in the same prison. In the poorhouse were above twenty insane and idiots; four chained to the floor. In the adjacent county were above fifty insane and epileptics; several cases of misery through brutal usage, by "kicks and beating," in private families.

Illinois, visited also in its whole extent in 1846, has more than four hundred insane, at the most moderate estimate. . . . I found crazy men and women in all sorts of miserable conditions; sometimes, as in Georgia, &c., &c., strapped upon beds with coarse, hard strips of leather; sometimes chained to logs, or to the floor of wretched hovels; often exposed to every vicissitude of the climate; but I limit myself to one more example. It was an intensely hot day when I visited F.—He was confined in a roofed *pen,* which enclosed an area of about eight feet by eight. The interstices between the unhewn logs admitted the scorching rays of the sun then, as they would open way for the fierce winds and drenching rains and frosts of the later seasons. The place was wholly bare of furniture—*no bench, no bed, no clothing.* His food, which was of the coarsest kind, was pushed through spaces between the logs; "fed like the hogs, and no better," said a stander-by. His feet had been frozen by exposure to cold in the winter past. Upon the shapeless stumps, aided by his arms, he could raise himself against the logs of the pen. In warm weather this wretched place was cleansed once a week or fortnight; not so in the colder seasons. "We have men called," said his sister, "and they go in and tie him with ropes, and throw him out on the ground, and throw water on him, and my husband cleans out the place." But the expedient to prevent his freezing in winter was the most strangely horrible. In the centre of the pen was excavated a pit, six feet square and deep; the top was closed over securely; and into this ghastly place, entered through a trap-door, was cast the maniac, there to exist till the returning warm weather induced his care-taker to withdraw him; there, without heat, without light, without pure air, was left the pining, miserable maniac, whose piteous groans and frantic cries might move to pity the hardest heart.

Forty-five years after Dorothea Dix made her report to Congress, social reformer Helen Campbell visited the insane asylum on one of the New York islands.

Twenty acres of land belong to the asylum, and are cultivated to the highest pitch by the patients. Flowers are everywhere, and the greenhouse is another source of pleasure to the workers in it. The water-supply flows through submarine pipes from the Croton reservoir and is abundant. In the new cook-house, soup is boiled in set kettles through which steam pipes pass, and is carried to the dining-room in huge pails. The dietary is a generous one. Soup predominates, but it is of the most nourishing order, and there is no limit as to quantity. Knives and forks are allowed to very few, and tin plates have proved the best form of dish, as they cannot be broken. . . .

Till very lately there was small provision for amusement, but the attendant physicians realized long ago how vital a factor this was in cure, and begged for larger quarters. A large and airy hall has at last been built, and here at least once a week all who are not too excited by numbers gather together, dance, sing, or are given some light entertainment. The delight in this is a thing that passes on from one week to the next.

As in every asylum, there is one who believes herself the Queen of Heaven, and daily receives dispatches from God; and one who owns it and everything in it, doctors included. Across the room sits a patient who receives guests affably and announces herself as the widow of President Garfield. A rag doll on the little table by her bed is one of her forty-five children, all of whom are grown up and doing well,— most of them, she says, in fine positions.

Near her is a little woman with twinkling blue eyes and a particularly merry laugh, who dances with delight, but pauses at intervals to whisper of the horrors she could tell if she were disposed.

"Murders by the score,—yes, by the score," she says, looking suspiciously about her; "but the victims are thrown into the river at once, so that no one has to mention it. Take care; I shall be heard,"—and she laughs again and nods to her partner, a silent man, who chuckles to himself at intervals and moves his lips noiselessly.

Under the trees sits a one-armed French soldier who believes he is one of Napoleon's marshals and that the Emperor is to come again. An Irish philosopher, a graduate of Dublin University, and here from drink and opium, owns the island, but lends it by the day to the institutions.

"To-morrow, may be, I'll have 'em all pulled down," he says reflectively. "I'm thinking foine gyardens would look better and more cheerful like, but there's no hurry. Whin the time comes there's enough to carry out me orders and no bother to meself. There's no hurry at all, and I wouldn't be discommoding the Doctors, not I."

Down the long walk comes a group of women out with an attendant, all of them in the asylum uniform of calico, less unpleasant than the bed-ticking dresses of the Workhouse prisoners, a detachment of whom are working here. One little woman, walking with bent head, raises it suddenly and emits a piercing toot. She thinks herself a steam engine and whistles periodically, to the rage of the others, who recognize her delusion but are wholly unconscious of their own.

So it goes, and for each is the story of a blighted life and often the ruin of other lives closely bound to theirs. It is a pauper asylum, and fifty years ago all know what fate would have been theirs.

Cholera was largely the result of slum conditions and
poor sanitation; but in this engraving by Kendrick, from
Life, August 2, 1883, it is depicted as a ghoul from Europe.

CHOLERA. *Extracts from two New York diaries, those of George Templeton
Strong and Philip Hone, about the cholera epidemic of the summer of 1849. In
the first, after a brief visit to West Point to rent summer accommodation for his
family, Strong is returning to the city on one of the Hudson River steamboats.*

July 14. Up at six—things looked very bright and beautiful, for
though it was still hot, there was a lively wind sweeping down the
river. On board the *Roger Williams* at eight. As we passed Piermont,
Alexander Wyckoff of the Hudson River R. R. Co. came to me and

said he was very sick and wanted me to take care of him. Swore he had the cholera, which I doubted; but when I found he could scarcely stand, his hands cold, scarcely any pulse at the wrist, eyes muddy, mouth filled with ropy saliva that one could plainly see in strings when he opened it to speak, and when he told me he'd had seventeen passages since three in the morning, I began to consider it not impossible he was right. So I made him as comfortable on some chairs as I could and went racing about the boat for a doctor. None on board, and what in Heaven's name was I to do, for that he was desperately ill there was no question, and he'd not an acquaintance on board but myself. Resolved to take the responsibility; got him into the cabin with some pillows, gave him a horn of brandy, had my pocket handkerchief converted into a colossal mustard plaster, and then fired away with camphor (which I had with me) and laudanum (which I got from the bar) at short intervals. This stopped the diarrhea, and then he began vomiting pailfulls. Kept on, and the mustard plaster on his abdomen seemed to give relief. Reached New York, sent for a carriage, had him carried ashore, and drove uptown with all convenient speed. Stopped at Kearny Rodgers's—out; Neilson ditto, Johnston ditto, Robeson ditto [these four were all physicians], and all this time he was lying in the carriage pretty near collapse almost convulsed with cramps, and as I thought like enough to die at any minute, which was not pleasant, for independently of other considerations, I didn't want to be indicted for unlicensed medical practice and perhaps for manslaughter. Caught Robeson by good luck at Mersereau's shop and then got Wyckoff to his house. All his family out of town and everything out of the way and inconvenient. Stayed till one, when some of his friends and Dr. Dubois appeared. The doctors said it was a full-blooded case of Asiatic cholera and they fully approved of what I did for him. When I left, the cramps continued and total prostration, but the corrugated blue look of his hands was diminished and they said the pulse was better.

July 26. Cholera the all-pervading subject and has been so for the past fortnight. Increase considerable, especially as shown by the Inspector's Weekly Report, the only reliable authority. That report shows a hundred deaths and upwards daily for the week ending Saturday last.

Poor Wyckoff died between four and five in the afternoon of the day I brought him to town. There was a partial reaction, but he began to sink about an hour after I left him and went straight down. The doctors approved of what I did for him, and his family have been pleased to be very grateful for my attention and care, though I did nothing more than the merest common humanity required.

Philip Hone picks up the story.

Saturday, July 28.—Poor New York has become a charnel house; people die daily of cholera to the number of two or three hundred—that is, of cholera and other cognate diseases. But this mortality is principally among the emigrants in the eastern and western extremities of the city, where hundreds are crowded into a few wretched hovels, amidst filth and bad air, suffering from personal neglect and poisoned by eating garbage which a well-bred hog on a Westchester farm would turn up his snout at.

Friday, August 3.—This is a day of fasting, humiliation, and prayer, ordered by the President of the United States. May the voice of a nation punished for the sins of the people be heard by the Almighty and serve to avert the dreadful infliction under which we are suffering. It is a sublime and solemn subject of reflection. Millions of people in this vast country, of different sexes, all ages, ranks and professions, and religions and political opinions, simultaneously offering their penitential appeals to heaven for pardon and forgiveness of their sins and a removal of the chastening hand which lies heavy on the nation.

DENTIST. *From the* Itinerarium *of Dr. Alexander Hamilton, a Maryland physician, who is traveling north and has just arrived at Tradaways, an inn near the ferry over the Susquehanna, in 1744.*

I supped upon fry'd chickens and bacon, and after supper the conversation turned upon politicks, news, and the dreaded French war; but it was so very lumpish and heavy that it disposed me mightily to sleep. This learned company consisted of the landlord, his overseer and miller, and another greasy thumb'd fellow who, as I understood, professed physick and particularly surgery. In the drawing of teeth, he practiced upon the house maid, a dirty piece of lumber, who made such screaming and squalling as made me imagine there was murder going forwards in the house. However, the artist got the tooth out att last with a great clumsy pair of black-smith's forceps; and indeed it seemed to require such an instrument, for when he showed it to us, it resembled a horsenail more than a tooth.

DIET: TWO ACCOUNTS. *William Wood, author of* New England's Prospect, *published in 1634, explains why the Indians north of Massachusetts Bay, whom he calls Aberginians, were so healthy.*

First of their stature, most of them being between five or six foot high, straight bodied, strongly composed, smooth-skinned, merry countenanced, of complexion something more swarthy than Spaniards,

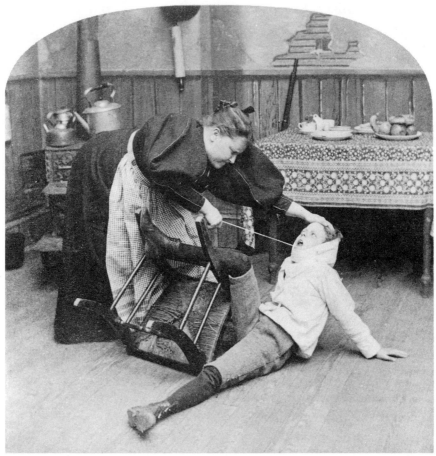

"Domestic Dentistry," 1897, a "humorous" stereoscopic photograph of a boy having
a bad tooth pulled using the string method.

black haired, high foreheaded, black eyed, out-nosed, broad shouldered, brawny armed, long and slender handed, out breasted, small
waisted, lank bellied, well thighed, flat kneed, handsome grown legs,
and small feet. In a word, take them when the blood brisks in their
veins, when the flesh is on their backs and marrow in their bones,
when they frolic in their antic deportments and Indian postures, and
they are more amiable to behold (though only in Adam's livery) than
many a compounded fantastic in the newest fashion.

It may puzzle belief to conceive how such lusty bodies should have
their rise and daily supportment from so slender a fostering, their
houses being mean, their lodging as homely, commons scant, their
drink water, and nature their best clothing. In them the old proverb
may well be verified: *Natura paucis contenta* [nature is satisfied with lit-
tle], for though this be their daily portion, they still are healthy and

lusty. I have been in many places, yet did I never see one that was born either in redundance or defect a monster, or any that sickness had deformed, or casualty made decrepit, saving one that had a bleared eye and another that had a wen on his cheek. The reason is rendered why they grow so proportionable and continue so long in their vigor (most of them being fifty before a wrinkled brow or gray hair bewray their age) is because they are not brought down with suppressing labor, vexed with annoying cares, or drowned in the excessive abuse of overflowing plenty, which oftentimes kills them more than want, as may appear in them. For when they change their bare Indian commons for the plenty of England's fuller diet, it is so contrary to their stomachs that death or a desperate sickness immediately accrues, which makes so few of them desirous to see England.

Looking back to the years 1760 to 1766, Dr. Benjamin Rush explains why the Philadelphians of that period were so unhealthy.

The diet of the inhabitants of Philadelphia, during those years, consisted chiefly of animal food. It was eaten, in some families, three times, and in all, twice a day. A hot supper was a general meal. To two and three meals of animal food in a day, many persons added what was then called "a relish," about an hour before dinner. It consisted of a slice of ham, a piece of salted fish, and now and then a beef-steak, accompanied with large draughts of punch or toddy. Tea was in the interval between dinner and supper. In many companies, a glass of wine and bitters was taken a few minutes before dinner, in order to increase the appetite. The drinks, with dinner and supper, were punch and table beer.

Besides feeding thus plentifully in their families, many of the most respectable citizens belonged to clubs, which met in the city in winter, and in its vicinity, under sheds, or the shade of trees, in summer, once and twice a week, and, in one instance, every night. They were drawn together by suppers in winter, and dinners in summer. Their food was simple, and taken chiefly in a solid form. The liquors used with it were punch, London porter, and sound old Madeira wine.

Death was . . . common between the 50th and 60th years of life from gout, apoplexy, palsy, obstructed livers, and dropsies. A club, consisting of about a dozen of the first gentlemen in the city, all paid, for their intemperance, the forfeit of their lives between those ages, and most of them with some one, or more of the diseases that have been mentioned. I sat up with one of that club on the night of his death. Several of the members of it called at his house, the evening before he died, to inquire how he was. One of them, upon being informed of his extreme danger, spoke in high and pathetic terms of his convivial talents and virtues, and said, "he had spent 200 evenings a year with him, for the last twenty years of his life." These evenings were all spent at public houses.

DOCTOR'S BILL. *An entry from the diary of William Johnson, a free black living in Natchez, Mississippi, in the 1830s, a town and a time in which dueling was common and doctors carried sword-sticks.*

1836. June 24. Roberson and Dr Hogg has a kind of a fight, old Dr Hogg made him Travell prety fast. Particulars are those, Roberson Owed the Dr 12 dollars for Medical Services. The Dr gave his account to Whiting to Collect for him so he presented the Acct. to Roberson & R. said that he was not the man, so Dr suied on it, & Robs. Came to his office to abuse him about it, and the old Dr told him to Leave his office. The Dr and him came to Blowes, and the Dr struck him with a chair & R. ran in the Street and struck him in the Breast with a Brick, then ran up Street as Hard as he could split and the old Dr after him. So Roberson run through Thistles Stable and came out at the Back side of the Stable and went Home. The Dr & Maj Miller went around to Robs House. Dr went in & struck him with his cane and R. caught the stick and the sword came out, and the Dr would have killed him if his arm had not been caught by Mr Ross—Roberson then Broke and run as hard as he could split to the Jail, and went in for Safe Keeping—In time of the fight Robs Brother Struck Maj Miller on the head with a Brick Bat and then Run and the old Maj after him as hard as he could split. The Maj stumbled and fell and as he fell he made a cut at Robison and Cut him in the Butt.

DRAPETOMANIA. *In* The Cotton Kingdom, *published in 1861, Frederick Law Olmsted quotes from an 1850s work,* Report on the Diseases and Physical Peculiarities of the Negro Race, *a supposedly scientific work by an antebellum southern physician, Dr. Samuel A. Cartwright.*

The learned Dr. Cartwright, of the University of Louisiana, believes that slaves are subject to a peculiar form of mental disease, termed by him *Drapetomania,* which, like a malady that cats are liable to, manifests itself by an irrestrainable propensity to *run away;* and in a work on the diseases of negroes, highly esteemed at the South for its patriotism and erudition, he advises planters of the proper preventive and curative measures to be taken for it.

He asserts that, "with the advantage of proper medical advice, strictly followed, this troublesome practice of running away, that many negroes have, can be almost entirely prevented." Its symptoms and the usual empirical practice on the plantations are described: "Before negroes run away, unless they are frightened or panic-struck, they become sulky and dissatisfied. The cause of this sulkiness and dissatisfaction should be inquired into and removed or they are apt to run away or fall into the negro consumption." When sulky or dissatisfied without cause, the experience of those having most practice with *drapetomania*, the Doctor thinks, has been in favour of "whipping them *out of it.*" It is vulgarly called, "whipping the devil *out of them,*" he afterwards informs us.

DRUNKEN DRIVING. *From* The Drunkard's Looking Glass, *by the clergyman and book agent Mason Locke Weems, published in 1813. Here he is describing the first of the three stages of drunkenness: "The frisky, or Foolish Stage."*

At this stage of the disease, the patient goes by a variety of nick-names, all of them well befitting the contemptibleness of his character, such as BOOZY—GROGGY—BLUE—DAMP—TIPSY—FUDDLED—HAILY GAILY—HOW CAME YOU SO—HALF SHAVED—SWIPY—HAS GOT A DROP IN HIS EYE—CUT—HAS GOT HIS WET SHEET ABROAD—CUT IN THE CRAW—HIGH UP TO PICKING COTTON (Georgia.) But tho' so different in name, 'tis the same in nature, all but *one disease* still . . . If he happens to be on horseback, he is just an hundred per cent. more of a brute than before; he presents you with a living likeness of what the ancients called a CENTAUR, i.e. a Monster, half man, and half beast. He reins up his horse, cracks his whip, gives the spur, and after much rearing and prancing, dashes up along side and challenges you to *run* with him, swearing that he can beat any thing that *ever went upon four legs.* Then wo be to the Cow, Calf, or Pig, that comes in his way: instantly he gives chase after them as hard as he can drive; and if to use his own elegant language, he don't break their *d—n'd backs for them,* it must be because they are lucky enough to outrun him.

"Hurra boys! D—n me, now you shall see fun," exclaimed Sam, as in his SKY BLUE and GOLD LACE, with an *elegant new Gig and Horse,* he was dashing home accompanied by a squad of YOUNKERS from the house of the good Mrs. H—s and her fair daughters, where they had been jollyfying on apple toddy until they were all quite *frisky.* "Hurra, Boys! Now you shall see fun!" thus chuckled Sam with looks quite big with some choice mischief. His *fun,* it seems, was to run his gig full tilt over one of his father's old cows that lay in the lane which they had just entered. Many a rich bowl of milk, and cream, many a heaping plate of butter and of cheese-curds, had that poor old animal given Sam in her time. But that's all forgotten; and Sam must have out his frolic, cost what it will . . . Off went his horse and gig, rising a cloud of dust along the lane. Unfortunately, the old cow was so sound asleep that she did not hear a syllable of the gig until it was close upon her. The horse, more humane than his master, would have given the old creature the *go-by;* but a sudden jerk of the rein, turned his course right over her neck and head. In that luckless moment, just started from her sleep, and frightened out of her seven senses, she fetched a violent leap, as from the clutches of a lion; and in that fatal leap, struck her horn up to the hub in the horses belly. Too weak to raise the horse, she herself, poor old creature, was thrown back sprawling, and bellowing on the ground; one of the wheels crossing her carcase, the gig was overset, and Sam with all his fine clothes tumbled in the dirt. The horse, though mortally wounded, and bleeding fast to death, was yet so distracted with pain and fright, that he never ceased leaping and bounding in the most furious manner, until he had completely demolished the gig. Then to finish the tragedy, he laid down, and falling into convulsions, presently expired.

DYSENTERY. *Two cures recorded by Swedish naturalist Peter Kalm in the 1740s.*

The following prescription was regarded as an infallible cure for dysentery: Boil some cinnamon bark in water; take a quantity of this water and pour it with some brandy in a bowl; over it place a couple of splinter (or pipe-stems) close beside each other, with a piece of sugar on top of them; set fire to the brandy and let it burn until the sugar is quite burnt. Let the patient then eat this sugar and drink some of the brandy and the cinnamon water. It is claimed that one dose was often enough for an immediate cure. Another excellent remedy was said to be fried red English cheese eaten on a sandwich.

FADS. *Thomas Low Nichols, author of* Forty Years of American Life, *describes some that were popular in the middle part of the nineteenth century.*

Freedom from prejudice, disregard of precedents . . . a love of novelty, a striving after progress, make the Americans ready listeners to every new doctrine, pretended science, or would-be philosophy.

When Dr. Spurzheim, the associate of Gall in the elaboration of the system of phrenology, came to America, about 1834, he was received with enthusiasm. Phrenology became the rage. Plaster casts of heads, and lithographs marked with the organs, were sold by the thousands. There was a universal feeling of heads. Lecturers went from town to town, explaining the new science, and giving public and private examinations. Periodicals were published to promulgate the new philosophy, and a library of books was rapidly published. I have no doubt that in five years after the advent of Dr. Spurzheim, there were more phrenologists, or believers of phrenology, in the United States than in all the world beside.

Animal magnetism trod closely on the heels of phrenology. . . . Monsieur Poyen, a French Creole, from one of the West India Islands, came to Boston, and introduced the new science to the American public. He was listened to with eager curiosity. I chanced to be present at one of Dr. Poyen's first lectures. His health was too feeble, as he said, to allow him to operate; but after the lecture, and in presence of a portion of the audience, a young man who volunteered to try the experiment succeeded in putting one of his companions to sleep. A few days afterwards he accompanied some physicians to a city hospital, and magnetized a patient selected for the experiment so thoroughly that she remained asleep forty-eight hours, though suffering from an acute disease of the heart that usually deprived her of rest. During the mesmeric sleep or trance, she appeared placid and free from pain, but it was found impossible to awaken her by ordinary means. At the end of forty-eight hours, she awoke herself, and seemed much refreshed, and said she was better than she had been for months. The publication of this and a few similar cases, of course set the whole people to mesmerising each other. There were medical mesmerists and clairvoyants everywhere. Distinguished surgeons performed operations on patients who were insensible to pain during the magnetic sleep. Clairvoyants professed to inspect the internal organs of patients, describe their diseases, and prescribe remedies, which were not more varied or dangerous than those given by the regular and irregular faculty.

Then came psychometrists, who could tell the lives, characters, fortunes, and diseases of people they had never seen, by holding a sealed letter, scrap of writing, lock of hair, or other connecting relic, in their hands. There was one who, when a fossil of some remote geological period was placed in contact with her forehead, would give an animated description of the appearance of the planet at that period, which she professed to see in a kind of vision.

The spread of hydropathy was another example of the readiness of Americans to accept anything new. The system of Priessnitz had scarcely been heard of before several large water-cure establishments were opened in America, five or six water-cure journals were published, two medical schools of hydropathy opened, and in a few years a hundred or more practitioners, male and female, of course, were dispensing packs and douches with much desirable cleanliness, and, it is probable, much sanitary improvement also, to the American public.

HYSTERIA. *By Helen Hunt Jackson, author of* A Century of Dishonor, Ramona, *and other works, including* Bits of Talk About Home Matters, *1873, from which this is taken.*

All physicians know what a disastrous effect one hysterical patient will produce upon a whole ward in a hospital. We remember hearing a young physician once give a most amusing account of a woman who was taken to Bellevue Hospital for a hysterical cough. Her lungs, bronchia, throat, were all in perfect condition; but she coughed almost incessantly, especially on the approach of the hour for the doctor's visit to the ward. In less than one week half the women in the ward had similar coughs. A single—though it must be confessed rather terrific—application of cold water to the original offender worked a simultaneous cure upon her and all of her imitators.

INFIRMARY. *In 1838–39 Fanny Kemble, an English-born actress, paid her first visit to her husband's slave plantation on the Georgia Sea Islands. Here she writes to her New England friend, Elizabeth Sedgwick, about her recent visit to the plantation infirmary.*

Stretched upon the ground, apparently either asleep or so overcome with sickness as to be incapable of moving, lay an immense woman; her stature, as she cumbered the earth, must have been, I should think, five feet seven or eight, and her bulk enormous. She was wrapped in filthy rags, and lay with her face on the floor. As I approached, and stooped to see what ailed her, she suddenly threw out her arms, and, seized with violent convulsions, rolled over and over upon the floor, beating her head violently upon the ground, and throwing her enormous limbs about in a horrible manner. Immediately upon the occurrence of this fit, four or five women threw themselves literally upon her, and held her down by main force; they even proceeded to bind her legs and arms together, to prevent her dashing herself about; but this violent coercion and tight bandaging seemed to me, in my profound ignorance, more likely to increase her illness by impeding her breathing and the circulation of her blood, and I bade them desist, and unfasten all the strings and ligatures not only that they had put round her limbs, but which, by tightening her clothes round her body, caused any obstruction. How much I wished that, instead of music, and dancing, and such stuff, I had learned something of sickness and health, of the conditions and liabilities of the human body, that I might have known how to assist this poor creature, and to direct her ignorant and helpless nurses!

The fit presently subsided, and was succeeded by the most deplorable prostration and weakness of nerves, the tears streaming down the poor woman's cheeks in showers, without, however, her uttering a single word, though she moaned incessantly. After bathing her forehead, hands, and chest with vinegar, we raised her up, and I sent to the house for a chair with a back (there was no such thing in the hospital), and we contrived to place her in it.

I have seldom seen finer women than this poor creature and her younger sister, an immense strapping lass called Chloe—tall, straight, and extremely well made—who was assisting her sister, and whom I had remarked, for the extreme delight and merriment which my cleansing propensities seemed to give her, on my last visit to the hospital. She was here taking care of a sick baby, and helping to nurse her sister Molly, who, it seems, is subject to those fits, about which I spoke to our physician here—an intelligent man residing in Darien, who visits the estate whenever medical assistance is required. He seemed to attribute them to nervous disorder, brought on by frequent childbearing. This woman is young, I suppose at the outside not thirty, and her sister informed me that she had had ten children—ten children, Elizabeth! Fits and hard labor in the fields, unpaid labor, labor exacted with stripes—how do you fancy that? I wonder if my mere narration can make your blood boil as the facts did mine?

INOCULATION. *As with many innovations, smallpox inoculation met heavy resistance when first introduced. The Reverend Cotton Mather, a vigorous champion of the method, records an extreme instance.*

1721, November 13. My Kinsman, the Minister of *Roxbury*, being Entertained at my House, that he might there undergo the *Small-Pox Inoculated,* and so Return to the Service of his Flock, which have the Contagion begun among them; Towards three a Clock in the Night, as it grew towards Morning of this Day, some unknown Hands, threw a fired Granado into the Chamber where my Kinsman lay, and which used to be my Lodging-Room. The Weight of the Iron Ball alone, had it fallen upon his Head, would have been enough to have done Part of the Business designed. But the *Granado* was charged, the upper part with dried Powder, the lower Part with a Mixture of Oil of Turpentine and Powder and what else I know not, in such a Manner, that upon its going off, must have splitt, and have probably killed the Persons in the Room, and certainly fired the Chamber, and speedily laid the House in Ashes. But, *this Night there stood by me the Angel of the* GOD, *whose I am and whom I serve;* and the merciful Providence of GOD my SAVIOUR, so ordered it that the Granado passing thro' the Window, had by the Iron in the Middle of the Casement, such a Turn given to it, that in falling on the Floor, the fired Wild-fire in the Fuse was violently shaken out upon the Floor, without firing the Granado. When the *Granado* was

Vaccinating the baby against smallpox, in an age when doctors
still made house calls, from *Harper's Weekly*, February 19, 1870.

taken up, there was found a Paper so tied with String about the Fuse,
that it might out-Live the breaking of the Shell, which had these words
in it; COTTON MATHER, *You Dog, Damn you: I'l inoculate you with this, with
a Pox to you.*

LAND TURTLE. *Writing in 1672, John Josselyn, an English naturalist, lists
some of the creature's medical uses.*

The shell of a land-*Turtle* burnt and the ashes dissolved in white wine
and oyl to an unguent healeth chaps and sores of the feet: the flesh
burnt and the ashes mixt with wine and oyl healeth sore legs: the ashes
of the burnt shell and the whites of eggs compounded together
healeth chaps in womens nipples; and the head pulverized with it prevents the falling of the hair, and will heal the Hemorrhoids, first washing of them with white-wine, and then strewing on the powder.

LANGUAGES. *Mary Boykin Chesnut, a southern lady who kept a diary throughout the Civil War, made this entry in June 1862 while in Columbia, South Carolina.*

One of our boarders here at lodgers is a German woman. She has been very ill. Dr. Fair attended her. She is still very feeble. Mem says that Dr. Fair advised her today to try and speak English—German was a very heavy language for one as weak as she was. "A very difficult language to speak," he said, turning to Mem. "She had better try French until she gains some strength—if she does not understand English." And the woman meekly responded, "My own tongue is lighter for me."

LUNACY. *Asa Sheldon, a Massachusetts-born jack-of-all-trades looks back to the years 1803–04 when he was a fifteen-year-old farm boy. Raynor, another hired hand, has just quit; Parker is the farmer, and Dave is his son.*

Soon after Raynor left, a traveller came along, and Dave took him in. He was a man of middle age. We never knew where he came from; if asked the question, he would not answer, but change the topic of conversation. He was no epicure, but would eat whatever was set before him. He slept in an attic chamber, with his door fastened. He was deranged in mind, and like other maniacs, when most crazy, would manifest a terrible temper. His name was Jeremiah Powers, and he could do a great amount of work, such as forking manure, hoeing, pitching hay, grain, &c; in doing any of these things, no man could beat him. He was exceedingly withy and spry. I have seen him stand with both feet together, and jump twelve feet ahead at a leap. Few men can do that.

In his worst spells, he would receive no directions about the work from any one except me, and would frequently urge me to join him to kill Parker and Dave, for he had a lunatic idea that if they were killed we could do as we pleased with the farm and stock.

Once on going into Dave's house, I found him sitting on a block in the corner, pale with terror, while Powers was standing over him, axe in hand, telling him if he moved he would split his brains out. And I believe he would have done so.

"Captain," said I, for we were used to calling him by that title, "what are you going to do with Dave?"

"Kill this old d—d regular," said he, "and take off his scalp."

"What are you going to do with it?"

"Sell it," said he.

"You can't get one cent for it; besides we want him to help get our hay in; he is a good mower you know."

He turned away with a demoniac laugh, and Dave was relieved from his terror-stricken embarrassment. I must confess I was frightened myself, but I made shift not to let Powers know it. "Asa," said he, "you are always right; I will let him go now."

He had a notion if any one hawked or spit, &c., they were mocking him. If a cock crowed within his reach, he would cut his head off if he could. Often while we were hoeing, the fowls would come round picking up worms, and he killed several in that way, when I would carry them into the house and have them cooked. As he was one day pitching hay, the horse, which was tied by a rope at the door, snuffed. Powers told her if she did it again he would let her guts out. The snuffing was immediately repeated, when Powers sprang to the ground, pitchfork in hand. I screamed out, "don't kill her, we want her to go fishing with, we can't go on foot." He stopped short, saying, "You are always right; I will let her live."

MALPRACTICE. *Some extracts from the diary of a young Englishman, Nicholas Cresswell. Shortly after his arrival in this country, Cresswell had this unhappy experience.*

Piscataway, Maryland—Tuesday, June 7th, 1774. This morning Captn. Knox and I left Annapolis. Dined at Marlbro, Lodged at Piscataway. A most violent pain in my Head attended with a high Fever, obliged to stop and rest myself at several houses on the road. Captn. Knox behaves exceedingly kind to me. *Wednesday, June 8th.* Got to Port Tobacco with great difficulty. Captn. Knox insists on me applying to Doctor Brown. I have taken his advice and he told me it is a Fever with some cussed physical name. He has given me some slops and I am now going to bed very ill.

Nanjemoy, Maryland—Thursday, June 9th. Find myself no better, However, the Doctor has given me more physic. Got to Nanjemoy. Almost dead with pain and fatigue, added to the excessive heat, which caused me to faint twice. *Wednesday, June 15th.* Very ill, confined to my room. This is the first day I have been able to stir out of it. I am much reduced and very weak, but my spirits are good and I hope in God I shall get better. Captn. Knox, Mr. Bayley, and the whole neighbourhood behaves with the greatest kindness to me, some of them has attended me constantly all the time. *Friday, June 17th.* Much better. The Doctor tells me I am out of all danger, but advises me to take some physic to clear my body and to drink a little more Rum than I did before I was sick. In short, I believe it was being too abstemious that brought this sickness upon me at first, by drinking water. *Saturday, June 18th.* Able to walk about the house. It is such excessive hot weather or I should mend faster.

Sunday, June 19th. Dined at a certain Mr. Hambleton's. Supped and spent the evening at Mrs. Leftwiches with some young ladies from Virginia. After supper the company amused themselves with several diverting plays. *Monday, June 20th*. Gathering strength very fast, the Doctor sent me a Box of Pills with directions to take two at night and two in the Morning. *Wednesday, June 22nd*. Taking the Pills the Doctor gave me, but these don't seem to work, only cause a bad taste in my mouth. Will take three this evening. *Thursday, June 23rd*. This morning took 4 Pills which has caused a violent pain in my bowels all day, attended with a constant thirst and a very bad taste in my mouth. But affects me no other way. *Friday, June 24th*. Much worse, my throat and tongue much swollen. Have sent for the Doctor. Confined to my bed. Am afraid that I am poisoned with his confounded Pills. A continual thirst, but these people will not let me drink. *Saturday, June 25th*. Captn. Knox sent an express for the Doctor, who came about eight this morning. After he had examined the Pills, he came with a truly physical face to the bedside and felt my pulse. Began to beg pardon for the mistake he said his Prentice had inadvertently committed by sending me strong Mercurial Pills, in the room of cooling ones. I immediately gave him as hard a blow as I could with my fist over the face, and would have given him a good trimming had I been able. This discomposed his physical muscles a good deal, and made him contract them into a most formidable frown. He did not attempt to resent it. Begged I would moderate my passion, follow his directions, and in a short time I should be well again. I believed myself poisoned and grew desperate, abused him most unmercifully. However, he left me some Brimstone and Salts which I took immediately after he was gone, which worked very well and has given me a great deal of ease. Tho' I am still full of pain and much swelled, spitting and slavering like a mad dog, my teeth loose and mouth very sore. I believe I have little to trust to but the strength of my constitution for my life. Much difficulty to write, but if I happen to die I hope this will appear against the rascal. *Sunday, June 26th*. This morning took a dose of Brimstone, laid in bed all day and sweat abundantly. This has made me very weak and faint. Doctor came to enquire after me, but did not come into the room. Much easier. *Monday, June 27th*. A great deal better but much relaxed and very weak, able to sit up most part of the day. *Wednesday, June 29th*. Mending very fast, able to walk about the room. The swelling gone away, my throat got well, but my mouth is very sore, which I wash every two hours with Vinegar. I understand the Doctor sends every day to enquire how I do. Had it not been for the extraordinary care of Captn. Knox, I must certainly have died. *Thursday, June 30th*. Took a dose of Salts, able to walk into the Yard. *Saturday, July 2nd*. Continue mending, but very slowly. *Sunday, July 3rd*. Rode out with Mr.

Wallace to Colonel Taylor's Plantation. It is only two miles, but I find it has fatigued me too much. *Tuesday, July 5th.* Took another dose of Salts, which I hope will be the last I shall have occasion to take at this time. Find myself pretty well. Free from pain, but very weak and much reduced. My clothes hang about me like a skeleton. The Doctor has never come in my sight since I struck him. Intend to go and pay the rascal to-morrow. *Wednesday, July 6th.* Went to see the Doctor, who (contrary to my expectation) treated me with the greatest kindness and acknowledged that he had given me just cause of complaint, though inadvertently, and absolutely refused being paid till I am quite recovered. I understand their Doctors' Bills in this country are very extravagant. Returned to Nanjemoy much fatigued.

MEDICINE MAN. *As reported by Dr. Edwin James, in an appendix to John Tanner's narrative, published in 1830. Tanner, captured by the Shawnee as a child, became an adopted member of the Ojibwa tribe.*

The Song of Chi-ah-ba, a celebrated Ojibbeway Medicine man.

Ah-way-ah noan-dah-wug-ga muk-kud-da ge-na-beek goo-we-ah-we-aun nee-kaun. (Some one, I hear him; but I make myself black snake, my friend.)

The medicine man speaks in his own person. He hears some one; he knows who it is that has used bad medicine to break his patient's life; but he brings, to oppose it, the power and craftiness of the black snake.

Ain-dun wa-we-tum-maun o-ge-tah-kum-maig ke-he-a. Ain-dun wa-we-tum-maun, etc. (I myself speak, standing here on the ground.)

He takes a bold and open stand against his enemies, and those of his employer.

We-go-nain-wa-we-ow we-he-naun? O-ge-na-beek-o-ga wa-we-yah wee-he-nah. (What is this I put in your body? Snake skins I put in your body.)

The two first verses are sung on entering the lodge, and before he commences giving his medicine. The third accompanies the exhibition of the first dose, which consists either of eight snake skins tied together, and the foremost having a small frog fastened to the head of it, or of eight fathoms of a small cord, or thong of leather, and eight wild cat's claws fastened at equal intervals. Difficult as the swallowing of this prescription may appear to us, and as it doubtless is, the patient receives and swallows it, all the time on his knees, and the doctor stands by singing the above song, and occasionally aiding with his finger, or a little water, in the inglutition of his formidable remedy. After this has remained a shorter or longer time in the stomach, according to the inclination of the medicine man, it is to be withdrawn; and it is in this operation, particularly when the cat's claws are used, that the patient suffers the most excruciating torture. The end which is first

This reproduction of a watercolor by John White portrays a group of
medicine men on Roanoke Island, Virginia, 1585.

given up is put into the hand of some of the attendants, and they
dance and sing with it about the lodge, as the remainder is gradually
given back. Then the medicine man sings the following, while the
dance becomes general.

Ne-man-i-to-we-tah hi-yo-che-be-kun-na on-je-man-i-to-wee-yaun we-ug-usk.
(I am Manito, the roots of shrubs and weeds make me Manito.)

O-ge-na-beek-o-ga ne-kau-naug. (Snakes are my friends.)

NURSES. *The ideal, as described in the 1860s by Miss Ann Preston, who
was, according to Catharine Beecher, "one of the most refined as well as talented and learned female physicians."*

"The good nurse is an artist. O the pillowy, soothing softness of her
touch, the neatness of her simple, unrustling dress, the music of her

assured yet gentle voice and tread, the sense of security and rest inspired by her kind and hopeful face, the promptness and attention to every want, the repose that like an atmosphere encircles her, the evidence of heavenly goodness, and love that she diffuses!"

The real, from the diary of Louisa May Alcott.

November 1862.—Thirty years old. Decided to go to Washington as a nurse if I could find a place. Help needed, and I love nursing, and *must* let out my pent-up energy in some new way. Winter is always a hard and a dull time, and if I am away there is one less to feed and warm and worry over.

I want new experiences, and am sure to get 'em if I go. So I've sent in my name, and bide my time writing tales, to leave all snug behind me, and mending up my old clothes,—for nurses don't need nice things, thank Heaven!

December.—On the 11th I received a note from Miss Hannah M. Stevenson telling me to start for Georgetown next day to fill a place in Union Hotel Hospital. Mrs. Ropes of Boston was matron, and Miss Kendall of Plymouth was a nurse there, and though a hard place, help was needed. I was ready, and when my commander said "March!" I marched. Packed my trunk, and reported in Boston that same evening.

We had all been full of courage till the last moment came, then we all broke down. I realized that I had taken my life in my hand, and might never see them all again. I said, "Shall I stay, Mother?" as I hugged her close. "No, go! and the Lord be with you!" answered the Spartan woman, and till I turned the corner she bravely smiled and waved her wet handkerchief on the door-step. Shall I ever see that dear old face again?

So I set forth in the December twilight, with May and Julian Hawthorne as escort, feeling as if I was the son of the house going to war.

All went well, and I got to Georgetown one evening very tired. Was kindly welcomed, slept in my narrow bed with two other room-mates, and on the morrow began my new life by seeing a poor man die at dawn, and sitting all day between a boy with pneumonia and a man shot through the lungs. A strange day, but I did my best, and when I put mother's little black shawl round the boy while he sat up panting for breath, he smiled and said, "You are real motherly, ma'am." I felt as if I was getting on. The man only lay and stared with his big black eyes, and made me very nervous. But all were well behaved, and I sat looking at the twenty strong faces as they looked back at me,—hoping that I looked "motherly" to them; for my thirty years made me feel old, and the suffering round me made me long to comfort every one.

January 1863. I never began the year in a stranger place than this; five hundred miles from home, alone among strangers, doing painful duties all day long, & leading a life of constant excitement in this greathouse surrounded by 3 or 4 hundred men in all stages of suffering, disease & death. Though often home sick, heart sick & worn out, I like it—find real pleasure in comforting tending & cheering these poor souls who seem to love me, to feel my sympathy though unspoken, & acknowledge my hearty good will in spite of the ignorance, awkwardness, & bashfulness which I cannot help showing in so new & trying a situation. The men are docile, respectful, & affectionate, with but few exceptions, truly lovable & manly many of them. John Suhre a Virginia blacksmith is the prince of patients, & though what we call a common man, in education & condition, to me is all that I could expect or ask from the first gentleman in the land. Under his plain speech & unpolished manner I seem to see a noble character, a heart as warm & tender as a woman's, a nature fresh & frank as any child's. He is about thirty, I think, tall & handsome, mortally wounded & dying royally, without reproach, repining, or remorse. Mrs. Ropes & myself love him & feel indignant that such a man should be so early lost, for though he might never distinguish himself before the world, his influence & example cannot be without effect, for real goodness is never wasted.

Monday 4th—I shall record the events of a day as a sample of the days I spend:—

Up at six, dress by gaslight, run through my ward & fling up the windows though the men grumble & shiver, but the air is bad enough to breed a pestilence & as no notice is taken of our frequent appeals for better ventilation, I must do what I can. Poke up the fire, add blankets, joke, coax, & command, but continue to open doors & windows as if life depended on it, mine does, & doubtless many another, for a more perfect pestilence-box than this house I never saw—cold, damp, dirty, full of vile odors from wounds, kitchens, wash rooms, & stables. No competent head, male or female, to right matters, & a jumble of good, bad, & indifferent nurses, surgeons & attendants to complicate the Chaos still more.

After this unwelcome progress through my stifling ward I go to breakfast with what appetite I may, find the inevitable fried beef, salt butter, husky bread & washy coffee, listen to the clack of eight women & a dozen men, the first silly, stupid or possessed of but one idea, the last absorbed in their breakfast & themselves to a degree that is both ludicrous and provoking.

Till noon I trot, trot, giving out rations, cutting up food for help-less "boys", washing faces, teaching my attendants how beds are made or floors swept, dressing wounds, taking Dr. Fitz Patrick's orders, (pri-vately wishing all the time that he would be more gentle with my big babies,) dusting tables, sewing bandages, keeping my tray tidy, rush-ing up & down after pillows, bed linen, sponges, books & directions, till it seems as if I would joyfully pay down all I possess for fifteen minutes rest.

At twelve the big bell rings & up comes dinner for the boys who are always ready for it & never entirely satisfied. Soup, meat, potatoes & bread is the bill of fare. Charley Thayer the attendant travels up & down the room serving out the rations, saving little for himself yet always thoughtful of his mates & patient as a woman with their help-lessness. When dinner is over some sleep, many read, & others want letters written. This I like to do for they put in such odd things & express their ideas so comically I have great fun interiorly while as grave as possible exteriorly. A few of the men word their paragraphs well & make excellent letters. John's was the best of all I wrote. The answering of letters from friends after some one has died is the sad-dest & hardest duty a nurse has to do.

Supper at five sets every one to running that can run & when that flurry is over all settle down for the evening amusements which consist of newspapers, gossip, Drs last round, & for such as need them the final doses for the night. At nine the bell rings, gas is turned down & day nurses go to bed.

Night nurses go on duty, & sleep & death have the house to themselves.

POISON. *Frances Trollope, the acerbic English author of* Domestic Manners of the Americans, *condemns slavery and saves a life.*

Among the poorer class of landholders, who are often as profoundly ignorant as the negroes they own, the effect of this plenary power over males and females is most demoralising; and the kind of coarse, not to say brutal, authority which is exercised, furnishes the most disgusting moral spectacle I ever witnessed. In all ranks, however, it appeared to me that the greatest and best feelings of the human heart were para-lyzed by the relative positions of slave and owner. The characters, the hearts of children, are irretrievably injured by it. In Virginia we board-ed for some time in a family consisting of a widow and her four daugh-ters, and I there witnessed a scene strongly indicative of the effect I have mentioned. A young female slave, about eight years of age, had found on the shelf of a cupboard a biscuit, temptingly buttered, of which she had eaten a considerable portion before she was observed.

The butter had been copiously sprinkled with arsenic for the destruction of rats, and had been thus most incautiously placed by one of the young ladies of the family. As soon as the circumstance was known, the lady of the house came to consult me as to what had best be done for the poor child; I immediately mixed a large cup of mustard and water (the most rapid of all emetics) and got the little girl to swallow it. The desired effect was instantly produced, but the poor child, partly from nausea, and partly from the terror of hearing her death proclaimed by half a dozen voices round her, trembled so violently that I thought she would fall. I sat down in the court where we were standing, and, as a matter of course, took the little sufferer in my lap. I observed a general titter among the white members of the family, while the black stood aloof, and looked stupified. The youngest of the family, a little girl about the age of the young slave, after gazing at me for a few moments in utter astonishment, exclaimed, "My! If Mrs. Trollope has not taken her in her lap, and wiped her nasty mouth! Why I would not have touched her mouth for two hundred dollars!"

The little slave was laid on a bed, and I returned to my own apartments; some time afterwards I sent to enquire for her, and learnt that she was in great pain. I immediately went myself to enquire farther, when another young lady of the family, the one by whose imprudence the accident had occurred, met my anxious enquiries with ill-suppressed mirth—told me they had sent for the doctor—and then burst into uncontrollable laughter. The idea of really sympathising in the sufferings of a slave, appeared to them as absurd as weeping over a calf that had been slaughtered by the butcher. The daughters of my hostess were as lovely as features and complexion could make them; but the neutralizing effect of this total want of feeling upon youth and beauty, must be witnessed, to be conceived.

POSTWAR STRESS. *As diagnosed and cured by Dr. D. G. Brinton and Dr. G. M. Napheys and recorded in their 1870 book* The Laws of Health in Relation to the Human Form.

We have recently been consulted by several ladies from the Southern States for a peculiar condition of the system which they say is not unusual there, and which they attribute to the mental anxiety, the prostration of hopes, the losses, and the change in social condition, brought about by our civil war. This is a general relaxation of the muscular system. They were not emaciated, nor did they suffer any pain, or appear in bad health. But the muscles were soft and ill-defined, the gait shambling and irregular, and the motions awkward, and made with disproportionate effort of the will. They had taken quantities of the usual tonics without avail, and were almost in despair. We prescribed the daily use of electricity, medicated douche baths, warm and cold, friction, a regulated diet, and no medicine. These means, together with change of air, resulted satisfactorily in all from whom we have since heard.

SCARLET FEVER. *In his autobiography, the Reverend John Barnard—who, like his father, was a Congregationalist minister in New England—tells how he was cured.*

In June, 1693, in my twelfth year, Sir Francis Wheeler, with his fleet, which had in vain made an attempt upon Martinique, came to Boston, and brought with him a violent and malignant distemper called the scarlet fever, by which he lost many hundreds of his men. The distemper soon spread in Boston, of which many persons died—and that within two or three days of their being taken ill. It pleased God I was seized with it, and through the rampancy of the fever and a violent pain at my heart, which rendered every breath I drew to be as though a sword had pierced me, I was so bad that life was despaired of. On the third night (I think) it seemed to me that a certain woman, wife of a doctor, who used to supply my father's family with plasters upon occasion, came and brought me some small dark-colored pills, and directed me to put one in my mouth and hold it there till it grew mellow, then squeeze it flat betwixt my thumb and finger and apply it to my right nipple; it would soak in, and before I had used them all so, I should be well. I followed the prescription, and when I had used the third pill, my pain and fever left me, and I was well. My tender father, very early the next morning, came into my bedchamber to inquire how it was with me. I told him I was quite well, and intended to get up presently, and said the pills Mrs. (naming her) had given me last night had perfectly cured me. He said to me, "Child, I believe she was not here; I heard nothing of it." To confirm him I said, "Sir, I have the remaining four pills now in my hand," and put my hand out of the bed to show them, but they dropped out of my hand into the bed. I then raised myself up to look for them, but could not find them. He said to me, "I am afraid, child, you are out of your senses." I said to him, "Sir, I am perfectly awake and in my senses, and find myself truly well." He left the room with the supposition that I was delirious, and I saw by his countenance that he was ready to give me over for lost. He then inquired of all the house whether that woman had been at the house the day or evening before. They all let him know that they had not seen her here. He betook himself to his closet [study], and in about an hour came to me again; I continued firm in the story I had told him. He talked to me of some other things, and found by my answers that I was thoroughly awake and, as he now thought, under the power of no distraction; he was better satisfied, and left me with a more placid countenance. By noon I got up, and was perfectly recovered from my sickness. I thought I would have given ever so much to know what the pills were, that others might receive the benefit of them. Finding that the abovesaid woman had not been at our house, and I was perfectly healed, I could not help thinking that a merciful God had sent an angel, as He did Isaiah to Hezekiah, to heal me; and to this very day I cannot but esteem it more than an ordinary dream or the wild ramblings of a heated imagination.

SCURVY. *In his book* Six Months in the Gold Fields, *E. Gould Buffum, ex-journalist and ex-soldier, tells how he joined the California gold rush and with a few companions went to seek his fortune on the Middle Fork River.*

The soil of this bar was exceedingly sandy, and the surface was covered with huge imbedded rocks, which required an immense amount of severe manual labor to remove. Below this was a red gravel, which was united with gold, the washing of which turned out about four ounces per day to each man. I was again dreaming of fortune and success, when my hopes were blasted by an attack of a terrible scourge which wrought destruction through the northern mines during the winter of 1848. I allude to the land scurvy. The exposed and unaccustomed life of two-thirds of the miners, and their entire subsistence upon salt meat, without any mixture of vegetable matter, had produced this disease, which was experienced more or less by at least one-half of the miners within my knowledge.

I noticed its first attack upon myself by swelling and bleeding of the gums, which was followed by a swelling of both legs below the knee, which rendered me unable to walk; and for three weeks, I was laid up in my tent, obliged to feed upon the very articles that had caused the disease, and growing daily weaker, without any reasonable prospect of relief. There were, at that time, about eight hundred persons at work on the river, and hoping to get some medicine, I despatched one of my companions one morning, with instructions to procure me, if possible, a dose of salts, and to pay for it any price that should be asked. He returned at night with the consoling news that he had failed, having found only two persons who had brought the article with them, and they refused to sell it at any price.

I was almost in despair: with only a blanket between myself and the damp, cold earth, and a thin canvas to protect me from the burning sun by day, and the heavy dews by night, I lay day after day enduring the most intense suffering from pain in my limbs, which were now becoming more swollen, and were turning completely black. Above me rose those formidable hills which I must ascend ere I could obtain relief. I believe I should have died, had not accident discovered the best remedy that could have been produced. In the second week of my illness, one of our party, in descending the hill on which he had been deer-hunting, found near its base, and strewn along the foot-track, a quantity of beans which sprouted from the ground, and were in leaf. Some one, in descending the hill with a bag of them on his back, had probably dropped them. My companion gathered a quantity and brought them into camp. I had them boiled, and lived entirely on them for several days, at the same time using a decoction of the bark of the spruce tree. These seemed to operate magically, and in a week after commencing the use of them, I found myself able to walk,—and as soon as my strength was partially restored, I ascended the hill, and with two companions walked into Culoma, and by living principally upon a vegetable diet, which I procured by paying three dollars per pound for potatoes, in a very short time I recovered.

SIMPLE REMEDIES. *Some extracts from a chapter with this title in* The American Frugal Housewife, *by Lydia Maria Child, first published in 1828.*

A good quantity of old cheese is the best thing to eat, when distressed by eating too much fruit, or oppressed with any kind of food. Physicians have given it in cases of extreme danger.

Honey and milk is very good for worms; so is strong salt water; likewise powdered sage and molasses taken freely.

For a sudden attack of quincy or croup, bathe the neck with bear's grease, and pour it down the throat. A linen rag soaked in sweet oil, butter, or lard, and sprinkled with yellow Scotch snuff, is said to have performed wonderful cures in cases of croup: it should be placed where the distress is greatest. Goose-grease, or any kind of oily grease, is as good as bear's oil.

A poultice of wheat bran, or rye bran, and vinegar, very soon takes down the inflammation occasioned by a sprain. Brown paper, wet, is healing to a bruise.

A rind of pork bound upon a wound occasioned by a needle, pin, or nail, prevents the lock-jaw.

Cork burnt to charcoal, about as big as a hazel-nut, macerated, and put in a tea-spoonful of brandy, with a little loaf sugar and nutmeg, is very efficacious in cases of dysentery and cholera-morbus. If nutmeg be wanting, peppermint-water may be used. Flannel wet with brandy, powdered with Cayenne pepper, and laid upon the bowels, affords great relief in cases of extreme distress.

Blackberries are extremely useful in cases of dysentery. To eat the berries is very healthy; tea made of the roots and leaves is beneficial; and a syrup made of the berries is still better.

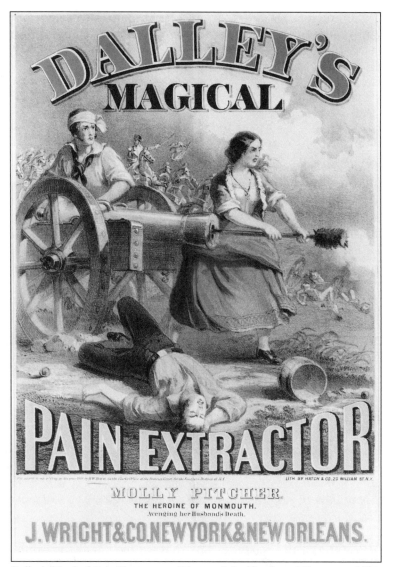

Dalley's Magical Pain Extractor, a lithograph by Hatch and Company, 1860.

Loaf sugar and brandy relieves a sore throat; when very bad, it is good to inhale the steam of scalding hot vinegar through the tube of a tunnel. This should be tried carefully at first, lest the throat be scalded.

A stocking bound on warm from the foot, at night, is good for the sore throat.

An ointment made from the common ground-worms, which boys dig to bait fishes, rubbed on with the hand, is said to be excellent, when the sinews are drawn up by any disease or accident.

If a wound bleeds very fast, and there is no physician at hand, cover it with the scrapings of sole-leather, scraped like coarse lint. This stops blood very soon.

Half a spoonful of *citric acid,* (which may always be bought of the apothecaries,) stirred in half a tumbler of water, is excellent for the head-ache.

Boiled potatoes are said to cleanse the hands as well as common soap; they prevent *chaps* in the winter season, and keep the skin soft and healthy.

Nothing is so good to take down swellings, as a soft poultice of stewed white beans, put on in a thin muslin bag, and renewed every hour or two.

The thin white skin, which comes from suet, is excellent to bind upon the feet for chilblains.

The common dark-blue violet makes a slimy tea, which is excellent for the canker.

Tea made of slippery elm is good for the piles, and for humors in the blood; to be drank plentifully.

Chalk wet with hartshorn [ammonia] is a remedy for the sting of bees; so is likewise table-salt kept moist with water.

Boil castor-oil with an equal quantity of milk, sweeten it with a little sugar, stir it well, and, when cold, give it to children for drink. They will never suspect it is medicine; and will even love the taste of it.

SMALLPOX. *From the diary of Francis Chardon for the year 1837. Chardon was in charge of the fur-trading post at Fort Clark, near Bismarck, North Dakota. The smallpox was probably brought to Fort Clark by a river steamer that stopped there in June. Several Indian tribes, some on very bad terms with one another, were encamped near the fort.*

14 [July]—One of the warmest days that we have had this summer—weather smokey—A young Mandan died to day of the Small Pox—several others has caught it—the Indians all being out Makeing dried Meat has saved several of them.

25—Several Young Men arrived from the dried Meat Camp, bringing With them each, one piece of Meat for those who remained at the Village. They will all be in tomorrow—they say that the small pox has broke out at the Camp.

27—Indians all out after berries. No News from any quarter. The small pox is Killing them up at the Village, four died to day.

28—Rain in the morning—This day was very Near being my last—a Young Mandan came to the Fort with his gun cocked, and secreted under his robe, with the intention of Killing me, after hunting me in 3 or 4 of the houses he at last found me, the door being shut, he waited some time for me to come out, just as I was in the act of going out, Mitchel caught him, and gave him in the hands of two Indians who conducted him to the Village. Had not Mitchel perceived him the instant he did, I would not be at the trouble of Makeing this statement—I am upon my guard.

The Mandans & Rees [Arickaree Indians] gave us two splendid dances, they say they dance, on account of their Not haveing a long time to live, as they expect to all die of the small pox—and as long as they are alive, they will take it out in dancing—

31—Mandans are getting worse, Nothing will do them except revenge—

Speech of the 4 Bears a Mandan Warrior to the Arricarees and Mandans, 30th July 1837—

My Friends one and all, Listen to what I have to say—Ever since I can remember, I have loved the Whites, I have lived With them ever since I was a Boy, and to the best of my Knowledge, I have never Wronged a White Man, on the Contrary, I have always Protected them from the insults of Others, Which they cannot deny. The 4 Bears never saw a White Man hungry, but what he gave him to eat, Drink, and a Buffaloe skin to sleep on, in time of Need. I was always ready to die for them, Which they cannot deny. I have done every thing that a red Skin could do for them, and how have they repaid it! With ingratitude! I have Never Called a White Man a Dog, but to day I do Pronounce them to be a set of Black harted Dogs, they have deceived Me, them that I always considered as Brothers has turned out to be My Worst Enemies. I have been in Many Battles, and often Wounded, but the Wounds of My enemies I exhalt in, but to day I am Wounded, and by Whom, those same White Dogs that I have always Considered and treated as Brothers. I do not fear *Death*, my friends. You know it, but to *die* with my face rotten, that even the Wolves will shrink with horror at seeing Me, and say to themselves, that is the 4 Bears the Friend of the Whites—

Listen well what I have to say, as it will be the last time you will hear Me. Think of your Wives, Children, Brothers, Sisters, Friends, and in fact all that you hold dear, are all Dead, or Dying, with their faces all rotten, caused by those dogs the whites, think of all that My friends, and rise all together and Not leave one of them alive.

[August] 1st—The Mandans are Makeing their Medicine for rain, As their Corn is all drying up—to day we had several light showers.

5—Indians out after berries, others out after Meat—News from the Gros Ventres, they say that they are encamped this side of Turtle Mountain, and that a great many of them have died of the small pox—several cheifs among them. They swear vengence against all the Whites, as they say the small pox was brought here by the Steamboat.

8—Four More died to day—the two thirds of the Village are sick, to day I gave six pounds of Epsom salt in doses to Men, Women, and children. The small pox has broke out at the Little Mandan Village—three died yesterday, two cheifs.

9—Seven More died to day—

14—The Rees are Makeing medicine for their sickness. Some of them have made dreams, that they talked to the Sun, others to the Moon, several articles has been sacrifised to them both—the Principal Chief of the Mandans died to day—The Wolf Chief—An other dog, from the Little Village came to the Fort naked with his gun cocked, to Kill one of us. We stopped him—

15—Gardepie with an other half breed arrived last evening from the North bringing with them 200 Muskrats and 50 lb Beaver. Sold him two horses. They left here early this Morning, the small pox scared them off—J. Be Joncá a half breed Kanza who has been liveing with the Gros Ventres several years, came on horse back at full speed to inform us that the Mandans went up to the Gros Ventres with a pipe, to Make them smoke, to try to get them to help Murder us, the Gros Ventres refused to smoke with them, saying that they were friendly to the Whites and that they would not take part with them. Joncá started back immediately.

The War Party of Rees and Mandans that left here the 26th of June, all came back to day, haveing Killed seven Sioux, Men, Women, and children, two lodges that were camped at the mouth of White River, it appears that the small pox has broke out amongst the Sioux, as some of the Party, on their way back, was taken sick at Grand River, haveing caught the disease from those that they butchered.

16—Several Men, Women, and Children that has been abandoned in the Village, are laying dead in the lodges, some out side of the Village, others in the little river not interred, which creates a very bad smell all around us—A Ree that has lost his wife and child threatened us to day—We are beset by enemies on all sides—expecting to be shot every Minute.

17—The Rees started out after Buffaloe, the Indians dying off every day—Were the disease will stop, I know not—We are badly situated, as we are threatened to be Murdered by the Indians every instant, however we are all determined, and Prepared for the worst—A Young Ree for several days has been lurking around the Fort, watching a good opportunity to Kill me, but not finding a good chance, this

Morning he came, full intent to sit himself down in front of the Fort gate, on the press, and waited a few Minutes for me to go out, in the Mean time one of my Men a Dutchman, John Cliver—stepped Out and sat himself down a long side of the Indian, after setting a few Minutes, he got up to come in the Fort, he only Made five paces, when the Indian shot him in the back bone and Killed him instantaneously, he made off immediately—We pursued after him shooting at him, but without effect—he got as far as the little river, where one of his Brothers is interred, on arriving there he made a stop, and hollowed to us that that was the place he wanted to die. Garreau approached in 15 paces of him and shot, the contents Knocked him over, he then rushed on him with his large Knife and ripped his body open.

Garreau deserves the highest praise from us all, he acted manfully although against his own nation—he always told me that he would always act as he has done—the Mother of the fellow we Killed came to the Fort crying, saying that she wanted to die also, and wished for us to Kill her. Garreau stepped up, and with his tommahawk would of Made short work of the Old Woman, but was Prevented—

18—Nothing but an occasional glass of grog Keeps me alive as I am worried almost to death by the Indians and Whites, the latter (the men) threaten to leave me. Put up some tobacco to send to the Gros Ventres—

19—Charboneau and his family started for the Gros Ventres last night, being afraid to trust himself in the day time—a Mandan and his Wife Killed themselves yesterday, to not Outlive their relations that are dead—I was in hopes that the disease was almost at an end, but they are dying off 8 and 10 every day—and new cases of it daily—Were it will stop, God only Knows—In the hurry and confusion on the 17th some dog made way with one of my guns—the disease broke out in the Fort six days ago—

20—Three more died in the Village last night—The Wife of a young Mandan that caught the disease was suffering from the pain, her husband looked at her, and held down his head, he jumped up and said to his wife, When you was young, you were hansome, you are now ugly and going to leave me, but no, I will go with you, he took up his gun and shot her dead, and with his Knife ripped open his own belly— two young men (Rees) Killed themselves to day, one of them stabbed himself with a Knife and the other with an arrow—A young Ree that has been sick for some time with the small pox, and being alone in his lodge, thought that it was better to die than to be in so much pain, he began to rub the scabs untile blood was running all over his body, he rolled himself in the ashes, which almost burnt his soul out of his body—two days after he was perfectly well, it is a severe operation, but few are disposed to try it—however, it proved beneficial to him—

22—Cool pleasant weather. The disease still Keeps ahead, 8 and 10 die off daily. Thirty five Mandans have died, the Women and Children I Keep no account of—Several Mandans have came back to remain in the Village. One of my Soldiers—(Ree) died to day—Two young Mandans shot themselves this morning—News from the Little Village that the disease is getting worse and worse every day, it is now two months that it broke out—A Ree that has the small pox, and thinking that he was going to die, approached near his wife, a young woman of 19—and struck her in the head with his tommahawk, with the intent to Kill her, that she might go with him in the Other World—she is badly wounded, a few Minutes after he cut his throat, a report is in circulation that they intend to fire the Fort—Stationed guard in the Bastion.

25—An other Mandan cheif died to day—(The long fingers) total Number of Men that has died—50. I have turned out to be a first rate doctor St. Grādo, An Indian that has been bleeding at the Nose all day, I gave him a decoction of all sorts of ingredients Mixed together, enough to Kill a Buffaloe Bull of the largest size, and stopped the effusion of Blood, the decoction of Medicine was, a little Magnisia, peppermint, sugar lead, all Mixed together in a phial, filled with Indian grog—and the Patient snuffing up his nose three or four times—I done it out of experiment, and am content to say that it proved effectual—the Confidence that an Indian has in the Medicine of the whites is half the cure.

26—The Indians all started Out on the North side in the quest of Buffaloe, as they had Nothing to eat—A young Ree, the nephew of Garreau, died at the Village last night—A young Ree that has the small pox, told his Mother to go and dig his grave, she accordingly did so— after the grave was dug, he walked with the help of his Father to the grave. I Went Out with the Interpreter to try to persuade him to return back to the Village—but he would not, saying for the reason that all his young friends were gone, that he wished to follow them, towards evening he died—

28—Wind from the North, rain, disagreeable weather, Several more Indians arrived with fresh Meat—gave us a small quantity which we found very good—Three more fell sick in the Fort to day—My Interpreter for one, if I lose him I shall be badly off—

29—Last Night I was taken very sick with the Fever, there is six of us in the Fort that has the Fever, and one the small pox—An Indian Vaccinated his child by cutting two small pieces of flesh out of his arms, and two on the belly—and then takeing a Scab from one that was getting well of the disease, and rubbing it on the wounded part. Three days after, it took effect, and the child is perfectly well—

30—All those that I thought had the small pox turned out to be true, the fever left them yesterday, and the disease showed itself. I am perfectly well, as last night, I took a hot whiskey punch, which made me sweat all last night, this Morning I took my daily Bitters as usual.

31—A young Mandan that died 4 days ago, his wife haveing the disease also—Killed her two children, one a fine Boy of eight years, and the other six, to complete the affair she hung herself—

The Number of Deaths up to the Present is very near five hundred—the Mandans are all cut off, except 23 young and Old Men.

September 1—This Morning two dead bodies, wrapped in a White skin, and laid on a raft passed by the Fort, on their way to the regions below. May success attend them.

2—But one death to day, although several are sick, those that catch the disease at Present seldom die.

4—A young Mandan that was given over for dead, and abandoned by his Father, and left alone in the bushes to die, came to life again, and is now doing well. He is hunting his Father, with the intent to Kill him, for leaveing him alone.

19—All quiet to day—nothing worth relating has transpired, except that the day pleasant—I was visited by a young fellow from the Little Village, he assures Me that there is but 14 of them liveing, the Number of deaths Cannot be less than 800—What a bande of RASCALS has been used up—

SNAKEBITE. *Some case histories from* The Prairie Traveler, *an 1859 guidebook for pioneers heading west, written by Captain Randolph Marcy, of the U.S. Army, at the request of the War Department.*

I knew of another instance near Fort Towson, in Northern Texas, where a small child was left upon the earthen floor of a cabin while its mother was washing at a spring near by. She heard a cry of distress, and, on going to the cabin, what was her horror on seeing a rattlesnake coiled around the child's arm, and striking it repeatedly with its fangs. After killing the snake, she hurried to her nearest neighbor, procured a bottle of brandy, and returned as soon as possible; but the poison had already so operated upon the arm that it was as black as a negro's. She poured down the child's throat a huge draught of the liquor, which soon took effect, making it very drunk, and stopped the action of the poison. Although the child was relieved, it remained sick for a long time, but ultimately recovered.

A man was struck in the leg by a very large rattlesnake near Fort Belknap, Texas, in 1853. No other remedy being at hand, a small piece of indigo was pulverized, made into a poultice with water, and applied to the puncture. It seemed to draw out the poison, turning the indigo white, after which it was removed and another poultice applied. These applications were repeated until the indigo ceased to change its color. The man

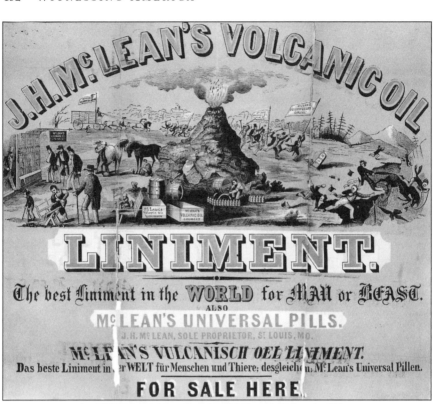

An 1855 broadside advertises McLean's Volcanic Oil—
"The best liniment in the world for man or beast."

was then carried to the hospital at Fort Belknap, and soon recovered, and the surgeon of the post pronounced it a very satisfactory cure.

A Chickasaw woman, who was bitten upon the foot near Fort Washita by a ground rattlesnake (a very venomous species), drank a bottle of whisky and applied the indigo poultice, and when I saw her, three days afterward, she was recovering, but the flesh around the wound sloughed away.

A Delaware remedy, which is said to be efficacious, is to burn powder upon the wound, but I have never known it to be tried excepting upon a horse. In this case it was successful, or, at all events, the animal recovered.

TOBACCO: TWO VIEWS. *John Josselyn, a seventeenth-century English traveler, after describing how the Indians smoked a tobacco called "Fishermen Poke," has this to say.*

The vertues of Tobacco are these, it helps digestion, the Gout, the Toothach, prevents infection by scents, it heats the cold, and cools them that sweat, feedeth the hungry, spent spirits restoreth, purgeth the stomach, killeth nits and lice, the juice of the green leaf healeth green wounds although poysoned, the Syrup for many diseases, the smoak for the Phthisick, cough of the lungs, distillations of Rheume, and all diseases of a cold and moist cause, good for all bodies cold and moist taken upon an emptie stomach . . .

Writing at the end of the nineteenth century, the crusading prohibitionist, Carry Nation, gives another view.

I am not only a reformer on the line of the licensed or unlicensed saloon, but on other evils. I believe that, on the whole, tobacco has done more harm than intoxicating drinks. The tobacco habit is followed by thirst for drink. The face of the smoker has lost the scintillations of intellect and soul it would have had if not marred by this vice. The odor of his person is vile, his blood is poisoned, his intellect is dulled.

A smoker is never a healthy man, either in body or mind, for nicotine is a poison. Nicotine poisons the blood, dulls the brain, and is the cause of disease. The lungs of the tobacco user are black from poison, his heart action is weak, and the worst thing to contemplate in the whole matter is that these tobacco users transmit nervous diseases, epilepsy, weakened constitutions, depraved appetites and deformities of all kinds to their offspring.

The tobacco user can never be the father of a healthy child. Therefore he is dangerous for a woman to have as a husband. If I were a young woman, I would say to the men who use tobacco and who would wish to converse with me: "Use the telephone; come no closer!" I would as soon kiss a spittoon as to kiss such a mouth.

YELLOW FEVER. *Samuel Breck, a Philadelphia merchant, on the epidemic of 1793, when more than four thousand people died.*

I had scarcely become settled in Philadelphia when in July, 1793, the yellow fever broke out, and, spreading rapidly in August, obliged all the citizens who could remove to seek safety in the country. My father took his family to Bristol on the Delaware, and in the last of August I followed him. Having engaged in commerce, and having a ship at the wharf loading for Liverpool, I was compelled to return to the city on the eighth of September and spend the ninth there. My business took me down to the Swedes' church and up Front street to Walnut street wharf, where I had my countinghouse. Everything looked gloomy, and forty-five deaths were reported for the ninth. In the afternoon, when I was about returning to the country, I passed by the lodgings of the Vicomte de Noailles, who had fled from the Revolutionists of France.

He was standing at the door, and calling to me, asked what I was doing in town. "Fly," said he, "as soon as you can, for pestilence is all around us." And yet it was nothing then to what it became three or four weeks later, when from the first to the twelfth of October one thousand persons died.

The public journals were engrossed by it, and related many examples of calamitous suffering. One of these took place on the property adjacent to my father's. The respectable owner, counting upon the comparative security of his remote residence from the heart of the town, . . . told me that in the height of the sickness, when death was sweeping away its hundreds a week, a man applied to him for leave to sleep one night on the stable floor. The gentleman, like every one else, inspired with fear and caution, hesitated. The stranger pressed his request, assuring him that he had avoided the infected parts of the city, that his health was very good, and promised to go away at sunrise the next day. Under these circumstances he admitted him into his stable for that night. At peep of day the gentleman went to see if the man

Columbia trying to save Florida from
strangulation by "Yellow Jack" yellow fever.
Drawing by Matt Morgan.

was gone. On opening the door he found him lying on the floor delirious and in a burning fever. Fearful of alarming his family, he kept it a secret from them, and went to the committee of health to ask to have the man removed.

That committee was in session day and night at the City Hall in Chestnut street. The spectacle around was new, for he had not ventured for some weeks so low down in town. The attendants on the dead stood on the pavement in considerable numbers soliciting jobs, and until employed they were occupied in feeding their horses out of the coffins which they had provided in anticipation of the daily wants. These speculators were useful, and, albeit with little show of feeling, contributed greatly to lessen, by competition, the charges of interment. The gentleman passed on through these callous spectators until he reached the room in which the committee was assembled, and from whom he obtained the services of a quack doctor, none other being in attendance. They went together to the stable, where the doctor examined the man, and then told the gentleman that at ten o'clock he would send the cart with a suitable coffin, into which he requested to have the dying stranger placed. The poor man was then alive and begging for a drink of water. His fit of delirium had subsided, his reason had returned, yet the experience of the *soi-disant* doctor enabled him to foretell that his death would take place in a few hours; it did so, and in time for his corpse to be conveyed away by the cart at the hour appointed.

Tombstone of Susanna Jayne, Marblehead, 1776. Death, crowned with a triumphal wreath, holds the sun in one hand and the moon in the other.

CHAPTER 11

DEPARTING

U NTIL RECENTLY, DEATH was a prominent part of daily life, a constant presence that was rarely welcome but also rarely denied. How could it be, when people died so easily and so early—when death, like doctors, still made house calls and people died at home in their beds rather than in hospitals? And then there were all those reminders: obituaries, eulogies, graveside orations, epitaphs, black veils for women and black hatbands and armbands for men, the tolling of the passing bell, the empty chair, the locket of hair . . .

So, a grim and constant presence. But for most people there have also been consolations: for some, the faith that they will meet again in heaven; for others, the prospect of being buried back home in their native country; and, for at least one Indian, a system of rewards and punishments that included, for those who have erred in this life, the chance of a second time around.

This chapter falls into two parts: The Departed, consisting of selected obituaries, and Aftermath, which tells of various burial customs and beliefs in the hereafter.

THE DEPARTED

PILGRIMS. *Governor William Bradford tells of the "Starving Time" in the winter of 1620–21, just after the Pilgrims had arrived at Plymouth.*

But that which was most sad and lamentable was, that in two or three months' time half of their company died, especially in January and February, being the depth of winter, and wanting houses and other comforts; being infected with scurvy and other diseases which this long voyage and their inaccommodate condition had brought upon them. So as there died some times two or three of a day in the foresaid time, that of 100 and odd persons, scarce fifty remained. And of these, in the time of most distress, there was but six or seven sound persons who to their great commendations, be it spoken, spared no pains night nor day, but with abundance of toil and hazard of their own health, fetched them wood, made them fires, dressed them meat, made their beds, washed their loathsome clothes, clothed and unclothed them. In a word, did all the homely and necessary offices for them which dainty and queasy stomachs cannot endure to hear named; and all this willingly and cheerfully, without any grudging in the least, showing herein their true love unto their friends and brethren; a rare example and worthy to be remembered. Two of these seven were Mr. William Brewster, their reverend Elder, and Myles Standish, their Captain and military commander, unto whom myself and many others were much beholden in our low and sick condition. And yet the Lord so upheld these persons as in this general calamity they were not at all infected either with sickness or lameness. And what I have said of these I may say of many others who died in this general visitation, and others yet living; that whilst they had health, yea, or any strength continuing, they were not wanting to any that had need of them. And I doubt not but their recompense is with the Lord.

YOUNG SYLVESTER. *From John Winthrop's journal, 1642.*

There fell out a very sad accident at Weymouth. One Richard Sylvester, having three small children, he and his wife going to the assembly, upon the Lord's day, left their children at home. The eldest was without doors looking to some cattle; the middle-most, being a son about five years old, seeing his father's fowling piece, (being a very great one,) stand in the chimney, took it and laid it upon a stool, as he had seen his father do, and pulled up the cock, (the spring being weak,) and put down the hammer, then went to the other end and blowed in the mouth of the piece, as he had seen his father also do, and with that stirring the piece, being charged, it went off, and shot the child into the mouth and through his head. When the father came home he found his child lie dead, and could not have imagined how he should have been so killed, but the youngest child, (being but three years old, and could scarce speak,) showed him the whole manner of it.

ELDER BREWSTER. *Governor William Bradford of Plymouth records the passing of his friend and fellow Pilgrim, Elder Brewster, in 1643.*

I am to begin this year with that which was a matter of great sadness and mourning unto them all. About the 18th of April died their

"Attack of Indians upon Daniel and Squire Boone and John Stewart, the last of whom was killed and scalped." Engraving by G. Murray in Humphrey Marshall's *History of Kentucky*, 1812.

Reverend Elder and my dear and loving friend Mr. William Brewster, a man that had done and suffered much for the Lord Jesus and the gospel's sake, and had borne his part in weal and woe with this poor persecuted church about 36 years in England, Holland and in this wilderness, and done the Lord and them faithful service in his place and calling. And notwithstanding the many troubles and sorrows he passed through, the Lord upheld him to a great age. He was near fourscore years of age (if not all out) when he died. He had this blessing added by the Lord to all the rest; to die in his bed, in peace, amongst the midst of his friends, who mourned and wept over him and ministered what help and comfort they could unto him, and he again recomforted them whilst he could. His sickness was not long, and till the last day thereof he did not wholly keep his bed. His speech continued till somewhat more than half a day, and then failed him, and about nine or ten a clock that evening he died without any pangs at all. A few hours before, he drew his breath short, and some few minutes before his last, he drew his breath long as a man fallen into a sound sleep without any pangs or gaspings, and so sweetly departed this life unto a better.

EYRE AND MAXWELL. *In his autobiography, the Reverend John Barnard tells of what happened soon after he entered Harvard in 1696.*

There were two accidents which happened while I was an undergraduate, that somewhat startled and awakened me. The one in the winter of my freshmanship, when a number of us went a skating upon what is called Fresh Pond in Watertown. Two lovely young gentlemen, John Eyre, of our class, son of Justice Eyre of Boston, and Maxwell, the class above me, a West Indian (which two only of all the company had asked leave of the Tutors to go out of town upon the diversion), being both good skaters, joined hand in hand, and flew away to the farther end of the pond; and as they were in like manner returning, they ran upon a small spot in the middle of the pond called the boiling hole (because rarely frozen over), which was open the day before but now had a skim of ice upon it about half an inch thick; and both of them broke the thin ice and plunged into the water. Maxwell rose not again, it being supposed he rose under the ice; Eyre rose in the hole they had broken, attempted to get upon the ice, but it gave way under him and plunged him anew. I, who happened to be nearest to them, ran towards the hole, called to Eyre only to keep his head above water by bearing his arms upon the thin ice, and we would help him with boards, which the rest of the company ran to fetch from a new house building by the edge of the pond, not twenty rods off; but he kept on his striving to get up, till it so worried him he sunk and rose no more; and thus both were drowned. It threw me into grievous anguish of mind to think I was so near my dear friend, within two rods, and yet it was impossible for me to help him. I went to the utmost edge of the thick ice, and raised my foot to take another step, but saw I must fall in as they had done. The boards arrived to the place within five minutes of Eyre's last sinking. The sight was truly shocking to me, and I plainly saw how soon and suddenly the providence of God might, by one means or another, snatch me out of the world, and what need I had to be always ready.

ROOSEVELT'S QUACK, PHILIPSE'S CUFFEE, JOHN HUGHSON, VAARCK'S CAESAR, AND OTHERS. *Following several major fires in the winter of 1740–41, a large number of blacks and a small number of whites were put on trial for conspiring to burn New York and massacre its citizens. This was known as The Great Negro Plot.*

Quack, Cuffee, and Caesar were slaves, identified by their owners' names. John Hughson, a white tavern keeper, was suspected of being a ringleader. He, his wife, and Caesar were hanged. This selection from the official account of the trial begins just after the attorney general has completed his case against Quack and Cuffee; there was no counsel for the defense.

Then the jury were charged, and a constable was sworn to attend them as usual; and they withdrew; and being soon returned, found the prisoners guilty of both indictments.

The prisoners were asked, what they had to offer in arrest of judgment, why they should not receive sentence of death? and they offered nothing but repetitions of protestations of their innocence; the third justice proceeded to sentence, as followeth.

Quack and Cuffee, the criminals at the bar,
You both now stand convicted of one of the most horrid and detestable pieces of villainy, that ever satan instilled into the heart of human creatures to put in practice: ye, and the rest of your colour, though you are called slaves in this country; yet are you all far, very far, from the condition of other slaves in other countries; nay, your lot is superior to that of thousands of white people. You are furnished with all the necessaries of life, meat, drink, and clothing, without care, in a much better manner than you could provide for yourselves, were you at liberty; as the miserable condition of many free people here of your complexion might abundantly convince you. What then could prompt you to undertake so vile, so wicked, so monstrous, so execrable and hellish a scheme, as to murder and destroy your own masters and benefactors? nay, to destroy root and branch, all the white people of this place, and to lay the whole town in ashes.

I know not which is the more astonishing, the extreme folly, or wickedness, of so base and shocking a conspiracy; for as to any view of liberty or government you could propose to yourselves, upon the success of burning the city, robbing, butchering and destroying the inhabitants; what could it be expected to end in, in the account of any rational and considerate person among you, but your own destruction? And as the wickedness of it, you might well have reflected, you that have sense, that there is a God above, who has always a clear view of all your actions, who sees into the most secret recesses of the heart, and knoweth all your thoughts; shall he not, do ye think, for all this bring you into judgment, at that final and great day of account, the day of judgment, when the most secret treachery will be disclosed, and laid open to the view, and every one will be rewarded according to their deeds, and their use of that degree of reason which God Almighty has entrusted them with?

Here ye must have justice, for the justice of human laws has at length overtaken ye, and we ought to be very thankful, and esteem it a most merciful and wondrous act of Providence, that your treacheries and villainies have been discovered; that your plot and contrivances, your hidden works of darkness have been brought to light, and stopped in their career; that in the same net which you have hid so privily for others your own feet are taken; that the same mischief which you have contrived for others, and have in part executed, is at length fallen upon your own pates, whereby the sentence which I am now to pronounce will be justified against ye; which is,

That you and each of you be carried from hence to the place from whence you came, and from thence to the place of execution, where you and each of you shall be chained to a stake, and burnt to death; and the lord have mercy upon your poor, wretched souls.

May 30, 1741. This day Quack and Cuffee were executed at the stake according to sentence. The spectators at this execution were very numerous; about three o'clock the criminals were brought to the stake, surrounded with piles of wood ready for setting fire to, which the people were very impatient to have done, their resentment being raised to the utmost pitch against them, and no wonder. The criminals shewed great terror in their countenances, and looked as if they would gladly have discovered all they knew of this accursed scheme, could they have had any encouragement to hope for a reprieve. But as the case was, they might flatter themselves with hopes: They both seemed inclinable to make some confession; the only difficulty between them at last being, who should speak first.

After the confessions were minuted down (which were taken in the midst of great noise and confusion) Mr. Moore desired the sheriff to delay the execution until the governor be acquainted therewith, and his pleasure known touching their reprieve; which, could it have been effected, it was thought might have been a means of producing great discoveries; but from the disposition observed in the spectators, it was much to be apprehended, there would have been great difficulty, if not danger in an attempt to take the criminals back. All this was represented to his honour [the governor]; and before Mr. Moore could return from him to the place of execution, he met the sheriff upon the common, who declared his opinion, that the carrying the negroes back would be impracticable; and if that was his honour's order it could not be attempted without a strong guard, which could not be got time enough; and his honour's directions for the reprieve being conditional and discretionary, for these reasons the execution proceeded.

July 3, 1741. This day Duane's Prince, Latham's Tony, Shurmur's Cato, Kip's Harry, and Marschalk's York, negroes, were executed at the gallows, according to sentence; and the body of York was afterwards hung in chains, upon the same gibbet with John Hughson.

Some few days after this the town was amused with a rumour, that Hughson was turned negro, and Vaarck's Caesar a white; and when they came to put up York in chains by Hughson (who was hung upon the gibbet three weeks before) so much of him as was visible, viz. face, hands, neck, and feet, were of a deep shining black, rather blacker than the negro placed by him, who was one of the darkest hue of his kind; and the hair of Hughson's beard and neck (his head could not be seen for he had a cap on) was curling like the wool of a negro's beard and head, and the features of his face were of the symmetry of a negro beauty; the nose broad and flat, the nostrils open and extended, the mouth wide, lips full and thick, his body (which when living was tall, by the view upwards of six feet, but very meagre) swelled to a gigantic size; and as to Caesar (who, though executed for a robbery, was also one of the head negro conspirators, had been hung up in chains a month before Hughson, and was also of the darkest complexion) his face was at the same time somewhat bleached or turned whitish, insomuch that it occasioned a remark, that Hughson and he had changed colours. The beholders were amazed at these appearances; the report of them engaged the attention of many, and drew numbers of all ranks, who had curiosity, to the gibbets, for several days running, in order to be convinced by their own eyes, of the reality of things so confidently reported to be, at least wondrous phenomenons, and upon the view they were found to be such as have been described; many of the spectators were ready to resolve them into miracles; however, others not so hasty, though surprized at the sights, were willing to account for them in a natural way, so that they administered matter for much speculation.

The sun at this time had great power, and the season as usual very hot, that Hughson's body dripped and distilled very much, as it needs must, from the great fermentation and abundance of matter within him, as could not but be supposed at that time, from the extraordinary bulk of his body; though considering the force of the sun, and the natural meagreness of his corpse, one would have been apt to imagine that long ere this it would have been disencumbered of all its juices. At length, about ten days or a fortnight after Hughson's mate, York, was hung by him, Hughson's corpse, unable longer to contain its load, burst and discharged pail fulls of blood and corruption; this was testified by those who were near by, fishing upon the beach when the irruption happened, to whom the stench of it was very offensive.

M. DE MEAUX. *Moreau de St. Méry, an aristocrat who fled the French Revolution and set up as a bookseller in Philadelphia, tells how lightning struck in that city.*

Violent thunder is often heard, but thanks to the remedy recommended by the immortal Franklin, Philadelphia is preserved from the misfortunes resulting from it. On the other hand, also, it seems to be a greater threat to houses where the preservative is neglected. Wednesday, March 27, 1782, lightning struck the house of the Minister of France in three places. It knocked down M. le Chevalier de la Luzerne's chimney to the level of the roof, broke the cast-iron stove which closed the opening of the chimney, broke all adjacent plaster, smashed furniture and windowpanes. It started a fire on the roof, set the curtains ablaze, entered the dining room, split two mahogany sideboards, and broke all the porcelain. Papers were burned in another room. Lastly it wounded M. de Meaux, officer of the French artillery, breaking his left arm and burning the lower part of his belly and his genital organs, so that he died of it the seventh day afterwards.

WILLIAM HARVERSON AND DAVID RUSSELL. *A cautionary tale by Parson Mason Locke Weems from his book* The Drunkard's Looking Glass, *circa 1810.*

CASE XXIV. Of William Harverson, who, in the demoniac of drunkenness, murdered David Russell; for which he was hung. Communicated by an *eye witness* of his execution.

William Harverson was born in the neighborhood of Camden, S. Carolina. Nature had been much more liberal to his *person* than his parents had been to his *mind:* for, while the former was erect and handsome as an angel, the latter, from defect of education, was deformed and grovelling as the beast that perisheth. For some offence, not well known to the writer, nor very important to the reader, he was confined in prison bounds in Camden. The bounds were large, extending nearly to Pinetree creek, a quarter of a mile south and east of the town. In the same prison was a poor little man, David Russell by name, and by profession a taylor; but being, as perhaps all taylors ought to be, of very diminutive size, he was generally called, not David Russell, but *"the little taylor."* The reader will please to take notice, that this little man was not in prison for debts, or misdemeanor, but from choice, working very honestly for the jailor and his family.

Placed together in this situation, with scarcely any other society than themselves, Harverson and the little taylor soon contracted a friendship.

After some time, the taylor's work being done in Camden, he took it into his head to go down to Statesburgh. *'Well, Mr. Harverson,'* said he, 'I am going down to Statesburgh to look for work; suppose you go with me as far as the creek, and we'll take a parting drink together; for God only knows when we shall see each other again.'

'*With all my heart,*' replied Harverson. Accordingly, soon as dinner was over, they went down to the creek, and sitting on an old tree, began to drink, from a bottle of rum, which the little taylor had brought with him. The little taylor was soon quite tipsey, rocking and reeling on the log where he sat; Harverson too was quite groggy, but not deprived of the power to move. Now, here comes the dreadful part of the story, and sufficient, God knows, to cause all drunkards to tremble for themselves. Harverson, all at once, conceives the horrible idea to murder his companion! With this bloody view, he staggers across the creek to an old indigo vat, where he found a rusty sledge hammer that had been left there by the workmen!! Oh, awful proof, that if the devil can but engage a wretched soul to do his work, he will soon put a fit instrument into his hand. With the sledge hammer on his shoulder, Harverson staggers back to his ill-fated comrade, and finding him still sitting on his log, quite silly, and reeling with his liquor, he lifted his cruel iron, and gave him a blow direct on his forehead.

Down fell the poor little taylor, but not killed, as might have been expected, by the blow, but on the contrary, as if roused by it to his recollection, he stretched his hands to his murderer, and cried out, though but with a feeble voice, '*Oh Harverson! don't kill me! don't kill me! If I have any thing that you want, take it, but oh spare my life!*'

This brought the wretch to a pause; but being drunk, and brutish as the swine that devours its own young, he regarded not the cries of the poor fallen supplicant, but lifting his blood-stained hammer, he dashed out his brains. He then took the dead body, and dragging it down the steep bank of the creek, covered it with leaves.

No suspicion was awakened concerning the little taylor, as it was supposed by his acquaintance in Camden that he was gone down to Statesburgh. However, in a few days, some young men passing that way to shoot ducks, and seeing a gang of buzzards fly up, went to the spot, and found the dead body, which was immediately known. From the ghastly marks on the skull, the jury reported it a *murder case.* A hot search was commenced after the murderer, who was presently found; for learning that Harverson was the last person seen in the company of the deceased, the officers of justice arrested him on the spot, and charged him with the crime. He made no scruple to confess the deed; and also confessed that he knew not *why he had done it.* '*He had no manner of ill-will against the little taylor,*' he said, but on the contrary liked him well; and, after striking him the first blow, felt as if he would have given as many worlds as there are stars in the heavens, if he had never done it. But seeing him pale, and trembling all over as in great misery, and concluding from his gushing blood, that he could never recover, he thought it would be mercy to kill him at once, and thereupon gave him the second blow, which put him to rest.

A gallows was erected for the miserable Harverson, on the very spot where he committed the murder, and his grave was dug by the side of the little taylor; but he was not buried there; for his brother John Harverson, with a coffin in his cart, came and begged the body, which was given him. At sight of his brother William, with a rope around his neck, John could not speak, and fell into a severe ague. His sister, a poor woman with a little child in her arms, came to see him die. He took her tenderly by the hand, and with tears told her that in their former innocent days, when they played so happily together, how little he thought of bringing upon her the pain of seeing him die in such a way *as that.* 'But *drink, drink,'* continued he, lifting up his hands and eyes to heaven, *'drink,* is that *accursed D—l,* that has undone me.' At this she wept bitterly. Her child lay asleep in his mother's arms; but waked by her scalding tears, he started up, and with the looks of an infant angel waking, he crowed and jumped, and stretched his little arms to his uncle, as if he wished to go to him. What it was that passed through the mind of the unhappy man I know not; but at sight of that dear innocent with shining face and sweet blue eyes, reaching towards him, he looked much troubled,—He took the child by the hand and said—'poor little nephew, I ought to have lived to be a friend to you; but my sins have cut me off. This moment we meet, and now we are going to part again, perhaps for ever. Oh! had God but taken me out of the world when I was young and innocent, like you, I might have been happy! But poor miserable me! what is to become of me now, I don't know.' Here he uttered a deep groan, and lifting his eyes, saddened with penitence, to heaven, he cried *'Lord Jesus Christ have mercy on my soul!'* He then begged his sister never to mention *his name* to her child. 'But,' continued he with a sigh, 'I suppose he must hear of it; some wicked boy or other will throw it in his teeth. And that is what grieves *me,* to think that the accursed fruits of my sins cannot die with me, but must live to grieve my poor unoffending relations when I am dead and gone.'

He then asked the sheriff if he might be *allowed to pray.* The sheriff said, *'to be sure.'* Whereupon, looking round upon the people, he asked them if they would join a *poor dying Sinner in his last prayer.* At this the looks of the people became like the soft clouds of spring melting into showers. Seeing their fellow feeling for him in their tearful eyes, and closer gathering round him, he fell upon his knees, and made one of the most moving and powerful prayers ever heard. At the close of his prayer, there appeared on his countenance a *serenity* so divine as utterly astonished the beholders. Several Christian people who were present declared openly, that they could see in his looks that he had heard that voice which once said to the dying penitent— *This day thou shalt be with me in Paradise.'* On rising from his knees, he said to the sheriff, *'well, I believe my hour is come.'* Then looking round the crowd, he cried, *'God bless you all! and preserve you and your children from the curses of drunkenness.'* These were the last words that he was heard to say, for instantly thereafter he let *drop his handkerchief* which was the sign agreed upon betwixt himself and the sheriff, and the cart drove from under him.

MAJOR ANTHONY. *As recorded by the New York merchant Philip Hone in his diary, June 14, 1838.*

Some time last winter a personal dispute occurred, during the session of the House of Representatives of the State of Arkansas, between a Mr. Wilson, the Speaker then presiding, and Major Anthony, a member, in the course of which the former came down from his chair, drew a large knife (a weapon which it appears these modern barbarians carry about their persons), attacked his adversary and killed him on the spot. Anthony endeavoured to defend himself (he had also his knife); but the movement of the honourable Speaker was so sudden as to render his efforts ineffectual, and I suppose it was "out of order" for other members to interfere in the parliamentary discipline of their presiding officer.

Wilson has been tried for this flagrant outrage. There is a full account of the trial in the newspapers, taken from the Arkansas "Gazette." From the testimony it does not appear that any violent provocation was offered by the deceased, and the facts above-stated were substantially proved, notwithstanding which the verdict of the jury was as follows: "Guilty of excusable homicide, and not guilty in any manner or form as charged in the indictment;" and the prisoner was discharged from custody. Further accounts state that immediately after this mockery of justice, the jurors, with the sheriffs and witnesses, had a grand drinking frolic at the expense of the defendant.

PRESIDENT WILLIAM HENRY HARRISON AND OTHERS. *Some selections from the* New-Yorker *issues of April and May 1841. The* New-Yorker *was a weekly newspaper edited by Horace Greeley, who later converted it into the* Tribune.

April 3 The Steamboat Creole, Captain Balman, on her passage down the Mississippi, caught fire near the mouth of Red River, and was immediately wrapped in flames. *Her tiller-ropes were instantly burnt off,* (she being unprovided with the tiller chains expressly required by act of Congress,) when she of course became unmanageable, and, directed by the current, was hurled forward by the doubled power of her red-hot boilers and machinery. She soon struck the shore, and many passengers jumped to reach it, but very few succeeded—the rest were drowned and the boat rebounded into the current. The number of persons on board was about seventy, of whom about thirty are missing—drowned. The officers all escaped. The cause of the fire is not stated.

DEATH OF THE PRESIDENT!
City of Washington, April 4, 1841.

An all-wise Providence having suddenly removed from this life, WILLIAM HENRY HARRISON, late president of the United States, we have thought it our duty, in the recess of Congress, and in the absence of the Vice President from the Seat of Government, to make this afflicting bereavement known to the country, by this declaration under our hands.

He died at the President's House, in this city, this fourth day April, Anno Domini, 1841, at thirty minutes before one o'clock in the morning.

The People of the United States, overwhelmed, like ourselves, by an event so unexpected and so melancholy, will derive consolation from knowing that his death was calm and resigned, as his life has been patriotic, useful and distinguished; and that the last utterance of his lips expressed a fervent desire for the perpetuity of the Constitution, and the preservation of its true principles. In death, as in life, the happiness of his country was uppermost in his thoughts.

DANIEL WEBSTER, Secretary of State.

THOMAS EWING, Secretary of the Treasury.

JOHN BELL, Secretary of War.

J.J. CRITTENDEN, Attorney General.

FRANCIS GRANGER, Postmaster General.

The Nation's Calamity.—We have hardly words to express our sense of the great affliction which has this week befallen the American People in the death of WILLIAM HENRY HARRISON, so lately inaugurated President of the United States. It seems like a dream—a sad and fearful illusion of the fancy—that he who was but yesterday called by a vast majority of the popular suffrages to the highest station in the People's gift—whose route from Ohio to Washington was marked by all the honors of a Roman triumph—who was inducted into the Chief Magistracy of this great and free Nation amid the joyous acclamations of an immense concourse of citizens—that he who had passed through so many perils and trials in the course of a long and eventful life, should have attained at last the summit of human ambition only to fold his robes around him and lie down in the unwaking slumber of Death! Why, what a bubble is Ambition!—what a mockery is Fame!—

One little week since, and thousands would have walked over burning ploughshares to exchange positions with the man; and now he is but dust and ashes, on which the clods are heavily closing! Who can ever struggle for power, save for noble ends and holiest uses?

April 10. William Boyd, Esq. Superintendent of the Susquehanna and Tide Water Canal, was drowned at Havre-de-Grace, Md., on the 18th inst. He was riding with a lady on the tow-path, when his horse took fright and leapt with him into the basin. Before medical aid could be procured he was past recovery.

Accidental Death.—A ship carpenter, named Horatio Doughty, fell from the sloop of war Fairfield, at the Brooklyn Navy Yard, on the 6th inst. into the water and was drowned.

In the conflagration of a dwelling-house on the 20th. ult in Jefferson Co. La., twelve negroes were burnt to death.

A Riot occurred at the Twelfth Ward of this City on Monday evening, on the occasion of the meeting of the Van Buren party to confirm the nomination of its Ward Committee. Two parties appeared on the spot, and the friends of the 'regular' ticket were overpowered and dreadfully beaten. One man was taken up for dead; another had his arm broken. The actors in this disgraceful fracas were nearly all Irishmen, and the grounds of dispute were entirely local and personal in their character.

April 17. Tragical Development.—Great excitement prevails in Owego, Tioga Co., in consequence of the mysterious disappearance of a female named Jane M'Allister and the subsequent discovery of her dead body. It appears that she was a servant in the family of a Mr. Truman, where she had been treated with uniform kindness. On the evening of Nov. 27, 1840, she was rebuked for some negligence, at which she took great offence. She retired to bed at about 10 o'clock; the next morning all the doors leading from her chamber to the outer door were found open, and she had disappeared. From that time no trace of her could be gained, until the 27th ult., when her body was found floating in the river at Skinner's Eddy, Pa. about sixty miles below Owego. On her head were discovered several wounds, although it was impossible to ascertain with certainty whether they were inflicted before or after her death. The verdict of the Coroner's Jury was 'that she came to her death from causes unknown to the Jury, probably by violence.' It is said that on the night of her disappearance screams were heard on the bridge at Owego, and that the planks were disarranged, as if they had been taken up and badly replaced. The whole affair remains a subject of the vaguest conjecture.

Shocking Accident.—While Mr. Martin Mikesell of Cambria Co. Penn. and his wife were absent from home at a sugar camp, their house took fire and was totally destroyed, with all its contents. When they returned they found their dwelling in ruins, and that three little children left in it had perished in the flames.

Another Shocking Steamboat Accident.—A little past 6 o'clock last Tuesday evening, 27th inst., as the steam towboat HENRY ECKFORD, Capt. Tice, was leaving the dock at the foot of Cedar-street, North River, and just as the escape of steam through the chimney had been stopped, her boiler burst with a tremendous explosion, tearing her machinery and upper works to fragments, and killing or wounding nearly every one on board—as follows:

Capt. Tice, blown 69 feet across the slip, over the lake-boat in tow, into the water: one leg broken, and otherwise severely injured—not scalded. His recovery is doubtful.

Mr. Belshow, of the lake-boat in tow, was killed outright; struck by a piece of the cylinder, and terribly mangled.

A fireman nearly killed; limbs broken, &c. The captain of an Eastern schooner alongside was knocked over by the water from the boiler, and one side of his face slightly scalded. The captain's wife (in the cabin) was immersed in water from the feeding cylinder, but not scalded.

The engine, piston, smoke-pipe, shafts, and upper work, wheel, pilot-house, deck-cabin, &c. were blown completely away—most of them into the river, so that they cannot be found. One-half the boiler is pushed forward, and remains on the boat; the other half was blown into the river. The steam and contents of the boiler were blown out aft, so that very little injury by scalding was experienced. The wreck was taken in tow by the Citizen for the foot of Seventeenth street, East River; but she was sinking so fast that it was by no means probable that she would reach her destination.

The Henry Eckford was probably the oldest steamboat running in the vicinity of New-York. She was built some seventeen years ago by Eckford, and has been used as a tow-boat on the River and in the Harbor.

The customary stereotype phrase on such occasions imports that "No blame can be attached to any one." We cannot use it here. It seems to us that there was gross recklessness of life evinced in the running of so old and worn-out a boat—that her engineer must have been unqualified for his station—and that the *United States Inspector* who examines and licenses boats has been grossly unfaithful to his duty. We will not pursue this subject now, but await farther developments.

A man who was on the wharf at the time, remarked to us that he was looking at the Eckford as she started, and heard her *squeal* when the

"Finale." Sheriff Pat Garrett fells Billy the Kid with a single shot in this woodcut from *Beadles Half-Dime Library*. The event took place at Fort Sumner, New Mexico in 1881.

escaping steam was shut off. He instantly observed—"There is too much steam on—we had better get away from here." The next instant a roar as of cannon was heard, and a cloud of steam, pierced by flying fragments of boiler, engine, works, &c. proclaimed that the boat was a ruin.

We understand that three or four persons are missing in addition to those above mentioned—possibly escaped, but more probably blown into the river—dead.

May 1. Murder and Robbery at St. Louis. A correspondent of the Commercial Advertiser, in a letter dated St. Louis, April 18th inst. says:

"The city is this morning in the greatest state of excitement that I ever saw. Some robbers last night entered the store of Muns, Simmons & Robinson, and murdered two clerks, after which they took what they could find and set fire to the building; this morning that elegant store lies a heap of smoking ruins. Collier & Pettis's banking house, being in the same building, is also consumed.

The two young men were highly respectable, and their loss is mourned by all. Several thousand people are at this moment standing round the ruins, hoping to find the remains of Mr. Baker; the other, Mr. Weaver, was found with his face much cut by a Bowie knife, and a pistol shot over the eye. They were both, I believe, from New-York.

Another man was killed by the falling of walls. The citizens met this morning and offered a reward of $5000. Every boat leaving the port is boarded by the police officers; one has just returned with a suspected man."

May 12. Trouble at Fort Snelling.—The Galena Gazette says:—"There have been rumors in town for several days past of difficulty between the Sioux and the United States troops at Fort Snelling. The following comes from a gentleman from Prairie du Chien, and is most likely nearly correct. He says, an Indian attempting to get into the garrison at night was shot by a soldier. The Indians, upon this, demanded the surrender of the sentinel for punishment. Upon the demand being refused, they surrounded the Fort, and exhibited such indications of hostility as to induce the commandant to send an express to Fort Crawford (Prairie du Chien) for reinforcements, which went up on the Chippewa. We apprehend no serious difficulty from this source. There are several boats above, and we expect to hear later news in a day or two."

Gen. Leigh Read killed!—The Tallahasee (Florida) Sentinel of April 30th says: "We regret to state that Gen. Leigh Read, of this place, was shot in the street on Monday morning last, by Mr. Willis Alston. He expired in about fourteen hours afterward. We forbear making any comments, as the affair will undergo a legal investigation. Two other persons were (accidentally, we presume) wounded—one severely, though we trust not mortally."

BRIDGET SUCH-A-ONE. *Henry David Thoreau and a friend witness the aftermath of a shipwreck.*

We left Concord, Massachusetts, on Tuesday, October 9th, 1849. On reaching Boston, we found that the Provincetown steamer, which should have got in the day before, had not yet arrived, on account of a violent storm; and, as we noticed in the streets a handbill headed, "Death! one hundred and forty-five lives lost at Cohasset," we decided to go by way of Cohasset. We found many Irish in the cars, going to identify bodies and to sympathize with the survivors, and also to attend the funeral which was to take place in the afternoon; and when we arrived at Cohasset, it appeared that nearly all the passengers were bound for the beach, which was about a mile distant, and many other persons were flocking in from the neighboring country. There were several hundreds of them streaming off over Cohasset common in that direction, some on foot and some in wagons, and among them were some sportsmen in their hunting-jackets, with their guns, and game-bags, and dogs. As we passed the graveyard we saw a large hole, like a cellar, freshly dug there, and, just before reaching the shore, by a pleasantly winding and rocky road, we met several hay-riggings and farm-wagons coming away toward the meeting-house, each loaded with three large, rough deal boxes. We did not need to ask what was in them. The owners of the wagons were made the undertakers. Many horses in carriages were fastened to the fences near the shore, and, for a mile or more, up and down, the beach was covered with people looking out for bodies, and examining the fragments of the wreck. There was a small island called Brook Island, with a hut on it, lying just off the shore. This is said to be the rockiest shore in Massachusetts, from Nantasket to Scituate,—hard sienitic rocks, which the waves have laid bare, but have not been able to crumble. It has been the scene of many a shipwreck.

The brig St. John, from Galway, Ireland, laden with emigrants, was wrecked on Sunday morning; it was now Tuesday morning, and the sea was still breaking violently on the rocks. There were eighteen or twenty of the same large boxes that I have mentioned, lying on a green hill-side, a few rods from the water, and surrounded by a crowd. The bodies which had been recovered, twenty-seven or eight in all, had been collected there. Some were rapidly nailing down the lids, others were carting the boxes away, and others were lifting the lids, which were yet loose, and peeping under the cloths, for each body, with such rags as still adhered to it, was covered loosely with a white sheet. I witnessed no signs of grief, but there was a sober despatch of business which was affecting. One man was seeking to identify a particular body, and one undertaker or carpenter was calling to another to know in what box a certain child was put. I saw many marble feet and matted heads as the cloths were raised, and one livid, swollen, and mangled body of a drowned girl,—who probably had intended to go out to service in some American family,—to which some rags still adhered, with a string, half concealed by the flesh, about its swollen neck; the coiled-up wreck of a human hulk, gashed by the rocks or fishes, so that the bone and muscle were exposed, but quite bloodless,—merely red and white,—with wide-open and staring eyes, yet lustreless, dead-lights; or like the cabin windows of a stranded vessel, filled with sand. Sometimes there were two or more children, or a parent and child, in the same box, and on the lid would perhaps be written with red chalk, "Bridget such-a-one, and sister's child." The surrounding sward was covered with bits of sails and clothing. I have since heard, from one who lives by this beach, that a woman who had come over before, but had left her infant behind for her sister to bring, came and looked into these boxes, and saw in one,—probably the same whose superscription I have quoted,—her child in her sister's arms, as if the sister had meant to be found thus; and within three days after, the mother died from the effect of that sight.

We kept on down the shore as far as a promontory called Whitehead, that we might see more of the Cohasset Rocks. In a little cove, within half a mile, there were an old man and his son collecting, with their team, the sea-weed which that fatal storm had cast up, as serenely employed as if there had never been a wreck in the world, though they were within sight of the Grampus Rock, on which the St. John had struck. The old man had heard that there was a wreck, and knew most of the particulars, but he said that he had not been up there since it happened. It was the wrecked weed that concerned him most, rock-weed, kelp, and sea-weed, as he named them, which he carted to his barn-yard; and those bodies were to him but other weeds which the tide cast up, but which were of no use to him. We afterwards came to the life-boat in its harbor, waiting for another emergency,— and in the afternoon we saw the funeral procession at a distance, at the head of which walked the captain with the other survivors.

HIRAM MALICK. *From a letter written to the rest of her family back East by Abigail Malick in October 1850. The family were on their way to the Oregon Territory. Her son Hiram was seventeen years old.*

I never shal see eney of you eny More in this world. We Are Almost three thousand Miles apart. I would like to se My sweet littl Ann And Homer And the other two but I never Shall. . . . And you never Will see Hiram. . . . Hiram drounded in the Plat River At the Mouth of Dear Krick. He went Aswiming with some other boys of the Compeny that we Trailed with And he swum Acrost the river and the Water run very fast And he could not reach this side. The young Men tried to save him but he had the Cramp And Could swim no more. And they Said o hiram do swim but he said I cannot swim eney More. And one young Man took A pole And started to him And the water ran so fast that he thought he Could not swim eney more so he returned And left him to his fate. And the other boys Called to him and said O hiram O swim. And he said o my god I cannot eney More. They said that he went down in the water seven or eight times before he drounded. And then he said o my god O lord gesus receive My Soul for I am no More. O yes I think that if ever A young Man went to their lord gesus that hee Did for he Always Was A very good boy and that knew him liked him. So you know All about Hiram's death now. So you need not ask eneything About him eney More. It has Almost kild Me but I have to bear it. And if we Are good perhapes then we can meete him in heven.

ESCAPED SLAVE. *This story appears as a footnote to* The Cotton Kingdom *by Frederick Law Olmsted. The year is 1854.*

From the *West Feliciana Whig.*—On Saturday last, a runaway negro was killed in the parish of East Baton Rouge, just below the line of this parish, under the following circumstances: Two citizens of Port Hudson, learning that a negro was at work on a flat boat, loading with sand, just below that place, who was suspected of being a runaway, went down in a skiff for the purpose of arresting him.

Having seized him and put him into the skiff they started back, but had not proceeded far when the negro, who had been at the oars, seized a hatchet and assaulted one of them, wounding him very seriously. A scuffle ensued, in which both parties fell overboard. They were both rescued by the citizen pulling to them with the skiff. Finding him so unmanageable, the negro was put ashore, and the parties returned to Port Hudson for arms and a pack of negro dogs [dogs trained to track runaway slaves], and started again with the intention to capture him. They soon got on his trail, and when found again he was standing at bay upon the outer edge of a large raft of drift wood, armed with a club and pistol.

In this position he bade defiance to men and dogs—knocking the latter into the water with his club, and resolutely threatening death to any man who approached him. Finding him obstinately determined not to surrender, one of his pursuers shot him. He fell at the third fire, and so determined was he not to be captured, that when an effort was made to rescue him from drowning he made battle with his club, and sunk waving his weapon in angry defiance at his pursuers. He refused to give the name of his owner.

IRISH LABORERS. *From the diary of George Templeton Strong, a New York lawyer.*

July 7, 1857. Yesterday morning I was spectator of a strange, weird, painful scene. Certain houses of John Watts DePeyster are to be erected on the northwest corner of this street and Fourth Avenue, and the deep excavations therefor are in progress. Seeing a crowd on the corner, I stopped and made my way to a front place. The earth had caved in a few minutes before and crushed the breath out of a pair of ill-starred Celtic laborers. They had just been dragged, or dug, out, and lay white and stark on the ground where they had been working, ten or twelve feet below the level of the street. Around them were a few men who had got them out, I suppose, and fifteen or twenty Irish women, wives, kinfolk or friends, who had got down there in some inexplicable way. The men were listless and inert enough, but not so the women. I suppose they were "keening"; all together were raising a wild, unearthly cry, half shriek and half song, wailing as a score of daylight Banshees, clapping their hands and gesticulating passionately. Now and then one of them would throw herself down on one of the corpses, or wipe some trace of defilement from the face of the dead man with her apron, slowly and carefully, and then resume her lament. It was an uncanny sound to hear, quite new to me.

ELIZABETH ALCOTT. *From the journal of Louisa May Alcott. Elizabeth was known in the family as Betty, Lizzie, and Beth.*

1857 July.—Grandma Alcott came to visit us. A sweet old lady; and I am glad to know her, and see where Father got his nature. Eighty-four; yet very smart, industrious, and wise. A house needs a grandma in it.

August.—A sad, anxious month. Betty worse; Mother takes her to the seashore. Father decides to go back to Concord; he is never happy far from Emerson, the one true friend who loves and understands and helps him.

September.—An old house near R.W.E.'s is bought with Mother's money, and we propose to move. Mother in Boston with poor Betty, who is failing fast.

October.—Move to Concord. . . . Find dear Betty a shadow, but sweet and patient always. Fit up a nice room for her, and hope home and love and care may keep her.

November.—Father goes West, taking Grandma home. We settle down to our winter, whatever it is to be. Lizzie seems better, and we have some plays. Sanborn's school makes things lively, and we act a good deal.

Twenty-five this month. I feel my quarter of a century rather heavy on my shoulders just now. I lead two lives. One seems gay with plays, etc., the other very sad,—in Betty's room; for though she wishes us to act, and loves to see us get ready, the shadow is there, and Mother and I see it. Betty loves to have me with her; and I am with her at night, for Mother needs rest. Betty says she feels "strong" when I am near. So glad to be of use.

December.—Some fine plays for charity.

January, 1858.—Lizzie much worse; Dr. G. says there is no hope. A hard thing to hear; but if she is only to suffer, I pray she may go soon. She was glad to know she was to "get well," as she called it, and we tried to bear it bravely for her sake. We gave up plays; Father came home; and Anna took the housekeeping, so that Mother and I could devote ourselves to her. Sad, quiet days in her room, and strange nights keeping up the fire and watching the dear little shadow try to while away the long sleepless hours without troubling me. She sews, reads, sings softly, and lies looking at the fire,—so sweet and patient and so worn, my heart is broken to see the change. I wrote some lines one night on "Our Angel in the House."

February.—A mild month; Betty very comfortable, and we hope a little.

Dear Betty is slipping away, and every hour is too precious to waste, so I'll keep my lamentations over Nan till this duty is over.

Lizzie makes little things, and drops them out of windows to the school-children, smiling to see their surprise. In the night she tells me to be Mrs. Gamp, when I give her her lunch, and tries to be gay that I may keep up. Dear little saint! I shall be better all my life for these sad hours with you.

March 14th.—My dear Beth died at three this morning, after two years of patient pain. Last week she put her work away, saying the needle was "too heavy," and having given us her few possessions, made ready for the parting in her own simple, quiet way. For two days she suffered much, begging for ether, though its effect was gone. Tuesday she lay in Father's arms, and called us round her, smiling contentedly as she said, "All here!" I think she bid us good-by then, as she held our hands and kissed us tenderly. Saturday she slept, and at midnight became unconscious, quietly breathing her life away till three; then, with one last look of the beautiful eyes, she was gone.

A curious thing happened, and I will tell it here, for Dr. G. said it was a fact. A few moments after the last breath came, as Mother and I sat silently watching the shadow fall on the dear little face, I saw a light mist rise from the body, and float up and vanish in the air. Mother's eyes followed mine, and when I said, "What did you see?" she described the same light mist. Dr. G. said it was the life departing visibly.

For the last time we dressed her in her usual cap and gown, and laid her on her bed,—at rest at last. What she had suffered was seen in the face; for at twenty-three she looked like a woman of forty, so worn was she, and all her pretty hair gone.

On Monday Dr. Huntington read the Chapel service, and we sang her favorite hymn. Mr. Emerson, Henry Thoreau, Sanborn, and John Pratt, carried her out of the old home to the new one at Sleepy Hollow chosen by herself. So the first break comes, and I know what death means,—a liberator for her, a teacher for us.

CAL SURCEY. *While driving a herd of cattle from Mexico to Wyoming in 1873, Nat Love and his fellow cowboys were subjected to a night attack while crossing Indian Territory (now eastern Oklahoma). In his memoirs, Love—born a slave and now known as Deadwood Dick—tells what happened the next day.*

We thought it advisable to move our herd on to a more desirable and safe camping place, not that we greatly feared any more trouble from the Indians, not soon at any rate, but only to be better prepared and in better shape to put up a fight if attacked. The second night we camped on the open plain where the grass was not so high and where the camp could be better guarded. After eating our supper and placing the usual watch the men again turned in, expecting this time to get a good night's rest. It was my turn to take the first watch and with the other boys, who were to watch with me, we took up advantageous positions on the lookout. Everything soon became still, the night was dark and sultry. It was getting along toward midnight when all at once we became aware of a roaring noise in the north like thunder, slowly growing louder as it approached, and I said to the boys that it must be a buffalo stampede. We immediately gave the alarm and started for our herd to get them out of the way of the buffalo, but we soon found that despite our utmost efforts we would be unable to get them out of the way, so we came to the conclusion to meet them with our guns and try to turn the buffalo from our direction if possible, and prevent them from going through our herd. Accordingly all hands rode to meet the oncoming stampede, pouring volley after volley into the almost solid mass of rushing beasts, but they paid no more attention to us than they would have paid to a lot of boys with pea shooters. On they came, a maddened, plunging, snorting, bellowing mass of horns and hoofs. One of our companions, a young fellow by the name of Cal Surcey, who was riding a young horse, here began to have trouble in controlling his mount and before any of us could reach him his horse bolted right in front of the herd of buffalo and in a trice the horse and rider went down and the whole herd passed over them. After the herd had passed we could only find a few scraps of poor Cal's clothing, and the horse he had been riding was reduced to the size of a jack rabbit.

THE DESPERADO "CHUNK." *Miguel Otero, at the time (1876) a young man working for his family's dry goods and commission business, writes of Clay Allison in* My Life on the Frontier.

My stay in the vicinity of La Junta, El Moro and Trinidad brought me into contact with Clay Allison, who deserves to rank with the famous killers of the period. He was born in Tennessee in 1835 or thereabouts, and as a young man had moved to Texas to enter the cattle business. He was well on the road to becoming one of the cattle kings of the Texas Panhandle, when he became involved in a terrible fight with an old friend and neighbor. The trouble was so deep-rooted that it could not be settled amicably. So the two men agreed to fight it out—and here appears that grim humor that characterized Clay Allison.

It was agreed that a grave should be dug, six feet deep, six and a half feet long, and two feet wide. They were to strip themselves to the waist, sit down at the two ends of the grave with a bowie knife in the right hand of each. At a given signal they were to begin fighting and were not to stop till one or the other was dead. Finally, the survivor was to cover the victim with the earth removed in digging the grave. The story went that Allison killed his man but was himself so severely wounded in one of the legs that he was thereafter lame. It was also averred that Allison kept to the agreement and buried his dead enemy.

Another famous story concerns Clay Allison's killing of the desperado "Chunk." One day at a horse race meeting, Chunk and Allison met. They bore a mutual dislike for each other, so it was not long before they quarrelled and arranged a death duel.

Allison, with his flair for the bizarre, was contending that they mount horses, face each other at a distance of a hundred yards, and at a given signal run their horses toward each other, firing at pleasure, until one or both had dropped to the ground. But before an agreement could be reached the dinner bell rang, and Chunk suggested that they eat first and fight afterwards, saying that it would be better for the dead man to go to hell with a full belly. Allison agreed, and the two men went into the dining-room together taking seats at opposite ends of the long table, around the sides of which were seated several other guests. Allison placed his pistol beside his soup plate; Chunk laid his in his lap. As Allison was lifting his spoon to his mouth, Chunk quickly raised his pistol from his lap and fired. Allison, who had detected the move, dropped his spoon and dodged to one side, thus getting out of the line of fire. At the same time, he grabbed his pistol and fired. Chunk was hit in the center of the forehead, his head fell forward into his dish of soup.

Allison cooly replaced his pistol in its scabbard and resumed eating his soup. He then ate a full dinner leisurely and when he had finished arose and, taking the dinner bell from the shelf, went to the door and began to ring it vigorously, announcing: "Gentlemen, the proposed horse duel is now declared off, owing to an accident to one of the principals." All this time Chunk's body remained where it had fallen, and all who sat at the table were forced to go on with the meal as though nothing unusual had taken place.

IRISH CHILD. *From* How the Other Half Lives, *by Jacob Riis, a Danish-born journalist and photographer whose 1890 exposure of slum conditions did much to help the reform movement.*

That ignorance plays its part, as well as poverty and bad hygienic surroundings, in the sacrifice of life is of course inevitable. They go usually hand in hand. A message came one day last spring summoning me to a Mott Street tenement in which lay a child dying from some unknown disease. With the "charity doctor" I found the patient on the top floor stretched upon two chairs in a dreadfully stifling room. She was gasping in the agony of peritonitis that had already written its death-sentence on her wan and pinched face. The whole family, father, mother, and four ragged children, sat around looking on with the stony resignation of helpless despair that had long since given up the fight against fate as useless. A

"End of the poor," a funeral from a tenement house on Baxter Street, Five Points, New York. Wood engraving in *Frank Leslie's Illustrated Newspaper,* July 1, 1865.

glance around the wretched room left no doubt as to the cause of the child's condition. "Improper nourishment," said the doctor, which, translated to suit the place, meant starvation. The father's hands were crippled from lead poisoning. He had not been able to work for a year. A contagious disease of the eyes, too long neglected, had made the mother and one of the boys nearly blind. The children cried with hunger. They had not broken their fast that day, and it was then near noon. For months the family had subsisted on two dollars a week from the priest, and a few loaves and a piece of corned beef which the sisters sent them on Saturday. The doctor gave direction for the treatment of the child, knowing that it was possible only to alleviate its sufferings until death should end them, and left some money for food for the rest. An hour later, when I returned, I found them feeding the dying child with ginger ale, bought for two cents a bottle at the pedlar's cart down the street. A pitying neighbor had proposed it as the one thing she could think of as likely to make the child forget its misery. There was enough in the bottle to go round to the rest of the family. In fact, the wake had already begun; before night it was under way in dead earnest.

AFTERMATH

THE CONSOLATION OF FAITH. *A letter from the Reverend John Cotton to Mary Hinckley, Plymouth, January 10, 1683.*

Hearing that you are deeply dejected under the late bereaving stroke of God's hand in your family, I cannot but, in conscience of my duty to God and in compassion to you—whom my blessed father loved, and whom I much respect in the Lord—speak a few words, that may by divine blessing tend to allay that excessive grief that hath taken hold of you. Consider, I beseech you, what is done and who hath done it and why is it done. You have lost a dear grandchild by an ordinary disease. What is there in this more than the common portion of the children of men—yea, and of the children of God?

If God deals with you as with a child, you have hereby an evidence of your adoption. You will not be cast down because God seals His fatherly love to your soul by this correction. God hath done what is done, and He did you no wrong. His right was greater to that little one than yours. It was covenant-seed, and God hath made haste to accomplish all covenant-mercy to it. I hope this will not grieve you. A babe embraced in the arms of Jesus Christ, the redeemer and shepherd of these lambs, lies safer and more comfortably than in the bosom of the most tender-hearted grandmother. Will this grieve you? What did you intend in the keeping of this child, if it had lived? Certainly you meant, while it was with you, to train it up for the Lord; and did you not often pray for it, that its soul might be accepted in the covenant of grace? All your good purposes, desires, and prayers are answered in this, that it is safe in Heaven. Your work is rewarded to the utmost of the wishes of your heart; and who can tell (but He that knows all our hearts) how much you needed this affliction, and how much spiritual good God intends to your soul hereby? Weaning dispensations are very merciful to a child of God. Our hearts cleave too close to earthly enjoyment. God, who is well worthy, would have more of our affections; and happy is that affliction that is sanctified to cause the heart to be more in love with God.

GHOST. *From the* American Weekly Mercury *of Newport, Rhode Island, March 30, 1722.*

This last winter there was a woman died at Narraganset of the small pox, and since she was buried, there has appeared, upon her grave chiefly, and in various other places, a bright light as the appearance of fire. This appearance commonly begins about 9 or 10 of the clock at night, and sometimes as soon as it was dark. It appears variously as to time, place, shape and magnitude, but commonly on or about the grave, and sometimes about and upon the barn and trees adjacent; sometimes in several parts, but commonly in one entire body. The first appearance is commonly small, but increases to a great bigness and brightness, so that in a dark night they can see the grass and bark of the trees very plainly; and when it is at the height, they can see sparks fly from the appearance like sparks of fire, and the likeness of a person in the midst wrapt in a sheet with its arms folded. This appearance moves with incredible swiftness, sometimes the distance of half a mile from one place to another in the twinkling of an eye. It commonly appears every night, and continues till break of day. A woman in that neighbourhood says she has seen it every night for these six weeks past.

EPITAPHS. *For some reason, writers of epitaphs have often been moved to express themselves in verse.*

From Oxford, New Hampshire.

> To all my friends I bid adieu
> A more sudden death you never knew
> As I was leading the old mare to drink
> She kicked and killed me quicker'n a wink.

From Vernon, Vermont: inscription for Jonathan Tute, who died after being inoculated for smallpox.

> Here lies cut down like unripe fruit
> A son of Mr. Amos Tute.
>
> To death he fell a helpless prey
> On April V and Twentieth Day
> In Seventeen Hundred Seventy-Seven
> Quitting this world we hope for heaven.
>
> But tho' His Spirits fled on high
> His body mould'ring here must lie.
>
> Behold the amazing alteration
> Effected by inoculation
> The means employed his life to save
> Hurried him headlong to the grave.

From Pelham, Massachusetts.

> Warren Gibbs
> Died by arsenic poison
> March 23 1860 Aged 36 years
> 5 months and 23 days
> Think my friends when this you see
> How my wife has dealt by me
> She in some oysters did prepare
> Some poison for my lot and share
> Then of the same I did partake
> And nature yielded to its fate
> Before she my wife became
> Mary Felton was her name.
>
> Erected by his brother
> Wm Gibbs

From the diary of Philip Hone, December 5, 1840. A monument has been erected at Rockaway over the remains of the unhappy sufferers on board the ships "Bristol" and "Mexico," wrecked on the Long Island shore in the winter of 1836–7. The Hempstead people have done well to evince their sympathy in this manner; but it was too bad, after the cruel suffering and miserable deaths of these poor strangers, that their memory should be handed down to posterity in such wretched poetry as the following inscription, which graces one side of the monumental stone:—

> "In this grave from the wide ocean doth sleep
> The bodies of those that had crossed the deep,
> And instead of being landed safe on the shore,
> On a cold frosty night they all were no more."

From the Methodist Cemetery in St. Louis, Missouri.

> Here lize a stranger braiv
> Who died while fightin the Suthern Confederacy to save
> Piece to his dust.
> Braive Suthern friend
> From iland 10
> You reach a Glory us end.
> We plase these flowrs above the stranger's hed
> In honor of the shiverlus ded.
> Sweet spirit rest in Heven
> There'll be know Yankis there.

PASSING BELL. *Lucy Larcom, author of* A New England Girlhood, *was born in 1821 in Beverly, Massachusetts, a small seafaring town.*

My brother's vigilant care of his two youngest sisters was once the occasion to them of a serious fright. My grandfather—the sexton—sometimes trusted him to toll the bell for a funeral. In those days the bell was tolled for everybody who died. John was social, and did not like to go up into the belfry and stay an hour or so alone, and as my grandfather positively forbade him to take any other boy up there, he one day got permission for us two little girls to go with him, for company. We had to climb up a great many stairs, and the last flight was inclosed by a rough door with a lock inside, which he was charged to fasten, so that no mischievous boys should follow.

It was strange to be standing up there in the air, gazing over the balcony-railing down into the street, where the men and women looked so small, and across to the water and the ships in the east, and the clouds and hills in the west! But when he struck the tongue against the great bell, close to our ears, it was more than we were prepared for. The little sister, scarcely three years old, screamed and shrieked,—

"I shall be stunned-ded! I shall be stunned-ded!" I do not know where she had picked up that final syllable, but it made her terror much more emphatic. Still the great waves of solemn sound went eddying on, over the hills and over the sea, and we had to hear it all, though we stopped our ears with our fingers. It was an immense relief to us when the last stroke of the passing-bell was struck, and John said we could go down.

He took the key from his pocket and was fitting it into the lock, when it slipped, dropping down through a wide crack in the floor, beyond our reach. Now the little sister cried again, and would not be pacified; and when I looked up and caught John's blank, dismayed look, I began to feel like crying, too. The question went swiftly through my mind,—How many days can we stay up here without starving to death?—for I really thought we should never get down out of our prison in the air: never see our mother's face again.

But my brother's wits returned to him. He led us back to the balcony, and shouted over the railing to a boy in the street, making him understand that he must go and inform my father that we were locked into the belfry. It was not long before we saw both him and my grandfather on their way to the church. They came up to the little door, and told us to push with our united strength against it. The rusty lock soon yielded, and how good it was to look into those two beloved human faces once more! But we little girls were not invited to join my brother again when he tolled the bell.

FUNERAL IN THE GOLD MINES. *From a letter home written by Louise Clappe in California. "Mrs. B" was Nancy Ann Bailey, aged twenty-six.*

Rich Bar,
East Branch of the North Fork of Feather River,
September 22, 1851

It seems indeed awful, dear M., to be compelled to announce to you the death of one of the four women forming the female population of this Bar. I have just returned from the funeral of poor Mrs. B., who died of peritonitis, (a common disease in this place) after an illness of four days only.

Her funeral took place at ten this morning. The family reside in a log-cabin at the head of the Bar; and, although it had no window—all the light admitted, entering through an aperture where there *will* be a door when it becomes cold enough for such a luxury—yet I am told, and can easily believe that it is one of the most *comfortable* residences in the place. I observed it particularly, for it was the first log-cabin that I had ever seen. Everything in the room, though of the humblest description, was exceedingly clean and neat.

On a board, supported by two butter-tubs, was extended the body of the dead woman, covered with a sheet; by its side stood the coffin of unstained pine, lined with white cambric.

The bereaved husband held in his arms a sickly babe ten months old, which was moaning piteously for its mother. The other child, a handsome, bold-looking little girl six years of age, was running gaily around the room, perfectly unconscious of her great bereavement. A sickening horror came over me, to see her every few moments, run up to her dead mother, and peep laughingly under the handkerchief, that covered her moveless face. Poor little thing! It was evident that her baby-toilet had been made by men; she had on a new calico dress, which, having no tucks in it, trailed to the floor, and gave her a most singular and dwarf-womanly appearance.

About twenty men, with the three women of the place, had assembled at the funeral. An *extempore* prayer was made, filled with all the peculiarities usual to that style of petition. Ah! how different from the soothing verses of the glorious burial service of the church.

As the procession started for the hill-side grave-yard—a dark cloth cover, borrowed from a neighboring monte-table, was flung over the coffin. Do not think that I mention any of these circumstances in a spirit of mockery; far from it. Every observance, usual on such occasions, that was *procurable,* surrounded this funeral. All the gold on Rich Bar could do no more; and should I die to-morrow, I should be marshaled to my mountain grave beneath the same monte-table cover pall, which shrouded the coffin of poor Mrs. B.

I almost forgot to tell you, how painfully the feelings of the assembly were shocked by the sound of the nails—there being no screws at any of the shops—driven with a hammer into the coffin, while closing it. It seemed as if it *must* disturb the pale sleeper within.

NEGRO BURIAL. *As observed by Frederick Law Olmsted during his travels gathering material for* The Cotton Kingdom; *this episode took place in Richmond, Virginia, in 1852.*

On a Sunday afternoon I met a negro funeral procession, and followed it to the place of burial. There was a decent hearse, of the usual style, drawn by two horses; six hackneyed coaches followed it, and six well-dressed men, mounted on handsome saddle-horses, and riding them well, rode in the rear of these. Twenty or thirty men and women were also walking together with the procession, on the side walk. Among all there was not a white person.

Passing out into the country, a little beyond the principal cemetery of the city (a neat, rural ground, well filled with monuments and evergreens), the hearse halted at a desolate place, where a dozen coloured people were already engaged heaping the earth over the grave of a child, and singing a wild kind of chant. Another grave was

"A Negro Funeral." Preceded by the gravediggers, a small funeral procession heads into the shadows of rural Virginia. Illustration by A. B. Frost, 1880.

already dug immediately adjoining that of the child, both being near the foot of a hill, in a crumbling bank—the ground below being already occupied, and the graves advancing in irregular terraces up the hill-side—an arrangement which facilitated labour.

The new comers, setting the coffin—which was neatly made of stained pine—upon the ground, joined in the labour and the singing, with the preceding party, until a small mound of earth was made over the grave of the child. When this was completed, one of those who had been handling a spade, sighed deeply and said—

"Lord Jesus, have mercy on us—now! you Jim—you! see yar! you jes lay dat yar shovel cross dat grave—so fash—dah—yes, dat's right."

A shovel and a hoe-handle having been laid across the unfilled grave, the coffin was brought and laid upon them, as on a trestle; after which, lines were passed under it, by which it was lowered to the bottom.

Most of the company were of a poor appearance . . . but there were several neatly-dressed and very good-looking men. One of these now stepped to the head of the grave, and, after a few sentences of prayer, held a handkerchief before him as if it were a book, and pronounced a short exhortation, as if he were reading from it. His manner was earnest, and the tone of his voice solemn and impressive, except that, occasionally, it would break into a shout or kind of howl at the close of a long sentence. I noticed several women near him, weeping, and one sobbing intensely. I was deeply influenced myself by the unaffected feeling, in connection with the simplicity, natural, rude truthfulness, and absence of all attempt at formal decorum in the crowd.

The speaker . . . concluded by throwing a handful of earth on the coffin, repeating the usual words, slightly disarranged, and then took a shovel, and, with the aid of six or seven others, proceeded very rapidly to fill the grave. Another man had in the mean time stepped into the place he had first occupied at the head of the grave; an old negro, with a very singularly distorted face, who raised a hymn, which soon became a confused chant—the leader singing a few words alone, and the company then either repeating them after him or making a response to them, in the manner of sailors heaving at the windlass. I could understand but very few of the words. The music was wild and barbarous, but not without a plaintive melody. A new leader took the place of the old man, when his breath gave out (he had sung very hard, with much bending of the body and gesticulation), and continued until the grave was filled, and a mound raised over it.

A man had, in the mean time, gone into a ravine near by, and now returned with two small branches, hung with withered leaves, that he had broken off a beech tree: these were placed upright, one at the head, the other at the foot of the grave. A few sentences of prayer were then repeated in a low voice by one of the company, and all dispersed. No one seemed to notice my presence at all. There were about fifty coloured people in the assembly, and but one other white man besides myself. This man lounged against the fence, outside the crowd, an apparently indifferent spectator, and I judged he was a police officer, or some one procured to witness the funeral, in compliance with the law which requires that a white man shall always be present at any meeting, for religious exercises, of the negroes.

THE PEARLY GATES. *An 1880s story attributed to "Marse Henry"— Henry Watterson, southern journalist and politician. Horace Greeley and Charles Sumner had been leaders in the abolition movement.*

Shortly before election, a colored political barbecue was held near Louisville and old Abram Jasper was asked to speak.

"Feller freemen," said he, "you all knows me. I is a Republican from way back. When dar has been any work to do, I has done it. When dar's been any votin to do, I has been in de thick of it. I is old line and tax-paid. I has seed many changes, too. I has seed de Republicans up. I has seed de Democrats up. But I is *yit* to see de nigger up.

"De other night I had a dream. Dremp I died and went to heaven. When I got to de Pearly Gate, old Saint Peter he say:

"'Who dar?' says he.

"'Abram Jasper,' says I.

"'Is you mounted or is you afoot?' says he.

"'I is afoot,' says I.

"'Well, you kain't git in here,' says he. 'Nobody lowed in here cept dem as comes mounted,' says he.

"'Dat's hard on me,' says I, 'atter comin all dat distance.' But he never say nothin to me, an I starts back, an about halfway down de hill, who does I meet but Charles Sumner an dat good old Horace Greeley!

"'Whar you gwine, Mr. Greeley?' I says.

"'I is gwine to heaven wid Mr. Sumner,' says he.

"'Mr. Greeley,' says I, ''tain't no use. I is jes been up dar, an nobody's lowed to git in cept dey comes mounted, an you is afoot.'

"'Is dat a fack?' says he.

"Mr. Greeley sorter scratch his head, an atter awhile he says, says he, 'Abram, I tell you what less do. Supposin you gits down on all fours an Sumner an me will mount an ride you in, and in dat way we kin all git in.'

"'Gentlemen,' says I, 'do you think you kin work it?'

"'I *know* I kin,' says bof of dem.

"So down I gits on all fours, and Greeley an Sumner gits astraddle, and we ambles up de hill agin, an prances up to de Gate, and old Saint Peter say:

"'Who dar?'

"'We is, Charles Sumner an Horace Greeley,' says Mr. Greeley.

"'Is you bof mounted or is you afoot?' says Peter.

"'We is bof mounted,' says Mr. Greeley.

"'All right,' says Peter, 'All right,' says he, 'jes hitch yo hoss outside, gentlemen, an come right in.'"

CHINESE CUSTOMS. *From* A Visit to Chinatown *by Mark Twain, 1872.*

A Chinaman hardly believes he could enjoy the hereafter except his body lay in his beloved China; also, he desires to receive, himself,

Chinese funeral service for the late High Lee in Deadwood, South Dakota, photographed by J. C. H. Grabill in 1891. Wild Bill Hickok and Calamity Jane were also buried there.

after death, that worship with which he has honored his dead that preceded him. Therefore, if he visits a foreign country, he makes arrangements to have his bones returned to China in case he dies; if he hires to go to a foreign country on a labor contract, there is always a stipulation that his body shall be taken back to China if he dies; if the government sells a gang of coolies to a foreigner for the usual five-year term, it is specified in the contract that their bodies shall be restored to China in case of death. On the Pacific coast the Chinamen all belong to one or another of several great companies or organizations, and these companies keep track of their members, register their names, and ship their bodies home when they die. The See Yup Company is held to be the largest of these. The Ning Yeong Company is next, and numbers eighteen thousand members on the coast. Its headquarters are at San Francisco, where it has a costly temple. . . . In it I was shown a register of its members, with the dead and the date of their shipment to China duly marked. Every ship that sails from San Francisco carries away a heavy freight of Chinese corpses—or did, at least, until the legislature, with an ingenious refinement of Christian cruelty, forbade the shipments, as a neat underhanded way of deterring Chinese immigration.

INDIAN WAYS: THREE OBSERVATIONS ON INDIAN RITUALS.
Roger Williams on the customs of the Narragansetts; from A Key into the Language of America, *published in 1643.*

Sequttôi—*He is in blacke.* That is, He hath some dead in his house (whether wife or child) for although at the first being sicke, all the Women and Maides blacke their faces with soote and other blackings; yet upon the death of the sicke, the father, or husband, and all his neighbours, the Men also (as the *English* weare blacke mourning clothes) weare blacke *Faces,* and lay on soote very thicke, which I have often seene clotted with their teares. This blackening and lamenting they observe in most dolefull manner, divers weekes and moneths; yea, a yeere, if the person be great and publike.

Nnowantam, nloasin—*I am grieved for you.*
As they abound in lamentations for the dead, so they abound in consolation to the living, and visit them frequently, using this word *Kutchimmoke, Kutchimmoke,* Be of good cheere, which they expresse by stroaking the cheeke and head of the father or mother, husband, or wife of the dead.

Yo apapan—*He that was here.*

Sachimaupan—*He that was prince here.*

These expressions they use, because, they abhorre to mention the dead by name, and therefore, if any man beare the name of the dead he changeth his name; and if any stranger accidentally name him, he is checkt, and if any wilfully name him he is fined; and amongst States, the naming of their dead *Sachims,* is one ground of their warres; so terrible is the King of Terrors, Death, to all naturall men.

The naturalist William Bartram on the Muscogulges and Chactaws, 1791.

The Muscogulges bury their deceased in the earth; they dig a foursquare deep pit under the cabin or couch which the deceased lay on, in his house, lining the grave with Cypress bark, where they place the corpse in a sitting posture, as if it were alive; depositing with him his gun, tomahawk, pipe and such other matters as he had the greatest value for in his life time. His eldest wife, or the queen dowager, has the second choice of his possessions, and the remaining effects are divided amongst his other wives and children.

The Chactaws pay their last duties and respect to the deceased in a very different manner. As soon as a person is dead, they erect a scaffold eighteen or twenty feet high, in a grove adjacent to the town, where they lay the corpse, lightly covered with a mantle; here it is suffered to remain, visited and protected by the friends and relations, until the flesh becomes putrid, so as easily to part from the bones, then undertakers, who make it their business, carefully strip the flesh from the bones, wash and cleanse them, and when dry and purified by the air, having provided a curiously wrought chest or coffin, fabricated of bones and splints, they place all the bones therein; which is deposited in the bone-house, a building erected for that purpose in every town. And when this house is full a general solemn funeral takes place. When the nearest kindred or friends of the deceased, on a day appointed, repair to the bone-house, take up the respective coffins, and following one another in order of seniority, the nearest relations and connections attending their respective corpse, and the multitude following after them, all as one family, with united voice of alternate Allelujah and lamentation, slowly proceeding on to the place of general interment, where they place the coffins in order, forming a pyramid, and lastly, cover all over with earth, which raises a conical hill or mount. Then they return to town in order of solemn procession, concluding the day with a festival, which is called the feast of the dead.

"Tribute to the Dead." Indian burial platform, photographed by Roland Reed in 1912.

A Menomonie ceremony as witnessed by John Tanner, who had been captured by the Shawnee as a boy, and was later adopted by an Ojibwa family.

In the spring of the year 1826, a man of the Menomonies died and was buried very near the encampment of a part of the fifth regiment of United States infantry, on the high prairie in the rear of the village of Prairie Du Chien, on the Mississippi. The body was attended to the grave by a considerable number of the friends and relatives, and when it was let down into the shallow grave, the wife of the deceased approached the brink, and after looking down on the rude coffin, she stepped upon it, and immediately across, taking her course over the plains, towards the bluffs there, about a mile distant. This is a common practice of the women of that tribe; and the mourner is careful, if she contemplates a second marriage, never to look back towards the grave she has left, but returns to her lodge by some devious and circuitous route. It is done, as they say, that the Cha-pi (Je-bi of the Ojibbeways,) of the dead person, may not be able to follow them afterwards. If the woman should look back, they believe she would either fall dead immediately, or become insane, and remain so ever after. On some occasions, but rarely, another person accompanies the mourner, carrying a handful of small twigs, and following immediately after her, flourishes it about her head, as if driving away flies. . . .

In the instance above mentioned, the woman walked rapidly, and without looking back, across the wide prairie, in a direction almost opposite that leading to her lodge; but her loud and bitter lamentings could be heard at a great distance, seeming to contradict the action by which she professed to seek an everlasting separation from the deceased.

HEAVEN AND HELL. *While leading the survey party that was to establish the dividing line between Virginia and North Carolina, the aristocratic William Byrd II, noted down some of the religious beliefs of their Indian guide.*

October 13, 1728. This being Sunday we rested from our Fatigue, & had a Sermon. Our Weather was very louring with the Wind hard at N W with great liklihood of Rain.

In the Evening I examin'd our Indian Ned Bearskin concerning his Religion, & he very frankly gave me the following Account of it. That he believ'd there was a Supream Being, that made the World & every thing in it. That the same Power that made it still preserves & governs it. That it protects and prospers good People in this World, & punishes the bad with Sickness & Poverty. That after Death all Mankind are conducted into one great Road, in which both the good & bad travel in Company to a certain Distance when this great Road branches into 2 Paths the One extremely Levil, & the other Mountainous. Here the good are parted from the bad, by a flash of Lightening, the first fileing to the Right, the other to the Left.

The Right hand Road leads to a fine warm country, where the Spring is perpetual, & every Month is May, And as the Year is always in its Youth, so are the People, and the Women beautifull as Stars, & never scold. That in this happy Climate there are Deer innumerable perpetually fat, & the Trees all bear delicious Fruit in every Season. That the Earth brings forth Corn spontaneously without Labour, which is so very wholesome, that none that eat of it are ever Sick, grow Old or Die. At the Entrance into this blessed Land sits a venerable Old Man who examines every One before he is admitted, & if he has behav'd well the Guards are order'd to open the Chrystal Gates & let him into this Terrestrial Paradise.

The left hand Path is very rough & uneven, leading to a barren Country, where 'tis always Winter, the Ground was cover'd with Snow, & nothing on the Trees but Icicles. All the People are old, have no teeth, & yet are very hungry. Only those who labour very hard make the Ground Produce a Sort of Potato pleasant to the Tast, but gives them the dry Gripes, & fills them full of Sores, which stink and are very painfull. The Women are old & ugly arm'd with sharp Claws like a Panther, & with those they gore the Men that slight their passion. For it seems these haggard old Furies are intollerably fond [amorous]. They talk very much, & very shrill, giving most exquisite pain to the Drum of the Ear, which in that horrid Climate grows so tender, that any sharp Note hurts it. On the Borders sits a hideous Old Woman whose Head is cover'd with Rattle-Snakes instead of Tresses, with glaring white Eyes, sunk very deep in her Head. Her Tongue is 20 cubits long arm'd with sharp Thorns as strong as Iron. This Tongue besides the dreadfull Sound it makes in pronouncing Sentence, serves the purpose of an Elephant's Trunk, with which the Old Gentlewoman takes up those she has convicted of Wickedness & throws them over a vast high wall hewn out of one Solid Rock, that Surrounds this Region of Misery, to prevent Escapes. They are receiv'd on the inside by another Hideous Old Woman who consigns them over to Punishments proper for their Crimes.

When they have been Chastiz'd here a certain Number of Years according to their degrees of Guilt, they are thrown over the Wall again, & drawn once more back into this World of Trial, where if they mend their Manners they are conducted into the abovemention'd fine Country after their Death.

BIBLIOGRAPHY

CHAPTER 1

IN THE BEGINNING: THREE NATIVE AMERICAN MYTHS. Megalopensis's account is included in *Narratives of New Netherland 1609–1664*, published by Charles Scribner's Sons in 1909; this book was part of the series Original Narratives of Early American History, edited by J. Franklin Jameson. Many books in the series have been reissued by Barnes & Noble. *The Homes of the New World*, by Fredrika Bremer, first published in English by Harper & Brothers in 1853, was reprinted in 1968 by Negro Universities Press. John Josselyn's *An Account of Two Voyages to New England*, first published in London in 1674, was reprinted in 1988 by University Press of New England under the title *John Josselyn, Colonial Traveler*.

THE WHITE MAN ARRIVES. Heckewelder's *Account of the History, Manners and Customs of the Indian Nations*, was published in Philadelphia by Abraham Small in 1819.

THE PILGRIMS SET FORTH. William Bradford's journals have been published under the title *Of Plymouth Plantation 1620–1647*, edited by Samuel Eliot Morison, Alfred A. Knopf, 1952.

GOD'S PROVIDENCE. See preceding entry.

THE HAND OF GOD. *A History of New-England from the English Planting in the Yeere 1628 untill the Yeere 1652*, is generally known as Edward Johnson's *Wonder-Working Providence of Sion's Saviour in New England*; it was published under this title by Charles Scribner's Sons in 1910 as part of the series Original Narratives of Early American History, edited by J. Franklin Jameson.

TAKING NO RISKS. This letter by Isaack de Rasieres appears in *Narratives of New Netherland 1609–1664* (see above, "In the Beginning")

MASSACRE IN VIRGINIA. From John Smith's *General Historie of Virginia*, first published in 1624, and reprinted in *Narratives of Early Virginia* by Charles Scribner's Sons as part of the series Original Narratives of Early American History.

THE CONQUISTADORS. From *The Journey of Francisco Vázquez de Coronado, 1540–1542,* translated by George Parker Winship, published by The Grabhorn Press, 1933, and reissued by Dover Publications in 1990.

THE NEW WORLD. For Megalopensis, see above, "In the Beginning."

THE WONDERS OF NEW ENGLAND. John Josselyn's *New England's Rarities Discovered* was first published in London in 1672; a facsimile edition has been put out by Applewood Books. For Josselyn's *An Account of Two Voyages to New England,* see above, "In the Beginning."

A HEALTHFULL PLACE. This extract from Higginson's *New-England's Plantation* comes from *The Puritans,* by Perry Miller and Thomas H. Johnson, American Book Company, 1938.

FREE LAND. "The Conditions propounded by the Lord Baltemore" are included in *Narratives of Early Maryland 1633–1684,* edited by Clayton Colman Hall and published by Charles Scribner's Sons in 1910 as part of the series Original Narrratives of Early American History.

SOME MORE WELCOME THAN OTHERS. For Megalopensis, see above, "In the Beginning."

PROSPERITY IN NEW YORK. Daniel Denton's *A Brief Description of New York* was first published in London in 1670 and reissued in New York by William Gowans in 1845.

THE CHARMS OF PENNSYLVANIA. From *Account of the Province and Country of Pensilvania* by Gabriel Thomas; the text used here is taken from *An American Primer,* edited by Daniel Boorstin, University of Chicago Press, 1966.

A BONNY COUNTRY. James Murray's letter was first published in Bradford's New York *Gazette* in 1737; it was reproduced in *Irish-American Historical Miscellany,* by John D. Crimmins, privately printed in 1905.

A WARNING. *Reise nach Pennsylvanien* by Gottlieb Mittelberger was first published in Germany in 1756. The extract used here was translated by the editor (there are full-length translations by Oscar Handlin and John Clive, and by Carl Theo Eben).

THE SLAVE TRADE. *An Account of the Slave Trade on the Coast of Africa,* by Alexander Falconbridge, late Surgeon in the African Trade, was first published in London in 1788.

AN ARISTOCRAT EMIGRATES. From *Journal d'une femme de cinquante ans, 1778–1815,* by La Marquise de La Tour du Pin; this extract was translated by the editor from the edition published in Paris by Berger-Levrault.

FACTORY WORKERS. *The Hollingworth Letters: Technical Change in the Textile Industry, 1826–1837,* edited by Thomas W. Leavitt, published by the Massachusetts Institute of Technology, 1969.

WHO ARE WANTED IN MINNESOTA. This editorial from the *St. Anthony Express* is reproduced in *Bring Warm Clothes, Letters and Photos from Minnesota's Past,* collected by Peg Meier and published by the *Minnesota Tribune,* 1981.

STEPS FORWARD. This editorial from the *New Mexican* is reproduced in *Santa Fe: The Autobiography of a Southwestern Town,* edited by Oliver LaFarge, University of Oklahoma Press, 1959.

IOWA FARMERS. Mary Stephenson's letter is taken from *Letters from the Promised Land, Swedes in America, 1840–1914,* edited by H. Arnold Barton and published by the University of Minnesota Press, 1975.

NO CHINESE. This text is quoted in *Chink! A Documentary History of Anti-Chinese Prejudice in America*, by Cheng-Tsu Wu, World Publishing, 1972.

LATTER-DAY PILGRIMS. From *The Promised Land*, by Mary Antin (Grabau), published by Houghton Mifflin in 1912.

CHAPTER 2

SOME PROS AND CONS. The Jeremiah Wise quotation comes from *The First Frontier*, by John C. Miller, published in 1966 by Delacorte Press. The Berkeley quotation comes from Daniel Boorstin's *The Americans, the Colonial Experience*, published in 1958 by Vintage Books. The John Winthrop story comes from *The History of New England 1630 to 1649*, first published in 1790 and reissued by Charles Scribner's Sons in 1908, edited by James Kendall Hosmer and published as part of the series Original Narratives of Early American History. The Daniel Gookin piece is from his *Historical Collections of the Indians in New England*, first published in 1792, reprinted in 1970 by Towtaid, edited by Jeffrey H. Fiske.

LAWS NORTH AND SOUTH. From *An Abridgment of the Laws and Ordinances of New-England, to the Year 1700*. A facsimile edition was published in 1991 by the Carrollton Press. The North Carolina law is reproduced in *The Black American, A Documentary History*, by Leslie H. Fishel, Jr., and Benjamin Quarles, published by William Morrow & Company, 1970.

EDUCATION FOR YOUNG FEMALES. From the Penguin Classics edition of *The Autobiography of Benjamin Franklin*.

MOTIVATION. *Forty Years of American Life*, by Thomas Low Nichols, first published in 1864 and reprinted in 1968 by Negro Universities Press.

TRUE INDEPENDENCE. *The American Woman's Home, or Principles of Domestic Science*, by Catharine Beecher and Harriet Beecher Stowe, first published in 1869 and reissued in facsimile in 1991 by the Stowe-Day Foundation, Hartford, Connecticut.

ADMISSION TO LAW SCHOOL. From the *Diary of George Templeton Strong*, edited by Allen Nevins and Milton Halsey Thomas, Macmillan & Company, 1952.

THE ACADEMIC MELTING POT. This quotation from the *New York Tribune* appears in *Underfoot*, by David Weitzman, published in 1976 by Charles Scribner's Sons.

HOME EDUCATION. From the *Diary of Cotton Mather 1681–1708*, published by the Massachusetts Historical Society, Boston, 1911.

THE SCHOOL OF MANNERS. A facsimile of the 1701 edition has been published by the Victoria and Albert Museum, London.

TOO TRUE TO BE DOUBTED. *The Life and Memorable Actions of George Washington*, by Mason Locke Weems, was first published in 1800; a revised edition appeared in 1806.

BOARDING OUT. For Thomas Low Nichols, see above, "Motivation."

END OF A TYRANT. For George Templeton Strong, see above, "Admission to Law School".

A THUNDERBOLT FROM THE PULPIT. *Social Dynamite; or, The Wickedness of Modern Society*, by Thomas De Witt Talmage, first published in Chicago in 1889.

LADY'S ETIQUETTE. *The Lady's Guide to Perfect Gentility*, by Emily Thornwell, published by The Burrows Brothers Company, Cleveland, 1887.

SUMMER SCHOOL TEACHER. *The Autobiography of W. E. B. Du Bois*, International Publishers, 1968.

PRAIRIE SCHOOL. From *Pioneer Women: Voices From the Kansas Frontier*, by Joanna L. Stratton, Simon & Schuster, 1981.

DAME'S SCHOOL. From *Laura Russell Remembers*, privately printed in Plymouth, Massachusetts, undated.

ROLE MODEL. *Twenty Years at Hull-House*, by Jane Addams, first published in 1910, reissued by Signet and New American Library.

COUNTRY SCHOOL. From *The Autobiography of Mark Twain*, published posthumously in 1924.

BUGLER BOY. From *My Life on the Plains*, by George Armstrong Custer, reissued in 1962 by The Citadel Press.

COUNTING COUP. Quoted in *Cry of the Thunderbird, The American Indians' Own Story*, edited by Charles Hamilton, published by the University of Oklahoma Press, 1972.

PRIVATE SCHOOL. From Richard Henry Dana's *Journal*, published in 1968 by Harvard University Press.

SCHOOL IN ANTEBELLUM SAVANNAH. *Reminiscences of My Life in Camp...* by Susie King Taylor, first published by the author in 1902, reissued in 1988 by Markus Wiener Publishing under the title *A Black Woman's Civil War Memoirs*.

ROSE AND SPOOKENDYKE. From *A Little House Sampler*, edited by William T. Anderson, published in 1989 by Perennial Library.

INDIAN SCHOOL. From *The Life Stories of Undistinguished Americans, As Told by Themselves*, edited by Hamilton Holt and published by James Pott & Company, New York, in 1906.

LIFE AT HARVARD. For the first piece, from John Winthrop, see above, "Some Pros and Cons." The second piece is from *The Journal of Jasper Danckaerts 1679–1680*, edited by Bartlett Burleigh James and J. Franklin Jameson, republished by Barnes & Noble in 1952.

THE ACADEMIC YEAR. *Joseph Cleaver, Jr: Diary of a Student at Delaware College*, edited by William Lewis. The text used here is from *Diary of America*, edited by Josef and Dorothy Berger, published by Simon & Schuster, 1957.

CHAPTER 3

PRIVATE PRAYER. For John Winthrop, see Chapter 2, "Some Pros and Cons."

THE LADIES OF BOSTON. Alexander Hamilton's *Itinerarium* is included in *Colonial American Travel Narratives*, published by Penguin, 1994.

BUNDLING. *Travels Through the Middle Settlements in North America*, by the Reverend Andrew Burnaby, published in London in 1775 and reissued by Cornell University Press in 1960.

BENJAMIN FRANKLIN AND THE PASSION OF YOUTH. For Benjamin Franklin see Chapter 2, "Education for Young Females."

SPARKING IN VIRGINIA. *Journal and Letters 1773–1774*, by Philip Vickers Fithian, edited by Hunter Dickinson Farish and published in 1943 by Colonial Williamsburg.

VENUS AND MARS. *The Journal of Nicholas Cresswell, 1774–1777*, published by Dial Press, 1924.

THE IRISH APPROACH. For Fredrika Bremer, see Chapter 1, "In the Beginning."

FARMER'S COURTSHIP. First published as *Life of Asa G. Sheldon, Wilmington Farmer*, in 1862 and reissued in 1988 under the title *Yankee Drover* by University Press of New England.

TWO WORLDS. For Richard Henry Dana, see Chapter 2, "Private School."

LOVE ON THE TRAIL. This interview is from *First-Person America*, edited by Ann Banks, published by Alfred A. Knopf in 1980.

COWBOY'S COURTSHIP. *A Texas Cow Boy*, by Charles A. Siringo, first published in 1885 and reissued in facsimile in 1991 by Indian Head Books.

BUXBY THE WOLF. *The Whole Art of Correct and Elegant Letter-Writing* is included in *The Lady's Guide to Perfect Gentility* (see Chapter 2, "Lady's Etiquette").

A SIOUX COURTSHIP. From *Black Elk Speaks, As Told Through John G. Neihardt*, University of Nebraska Press, 1961.

"ASKING PA." From *Sarah Morgan: The Civil War Diary of a Southern Woman*, edited by Charles East, Touchstone, 1992.

TWO SLAVE WEDDINGS. The multivolume *Slave Narratives*, compiled in the 1930s by the Federal Writers' Project (part of the WPA), have not been published in their entirety, but at least two books offer selections: *Lay My Burden Down*, edited by B. A. Botkin and published by Dell, and *Bullwhip Days*, edited by James Mellon and published by Avon Books.

PIONEER WEDDING. This is reproduced in *Pioneer Women*. See Chapter 3, "Prairie School."

A WORD OF WARNING. *A Lecture to Young Men*, by Sylvester Graham, 1834, was reprinted in 1974 by Arno Press.

A PURITAN TO HIS WIFE. John Winthrop's letter appears in *The Puritans*, by Perry Miller and Thomas H. Johnson, published by American Book Company, 1938.

A BIGAMIST. Thomas Dudley's letter appears in *Living Documents in American History*, edited by John A. Scott, published by Washington Square Press, 1963.

ADULTERY PUNISHED. This piece comes from John Winthrop. See Chapter 2, "Some Pros and Cons."

A LUSTFUL STRUMPET. *New England's Prospect*, by William Wood, was first published in London in 1634; it was reissued in 1977 by the University of Massachusetts Press, edited by Alden T. Vaughan.

DIVORCE IN NEW NETHERLAND. For Isaack de Rasieres, see Chapter 1, "Taking No Risks."

PURITAN PATERFAMILIAS. From *The Diary of Samuel Sewall, 1674–1729*, edited by M. Halsey Thomas, and published in 1973 by Farrar, Straus & Giroux.

MARRIAGE À LA MODE. *The Secret Diary of William Byrd of Westover 1709–1712*, edited by Louis B. Wright and Marion Tinling, 1941, and published by The Dietz Press, Richmond, Virginia.

TWO MARRIAGES. *Journal of a Residence on a Georgian Plantation in 1838–1839*, by Frances Anne Kemble, was first published in 1863 and reissued by the University of Georgia Press in 1984, edited by John A. Scott.

MINISTER'S WIFE. *A Red Record: Lynchings in the United States 1892–1893–1894,* by Ida B. Wells, is included in a volume titled *On Lynchings,* published in 1969 by Arno Press.

ALL FOR THE CAUSE. *Living My Life,* by Emma Goldman, was published in 1931, and reprinted by Dover Publications in 1970.

CHAPTER 4

INDENTURED SERVANTS. For John Winthrop, see Chapter 2, "Some Pros and Cons."

TROUBLEMAKERS. This text appears in *Remarkable Providences, Readings on Early American History,* by John Demos, published in 1972 by Northeastern University Press.

SLUGGARDS. *The History of the Dividing Line Betwixt Virginia and North Carolina Run in the Year of Our Lord 1728,* by William Byrd II, was first published in 1841 and reissued by Dover Publications in 1967.

RUNAWAYS. This text appears in *Voyagers to the West,* by Bernard Bailyn, published by Alfred A. Knopf, 1986.

SENTRY DUTY. From *A Narrative of Some of the Adventures, Dangers and Sufferings of a Revolutionary Soldier,* by Joseph Plumb Martin, republished in 1962 by Arno Press under the title *Private Yankee Doodle.*

PHILADELPHIA DOCTOR. *Medical Inquiries and Observations,* by Dr. Benjamin Rush, 4th edition, was published in Philadelphia in 1815, and reissued in facsimile by Arno Press.

YANKEE PEDDLER. *Retrospectives of America 1797–1811,* by John Bernard, first published by Harper & Brothers in 1887, has been reissued by Heritage Books of Bowie, Maryland.

TRADING WITH THE INDIANS. From *The Journals of Lewis and Clark,* edited by Bernard De Voto, Houghton Mifflin, 1953; there are numerous other editions of this book.

FIREWOOD. For Asa Sheldon, see Chapter 3, "Farmer's Courtship."

FARM WORKERS. *A Year's Residence in the United States of America,* by William Cobbett; a facsimile of the 1818–1819 edition was published in 1969 by Augustus M. Kelley, New York.

BUDDING ARTIST. *The Travel Diary of James Guild,* Vermont Historical Society Proceedings, 1937; the text is included in *Quest for America, 1810–1824,* edited by Charles L. Sanford, published by Doubleday Anchor Books, 1964.

YOUNGEST SON. For Hollingworth, see Chapter 1, "Factory Workers."

MILL GIRL. *A New England Girlhood,* by Lucy Larcom, first published in 1889, has been reissued by Northeastern University Press, edited by Nancy F. Cott.

LOADING HIDES. From *Two Years Before the Mast,* by Richard Henry Dana, first published in 1840 by Harper & Brothers and often reissued.

JOURNALIST. For Richard Henry Dana's *Journal,* see Chapter 2, "Private School."

APPRENTICE CAULKER. *Narrative of the Life of Frederick Douglass,* first published in 1845 by The Anti-Slavery Society, is included in *The Classic Slave* narratives, edited by Henry Louis Gates, Jr., published in 1987 by the New American Library.

TAVERN KEEPER. *Ten Nights in a Bar-room, and What I Saw There,* by Timothy Shay Arthur, was first published in 1854 and often reprinted.

LIGHTHOUSE KEEPER. From *Henry David Thoreau,* edited by Robert F. Sayre, published by Literary Classics of the United States.

COTTON PLANTATION. *The Cotton Kingdom,* by Frederick Law Olmsted, 1861, was a compendium of three earlier books; the text used here is from the 1969 Modern Library edition, edited by Arthur Schlesinger, Jr.

STOREKEEPER. Isaac Meyer's story is taken from *Memoirs of American Jews,* edited by Jacob Rader Marcus, The Jewish Publication Society of America, 1955.

GOVERNESS. From *Selected Letters of Louisa May Alcott,* edited by Joel Myerson and Daniel Shealy, Little, Brown & Company, 1987.

FUR TRAPPER. *An Autobiography of Buffalo Bill* (Colonel W. F. Cody); the text used here is from the Holt, Rinehart & Winston edition.

MINING ON THE HUMBOLDT. Mark Twain's *Roughing It* was first published by the American Publishing Company in 1872.

TOWN MARSHAL. *My Life on the Frontier,* by Miguel Otero, was published in 1935 by The Press of the Pioneers.

FARMER'S WIFE. From *The Life Stories of Undistinguished Americans, As Told By Themselves* (see Chapter 2, "Indian School").

SANDHOG. *My Life and Loves,* by Frank Harris, once banned, was privately printed by the author and reissued by Grove Press in 1963.

COWBOY. *Up the Trail in '79,* by Baylis John Fletcher, was reissued in 1968 by the University of Oklahoma Press.

CHILD LABOR. *Darkness and Daylight* or *Lights and Shadows of New York Life,* was first published in 1891 by The Hartford Company and republished in 1969 by Singing Tree Press, Detroit. Helen Campbell and Thomas Knox were co-authors.

CRUSADER. *The Use and Need of the Life of Carry A. Nation,* was published in 1908 by F. M. Steves & Sons, Topeka.

CHAPTER 5

ADOBE HOUSES. For Pedro de Castañeda, see Chapter 1, "The Conquistadors."

WIGWAM. *A Relation or Journal of the Beginning and Proceedings of the English Plantation Setled at Plimoth in New England,* generally known as *Mourt's Relation,* first published in England in 1622, has been reissued in facsimile by Applewood Books.

MOVABLE HOUSES. *A Key into the Language of America,* by Roger Williams, was reissued in 1973 by Wayne State University Press, edited by John J. Teunissen and Evelyn J. Hinz.

CELLARS. This extract from *Information Relative to Taking Up Land in New Netherland,* by Cornelis van Tienhoven, is taken from *Remarkable Providences,* by John Demos, Northeastern University Press.

FRONTIER HOUSING. *The Soveraignty and Goodness of God...,* by Mrs. Mary Rowlandson, also known as *The Narrative of the Captivity and Restoration of Mrs. Mary Rowlandson,* first printed in 1682, and often reissued.

ALBANY, NEW YORK. For Alexander Hamilton, see Chapter 3, "The Ladies of Boston."

PROSPEROUS FARMS. From *A Year's Residence in the United States of America*, by William Cobbett, 1818–1819.

LOG HOUSE. Alexis de Tocqueville's *Journal* was republished in 1960 by Yale University Press, edited by J. P. Mayer.

REBUILDING NEW YORK. *The Diary of Philip Hone 1828–1851*, edited by Bayard Tuckerman, was published by Dodd, Mead & Company in 1889.

BOOM TOWN. Bayard Taylor's reports for the *New York Tribune* were later incorporated in his book *Eldorado*, published in 1850. The story by Morris Shloss appears in *Memoirs of American Jews* (see Chapter 4, "Storekeeper").

POOR WHITES. For Frederick Law Olmsted, see Chapter 4, "Cotton Plantation."

OGLALA CAMP. *Narrative of My Captivity Among the Sioux Indians*, by Fanny Kelly, 1871, has been reissued by Carol Publishing Group.

ORPHANAGE AND ASYLUM. For Louisa May Alcott, see Chapter 4, "Governess."

COWBOYS AND SETTLERS. "Tearing Down of Settlers' Houses by Cowboys" appears in *Pioneer History of Custer County, Nebraska*, by Solomon D. Butcher, republished in 1976 by Purcell's, Broken Bow, Nebraska.

LIFE IN THE STOCKADE. For *The Life Stories of Undistinguished Americans, As Told By Themselves*, see Chapter 2, "Indian School."

A DUG-OUT. For Charles Siringo, see Chapter 3, "Cowboy's Courtship."

LIFE AT THE BOTTOM. For Helen Campbell, see Chapter 4, "Child Labor."

CLEANING THE STREETS OF CHICAGO. For Jane Addams, see Chapter 2, "Role Model."

STEAM BATH. This piece by David de Vries appears in *Narratives of New Netherland* (see Chapter 1, "In the Beginning").

MAN'S BEST FRIEND. For John Winthrop, see Chapter 2, "Some Pros and Cons."

NEIGHBORS. This text comes from *Dutch New York*, by Esther Singleton, published by Dodd, Mead, 1909.

EXPLOSION. For Samuel Sewall, see Chapter 3, "Puritan Paterfamilias."

PET. *Travels in North America*, by Peter Kalm, was variously translated by J. R. Foster, F. Elfving, and A. Benson, and was published by Wilson-Erickson, New York, in 1937.

HOUSEWIFE. *The American Frugal Housewife*, by Lydia Maria Child, has been reissued in facsimile by Applewood Books.

PIANO LEGS. *A Diary in America*, by Frederick Marryat, first published in 1838, has been reissued by Alfred A. Knopf, edited by Sydney Jackson.

FIRE. For George Templeton Strong, see Chapter 2, "Admission to Law School."

VOLUNTEER FIREMAN. For Thomas W. Knox, see Chapter 4, "Child Labor."

FEATHER BED. For *Slave Narratives*, see Chapter 3, "Two Slave Weddings."

THE EARTH CLOSET. For *The American Woman's Home*, see Chapter 2, "True Independence."

URBAN PASTORALE. "The First Spring Day on Chestnut Street" comes from the Library of America edition of Walt Whitman.

CHAPTER 6

JAMESTOWN AND JOHN SMITH. For John Smith, see Chapter 1, "Massacre in Virginia."

NEW ENGLAND. For *Mourt's Relation,* see Chapter 5, "Wigwam." For Isaack de Rasieres, see Chapter 1, "Taking No Risks." For Roger Williams, see Chapter 5, "Movable Houses." For Daniel Gookin, see Chapter 2, "Some Pros and Cons." For John Josselyn, see Chapter 1, "In the Beginning."

COLONIAL RECIPES. The 1683 edition of *The Housewife's Skill in Cookery,* by Gervase Markham, was reprinted by Story Press in 1991.

IN THE WOODS. Paul Dudley's letter to the Royal Society is included in *The Puritans* (see Chapter 3, "A Puritan to his Wife"). For William Byrd, see Chapter 4, "Sluggards."

HUNTER'S TALES. William Bartram's *Travels through North & South Carolina, Georgia, East & West Florida...* first published in Philadelphia in 1791, has been reissued by Yale University Press and Dover Publications and Penguin, in 1988. *A Narrative of the Captivity and Adventures of John Tanner,* first published in 1830, has been reissued by Penguin Books under the title *The Falcon.*

IN KENTUCKY. John James Audubon's *Ornithological Biographies* is sometimes also called the *Episodes* (the text that accompanied *Birds of America*).

ON THE PLAINS. For Lewis and Clark, see Chapter 4, "Trading with the Indians." *Across the Plains in Forty-Nine,* by Reuben Cole Shaw, was reissued in 1948 by Lakeside Press, Chicago. *The Prairie Traveler, A Handbook for Overland Expeditions,* by Captain Randolph Marcy, 1859, has been reissued in facsimile by Applewood Books.

THE WEST COAST. *Life Among the Modocs,* by Joaquin Miller, was first published in London in 1873 and reprinted in 1982 by Urion Press, Eugene, Oregon.

MARKETS. Mrs Royall's *Southern Tour* was first published in 1830. Nathaniel Hawthorne's *Passages from the American Notebooks* was first published in 1868. *Ten Years of Preacher Life,* by William Henry Milburn, was published in 1859.

IN THE KITCHEN. "Common Cooking" is included in *The American Frugal Housewife* (see Chapter 5, "Housewife").

A FAMOUS DINNER. Edward Winslow's letter is included in *Mourt's Relation* (see Chapter 5, "Wigwam").

STARVING TIME IN EARLY JAMESTOWN. *The Tragical Relation of the Virginia Assembly* is included in *Narratives of Early Virginia* (see Chapter 1, "Massacre in Virginia").

GOURMET FOOD. This advertisement from the *Boston Gazette* is reproduced in *Underfoot,* by David Weitzman, Scribner's, 1976.

ON PAROLE. Baroness von Riedesel's story appears in *Narratives of the American Revolution,* edited by Hugh Rankin and published in 1976 by The Lakeside Press, Chicago.

SOUTHERN COMFORT. Henry Barnard's letter is included in *The Leaven of Democracy*, edited by Clement Eaton and published by George Braziller, 1963.

A TOLERABLE GOOD DINNER. William Johnson's *Natchez: The Ante-Bellum Diary of a Free Negro*, edited by William Ransom Hogan and Edwin Adams Davis, published in 1951 by Louisana State University Press.

BREAKFAST. *Six Months in the Gold Mines*, by E. Gould Buffum, was published in 1850.

DAKOTA TREAT. *The Oregon Trail*, by Francis Parkman, was first published in 1849.

NEW YEAR'S DAY DINNER. Abigail Malick's letter is quoted in *Far From Home*, edited by Lillian Schlissel, Byrd Gibbens, and Elizabeth Hampsten, and published by Schocken Books, New York.

BLIZZARD. From *A Little House Sampler* (see Chapter 2, "Rose and Spookendyke").

PRISON FARE. *The Road* is included in the Library of America edition of Jack London.

THE GILDED AGE. Ward McAllister's *Society As I Have Found It* was first published in 1890 by Cassell Publishing Co.

CHAPTER 7

NEW YEAR'S DAY AND MAY DAY IN NEW AMSTERDAM. Peter Stuyvesant's ordinance is quoted in *Dutch New York* (see Chapter 5, "Neighbors").

FANDANGO. The *Personal Narrative of James O. Pattie of Kentucky*, first published in 1831, was reissued by J. B. Lippincott in 1962.

ELECTION DAY IN KENTUCKY, 1830. George Prentice was writing for the *New England Review*, published in Hartford, Connecticut.

JULY 4, 1837. For Frederick Marryat, see Chapter 5, "Piano Legs."

JULY 4 IN OREGON. This interview is reproduced in *First-Person America* (see Chapter 3, "Love on the Trail").

CHRISTMAS IN EDENTON, NORTH CAROLINA. *Incidents in the Life of a Slave Girl*, by Harriet Jacobs (also known as Linda Brent), was first published in 1861.

CHRISTMAS IN KANSAS. Ida Lindgren's letter appears in *Letters from the Promised Land, 1840–1914*, published by the University of Minnesota Press for the Swedish Pioneer Historical Society, 1975.

INDIAN GAMES. For Roger Williams, see Chapter 5, "Movable Houses."

OTHELLO BY ANY OTHER NAME. This playbill appears in *Retrospectives of America, 1797–1811* (see Chapter 4, "Yankee Peddler").

RARE PIG. Dr. Rush's *Commonplace Book, 1792–1813*, is included in *The Autobiography of Benjamin Rush*, published in 1948 by the Greenwood Press, Westport, Connecticut.

A DELIGHTFUL SPORT. From Audubon's *Ornithological Biographies* (see Chapter 6, "In Kentucky").

STAG HUNT. For John Bernard, see Chapter 4, "Yankee Peddler."

FOOTBALL. For Laura Russell, see Chapter 2, "Dame's School."

CHILDREN'S GAMES. From *The Girl's Own Book*, by Lydia Maria Child, first published in 1834 and reissued in facsimile by Applewood Books.

MINSTREL SHOW. From *The Autobiography of Mark Twain*, edited by Charles Neiden.

CELEBRITY-WATCHING. Charles Dickens's letter is quoted by John Forster in *The Life of Charles Dickens*, published 1872–1874.

AN AVID READER. See preceding entry.

MELODRAMA. For George Templeton Strong, see Chapter 2, "Admission to Law School."

CUSTER HUNTS A BUFFALO. *My Life on the Plains*, by George Armstrong Custer, first published in 1874, has recently been reissued by Citadel Press.

POCAHONTAS THROWS A PARTY. For John Smith, see Chapter 1, "Massacre in Virginia."

NOT IN NEW ENGLAND. Increase Mather's essay is included in *The Puritans* (see Chapter 3, "A Puritan to his Wife").

VIRGINIA REELS. For Philip Vickers Fithian, see Chapter 3, "Sparking in Virginia."

A MEMORABLE ADVENTURE. For Nicholas Cresswell, see Chapter 3, "Venus and Mars."

HUSKING BEE. This excerpt from *Recollections of Life in Ohio, 1813–1840*, by William Cooper Howells, is included in *Voices from America's Past*, edited by Richard Morris and James Woodress, published by E. P. Dutton.

MRS. BREVOORT'S BAL COSTUMÉ. For Philip Hone, see Chapter 5, "Rebuilding New York."

RUSTIC IDYLL. *Social Relations in Our Southern States*, by Daniel R. Hundley, was published by H. B. Price in 1860.

THE WILD WEST: A VISIT TO DODGE CITY. *The Log of a Cowboy*, by Andy Adams, first published in 1903, has been reissued as a Bison Book by the University of Nebraska Press.

CHAPTER 8

NEW ENGLAND PURITANISM AND WITCHCRAFT. For William Bradford, see Chapter 1, "The Pilgrims Set Forth." For John Winthrop, see Chapter 2, "Some Pros and Cons." For Edward Johnson, see Chapter 1, "The Hand of God." *Wonders of the Invisible World*, by Cotton Mather, first published in 1692, has been reissued in facsimile by Dorset Press, New York, under the title *On Witchcraft*. *More Wonders of the Invisible World*, by Robert Calef, was first published in 1700; the 1861 edition was recently reissued by Heritage Books, of Bowie, Maryland, and retitled *Salem Witchcraft*.

THE SHAKERS. This anonymous account appears in *History of American Socialisms* by John Humphrey Noyes, 1870, reissued by Dover Publications under the title *Strange Cults and Utopias of 19th-Century America*.

SLAVE RELIGION. The Virginia law is taken from Volume 1 of *The Annals of America*, published by Encyclopaedia Britannica, Inc. The catechism was published in the *Southern Episcopalian*, 1854. For the *Slave Narratives*, see Chapter 3, "Two Slave Weddings."

CATHOLICS. For Megalopensis, see Chapter 1, "In the Beginning." For *The Laws of New England...*, see Chapter 2, "Laws North and South." *The New York Conspiracy, or A History of the Negro Plot..., 1741–2*, by Daniel Horsmanden, was published in 1810 by Southwick and Pelsue, New York. *Awful Disclosures of the Hotel Dieu Nunnery of Montreal*, by Maria Monk, was first published in 1836, and reprinted by Arno Press, New York, in 1977. The letter by Walter T. Post is taken from *Bring Warm Clothes...* (see Chapter 1, "Who Are Wanted in Minnesota").

SPIRITUALISM. For Thomas Low Nichols, see Chapter 2, "Motivation."

HEBREW SUNDAY SCHOOL. Rosa Mordecai's memoir is taken from *Memoirs of American Jews 1775–1865*, edited by Jacob Rader Marcus, published by the Jewish Publication Society of America, Philadelphia, 1955.

WITH THE JESUITS. From *Luz de Tierra Incognita*, by Juan Mateo Manje.

JOHN ELIOT. For Daniel Gookin, see Chapter 2, "Some Pros and Cons."

A HELLFIRE SERMON. This text is taken from *Jonathan Edwards: Basic Writings*, edited by Ola Elizabeth Winslow, published by Signet Classic in 1966.

A BAPTIST AND A MOB. This text appears in *The Rising Glory of America*, edited by Gordon S. Wood, published in 1971 by George Braziller.

A METHODIST AT WORK. Peter Cartwright's *Autobiography* was first published in 1856.

WOODLAND WORSHIP. *Domestic Manners of the Americans*, by Frances Trollope, first published in 1832, has been frequently reissued.

MORMON SERMON. *Across the Continent: A Summer's Journey to the Rocky Mountains...* was published in 1865.

ALL-NIGHT MISSIONARY GIBBUD'S STORY. For Helen Campbell, see Chapter 4, "Child Labor."

CHAPTER 9

HARSH PUNISHMENT. For John Smith, see Chapter 1, "Massacre in Virginia."

PILLORY. *Proceedings of the Virginia Assembly* appear in *Narratives of Early Virginia* (see Chapter 1, "Massacre in Virginia").

HOLDUP, 1631. For William Bradford, see Chapter 1, "The Pilgrims Set Forth."

ANOTHER SCARLET LETTER. For John Winthrop, see Chapter 2, "Some Pros and Cons."

A SHIFTLESS MAID. See preceding entry.

SIN IN PLYMOUTH. For William Bradford, see Chapter 1, "The Pilgrims Set Forth."

ATTEMPTED MURDER IN CONNECTICUT. For John Winthrop, see Chapter 2, "Some Pros and Cons."

SILENCER. See preceding entry.

OTHER CRIMES AND PUNISHMENTS. For John Josselyn, see Chapter 1, "In the Beginning."

INFANTICIDE. For John Winthrop, see Chapter 2, "Some Pros and Cons."

PIRATES. For Samuel Sewall, see Chapter 3, "Puritan Paterfamilias."

SATURDAY-NIGHT ROWDIES. See preceding entry.

SLAVE LAW. This text is taken from *The Black American* by Leslie H. Fishel, Jr. and Benjamin Quarles, published by William Morrow & Company.

EX-GOVERNOR. This extract from *North Carolina Historical and Genealogical Register, III* is quoted in *Remarkable Providences* (see Chapter 4, "Troublemakers").

SOME PENNSYLVANIA LAWS. For Peter Kalm, see Chapter 5, "Pet."

A BAD HAT. This text appears in *The Rising Glory of America* (see Chapter 8, "A Baptist and a Mob.")

MAKING AMENDS. For John Tanner, see Chapter 6, "Hunter's Tales."

LIFE IN ANTEBELLUM NATCHEZ. For William Johnson, see Chapter 6, "A Tolerable Good Dinner."

CHEATING THE GALLOWS. For George Templeton Strong, see Chapter 2, "Admission to Law School."

JUSTICE IN THE GOLD MINES. *The Shirley Letters*, by "Dame Shirley" (Louise Clappe), first published in *Pioneer Magazine*, 1854–1855, was reissued by Alfred A. Knopf in 1949.

MARTIAL LAW IN BOSTON. For Richard Henry Dana, see Chapter 2, "Private School."

THE KLAN AT WORK. For the *Slave Narratives*, see Chapter 3, "Two Slave Weddings."

DANGEROUS TIMES IN SANTA FE. For the *New Mexican*, see Chapter 1, "Steps Forward."

TEXAS RANGERS. *A Texas Ranger*, by N. A. Jennings, first published in 1898, was reissued in 1992 by The Lakeside Press, Chicago.

VIGILANTES IN KANSAS. This story appears in *A Little House Sampler* (see Chapter 2, "Rose and Spookendyke").

MAIL FRAUD. *Frauds Exposed*, by Anthony Comstock, first published in 1880, was reissued in 1969 by Patterson, Smith of Montclair, New Jersey.

CIVIL RIGHTS. *Crusade for Justice*, by Ida B. Wells, was reissued in 1970 by the University of Chicago Press.

VICE-BUSTER. For Anthony Comstock, see "Mail Fraud" above.

LYNCH LAW. *Mob Rule in New Orleans*, by Ida B. Wells, first published in 1900, is included in *On Lynchings*, published in 1969 by Arno Press.

VAGRANT. For Jack London, see Chapter 6, "Prison Fare."

CHAPTER 10

ACCIDENTS. For John Winthrop, see Chapter 2, "Some Pros and Cons." For Samuel Sewall, see Chapter 3, "Puritan Paterfamilias." For Joseph Plumb Martin, see Chapter 4, "Sentry Duty."

AGUE. For Peter Kalm, see Chapter 5, "Pet."

AMPUTATION. For John Tanner, see Chapter 6, "Hunter's Tales."

ASYLUMS. Memorial of Dorothea Dix asking for a grant of land, is cataloged as Series: 30th Cong, First Sess. Senate Miscellaneous Document 150. For Helen Campbell, see Chapter 4, "Child Labor."

CHOLERA. For George Templeton Strong, see Chapter 2, "Admission to Law School." For Philip Hone, see Chapter 5, "Rebuilding New York."

DENTIST. For Alexander Hamilton, see Chapter 3, "The Ladies of Boston."

DIET: TWO ACCOUNTS. For William Wood, see Chapter 3, "A Lustful Strumpet." For Dr. Rush, see Chapter 4, "Philadelphia Doctor."

DOCTOR'S BILL. For William Johnson, see Chapter 6, "A Tolerable Good Dinner."

DRAPETOMANIA. For Frederick Law Olmsted, see Chapter 4, "Cotton Plantation."

DRUNKEN DRIVING. The 1816 edition of *The Drunkard's Looking Glass*, by Mason Locke Weems, was reissued in 1929 by Random House.

DYSENTERY. For Peter Kalm, see Chapter 5, "Pet."

FADS. For Thomas Low Nichols, see Chapter 2, "Motivation."

HYSTERIA. *Bits of Talk About Home Matters*, by H. H. (Helen Hunt Jackson), was published in 1873 by Roberts Brothers, Boston.

INFIRMARY. For Fanny Kemble, see Chapter 3, "Two Marriages."

INOCULATION. For Cotton Mather's *Diary*, see Chapter 2, "Home Education."

LAND TURTLE. For John Josselyn, see Chapter 1, "In the Beginning."

LANGUAGES. *Mary Chesnut's Civil War*, edited by C. Vann Woodward, was published by Yale University Press in 1981.

LUNACY. For Asa Sheldon, see Chapter 3, "Farmer's Courtship."

MALPRACTICE. For Nicholas Cresswell, see Chapter 3, "Venus and Mars."

MEDICINE MAN. For John Tanner, see Chapter 6, "Hunter's Tales."

NURSES. For Catharine Beecher, see Chapter 2, "True Independence." *The Journals of Louisa May Alcott*, edited by Joel Myerson and Daniel Shealy, were published by Little, Brown in 1989.

POISON. For Frances Trollope, see Chapter 8, "Woodland Worship."

POSTWAR STRESS. *The Laws of Health in Relation to the Human Form*, by D. G. Brinton and G. M. Napheys, has been reissued by Applewood Books and retitled *Personal Beauty*.

SCARLET FEVER. Extracts from the autobiography of John Barnard appear in *Remarkable Providences* (see Chapter 4, "Troublemakers").

SCURVY. For E. Gould Buffum, see Chapter 6, "Breakfast."

SIMPLE REMEDIES. For Lydia Maria Child, see Chapter 5, "Housewife."

SMALLPOX. Francis Chardon's *Journal at Fort Clark 1834–1839*, edited by Annie Heloise Abel, was published by the Department of History, State of South Dakota, in 1932.

SNAKEBITE. For Randolph Marcy, see Chapter 6, "On the Plains."

TOBACCO: TWO VIEWS. For John Josselyn, see Chapter 1, "In the Beginning." For Carry Nation, see Chapter 4, "Crusader."

YELLOW FEVER. *Recollections of Samuel Breck*, edited by H. E. Scudder, was published by Porter & Coates, Philadelphia, in 1877.

CHAPTER 11

PILGRIMS. For William Bradford, see Chapter 1, "The Pilgrims Set Forth."

YOUNG SYLVESTER. For John Winthrop, see Chapter 2, "Some Pros and Cons."

ELDER BREWSTER. For William Bradford, see Chapter 1, "The Pilgrims Set Forth."

EYRE AND MAXWELL. For John Barnard, see Chapter 10, "Scarlet Fever."

ROOSEVELT'S QUACK... For *The New York Conspiracy*, see Chapter 8, "Catholics."

M. DE MEAUX. Moreau de St. Méry's *American Journey, 1793–1798,* translated by Kenneth and Anne Roberts, was published by Doubleday & Company in 1947.

WILLIAM HARVERSON AND DAVID RUSSELL. For *The Drunkard's Looking Glass,* see Chapter 10, "Drunken Driving."

MAJOR ANTHONY. For Philip Hone, see Chapter 5, "Rebuilding New York."

PRESIDENT WILLIAM HENRY HARRISON AND OTHERS. The *New-Yorker,* edited by Horace Greeley, was published as a weekly from 1834 to 1841.

BRIDGET SUCH-A-ONE. For Henry David Thoreau, see Chapter 4, "Lighthouse Keeper."

HIRAM MALICK. Abigail Malick's letter appears in *Far From Home* (see Chapter 6, "New Year's Day Dinner").

ESCAPED SLAVE. For Frederick Law Olmsted, see Chapter 4, "Cotton Plantation."

IRISH LABORERS. For George Templeton Strong, see Chapter 2, "Admission to Law School."

ELIZABETH ALCOTT. For Louisa May Alcott's *Journals,* see Chapter 10, "Nurses."

CAL SURCEY. *The Life and Adventures of Nat Love, by Himself,* was reissued by Arno Press in 1968.

THE DESPERADO "CHUNK." For Miguel Otero, see Chapter 3, "Town Marshal."

IRISH CHILD. *How the Other Half Lives,* by Jacob Riis, first published in 1890, was reissued in 1971 by Dover Publications.

THE CONSOLATION OF FAITH. John Cotton's letter appears in *Collections of the Massachusetts Historical Society, Fourth Series, V.*

GHOST. This story is quoted by Peter Kalm (see Chapter 5, "Pet").

EPITAPHS. The first three epitaphs appear in *It's an Old New England Custom,* by Edwin Valentine Mitchell, Vanguard Press, 1946. For Philip Hone, see Chapter 5, "Rebuilding New York." The Methodist Cemetery epitaph is taken from *American Epitaphs,* by Charles D. Wallis, Dover Publications.

PASSING BELL. For Lucy Larcom, see Chapter 4, "Mill Girl."

FUNERAL IN THE GOLD MINES. For Louise Clappe, see Chapter 9, "Justice in the Gold Mines."

NEGRO BURIAL. For Frederick Law Olmsted, see Chapter 4, "Cotton Plantation."

THE PEARLY GATES. The text is from *The American Treasury,* edited by Clifton Fadiman and Charles van Doren, published in 1955 by Harper & Brothers.

CHINESE CUSTOMS. For Mark Twain's *Roughing It,* see Chapter 4, "Mining on the Humboldt."

INDIAN WAYS: THREE OBSERVATIONS ON INDIAN RITUALS. For Roger Williams, see Chapter 5, "Movable Houses." For William Bartram, see Chapter 6, "Hunter's Tales." For John Tanner, see Chapter 6, "Hunter's Tales."

HEAVEN AND HELL. For William Byrd's *The History of the Dividing Line...,* see Chapter 4, "Sluggards."

INDEX